Public Administration and Public Affairs

Twelfth Edition

NICHOLAS **HENRY**

Georgia Southern University

PEARSON

Boston   Columbus   Indianapolis   New York   San Francisco   Upper Saddle River
Amsterdam   Cape Town   Dubai   London   Madrid   Milan   Munich   Paris   Montreal   Toronto
Delhi   Mexico City   São Paulo   Sydney   Hong Kong   Seoul   Singapore   Taipei   Tokyo

To Muriel

Assistant Editor: Stephanie Chaisson
Executive Marketing Manager: Wendy Gordon
Production Project Manger: Clara Bartunek
Full Service Vendor: Kiruthiga Anand, Integra Software Services Pvt. Ltd.
Manager Central Design: Jayne Conte
Cover Designer: Karen Noferi
Cover Illustration: Alamy
Printer and Binder: Courier Companies
Cover Printer: Lehigh / Phoenix, Hagerstown, PA

Library of Congress Cataloging-in-Publication Data
Henry, Nicholas
    Public administration and public affairs / Nicholas Henry.—12th ed.
        p.   cm.
    Includes bibliographical references and index.
    ISBN-13: 978-0-205-85586-5 (alk. paper)
    ISBN-10: 0-205-85586-5 (alk. paper)
    1. Public administration.   I. Title.
    JF1351.H45 2013
    351—dc23   2011043727

3 4 5 6 7 8 9 10 V092 17 16 15 14 13 12

PEARSON

ISBN-10: 0-205-85586-5
ISBN-13: 978-0-205-85586-5

CONTENTS

CHAPTER 12
Intergovernmental Administration   411

PREFACE

*P*ublic Administration and Public Affairs is, at root, about the public interest. It explains both the means used to fulfill the public interest, and the human panoply that is the public interest.

Public Administration and Public Affairs, despite its orientation toward U.S. readers, has been translated and published in Chinese, Japanese, Romanian, and portions of it in Spanish. There is also an Indian edition and other international editions in English. We relate this polyglot publishing history to demonstrate that, with accelerating appreciation, public administration is seen around the globe as central to "good government," and good government, as we explain in the introduction to Part I, is seen by the world's people as central to the good life.

NEW TO THIS EDTION

The twelfth edition of *Public Administration and Public Affairs* has been significantly revised, expanded, and updated. Most notably, we have concentrated on three developments of singular consequence. They are:

- Public administration's reinvigorated concern with curbing corruption.
- The rise of the nonprofit sector in governing and administering the state.
- And the current, and likely long-term, crisis in public finance.

In addition, there is a *great* deal of brand new information in this edition. Each chapter has been updated with current examples and new material. Some highlights include:

- Coverage of the BP oil spill, the onset of the "Great Recession" and the biggest Ponzi scheme in history as examples of the failure of government have been added to Part I.
- New information has been added to Chapter 1 about Americans' unique views, relative to other cultures, on the role of government as well as their deep and growing distrust of elected leaders and the institution of government.
- A new box in Chapter 2 shows the differing logics of politics and administration, featuring the case of Shirley Sherrod's resignation, in 2010, from the U.S. Department of Agriculture.
- Increased information on nonprofit organizations has been added to Part II, and Chapter 3 now covers incivility and bullying in the workplace, particularly the public workplace, including the intriguing case of National Security Adviser Condoleeza Rice and Defense Secretary Donald Rumsfeld.
- Chapter 5 has new information on the role of "emotional intelligence" in public policy and the increasing decline of employee engagement.
- Chapter 7 now includes a discussion on the biggest little bill that nobody ever heard of: The Government Performance and Results Act Modernization Act of 2010 as well as performance reporting in the federal, state, and local governments.

- Chapter 8 now addresses Americans' demand for transparent and accountable public financial management and the numerous shifts in federal tax policies.
- Chapter 11 has added coverage on Frannie Mae and Freddie Mac and surrounding financial issues.
- Finally, among countless other new subjects and more updated material, Appendix A provides students with resume writing tips, interviewing skills, information on advanced degrees, and advice for beginning their careers in public policy.

WHAT'S OLD?

What's old? This book. It is now in its fifth decade, a number that struck us when we read a gratifyingly positive review of it and four other texts in the field's major journal, *Public Administration Review*. The last time that *Public Administration Review* reviewed introductory textbooks (four of them) was thirty-three years earlier. *Public Administration and Public Affairs*, uniquely, was reviewed then, too.[1]

Writing textbooks also is unique. Paul Krugman, Nobel laureate and a columnist for the *New York Times*, and Robin Wells, also a distinguished economist, wrote a textbook that consumed "five years of intense work." Wells described writing it as "excruciatingly hard" because, as Krugman explained, a textbook "has to be impeccable. If you're writing an academic paper, if you have some stuff that's blurrily written, that won't do much harm. If you write a newspaper article, and a third of your readers don't get it, that's a success. But a textbook has to be perfect."[2]

As one who also has written academic papers, newspaper articles, and textbooks (alas, the Nobel has stubbornly eluded us), we concur that a textbook should be perfect. A textbook has a far longer reach, a far larger audience, and a far deeper impact than virtually any other intellectual medium.

We doubt, frankly, that *Public Administration and Public Affairs* is perfect. But we keep trying.

NICHOLAS HENRY
SAVANNAH, GEORGIA

GIVE YOUR STUDENTS CHOICES

In addition to the traditional printed text, *Public Administration and Public Affairs* 12/e is available in the following format to give you and your students more choices—and more ways to save.

The **CourseSmart eText** offers the same content as the printed text in a convenient online format—with highlighting, online search, and printing capabilities. Visit **www.coursesmart.com** to learn more.

MySearchLab® WITH PEARSON eTEXT

MySearchLab is an interactive website that features an eText, access to the EBSCO ContentSelect database and multimedia, and step-by-step tutorials which offer complete overviews of the entire writing and research process. MySearchLab is designed to amplify a traditional course in numerous ways or to administer a course online. Additionally, MySearchLab offers course specific tools to enrich learning and help students succeed.

■ **eText:** Identical in content and design to the printed text, the Pearson eText provides access to the book wherever and whenever it is needed. Students can take notes and highlight, just like a traditional book. The Pearson eText also is available on the iPad for all registered users of MySearchLab.

■ **Flashcards:** These review important terms and concepts from each chapter online. Students can search by chapters or within a glossary and also access drills to help them prepare for quizzes and exams. Flashcards can be printed or exported to your mobile devices.

■ **Chapter-specific Content:** Each chapter contains Learning Objectives, Quizzes, and Flashcards. These can be used to enhance comprehension, help students review key terms, prepare for tests, and retain what they have learned.

Learn more at **www.mysearchlab.com**

NOTES

1. The reviews are Jane Beckett-Camarata and Larkin Dudley, "Educating American Public Administrators: Texts for the Introductory Course," *Public Administration Review* 70 (July/August 2010), pp. 634–636; and William H. Harader, "Whither Public Administration?" *Public Administration Review* 37 (January/February 1977), pp. 97–102.
2. Larissa MacFarquhar, "The Deflationist," *The New Yorker* (March 1, 2010), pp. 38–49. The quotations are on p. 47.

ACKNOWLEDGMENTS

I owe an unpayable intellectual debt to at least three of my teachers, Lynton Keith Caldwell, Jack T. Johnson, and York Y. Wilbern. Later, Frank J. Sackton introduced me to the classroom of the practical world. All, regrettably, are deceased, but their beneficent influence lives on.

I also am indebted to my colleagues, students, and the book's reviewers, who have had such a constructive influence on the continuing evolution of *Public Administration and Public Affairs*. As always, my wife, Muriel, and my children, Adrienne and Miles, and their spouses, Kevin and Anna, provided the deepest level of support. The book is for them, and, much to my gratification, my grandchildren, Callum, Margaret, and Charlotte.

NICHOLAS HENRY
SAVANNAH, GEORGIA

In Defense
of Governing Well

Bureaucracy is in our bones. Prehistoric evidence unearthed at archeological digs suggests that the rudiments of a bureaucratic social order were in place 19,000 years ago.[1]

DO WE NEED GOVERNMENT?

Not everyone agrees that bureaucracy and government are basic to society. Some contend, in a distorted extension of Thomas Paine's dictum, "that government is best which governs least," that the very best government is no government at all. As a prominent conservative explains, "What holds together the conservative movement" is that conservatives "want the government to go away."[2]

The Wrecking-Crew View

It has been argued that when those who want the government to go away are in power, they deliberately delegitimize government in the eyes of the public. Restrained by only what is politically infeasible, they act as a "wrecking crew" that sabotages governmental competence; tolerates, even encourages, corruption; and privatizes or sheds altogether core public responsibilities.[3]

Perhaps the clearest and most critical example of the wrecking-crew mentality is that of regulation, an area often touted by these advocates as a burden from which Americans demand relief. It is true, certainly, that, when asked the general (and, some would suggest, somewhat loaded) question, "Has government 'gone too far in regulating business and interfering with the free enterprise system?'"

most Americans reply, "Yes."[4] Yet, when queried about regulating specific industries, three times more citizens, on average, want more regulation than those who want less.[5]

Wrecking Government and Wrecking America

That the public could benefit from more responsible regulation of some industries seems plausible. Consider some evidence.

Wrecking the Environment On April 20, 2010, BP's (formerly British Petroleum) thirty-story-tall Deepwater Horizon oilrig in the Gulf of Mexico exploded, listed, and sank. Eleven crewmen's lives ended, and the most disastrous oil spill in American history began. Ultimately, nearly 5 million barrels of crude polluted the Gulf.

The company could not have been drilling in the Gulf had it not received a federal permit to do so, which BP had indeed received, despite its spectacularly tawdry safety record. Over the three years preceding the spill, the Occupational Health and Safety Administration cited BP for 760 "egregious willful" safety violations. These are the agency's most severe violation out of five types and apply only to violations of those rules that are "designed to prevent catastrophic events." How many citations for egregious willful violations had all other oil companies combined accumulated over the same period? One.[6]

The regulatory agency that had licensed BP to drill in the Gulf was the Minerals Management

Service (MMS), a little-known bureau of 1,700 employees created by the interior secretary in 1982. It is charged with issuing permits to, and collecting royalties from, companies that drill offshore.

MMS's regulatory record was at least as tawdry as BP's safety record. During the 1990s, it was revealed that the agency was failing to collect all royalties owed, losses amounting to billions of dollars, a major failure that continued unabated throughout the 2000s.[7]

Its administrators "routinely overruled staff scientists whose findings highlight the environmental risks of drilling," and scientists "repeatedly had their scientific findings changed to indicate no environmental impact."[8]

It would slander boilerplate to apply that term to the company's 582-page "oil spill response plan" that it submitted to MMS to establish the Deepwater Horizon. Besides stating that "no significant adverse impacts are expected" from a spill, it notes that walruses (which have not wallowed in the Gulf since the Ice Age) would be protected; provides an address for the "rapid deployment of spill response resources" that turned out to be that of a Japanese home shopping network; and "never once discusses how to stop a deepwater blowout.... Nobody" at MMS "read it."[9]

Nor, apparently, had anyone read any of the nearly identical plans, "all written by the same tiny Texas subcontractor," submitted by the four other major offshore drillers, all but one of which also referenced those walruses in the Gulf.[10] All five of the major companies' spill response plans amounted to the longest works of maritime fiction since *Moby-Dick*.

MMS also was riddled with corruption. According to a federal report, the agency had a "culture of ethical failure." "More than a dozen" of its current and past officials in Louisiana were implicated in steering contracts to; accepting gifts of holidays, tickets, and illegal drugs from; and having illicit sex with industry representatives (giving new meaning to regulators "being in bed" with industry).[11]

None of this should be surprising in light of the fact that three out of every four of the more than 600 lobbyists who lobby for the oil and gas industry are former federal employees, including two former directors of MMS. "Nowhere has

government and industry coziness been on display more clearly than at MMS."[12]

Besides being incompetent and corrupt, MMS's administrators were just plain dumb. During the week following the president's declaration of a moratorium on offshore drilling and the issuance of waivers, with oil still gushing into the Gulf, MMS granted seven permits and five waivers.[13]

In the midst of the spill, MMS was hastily renamed the Bureau of Ocean Energy Management, Regulation and Enforcement, an exhaustingly long moniker that should discourage future journalistic coverage of the agency. In 2011, the Government Accountability Office belatedly declared the management of oil and gas resources, a program that generates more nontax revenue—$9 billion per year—than any other, to be a "high-risk area" that required extra federal attention to prevent waste, fraud, and abuse.[14]

Wrecking the Economy Three decades after the steady deregulation of the financial sector that began in the early 1980s, America's foremost business magazine stated that "It is chillingly clear that U.S. financial institutions have for a good while been regulated no more stringently than, say, demolition derby drivers."[15]

Demolition is a fitting word. In the late 2000s, the United States narrowly escaped economic collapse. Near, or perhaps at, the heart of that barely missed meltdown were over-the-counter derivatives, which are highly leveraged financial exotica, such as mortgage-backed securities, that many analysts think caused the crisis. In 2003, the legendary investor Warren Buffet dubbed these derivatives "weapons of mass financial destruction" and warned that they involved "huge-scale fraud."[16]

Over-the-counter derivatives were introduced in the 1980s and flourished in a secretive, "completely dark market" about which regulators were also in the dark.[17] When the derivatives market peaked in June 2008, its face (or "notional") value was an absurd and inconceivable $683 *trillion*,[18] a sum that was more than eleven times the combined gross domestic products of every nation in the world, and almost all of it was owned by America's biggest banks.

When the head of a small regulatory agency attempted, in the late 1990s, to persuade Washington to regulate over-the-counter derivatives, she ran into rock-hard resistance. She was stunned when the chair of the Federal Reserve, Alan Greenspan, informed her that he did not "believe that fraud…was something that regulators should worry about" because "the free market self-corrects and takes care of fraudulent actors."[19]

In 2000, at the urging of Greenspan, the treasury secretary, and the financial industry (which has five lobbyists on its payroll for every member of Congress[20]), Congress passed the Commodity Futures Modernization Act, which declared illegal any federal *or state* regulation of over-the-counter derivatives.

Nearly a year and a half after the resultant "Great Recession" struck, the stock market had lost an astounding 56 percent of its value, more than had been lost over the same period during the Great Depression.[21] Two years following its start, 8.7 million jobs were gone,[22] four times more than in the severe, double-dip recession of 1980–1982.[23]

Special interests (such as the financial industry) appear to have unusually destructive effects on the economy. A study of lobbyists found that the deeper the influence of interest groups, the steeper the decline in the economy's growth rate and the greater the rise in its inflation rate.[24]

Equal Opportunity Wreckage   The wrecking-crew mentality is an equal-opportunity ideology. It hurts rich and poor alike.

Here is an example of the former: The chief business regulator, the Securities and Exchange Commission (SEC), received, over the course of sixteen years, "more than ample information," including "six substantive complaints that should have raised significant red flags" and two articles that "appeared in reputable publications," that financier Bernard Madoff was swindling his wealthy investors, including several charities. Yet, "a thorough and competent investigation…was never performed."[25] Not that one was really needed; a whistle blower tried in vain to convince the SEC that Madoff was a crook, showing its inept staff that, if Madoff were a baseball player, he would have a batting average of 960 each and every year and hit only doubles—no singles, triples, or home runs, ever—a pair of statistical impossibilities.[26] Madoff's machinations eventually were ratted out

by his own sons, and, by the time he was sentenced to 150 years in prison, Madoff had "made off" with an estimated \$65 billion, marking it the biggest Ponzi scheme in the history of the Milky Way Galaxy—well, at least of Planet Earth.

Here is an example of the latter: The federal Wage and Hour Division, which is charged with assuring that employers do not steal their employees' wages, is "an ineffective system" that "discourages wage theft complaints"; is beset with "sluggish response times" of "months to years"; is characterized by a refusal to "compel employers to pay" their employees what they owe them; and is rife with "inadequately investigated" cases in which some investigators "lied about investigative work performed and did not investigate." The Division "instructed many offices" to alter their databases to hide the fact that they had made "low wage workers vulnerable to wage theft."[27]

All the quotations and findings in the foregoing examples appeared not in lurid press accounts, but in official government reports. These reports draw short of charging the agencies with corruption, but whether they are corrupt or merely incompetent (if staggeringly so), is either condition good for society? Some scholars think so.

IS GRAFT GOOD?

The contention that bad, even corrupt, government is good has two components: the political and the economic.

Fighting for Fraud: Corruption Improves Public Services

The political argument for corruption is an old chestnut originated by a distinguished political scientist (the American Political Science Association's Prize for Excellence is named in his honor), who, ironically, was an ardent reformer.[28] His research outlived his political preferences, however, and, more than seven decades following its publication, his work still is cited, approvingly, in mainstream texts.

Graft's political justification is that corrupt political machines "work" and perform "many important social functions." In exchange for votes and the public's tolerance for politicians and their toadies who plunder the public till, ward heelers fix their constituents' traffic tickets, get them jobs, lower their tax bills, waive zoning and building codes, and attend their funerals, among a slew of other services, some more licit than others. When an "upper-class elite" of "reformers and do-gooders," this argument implicitly continues, replaces responsive political machines with lumbering, lethargic, legalistic public bureaucracies, the needs of the poor, and even of better-off taxpayers, are seldom met.[29]

This romanticized defense of corruption has scant evidentiary support. Corruption slashes governments' legitimate revenue by as much as half, and, with it, public services, and adds from 3 to 10 percent to the cost of legitimate services because citizens must bribe officials to acquire them.[30] As we document in Chapter 2, uncorrupted, reformed government in the twenty-first century correlates strongly and positively with better governing— that is, more efficient, effective, and responsive governments.

Fighting for Fraud: Corruption Brings Prosperity

The other argument for corruption, though originated by a sociologist,[31] is economic; it holds that graft munificently paves the way for longer-term prosperity. "Grease money" amounts to "speed money," in that bribes used to circumvent a blocking bureaucracy accelerate a nation's economic development.[32]

Ideas have power. The "efficient grease hypothesis" long has been a factor in justifying the international development community's policy of ignoring rampant corruption in allocating its funds. According to the World Bank, corruption has been "treated as a taboo subject" by the development community for decades.[33]

Fortunately, this ideology is fading, largely because it is increasingly clear that "efficient grease" actually retards prosperity. Not one of the nineteen impoverished nations that have been granted debt service relief through the Heavily Indebted Poor Countries Initiative is rated as having anything better than "serious to severe" governmental corruption.[34]

The rate of investment in countries with high and unpredictable rates of corruption is almost half of that in low-corruption countries.[35] An analysis of more than a hundred countries over thirteen years found that, when corruption increases by about two points on a ten-point scale, investment decreases by 4 percent, and gross domestic product falls by half a percent.[36] Corruption inflates the prices of goods by as much as a fifth,[37] and severely curtails personal income growth for just about everyone, but especially for the poor.[38]

The dollars lost to global corruption roughly match the annual budget of the federal government,[39] so obviously some people—the corruptors—are making a ton of money, right?

Well, no. Bribery costs even the bribers. Three surveys of 2,400 businesses in fifty-eight nations found that "firms that pay more bribes are also likely to spend more, not less, management time with bureaucrats negotiating regulations, and face higher, not lower, costs of capital."[40] The more that firms pay in bribes, the lower their annual growth rates.[41]

The United States is not immune. Long-term state-government corruption, in tandem with high state unemployment rates, produces greater income inequality among citizens and reduces real personal incomes, education levels, and unionization rates, all to statistically significant degrees.[42]

When countries curb corruption, good things happen: Poverty and child mortality rates decline, and per capita income and literacy rates rise, among other benefits.[43]

WHAT IS GOOD GOVERNMENT?

The inarguable harm brought by bad government leads us to our second inquiry: What is good government?

Good government is uncorrupted, democratic, and competent.

Good Government Is Uncorrupted

Aside from a few intellectuals who mud-wrestle on the slippery slopes of "corruption that 'works'" and "efficient grease," everyone knows that honest governance is good government. Globally, the leading "very big problem" is corrupt political leaders.[44]

Good Government Is Democratic

Democracy is good government. A massive and ongoing study finds that "the basic ideas of democracy are virtually universally accepted around the world," regardless of culture, and that these ideas are "viewed as the only game in town," even by the residents of dictatorships.[45]

Good Government Is Able

Finally, there is a third component of good government: Competence.

As with uncorrupted and democratic government, well-managed government enhances the daily lives of people. An analysis of twenty-nine nations found that "the efficient delivery of public services can *directly* affect welfare, and good governance has been shown to be associated with higher rates of...growth in incomes."[46] A study of the American states found that a high level of "state management capacity" (*management capacity* is a mix of policies, resources, and adaptability that produces efficient and effective governing) "clearly...contributes *directly* to improving the overall quality of life for state citizens."[47]

Governments' often-heroic response to the terrorist attacks of 2001 brought a doubling in popular trust in government.[48] Conversely, the price of weak, brittle, and clumsy government can be steep. Governments' bungled response to Hurricane Katrina in 2005 resulted in a ten-point plummet in Americans' faith in their governments' ability to protect them.[49]

President Barack Obama, in his inaugural address, phrased the matter well: "The question we ask today is not whether government is too big or too small, but whether it works."[50] That is precisely what this book is about.

The Place of Public Administration

Good government, then, rests on three pillars: honesty, democracy, and competency. Public administrators, as we shall see throughout this book, are essential to each.

Public administration is a broad-ranging and amorphous combination of theory and practice that is meant to promote a superior understanding of government and its relationship with the society it governs, as well as to encourage public policies more responsive to social needs and to institute managerial practices attuned to effectiveness, efficiency, and the deeper human requisites of the citizenry. Admittedly, the preceding sentence is itself rather broad ranging and amorphous (although one reviewer of this book described our definition as "a classic"[51]), but for our purposes it will suffice.

In Chapter 1, we review the longstanding and everlasting tension between bureaucracy and democracy in the United States.

In Chapter 2, we review the intellectual evolution of public administration. How public administrators see themselves and their proper field of action in a democracy deeply affects the health of democracy itself.

So welcome to *Public Administration and Public Affairs*, and welcome to one of the most exciting and rewarding career possibilities on earth.

NOTES

1. Scott Van Nystrom and Luella C. Nystrom, "Bureaucracy in Prehistory: Case Evidence from Mammoth Bone Dwellers on the Russian Steppes," *International Journal of Public Administration* 21 (Winter 1998), pp. 7–23.
2. Newt Gingrich, former Republican Speaker of the House, as quoted in John Cassidy, "The Ringleader," *The New Yorker* (August 1, 2005), pp. 42–53. The quotation is on p. 46.
3. Thomas Frank, *The Wrecking Crew: How Conservatives Rule* (New York: Macmillan, 2008).
4. Pew Research Center for the People and the Press, *Distrust, Discontent, Anger, and Partisan Rancor: The People and Their Government* (Washington, DC: Author, 2010), http://people-press.org/report/?pageid=1699. Data are for 1964–2010.
5. As derived from data in Meg Bostrom, *By, or for, the People? A Meta-analysis of Public Opinion of Government* (New York: Demos, 2006), p. 33. Figures are for 2003.
6. Jim Morris and M. B. Pell, *Renegade Refiner: OSHA Says BP Has "Systemic Safety Problem"*

(Washington, DC: Center for Public Integrity, 2010), pp. 3, 1. Figures are for June 2007–February 2010.

7. U.S. Government Accountability Office, *Mineral Revenues: Data Management Problems and Reliance on Self-Reported Data for Compliance Efforts Put MMS Royalty Collections at Risk*, GAO-08-893R Mineral Revenues (Washington, DC: U.S. Government Printing Office, 2008).

8. Six MMS scientists as cited in Ian Urbina, "U.S. Said to Allow Drilling Without Needed Permits," *New York Times* (May 12, 2010).

9. Tim Dickinson, "The Spill, The Scandal and the President," *Rolling Stone* (June 8, 2010), http://www.rolingstone.com/politics/news/the-spill-the-scandal-and-the-president-20 100608.

10. Steven Mufson and Juliet Eilperin, "Lawmakers Attack Plans Oil Companies Had in Place to Deal with a Spill," *Washington Post* (June 15, 2010).

11. Office of the Inspector General, U.S. Department of the Interior, transmittal memorandum of September 9, 2008, *Investigative Report: Oil Marketing Group—Lakewood* (Washington, DC: Author, 2008).

12. Mufson and Eilperin "Lawmakers Attack Plans Oil Companies Had in Place to Deal with a Spill." Figures are for 2009.

13. Ian Urbina, "Despite Moratorium, Drilling Projects Move Ahead," *New York Times* (May 23, 2010).

14. U.S. Government Accountability Office, *High-Risk Series: An Update*, GAO-11-278 (Washington, DC: U.S. Government Printing Office, 2011), p. 36.

15. Carol J. Loomis, "Derivatives: The Risk That *Still* Won't Go Away," *Fortune* (July 6, 2009), pp. 55–60. The quotation is on p. 55.

16. Warren Buffett, quoted in "Buffett Warns on Investment 'Time Bomb,' " *BBC News* (March 4, 2003), http://news.bbc.co.uk/.

17. Public Broadcasting System, "The Warning," *Frontline* (October 20, 2009), http://www.pbs.org. Brooksley Born is quoted.

18. Stephen Feglewski, Roy C. Smith, and Ingo Walter, "Geithner's Plan for Derivatives," *Forbes* (May 18, 2009), http://www.forbes.com/2009/05/18/.

19. Public Broadcasting System, "The Warning." Michael Greenberger is quoted.

20. Ibid.

21. Henry Blodget, "Crash of 2008 Now Worse than the Crash of 1929," *Business Insider* (March 5, 2009), http://www.businessinsider.com. Great

Recession figure is for October 9, 2007–March 5, 2009, or 513 calendar days; Great Depression figure, 49 percent, also is for its first 513 days. Both figures refer to the S & P 500 index.

22. National Employment Law Project, *July's Job Report: Economy Faces Deficit of Over 11.0 Million Jobs* (August 5, 2011), http://www.nelp.org.

23. Don Lee, "U.S. Unemployment Rate Falls Unexpectedly, but Job Losses Continue," *Los Angeles Times* (February 6, 2010).

24. Daniel Horgos and Klaus Zimmermann, "Interest Groups and Economic Performance: Some New Evidence," *Public Choice* 138 (March 2009), pp. 301–315. This is a study of German lobbying.

25. Office of the Inspector General, U.S. Securities and Exchange Commission, *Report of Investigation, Case No. OIG-509, Investigation of Failure of the SEC to Uncover Bernard Madoff's Ponzi Scheme, Executive Summary* (Washington, DC: Author, 2009), p. 1.

26. Henry Markopolis, appearing on *Morning Joe*, MSNBC (August 24, 2011).

27. U.S. Government Accountability Office, *Department of Labor: Wage and Hour Division's Complaint Intake and Investigative Processes Leave Low Wage Workers Vulnerable to Wage Theft*, GAO-09-458T (Washington, DC: U.S. Government Printing Office, 2009), Highlights page.

28. Harold F. Gosnell, *Machine Politics: Chicago Model* (Chicago: University of Chicago Press, 1937).

29. Thomas R. Dye, *Politics in States and Communities*, 9th ed. (Upper Saddle River, NJ: Prentice-Hall, 1997), pp. 291–316. The quotations are on pp. 292, 299.

30. Rick Stapenhurst and Sahr Kpundeh, eds., *Curbing Corruption: Toward a Model for Building National Integrity* (Washington, DC: World Bank, 1999), http://publications.worldbank.org/ecommerce/catalog/product-detail?product_id=208301&.

31. Robert K. Merton, *Social Theory and Social Structures* (New York: Free Press, 1957).

32. Daniel Kaufmann and Shang-Jin Wei, *Does "Grease Money" Speed Up the Wheels of Commerce?* NBER Working Paper No. W7093 (Cambridge, MA: National Bureau of Economic Research, 1999).

33. Stapenhurst and Kpundeh, *Curbing Corruption.*

34. World Bank Institute, as cited in Transparency International, *Perceived Corruption Index, 2005* (Berlin: Author, 2005).

35. World Bank, *World Development Report, 1997* (Washington, DC: Oxford University Press, 1997), pp. 102–104.

36. Paolo Mauro, *Why Worry About Corruption?* Economic Issues No. 6 (Washington, DC: International Monetary Fund, 1997), pp. 9–10. Figures are for 1982–1995.

37. Stapenhurst and Kpundeh, *Curbing Corruption.*

38. Sanjeev Gupta, Hamid Davoodi, and Rosa Alonso-Terme, *Does Corruption Affect Income Inequality and Poverty?* IMF Working Paper 98-76 (Washington, DC: International Monetary Fund, 1998).

39. World Bank calculation as cited in John Ashcroft, *Prepared Remarks of Attorney General John Ashcroft at the World Economic Forum,* Davos, Switzerland, January 22, 2004 (Washington, DC: U.S. Department of Justice, 2004), p. 2. Global corruption costs countries $2.3 trillion in 2004 dollars per year.

40. Kaufmann and Wei, *Does "Grease Money" Speed Up the Wheels of Commerce?* Abstract page.

41. Jakob Fisman and Raymond J. Svensson, "Are Corruption and Taxation Really Harmful to Growth? Firm Level Evidence," *Journal of Development Economics* 83 (May 2007), pp. 63–75. This is a study of 173 Ugandan firms. A 1 percent rise in the rate of bribery payments correlated with a 3.3 percent drop in the firms' annual growth rate.

42. Nicholas Apergis, Oguzhan Dincer, and James Payne, "The Relationship between Corruption and Income Inequality in U.S. States: Evidence from a Panel Cointegration and Error Correction Model," *Public Choice* 145 (October 2010), pp. 125–135.

43. Stapenhurst and Kpundeh, *Curbing Corruption.*

44. Pew Global Attitudes Project, *Global Opinion Trends, 2002–2007* (Washington, DC: Author, 2008), p. 34. Figures are for 2007.

45. Pippa Norris, as quoted in Richard Morin, "Islam and Democracy," *Washington Post* (April 28, 2002).

46. Stephen Knack, *Social Capital and the Quality of Government: Evidence from the U.S. States*, World Bank Policy Research Working Paper No. 2504 (Washington, DC: World Bank Development Research Group, 2000), p. 24. Emphasis added.

47. Jerrell D. Coggburn and Saundra K. Schneider, "The Relationship between State Government Performance and State Quality of Life," *International Journal of Public Administration* 26 (December 2003), pp. 1337–1358. The quotation is on p. 1337. Emphasis added.

48. G. Calvin McKenzie and Judith M. Labiner, *Opportunity Lost: The Rise and Fall of Trust and Confidence in Government after September 11* (Washington, DC: Brookings, 2002), p. 3.

49. Kathy Frankovic, "Polls Show Skepticism of Katrina Recovery," *CBS News* (August 29, 2007), http://www.cbsnews.com/stories/2007/08/29/opinion/pollpositions/main3216082.shtml.

50. Barack Obama, *Inaugural Address* (Washington, DC: U.S. Government Printing Office, January 20, 2009).

51. William H. Harader, "Whither Public Administration?" *Public Administration Review* 37 (January/February 1977), pp. 97–102. The quotation is on p. 98.

Big Democracy, Big Bureaucracy

The public bureaucracy is the arm of the state's civil power. In the United States, that arm appears, at least, to be atrophied when compared with its counterparts in most other developed democracies. This apparent bureaucratic flaccidity is a consequence of an entrenched national culture and careful political design.

AN UNPROMISING PRECIS

The roots of Americans' profound suspicion of executive authority are deeply sunk, and are apparent in the nation's earliest influences and origins.

The Indians and the English

One such influence was the Native Americans, who surrounded the early European settlers for centuries. Hence, the "framers of the Constitution... were pervaded by Indian images of liberty."[1] The Iroquois Confederation, a vast alliance of tribes, was emblematic of executive constraint: "Their whole civil policy was averse to the concentration of power in any single individual."[2]

Another influence was the English, who governed their colonists with a firm hand, but resisted royal rule on their own sceptral isle. No less an authority than Woodrow Wilson, the acknowledged founder of American public administration, observed that, "The English race long and successfully studied the art of curbing executive power to the constant neglect of the art of perfecting executive methods."[3]

The Indians and the English set a governing tone that, in the eighteenth century, expressed itself in three formats that outlined Americans' enduring *social contract*, or that unwritten agreement between the governed and their governments, often more understood than expressed, that defines and limits the responsibilities of each.

Administration by Ambassadors: The Articles of Confederation

One such format was the woefully misnamed Articles of Confederation and Perpetual Union, which, from 1781 to 1789, provided the first framework for the new nation, and exemplified Americans' contempt for princely prerogatives.

There was no chief executive. In fact, the first draft of the Articles, written in 1776, was rejected by the Second Continental Congress on the specific grounds that it had proposed an executive, and this bias against executive authority extended to *every* national officeholder; under the Articles, every continental official had a one-year term, and each one was subject to term limits.[4]

The states reigned supreme under the Articles. Congress was less a legislature and more a convention of powerless state ambassadors, chosen by state assemblies, which could recall them at will. The Articles did set up a rudimentary civil service, but it reported directly to committees of the Continental Congress, which retained all authority over it.

To be fair, the nation's early political thinkers were wrestling with how to organize something truly new: big democracy. When Daniel Shays ignited his ill-conceived rebellion in 1786 (the country's first tax revolt), the nation's political leaders discovered that no arm of "American government," such as it was, could be authorized to put down the disturbance.

Administration by Legislators: The First State Constitutions

At about the same time that the Articles of Confederation were being written, the states were busily drafting their own constitutions. Between 1776 and 1780, eleven of the thirteen states (Connecticut and Rhode Island kept their royal charters until well into the next century) adopted constitutions.

These eleven states were notably aggressive in restraining the powers of the chief executive. Ten limited gubernatorial terms to only a single year, and, with the exceptions of New York and arguably Massachusetts, their appointment and veto powers were severely restricted or nonexistent. In the remaining nine states, all executive and most judicial powers were placed squarely within the legislatures.

Civil services were present, but only rarely so in governments' executive branches, which were themselves, typically, withered appendages. Public administrators usually were appointed by legislatures or by "privy councils" composed of elected officials, and reported to these councils, or to legislatures, or to the courts, or to some combination thereof. State administrators often reported not only to state political bodies, but to local ones, too![5]

Did this anti-executive mishmash amount to true, natural, Rousseauist democracy? Hardly. Passing few people, about 5 percent of the population, were allowed to vote on anything or anyone.[6] Only three states permitted their governors to be elected even by those few people who were qualified to vote; in the remaining ten states, governors were appointed by legislators or judges. Big democracy was not only new, it was distrusted, and the public executive bore the brunt of that distrust.

At least one petulant English observer foresaw the impossibility of his former colonies to ever found a government worthy of the name, and he attributed this failure to Americans' fixation on a weak executive: "As to the future grandeur of America, and its being a rising empire under one head, whether Republican or Monarchial, it is one of the idlest and most visionary notions that was ever conceived even by writers of romance."[7]

Administration by Enfeebled Executives: Jefferson Prevails

Layering and striating all of this early American activity in drafting confederations and constitutions was our third expression of the emerging social contract: the massive brilliance of America's founders, but particularly that of Alexander Hamilton and Thomas Jefferson.

Hamiltonian Energy Hamilton was not only, like Jefferson, one of America's first public administrators (he was its first treasury secretary), but likely its first scholar of public administration, too. Hamilton displayed a strong interest in understanding the administrative apparatus of the state, and was contemplating a "full investigation of the history and science of civil government and...practical results of various modifications of it upon the freedom and happiness of mankind."[8] In other words, Hamilton was about to write the world's first textbook in public administration.

Hamilton extolled a strong chief executive, equating a strong executive with the "energy" needed to make a government function: "A feeble executive [by contrast] implies a feeble execution of government. A feeble execution is but another phrase for a bad execution; and a government ill executed...must be, in practice, a bad government."[9] Things, in sum, had to get done.

Even more than a strong chief executive, Hamilton advocated a *very* strong bureaucracy. He urged that department heads be paid exceptionally well, that they possess substantial powers, and that their tenure in office should extend beyond that of the chief executive who appointed them. Congress balked at Hamilton's recommendations, and still does.

Jeffersonian Constraint In stark contrast to Hamilton, Jefferson held a "profound distrust of bureaucracy," and "was no friend...to professionalism in public administration."[10]

As we explain in Chapters 7 and 9, the founders were concerned about governmental honesty and efficiency, two values that gave birth to American public administration. Nevertheless, the word, "administration," is nowhere to be found in the Constitution that Madison largely framed, an absence reflective of Jefferson's victory over Hamilton in the nation's earliest culture war: the formulation of the American social contract itself.

Ironically, the more experience that Jefferson gained as a public official, the more he forsook this position, ultimately reversing his views and advocating far greater powers for public executives. After he retired from government service, Jefferson even argued that the "laws of necessity...are of higher obligation" than "a scrupulous adherence to written law,"[11] a statement that is almost as disquieting as Richard Nixon's, uttered more than 150 years later: "If the president does it, that means it's not illegal."[12] Jefferson's conversion arrived too late, however, and his damage to a legitimately powerful public administration in America still stands.

A CULTURE OF CONSTRAINT

These eighteenth-century expressions of government's role reflected an already-formed American political culture that continues unabated today.

Americans and Their Governments

Americans' perspective on the proper place of government differs radically from that of Europeans. Almost six out of ten Americans believe that it "is more important for government to provide freedom to pursue [individual] goals," compared with about four out of ten French and Germans, and approximately three out of ten Britons and Italians. Some six out of ten citizens in each of these countries, compared to fewer than three out of ten Americans, say that it "is more important for government to guarantee no one is in need."[13] Large majorities of Americans of all races believe that "poor people have become too dependent on government assistance programs."[14] Not for nothing has Europe been called America's biggest blue state.

More broadly, the greatest governmental gap between Americans—who, as we elaborate in

Chapter 5, are measurably more independent and confident than virtually any other people—and the rest of the world is their relationship with the state.

Allow us some gross generalizations of continental dimensions that we offer solely for purposes of contrast. The African social contract has been described as a familial "half enlarged household, half enlarged state."[15] In Asia, the citizens' relationship with their governments often is based on Confucian principles, with governments headed by father figures who are, presumably, compassionate and wise, but certainly authoritative. In Europe, the relationship is a covenant, subject to adjustment, in which the rulers and the ruled are equals. And in Latin America, the relationship between state and citizen appears to be an authoritarian, paternal compact.

Not so in the United States, where the social contract, forged in revolution, leashes government with a taut tether. Those who govern are, in every sense, the citizenry's "servants," and, consequently, the American social contract may be reduced to a word. That word is *constraint*.

Such phrases as "the hollow government,"[16] "government by gridlock,"[17] and "demosclerosis"[18] all suggest a governance jammed by malfunctioning political mechanisms. In reality, however, turbid governance is a consequence of an American culture that places a high premium on constraining what governments do. So ingrained is this culture of constraint that serious scholars of American public administration have been known to argue against administrative reforms precisely because they could displace "prudential judgment" by "discreet 'mandarins.'"[19]

An American culture of administrative constraint is unique to the public sector, and is quite the opposite from that of the private sector, with its rapacious, robber-baron roots. Consider the assessment by Ted Turner, the spectacularly innovative and candid entrepreneur who founded CNN and other cable networks: "You play to win. And you know you've won when the government stops you."[20]

Governing in a Distrusting Culture

Constrained governance is inextricably enmeshed in Americans' distrust of politics and government. As Figure 1-1 shows, only 26 percent of Americans

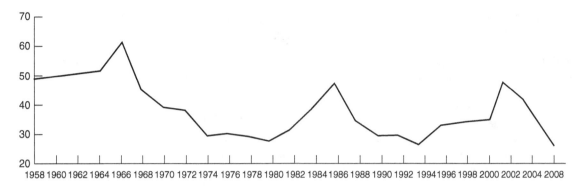

FIGURE 1-1
Trust in Government Index 1958–2008

Source: The National Election Studies, University of Michigan. *The NES Guide to Public Opinion and Behavior* (Ann Arbor, MI: Author. 2010).

Note: Index constructed using data from the following questions:

"How much of the time do you think you can trust the government in Washington to do what is right—just about always, most of the time or only some of the time?"

"Would you say the government is pretty much run by a few big interests looking out for themsleves or that it is run for the benefit of all the people?"

"Do you think that people in the government waste a lot of money we pay in taxes, waste some of it, or don't waste very much of it?"

"Do you think that quite a few of the people running the government are (1958–1972: a little) crooked, not very many are, or do you think hardly any of them are crooked (1958–1972: at all)?"

trust political leaders and the governments that they run. This is the lowest percentage ever recorded in the fifty-year history of the poll.

Distrust of Elected Leaders More than nine out of ten Americans think that their elected officeholders are "influenced by special interest money," "care only about their own careers," and "are out of touch with regular people." Well over four-fifths of those voicing these opinions consider each one of these issues to be a "major problem."[21]

Public administrators themselves reflect these currents. "The confidence levels of government employees" in those heading the federal executive branch and Congress, "almost perfectly reflect those of the general citizenry," although "top bureaucrats differ more substantially from the general public, usually in the direction of greater cynicism, but their rankings of the people running institutions are quite similar to the general public's."[22]

Distrust of Government Americans trust their governments no more than the officials they elect to run them. Their distrust focuses on government's size,

direction, performance, and power.[23] They reserve their deepest distrust for those parts of government that house elected officials and display their highest trust for agencies with public safety or military missions, findings that "are consistent to a large extent with findings in other Western countries."[24]

Those Americans who trust government "to do what is right" only "some of the time" or "never" tend to be white, Republican, thirty or older, and did not graduate from college.[25] Over thirteen years, the number of Americans who thought that the federal, state, and local governments have a "negative impact" on their day-to-day lives grew, on average, by more than three-fifths, a startling increase, and those who felt that governments' impact was positive plummeted by a fourth.[26] Not even half, a declining proportion, of Americans think that the government is "really run for the benefit of all the people."[27] Fifty-three percent of the public, an increase of more than two-fifths over thirteen years, is convinced that the federal government requires "very major reform."[28]

Again, public administrators' opinions track those of the general public. Top federal, state, and local executives believe that "there is a deeply systemic problem with our governance system," which "is not performing the way it should."[29]

Why Trust Matters Popular trust in and esteem for government are important, perhaps vitally so.

Some Diverse and Unexpected Correlations High levels of trust in government correlate, positively and internationally, with less political corruption;[30] better "government performance on the economy";[31] greater economic growth and opportunity;[32] superior "perceived outcomes" by networks of governments;[33] less "negative" popular evaluations of the performance of the entire political system;[34] and even with lower rates of street crime.[35] Public esteem, a corollary of trust, for government also associates with lower corruption.[36]

In the United States, high levels of trust in, and esteem for, government not only associate with lower levels of corruption[37] and street crime,[38] but also with more energetic and widespread public policy innovation.[39] In the view of local officials, there is a very robust connection between high trust and deeper engagement by citizens in local policymaking.[40]

High Trust Equals High Performance Of greatest importance, public trust and esteem are "positively related" with high performance by public agencies and greater citizen satisfaction with public services, a "strong correlation" that is "not unusual and is acknowledged in the literature."[41] This strong correlation appears to be universal in democracies,[42] and it exists because trust "helps determine how much power citizens grant" to their governments, which, in turn, "is what allows citizens to grant the flexibility required for bureaucrats to effectively govern."[43] Indeed, trust trumps public participation in agency decision making, accessibility of services, and even equality of treatment as a correlate with higher public performance.[44]

Certainly, these patterns are found in the United States. There is a clear correlation, for example, between plentiful *social capital* (an index composed of "generalized trust and strong civic norms") and high-performing state governments.[45] A study of the thirty-five largest American cities found that a 5 percent increase in popular trust in their government resulted in a 1 percent hike in that government's performance.[46]

THE CONSEQUENCES OF CONSTRAINT

Constraint. What are its consequences in the context of American government?

Hobbled Elected Chief Executives

A notable consequence is the hobbling of elected chief executives at every level of government.

The Domesticated Presidency Congress imposes an immense number of legal limitations on executive action. Here is what a cabinet secretary said about it: "The Congress has, for whatever reason, decided that they want to put literally thousands of earmarks on the legislation—that you can't do this, that you can't do that.... Well, your flexibility is just—it's like Gulliver with a whole bunch of Lilliputian threads over them: No one thread keeps Gulliver down, but in the aggregate he can't get up."[47]

Largely as a consequence of these Lilliputian leashes, there is a historic "presidential tendency" to be "reactive" in domestic politics, where power must be shared with Congress and often is reigned in by the courts, but to be "proactive.... powerful, costly...energetic," and interventionist in foreign affairs.[48]

Certainly this assessment applies to the president who was so critical in creating a culture of governmental constraint, Thomas Jefferson. In domestic matters, Jefferson is one of only seven presidents, and the sole two-term president, who never vetoed an act of Congress. Yet, in foreign affairs, he acted with stunning boldness.

A case-in-point is the Louisiana Purchase. With no consultation whatsoever with Congress, Jefferson assigned two of his public administrators to "merely inquire" about buying from France "The Floridas"—which were Spain's, but who knew?—and New Orleans. When France unexpectedly offered the entire Louisiana Territory, Jefferson's administrators snapped it up—without, in turn, consulting Jefferson. This unilateral act doubled the size of the nation—hardly a dilettantish dabbling in diplomacy. So controversial was "this extraordinary example of administrative discretion" that a band of respected political leaders tried to organize a secession of *Northern* states![49]

A more recent example of this strange duality is the surreal spectacle that unfolded in 1998, when the House of Representatives voted to impeach the president (for only the second time in history) on charges pertaining entirely to domestic affairs, while the president simultaneously launched a major and sustained air war on Iraq because it refused to cooperate with weapons inspectors from the United Nations.

In the administration of the nation, Jeffersonian constraint prevails—but only in domestic affairs. In foreign ones, Katy bar the door; Hamiltonian energy is rampant. This queer combination is schizoid: an enfeebled executive for the country, but an energetic one for the planet.

Constraining Governors

Governors gradually have gained executive power over the last three centuries—since 1960, state constitutional revisions have lengthened their terms of office and strengthened their powers of appointment, budgeting, and the veto[50]—but they still remain tightly constrained. For example, state agency heads accord their governors and legislators essentially identical levels of influence in agency "rulemaking," which is a pseudonym for agency policymaking, and this has been consistently the case for more than a quarter century; "legislators exert major influence on agency rules."[51]

An Insipid Appointment Power Out of six "institutional powers" available to the governors, the power to appoint ranks as the weakest.[52] More than half of key state administrators are not appointed by the governor. Of the almost 2,000 major administrative officers in the fifty states, 750 are appointed by someone or some body other than the governor, and nearly 300 are elected directly by the people.[53] When we add in those state administrators who are less than major, the total number who are elected separately surpasses 500, or more than ten per state, on average, a number that has "changed little" since 1955. The number of *agencies* that are headed by elected administrators, however, has declined by a fourth over nearly four decades, and now averages a bit more than five such agencies per state. But, "as with separately elected officials, there appears to be a bottoming out of the ability to reduce this number across the states."[54]

When agency heads are "outside the orbit of control by the governor via appointment," not-so-good things happen. Compared with those appointed by the governor, these state executives not only are somewhat more attuned to legislators than to their governors, they also attribute a significantly "higher level of influence" to special interests when making policy, and lobbyists' access to their agencies is "definitely greater."[55]

Lieutenant Governors, Term Limits, and Recalls There are additional constraints on executive power in the states.

One is the fact that, in nineteen of the forty-five states with lieutenant governors, the governor and lieutenant governor are elected independently,[56] and, presumably, have political agendas that differ. (In 1804, Americans relieved the federal government of this potentially destabilizing conflict, as it applied to the president and vice president, by ratifying the Twelfth Amendment.)

Another is term limits—or the lack of them. Most elected state administrators—from more than half to all, depending on the office[57]—and legislators in thirty-five states,[58] may be reelected without limit, a potentially huge political advantage. By contrast, governors in only eleven states have unlimited terms.[59]

Eighteen states also permit the recall of the governor and other state officials; a *recall* is a specially called election, initiated by voters signing petitions, that determines whether or not an elected officeholder may complete his or her term. Michigan and Oregon introduced the state recall in 1908, but it has turned out only two governors since its inception.[60] Nevertheless, the recall remains as yet one more potential executive constraint in those states that have it.

Constraining Local Elected Chief Executives

Local elected chief executives typically have powers barely worthy of the noun.

Puny Political Powers Almost three-quarters of county commission chairs,[61] roughly half of the mayors of towns and townships,[62] and nearly a fourth of municipal mayors[63] are not elected to office by popular vote. Instead, they are selected by their fellow council members or even by mindless rotation, thereby denying them their own electoral power bases. By contrast, legions of more specialized local executives, such as treasurers, tax collectors, coroners, and clerks, are voted into office. Virtually none of these officials have term limits, but close to a tenth of local elected chief executives do.[64]

That term limits are imposed on relatively few mayors and commission chairs reflects their unusually brief terms: only a minority has terms as long as four years. Well over four-fifths of county and municipal elected chief executives are part-timers, and few have the normal powers of the president and the governors, notably the veto, preparation of the budget, and appointment powers.[65]

The Rising Recall Thirty-eight states permit voters in at least some of their local jurisdictions to recall their elected chief executives and other elected officials.[66] Voters in six out of every ten cities and towns,[67] in nearly as many counties,[68] and in many school districts and special districts may initiate the recall.

The local recall was invented in 1903 by Los Angeles.[69] Until very recently, local recall campaigns almost never exceeded two or three per year nationally, and in most years there were none. Then, in 2009, something happened. There were 100 of them. In 2010, there were 180. More than a third were successful, and the remainder were either defeated or failed to make the ballot.[70]

Recall attempts against mayors more than doubled during the same period, and about a fourth resulted in mayors resigning or being voted out of office. Most recall campaigns are not based on allegations of criminal acts, but stem instead from public concerns over service cuts or tax hikes. The bases of some recall attempts, however, seem trivial, if not strange, such as voters' opposition to a mayor's proposal to switch from diagonal parking spaces to parallel ones (Johnstown, Colorado), or a mayor's firing of two lifeguards (Ogden, Kansas).[71]

Hobbled Governments

The constraints that Americans have imposed on their elected chief executives extend to the institution of government itself.

Constraining the Federal Government The American founders created a Constitution that divides power between the national and state governments, and checks and balances federal power among its executive, legislative, and adjudicative branches. More contemporaneously, as we elaborate in Chapter 11, the federal government has ceded significant power to private and nonprofit organizations, whose costs account for 40 percent of federal discretionary spending, and on which core federal policies have grown dependent.

Constraining State Governments States constrain themselves. As we detail in Chapter 8, thirty legislatures have inflicted taxation or expenditure limitations upon their governments (including three states that limit both), and sixteen require legislative "supermajorities," three of which *also* demand voter approval, to raise some or all taxes.

The people have imposed on their state governments the constraining devices of direct democracy. One such device is the *referendum*, or a legislatively authorized popular vote to approve or disapprove a proposed policy. Invented by South Dakota in 1898, it has since spread to all the states,[72] and voters typically approve from three-quarters to four-fifths of them.[73] South Dakota, also in 1898, gave us the *initiative*, or *initiative petition*, which places an issue on the ballot by gathering a stipulated percentage of registered voters' signatures on a petition. Two dozen states now have it.[74] The states' use of the initiative has nearly quadrupled since the decade of the 1960s, when fewer than a hundred were on state ballots, to a record 377 in the 1990s and 374 in the 2000s, a number second only to the 1990s.[75] Slightly more than two-fifths of all 2,360 state initiatives, beginning with the first one in 1904, have been approved by voters.[76]

Constraining Local Governments Local governments are the most institutionally limited of all governmental levels. In metropolitan areas, where 80 percent of Americans dwell, public power still is shared, divided, and parsed among many governments operating at multiple levels, much as it was in the eighteenth century. During the twenty-first century, however, swarms of nongovernmental entities, such as private companies and nonprofit organizations, and sprawling special purpose governments, such as public authorities and special districts, are infusing this inchoate administrative stew.

As we elaborate in Chapter 8, almost all state legislatures, whose thirst to curb taxing and spending remains apparently unquenched by the limitations that they have imposed on their own governments, have extended these constraints to their local governments as well, and voters in one out of every eight cities have mandated even stricter limitations on their own municipal governments.

Local governments use most of the devices of direct democracy even more liberally than do states. More than three-quarters of municipalities and towns permit the referendum, and all allow the initiative or variations of it.[77] More than seven out of ten counties allow the referendum and the initiative.[78]

The Unclear Outcomes of Imposed Constraints. Although, as we detail in Chapter 8, the tax and expenditure limitations that state and local governments have imposed correlate with reduced spending (marginally, or even negatively, for the states, more so for localities), the devices of direct democracy evidence quite mixed patterns.

In those states with initiatives (which typically permit local as well as state initiatives), state spending is 12 percent lower, but local spending is 10 percent higher, suggesting that voters support services that are closer to themselves, and resist those that are delivered from afar to others (as well as to themselves).[79] In local governments with initiatives, "their mere presence is an insufficient factor" in influencing the "decision making of local legislative bodies."[80]

Although there is a positive and robust cross-country correlation between direct democracy at the local level and lower total public spending and taxation,[81] it is unclear, at best, that the referendum and initiative associate with wise governance. The thirty-four countries that require their citizens to vote on national referenda spend less than nations without them. Those eighteen countries with national initiatives spend more overall, but also are more corrupt. Neither the referendum nor the initiative appears to be related to sound, or unsound, budgeting, effective and productive governing, and public happiness.[82]

INFERNAL VERNON

A Case of Unconstrained Public Administration

We have been suggesting that local governments are constrained especially tightly. But there are exceptions. Here is one.

The City of Vernon, in Los Angeles County, California, has an official population of ninety-one, mostly very economically secure, souls. Sixty of these residents have been registered voters for many years, and almost all them are city employees or are related to a city official. Most live in heavily-subsidized housing provided by the city, which owns almost all the residences in Vernon, with some houses renting for less than $150 per month.

The city, which bills itself as "Exclusively Industrial," supplies electricity and gas to firms—and to their 46,000 employees—doing business in Vernon

with remarkably lucrative results. Vernon has more than $100 million in cash and investments, an amount more than double its general operating budget. Its city administrator commands a salary of $875,000, more than twice that of the president of the United States, and at least one of Vernon's retired officials is paid more than $1 million a year in consulting fees. From the 1970s to the present, the city clerk typically has been the highest-paid municipal employee in California.

In 1978, Vernon's city clerk disqualified enough challenger ballots to assure that the grandson of the city's founder was elected mayor. In 1980, he did it again. For the next quarter-century, the city

(*continued*)

(*continued*)

simply canceled all elections. The next election was scheduled, ostensibly, for April 2006.

Then, in January 2006, eight newcomers moved into an empty building in town, and promptly registered to vote. Three of them filed petitions to run for city council. Their apparent leaders were a disbarred lawyer who had been convicted on charges of embezzlement and forgery, and a disgraced and deposed city treasurer of nearby South Gate, who was facing a federal prison sentence after being convicted a year earlier for corruption that had almost bankrupted that city.

More newbies followed, and, in a matter of weeks, Vernon's electorate burgeoned by more than two-fifths to eighty-six registered voters. Vernon's five city council members, each of whom had served in office from thirty to fifty years, were not pleased. The council rescinded the voting registrations of the eight new residents, and, for good measure, cut off their power, condemned their building, and evicted them. Private investigators, cruising in cars with tinted windows and no license plates, followed and videotaped suspected "ringer residents," and not only in Vernon, but in other communities as well. In one incident, a pistol was drawn.

True to tradition, the city disqualified the three new candidates' voter registrations and cancelled its election for 2006. Charges were duly filed, and the Los Angeles Superior Court ruled that Vernon reinstate the voters' registrations and actually hold an election. These it did. At the close of voting, however, the city clerk (who, coincidentally, was the son of the recently retired city administrator) confiscated the ballots and locked them away in City Hall, an unprecedented act that, at the very least, was questionable under state law.

The clerk's justification was that the ballots should not be tallied until Vernon's swelling court docket was decided. And Vernon did indeed have a large lump of lawsuits. The three challengers had brought suit to disenfranchise more than eight out of ten of Vernon's voters on the grounds of conflict of interest. Moreover, a dozen voters, including the mayor, claimed residence in Vernon, but allegedly lived elsewhere, thereby disqualifying them as voters. The District Attorney for Los Angeles County was investigating corruption charges that centered on the city clerk. Vernon, in turn, was embroiled in its own suit to seal its records from review by prosecutors.

Six months following the election, the Superior Court ruled that the election could not be nullified by the City, and described Vernon as being "run like a fiefdom." Vernon promptly appealed.

An administrator in the county's registrar's office mused, "You know, Vernon kind of keeps falling into this category you just don't find legal citations for.... It's very, very strange...They're one the most unusual little jurisdictions I've ever encountered."

Or, as another seasoned observer put it, "Vernon acts more like a for-profit company...than a city" (White). ■

Sources: The following articles were published in 2006 by the *Los Angeles Times* and written by Hector Becerra: "Vernon Shoo-Ins Shoo Outsiders" (February 12); "In Tiny Vernon, a Surge in Voters" (April 7); "Judge Is to Have Key Role As Vernon Casts Votes" (April 11); "Vernon's Inaction on Vote Stumps Experts" (April 13); "S. Pasadena Is Tired of Vernon Politics" (April 15); "Vernon Fights to Keep Records Private" (April 26); and "Attempt to Nullify Vernon Election Defeated" (August 4); "Infernal Vernon" (editorial), *Los Angeles Times* (April 14, 2006); Kim Christensen and Sam Allen, "Hefty Paychecks for Vernon Officials Rival Those in Bell," *Los Angeles Times* (August 20, 2010); "Otis White's Urban Notebook," *Governing* (April 2006), p. 19.

Hobbled Governmental Growth

Most crucially, a culture of constraint restrains governmental growth.

American governments do grow. By the close of the 1800s, federal, state, and local government workers accounted for not even 2 percent of the population, and government revenues at all levels amounted to about 8 percent of the economy.[83] The proportion of all government workers since has more than tripled, accounting for more than 7 percent of the resident population, and total public revenues have nearly quadrupled their share of the economy and amount to more than a third of the gross domestic product (GDP).[84]

The heart of our matter, however, is this: Do American governments grow as fast and as big as governments elsewhere?

No, they do not. Constrained governmental growth has been particularly evident since 1978, when California's notorious initiative, Proposition 13, was voted in by a two-to-one popular margin. Proposition 13 slashed, and effectively capped, all local property taxes and made California the only state that requires a two-thirds vote in the legislature both to adopt a budget and to raise any tax. The initiative became the enduring and iconic symbol of the revolt against governmental growth.

Between 1946 (the year following the end of World War II) and 1978 (the year of Proposition 13, which most observers peg as the year of the tax revolt's first shot heard around the nation), the revenue collected by the federal government as a percentage of personal income grew by about one-half of 1 percent per year (17 percent over thirty-two years), and the revenues of state and local governments as a percentage of personal income grew by 4 percent per year, nearly doubling over the same period. But *after* 1978, federal revenue as a percentage of personal income essentially held flat, and after 2001, as a consequence of unprecedented federal tax cuts, it actually declined.[85] Similarly, after 1978, the growth of state and local revenues as a percentage of personal income was slashed by three-fourths to a growth rate of about 1 percent per year.[86] Today, all taxes imposed by all governments are at their lowest levels as a percentage of personal income since the 1950s, "before the advent of the most expensive transfer programs," such as Medicare.[87]

Because Americans resist governmental growth, American governments are substantially smaller than are governments in other developed democracies. Whereas the revenue collected by all American governments amounts to 30 percent of GDP, those collected by the governments of eighteen Western and Central European democracies, Australia, Canada, Japan, New Zealand, and South Korea amount to 46 percent of their respective GDPs, on average—a third higher take than in the United States.[88] Not only does the United States have a lower *overall* tax rate than comparable countries, but, remarkably, *each type* of American tax—income, sales, property, and payroll tax—is lower than its counterpart tax in these nations.[89]

Perhaps more than any other measures, the relatively slow rate of America's long-term governmental growth and the comparatively small size of American governments stand as testaments to America's culture of governmental constraint. Whether this is good or bad for Americans is an open question. A massive global analysis found that, while there is "a significant positive association" between higher personal income and greater personal happiness, there is no relationship between higher government spending and happiness: "increased government spending does not lower [or raise] happiness in broad cross-country contexts."[90]

THE BUREAUCRAT: BRAINED, BLAMED, AND BOUNCING BACK

America's culture of constrained governance has unique effects on its public administrators.

Bashing Bureaucrats

Perhaps the most obvious cultural manifestation of Americans' suspicion of executive authority is bureaucrat bashing. Wide swaths of American institutions single out the bureaucrat as the craven cause of governmental failure.

Politicians' Pandering Politicians routinely run against the bureaucracy in their ceaseless grubbing for votes. The campaign mantra of bureaucratic "waste, fraud, and abuse" has been a self-serving rhetorical standard of office seekers for more than a generation.[91] Once elected to office, politicians are measurably and radically more contemptuous of public administrators than are the voters whose support they sought. The proportions of elected officials who characterize public administrators as "dull" or who "make red tape" are twice those of the general public, and the percentage of politicians who describe them as "bureaucratic" is three times that of the citizenry.[92] When speaking on the floor of the U.S. House, representatives call public administrators "bureaucrats" 70 percent of the time, and 84 percent of these references are clearly pejorative.[93]

Academia's Undercutting Intellectuals foster an image of bureaucracy that ranges from its being merely unresponsive to dangerously undemocratic. This anti–public administration propaganda begins at an early age. American children's literature portrays public servants as measurably less benevolent and competent than does British children's literature.[94]

Over three-fourths of introductory college textbooks on American government portray public administrators as "government employees who stay on forever," and two-thirds demonize governmental bureaucracy as "all powerful and out of control."[95] "The most deeply rooted and persistent misconception" of these texts is that public administrators "are not accountable."[96]

Media's Mordancy Judging by what evidence we have, the news media's coverage of the public bureaucracy is not good. Over the course of two decades, 80 percent of the televised news stories about the federal government, and 70 percent of the printed ones, focused on the executive branch, and only a third or, more commonly, depending on the medium, less, of those that focused on the executive branch's "job performance" were positive in tone.[97]

Media's mordancy is not confined to the news. Although nearly two-thirds of twenty movies released since 1990 present public administrators in a mostly favorable light,[98] federal administrators often are portrayed as "the baddest villains in Hollywood films."[99]

Thirty percent of television's prime-time entertainment episodes present civil servants in a positive light and 22 percent in a negative one, figures that have remained fairly constant since the mid-twentieth century.[100] Most programs display a neutral tone toward civil servants, and, compared with other governmental officials and professionals—politicians, law enforcers, and teachers—bureaucrats are cast in "unmemorable roles."[101] They are "frequently shown as robotic paper shufflers or abrasive malcontents who were too lazy, apathetic or self-absorbed to serve the public."[102]

Perhaps we should not be surprised that young adults' "favorite TV public servant" is the casually corrupt, and definitively dumb, animated Mayor Joe Quimby of *The Simpsons*.[103]

Are Bureaucrats to Blame?

Do Americans really believe that their public administrators are against them?

The Public Likes Public Administrators Evidently not. Overall, "the American public does not appear as disdainful of bureaucrats as the projected media image would indicate."[104] About seven out of every ten Americans, a rising proportion, have a favorable opinion of government workers.[105] Only 6 percent of Americans blame government employees for "what is wrong with government," compared with four times that number, 24 percent, who say elected office holders are responsible for government's failures.[106]

Why the disconnect? Why do Americans like public administrators *in spite of* their deepening distrust of elected leaders and government, and the unremitting bombardment blasting bureaucrats fired by politicians, professors, reporters, and entertainers?

Encountering Bureaucrats Because bureaucrats deliver. Polls prove it.[107]

American bureaucrats are helpful, efficient, fair, and courteous in dealing with people. About two-thirds of Americans who have asked federal, state, or local bureaucrats to do something unusual for them—that is, their request was not a routine matter—found their civil servants to be helpful,[108] a striking proportion that belies the stereotype of inflexible, impersonal bureaucrats. Nearly three-quarters of Americans report that "the people at the [government] office" are very efficient (43 percent) or fairly efficient (31 percent) in handling their problems, and more than three-fourths feel that they are treated fairly; indeed, only 12 percent think that they are treated unfairly.[109]

American bureaucrats give good service, too. In annual surveys that have been conducted for more than a decade, from 65 to 72 percent of Americans say that they are satisfied with the services that they receive from federal agencies, and have a favorable view of them.[110] From three-fifths to over four-fifths of the public report that they are satisfied or highly satisfied with state governmental services,[111] and local services garner "generally favorable assessments" from more than 200,000 citizens in forty states.[112]

The Bureaucrat: Government's Savior?

Ironically, those battered and bruised bureaucrats may be leading the way in restoring Americans' trust in government.

Seventy percent of Americans have low expectations about obtaining good governmental services, but more Americans, 77 percent, who actually experience public services feel that they receive services of high quality.[113] This holds true even for two of the most widely belittled government agencies, the U.S. Postal Service[114] and local public schools.[115]

The consequences of these positive experiences for governments are varied. Overall, Americans who have had good experiences with an agency (32 percent, *versus* 18 percent who have not) are "three times more likely to give a positive performance rating" to "government in general" (41 percent *versus* 14 percent).[116] Those citizens who have had positive personal dealings with an agency, but who hold a deeply negative view about government in general, express highly positive opinions about that particular agency but their negative view of the *institution* of government persists.[117]

The high regard that Americans have for bureaucrats with whom they have dealt is significant because "the impact of a negative experience with a public agency is much more pronounced than the effect of a positive one.... Decreasing the number of disappointed clients will have a stronger effect on increasing trust in...government than increasing the number of already well-pleased clients."[118] Because relatively few citizens have a bad bureaucratic experience, bureaucrats may be leading a restoration of trust in government.

A PARADOXICAL POWER: THE GRAY EMINENCE OF THE PUBLIC ADMINISTRATOR

So what does all this mean for the American public administrator? It means that the United States has produced a paradoxical public administration characterized by cultural, institutional, and legal limits on executive action, and by a nonetheless powerful public administrative class. "The fragmented managerial climate of government" actually grants public administrators more opportunities for acquiring power than are available to their corporate counterparts.[119]

Staying Power

Of considerable, but often underappreciated, importance is the staying power of bureaucracies and the bureaucrats in them, a power that permits them to wait out and outlast elected officeholders and the policies that they push.

Of 175 federal agencies, only 15 percent disappeared over a half century, a "death rate" that was far below that of business failures during the same period, leading to the conclusion that, by and large, government organizations are "immortal."[120] Examples include the Commission for the Standardization of Screw Threads, formed in 1918 with a sixty-day life span, the "commission that will not die";[121] the Rural Electrification Administration, chartered in 1935 to electrify backwoods America, had accomplished its mission by the 1950s; and the Federal Helium Reserve, created by Congress in 1925 to assure the Army Air Corps a continuing supply of fuel for its cutting-edge (at the time) aeronautical technology—blimps.[122] All, if differently titled, are with us today.

Just as bureaucracies stay on, so do bureaucrats. The median job tenure of all government employees is four-fifths longer than that of private-sector employees, and, depending on the level of government, top public careerists average from seventeen to twenty-six years on public payrolls.[123] Forty-three percent of federal civilian workers, 38 percent of state government employees, and 37 percent of the local workforce are fifty years old or older; for the private sector, this figure is just 29 percent of all employees.[124]

Bureaucracies and bureaucrats endure.

Discretionary Power

Discretionary power refers to a public administrator's authority to decide how to implement public policies. In the American states, for example, "greater managerial discretion," in tandem with deregulation, "drove reforms" in the critical areas of budgeting, procurement, and personnel, and, in all three areas, these reforms left "a deep and long legacy."[125]

Legislatures frequently enable bureaucratic discretion. For instance, Congress in 1988 effectively granted the Federal Emergency Management Agency total authority to determine not only how much assistance is *needed* in a disaster, but even how much aid is *desirable*.[126]

Often, however, administrators exercise discretion sans specific legislative instructions. Federal administrators "fill out" 71 percent of new laws by appending proscriptions and procedures that have the force of law.[127] The U.S. Department of Education has enacted rules that prohibit schools from expelling special education students who have discipline problems (including those who bring guns and drugs to school), despite the absence of any legislation requiring such policies. The Army Corps of Engineers has elected to interpret "navigable waters" to mean "wetlands" in a law that does not mention "wetlands," which, of course, are neither navigable nor waters.[128]

In 1983, the Supreme Court tucked the bureaucracy's discretionary powers into a warm, protective blanket by ruling as unconstitutional the *legislative veto*, or the repeal by the legislature of an executive action taken in the course of administering a law.[129] The legislative veto emerged in 1932, and, by 1980, Congress had inserted legislative vetoes into 555 provisions in 355 legislative acts, most of which were enacted during the 1970s.[130] That intrusive congressional practice disrupts agencies' discretion no longer.

Policymaking Power

Aside from the actual decision to select a public policy (a decision that, as we detail in Chapter 10,

is uniquely idiosyncratic for each policy process), policymaking is composed of three main steps: *Setting the policy agenda*, or discovering and expressing social problems that need addressing; *developing options* about how to resolve those problems; and *implementing the policy*.[131]

Policymaking by Federal Administrators Although "no one set of actors dominates the process" of federal agenda setting, "elected politicians *and their appointees* come closer than any other."[132] Top presidential appointees rank higher than the president and members of Congress in setting the agenda, and are closely followed by staffers in the White House and Congress.

Career civil servants in the executive branch are less involved in agenda setting, but they are extremely significant—more so than political appointees—in structuring alternative policies. Careerists have "yet more" impact on the final policy process, that of implementing policy, as implementation is a "major preoccupation" of theirs.[133]

There are about 30,000 unelected employees in the institutional center of national policymaking, Congress,[134] a number that includes some 21,000 personal and committee staffers (up from fewer than 2,500 in 1948),[135] and the employees of the Government Accountability Office, Library of Congress, and Congressional Budget Office. These professionals, but particularly staffers, wield significant power in the policymaking process.[136]

Policymaking by State Administrators Public administrators play comparable policymaking roles in the states.[137] A five-decade-long study of state agency heads finds that these executives consistently allocate half their time to "policy development" and "building political support"; the other half is spent on "internal management."[138] In state executive offices, administrative professionalism itself ranks "as an important influence" in state policy formation, equaling "other more commonly studied state characteristics," including the most powerful political forces, such as special interests and ideologies.[139]

The nation's more than 7,300 state legislators[140] employ 28,000 full-time legislative staffers and another 5,000 when the legislatures are in session.[141] Just three legislatures fail to provide their standing committees with professional staffs;[142] none did so in 1960.[143]

As with Congress, the role of these staffs is a powerful one. As a former state legislative staffer put it, "The most remarkable discovery that I made during my tenure as a staff member was the amount of power I had over bills on which I worked."[144]

Policymaking by Local Administrators   There is a small raft of research substantiating that top local administrators are their governments' *de facto* policymakers. As we detail in Chapters 9 and 11, nearly nine out of ten cities and towns, more than half of counties, and essentially all independent special purpose governments have chief administrative officers whose growing budgetary and appointive powers render them, in general, the single most powerful actors in local governments.

Most of the research on policymaking power in local governments focuses on city and town managers. "The policy role" of these appointed chief administrators "consumes approximately one-third" of their time,[145] a share that has held steady since the mid-1980s.[146] "Virtually all" of them "always or nearly always participate in the formulation of policy and set the council agenda,"[147] with a stunning 96 percent *initiating* policy proposals.[148] The rise of the local manager as a policymaker is not without its tensions: As the managers' "external" policymaking leadership deepens, their "internal" administrative authority lessens.[149]

Lethargic Local Legislators   Most city council members are "are ambivalent about making policy decisions," are uninvolved in policymaking and mission development, and *approve* of their managers' taking over these responsibilities that, legally, are theirs.[150] The longer that a city council member has served on the council, the greater the deference that he or she has for city administrators.[151]

Other local councils demonstrate a comparable lack of interest in policymaking. Virtually all researchers who have addressed this issue in county governments also find that county commissioners also "are relatively uninvolved in policy formation," a vacuum that is typically filled by county administrators.[152] Special purpose governments may cede even greater policymaking powers to their bureaucrats. In school districts, for example,

the school superintendent is the major formulator of educational policy, and school boards adopt the policies recommended by their superintendents an astonishing 99 percent of the time. "The superintendent—far more than the board—is identified publicly as the 'governor' of education."[153]

Is this accretion by bureaucrats of local policymaking power a good thing? It likely is. An extensive investigation found that "democratic accountability" is greatly enhanced by city managers who actively involve themselves in local policymaking, and this is particularly true in light of "the diminishing role of elected officials in providing political guidance."[154]

The Demise of Democracy?   Local managers are not merely making public policy. They are replacing local legislators as the effective political representatives of the people. "This finding represents a significant departure" from previous research, and marks a new nadir for local democracy.[155]

A remarkable 70 percent of city managers spend "more than half their time.... on self-selected tasks [rather] than on tasks imposed by others," such as by council members, leaving them free "to work on tasks that they find most appealing." What these managers find most appealing is taking "a more active political role" in their communities; exhibiting "a strong preference" to communicate directly with citizens (another analysis found that city managers "have not taken advantage of the Internet to bring citizens closer to their governments because these officials strongly prefer traditional citizen participation"[156]); and considering "citizen input in their decision making." City managers "more directly and visibly influence the development of public policy by working more closely with citizens and assuming the mantle of community leadership."[157]

Is there any remaining rationale to elect local legislators to office?

Stopping Power

Bureaucrats, in brief, have the power to do things. They also possess the power to not do things.

Consider the case of John R. Bolton as arms-control chief in the State Department. During President George W. Bush's first term, Bolton allegedly stymied for two years the disposal of sixty-eight tons of Russian plutonium capable of fueling 8,000 nuclear bombs (a task that he was charged with facilitating, not undermining); withheld American support from Europe for a joint approach regarding Iran's nuclear plans; and blocked a new initiative concerning the sharing of civilian nuclear technology with India.

In 2005, the president appointed a new secretary of state and Bolton as ambassador to the United Nations, moves that effectively cut Bolton out from these policymaking loops. Almost immediately, the logjams on these and other issues broke. As a former official at Foggy Bottom put it, "throughout his career...he was always playing the stopper role.... Even when there was an obvious interest by the president to move things forward, Bolton often found ways of stopping things by tying the interagency process in knots."[158] Or, as a federal administrator phrased it when addressing another incident of bureaucratic stopping power, "policy is not what the president says in speeches. Policy is what emerges from interagency meetings."[159]

The Contest for Control

In light of the impressive quantum of power that bureaucrats have accrued in both the executive and legislative branches of governments, how do elected chief executives control "their" bureaucracies? In local governments, as we have seen, the battle for bureaucratic control is largely over, and has been won—with the blessings of their elected officials—by the bureaucrats themselves. In the national and state governments, however, the contest continues. In Washington, that fight is waged between the president and the bureaucracy itself. In the states, the battle is fought between governors and legislators.

Presidents *versus* Bureaucrats: Mobilizing the Bureaucracy

Nowhere is this challenge more daunting than in that biggest bureaucracy of all, the federal service.

Presidential Frustration Consider the following comments made by presidents about "their" bureaucracy.

- Harry Truman: "I thought I was the president, but when it comes to these bureaucrats, I can't do a damn thing."[160]
- John F. Kennedy told a caller, "I agree with you, but I don't know if the government will."[161]
- Richard Nixon: "We have no discipline in this bureaucracy! We never fire anybody! We never reprimand anybody! We never demote anybody!"[162]
- Jimmy Carter, in the final year of his presidency: "Before I became president, I realized and was warned that dealing with the federal bureaucracy would be one of worst problems I would have to face. It has been worse than I had anticipated."[163]

Why do presidents feel this way? We offer a couple of small but revealing examples:

Some years ago, President John F. Kennedy was pestered by his brother, Attorney General Robert Kennedy, over the fact that, during his daily commute, he could see a large sign directing drivers to the Central Intelligence Agency's headquarters, which, in his view, should not be advertised. President Kennedy ordered an aide to have the sign removed; the aide, in turn, directed the Interior Department to remove it. Nothing happened. A few days later, the president repeated his order. Again, nothing happened. Aggravated by both the bureaucracy and his brother's badgering, the president personally called the official in charge of signs: "This is Jack Kennedy. It's eleven o'clock in the morning. I want that sign down by the time the attorney general goes home tonight, and I'm holding you personally responsible." The sign was removed and the president had learned a lesson: "I now understand that for a president to get something done in this country, he's got to say it three times."[164]

Such an understanding of supposed bureaucratic inertia is held by most presidents. But quite the opposite can occur. President Carter's daughter, Amy, was having difficulty one Friday afternoon on a homework problem about the industrial revolution. Amy asked her mother for help, who asked an aide if she knew the answer. The aide called the Labor Department for assistance. Labor was pleased to oblige. On Sunday, a truck pulled up to the White House with Amy's answer: a massive computer printout, costing an estimated $300,000 and requiring a special team of analysts to work overtime. The Department thought it was responding to an order from the president. Amy received a "C" for her homework assignment.[165]

Bringing Bureaucracy to Heel? As these incidents reveal, gaining presidential control over a colossal bureaucracy involves clarity and communication, skill and will. Some presidents have no clear vision of what they want to do (George H. W. Bush,[166] Bill Clinton[167]). Others do not comprehend the criticality of the bureaucracy in securing their place in history (Richard Nixon, at least in his first term,[168] and Clinton,[169] who imprudently kept his naïve and rash campaign promise to cut the White House staff by a fourth, filled the resultant vacuum with unpaid interns, one of whom he had an affair with, leading to his disbarment and impeachment[170]). Hence, not much gets done. Other presidents, however, do have goals, and appreciate the civil service's importance in attaining them, but lack the skills needed to master the bureaucracy.[171] Lyndon Baines Johnson,[172] Nixon in his second term,[173] and Jimmy Carter[174] are exemplary.

We offer two opposing and extreme examples of presidents' attitudes and actions in bringing their bureaucracies to heel.

Executive Expertise The president who was most skilled in mobilizing his bureaucracy behind his vision was Ronald Reagan. So devoted were Reagan's appointees that they served 52 percent longer in their offices than did those appointed by Bill Clinton, and there is "no statistically significant difference in duration of appointee service for the two Bush administrations relative to the Clinton administration."[175]

"Few if any presidential administrations come to Washington with as clear a game plan as the Reagan administration had," and this clarity was critical to its relative bureaucratic success.[176] Reagan centralized personnel selection in the White House; appointed loyal fellow ideologues not only as Cabinet secretaries, but, of even greater importance, to operational positions deep in the bureaucracy (often, long before he appointed

the secretaries to whom they reported); and then decentralized power to them.[177]

Crucially, Reagan did not eschew competence in his appointments. "Ronald Reagan pursued managers," but he "shrewdly coupled loyalty to the Reagan agenda with federal management experience."[178]

Presidential Indifference President George W. Bush seems to have had neither a program, other than cutting taxes and responding to 9/11, nor an ability to manage the bureaucracy—or even an interest in doing so. Former insiders portray him not as the self-declared "decider," but rather as a dissociated ditherer on most important issues, allowing them to fester among his executives. When a policy eventually was chosen, he typically failed to marshal his bureaucracy behind it.[179]

Here is how Bush's National Security Adviser, in an "extraordinary remark," put it: Bush "will talk with great authority and assertiveness.... 'This is what we are going to do.' And he won't mean it. Because he will not have gone through the considered process where he finally is prepared to say, 'I've decided.'" Historians will conclude from the written record that, "'Well, he decided on this day to do such and such.' It's not true. It's not history. It's a fact, but it's a misleading fact."[180]

We offer a small, but revealing, example. An obsolete relic of the Cold War (and one that remains supremely annoying to Russia) is the Jackson–Vanik amendment to the Trade Act of 1974, which links trade with free emigration, an issue that expired with the Soviet Union. In 2002, officials determined that the president needed to make just four phone calls to congressional leaders to end Jackson-Vanik, "but they found that getting the president to schedule the calls was impossible, no matter how hard they tried."[181]

Control and Autonomy There can be little doubt that the immensity, complexity, and publicness of the federal service are unique presidential challenges, but an irony in presidents' exertions to bring their bureaucracy to heel is that the problem often resides not with the bureaucrats, but with them. Many presidents do not have a concrete mission in mind, and, without one, coherent policy directives, other than a demand for loyalty, are often absent.

When the president's program is clear, top federal careerists are extraordinarily responsive, even by White House standards. For more than forty years, from almost four-fifths to more than nine-tenths, depending on the administration, of all presidential appointees have fulsomely praised the competence and responsiveness of career public administrators.[182] The "evidence is overwhelming that experienced political appointees, regardless of administration, party, or ideology, believe that career executives are both competent and responsive."[183]

The central question is less one of presidential dominance of their bureaucracies *versus* the bureaucrats' drive for autonomy, and more of a recognition that "democratic control and bureaucratic autonomy are not incompatible." When elected executives and administrators respect each other and work together, the governed benefit.[184]

A Bureaucracy Newly Girded Bureaucratic sabotage of presidential policies, while not utterly absent,[185] is so rare as to be almost nonexistent. Federal administrators, however, do resist the politicization of their agencies, and they are getting better at it. Over time, "the capacity of the bureaucracy to fight back" presidential attempts to undermine its professionalism "has improved substantially—because of shifting cultural attitudes about the legitimacy of bureaucratic dissent, better legal protections for whistle-blowers...technological changes that have made it easier to broadcast leaks.... [and] a lucrative market for insider accounts of the administration's decision making." These add up "to a significant new check on presidential authority."[186]

Governors *versus* Legislators: The Battle for the Bureaucracy

"The struggle to control state bureaucracy is one of the long-standing conflicts of state politics,"[187] and it pits governors against legislators.

In 1964, only 32 percent of state agency heads reported that their governors had greater control over their agencies than the legislature, and 44 percent said that the legislature had more control. Today, these figures have reversed: 45 percent of agency chiefs say that the governor

exercises more control than the legislature, and those who report that the legislature has greater control has slipped to 32 percent; a fourth say that they are "each the same," a proportion that has held remarkably constant over forty-four years.[188] However, only about a third of state budget chiefs think that their governors are their states' principal budget shapers, a decline of almost two-fifths over twelve years.[189]

Empirical research finds that governors and legislatures are essentially dead even in their control of executive agencies. The governors' influence over their agencies in four vital areas dealing with policy development is statistically the same as that of the legislatures' influence over the agencies.[190]

Over time, governors have gained some power over their bureaucracies, but it is indisputable that their authority remains severely constrained. A half-century-long study of some 1,000 state agencies concludes that "the degree of executive control in the American states is modest at best."[191]

KNOWLEDGE: THE BASE OF BUREAUCRATIC POWER

How has the bureaucracy grown so in political importance and independence?

Knowledge Is Power

The old saw "knowledge is power" has never been more salient than it is today. "Administration is knowledge. Knowledge is power. Administration is power." This "simplistic syllogism"[192] has been reduced to the phrase, *noetic authority*, or the power that derives from knowledge.[193]

Public administrators work in bureaucracies, and bureaucracies are more likely to be found in big, complicated systems and societies, where knowledge is critical to success and often to survival. The more economically and socially complex states, for instance, also have the more advanced, informed, and well-developed legislative bureaucracies.[194] The larger the city, the likelier the city manager will be intensely involved in municipal policymaking.[195] School superintendents have far more power relative to their school boards in big cities, substantially less power in the suburbs, and even less power in small towns.[196]

Max Weber, the famous theorist on bureaucracy, noted a century ago: "In facing a parliament, a bureaucracy, out of a sure power instinct, fights every attempt of the parliament to gain knowledge by means of its own experts or from interest groups…. bureaucracy naturally welcomes a poorly informed and hence a powerless parliament—at least insofar as ignorance somehow agrees with the bureaucracy's interests."[197]

Public administrators, who fully comprehend the connection between knowledge and power, are quick to defend their monopoly on knowledge. Because they might threaten their knowledge monopolies, most city managers oppose the provision of a full-time separate staff for the mayor, 60 percent strongly object to a full-time, paid city council ("This item evoked the strongest expression of opinion in the entire series of questions"), and 77 percent always or nearly always resist council involvement in "management issues" (which can be, in reality, policy issues).[198]

When forces external to the executive branch do gain knowledge, they also gain power at its expense; often, they institutionalize their new knowledge by creating their own counter-bureaucracies. Usually, state agency heads possess "bureaucratic information asymmetry"—that is, they have the most access to the most knowledge about their programs—but not always. When governors, legislators, or lobbyists "have informational advantages over estimated program costs" they "significantly affect agency budget requests."[199] The more highly professionalized the state legislature, and the larger its staff, the lower the influence of the executive agencies in their own policy areas.[200]

As a matter of course, bureaucracy and knowledge reside most frequently in the executive branch. Potentially, however, any branch of government, and any special interest, can create its own bureaucratic knowledge base, and when it does, power follows.

Knowledge, Power, and the Public Interest

As we all know, power can be misused, and, because knowledge is power, knowledge sometimes is deliberately distorted to serve the powerful. Consider some examples:

- President Nixon ordered his Bureau of Labor Statistics to stop holding news conferences in which politically embarrassing monthly unemployment figures were released and interpreted.[201]
- Vice President Al Gore "drove some environmental researchers out of government positions because their views on global warming and ozone depletion clashed with his own."[202]
- In 2004, the chief actuary of the Medicare program calculated (accurately, as it turned out) that the proposed new benefit of adding prescription drugs would cost about $150 billion more than the White House said it would cost, and reported that his politically appointed boss, the head of Medicare, had threatened to fire him if he released his analysis, an act that has been illegal since 1912.[203]
- Toward the close of President George W. Bush's second term, the Associated Press noted "a pattern by the Bush administration not to seek input from its scientists" concerning science-based policy, relying instead on lawyers and ideologues.[204] Sixty percent of nearly 1,600 scientists in the Environmental Protection Agency[205] and 58 percent of more than 1,600 climate scientists in seven federal agencies[206] reported that they had experienced "political interference" with their work over the past five years.
- A parallel pattern of ignoring or misrepresenting informed sources was evident regarding 9/11 and the subsequent decision to invade Iraq. The White House scotched the 9/11 Commission's conclusion that officials of the Federal Aviation Administration ignored numerous advanced warnings concerning possible airline hijackings and suicide missions by Al Qaeda terrorists.[207] In an apparent effort to drum up support for the invasion of Iraq, the under secretary of defense for policy, according to the Defense Department's own

inspector general, manufactured a case for an Iraq–Al Qaeda relationship that was never vetted by the intelligence community and not supported by intelligence. A "Senior Intelligence Analyst…countered, point-by-point, each instance of an alleged tie between Iraq and al-Qaida" pushed by the under secretary.[208]

- And, in a sad reprise of an earlier presidency, the Bureau of Labor Statistics in 2005 was ordered to stop reporting mass layoffs.[209]

Fortunately, these incidents are the exception, not the rule. "Politics as usual? Not really. Hard as it may be to believe…the executive branch has traditionally succeeded at hewing to the ideals of objectivity and nonpartisanship." Government agencies "have produced reliable numbers, even when those numbers have made sitting Presidents look worse…. The people who have made this possible are among the most heavily scorned figures in American life—George Wallace's 'pointy-headed bureaucrats.'" Yet, these bureaucrats are "the only professionals in government—the only ones to say what they think instead of what they believe their bosses and voters want them to. Would we trust the unemployment numbers if, every time a new President came along, he replaced the entire Bureau of Labor Statistics with a new crop of cronies and campaign aides?"[210]

Therein lies the power—and the honor—of the public administrator.

NOTES

1. Charles C. Mann, "The Founding Sachems," *New York Times* (July 4, 2005).
2. Ethnographer Lewis Henry Morgan, as quoted in ibid.
3. Woodrow Wilson, "The Study of Administration," *Political Science Quarterly* 2 (June/July 1887), pp. 197–222, especially pp. 206–219; the quotation is on p. 206.
4. Garry Wills, *A Necessary Evil: A History of American Distrust of Government* (New York: Simon & Schuster, 1999), p. 66.
5. John C. Beach, Elaine D. Carter, Martha J. Dede, *et al.*, "State Administration and the Founding Fathers During the Critical Period," *Administration & Society* 28 (February 1997), pp. 511–530.
6. Steven Hill, as cited in Patrick Garvin, "American Democracy: Can It Be Repaired?" *American Examiner* (August 3, 2006). In 1790, about 200,000 people in a population of 3,929,214 could vote. Voters had to be propertied white men, although free black men could vote in three states.
7. Josiah Tucker, as quoted in Page Smith, *The Constitution: A Documentary and Narrative History* (New York: Morrow Quill, 1980), p. 82.
8. William Kent, *Memoirs and Letters of James Kent* (Boston: Little, Brown, 1898), pp. 327–328. Kent was a contemporary of Hamilton's.
9. Alexander Hamilton, "No. 70," *The Federalist Papers*, Clinton Rossiter, ed. (New York: New American Library, 1961), p. 423.
10. Lynton K. Caldwell, "The Administrative Republic: The Contrasting Legacies of Hamilton and Jefferson," *Public Administration Quarterly* 13 (Winter 1990), pp. 470–494. The quotation is on p. 482.
11. Thomas Jefferson, writing in 1810, as quoted in Wills, *A Necessary Evil*, p. 53.
12. Richard Nixon, as quoted from his interview of April 6, 1977, with David Frost, in http://www.historycommons.org.
13. Allensbach Opinion Research Institute, National Opinion Research Center, and Pew Research Center for the People & the Press, as cited in "A Nation Apart," *The Economist* (November 6, 2003), http://www.economist.com. Data are for 2003.
14. Pew Research Center for the People and the Press, *Independents Take Center Stage in Obama Era* (May 21, 2009), Section 2, http://people-press.org/report/517/political-values-and-core-attitudes. In 2009, 76 percent of whites, 63 percent of blacks, and 62 percent of Hispanics agreed with the statement, percentages that were much the same in 2007.
15. Aidan W. Southall, *Alur Society: A Study in Processes and Types of Domination* (Cambridge: Cambridge University Press, 1953), p. 195.

16. Mark L. Goldstein, *America's Hollow Government: How Washington Has Failed the People* (Homewood, IL: Business One Irwin, 1992).

17. Sarah A. Binder, "Going Nowhere: A Gridlocked Congress," *Brookings Review* 18 (Winter 2000), pp. 16–19.

18. Jonathan Rauch, *Demosclerosis: America's Silent Killer* (New York: Time Books, 1994).

19. John Kane and Haig Patapan, "In Search of Prudence: The Hidden Problem of Managerial Reform," *Public Administration Review* 66 (September/October 2006), pp. 711–724. The quotation is on p. 711.

20. Quoted in Ken Auletta, "The Lost Tycoon," *The New Yorker* (April 23 and 30, 2001), pp. 138–163. The quotation is on p. 154.

21. Pew Research Center for the People and the Press, *Distrust, Discontent, Anger and Partisan Rancor: The People and Their Government* (Washington, DC: Author, 2010), Section 4, http://people-press.org/report/606/trust-in-government. Data are for 2010, and apply only to elected federal officials.

22. Gregory B. Lewis, "In Search of Machiavellian Milquetoasts: Comparing Attitudes of Bureaucrats and Ordinary People," *Public Administration Review* 50 (March/April 1990), pp. 220–227. The quotation is on p. 223.

23. Pew Research Center for the People and the Press, *Deconstructing Distrust: How Americans View Government* (Washington, DC: Author, 1998), p. 2.

24. Shlomo Mizrahi, Eran Vigoda-Gadot, and Gregg Van Ryzin, "Public Sector Management, Trust, Performance, and Participation," *Public Performance & Management Review* 32 (December 2010), pp. 268–312. The quotation is on p. 268.

25. Pew Research Center for the People and the Press, *Distrust, Discontent, Anger and Partisan Rancor*, Sections 2 and 1.

26. As derived from data in ibid., Section 3. Figures are for 1997–2010. Growth figure is 61 percent.

27. Pew Research Center for the People and the Press, *Independents Take Center Stage in Obama Era*, Section 2. Figure, 49 percent, is for 2010. In 1987, 57 percent thought this.

28. Pew Research Center for the People and the Press, *Distrust, Discontent, Anger and Partisan Rancor*, Sections 2 and 1. Those who favored

29. National Academy of Public Administration, *Key Issues of Governance, Public Management, and Public Administration* (Washington, DC: Author, 1999), p. 6. This is a survey of the Fellows of the National Academy of Public Administration, 1998–1999.

30. Richard Wike and Kathleen Holzwart, *Where Trust Is High, Crime and Corruption Are Low* (Washington, DC: Pew Global Attitudes Project, Pew Research Center for the People and the Press, 2008). Data were collected in thirty-nine countries on five continents in 2007.

31. Akira Nakamura and Soonhee Kim, "Public Trust in Government in Japan and South Korea: Does the Rise of Critical Citizens Matter?" *Public Administration Review* 70 (September/October 2010), pp. 801–810. The quotation is on p. 801.

32. Vadim Radaev, "Coping with Distrust in Emerging Russian Markets," *Distrust*, Russell Hardin, ed. (New York: Russell Sage Foundation, 2004), pp. 233–245.

33. Erik-Hans Klijn, Jurian Edelenbos, and Bram Steijn, "Trust in Governance Networks: Its Impact on Outcomes," *Administration & Society* 42 (April 2010), pp. 193–221. The quotation is on p. 193.

34. Christopher J. Anderson and Yuliya V. Tverdova, "Corruption, Political Allegiances, and Attitudes Toward Government in Contemporary Democracies," *American Journal of Politics* 47 (January 2003), pp. 91–109. Data are for 1996. This is an analysis of surveys conducted in sixteen "mature and newly established democracies around the globe."

35. Wike and Holzwart, *Where Trust Is High, Crime and Corruption Are Low*.

36. Geoffrey Brennan and Philip Pettit, *The Economy of Esteem* (New York: Oxford University Press, 2004).

37. Ibid.; and Daniel Carpenter, *Reputation and Power: Organizational Image and Pharmaceutical Regulation at the FDA* (Princeton, NJ: Princeton University Press, 2010).

38. Gary LaFree, *Losing Legitimacy: Street Crime and the Decline of Social Institutions in America* (Boulder, CO: Westview Press, 1998).

39. Marc J. Heatherington, *Why Trust Matters: Declining Political Trust and the Demise of*

major reform increased from 37 to 53 percent, 1997–2010.

Liberalism (Princeton, NJ: Princeton University Press, 2004).

40. William Barnes and Bonnie Mann, *Making Local Democracy Work: Municipal Officials' Views about Public Engagement* (Washington, DC: National League of Cities, 2010), p. 18. Data are for 2009.

41. Shlomo Mizrahi, Eran Vigoda-Gadot, and Nissim Cohen, "Trust, Participation, and Performance in Public Administration: An Empirical Examination of Health Services in Israel," *Public Performance & Management Review* 33 (September 2009), pp. 7–33. The quotations are on pp. 7, 27.

42. Stephen Knack and Philip Keefer, "Does Social Capital Have an Economic Payoff? A Cross-Country Investigation," *Quarterly Journal of Economics* 102 (November 1997), pp. 1251–1288. This is an analysis of twenty-nine market economies.

43. Christopher A. Cooper, H. Gibbs Knotts, and Kathleen M. Brennan, "The Importance of Trust in Government for Public Administration: The Case of Zoning," *Public Administration Review* 68 (May/June 2008), pp. 459–467. The quotations are on pp. 459, 464.

44. Mizrahi, Vigoda-Gadot, and Cohen, "Trust, Participation, and Performance in Public Administration."

45. Stephen Knack, *Social Capital and the Quality of Government: Evidence from the U.S. States,* World Bank Policy Research Working Paper No. 2504 (Washington, DC: World Bank Development Research Group, 2000).

46. Johnny Goldfinger and Margaret R. Ferguson, "Social Capital and Governmental Performance in Large American Cities," *State and Local Government Review* 41 (Winter 2009), pp. 25–36. The data are on p. 32.

47. Remarks made in 2002 by Secretary of Defense Donald Rumsfeld, as quoted in Jonathan D. Breul, "Three Bush Administration Management Reform Initiatives: The President's Management Agenda, Freedom to Manage Legislative Proposals, and the Program Assessment Rating Tool," *Public Administration Review* 67 (January/February 2007), pp. 21–27. The quotation is on p. 23.

48. Caldwell, "The Administrative Republic," pp. 483–484.

49. Stephanie P. Newbold, "Statesmanship and Ethics: The Case of Thomas Jefferson's Dirty Hands," *Public Administration Review* 65 (November/December 2005), pp. 669–677. The quotations are on p. 671.

50. Thad Beyle, "The Governors," *Politics in the American States: A Comparative Analysis,* 6th ed., Virginia Gray and Herbert Jacob, eds. (Washington, DC: CQ Press, 1996), pp. 207–252.

51. Chreyl M. Miller and Deil S. Wright, "Who's Minding Which Store? Institutional and Other Actors' Influence on Administrative Rulemaking in State Agencies, 1978–2004," *Public Administration Quarterly* 33 (Fall 2009), pp. 397–428. The quotation is on p. 403. Six surveys of agency heads were conducted over the period.

52. Thad L. Beyle, "Enhancing Executive Leadership in the States," *State and Local Government Review* 27 (Winter 1995), pp. 18–35. The quotation and data are on p. 29.

53. National Commission on the State and Local Public Service, *Hard Truths/Tough Choices: An Agenda for State and Local Government Reform,* First Report (Albany, NY: Nelson A. Rockefeller Institute of Government, State University of New York, 1993), pp. 16–17.

54. Beyle, "Enhancing Executive Leadership in the States," pp. 20–21. Figures are for 1955–1994.

55. Miller and Wright, "Who's Minding Which Store?" p. 410.

56. As derived from data in Council of State Governments, *Book of the States, 2010,* (Lexington, KY: Author, 2010), Table 4.12. Figures are for 2010.

57. As derived from data in ibid. Table 4.10. Data are for 2010.

58. National Conference of State Legislatures, *Legislative Term Limits: An Overview* (Washington, DC: Author, 2010). Figure is for 2010.

59. As derived from data in Council of State Governments, *Book of the States, 2010,* Table 4.9. Figure is for 2010.

60. National Council of State Legislators, *Recall of State Officials* (Washington, DC: Author, 2006).

61. Tanis J. Salant, "Trends in County Government Structures," *Municipal Year Book, 2004* (Washington, DC: International City/County Management Association, 2004), p. 39. Figure is for 2002.

62. U.S. Bureau of Census, *Census of Governments, 1992,* Vol. 1, No. 2 (Washington, DC: U.S. Government Printing Office, 1995), pp. 9–19. Figure is for 1992, and includes council presidents.

63. Evelina R. Moulder, "Municipal Form of Government: Trends in Structure, Responsibility, and Composition," *Municipal Year Book, 2008* (Washington, DC: International City/County Management Association, 2008), p. 38. Figure is for 2006, and includes council presidents.

64. Ibid., p. 39, and Salant, "Trends in County Government Structures," p. 40. In 2006, 9 percent of mayors had term limits, and in 2002, 4 percent of county commission chairs had them.

65. Ibid.; Salant, "Trends in County Government Structures"; and Susan A. MacManus and Charles S. Bullock, III, "The Form, Structure, and Composition of America's Municipalities in the New Millennium," *Municipal Year Book, 2003* (Washington, DC: International City/County Management Association, 2003), pp. 3–18.

66. Ryan Holeywell, "Recall Fever," *Governing* (April 2011), pp. 44–48. Figure is for 2011.

67. Moulder, "Municipal Form of Government," p. 5. Figure, 60 percent, is for 2006.

68. Edgar E. Ramirez de la Cruz, "County Form of Government: Trends in Structure and Composition," *Municipal Year Book, 2009* (Washington, DC: International City/County Management Association, 2009), pp. 21–27. Figure, 55 percent (p. 26), is for 2007.

69. National Council of State Legislators, *Recall of State Officials.*

70. As derived from data in *Political Recall Efforts,* Ballotpedia, http://www.ballotpedia.org/wiki/index.php/Political_recall_efforts. In 2008, there were eight recall efforts; in 2007, three; and in 2006, two. Figures for success, defeat, and failure to make the ballot are for 2009.

71. Holeywell, "Recall Fever," pp. 45, 46. Mayoral recall attempts rose from twenty-three (of which five were successful) to fifty-seven (fifteen succeeded), 2009–2010.

72. National Conference of State Legislatures, *Initiative, Referendum and Recall* (Washington, DC: Author, 2010). Figure is for 2010.

73. Initiative and Referendum Institute, *Ballotwatch* (Los Angeles: Author, 2010), p. 1.

74. National Conference of State Legislatures, *Initiative, Referendum and Recall.* Figure is for 2010.

75. Initiative and Referendum Institute, *Overview of Initiative Use, 1904–2009* (Los Angeles: Author, 2010), p. 1. Figures exclude initiatives seeking to repeal laws and refer only to those seeking to enact new laws or constitutional amendments.

76. As derived from data in ibid.; and Initiative and Referendum Institute, *Ballotwatch*, p. 1. Forty-one percent of state initiatives have been approved by voters, 1904–2010. Figure excludes initiatives seeking to repeal laws and refers only to those seeking to enact new laws or constitutional amendments.

77. Moulder, "Municipal Form of Government," p. 5. Figures are for 2006.

78. Ramirez de la Cruz, "County Form of Government," p. 26. Figures, 71 and 72 percent, respectively, are for 2007. Initiatives include popular referenda; both devices require citizens to collect signatures on petitions.

79. John G. Matsusaka, "Fiscal Effects of the Voter Initiative: Evidence from the Past 30 Years," *Journal of Political Economy* 103 (June 1995), pp. 587–623.

80. Carl J. Gabrini, "Do Institutions Matter? The Influence of Institutions of Direct Democracy on Local Government Spending," *State and Local Government Review* 42 (December 2010), pp. 210–225. The quotation is on p. 222.

81. Silika Prohl and Friedrich Schneider, "Does Decentralization Reduce Government Size? A Quantitative Study of the Decentralization Hypothesis," *Public Finance Review* 37 (November 2009), pp. 639–664.

82. Lorenz Blume, Jens Muller, and Stefan Voigt, "The Economic Effects of Direct Democracy—A First Global Assessment," *Public Choice* 140 (September 2009), pp. 431–461. Numbers of countries with mandatory national referenda and national initiatives were derived from data on p. 439.

83. U.S. Advisory Commission on Intergovernmental Relations, *The Federal Role in the Federal System: The Dynamics of Growth, A Crisis of Confidence and Competence,* A-77 (Washington, DC: U.S. Government Printing Office, 1980), pp. 131, 111.

84. As derived from data in U.S. Bureau of the Census, *Statistical Abstract of the United States, 2011,* 130th ed. (Washington, DC: U.S. Government Printing Office, 2011), Tables 2, 459, 428, and 1358. The government employment-to-population ratio is for 2008. Government receipts as a percentage of GDP are for 2009.

85. As derived from data in American Council on Intergovernmental Relations, *Significant Features of Fiscal Federalism, 1995,* Vol. 2 (Washington, DC: Author, 1998), p. 54, for 1978–1994 growth rates, and David Osborne and Peter Hutchinson, *The Price of Government: Getting the Results We Need in an Age of Permanent Fiscal Crisis* (New York: Basic Books, 2004), pp. 44–47, for subsequent growth rates.

86. As derived from data in American Council on Intergovernmental Relations, *Significant Features of Fiscal Federalism, 1995*, Vol. 2, p. 54. Current growth rates are for 1978–1994. State and local revenue growth refers to revenue derived from these governments' own revenue sources and does not include intergovernmental revenue transferred to them by other governments.

87. John E. Petersen, "Debtor's Dilemma," *Governing* (May 2004), p. 78.

88. As derived from data in U.S. Bureau of the Census, *Statistical Abstract of the United States, 2011,* Table 1359. Figures are for 2009. The United States ranks lowest out of all twenty-four countries.

89. Sven Steinmo, "Why Is Government So Small in America?" *Governance* 8 (July 1995), pp. 303–334.

90. Rati Ram, "Government Spending and Happiness of the Population: Additional Evidence from Large Cross-Country Samples," *Public Choice* 138 (March 2009), pp. 483–490. The quotations are on p. 483.

91. Annenberg Campaign Data Base, as cited in Paul C. Light, *The True Size of Government* (Washington, DC: Brookings, 1999), p. 88.

92. Subcommittee on Intergovernmental Relations, Committee on Government Operations, U.S. Senate, *Confidence and Concern: Citizens View American Government, A Survey of Public Attitudes, Part 2,* 93rd Congress, 1st Session (Washington, DC: U.S. Government Printing Office, 1973), p. 310. This reports a national Harris poll conducted in 1973. The precise percentages, in order of their citation, are: 14 *versus* 6 percent ("dull"); 25 *versus* 12 percent ("red tape"); and 58 *versus* 14 percent ("bureaucratic").

93. Thad E. Hall, "Live Bureaucrats and Dead Public Servants: How People in Government Are Discussed on the Floor of the House," *Public Administration Review* 62 (March 2002), pp. 242–251. This is an analysis of House of Representatives in the 104th Congress.

94. Marc Schwerdt, "Stories of Service: Public Service in the Children's Literature of United States and Great Britain," *Politics and Policy* 31 (June 2003), pp. 195–214.

95. Beverly A. Cigler and Heidi L. Neiswender, "Bureaucracy in the Introductory American Government Textbook," *Public Administration Review* 51 (September/October 1991), pp. 442–450. The quotation is on p. 444.

96. David J. Lorenzo, "Countering Popular Misconceptions of Federal Bureaucracies in American Government Classes," *Political Science and Politics* 32 (December 1999), pp. 743–747. The quotation is on p. 744.

97. Council for Excellence in Government and Center for Media and Public Affairs, *Government: In and Out of the News* (Washington, DC: Authors, 2003), pp. 6, 5, 36, 125, 75.

98. Beth A. Wielde and David Schultz, "Public Administration and Pop Culture," *PA Times* (November 2007), pp. 3, 6. Figure is for 1990–2007.

99. Carrie Rickey, "Hollywood Movies Cast Government as Bad Guy," *Philadelphia Inquirer* (July 7, 1996). The review covered 1990–1995.

100. S. Robert Lichter, Linda S. Lichter, and Dan Amundson, *Changing Images of Government in TV Entertainment* (Washington, DC: Center for Media and Public Affairs and Council for Excellence in Government, 2002), p. 8. Figures are for 1999–2001.

101. S. Robert Lichter, Linda S. Lichter, and Dan Amundson, *Government Goes Down the Tube: Images of Government in TV Entertainment* (Washington, DC: Center for Media and Public Affairs and Council for Excellence in Government, 1999), p. 19.

102. Lichter, Lichter, and Amundson, *Changing Images of Government in TV Entertainment*, p. 12.

103. Council for Excellence in Government, Gallup, and Accenture, *The Appeal of Public Service: Who…What…and How?* (Washington, DC: Authors, 2008), p. 6. In 2008, about one out of three Americans aged eighteen to twenty-nine cited Mayor Quimby. Those thirty and older preferred Detective Olivia Benson of *Law and Order, SVU.*

104. Charles T. Goodsell, *The Case for Bureaucracy: A Public Administration Polemic,* 2nd ed. (Chatham, NJ: Chatham House, 1985), p. 106. This is the conclusion drawn from a review of surveys on the topic.

105. Pew Research Center for the People and the Press, *Deconstructing Distrust*, p. 2. In 1997, 69 percent of respondents had a favorable opinion of government workers, and in 1981, 55 percent did.

106. Council for Excellence in Government and Hart-Teeter Poll, *America Unplugged: Citizens and Their Government* (Washington, DC: Authors, 1999), p. 4. Figures are for 1999.

107. Steven A. Peterson, "Sources of Citizens' Bureaucratic Contacts: A Multivariate Analysis," *Administration & Society* 20 (August 1988), pp. 152–165; and Charles T. Goodsell, *The Case for Bureaucracy: A Public Administration Polemic*, 4th ed. (Washington, DC: CQ Press, 2004), Chapter 2.

108. Subcommittee on Intergovernmental Relations, Committee on Government Operations, U.S. Senate, *Confidence and Concern, Part 1*, pp. 173–175, and *Part 2*, pp. 301, 303, 305, 311, 313, 315, 319, 321. Data are for 1973.

109. Daniel Katz, Barbara A. Gutek, Robert L. Kahn, and Eugenia Barton, *Bureaucratic Encounters* (Ann Arbor, MI: Institute for Social Research, University of Michigan, 1975), pp. 64, 68, 69, and 221. Data are for 1973.

110. American Customer Satisfaction Index, *Special Report on Government Services* (Ann Arbor, MI: Author, 2011), p. 1. Figures are averages for all federal agencies, 1999–2010.

111. As derived from data in Subcommittee on Intergovernmental Relations, Committee on Government Operations, U.S. Senate, *Confidence and Concern, Part 1*, pp. 173–175, and *Part 2*, pp. 301, 303, 305, 311, 313, 315, 319, and 321; Barbara J. Nelson, "Clients and Bureaucracies: Applicant Evaluations of Public Human Service and Benefit Programs," Paper Presented at the Annual Meeting of the American Political Science Association (Washington, DC, 1979), pp. 6–8; and Stuart M. Schmidt, "Client-Oriented Evaluation of Public Agency Effectiveness," *Administration & Society* 8 (February 1977), pp. 412, 421–422.

112. Thomas I. Miller and Michelle A. Miller, "Standards of Excellence: U.S. Residents' Evaluations of Local Government Services," *Public Administration Review* 51 (November/December 1991), pp. 503–514. The quotation is on p. 503. This is a "meta-analysis" of 261 citizen surveys.

113. Claes Fornell, *ACSI Commentary: Government Scores (Ann Arbor, MI: American Customer Satisfaction Index, December 14, 2006), http://www.theacsi.org/index.* Figures pertain to federal services, and are for 2006.

114. John T. Tierney, *The U.S. Postal Service: Status and Prospects of a Public Enterprise* (Dover, MA: Auburn House, 1988), pp. 5–6; and Associated Press, "Postal Service Really Delivers, Most in Poll Say," *Washington Post* (January 23, 1999).

115. Susan M. Willis-Walton and Alan E. Bayer, *Quality of Life in Virginia: 2003* (Blacksburg, VA: Center for Survey Research, Virginia Polytechnic Institute and State University, 2003), pp. D9–D10.

116. Partnership for Public Service and Gallup Consulting, *In the Public We Trust: Renewing the Connection between the Federal Government and the Public* (Washington, DC, and New York: Authors, 2008), p. 3. Figures are for 2008.

117. As derived from data in Pew Research Center for the People and the Press, *Performance and Purpose: Constituents Rate Government Agencies* (Washington, DC: Author, 2000). Data are for federal agencies in 2000.

118. Jarl K. Kampen, Steven Van de Walle, and Geert Bouckaert, "Assessing the Relation Between Satisfaction with Public Service Delivery and Trust in Government: The Impact of the Predisposition of Citizens Toward Government on Evaluation of Its Performance," *Public Performance & Management Review* 29 (June 2006), pp. 387–404. The quotation is on pp. 399–400.

119. Richard A. Loverd, "Gaining the Power to Lead," *Leadership for the Public Service: Power and Policy in Action*, Richard A. Loverd, ed. (Upper Saddle River, NJ: Prentice-Hall, 1997), p. 7.

120. Herbert Kaufman, *Are Government Organizations Immortal?* (Washington, DC: Brookings, 1976). The years covered were 1923–1973. Subsequent research has questioned Kaufman's methodology, but not his conclusion, at least not definitively. See B. Guy Peters and Bryan W. Hogwood, "The Death of Immortality: Births, Deaths, and Metamorphoses in the U.S. Federal Bureaucracy, 1933–1983," *American Review of Public Administration* 18 (June 1988), pp. 119–133.

121. Jim Clark, "The International Screw Thread Commission," *Washington Monthly*, as reprinted in *Doing Public Administration: Exercises, Essays, and Cases*, Nicholas Henry, ed. (Boston: Allyn and Bacon, 1978), pp. 41–42. The quotation is on p. 42.
122. "Bureaucratic Vampires," *Wall Street Journal* (May 6, 1994).
123. Sources and details are in Chapter 9.
124. As derived from data in Partnership for Public Service and Booz Allen Hamilton, *Unrealized Vision: Reimagining the Senior Executive Service* (Washington, DC; Herndon, VA: Authors, 2009), p. 7. Data are for 2008.
125. Jeffrey L. Brudney, Brendan Burke, Chung-Lae Cho, and Deil S. Wright, "No 'One Best Way' to Manage Change: Developing and Describing Distinct Administrative Reform Dimensions Across the Fifty American States, *Public Administration Quarterly* 33 (Summer 2009), pp. 197–222. The quotations are on p. 206.
126. Rutherford H. Platt, *Disasters and Democracy: The Politics of Extreme Natural Events* (Washington, DC: Island Press, 1999), pp. 19–20. The legislation is the Robert T. Stafford Disaster Relief and Emergency Assistance Act of 1988.
127. Kenneth J. Meier and Laurence J. O'Toole, Jr., *Bureaucracy in a Democratic State: A Governance Perspective* (Baltimore, MD: Johns Hopkins University Press, 2006), p. 60.
128. Robert Kasten, "It's a Tough Competition for the Worst Regulation," *Washington Times* (July 23, 1996). The navigable waters legislation is the 1972 amendments to the Federal Water Pollution Control Act of 1956.
129. The case is *U.S. Immigration and Naturalization Service v. Chadha*.
130. As derived from data in Cornelius M. Kerwin and Scott R. Furlong, *Rulemaking: How Government Agencies Write Law and Make Policy*, 4th ed. (Washington, DC: CQ Press, 2011), p. 230.
131. John W. Kingdon, *Agendas, Alternatives, and Public Policies* (Boston: Little, Brown, 1984).
132. Ibid., p. 7. Emphasis added.
133. Ibid., pp. 46, 34.
134. U.S. Bureau of the Census, *Statistical Abstract of the United States, 2011*, Table 494. Figure is for 2009.
135. Mike Causey, "Hill Staff, Then and Now," *Washington Post* (September 30, 1991); and "Washington Pots and Kettles," *Baltimore Sun* (October 27, 1991).
136. Kingdon, *Agendas, Alternatives, and Public Policies*, p. 34.
137. For a good review of this research, as well as some original findings, see Virginia Gray and David Lowery, "Where Do Policy Ideas Come From? A Study of Minnesota Legislators and Staffers," *Journal of Public Administration Research and Theory* 10 (July 2000), pp. 573–597.
138. Jeffrey L. Brudney, Cynthia J. Bowling, and Deil S. Wright, *Continuity and Change in Public Administration Across the 50 States: Linking Practice, Theory, and Research through the American State Administrators Project, 1964–2008* (Auburn, AL: Center for Governmental Services, Auburn University, 2010), p. 6. Figures are for 1964–2008.
139. Jerrell D. Coggburn and Saundra K. Schneider, "The Quality of Management and Government Performance: An Empirical Analysis of the American States," *Public Administration Review* 63 (March/April 2003), pp. 206–213. The quotations are on p. 206.
140. As derived from data in Council of State Governments, *Book of the States, 2010*, Table 3.3. Figure, 7,333 state legislative positions, is for 2010.
141. Karl Kurtz and Brian Weberg, "The State of Staff," *State Legislatures* (July/August 2009), pp. 42–45. Figures are for 2009.
142. As derived from data in Council of State Governments, *Book of the States, 2010*, Table 3.22. Figure is for 2010. The three states are Connecticut, Idaho, and Wyoming.
143. Herbert L. Wiltsee, "Legislative Service Agencies," *Book of the States, 1961–62* (Lexington, KY: Council of State Governments, 1962), p. 67.
144. Michael J. BeVier, *Politics Backstage: Inside the California Legislature* (Philadelphia: Temple University Press, 1979), p. 229.
145. Jerri Killian and Enamul Choudhury, "Continuity and Change in the Role of City Managers," *Municipal Year Book, 2010* (Washington, DC: International City/County Management Association, 2010), pp. 10–18. The quotation is on p. 16. Figure is for 2010.
146. Charldean Newell and David M. Ammons, "Role Emphases of City Managers and Other Municipal Executives," *Public Administration*

Review 47 (May/June 1987), pp. 246–253. Datum (p. 249) is for 1985.

147. James H. Svara, "Council and Administrator Perspectives on the City Manager's Role: Conflict, Divergence, or Congruence?" *Administration & Society* 23 (August 1991), p. 231. This is a review of the literature.

148. Robert T. Golembiewski and Gerald Gabris, "Today's City Managers: A Legacy of Success-Becoming-Failure," *Public Administration Review* 54 (November/December 1994), pp. 525–530.

149. Yahong Zhang and Richard C. Feiock, "City Managers' Policy Leadership in Council-Manager Cities," *Journal of Public Administration Research and Theory* 20 (April 2010), pp. 461–476. This is a study of Florida's cities.

150. James H. Svara, "The Shifting Boundaries between Elected Officials in Large Council-Manager Cities," *Public Administration Review* 59 (January/February 1999), pp. 44–53. The quotation is on p. 50.

151. John Nalbandian, "Politics and Administration in Council-Manager Government: Differences between Newly Elected and Senior Council Members," *Public Administration Review* 64 (March/April 2004), pp. 200–209. Only council-manager cities were analyzed.

152. James H. Svara, "Leadership and Professionalism in County Government," *The American County: Frontiers of Knowledge*, Donald C. Menzel, ed. (Tuscaloosa, AL: University of Alabama Press, 1996), pp. 109–127. The quotation is on p. 118.

153. Harvey J. Tucker and L. Harmon Ziegler, *Professionals versus the Public: Attitudes, Communication, and Response in School Districts* (New York: Longman, 1980), p. 143.

154. Tansu Demir and Ronald C. Nyhan, "The Politics-Administration Dichotomy: An Empirical Search for Correspondence between Theory and Practice," *Public Administration Review* 68 (January/February 2008), pp. 81–96. The quotation is on p. 92. This is a survey of 1,000 city managers in the United States conducted in 2005.

155. Killian and Choudhury, "Continuity and Change in the Role of City Managers," pp. 16–17.

156. Stephen Kwamena Aikens and Dale Krane, "Are Public Officials Obstacles to Cintizen-Centered E-Government? An Examination of Municipal Administrators' Motivations and Actions," *State and Local Government Review* 42 (Spring 2010), pp. 87–103. The quotation is on p. 87. This is a survey of city managers in five Midwestern states.

157. Killian and Choudhury, "Continuity and Change in the Role of City Managers," pp. 15–18.

158. Peter Baker and Dafnia Linzer, "Policy Shifts Felt after Bolton's Departure from State Dept.," *Washington Post* (June 20, 2005). Rose Gottemoeller, a Clinton administration official who worked on nonproliferation issues, is quoted.

159. Peter Baker, "As Democracy Push Falters, Bush Feels Like a 'Dissident,'" *Washington Post* (August 20, 2007).

160. Quoted in Clinton Rossiter, *The American Presidency* (New York: New American Library, 1956), p. 42.

161. Quoted in Richard P. Nathan, *The Administrative Presidency* (New York: Macmillan, 1983), p. 1.

162. Quoted in Richard P. Nathan, *The Plot That Failed: Nixon and the Administrative Presidency* (New York: John Wiley and Sons, 1975), p. 69.

163. Quoted in Haynes Johnson, "Tests," *Washington Post* (April 30, 1978).

164. Quoted in Peter Goldman, *et al.*, "The Presidency: Can Anyone Do the Job?" *Newsweek* (January 26, 1981), p. 41.

165. United Press International, "Amy's Homework Aid Likely Costs Thousands," *Arizona Republic* (February 9, 1981).

166. David Mervin, *George Bush and the Guardianship Presidency* (New York: Macmillan, 1996).

167. Joel D. Aberbach and Bert A. Rockman, *In the Web of Politics: Three Decades of the U.S. Federal Executive* (Washington, DC: Brookings, 2000), pp. 39–40.

168. Nathan, *The Plot That Failed.*

169. Aberbach and Rockman, *In the Web of Politics*, pp. 39–40.

170. Norman Ornstein, "Blunders That Backfired," *Washington Post* (June 20, 1996).

171. Nathan, *The Administrative Presidency*, p. 93.

172. Randall B. Woods, *LBJ: Architect of American Ambition* (New York: Free Press, 2006).

173. Nathan, *The Plot That Failed.*

174. Aberbach and Rockman, *In the Web of Politics,* pp, 32–35; Dom Bonafede, "Carter Sounds Retreat from 'Cabinet' Government," *National Journal* (November 18, 1978), p. 1852; and James Fallows, "The Passionless President," *Atlantic Monthly* (May 1979), pp. 33–48.

175. B. Dan Wood and Miner P. Marchbanks, III, "What Determines How Long Political Appointees Serve?" *Journal of Public Administration Research and Theory* 18 (July 2008), pp. 375–396. The figure and quotation are on p. 392.

176. Aberbach and Rockman, *In the Web of Politics,* p. 35.

177. Ibid., pp. 35–37; and Shirley Anne Warshaw, "White House Control of Domestic Policy Making: The Reagan Years," *Public Administration Review* 55 (May/June 1995), pp. 247–253.

178. Warshaw, "White House Control of Domestic Policy Making," p. 250.

179. Douglas J. Feith, *War and Decision: Inside the Pentagon at the Dawn of the War on Terrorism* (New York: HarperCollins, 2008); and Scott McClellan, *What Happened: Inside the Bush White House and Washington's Culture of Deception* (Washington, DC: PublicAffairs, 2008).

180. Bob Woodward, "10 Take Aways From the Bush Years," *Washington Post* (January 18, 2009). Woodward is quoting Stephen J. Hadley's "extraordinary remark" of March 8, 2008.

181. Daniel Benjamin, "The Russians Moved Because They Know You Are Weak," *Brookings* (August 25, 2008), p. 2.

182. National Academy of Public Administration, *Leadership in Jeopardy: The Fraying of the Presidential Appointments System* (Washington, DC: Author, 1985), p. 67; and Paul C. Light and Virginia L. Thomas, *The Merit and Reputation of an Administration: Presidential Appointees on the Appointments Process* (Washington, DC: Brookings, 2000), pp. 9, 31, 32.

183. James P. Pfiffner, "Political Appointees and Career Executives: The Bureaucracy-Democracy Nexus in the Third Century," *Public Administration Review* 47 (January/February 1987), pp. 57–65. The quotation is on p. 61.

184. Doo-Rae Kim, "Political Control and Bureaucratic Autonomy Revisited: A Multi-Institutional Analysis of OSHA Enforcement," *Journal of Public Administration Research and Theory* 18 (January 2008), pp. 33–55. The quotation is on p. 33.

185. B. Dan Wood and Richard W. Waterman, *Bureaucratic Dynamics: The Role of Bureaucracy in Democracy* (Boulder, CO: Westview Press, 1994); and Marissa Martino Golden, *What Motivates Bureaucrats? Politics and Administration during the Reagan Years* (New York: Columbia University Press, 2000). The Environmental Protection Agency and the Civil Rights Division of the Justice Department resisted Reagan administration efforts to pull back their initiatives.

186. Alasdair Roberts, as quoted in Donald Moynihan, "A Crisis of Authority? A Conversation with Alasdair Roberts about the Bush Years," *Public Administration Review* 68 (May/June 2008), pp. 516–522. The quotation is on p. 517.

187. Thad Beyle and Margaret Ferguson, "Governors and the Executive Branch," *Politics in the American States: A Comparative Analysis*, 9th ed. (Washington, DC: CQ Press, 2008), pp. 192–228. The quotation is on p. 217.

188. Brudney, Bowling, and Wright, *Continuity and Change in Public Administration Across the 50 States*, p. 17. Current figures are for 2008.

189. Figures are for 1982–1994. Sources and details are in Chapter 8.

190. F. Ted Hebert, "Governors as Chief Administrators and Managers," *Handbook of State Government Administration*, John J. Gargan, ed. (New York: Marcel Dekker, 2000), pp. 107–126. In 1994, gubernatorial influence over the agencies garnered a score of 9.47 out of a possible twelve points, but legislative influence was accorded a score of 9.40, a statistically insignificant difference.

191. Yoo-Sung Choi, Chung-Lee Cho, and Deil S. Wright, "Administrative Autonomy among American State Agencies: An Empirical Analysis of Fragmentation and Functionalism," *International Journal of Public Administration* 27 (January 2004), pp. 373–398. The quotation is on p. 394.

192. James D. Carroll, "Service, Knowledge, and Choice: The Future as Post-Industrial Administration," *Public Administration Review* 35 (November/December 1975), pp. 578–581. The quotations are on p. 578.

193. James D. Carroll, "Noetic Authority," *Public Administration Review* 29 (September/October 1969), pp. 492–500.

194. Stephanie Owings and Rainald Borck, "Legislative Professionalism and Government Spending: Do Citizen Legislators Really Spend Less?" *Public Finance Review* 20 (May 2000), pp. 210–225.

195. Robert J. Huntley and Robert J. McDonald, "Urban Managers: Managerial Style and

Social Roles," *Municipal Year Book, 1975* (Washington, DC: International City Management Association, 1975), pp. 149–159. The datum is on p. 153.

196. Harmon Ziegler and M. Kent Jennings, with the assistance of G. Wayne Peak, *Governing American Schools: Political Interaction in Local School Districts* (North Scituate, MA: Duxbury, 1974), pp. 177–178.

197. Max Weber, *From Max Weber: Essays in Sociology*, H. H. Gerth and C. Wright Mills, eds. (New York: Oxford University Press, 1946), p. 233.

198. Huntley and McDonald, "Urban Managers," p. 150.

199. Jay Eungha Ryu, Cynthia J. Bowling, Chung-Lae Cho, and Deil S. Wright, "Effects of Administrators' Aspirations, Political Principals' Priorities, and Interest Groups' Influence on State Agency Budget Requests," *Public Budgeting & Finance* 27 (Summer 2007), pp. 22–49. The quotations are on pp. 41, 43. Figures are for 1998.

200. Matthew Potoski and Neal Woods, "Designing State Clean Air Agencies: Administrative Procedures and Bureaucratic Autonomy," *Journal of Public Administration Research and Theory* 11 (April 2001), pp. 203–221.

201. David E. Rosenbaum, "Politics as Usual, and Then Some," *New York Times* (September 20, 2005).

202. Ibid.

203. Robert Pear, "Agency Sees Withholding of Medicare Data from Congress as Illegal," *New York Times* (May 4, 2004). The head of Medicare said he was just kidding when he threatened to fire the actuary, Richard S. Foster.

204. Dina Cappiello, Associated Press, "Bush Administration to Relax Protected-Species Rule," *Savannah Morning News* (August 12, 2008).

205. Union of Concerned Scientists, *Interference at the EPA: Science and Politics at the Environmental Protection Agency* (Cambridge, MA: USC Publications, 2008), p. 2. Figure is for 2007.

206. Union of Concerned Scientists, *Atmosphere of Pressure: Political Interference in Federal Climate Science* (Cambridge, MA: USC Publications, 2007), p. 2. Figure is for 2006.

207. Eric Lichtblau, "9/11 Report Cites Many Warnings about Hijackings," *New York Times* (February 10, 2005).

208. Deputy Inspector General for Intelligence, *Review of the Pre-Iraqi War Activities of the Office of the Under Secretary of Defense for Policy*, Report No. 07-INTEL-04 (Washington, DC: Office of the Inspector General, U.S. Department of Defense, February 9, 2007), p. 8.

209. James Surowiecki, "Hail to the Geek," *The New Yorker* (April 19 and 26, 2004), p. 70.

210. Ibid.

Paradigms of Public Administration

Public administration has developed as an academic and professional field through a succession of six paradigms—that is, how the field has "seen itself" in the past and present.

THE BEGINNING

That uniquely academic president, Woodrow Wilson, is commonly thought to be the founder of public administration in the United States. In 1887, Wilson introduced Americans to the field with an essay titled, "The Study of Administration."[1] In it, the future president observed that it "is getting harder to *run* a constitution than to frame one," and called for the bringing of more intellectual resources to bear in the management of the state.

Think Tanks for Public Service

Aside from Wilson's formative essay, public administration's intellectual roots were planted in practical ground—even in the streets. The reformist "public service movement" that was sweeping the American political landscape in the early twentieth century was a factor in John D. Rockefeller's decision, in 1906, to found, and fund, the New York Bureau of Municipal Research. The Bureau was a prototype of what we now know as "think tanks," and, although its focus was limited to New York City, it was extraordinarily creative in laying the intellectual groundwork of what public administration should be, producing some of the early guides for a wide variety of public administrative tasks.

Tammany Hall, the corrupt political machine that ran the City, felt directly threatened by the Bureau, referring to it as "The Bureau of Municipal Besmirch," and initiated a smear campaign designed to emasculate it. The campaign backfired, and encouraged reformers in other cities to emulate the Bureau's success.[2] By 1928, seventy-four cities had research bureaus, and they continued to multiply, both domestically and abroad, through the early 1940s.[3]

Public Administration and the Intellectuals: The Fortuitous Year of 1914

Prior to 1914, academia was openly disdainful of public administration.

Public Administration—"No Career for a Gentleman." Perhaps because professional public administration was being practiced solely in sordid city streets, the occupants of ivory towers had no interest in stooping to its level. During the first decade of the twentieth century, Ms. E. H. Harriman offered $250,000 to the presidents of Harvard, Yale, and Columbia to start a school of public administration. She found them to be "polite but amused" by her proposal, advising her that they had no intention of sending their "graduates into a blind alley" that led to "no career for a gentleman." Rejected by the Ivy League, Harriman gave her money to the New York Bureau of Municipal Research, stipulating that it create, in 1911, its Training School for Public Service, which produced the nation's first corps of trained public administrators. (Ultimately, Mary Harriman prevailed. In 1924, the Bureau gave its Training School, lock, stock, and students, to Syracuse University, where it became the Maxwell School of Citizenship and Public Affairs.)[4]

Turning Sharply: Academia's Reconsideration

Eventually, universities reconsidered. In 1912, an influential scholarly journal devoted an entire issue to municipal research bureaus,[5] and in 1914 academia's attitudes evidenced a sharp turnabout. In that year, the American Political Science Association's (APSA) Committee on Practical Training for Public Service, which had been founded only two years earlier, persuaded the reformist mayor of New York to welcome the nation's first "Conference on Universities as Related to Public Service." The conference recommended, with unusual foresight, that "professional schools," and possibly new degrees, be established to educate public administrators,[6] and its attendees founded the freestanding Society for the Promotion of Training for the Public Service. Although the Society ceased its activities in 1917 (it was effectively a casualty of World War I), it nonetheless served as an inspirational model in the founding, a generation later, of the field's principal professional association, the American Society for Public Administration.[7]

Also in 1914, the APSA's Committee on Instruction in Government specified that one of political science's four core missions was to educate "experts and to prepare specialists for governmental positions."[8] And it was in 1914 that the "first distinctly graduate, professional program in public administration" was founded by a university: The University of Michigan, which placed the program in its political science department, a precedent that quickly waxed over the next half century into a dominant tradition.[9]

By the early twentieth century, public administration stood as a prominent pillar of political science.

PARADIGM 1: THE POLITICS/ ADMINISTRATION DICHOTOMY, 1900–1926

In his groundbreaking book, *Politics and Administration*, published in 1900, Frank J. Goodnow contended that there were "two distinct functions of government," which he identified with the title of his tome. "Politics," wrote Goodnow, "has to do with policies or expressions of the state will," while administration "has to do with the execution of these policies."[10] Goodnow's point— that elected politicians and appointed public administrators do different things—eventually was labeled by academics as the *politics/administration dichotomy*.

The Uses of the Dichotomy

As a practical matter, the politics/administration dichotomy offered some protection for a fledgling profession.[11] It held that public administrators merely brought efficiency to the execution of policies made by elected politicians, and thus, in their bland, bloodless, apolitical, and clerical way, more than paid for themselves.

This is not to say that the dichotomy amounted to nothing more than a cynical defense of a nascent and threatened profession. It also was a deeply believed rationale for a profession of public administration, one that still has some salience to this day. Even though city managers, for instance, assume a highly activist leadership and policymaking role in their governments (recall Chapter 1), many, if not most, are still uncomfortable with this role because, as research indicates,[12] it is a passionate "article of faith among city managers that they are merely administrators and do not involve themselves in politics."[13]

The Dilemma of the Dichotomy

Because those who believed in the politics/administration dichotomy would not accept the reality that public administrators often make policy, it plagued the field for decades. In actuality, the field's first thinkers' were more interested in clarifying roles so that elected office holders and appointed public administrators could work together more effectively as civic leaders.

Nevertheless, such subtleties were overlooked as public administration sought its identity during this period. Leonard D. White's *Introduction to the Study of Public Administration* of 1926, the first textbook devoted to the field, expressed the Progressive values of public administration at the time: Partisan politics should not intrude on administration; the mission of public administration is efficiency; and administration in general is capable of becoming a "value-free" science in its own right.[14] These perspectives provided an intellectual base for public administration's next paradigm, which rested on the idea that, just as there were principles of science, there were principles of administration.

PARADIGM 2: PRINCIPLES OF PUBLIC ADMINISTRATION, 1927–1937

In 1927, W. F. Willoughby's book, *Principles of Public Administration*, appeared as the second fully fledged text in the field. Its title alone indicated the new thrust of public administration: That public administrators would be effective if they learned and applied scientific principles of administration.

Willoughby's textbook reflected intellectual trends that suffused the whole of management theory, and public administration was no exception. In this regard, the field's infatuation with principles of administration stood in stark contrast with its ongoing embrace of the politics/administration dichotomy, which was unique to public administration.

A Reputational Zenith

The status of public administration soared during the principles-of-administration period.

Money and Power Its rising stature can be attributed, at least in part, to the Rockefeller family, whose interest in the field remained undiminished following its success with the New York Bureau of Municipal Research. Rockefeller philanthropies poured millions of dollars into the profession, leaving "no important part of the public administration community...untouched.... A person could not have spoken about the field of public administration in 1925 and had confidence that the audience knew what was meant. In 1937, the situation was quite different."[15]

An Academic Backtrack By the late 1920s, there may have been thirty to forty universities with public administration programs, and "many were so subordinated to political science departments that their survival was in doubt."[16] This bleak condition soon changed. Between 1927 and 1936, the number of universities that offered public administration courses quadrupled.[17]

So rapid was public administration's rise that the academic community grew worried over traditional turfs. In 1935, Princeton University hosted a national conference that produced a report which differed radically from the one issued in 1914. Rather than advocating separate schools and degrees for budding bureaucrats, the 1935 conference found itself "unable to find any single formula which warrants the establishment of an isolated college or university program which alone will emphasize preparation exclusively for the public service."[18] "A logical consequence of this reasoning could have been the elimination of public administration as a discrete field of study within the universities."[19]

The Meaning of Principles

By the very fact that the principles of administration were indeed *principles*—that is, by definition, they "worked" in any administrative setting and without exception—it therefore followed that they could be applied successfully anywhere.

In 1937, the community of public administration expressed this perspective in a singular volume that has come to be called the field's "high–noon of orthodoxy":[20] Luther H. Gulick and Lyndall Urwick's *Papers on the Science of Administration*. Gulick and Urwick were confidantes of President Franklin D. Roosevelt; their *Papers* were a report to the President's Committee on Administrative Science.

Principles were important to Gulick and Urwick, but where those principles were applied was not. As they said in the *Papers*, "It is the general thesis of this paper that there are principles which...should govern arrangements for human association of any kind.... irrespective of the purpose of the enterprise, the personnel comprising it, or any constitutional, political, or social theory underlying its creation."[21]

Gulick and Urwick (though perhaps more so in Gulick's case) understood that their "principles" were not immutable facts of nature, but were simply helpful touch points in conveying an understanding of "What is the work of the chief executive?"[22] Nevertheless, Gulick and Urwick also were aware that their still-spindly profession needed nourishment if it were to survive, and realized that a "science of administration," based on scientific "principles," was a publicly appealing image—indeed, "science" amounted to an "unassailable principle" in its own right.[23] Whatever the merits might have been of promoting an unassailable public administration, however, casting the field as a pure science saddled it with an ultimately untenable paradigm.

THE CHALLENGE, 1938–1950

Dissent from mainstream public administration accelerated in the 1940s in two mutually reinforcing directions. One objection was that politics and administration could never be separated in any remotely sensible fashion. The other was that the principles of administration were something less than the final expression of managerial rationality.

Deflating the Dichotomy

Two subtle intellectual shifts were causing the politics/administration dichotomy to be questioned.

The Demise of the Dichotomy One was internal to public administration. Public administration scholars were shyly noting as early as the 1930s that making public policy remained, certainly, "a question for statesmen, but officials can effect in some manner the turning of the scales."[24] In other words, public administrators, like politicians, could mold public policy, too.

The second shift was external to the field and less positive. Over the years, a peculiar perversion had warped what likely was the original meaning of the politics/administration dichotomy. "Politics" initially had meant only partisan (and often corrupt) politics. By the 1930s, however, "politics" had been expanded in its scholarly meaning to include public policymaking, and public administrators, in accordance with the dichotomy, should not enter this forbidden "political" zone. It was at this point that the politics/administration dichotomy "became intellectually untenable, though difficult to shed."[25]

In 1946, a book of readings written by fourteen scholars, most of whom had extensive experience as public administrators, forcefully questioned the assumption that politics and administration could be cleanly and clearly sundered.[26] Were not what appeared to be neutral "administrative" decisions often heavily laden with policy preferences? The short answer was, "Yes."

The abandonment of the politics/administration dichotomy culminated in 1950 when a leading scholar wrote in the field's leading journal that, "A theory of public administration means in our time a theory of politics also."[27] With this declaration, the dichotomy died.

A Dead Dichotomy, a Diminished Field As a consequence, the nature of the field was fundamentally altered, and also, sadly, diminished. The field's founders had harbored no qualms about the wisdom of differentiating public administration from the hoi polloi of politics because they firmly believed that only a knowledgeable, noble elite (i.e., public administrators) could pull the people from their pestilent cistern of civic suffering, and into the light of prosperity and progress. Consider what Wilson wrote in this regard: "the many, the people.... are selfish, ignorant, timid, stubborn.... they are not the children of reason." Hence, "bureaucracy can exist only where" it is entirely "removed from the common political lives of the people."[28]

Wow. We forget, perhaps mercifully, just how arrogant the field's first thinkers could be. But it was an arrogance that, whatever its drawbacks, did imbue the public-administration pioneers with a sense of mission, leadership, superiority, and *élan* that was largely lost when public administration became as "common" as politics. With time, the revisionist ideology that politics and administration were inseparable—indeed, indistinguishable—took root and rigidified.

Puncturing the Principles

A simultaneous, and even more elemental, challenge was the contention that there could be no such thing as a "principle" of administration.

In the year following the publication of Gulick and Urwick's defining opus, Chester I. Barnard's *The Functions of the Executive* appeared,[29] which had a major impact on Herbert A. Simon when he was writing his devastating critique, *Administrative Behavior*, published in 1947. Although Simon was not alone in his questioning of managerial principles,[30] or what he dubbed dismissively as "the proverbs of administration,"[31] his volume had such intellectual force that it led to Simon's receiving the Nobel Prize in 1978.

Simon wrote that "a fatal defect of the current principles of administration" is that for "almost every principle one can find an equally plausible and acceptable contradictory principle," thus rendering the whole idea of principles moot.[32]

For example, the traditional administrative literature held that clear internal communication was essential to effective managerial control, but it promoted at least two contrary principles for achieving clarity of communication. One principle was *narrow span of control*—that is, a manager could manage only a limited number of subordinates if orders were to be communicated effectively. An organization that followed the principle of narrow span of control would have a "tall" hierarchy.

Span of control makes sense up to a point. Yet, the administrative literature argued with equal vigor for another principle that was vital for clear communication: minimal message handling. The fewer people who passed a message up or down the hierarchy, the clearer and less distorted the message would be.[33] This, too, makes sense up to a point. The hierarchy required to bring the bureaucracy in accord with this principle, however, would be "flat."

Obviously to Simon and now to us, the two "principles" are mutually contradictory, and therefore, by definition, cannot be principles. This dilemma drenched the whole of the management literature, including public administration, but it was never more than suspected of being so stark a case until Simon published his book.

Simon himself was rather mellow about the future of management theory, writing that, "Can anything be salvaged in the construction of an administrative theory? As a matter of fact, almost everything can be salvaged."[34] But the wreckage had been wrought. By mid-century, the two defining pillars of public administration—the politics/administration dichotomy and the principles of public administration—had been abandoned by creative intellects in the field. This abandonment left public administration bereft of a distinct intellectual identity.

Fearful Reactions

In the same year that Simon obliterated administrative principles as the foundation of management theory, and, with them, those of public administration as well, he offered an alternative to the old paradigms, proposing that there be two kinds of "public administrationists"[35] (i.e., the professors, in contrast to the public administrators) working in harmony: Those scholars concerned with developing "a pure science of administration" based on "a thorough grounding in social psychology," and those concerned with "prescribing for public policy," an enterprise that "cannot stop when it has swallowed up the whole of political science; it must attempt to absorb economics and sociology as well."[36]

Political science, which was the first field that Simon fingered for public administration to swallow up whole, had its own reasons for keeping public administration under its thumb. A distinguished political scientist of this period wrote that political science, "with the exception of public administration," its most prestigious subfield, was "almost generally stigmatized as the least advanced" social science by government and academia alike.[37] And political scientists had reason to fear that they might lose public administration:

The founding in 1939 of the American Society for Public Administration was "above all an attempt to loosen Public Administration from the restraints of political science."[38]

Political scientists' fears were further attenuated because public administration was not their only rebellious subfield; others, notably international relations ("the largest single specialty group in political science" at the time), threatened secession, too.[39] Should any subfield depart, others might follow, calling into question the very future of political science.

Political scientists were not about to ignore their looming dismemberment. In 1952, an article appeared in political science's preeminent journal that put the matter plainly, calling for the continued "dominion of political science over public administration," its "strange and unnatural child."[40]

PARADIGM 3: PUBLIC ADMINISTRATION AS POLITICAL SCIENCE, 1950–1970

As a result of these and related concerns, public administrationists wormed their way back into the warm and welcoming womb (or so they thought) of the mother discipline, political science. Some political scientists, however, tried to smother their "strange and unnatural" progeny in it.

Consternation and Contempt

Paradigm 3 began as an exercise in reestablishing the linkages between public administration and political science. But there were issues.

The public administrationists were no longer really sure what they should be doing. Public administration professors groped for answers to the point that "the study of public administration in the United States" during this period was "characterized by the absence of any fully comprehensive intellectual framework."[41]

For their part, political scientists were willing to absorb public administration into their larger and loftier realm, but the price of admission was steep: Public administration would shrivel to an "emphasis," an "area of interest," even a "synonym" of political science.[42] Observers commented that, "public administration stands in danger of . . . senescence,"[43] and "that lusty young giant of a decade ago, may now 'evaporate' as a field."[44]

And evaporation during this perilous period was not improbable. Over ten years, a meager 4 percent of all the articles published in the five major political science journals dealt with public administration,[45] and political scientists who identified public administration as their "primary field of interest" shrank by a shattering two-thirds, from 35 percent to just 12 percent.[46] During the 1960s, the American Political Science Association moved "officially or formally" to rid itself of public administration,[47] and, even as late as 1977, the APSA's president dismissed it as an "intellectual wasteland."[48] A leading public administrationist wrote during this period that political scientists' opinions of his field often dripped with "undisguised contempt or hostility. We are now hardly welcome in the house of our youth."[49]

The Impact of Political Science: Bureaucracy in the Service of Democracy

Political science—the presumptive "mother discipline" of public administration—clearly has had a profound effect on the character of the field. The fundamental precepts of American political science, such as the self-evident worth of democracy, political participation, and due process under law, continue to hold sway among even the most independently-minded public administrationists. Despite the disdain with which political science often treated public administration, political science likely was a salutary former of the field in laying some of its normative foundations.

Beyond providing a base of democratic values, however, political science seems to have less utility in the education of public administrators. Asks a scholar: "What can political science contribute to the improvement of practitioner skill? An overview of the major intellectual approaches within political science suggests the answer is 'not much.' "[50]

Or, to put the matter plainly, political science educates for (to quote one particularly lucid synopsis) "intellectualized understanding" of public administration, whereas public administration educates for "knowledgeable action,"[51] and these epistemologies—academic *versus* professional—are fundamentally different *Zeitgeists*.

PARADIGM 4: PUBLIC ADMINISTRATION AS MANAGEMENT, 1950–1970

Partly because of their second-class citizenship in a number of political science departments, a few public administrationists began searching for an alternative. They found it in *management*, sometimes called *administrative science* or *generic management*, which holds that sector, culture, institution, mission, whatever, are of little consequence to efficient and effective administration, and that "a body of knowledge"—statistics, economics, accounting, operations research, and organization theory are often cited—"exists that is common to the fields of administration."[52]

Paradigm 4 occurred roughly concurrently in time with Paradigm 3, although it never received the broadly based favor that political science once garnered from public administrationists. But in both the Political Science and Management paradigms, the essential thrust was one of public administration losing its identity within the confines of some "larger" concept.

Cornell University's Graduate School of Management, founded in 1948, is generally thought to be the first academic unit that embraced the idea of generic management. Public administrationists who toiled in these schools, while not as actively reviled as those in some political science departments, were treated, at best, with indifference, shivering in the drafty attic of an absentminded aunt who often forgot to serve meals.

The "Groundswell" of Management

During the 1950s and 1960s, a spate of scholars writing in a variety of journals accelerated the drumbeat of generic management as the logical successor to more "parochial" paradigms, such as public administration and business administration.[53] In 1956, an important journal, *Administrative Science Quarterly*, was founded on the premise that public, private, and other institutional distinctions of management were false.

By the early sixties, a national survey of graduate programs in public administration concluded that "management" was "a groundswell development that tends to pervade all others,"[54] and as many as a fifth of business administration programs also taught public administration or social sciences.[55] Suddenly it seemed that a number of public administrationists were rediscovering the line in Woodrow Wilson's seminal essay of 1887: "the field of administration is a field of business. It is removed from the hurry and strife of politics."[56]

"Fundamentally Alike in All Unimportant Respects"

Is public administration a subfield of management? Does public administration, at root, amount to little more than an understanding of civil service regulations, while the core administrative functions remain essentially the same, whether they are practiced in businesses, nonprofit organizations, or governments?

The Erratic Impact of the Intellectuals In light of the management scholars' contention that a singular body of knowledge exists that unites all administrative "fields," it is noteworthy that there is a "substantial amount of disagreement about the commonality of administrative tools and techniques" among generic management schools, and no fewer than thirty *different* courses in these schools comprise the "basic requirements" for a master's degree![57] If, indeed, management is management is management, then why is there no reasonably consistent curriculum among the nation's management schools?

Given the national incoherence of generic management curricula, it is reasonable to conclude that something is missing.

What Is Missing? Actually, quite a lot is missing. Specifically, function, institution, and sector are absent. Both experiential and empirical data support the contention that public administration is unique.

Those successful businesspeople who have become public executives are among the first to deny that there are significant similarities between the public and private sectors.[58] Public administrators who enter the corporate world experience comparable difficulties of transition.[59]

Some seminally significant research has found that the single most important key to managerial effectiveness in government is not wide-ranging experiences as executives in other sectors, but the depth of one's experience *as a public administrator*.[60] On a personal level, it appears that a substantial background in business may handicap a subsequent career in government. The longer the time spent working in the private sector before entering public service, the lesser the likelihood that public administrators will be promoted and supervise large numbers of employees.[61]

As we shall see in Part II, a burgeoning trove of research that empirically compares public, nonprofit, and private organizations casts grave doubt that management can be fruitfully approached as a seamless entity, except in the broadest strokes conceivable. The emerging consensus of both practitioners and scholars increasingly appears to be that public and private management are, to cite Wallace Sayre's old saw, "fundamentally alike in all unimportant respects."[62]

The Impact of Management: Understanding the "Public" in Public Administration

The unambiguously clear impact of the management paradigm is that it pushed public administration scholars into rethinking what the "public" in public administration really meant.

Defining the "public" in public administration has long been a knotty problem for academics, in part because Western culture has never completely sorted out the "complex-structured concept" of "publicness" and "privateness."[63] Publicness and privateness in society are composed of three dimensions: agency, interest, and access.

The Agency, or Institutional, Definition of "Public." "Agency" refers to the distinction between an institution that acts on behalf of everyone (i.e., it acts publicly) and an institution that acts only in its own behalf (i.e., it acts privately).

Traditionally, public administrationists have thought that the "public" in public administration refers to the institution of government and its agencies, and this definition still dominates thinking in the field. Seven out of ten books about public organization theory take an "agency" perspective, as opposed to an "interest" or "access" view.[64]

Regrettably, the real world renders this approach problematic. Privatization, the third sector, and similar phenomena blur institutional distinctions, and conspire to make an institutionally defined public administration an elusive entity.

The Interest, or Philosophic, Definition of "Public." *Interest* is concerned with who benefits. It is in the (public) interest of government to benefit everyone it governs; it is in the (private) interest of the for-profit firm to benefit only its owners. During the 1970s, public administrationists moved toward a meaning of "public" that focused less on agencies and more on whose interest was affected. Thus, rather than concentrating on the Department of Defense, for instance, and leaving, say, Boeing Corporation to business scholars, public administrationists explored the Pentagon's contractual relationships with Boeing because they involved the public interest.

The Access, or Organizational, Definition of "Public." Our final dimension of "publicness" and "privateness" is that of *access*, which addresses the degree of openness to the public found in an organization's *activities, space, information*, and *resources*.

As we explain in Part II, compared with private and nonprofit organizations, public agencies are outrageously accessible. In fact, an astounding 94 percent of cities and counties (up from 84 percent just three years earlier) *invite* such access, and proactively "*provide* citizens with the resources necessary to solve problems and implement decisions." Some four-fifths of these governments grant outsiders access to their staffers, data, and reports, and nearly two-fifths give them budgets.[65]

Three Interlocked Understandings of "Public." Our three definitions of *public* administration—institutional, interest, and organizational—are in no way mutually exclusive. Rather, they are mutually reinforcing. Of equal importance, these definitions clarify not only the "public" in public administration, but also demonstrate that "publicness," and hence public administration, is unique.

THE FORCES OF SEPARATISM, 1965–1970

Even at its nadir during the period of Paradigms 3 and 4, public administration was sowing, if unconsciously, the seeds of its own renaissance.

In the halls of academe, it was becoming increasingly clear to public adminstrationists that neither political science nor management addressed their interests, nor could they. Political science's intellectual focus is pluralist, specialized, and communal, whereas public administration's is elitist, synthesizing, and hierarchical. Management's focus is exclusively technical, whereas public administration's is both technical and normative.

In the corridors of power, practitioners' pride was emerging, as witnessed by the founding, in 1967, of the National Academy of Public Administration. Its founders purposely created an association of the nation's most distinguished public administrators and academics that could serve as a resource in the solution of public problems—much like the National Academy of Sciences serves as the nation's single most authoritative advisor to government on scientific matters. Both academies are the only ones chartered by Congress.

In sum, both the academic and practitioner communities of public administration were, in the last years of the sixties, moving toward an enhanced self-awareness. By 1970, the separatist movement was underway.

PARADIGM 5: PUBLIC ADMINISTRATON AS PUBLIC ADMINISTRATION, 1970–PRESENT

"Public administration as public administration" refers to public administration's successful break with both political science and management, and its emergence as an autonomous field of study and practice.

We shall provide ample evidence of this autonomy, but consider first a somewhat quirky, but revealing, example. A study of academic journals concluded that public administration is now "largely isolated" from the fields of law, management, and political science, "the three disciplines that are commonly believed to form its underlying foundation." Even though this analysis also found that these three fields are at least equally isolated from public administration, the researcher nevertheless bemoaned public administration's isolation.[66] Could not the argument be made, however, that "isolation" merely signals independence?

Independence brings a bounty of benefits. Paradigm 5 is, in many ways, a union—really, a reunion—of professors and practitioners that has not been seen since the 1930s. The bonds linking professors and public administrators, as well as students, may now be strengthened in a nurturing atmosphere, free from snide asides by political scientists about public administration's predilection for "nuts and bolts," and absent condescending comments by business faculties about the "sinecures" of gutless government bureaucrats.

NASPAA's Nascency

Academic programs in public administration have banded together since 1958, when the long-extinct Council on Graduate Education for Public Administration was founded in a depressing attempt to shield the field from being starved by political science and management. But it was only in 1970, when the National Association of Schools of Public Affairs and Administration (NASPAA) was birthed, that public administration definitively declared its epistemological independence.

NASPAA is composed of about 260 of America's Master of Public Administration (M.P.A.) and related degree programs—essentially all such programs in the United States. In 1983, NASPAA's members voted to become the nation's professional accrediting agency for these degrees.

About 160 M.P.A. and related degree programs have been accredited by NASPAA, and its accreditation associates with greater prestige, more effective programs, and an enhanced ability to recruit higher quality faculty and students.[67] NASPAA-accredited programs offer a consistent core curriculum nationally (in contrast to the chaotic core curricula found in schools of generic management[68]), and these programs are "generally more focused on professional skills" than are unaccredited programs. "NASPAA standards appear to work well."[69]

The Statistics of Secession

Public administration's secession is real. For more than three decades, the number of M.P.A. and related programs situated in business and management schools has withered by almost two-thirds and now stands at just 6 percent; those conducted in political science departments stands at roughly one out of every three, and is in slow but steady decline; and programs offered by freestanding units of public administration or public policy comprise about half of all programs.[70]

This move toward an autonomous academic field has been good for public administration. The most effective M.P.A. programs are those that are administered by freestanding schools and departments,[71] and these units are experiencing the fastest rates of student growth of all organizational types.[72]

There are more than 31,000 students enrolled in M.P.A. and related programs, up from fewer than 11,000 in 1973.[73] Nearly two-thirds of these students are women,[74] and almost four out of ten are students of color.[75]

From Politics/Administration Dichotomy to Political-Administrative Continuum

Central, perhaps, to Paradigm 5 is the resurrection of the politics/administration dichotomy that defined public administration's origins nearly a century ago. But the dichotomy has reemerged in a significantly new form—as a political–administrative continuum, rather than as a politics/administration division—that furnishes the field with an intellectual gravitas that is sensible, understandable, and workable.

Public administration rejects Paradigm 1's notion that public administration crouches, or ought to crouch, behind a dichotomizing firewall that protects it from politics. Nor does public administration accept the puckering premise of Paradigms 3 and 4—that public administration is nonexistent, amounting to nothing more than an unformed, indistinguishable blob, sliming the awesome architectures of politics and management.

In Paradigm 5, politics and public administration do co-exist on the same social continuum, but as separate and distinct "constellations of logic"[76] whose activities sometimes overlap. At the far ends of that continuum, political acts (such as appointing to government jobs unqualified nephews) can be distinguished from administrative acts (such as appointing to government jobs the most qualified applicants drawn from a competitive pool), and easily so. This is not rocket science. True, it may be less easy to separate the political from the administrative in the middle reaches of that continuum, but we nonetheless understand that politics' values relate more to power, community, pluralism, personality, loyalty, emotion, and ideology, whereas public administration's values relate more to fairness, hierarchy, elitism, impersonality, professionalism, analysis, and neutrality.

The Pioneers of Public Administration Were Right

New research suggests that the pioneering public administrationists seem to have gotten it pretty much right on several important counts.

Professional Public Administration Improves Governance   Perhaps the central insight of these early scholars is that professionalism improves governing, an insight that has turned out to be precisely on target.

Career federal executives are measurably and significantly more productive public administrators

LOGICS

Politics and Administration

Shirley Sherrod is the daughter of an African American farmer. In 1965, when she was seventeen, her father was fatally shot in the back by a white farmer. An all-white grand jury in Baker County, Georgia, filed no charges, so no one could be tried for his murder. Her mother and she remained in southwest Georgia and became dedicated civil rights activists.

Forty-five years later, in 2010, when Sherrod was the U.S. Department of Agriculture's director of rural development for Georgia, a conservative blogger released a portion of a videotape, broadcast by Fox News, of Sherrod addressing a banquet hosted by the National Association for the Advancement of Colored People (NAACP). In her address, Sherrod recounted an incident in which she said that, two dozen years earlier, she had not given a white farmer facing the loss of his farm "the full force of what I could do." The NAACP's national president and a heaving host of others denounced her remark as racist and, according to Sherrod, officials in her department and the White House intensely pressured her to resign.

Sherrod resigned. No more than ten hours and twenty-two minutes had elapsed from the blogger's initial release of the edited videotape to Sherrod's resignation.[*]

As Sherrod had tried in vain to explain, her comment had been ripped out of context. The entire tape of her speech revealed that Sherrod had gone on to state that she had rejected her first, admittedly prejudiced, instinct, recognizing that "there is no difference between us," and had in fact accorded the farmer her full force in successfully saving his farm. The farmer in question said that Sherrod had exhibited "no racist attitude. Heck no. . . . I was never treated nicer." His wife added that they have long been friends with Sherrod, in part because, "She helped us save our farm by getting in there and doing everything she could do."

---

[*]The blogger released the videotape at 11:18 on the morning of July 19, 2010, and "Fox News Alert" reported at 9:04 that evening that Sherrod "resigned just a short time ago."

The White House and the department apologized to Sherrod. The secretary of agriculture offered to reinstate her. Sherrod declined.

This episode epitomizes the logic of politics. It differs starkly from the logic of administration.

The logic of politics demands that, for reasons of personal professional survival, politicians rid themselves of harmful controversies (and all controversies are harmful politically) as quickly and as expeditiously as possible. Hence, Sherrod's (allegedly) forced resignation was instant; she *was* the harmful controversy.

By contrast, the logic of administration demands that, for reasons of personal professional survival, executives learn the relevant facts before acting. Had an impartial fact-finding inquiry been mounted, which would have quickly exposed the blogger's malicious misdirection, Sherrod would not have been pressured to resign.

The trick in *public* administration is to reconcile political and administrative reasoning, a reconciliation that often is difficult but is far from impossible. (In the foregoing fiasco, simply viewing the entire videotape, an undertaking that would have consumed less than an hour, would have aborted vast political embarrassment.) This is why public administration is uniquely complex and deeply fascinating. Public administration blends politics and management, and, as an intellectual and professional enterprise, supersedes both. ∎

Sources: Will Bunch, "The Story behind the 1965 Killing of Sherrod's Dad," *Huffington Post* (July 21, 2010); Karen Tumulty and Ed O'Keefe, "Fired USDA Official Receives Apologies from White House, Vilsak," *Washington Post* (July 22, 2010); and Media Matters for America, *Timeline of Breitbart's Sherrod Smear,* http://mediamatters.org/research/201007220004.

---

than are those who are political appointees.[77] Mayors who are greatly involved administratively, and who have high levels of education and deep job-related experience, put more pupils in schools,[78] collect more property taxes, and spend more on social programs than less educated and experienced mayors.[79] The professionalizing reforms of local government that were advocated by the first public administrationists—home-rule status, nonpartisan elections, few governmental jurisdictions, and short ballots, among others—all correlate positively with more efficient and responsive government.[80]

Public Administrators, Politicians, and Teamwork Recall that the founding scholars hoped that, even though elected politicians and appointed administrators do different things, they would more amply fulfill the public interest by working together. This, too, has come to pass.

"Elected officials and administrators...have extensive interactions,"[81] and there is a growing "complementarity" between them.[82] A densely careful study of local governments in fourteen Western countries, including the United States, found that mayors and city managers "are not engaged in a zero-sum contest for control," but instead have "interdependency and reciprocal influence." Although the form of government can favor one over the other, when this variable is removed, "the influence of the two officials rises and falls together."[83] Studies of American county governments similarly find that "county managers are adept at people skills and consensus building, perhaps even more so than city managers."[84]

Crucial to the connection between teamwork and better governing, at least in localities, is the presence of a council-manager form of government, which brings less conflict and more collaboration to governing than any other form. In fact, "form of government is the *only* statistically significant factor"—not population size, urban or suburban location, finances, socioeconomic conditions, or types of council elections—"to account for levels of conflict and cooperation in the decision-making process."[85]

That icon of council-manager government, the city manager, also enhances team-based governing. There is greater political-administrative teamwork in mayor-council cities with a city manager than there is in cities that lack one.[86]

Two Quiet Revolutions: The Pioneers' Prime Proposals Although the pioneers of public administration affected all governments, they brought most of their considerable intellect to bear on local ones. Their core proposals here were the council-manager plan and the

city manager. Without question, both of these intertwined reforms have improved local governing, and vastly so, in ways other than improving local teamwork.

Just as the field's first thinkers thought it would, the council-manager plan has curtailed corruption and has rendered local services far more efficient, effective, and responsive.

The plan "allows administrators and elected officers to more easily resist opportunistic behavior" (i.e., corrupt behavior) relative to mayor-council communities.[87] When a city most exemplifies the values of council-manager government, its citizens "are more likely to rate the quality of city services in the top category" than are citizens who are governed by any other type of local government.[88]

A contributing factor in this highest of approval ratings doubtless lies in council-manager cities' aggressive interest in learning what their residents think about their services. More than three-fourths of council-manager municipalities inquire, using various methods (nearly three-fifths of these cities use citizen surveys), about their citizens' satisfaction with specific services; no other governmental form comes even remotely close.[89] In fact, council-manager cities so satisfy their citizens that voting turnout in these "administrative cities" is much lower than in "political cities." "Voter turnout *is dependent* on the form of government" used by a community.[90]

City managers have comparable effects. When making decisions, city managers are much more responsive to citizens than are mayors of cities without city managers.[91] "The most consistent predictor" that a city council will agree to proposals for more efficient and effective governance is the presence of a city manager who has long been in office.[92]

PARADIGM 6: GOVERNANCE, 1990–PRESENT

"Sea changes in technology, communication, the global economy, and the power and role of government are causing self-assessments within the business, nonprofit, and government sectors. The roles of the sectors are changing."[93]

The Future of Governing

Most particularly, these sectoral "sea changes" metamorphose how we govern.

The Decline of Governments

We consider in greater detail the governmental consequences of these conditions in upcoming chapters, particularly Chapter 11, but, at root, globalization, the Internet, and related developments pressure governments to reduce their sovereignty.[94] American governments are relinquishing, by design or default, their traditional responsibilities to: individual citizens; groups of citizens; public-private partnerships; the nonprofit sector; the private sector; public authorities; associations of governments; and other governments.

As one scholarly wit winsomely asked, "Wither the state?"[95]

"Making a Mesh of Things": The Rise of Governance

We are, in sum, moving away from *government*, or the control over citizens and the delivery of public benefits by institutions of the state, and we are moving toward *governance*, or configurations of laws, policies, organizations, institutions, cooperative arrangements, and agreements that control citizens and deliver public benefits. Government is institutional; governance is institutional *and networked*.

Some seven decades ago, a distinguished scholar foretold of governing by network, defining public administration as "making a mesh of things."[96] The mesh of governance is amply documented. A unique analysis of more than 800 empirical studies, covering a range of disciplines, found a general shifting away from "hierarchical government" and a distinct movement toward "horizontal governing," involving "a gradual addition of new administrative forms."[97] Some types of local administrators spend one full working day out of five on "handling the interdependencies between their organizations and others," and city governments link their activities with an average of sixty other public, private, and nonprofit organizations.[98]

Does Governance Work?

A "meta-analytical study" of "137 cases of collaborative governance across a range of policy sectors" concluded that making a mesh of things seems to work reasonably well.[99] We offer three examples:

- There is a positive correlation between intense collaboration among public organizations and a high level of satisfaction held by clients.[100]
- "At a minimum, managerial networking boosts educational performance" in school districts.[101]
- *Focused deterrence* is a network-based method designed to reduce gang-related violence by coordinating police, prosecutors, social workers, clergy, outreach workers, victims, former gang members, social-network analysts, and public and private employers, among others. Used in about sixty diverse cities, the approach has often been spectacularly successful, with homicides in several cities cut by half or more in just two years. In High Point, North Carolina, focused deterrence eliminated in a single day an open-air drug market that had endured for decades, despite unremitting "cuff-and-stuff" attempts to close it, and it had yet to return five years later.[102]

Governance is not a panacea. No paradigm is, and other paradigms, depending on "the nature of the task" at hand, may be more useful, as "unexpected mismatches" of approach and task inevitably fail. "Insofar as researchers or politicians still believe in the superiority of one particular approach," their beliefs are "based on wishful thinking."[103] In fact, it appears that "networking overall, as an aggregate concept, has no impact on [governmental] performance." Rather, specific parts of networks interacting with one another is what boosts performance.[104]

Nevertheless, governing by partnering correlates, significantly and positively, with agencies that perform better than agencies that work alone.[105]

A large-scale analysis found that certain "critical variables" must be present for governance to succeed. They are trust; commitment; solid leadership; a history of cooperation; incentives to collaborate; balanced power and resources among the participants; face-to-face conversation among the collaborators; and a shared understanding of processes, people, and goals. When it comes to governing, "small wins" matter a lot.[106]

The Future of Public Administration: The Nonprofit Sector?

The future of public administration is one of less government. Americans who want to serve the public, and there are many, increasingly are turned off by government. Far more young adults express an interest in working for a community service organization than in working for government.[107]

Certainly this applies to students of public administration and public policy. Sixty-one percent of the directors of these programs report that they have seen an increase over the past year in student interest in working in a nonprofit organization.[108] A plurality, 21 percent, of these students state that their "ideal area of work" following graduation would be the nonprofit sector, followed by the federal and local governments, at 18 percent.[109] (Professors who teach in M.P.A. programs have responded to their students' interest: Fully half of all master's-level nonprofit management programs are found within M.P.A. degrees.[110])

Fewer than two-thirds of the graduates of all M.P.A. and similar programs are employed by governments on graduation,[111] and, at the twenty top programs, not even half are. Almost two-thirds of the top twenty programs' graduates who enter government service switch to other sectors, and nearly three-quarters of those who leave government depart for "more challenging work" (only a fourth leave for better salaries).[112]

We are not in the business of knocking government. We do want to illustrate, however, that the institutions which capture the imaginations and loyalty of those Americans who are among the most passionately committed to the public service are increasingly less likely to be governments.

PUBLIC ADMINISTRATION, HAPPY AT LAST

Public administration now straddles two paradigms. One asserts its independence as a stand-alone, self-aware field of study and practice. The other asserts its paramount purpose—creating and implementing social change for social good.

Both paradigms are complementary and mutually reinforcing. Without independence, public administration would be a sorry, surly supplicant, shorn of the capacity to chart its own course. Without purpose, independence would be irrelevant.

This joyful, codependent, paradigmatic merger has been a long time coming, but it has come. And it has arrived in style. Just as public administration was a prestigious model for managers in all sectors during the 1930s, so it is today: As a major business journal argued, "Public governance.... offers a distinct set of ideas for how corporate governance can be improved in practice," especially in the areas of "manager compensation, division of power within firms, rules of succession to top positions, and institutionalized competition in core areas of the corporation.... To an even larger extent," these ideas "could be applied to not-for-profit firms."[113]

Public administration, happy at last.

NOTES

1. Woodrow Wilson, "The Study of Administration," *Political Science Quarterly* 2 (June/July 1887), pp. 197–222.
2. Daniel W. Williams, "Evolution of Performance Measurement until 1930," *Administration & Society* 36 (May 2004), pp. 131–165.
3. As derived from data in Institute of Public Administration, http://www.theipa.org/aboutipa/history.html.
4. Luther Gulick, "George Maxwell Had a Dream: A Historical Note with a Comment on the Future," *American Public Administration: Past, Present,*

Future, Frederick C. Mosher, ed. (University, AL: University of Alabama Press, 1975), pp. 253–267. The quotation is on p. 257.

5. "Efficiency in City Government," *Annals of the American Academy of Political and Social Science* XLI (May 12, 1912).

6. Committee on Practical Training for Public Service, American Political Science Association, *Proposed Plan for Training Schools for Public Service* (Madison, WI: American Political Science Association, 1914), p. 3.

7. Hindy Lauer Schachter, "When Political Science Championed Public Service Training: The American Political Association Campaign for Professional Public Administration," *American Review of Public Administration* 37 (September 2007), pp. 362–375. The information cited is on pp. 369, 371.

8. *Proceedings of the American Political Science Association, 1913–1914*, p. 264, as cited in Lynton K. Caldwell, "Public Administration and the Universities: A Half Century of Development," *Public Administration Review* 25 (March 1965), pp. 52–64. The quotation is cited on p. 54.

9. Alice B. Stone and Donald C. Stone, "Appendix: Case Histories of Early Professional Education Programs," in *American Public Administration*, pp. 268–290. The quotation is on p. 272.

10. Frank J. Goodnow, *Politics and Administration* (New York: Macmillan, 1900), pp. 10–11.

11. Much of this discussion is based on James H. Svara, "The Politics-Administration Dichotomy Model as Aberration," *Public Administration Review* 58 (January/February 1998), pp. 51–58.

12. Robert T. Golembiewski and Gerald T. Gabris, "Today's City Managers: A Legacy of Success-Becoming-Failure," *Public Administration Review* 54 (November/December 1994), pp. 525–530.

13. Alan Ehrenhalt, "The Mayor-Manager Merger," *Governing* (October 2006), pp. 9–10. The quotation is on p. 9.

14. Dwight Waldo, "Public Administration," *Political Science: Advance of the Discipline*, Marian D. Irish, ed. (Englewood Cliffs, NJ: Prentice-Hall, 1968), pp. 153–189.

15. Alasdair Roberts, "Demonstrating Neutrality: The Rockefeller Philanthropies and the Evolution of Public Administration, 1927–1936," *Public Administration Review* 54 (May/June 1994), pp. 221–228. The quotations are on p. 222.

16. Alice B. Stone and Donald C. Stone, "Early Development of Education in Public Administration," in *American Public Administration*, pp. 11–48. The quotation is on p. 30.

17. Roberts, "Demonstrating Neutrality," p. 22.

18. Morris B. Lambie, ed., *Training for the Public Service: The Report and Recommendations of a Conference Sponsored by the Public Administration Clearing House* (Chicago: Public Administration Clearing House, 1935).

19. Caldwell, "Public Administration and the Universities," p. 57.

20. The famous phrase was first written by Wallace Sayre in "Premises of Public Administration: Past and Emerging," *Public Administration Review* 18 (March/April 1958), pp. 102–105. The quotation is on p. 104.

21. L. Urwick, "Organization as a Technical Problem," *Papers on the Science of Administration*, Luther Gulick and L. Urwick, eds. (New York: Institute of Public Administration, 1937), pp. 47–88. The quotation is on p. 49.

22. Luther H. Gulick, "Notes on the Theory of Organization," *Papers on the Science of Administration*, pp. 1–46. The quotation is on p. 9.

23. Alasdair Roberts, "The Unassailable Principle: Why Luther Gulick Searched for a Science of Administration," *International Journal of Public Administration* 21 (June 1998), pp. 235–274.

24. E. Pendleton Herring, *Public Administration and the Public Interest* (New York: McGraw-Hill, 1936), p. vii.

25. David Rosenbloom, "The Politics-Administration Dichotomy in U.S. Historical Context," *Public Administration Review* 68 (January/February 2008), pp. 57–60. The quotation is on p. 60.

26. Fritz Morstein Marx, ed., *Elements of Public Administration* (New York: Prentice-Hall, 1946).

27. John Merriman Gaus, "Trends in the Theory of Public Administration," *Public Administration Review* 10 (Summer 1950), pp. 161–168. The quotation is on p. 168.

28. Wilson, "The Study of Administration," pp. 501, 504.

29. Chester I. Barnard, *The Functions of the Executive* (Cambridge, MA: Harvard University Press, 1938).

30. See, for example, Robert A. Dahl, "The Science of Public Administration: Three Problems," *Public Administration Review* 7 (Winter 1947), pp. 1–11.

31. Herbert A. Simon, "The Proverbs of Administration," *Public Administration Review* 6 (Winter 1946), pp. 53–67.

32. Herbert A. Simon, *Administrative Behavior: A Study of Decision-Making Processes in Administrative Organization,* 3rd ed. (New York: Free Press, 1976), p. 20.

33. Ibid., p. 28.

34. Ibid., p. 38.

35. The term *public administrationist* apparently was coined by Dwight Waldo, in "Public Administration," p. 154. Waldo wrote that he could not think of a better title, and hence was forced to use "an awkward expression in lack of an adroit one."

36. Herbert A. Simon, "A Comment on 'The Science of Public Administration,'" *Public Administration Review* 7 (Summer 1947), pp. 200–203. The quotation is on p. 202.

37. David Easton, *The Political System* (New York: Knopf, 1953), pp. 38, 40.

38. Dwight Waldo, "Introduction: Trends and Issues in Education for Public Administration," *Education for Public Service, 1979,* Guthrie S. Birkhead and James D. Carroll, eds. (Syracuse, NY: Maxwell School of Citizenship and Public Affairs, Syracuse University, 1979), pp. 13–26. The quotation is on p. 15.

39. Harry Howe Ransom, "International Relations," *Political Science*, pp. 55–81. The quotation is on p. 55.

40. Roscoe Martin, "Political Science and Public Administration—A Note on the State of the Union," *American Political Science Review* 46 (September 1952), pp. 660–676. The quotations are on pp. 665, 661.

41. William J. Siffin, "The New Public Administration: Its Study in the United States," *Public Administration* 24 (Winter 1956), pp. 365–376. The quotation is on p. 367.

42. Martin Landau, "The Concept of Decision-Making in the 'Field' of Public Administration," *Concepts and Issues in Administrative Behavior*, Sidney Mailick and Edward H. Van Ness, eds. (Englewood Cliffs, NJ: Prentice-Hall, 1962), pp. 1–29.

43. Mosher, "Research in Public Administration." The quotation is on p. 171.

44. Landau, "The Concept of Decision-Making in the 'Field' of Public Administration," p. 2.

45. Jack L. Walker, "Brother, Can You Paradigm?" *PS* 5 (Fall 1972), pp. 419–422. Figure is for 1960–1970.

46. Albert Somit and Joseph Tanenhaus, *American Political Science: A Profile of a Discipline* (New York: Atherton, 1964), pp. 52, 54. Figures are for 1953–1963.

47. Waldo, "Public Administration," p. 154.

48. Heinz Eulau (1977), as quoted in Krishna K. Tummala, "Comparative Study and the Section on International and Comparative Administration (SICA)," *Public Administration Review* 58 (January/February 1998), p. 21.

49. Dwight Waldo, "Scope of the Theory of Public Administration," *Theory and Practice of Public Administration: Scope, Objectives, and Methods,* Monograph 8, James C. Charlesworth, ed. (Philadelphia: American Academy of Political and Social Sciences, 1968), pp. 1–26. The quotation is on p. 8.

50. David L. Weiner, "Political Science, Practitioner Skill, and Public Management," *Public Administration Review* 52 (May/June 1992), pp. 240–245. The quotation is on p. 241.

51. Caldwell, "Public Administration and the Universities," p. 57.

52. Kenneth L. Kraemer and James L. Perry, "Camelot Revisited: Public Administration Education in a Generic School," *Education for Public Service, 1980,* Guthrie S. Birkhead and James D. Carroll, eds. (Syracuse, NY: Maxwell School of Citizenship and Public Affairs, Syracuse University, 1980), pp. 87–102. The quotation is on p. 91. The authors examined twenty-two schools that they thought qualified as management schools.

53. One example among many is Edward H. Litchfield, "Notes on a General Theory of Administration," *Administrative Science Quarterly* 1 (June 1956), pp. 3–29.

54. Ward Stewart, *Graduate Study in Public Administration: A Guide to Graduate Programs*, Report to the U.S. Department of Health, Education, and Welfare (Washington, DC: U.S. Government Printing Office, 1961), p. 39.

55. Delta Sigma Pi, *Eighteenth Biennial Survey of Universities Offering an Organized Curriculum in Commerce and Business Administration* (Oxford, OH: Educational Foundation of Delta Sigma Pi, 1962).

56. Wilson, "The Study of Administration," p. 209.

57. Kraemer and Perry, "Camelot Revisited," p. 92. The core curricula of eight "illustrative generic schools" are analyzed.

58. See, for example, James M. Kouzes, "Why Businessmen Fail in Government," *New York Times* (March 8, 1987).

59. Donald Rumsfeld, "A Politician-Turned-Executive Surveys Both Worlds," *Fortune* (September 10, 1979), pp. 50–54.

60. David E. Lewis, *Political Appointments, Bureau Chiefs, and Federal Management Performance* (Princeton, NJ: Woodrow Wilson School of Public and International Affairs, Princeton University, 2005). Details are in Chapter 9.

61. Barry Bozeman and Branco Ponomariov, "Sector Switching from a Business to a Government Job: Fast-Track Career or Fast-Track to Nowhere?" *Public Administration Review* 69 (January/February 2009), pp. 77–91. Switching from business to government has "a positive effect on promotion and the number of employees supervised," but the longer one's tenure in the private sector, the "less likely" that either development will happen; "there is a strategic time to switch careers" (pp. 81, 89).

62. The original expression of Sayre's mythic and enduring *pronunciemento* is unclear. Graham T. Allison, Jr. reports that, after being a formative figure in the planning of the nation's first generic school of management, at Cornell University, Sayre departed for Columbia University and, evidently as a parting shot, issued his famous aphorism. See Allison's "Public and Private Management: Are They Fundamentally Alike in All Unimportant Respects?" in *Public Management*, pp. 72–92.

63. Stanley I. Benn and Gerald F. Gaus, "The Public and the Private: Concepts and Action," *Public and Private Social Life*, S. I. Benn and G. F. Gaus, eds. (New York: St. Martin's, 1983), pp. 3–27. The quotation is on p. 5. The following discussion is based on this book.

64. James L. Perry, Hal G. Rainey, and Barry Bozeman, "The Public-Private Distinction in Organization Theory: A Critique and Research Strategy," Paper presented by the 1985 Annual Meeting of the American Political Science Association (New Orleans, August 29–September 1, 1985), Table 1.

65. Evelina R. Moulder, "Citizen Engagement: An Evolving Process," *Municipal Year Book, 2010* (Washington, DC: International City/County Management Association, 2010), pp. 28–32. Emphasis added. Data (p. 30) are for 2009.

66. Bradley E. Wright, "Public Administration as an Interdisciplinary Field: Assessing Its Relationship with the Fields of Law, Management, and Political Science," *Public Administration Review* 71 (January/February 2011), pp. 96–101. The quotation is on p. 98.

67. Mark R. Daniels, "Public Administration as an Emergent Profession: A Survey of Attitudes About the Review and Accreditation of Programs," Paper presented at the National Conference of the American Society for Public Administration, New York, April 1983; and J. Norman Baldwin, "Comparison of Perceived Effectiveness of MPA Programs Administered Under Different Institutional Arrangements," *Public Administration Review* 48 (September/October 1988), pp. 876–884.

68. Kraemer and Perry, "Camelot Revisited," p. 92.

69. David A. Breaux, Edward J. Clynch, and John C. Morris, "The Core Curriculum Content of NASPAA-Accredited Programs: Fundamentally Alike or Different?" *Journal of Public Affairs Education* 9 (October 2003), pp. 261–276. The quotations are on pp. 271, 259.

70. As derived from data in National Association of Schools of Public Affairs and Administration, *Almanac* (Washington, DC: Author, 2008), and *1986 Directory: Programs in Public Affairs and Administration* (Washington, DC, Author, 1986), p. xix.

71. Baldwin, "Comparison of Perceived Effectiveness of MPA Programs Administered Under Different Institutional Arrangements," p. 876.

72. Robert A. Cleary, "Masters Programs in PA Continue to Expand," *PA Times*, 19 (December 1, 1996), pp. 2, 14.

73. National Association of Schools of Public Affairs and Administration, *Almanac*; and *1986 Directory*, p. xix. Current figure, 31,571, is for 2009 and includes 2,320 doctoral students. The response rates to NASPAA's surveys have declined significantly over time, from well over 90 percent in the 1970s through 1980s to less than 60 percent in the mid-2000s (although, in 2009, it hit 66 percent), artificially skewing the growth in public administration students for the worse. Our estimate is that there are from 40,000 to 45,000 students enrolled in M.P.A. and related programs.

74. National Association of Schools of Public Affairs and Administration, *Student Survey*,

2008 (Washington, DC: Author, 2008). Figure, 64 percent, is for 2008.

75. National Association of Schools of Public Affairs and Administration, *Almanac* (Washington, DC: Author, 2006). Figure is for 2006.

76. John Nalbandian, "Reflections of a 'Pracademic' on the Logic of Politics and Administration," *Public Administration Review* 54 (November/December 1994), pp. 531–536. The quotation is on p. 531.

77. Lewis, *Political Appointments, Bureau Chiefs, and Federal Management Performance.* Details are in Chapter 9.

78. Claudia N. Avellaneda, "Municipal Performance: Does Mayoral Quality Matter?" *Journal of Public Administration Research and Theory* 19 (April 2009), pp. 285–312. This is an analysis of forty Colombian municipalities and their elected mayors, 2000–2004. The Colombian constitution requires a "strong-mayor" form of municipal government, so mayors are deeply involved in local administration.

79. Claudia N. Avellaneda, "Mayoral Quality and Local Public Finance," *Public Administration Review* 69 (May/June 2009), pp. 469–486. See the preceding endnote for details.

80. Alejandro Rodriquez, "Reformed County Government and Service Delivery Performance: An Integrated Study of Florida Counties," *International Journal of Public Administration* 30 (10, 2007), pp. 973–994.

81. James H. Svara, "The Search for Meaning in Political-Administrative Relations in Local Government," *International Journal of Public Administration* 29 (12, 2006), pp. 1065–1090. The quotation is on p. 1065.

82. Tansu Demir, "The Complementarity View: Exploring a Continuum in Political-Administrative Relations," *Public Administration Review* 69 (September/October 2009), pp. 876–888.

83. Poul Erik Mouritzen and James H. Svara, *Leadership at the Apex: Politicians and Administrators in Western Local Governments* (Pittsburgh, PA: University of Pittsburgh Press, 2002), p. 258.

84. James H. Svara, "Leadership and Professionalism in County Government," *The American County: Frontiers of Knowledge*, Donald C. Menzel, ed. (Tuscaloosa, AL: University of Alabama Press, 1996), pp. 109–127. The quotation is on p. 124.

85. Karl Nollenberger, "Cooperation and Conflict in Governmental Decision Making in Mid-Sized U.S. Cities," *Municipal Year Book, 2008* (Washington, DC: International City/County Management Association, 2008), pp. 9–15. The quotation (emphasis added) is on p. 9.

86. Ibid.

87. Richard C. Feiock and Jaehoon Kim, "Credible Commitment and Council-Manager Government: Implications for Policy Instrument Choices," *Public Administration Review* 63 (September/October 2003), pp. 616–625. The quotation is on p. 616.

88. Curtis Wood and Yongmao Fan, "The Performance of the Adapted City from the Perspective of Citizens," *Public Performance & Management Review* 31 (March 2008), pp. 407–430. The quotation is on p. 407. The authors categorized governmental forms used by seventy-four cities in thirty states into five types, ranging from "political" to "administrative."

89. Moulder, "Citizen Engagement." Figures, 76 and 58 percent (p. 31), respectively, are for 2009.

90. Curtis Wood, "Voter Turnout in City Elections," *Urban Affairs Review* 38 (November 2002), pp. 209–231. The quotations are on p. 209. Emphasis added.

91. David H. Folz and P. Edward French, *Managing America's Small Communities: People, Politics, and Performance* (Lanham, MD: Rowman and Littlefield, 2005).

92. Timothy B. Krebs and John P. Peliserro, "What Influences City Council Adoption and Support for Reinventing Government? Environmental or Institutional Factors?" *Public Administration Review* 70 (March/April 2010), pp. 258–267. The quotation is on p. 263.

93. The Three Sector Collaborative Project of the Conference Board, Council on Foundations, Independent Sector, National Academy of Public Administration, National Alliance of Business, and National Governors' Association, *Changing Roles, Changing Relationships: The New Challenge for Business, Nonprofit Organizations and Government* (Authors: ND), p. iii.

94. Donald F. Kettl, "The Transformation of Governance: Globalization, Devolution, and the Role of Government," *Public Administration Review* 60 (November/December 2000), pp. 488–497.

95. Ira Sharkansky, *Wither the State? Politics and Public Enterprise in Three Countries* (Chatham, NJ: Chatham House, 1979).

96. Paul H. Appleby, *Policy and Administration* (Tuscaloosa, AL: University of Alabama Press, 1949), p. 15.

97. Carolyn J. Hill, "Is Hierarchical Government in Decline? Evidence from Empirical Research," *Journal of Public Administration Research and Theory* 15 (Spring 2005), pp. 173–196. The quotations are on p. 173.

98. Robert Agranoff and Michael McGuire, "American Federalism and the Search for Models of Management," *Public Administration Review* 61 (November/December 2001), pp. 671–681. The quotation is on p. 677. This is a study of local administrators charged with economic development responsibilities in 237 American cities.

99. Chris Ansell and Alison Gash, "Collaborative Governance in Theory and Practice," *Journal of Public Administration Research and Theory* 18 (October 2008), pp. 543–571.

100. Keith G. Provan and H. Brinton Milward, "A Preliminary Theory of Interorganizational Effectiveness: A Comparative Study of Four Community Mental Health Systems," *Administrative Science Quarterly* 40 (Spring 1995), pp. 1–33.

101. Laurence J. O'Toole, Jr. and Kenneth J. Meier, "Desperately Seeking Selznick: Cooptation and the Dark Side of Public Management in Networks," *Public Administration Review* 64 (November/December 2004), pp. 681–693. The quotation is on p. 690.

102. John Seabrook, "Don't Shoot," *The New Yorker* (June 22, 2009), pp. 32–41.

103. Jorgen Svensson, Willem Trommel, and Tineke Lantink, "Reemployment Services in the Netherlands: A Comparative Study of Bureaucratic, Market, and Network Forms of Organization," *Public Administration Review* 68 (May/June 2008), pp. 505–515. The quotations are on p. 514.

104. Richard M. Walker, Rhys Andrews, George A. Boyne, *et al.*, "Wakeup Call: Strategic Management, Network Alarms, and Performance," *Public Administration* Review 70 (September/October 2010), pp. 731–741. The quotation is on p. 738.

105. Rhys Andrews and Tom Entwistle, "Does Cross-Sectoral Partnership Deliver? An Empirical Exploration of Public Service Effectiveness, Efficiency, and Equity," *Journal of Public Administration Research and Theory* 20 (July 2010), pp. 679–701. Details are in Chapters 11and 12.

106. Ansell and Gash, "Collaborative Governance in Theory and Practice," p. 543.

107. Council for Excellence in Government and Peter D. Hart Research, *Calling Young People to Government Service: From "Ask Not…" to "Not Asked"* (Washington, DC: Authors, 2004), pp. 3–4. Details are in Chapter 9.

108. National Association of Schools of Public Affairs and Administration, *Nonprofit Survey Summary* (Washington, DC: Author, 2008). Figure is for 2008.

109. National Association of Schools of Public Affairs and Administration, *Student Survey, 2008.* Figure is for 2008.

110. As derived from data in Roseanne M. Mirabella, *Nonprofit Management Education* http://academic.shu.edu/npo/list.php?sort=degree&type=gnoc. In 2011, there were 185 master's degrees that were stand-alone nonprofit management degrees or degrees that offered concentrations in nonprofit management, ninety-two of which were housed within M.P.A. programs.

111. National Association of Schools of Public Affairs and Administration, *Almanac.*

112. Paul C. Light, *The New Public Service* (Washington, DC: Brookings, 1999), pp. 89–90.

113. Matthias Benz and Bruno S. Frey, "Corporate Governance: What Can We Learn from Public Governance?" *Academy of Management Review* 32 (January 2007), pp. 92–104. The quotations are on pp. 101, 92.

Public and Nonprofit Organizations

In the following chapters, we explain organizations—their threads of theory, fabric of forces, and fibers of people.

We focus, of course, on *public* and *public-serving nonprofit organizations*, which are collectivities of people whose mission emphasizes the delivery of goods and services that benefit people outside, rather than people inside, the organization. It is a realistic definition because it implicitly recognizes that these organizations are not necessarily peopled by would-be saints; hence, the purpose of public and nonprofit organizations only "emphasizes" benefiting others, a nuance which accepts that these organizations, like private ones, can legitimately benefit their own employees, too. Still, the emphasis on serving others is real, and it associates with some very real differences.

All organizations, whether public, private, or nonprofit, have some basic similarities, and we shall review these, but our real interest lies in revealing behavioral differences among organizations by sector. The *public sector* is composed of governments, government agencies, and government corporations. The *private sector* includes profit-seeking companies. The *nonprofit sector*, also known as the *independent, voluntary, emerging, hybrid*, or *third sector*, is made up of privately owned organizations that do not seek profits. Technically, the nonprofit sector is a part of the private sector, but we treat it as a stand-alone sector (one of its titles, after all, is the "third sector"). At the risk of getting ahead of ourselves, we refer the reader to Figure 11-1, in Chapter 11, for a breakdown of the characteristics of each of the three sectors.

Part II may be that portion of this book that will have the most lasting value for you. It discusses why bureaucrats behave in the ways they do, and attempts to help you gain a bit of insight about what to expect should you find yourself working in the public or nonprofit sector.

The Threads of Organization: Theories

Because organizations are different creatures to different people, organizations are "defined" according to the contexts and perspectives peculiar to the person doing the defining. Nevertheless, we can, at least, posit certain characteristics that are common to all organizations.

Organizations

- are purposeful, complex human collectivities;
- are characterized by secondary (or impersonal) relationships;
- have specialized and limited goals;
- are characterized by sustained cooperative activity;
- are integrated within a larger social system;
- provide services and products to their environment; and
- are dependent upon exchanges with their environment.

Organization theorists, using essentially this list of characteristics but stressing different items in it, have produced a vast body of literature on the nature of organizations. This literature can be viewed as a long lanyard plaited of two yarns, each with its own threads.

THE CLOSED MODEL OF ORGANIZATIONS

Our first yarn is the closed model of organizations, which goes by many names. *Bureaucratic, hierarchical, formal, rational,* and *mechanistic* are some of them.

Characteristics of the Closed Model of Organizations

We rely on a classic analysis in listing the principal features of the closed model of organizations:[1]

- Routine tasks occur in stable conditions.
- Task specialization (i.e., a division of labor) is central.
- Means (or the proper way to do a job) are emphasized.
- Conflict within the organization is adjudicated from the top.
- "Responsibility" (or what one is supposed to do, one's formal job description) is emphasized.
- One's primary sense of responsibility and loyalty is to the bureaucratic subunit to which one is assigned (such as the accounting department).
- The organization is perceived as a hierarchic structure (i.e., the structure "looks" like a pyramid).
- Knowledge is inclusive only at the top of the hierarchy (in other words, only the chief executive knows everything).
- Interaction between people in the organization tends to be vertical (i.e., one takes orders from above and transmits orders below), but not horizontal.
- The style of interaction is directed toward obedience, command, and clear superordinate/subordinate relationships.

- Loyalty and obedience to one's superior and the organization generally are emphasized, sometimes at the expense of performance.
- Prestige is "internalized," that is, personal status in the organization is determined largely by one's formal office and rank.

So runs our closed model of organizations. And it is just that—a model. No organization meets all twelve of its features in practice. Among organizations that are widely known, the Department of Defense likely comes closest to accomplishing the requisites of the closed model, but the Pentagon's exceptions to the model are obvious, such as highly *un*stable conditions during wartime.

There are at least three theoretical threads that have thrived within the closed model's framework.

Bureaucratic Theory

The earliest school of the closed model is that of *bureaucratic theory,* or the study of the impersonal organization, execution, and enforcement of legal rules in organizations. Its best-known representative is Max Weber, a remarkable German sociologist who wrote around the turn of the twentieth century. Although "bureaucracy" is common in all sectors, Weber cast his theory of bureaucracy squarely in the public one.

In what is perhaps a too-succinct summary, the features of bureaucracy are

- hierarchy,
- promotion based on professional merit and skill,
- the development of a career service,
- reliance on and use of rules and regulations, and
- impersonality of relationships among career-professionals in the bureaucracy and with their clientele.

To Weber, an impersonal, rule-abiding, efficient, merit-based career service provided the surest way of fulfilling the public interest in the face of a politically fragmented Germany and an arrogant, powerful, yet somewhat silly *Junker* class. Weber, in a large sense, was not anti-humanist in his thinking, as has been alleged, but the effects of the bureaucracy that he so loudly touted could be, both

to the citizens who were governed by the bureaucrats and to the bureaucrats themselves.

Weber's rigidly rational theory was warmly welcomed by the first public administrationists, who embraced it as an erudite justification of their values, all of which shared an abhorrence with messy politics. Woodrow Wilson's closest adviser, Colonel Edward House, anonymously wrote a novel that memorably expresses this revulsion. In it, the president is replaced by an omnipotent "Administrator of the Republic" who resides in a monastic barracks, spurning the distractive fripperies of the White House, and who ends the odious "rule of the bosses." Congress is disbanded in favor creating numerous "boards," each composed of five neutral experts who are charged with reforming the courts, taxes, railroads, "the unsanitary custom of burial in cemeteries," and anything else that could benefit from a dose of the Administrator's common sense—in other words, just about everything.[2] (This perspective remains remarkably persistent; nearly a third of Americans think that policymaking should be shorn from elected officials and turned over to "non-elected experts."[3])

Scientific Management

Another rivulet of research in the closed model is *scientific management,* which is the analysis of workflow processes as the means of raising organizational productivity. Scientific management refers to what are more popularly known as time-motion studies; it flourished at the beginning of the twentieth century and remains in use today in industry.

Workers as "Gear Wheels" Scientific management's overriding concern is to increase production, and it does this by making human beings as efficient as, and more like, machines. To quote one of the school's founders, "it is absolutely necessary for every man in an organization to become one of a train of gear wheels."[4]

Key representatives of the scientific management school include Frederick Taylor (who gave this school its name with his 1911 volume, *Principles of Scientific Management*),[5] and Frank and Lillian Gilbreth.[6] The person-as-machine perspective, replete with all its discomfiting overtones, is on clear display in Taylor's writings. A notorious example is Taylor's story of Schmidt, a pig-iron hauler, whom Taylor declared to be "stupid...phlegmatic...[and] more nearly resembles in his mental make-up the ox than any other type." After Taylor analyzed Schmidt's physical movements, he ordered him to change how he moved his body and, as a result of these "scientific" alterations, Schmidt's production went up from twelve and a half tons of pig-iron hauled per day to forty-seven tons.[7]

Similarly, the Gilbreths developed the concept of the "therblig," each one of which represented a category of eighteen basic human motions—all physical activity fell into a therblig class of one type or another.[8] (The scientific management crowd rarely was constrained by modesty, false or otherwise; try reading therblig backward.)

The person-as-machine perspective has a distasteful aura. People are not machines. Before dismissing the scientific managers as exploiters of the working class, however, keep in mind that efficiency can serve humane ends as well as any other, and this aspect sometimes is overlooked by critics. Frank Gilbreth, for example, applied his therbligs to surgery techniques in hospitals, and the sharply ordered "Scalpel! Sponge!" slapped into a surgeon's palm by a hyperefficient nurse is a direct result of Gilbreth's operating-room studies.[9] Prior to Gilbreth's analysis, surgeons rustled around for their own instruments with one hand, evidently holding open the incision with the other.

Frank Gilbreth's wife, Lillian, held a professorship at Purdue University that was split between its schools of Management and Home Economics and gave us kitchen islands, rolling kitchen carts, and cookery's "work triangle."[10] As "the mother" of scientific management[11] (Taylor is the "Father of Scientific Management"—it says so on his tombstone), she was featured on a U.S. postage stamp, advised six presidents of the United States, and bore Frank, at his request, six boys and six girls—two of whom wrote *Cheaper by the Dozen*, a rollicking account of life in a scientifically managed household.

The Lasting Impact of a Fraud? A deeper criticism of scientific management is that "there

was almost no science to it."[12] Taylor's Schmidt was likely fictional,[13] his methodologies were idiosyncratic at best, and he never published the actual data on which his theory was based.[14] Whether "Speedy Taylor," as he was called, was "a shameless fraud is a matter of some debate, but not, it must be said, much."[15] Taylor's sometimes-brutal applications of his theory (the Gilbreths were much more humane) brought about strikes by exhausted workers and a hostile congressional investigation. (Perhaps it should give us pause that Taylor thought public administration to be "on the whole good."[16])

Nevertheless, the impact of scientific management was stunning. Taylor was central in organizing America's first graduate school to offer a degree in business (at Harvard, in 1908); his theories underlay the Soviet Union's first five-year economic plan[17] and were given their "fullest application by Henry Ford, who," following Speedy Taylor's example, "measured his workers' movements on the assembly line with a stopwatch."[18] "The world of management"—including public management, where "Taylor's ghost" may "still haunt the halls of government"[19]—"remains deeply Taylorist in its foundations."[20]

Administrative Management

Our final literature of the closed model is administrative management. *Administrative management,* also called *generic management,* is the discovery and application of universal, scientific, administrative principles that can improve any organization's efficiency and effectiveness. Unfortunately for this school, as we explained in Chapter 2, there are no universal, scientific, administrative principles, but some of its adherents nevertheless made some contributions of consequence.

The scholars of administrative management devoted their energies to the discovery of managerial principles that worked in any and all institutional settings—from corporations and clubs, to governments and gulags—and in any and all cultural contexts—from Boston and Botswana, to Paris and Patagonia. Writers in this stream usually offered up very specific principles of administration: The public administration scholars, Luther Gulick and Lyndall Urwick (recall Chapter 2), listed seven "principles";[21] James D. Mooney and Alan C. Reiley, in their aptly-titled and influential work, *The Principles of Organization*, found four;[22] another, Henri Fayol, unearthed fourteen.[23] Among the premier scholars in the administrative management tradition, Mary Parker Follett was one of the few who fudged when it come to enumerating principles of administration, but then she was unusually ahead of her time, perhaps because her intellectual roots were deeply planted in public administration.[24]

With the emergence of administrative management, a hint surfaced that presaged a revolution in organization theory, one that ultimately would bluntly question a foundation of its two theoretical predecessors, bureaucratic theory and scientific management. That hint was that underlings and toilers in organizations conceivably might have minds of their own.

It was not much of an inkling, but it is intimated, if perversely, in Mooney and Reiley's contention that the "indoctrination" of workers is vital to well-managed organizations; they thought that the Catholic church had done a simply swell job of indoctrination over the preceding 2,000 years. The idea that workers could think is much more apparent in Follett's writing, who was suggesting power sharing, stakeholder theory, and team building in the 1920s!

Follett's ideas (as channeled through W. Edwards Deming, of total-quality-management fame) were implemented by Japanese automakers, who applied them with enormous success, at least up to a point. Japan's Toyota, after faithfully following Follett's philosophy for more than fifty years, abandoned it in favor of overtaking General Motors as the globe's biggest automaker (which it did) by embracing "disastrous policies adopted after 2000, when top management's thinking changed sharply in a direction that, while consistent with that of most other Western companies, would never have been tolerated at Toyota in the past."[25] One result: Toyota's global rolling recalls in 2010 and 2011 to correct safety issues in more than *fourteen million* vehicles, its largest number ever. (An unprecedented, ten-month federal investigation found no electronic problems, but did discover two mechanical malfunctions involving unanticipated acceleration.[26]) As Follett

exemplifies, the administrative management writers were among the first to express a dawning recognition that subordinates were people (like managers) and could think (almost like managers). This breakthrough provided a basis for organization theory's next paradigm, the open model.

THE OPEN MODEL OF ORGANIZATIONS

As with the closed model, the open model goes by many names. *Collegial, competitive, free market, informal, natural,* and *organic* are some of them.

The origins of the open model actually precede those of the closed model by more than a century and a half and can be traced to Count Louis de Rouvroy Saint-Simon, the brilliant French social thinker, and to his protégée Auguste Comte, the "father of sociology." Partly as a reaction to the social stultification of the last days of the French kings and the explosiveness of the resultant Revolution, Saint-Simon, and later Comte, speculated on what the administration of the future would be like. They thought that technology would spawn new professions; that administrators would be appointed on the basis of skill rather than heredity; and that organizations would be created spontaneously, evolve "naturally," and be a liberating force for humanity.[27]

Characteristics of the Open Model of Organizations

The principal features of the open model of organization are[28]

- Nonroutine tasks occur in unstable conditions.
- Specialized knowledge contributes to common tasks (thus differing from the closed model's specialized *task* notion in that the specialized *knowledge* possessed by any one member of the organization may be applied profitably to a variety of tasks undertaken by various other members of the organization).
- Ends (or getting the job done), rather than means, are emphasized.

- Conflict within the organization is adjusted by interaction with peers, rather than adjudicated from the top.
- "Shedding of responsibility" is emphasized (in other words, formal job descriptions are discarded in favor of all organizational members contributing to all organizational problems).
- One's sense of responsibility and loyalty is to the organization as a whole.
- The organization is perceived as a fluidic network structure (i.e., the organization "looks" like an amoeba).
- Knowledge can be located anywhere in the organization (in other words, everybody knows something relevant about the organization, but no one, including the chief executive, knows everything).
- Interaction between people in the organization tends to be horizontal (i.e., peers interact with peers), as well as vertical.
- The style of interaction is directed toward accomplishment, "advice" (rather than commands), and is characterized by a "myth of peerage," which envelops even the most obvious superordinate/subordinate relationships.
- Task achievement and excellence of performance in accomplishing a task are emphasized, sometimes at the expense of obedience to one's superiors.
- Prestige is "externalized" (i.e., personal status in the organization is determined largely by one's professional ability and reputation, rather than by office and rank).

So runs our open model of organizations, which, like the closed model, does not exist in actuality, although a major university might come close (which is why the open model occasionally is called the "collegial" model). But exceptions are apparent; for instance, in universities one is likely to find a higher degree of loyalty to the subunit (such as the academic department) than to the organization as a whole.

As with the closed model, three threads comprise the open model of organizations.

Human Relations

Human relations, the first of our three threads, is the study of people's problems, opportunities, and interactions in organizations. It focuses on organizational variables never considered in the closed model, such as personal motivations, among others. Ironically, this focus resulted from what originally was intended to be a research undertaking in scientific management, a literature at the opposite end of the continuum in terms of the views held by its theorists.

The Hawthorne Experiments

In 1924, Elton Mayo and Fritz J. Roethlisberger began a series of studies (later known as "the Hawthorne experiments," for the location of the plant) of working conditions and worker behavior at a Western Electric factory.[29] Their experiment was predicated on the then-plausible Taylorian hypothesis that workers would respond like "gear wheels" to changes in working conditions. To test it, they altered the intensity of light available to a group of selected workers, expecting that the dimmer the light the lower their productivity. The lights were turned down and production went up. Mayo and Roethlisberger were disconcerted. They dimmed the lights to near darkness, and production kept climbing.

Among the explanations of this phenomenon that later came forth were

- Human workers probably are not entirely like machines.
- The Western Electric workers were responding to some motivating variable other than the lighting, or despite the lack of it.
- They likely kept producing more in spite of poor working conditions because they had been told that they were being watched.

Mayo and his colleagues were so impressed by these initial findings that they ultimately conducted a total of six interrelated experiments over eight years. In part because of the massive size of the undertaking, the Hawthorne studies number among the most influential empirical research ever conducted by social scientists. Most notably, they produced the famous term "Hawthorne effect," or the tendency of people to change their behavior when they know that they are being observed. But of even greater importance, the studies were interpreted by succeeding generations of management scientists as validating the idea that unquantifiable relationships (or "human relations") between workers and managers, and among workers themselves, are significant determinants of workers' productivity.

Reinterpretations of the Hawthorne data conclude that human relations were *not* the reasons behind worker productivity, but other factors were explanatory, such as their fear of being laid off and that, unlike other workers, they were given rest periods and group pay incentives.[30] Other research suggests that the original lessons of the Hawthorne experiments remain valid.[31] In any case, the Hawthorne studies marked the continuation of the Saint-Simonian tradition after a century-long gap, and the beginning of human relations as we know it.

From Self-Actualization to Engagement The Hawthorne experiments inspired much research on job satisfaction, and an important contribution to this research is the "hierarchy of human needs" developed by A. H. Maslow. Maslow perceived human desires to be based, first, on *physiological* needs (such as eating), which provided the foundation for a person's next greatest need, *economic security*, then *love* or *belongingness*, followed by *self-esteem*, and ultimately *self-actualization*. *Self-actualization* refers to a person growing, maturing, and achieving a deep inner sense of self-worth as he or she relates to his or her job. Maslow wrote that these "highly evolved" self-actualized people assimilated "their work into the identity, into the self, *i.e.*, work actually becomes part of the self, part of the individual's definition of himself."[32]

The mildly melodramatic concept of self-actualization has evolved into the blander notion of "employee engagement." *Employee engagement* holds that workers who have an *emotional commitment* (i.e., the visceral pride and enjoyment that employees derive from their work and organization), as well as a *rational commitment* (i.e., employees' logical understanding that their employment benefits them financially and professionally), to their organization will exert their very best effort on their organization's behalf.[33] In contrast to self-actualization, engagement extends employees' psychic bonding with their work to their organization.

THE DISASTER OF DISENGAGEMENT

As we enter our discussion of employee engagement, it is illustrative to contrast it with employee disengagement. We offer an example of that disengagement — or, perhaps more precisely, the refusal of some public employees to become engaged in their jobs — and the tragedy that resulted.

Carl J. Jatho was a freewheeling entrepreneur in Kingman, Arizona, who headed a tax preparation business called The Bookkeeper. Ultimately, Jatho pled guilty to five counts of tax fraud that had cheated the federal government out of an estimated $45 million in taxes owed by some 3,800 taxpayers. So many of these bilked taxpayers appeared in federal court *en masse* during Jatho's trial that the press took to calling them The Jatho People. Ultimately, Jatho was sentenced to three years in prison. Jatho was imprisoned in September 1986.

Among Jatho's remaining assets were thirty-five to forty horses that Jatho kept fenced on his ranch in Kingman. Apparently, no one thought too seriously about the fate of the horses until early January, 1987, when officials from the Internal Revenue Service (IRS), the Arizona Livestock and Sanitary Board, and some local agencies met to discuss what to

(continued)

(*continued*)

do with them. What exactly occurred at this meeting is unclear. The IRS had the legal authorization to seize the horses as part of its civil case but decided not to do so because its officials believed that only seventeen of the horses actually belonged to Jatho, and no one was sure which of the beasts were his. The Mojave County Animal Control Board and the Mojave County Sheriff's Office thought that the animals fell under the jurisdiction of the State Livestock Board, but the Livestock Board decided not to act on the grounds that it believed the IRS had jurisdiction. It did appear from subsequent press reports, however, that neither the IRS nor the Livestock Board had any plans to take care of the horses, and that each agency knew that the other was not going to assume responsibility for them either.

It was at this juncture that Jatho's starving horses morphed into public employee disengagement gone wild.

Five days after the meeting, the press reported that four of the horses had died from starvation. When questioned by the press about how and why this had occurred, IRS agent William Bronson stated that the horses were in such poor condition that they could not be sold, adding, "We are a tax collecting agency, not a humane society."

At this point, the State Livestock Board acted and seized the horses, noting in the process that hay and other feed had been in the storage shed behind the Jatho house during the entire five months that had passed since Jatho entered prison. In an apparent effort to show that it was on top of the problem, the Livestock Board filed charges of willful neglect and cruelty to animals against Jatho, who had, of course, been in prison since September. Meanwhile, the

Phoenix office of the Internal Revenue Service was besieged with phone calls from irate citizens.

The IRS and the Livestock Board soon began trading charges. A member of the Livestock Board stated that, "It was the IRS that put the guy in jail. The IRS should have made some provision for the horses." The IRS contended, in turn, that it was the victim of a cheap shot by the media and other government agencies.

The senior Senator from Arizona soon got into the act by writing to the commissioner of the IRS that the incident in Kingman was the "result of either a severely flawed policy by the agency or negligent actions taken by IRS personnel" and launched his own inquiry. An aide to the Senator observed: "The word 'insane' is used rather frequently in news stories because news stories cover unusual and unexpected things, but I don't ever recall seeing a news story where the word 'insane' was more applicable.... You don't just leave forty horses there to die. It's crazy. There's nothing rational about it."

The state's largest newspaper editorialized that the explanations from both the IRS and the Livestock Board were "lame and ludicrous."

Mojave County Supervisor Becky Foster, after noting that a number of citizens had offered to donate food or money for the benefit of horses, stated, "This restores your faith in humanity." Then she broke into tears as she watched workers dump the dead horses into a truck. ∎

Sources: Steve Daniels, "Outraged Arizonans Rally to Rescue Starving Horses," *Arizona Republic* (January 14, 1987); Andy Hall and Steve Daniels, "Agencies Trade Blame for Abandoned Horses," *Arizona Republic* (January 15, 1987); and "The Cold Hands of the IRS," *Arizona Republic* (January 16, 1987).

Achieving Engagement: The Roles of Hygienic Factors and Motivator Factors How does an organization induce its employees to engage? Frederick Herzberg stimulated much of the empirical research on this question.[34] Herzberg's "motivation-hygiene theory" holds that there are two classes of phenomena that make people feel good or bad about their jobs and that lead to their engagement or disengagement with their organization.

One class relates to the *context* of the job, and includes such factors as working conditions, organizational policies, and salary. Herzberg called these "extrinsic" dimensions *hygienic factors*, so named because they are needed to avoid worker dissatisfaction, but fail, in and of themselves, to provide satisfaction and engagement. Hygienic factors correspond, more or less, with the base of Maslow's pyramid of human needs, where physiological and security needs are found, and with the employee-engagement researchers' idea of "rational commitment" to the organization.

Herzberg's second category relates to the *content* of the job, and includes such factors as professional and personal challenge, appreciation of a job well done by supervisors and peers, and a sense of being responsible for important matters. Herzberg called these "intrinsic" aspects *motivator factors.* Motivators relate, by and large, with the upper reaches of Maslow's pyramid—belongingness, self-esteem, and self-actualization—and with the notion of an employee's "emotional commitment" to the organization.

What Matters to Public and Nonprofit Employees?

What matters more to public and nonprofit employees, hygienic factors, such as pay and perks, or motivators, such as praise and producing?

Motivators Matter Without question, motivator factors and engagement dominate. And they appear to be more important to government and nonprofit workers than they are to other and larger working populations.

Motivating Public Workers Large-scale studies find that government workers are "significantly less motivated by salary" than are private-sector workers. Motivator factors and engagement have an even greater impact among top public administrators than among lower-level ones.[35]

For nearly three decades, roughly nine out of every ten federal employees have stated that "the work I do is meaningful,"[36] compared with about half of all Americans who state, in a similar vein, that "a feeling of accomplishment" is the "most important" single aspect of their jobs.[37] More than four-fifths of federal workers are engaged in their work, either fully (35 percent) or "somewhat" (47 percent), compared with 20–30 percent of the all North American workers, and only 18 percent are "not engaged," compared with 50 percent of North American employees.[38] Federal managers

are much more likely than their counterparts in business to "come to work" because of the "nature of their jobs."[39]

State government workers also display high engagement and "are more motivated to perform their work when they have clearly understood and challenging tasks that they feel are important and achievable."[40]

Motivating Independent Workers Motivators and engagement are even more pronounced in the independent sector: "The mean level of nonprofit managers' job involvement is significantly greater than for public managers."[41] More than two-thirds of nonprofit employees report that they are given the chance to do the things that they do best and that their colleagues are willing to help other employees learn new skills, compared with about half of federal and corporate employees.[42]

An important indicator of employee engagement is how many hours employees devote to their jobs, a behavior that correlates strongly and positively with greater satisfaction and pride in one's job.[43] One study found that nonprofit "managers" worked 14 percent longer hours per week (nearly fifty-one hours) than state "managers" (forty-five hours),[44] although other surveys have found that state agency heads,[45] city managers,[46] and assistant city managers[47] work, on average, more than fifty hours per week—figures have held steady for decades.

In sum, it is absolutely clear from this research that, when compared with corporate employees, public and nonprofit workers and administrators relish their jobs.

Friends Matter Having a "best friend at work" is a critical component of employee happiness.[48] A study of public and nonprofit employees found "strong support" for the proposition that "a strong social network" within the organization reduced employees' inclination to leave. Social networks outside the organization, by contrast, were only a negligible temptation in inducing them to quit and join another enterprise.[49]

While it is satisfying to know that "ability" is "the single most important" factor in accounting for employees' upward mobility in the public sector, the combined factors of "reputation, social credentials, and patronage...are at least equally as important" as ability.[50] Friends count.

Mentors Matter Mentors in the workplace are particularly powerful motivators of employee engagement,[51] and this is especially true in government, where mentoring is widespread. Almost three-fourths of "senior career executives in municipal, state, and federal governments" report that they had a mentor in their early years, a proportion that appears to be growing over time.[52] A fifth of senior federal administrators,[53] two-thirds of city managers,[54] and four-fifths of U.S. Army officers had mentors.[55] Formal "mentor-protégé programs" have spread to thirteen major federal agencies since the Pentagon initiated the first one, in 1991.[56]

There is empirical evidence that mentoring in government is positively linked to career success.[57] More than four-fifths of federal, state, and local administrators find the influence of mentors on themselves and their careers to be "substantial" to "extraordinary,"[58] with a remarkable 85 percent of federal employees each identifying their top two "career accelerators" as a "supportive supervisor" or a nonsupervisory "mentor."[59] The higher that one ascends in government, the more that public executives believe their mentors were critical to their success.[60]

What Matters to Organizations?

It may be comforting, in a bleeding-heart sort of way, to know that motivators and engagement matter most to employees, but do they, or hygienic factors, matter more in advancing the interests of the organization?

Hygienic factors count, but not much. There is no relationship—none—between progressive hygienic policies (such as shorter hours, generous vacations, and so forth) and more productive, competitive companies. Nor is there any correlation between stingy benefits and less, or more, competitive corporations.[61] Hygienic factors and satisfied but disengaged employees "are like tickets to the ballpark—they can get you into the game, but they can't help you win."[62]

Motivated, engaged employees, by contrast, help you win. A variety of large-scale analyses show that "employee engagement surpasses satisfaction as an indicator of productivity"[63] and "has an enormous impact on organizational outcomes. Multiple research studies have demonstrated the positive relationship between high levels of employee engagement and desired organizational outcomes."[64] Engaged employees are more likely to report misconduct, thereby reducing organizational risk.[65]

Six motivator factors are especially vital in engaging organizational members. When employees feel that they know what is expected of them at work, have what they need to do their jobs right, have the opportunity "to do what I do best every day," believe that someone at work cares about them as a person, receive recognition for work well done over the last seven days, and think that there is someone at work who encourages their development, then companies score markedly higher on the four critical measures of corporate strength: productivity, profit, employee retention, and customer satisfaction.[66]

What Matters to Governments?

The same holds true for governments. Mentoring, an important motivator, associates with a more positive commitment to the United States Army and a lower likelihood of leaving it.[67] Federal employees who are engaged with their jobs are up to three times less likely to perceive "prohibited personnel practices," such as discrimination, occurring in their agencies than are their disengaged colleagues, a perception that doubtless reduces organizationally costly complaints and litigation brought by employees.[68]

Those federal agencies with the highest proportions of engaged employees, in comparison to those with the lowest percentages, have much higher performance and accountability scores; far less likelihood that employees will leave the agency; much lower injury and sick leave rates; and far fewer discrimination complaints. These differences are not merely statistically significant; those agencies with many engaged employees frequently boast measures of agency quality that are *two or three times greater* than those of agencies with few.[69]

An analysis of state workers amplifies our understanding of those conditions that associate with more productive government workers. Public employee performance heightens when the worker's job role is clear ("role ambiguity negatively affects job performance"); the employee directly contributes to the fulfillment of the agency's mission; and the worker perceives that the agency not only is adequately funded but also spends those funds efficiently.[70]

Rude, Crude, and Lewd: The Impact of Negative Motivators
We can gain a fuller understanding of the importance of motivator factors and employee engagement in advancing organizational success when we contrast their positive impact with that of "negative motivators," or the presence of people who are not supportive and caring, but instead are uncivil and bullying.

Uncivil Actions *Organizational incivility* is "the exchange of seemingly inconsequential inconsiderate words and deeds that violate conventional norms of workplace conduct." Almost all American workers and executives—96 percent of them—in the private sector report that they have been direct targets of uncivil behavior. Employees who are "treated rudely" at least once a week have almost doubled over seven years, from a fourth to "nearly half." Three-fifths of perceived incivility is inflicted by supervisors on subordinates,[71] and its presence may veil deeper pathologies, such as racism and sexism.[72] Yet, from only 1 to 6 percent of employees who experience incivility report it.[73]

The organizational costs of incivility are considerable. Sixty-six percent of workers and executives who think that they were victims of uncivil acts report that their performance declined; 48 percent say that they intentionally decreased their "work effort," and 38 percent decreased their "work quality";[74] a third of workers spread unflattering rumors about uncivil executives;[75] 30 percent were less creative and produced a fourth fewer new ideas; a fifth of workers stalled in responding to requests from uncivil managers; and 12 percent voluntarily left the organization because of incivility. Empirical tests confirm that incivility results in less creativity, cooperation, collaboration, teamwork, and productivity.[76]

Bully Pulpits *Bullying* is incivility on steroids and refers to overbearing and intimidating behavior.

Bullies are not nice, nor even competent, employees. Supervisors who bully often perceive

their victims as threats, or just enjoy bullying.[77] Arrogance, often a component of bullying (its behavioral characteristics include anger and a desire to dominate), clearly correlates with low self-esteem, low verbal and numerical abilities, and low performance ratings.[78]

Thirty-seven percent of employees in all sectors report that they have been bullied at work. Seventy-two percent of bullies are supervisors; 57 percent of those bullied are women; and, when women are bullied, 71 percent of their bullies are women.[79] Bullying bosses also focus on minorities, employees with little job security, and even highly paid employees in high-pressure organizations or during downsizing.[80] Seventy-seven percent of bullies receive no reprimand of any sort from management.[81] Unsurprisingly, bullying by bosses occurs most frequently at workplaces that are characterized by poor procedures, inadequate planning, and incompetent managers.[82]

The organizational costs of bullying are far higher than those of incivility. An astonishing four-fifths of the victims of bullying voluntarily depart for other organizations (40 percent), are "terminated, driven out" (24 percent), or transfer to other departments (16 percent).[83] These departures tote up when we realize that turnover costs range from a third to two-and-a-half times the salary of each employee who leaves.[84] In those organizations where bullying is chronic, strong unions are often a consequence.[85]

Incivility, Bullying, and Government Governments may be leading the way down these rude roads and bullying byways. A fourth of government employees have observed "abusive or intimidating behavior" by co-workers over the past year (23 percent of federal workers and 26 percent each of state and local employees), compared with 21 percent of businesspeople and 19 percent of nonprofit employees.[86]

In the public sector, the costs of incivility and bullying can be quite a bit higher than in the other two, particularly when executives fail to actively squelch such behavior. When President George W. Bush and others were being briefed in 2002 about the Iraq war plan, Defense Secretary Donald Rumsfeld snatched a copy of the Pentagon's briefing slides from the hands of National Security

Adviser Condoleezza Rice, saying, "You won't be needing that." Bush responded with, "I'll let you two work it out," and left. "Instead of a team of rivals, Bush wound up with a team of back-stabbers with long-running, poisonous disagreements about foreign policy fundamentals."[87]

Organization Development

Another important subfield of the open model is *organization development* (*OD*), which is a planned, organization-wide attempt directed from the top that is designed to increase organizational effectiveness and viability through calculated interventions in the active workings of the organization, using knowledge from the behavioral sciences.[88]

OD: Mission and Methods The mission of OD is to:

- improve the individual member's ability to get along with other members,
- legitimate human emotions in the organization,
- increase mutual understanding among members,
- reduce tensions,
- enhance "team management" and intergroup cooperation,
- develop more effective techniques for conflict resolution through nonauthoritarian and interactive methods, and
- evolve less structured and more "organic" organizations.

"The basic value underlying all organization-development theory and practice is that of choice. Through...the collection and feedback of relevant data to relevant people, more choices become available and hence better decisions are made."[89]

OD owes its origins to the social psychologist Kurt Lewin and his groundbreaking "Harwood studies" of 1939–1947.[90] Researchers later developed techniques (such as sensitivity training, "interlocking group conferences," and employee surveys) that encourage people to be candid about their views about the organization. Outside consultants who specialize in OD (what the field calls "third party change agents") usually coordinate all these group-and-feedback activities, and their consultations are referred to as "interventions."

OD: The Public Experience Perhaps as many as half of all OD interventions occur in governments, and more than four-fifths of government workers who participated in them report positive and intended effects on their agencies; less than a tenth report negative effects.[91] These rates were quite comparable to the private sector's experience with OD.[92] OD interventions in public agencies "seem to be equally effective" as corporate interventions when it comes to "enhancing both individual development and organizational performance," but less so in affecting structures, goals, procedures, and rewards[93]—not surprising, as legislatures and civil service commissions, not agencies, usually control these factors.

The public sector (specifically, a metropolitan county's sheriff's department) has housed "the longest longitudinal study [over thirty years] of the effects of organization development interventions" on an organization. The findings have been gratifying and include "improved organization climate and leader effectiveness; decreased employment turnover, jail breaks, and citizen complaints; increased resources allocated to the organization, and [measurably] improved organizational effectiveness."[94]

OD: Crises and Caveats Despite its successes, however, as OD matures, its adherents grow less confident about their field. "A number of senior practitioners...believe that the profession has lost its way,"[95] and some think that OD may end up as "a historical artifact."[96]

OD's disarray may stem from its basics.

One such basic is the field's founding notion that the more choices available to employees, the more productive that they and their organizations are. (Recall that choice is "the basic value underlying all organization-development theory and practice."[97]) Researchers have found that when people have more, rather than fewer, options from which to choose, they are convinced that their choices will result in better performance. The OD scholars concur wholeheartedly with this belief, but, in fact, the reverse is true. "The costs of choice freedom outweigh its benefits.... As a result, those who have the option to choose exercise it, yet end up performing worse and feeling worse than those who do not have that option."[98]

What seems to be even more basic to the field is its premise that happier, friendlier, and more relaxed, open, and laid-back employees are more productive employees. But these qualities do not add up to employees who are actually engaged in their jobs and organizations. As we explained earlier, merely happy, or satisfied, workers are not necessarily productive workers. It takes employee engagement to improve organizational productivity.

OD's prime value seems to be less one of organizational effectiveness and more one of employee happiness. In fact, some of the field's adherents worry that the very idea of using OD to boost organizational performance is a sell-out of the field's mission of improving individual lives in the workplace. The bottom line and "the mind-set of management" have perverted OD; as a consequence, employees trapped in "the grubby realities of worklife soon figure out whose side [these] breezy, self-assured, and excessively articulate" OD consultants are truly on, and they are not on the employees' side.[99] They are, contemptibly (in this perspective), on management's side.

All this is, of course, fine. It is admirable that OD exists as a profession to help people lead happier organizational lives. Executives who hire OD consultants to enhance their organizations' performance, however, should be aware that their priority may not be shared by the consultants whom they hire.

The Organization as a Unit in Its Environment

Our third school of the open model can be traced at least as far back as the 1930s,[100] and this theoretical thread is undergoing a significant revitalization.

Adapting to the Environment This research is characterized by its use of the organization as a whole as its analytical unit (in contrast to the other schools' preference for the small group),

and its focus on pressures emanating from the environment. Organization theorists often refer to this literary stream as *adaptive systems* or *contingency theory*, which hold that organizations are themselves, and function in, dynamic, decentralized networks in which elements and forces act and react to one another, and are able to cohere and stabilize only when their competition and collaboration achieve a rough balance.

In this construct, the organization's environment is almost overwhelming, a "perpetually varying" and "ever-changing screen," through which the organization, by continually assuming "different shapes and sizes," must pass or be "swept away."[101] Hence, these researchers have found that more flexible organizations are more likely to endure in rapidly changing environments,[102] and that higher-performing organizations match the complexity of their environments.[103]

Theorists differ over precisely how organizations adapt to their environments.[104]

Adapting Biologically One school, known as *population ecology* or *organizational ecology*, holds that organizational adaptation is a biological, evolutionary process; organizations that cannot adapt die.

The blind spots in this view are several. It assumes that there is perfect competition in the social world, just as there is in the cellular one, but competition in society is far from perfect. The social sphere defines survival in terms of individual units (e.g., an organization), a definition that does not work in the natural sphere, where survival is defined in terms of collectivities (whole species). And, in society, survival is determined, in part, by rational action, a phenomenon not found in nature, where long-term survival is a product of genetic sport.

Adapting Rationally Other theorists hold that organizational survival and success are entirely attributable to human rationality, a perspective that flourishes in business schools and in the leadership literature. The problem here (and one that it shares with the organizational ecologists) is that, although the rationalists understand that organizations dwell in "conflict systems," or highly competitive environments, they fail to appreciate that organizations themselves are conflicted. Organizations are not happy families, but rather pastiches of passive and aggressive, astute and dumb, and ethical and unethical people, groups, and divisions, each with its own goals and methods.

Adapting Politically Luckily, there is a school that reconciles the biological and rational metaphors. It does so by focusing on political interactions. Neither biology nor rationality dominate—but both are present in a world of persons and coalitions that unremittingly cut political deals with each other, both inside and outside the organization.

This approach is realistic in that it recognizes that (1) most organizations are highly differentiated by divisions of labor, multiple professions, differing goals, and so forth; and (2) in most organizations, members are free to leave. This combination of many internal differences and few sanctions allows organizations to adapt both biologically, in that environmental forces affect discrete elements differently within the organization (and not just the "whole" organization), *and* rationally, in that each of these elements is dealing with those forces in logical ways that protect its own interests. In the political model, organizational adaptation combines heart and head—about as apt a description as we can imagine, and one that seems well suited to public and nonprofit organizations.

The Environment of the Public Organization

Perhaps the classic analysis of organizational adaptation in the public sector is Philip Selznick's study of the Tennessee Valley Authority (TVA).[105] In it, Selznick introduced the notion of *co-optation*, which occurred when TVA's directors won over hostile local interests by cajolery, flattery, veiled bribery, and token representation in policymaking. Some forty years later, however, those local interests that ostensibly had been co-opted had waxed considerably more powerful, and, in fact, could "foster new operative goals for TVA" and "prevent TVA initiated modifications of those goals."[106] Who had co-opted whom?

As the studies of the TVA imply, the task environment has an unusually heavy and distorting impact on the public organization. If the literature on the differences between public, nonprofit,

and private organizations agrees on anything, it is that *public organizations must deal with far more environmental constraints and pressures than nonprofit and private organizations*. This reality deeply affects every aspect of the public organization: processes, structure, decision making, effectiveness—everything.

THE CLOSED AND OPEN MODELS: THE ESSENTIAL DIFFERENCES

We have reviewed two eminently disparate models of organizations, but their fundamental differences may be reduced to five differing assumptions about how the world works.

Assumptions About the Organization's Environment

The closed model is predicated on the premise that organizations exist in a stable, routine environment, and the open model is based on the belief that organizations must function in an unstable environment, replete with surprises. Both models, however, assume that organizations are not suicidal. Organizations will act in order to survive and, ultimately, to thrive.

The beauty in these two differing perceptions is that each model works in the environment posited for it, but not in the other. A closed-model organization, with its tall, inflexible bureaucracy and rigid routines for dealing with predictable patterns in a stable environment, is superbly suited for that setting. It would wither if its environment's predictability and stability suddenly shattered and were replaced by swirling and confusing new forces; unfamiliar environmental contingencies that have no commonalities require that the organization "loosen up" and treat each one as the unique challenge that it is.

Conversely, an open-model organization—with its flat, streamlined hierarchy and nimble responses to fast-paced changes in its unstable environment in which everything is unremittingly new and fresh—is equally well tailored to its surroundings. It would "die" if its environment suddenly stabilized, and "inventing the wheel" for every environmental contingency no longer worked because such a response would be grotesquely inefficient; predictable and orderly environmental patterns require correspondingly predictable and orderly organizational procedures.

Assumptions About the Human Condition

The second difference between the closed and open models parallels the first, in that their respective models of human beings differ but are appropriate for each.

Theory X and Theory Y Douglas McGregor famously named these models "Theory X" and "Theory Y."[107] *Theory X* assumes that motivation to work is an individual matter, and that most people do not like work, prefer close and unrelenting supervision, cannot contribute creatively to the solution of organizational problems, and are motivated by the direct application of threat or punishment. It is apparent that organizations exemplifying the closed model not only would fit but possibly might be appealing, to Theory X people.

Theory Y, by contrast, assumes that motivation to work is a group matter, and, given the right conditions, most people can enjoy work as much as play, exercise self-control and prefer doing jobs in their own way, solve organizational problems creatively, and often are motivated by social and ego rewards. It is apparent that organizations predicated on the open model likely would attract Theory Y people.

The Riddle of Rational Interest A related facet of human nature posited by the two models is the problem of *rational interest*, or how people define their self-interest and the rationale that they use to fulfill it.

In the closed model, *rational interest* means that everyone in the organization has the same goal (i.e., the organization's official mission) and agrees on how to achieve that goal in an optimal fashion.

In the open model, however, *rational interest* means that each person in the organization has his or her own unique goals, and has his or her own personal way to achieve those goals. Each person's

real goals revolve around such values as getting ahead, enjoying one's work, and other kinds of social-psychological satisfaction that are not only disparate, but often in conflict with the goals of other members and possibly with the mission of their own organization. The way in which each person chooses to fulfill his or her goals also is unique; executives vying for a promotion, for instance, may employ entirely different means to win it, ranging from badgering their bosses to brown-nosing them.

Happily, in public organizations there is a close match between personal and organizational interests, and this match bodes well for good government. "In most cases, the self-interests" of public administrators "do not necessarily run counter to the organization's overall interests, in that they reflect a desire to make a useful contribution to the performance of their organization.... The assumption of an inherent conflict between self- and collective interests is not always valid, particularly in a public sector context."[108]

Assumptions About the Role and Legitimacy of Organizational Power

Power, in an organizational context, simply means getting people to do what you want them to do. The models divide not only on *how* to exercise organizational power but also on *whether* it should be exercised at all.

Power in the Closed Model The closed model has no qualms about employing power. Its theorists believe in orders and obedience, rules and regulations, punctuality and punctiliousness. It advocates "using" people for the sake of the organization's ends, and the callous use of authoritarian compulsion is seen as entirely legitimate.

Power in the Open Model In complete contrast to the closed model, the open model views coercion as reprehensible, and, indeed, the open model occasionally appears to argue against the presence of organizational power altogether. Relying on it is condemned as dehumanizing, "dematurizing," and not at all nice.[109]

Regrettably, the open modelists' distaste for power leads to a contradiction in their theory of organizational behavior. On the one hand, they argue that the exercise of authoritarian power makes people miserable, and misery undermines the attainment of organizational goals; ergo, terminate the use of power and unhappy-unproductive workers will blossom into "happy-productive" workers who will fulfill those goals.[110]

On the other hand, these same scholars also agree that even happy workers remain uniquely individual beings who still harbor their own personal objectives that may or may not coincide with organizational goals. But which one prevails, the worker or the organization? "Either the individual is autonomous or the organization is dominant, for the very notion of individualism wars against even benevolent organization"; reconciling the two may be a "hopeless task."[111]

The Quirk in Collective Action The open modelists' passionate, but perhaps "hopeless," commitment to reconcile each person's individual goals with the stated goals of his or her organization suggests that large organizations, such as governments, face severe challenges in motivating their employees to work for the benefit of the whole organization— that is, for the common collective good.

On the face of it, this is weird. If, for example, International Widget's employees all worked together and succeeded in fulfilling their company's mission of becoming the world's most profitable corporation, then they would, at least potentially, profit, too. So why do employees stubbornly and divisively persist in viewing their organization's official mission not as an end, but merely as one of several means to an end—their end? Why do they not join in the organizational equivalent of singing "Kumbaya" and get with the program?

Because doing so makes little sense. Even though all organizational members would benefit from attaining the collective good (i.e., by fulfilling their organization's mission), it is nonetheless irrational for any one member to voluntarily sacrifice to achieve that collective good. Why, for example, would an employee voluntarily work without compensation? Better to let other employees work for free so that the nonvolunteer can freeload. And, unless the organization is composed of "altruistic"

or "irrational" employees, no one else in the organization will volunteer, either.[112]

The Inescapability of Organizational Power If organizations depended on each member's unique rational interest to attain their common goals, as advocated in the open model, then organizations would be pushed toward actions that are collectively ruinous. Hence, coercion is mandatory in any organization whose members are rational and self-interested if the common good— that is, the organization's stated purpose—is to be realized.

Power is fundamental to the very idea of organization. Most open-model theorists seem to accept, poutingly, the immutable reality of organizational power. But some seem not to.

Assumptions About Manipulating Members of Organizations

Manipulation is the techniques employed to exercise organizational power. As with power itself, the two models part company on its use.

Manipulation in the Closed Model A manipulative technique occasionally used by public administrators in the Third Reich, about as closed-model an organization as one is likely to find, was leveling a Luger at a subordinate's neck to persuade him or her to execute an order.

In closed-model organizations, manipulation is obvious, coercive, and legitimate. The human and organizational dysfunctions of authoritarian manipulation are clear: rigidity, fear, alienation, secrecy, narrowness, lying, and stultification number among them. But there are also human advantages to the crudities of the closed model's manipulations: People in closed-model organizations "know where they stand." The coerciveness of the closed model is for people who like things straightforward and clear-cut.

Manipulation in the Open Model Manipulation in the open model is far paler in hue than the red-meat methods of the closed model, and its exercise is discreet, disguised, and obfuscated.

Recall our twelve characteristics of the open model; "myths of peerage," "advice," "adjustment," and supportive relationships number prominently among them. These and similarly insinuating subtleties comprise the manipulative methods of the open model. A distinguished scholar of organization development, for example, has written that one's "good mornings" must be "appropriately" tailored in tone to each of their recipients if one wishes to smooth the way for attaining organizational goals.[113]

The advantages of the open model's social-psychological manipulation are clear: humanism, openness, communication, teamwork, and innovation are some of them. But there are also liabilities. The open model's nuanced manipulative methods are "just a more subtle form of bureaucratic control.... to get each worker to participate in an ever more refined form of" his or her "enslavement."[114] Because they camouflage the unavoidable exercise of power in organizations, as they are meant to do, people in open-model organizations, unlike those in closed-model organizations, may never be sure "where they stand."

Of greater significance, if members think that they do know where they stand, their knowledge may be the end-product of a manipulation of their psyches so profound as to render them analogous to the "conditioned" human shell of the protagonist in George Orwell's *1984*, who uncontrollably shrieked "Long Live Big Brother!" even as he despised him. Eric Fromm expresses this idea with his concept of *willing submissiveness*; that is, even though organizational subordinates may appear to have "team spirit" (and actually may have been so successfully manipulated as to believe they have it), the psychological techniques used to create their willing submissiveness induces, in reality, a subliminal and deep resentment toward their superiors bordering on hatred.[115] There is, in fact, empirical research suggesting that this is precisely what happens in organizations that use the open model's manipulative techniques.[116]

Assumptions About the Moral Significance of Organizations in Society

Our final distinction between the closed and open models is particularly germane to the study of public administration, and centers on how their respective theorists have viewed the organization and its moral relationship with the larger society.

The Moral View of the Closed Model The *Ur* closed modelist Max Weber believed that bureaucracy, replete with its own internal injustices, dehumanizing rules, and monocratic arbitrariness, was vital, in its very rigidity and rationalism, in mitigating the unorganized societal lunacy that surrounded it. If Weber's notion of the bureaucracy's stand-alone station in society could be illustrated, it would look something like Figure 3-1.

Weber was not unsympathetic to the plight of the individual bureaucrat. In fact, he deplored what bureaucratic settings could do to the human spirit, sighing that the passion for bureaucracy among his German students "is enough to drive one to despair."[117] But, when all was said and done, Weber could accept the dehumanization of society's public servants, who were somehow apart from the other citizens, on the grounds that bureaucracy was essential to social progress and the elimination of injustice.

The Moral View of the Open Model In marked contrast, the open-model theorists hold that every citizen, bureaucrat and nonbureaucrat alike, is encased in some sort of bureaucratic organization. Society is a series of overlapping and interacting organizations, and there is no unorganized, irrational society "out there," roiling beyond organizational boundaries. The open model's concept that society *is* bureaucracy looks like Figure 3-2.

In this school, bureaucracy's domination of society is not a good thing. "Bureaucracy gives birth to a new species of inhuman beings.... incapable of

FIGURE 3-1
The Closed Model's View:
Organizations *and* Society

FIGURE 3-2
The Open Model's View: Organizations *as* Society

emotion and devoid of will. Rationalistic...control relations" replace "social relations."[118]

Thus, for the public bureaucracy to dehumanize its own bureaucrats in order to advance social justice is self-defeating because the bureaucrat and the citizen are one and the same. Indeed, to treat a member of an organization, particularly a subordinate, badly is immoral because there is no higher morality to excuse such treatment, as there is in the closed model. In the open model, what is good for the person is good for the people.

Who Must Be Sacrificed? This distinction between the closed and open models leads to starkly different ethical conclusions. When push comes to shove, someone must pay the price of advancing society, and a fundamental distinction between the two models pivots on just who must pay that price.

Those who advocate the closed model state that the organization's clerks and laborers must be sacrificed for the larger good of revolutionizing society. This revolution, which only bureaucratic organizations can achieve, is the creation of a more fair, honest, equitable, and transparent society. Because the organization's executives are the engines of this revolution, their chief revolutionary tool—the human spirit of the organization's clerks and laborers—can legitimately be sacrificed for the good of the larger cause.

Those who advocate the open model state that the creation of a more just society (which is cast in precisely the same terms as in the closed model) is not facilitated by organizations, as the closed model contends, but is blocked by them; hence, the organization itself must be sacrificed. If destroying the organization is impractical (as it likely is), then at least indoctrinating, transforming, and, if necessary, replacing (ideally with nonhierarchical teams of clerks and laborers) those "inhuman beings" who comprise its leadership, will suffice.

CONJOINING OPPOSITES: THE DRIVE TO REDUCE UNCERTAINTY

Students of organizations may be initially puzzled by the two fundamentally different paradigms of organization theory. The closed model assumes that people hate work, organizations are rational, their environments are stable, coercion is basic, bureaucrats are different from citizens, and bureaucracies are the saviors of society. The open model assumes that people love work, organizations are irrational, their environments are unstable, coercion is unacceptable, bureaucrats and citizens are one and the same, and bureaucracies are the bane of society. These are basic differences. Can they be reconciled?

Uncertainty Reduction: Reconciling the Open and the Closed

Yes, they can. Reconciling the open and closed models begins with the open model's world view—that is, organizations are spontaneous collectivities of people with their own goals and drives, who are operating uncertainly in an unstable environment. This is not a bad set of assumptions about any organization that is just getting started. But no organization can long last in a state of near nature. Nature is unpredictable and uncertain, and all organizations are extraordinarily averse to uncertainty. So organizations are possessed by an overpowering need to *reduce uncertainty*—that is, to routinize and rationalize the organization's internal workings and its relations with its environment whenever and wherever possible.

Uncertainty reduction is essentially a Darwinian notion: adapt or die. The need to reduce uncertainty runs deep in the human species. Psychologists tell us that the more certain we are, the happier we are,[119] and this correlation appears to hold for organizations as well.

Thus, the two models are conjoined, and the synthesis is predicated on three very reasonable assumptions:

- Organizations and their environments can and do change.
- Organizations and the people in them act to survive.
- Organizations and the people in them can and do learn from experience, including failures and successes.

Responding to Organizational Uncertainty

Organizational uncertainty may spring from sources inside and outside the organization, and whether the source is internal or external can shape organizational strategies in addressing uncertainty.

Responses to Internal Sources of Uncertainty

If the sources of organizational uncertainty are internal, then the organization will strive to reduce uncertainty by centralizing. Centralizing techniques include indoctrinating all members of the organization "to respond only to commands from the central leadership and from no other source"; controlling all communication involving "vexing suborganizations" in an effort to nip "nonconforming thought" and "deviant behavior"; intensifying surveillance of troublesome subunits; "detaching key operations," such as the control of funds, from deviating departments, "thus reducing their self-containment and increasing their vulnerability to central direction"; and, finally, expelling offending units, a radical act that amounts to "a contraction of boundaries constituting a withdrawal from internal sources of uncertainty."[120]

Responses to External Sources of Uncertainty

If, however, the sources of organizational uncertainty are external—that is, they are in the organization's task environment—then the organization will seek to reduce that uncertainty by absorbing the outside sources of uncertainty into the organization itself. It does this by expanding its boundaries—by growing. Co-optation, described earlier, is one form that this incorporation of external uncertainties might take; the effort by an organization to control some facet of the natural environment (e.g., to engage

in flood control) is another form; to merge or ally with competitive organizations is yet another. Ironically, decentralization often is required if an organization is to expand, and decentralization can result in new, internal sources of uncertainty.

If the expansion of an organization's boundaries is blocked, then the organization will seek to reduce its exchanges with its environment—"withdrawal from the source of uncertainty, as it were."[121] A firm uncertain about its future supplies might decide to stockpile or produce its own manufacturing components. Entire nations, particularly in Asia, have been known to reduce their external uncertainties by radically reducing exchanges with other nations and launching self-sufficiency policies; the invariable consequence, however, is an elevation of costs and a lowering of living standards.

The Public Organization and Environmental Uncertainty

In the public sector, those administrators who perceive high levels of political, social, and economic uncertainty in their organizations' environments also harbor concerns about their organizations' "inertia"; consult with citizens a lot; and, of greatest importance, maintain a responsive, curious, and exploratory "strategic stance" relative to their external environments.[122]

When these public administrators worry about environmental uncertainty, the public can benefit. Public agencies "that perceive high levels of uncertainty in their external political environment perform better than those that perceive that environment to be certain," and this linkage is "positive and statistically significant.... even when controlling for past performance, service expenditure, and external constraints." This correlation pertains, however, only to the public organization's *political* environment; "perceptions of the relative level of uncertainty in the social and economic circumstances are unrelated to their service achievements."[123]

ARE PUBLIC AND NONPROFIT ORGANIZATIONS DIFFERENT?

Historically, organization theorists have minimized, ignored, or denied that organizations can be usefully classified along behavioral and sectoral lines (the profoundly influential sociologist, Talcott Parsons, likely set the standard in this regard[124]), contending instead that organizations are organizations are organizations. "Virtually all the major contributions to the field were conceived to apply broadly across all types of organizations....The distinction between public and private organizations received short shrift."[125] As a consequence, there was, for at least three-quarters of the twentieth century, "not a single general work on organization theory that pays systematic attention to the distinctive features of the public bureaucracy."[126]

Researchers are now focusing more on the unique properties of public—and nonprofit—organizations than they have in the not-so-distant past. This new focus is still coming in fits and starts—what is arguably organization theory's most prestigious academic journal has slashed its articles that deal with public and nonprofit organizations by more than 70 percent over two decades[127]—but it is coming, and it has produced a respectable literature. As we shall learn in Chapters 4 and 5, governmental, independent, and private organizations do indeed differ from one another, and in highly important ways.

So, yes, public and nonprofit organizations are different.

NOTES

1. Tom Burns and G. M. Stalker, *The Management of Innovation* (London: Tavistock, 1961).

2. Edward Mandell House (anonymous), *Philip Dru: Administrator: A Story of Tomorrow, 1920–1935* (New York: B.W. Huebsch, 1912), pp. 262, 249.

3. John R. Hibbing and Elizabeth Theiss-Morse, "Americans' Desire for Stealth Democracy: How Declining Trust Boosts Political Participation," Paper Presented at the Annual Meeting of the Midwest Political Science Association (Chicago, April 2001), Table 1.

4. Frederick W. Taylor, quoted in Peter J. Boyer, "The Road Ahead," *The New Yorker* (April 27, 2009), pp. 44–57. The quotation is on p. 49.

5. Frederick W. Taylor, *Principles of Scientific Management* (New York: Harper & Row, 1911).

6. Frank B. Gilbreth, *Primer of Scientific Management* (New York: Van Nostrand, 1912).

7. Taylor, *Principles of Scientific Management*, p. 59.

8. Frank B. Gilbreth and Lillian M. Gilbreth, *Applied Motion Study: A Collection of Papers on the Efficient Method of Industrial Preparedness* (New York: Sturgis & Walton, 1917).

9. Frank B. Gilbreth, "Scientific Management in the Hospital," *The Modern Hospital* 3 (November 1914), pp. 321–324.

10. Jill Lepore, "Not So Fast," *The New Yorker* (October 12, 2009), pp. 114–122.

11. Susan Reverby, "The Search for the Hospital Yardstick: Nursing and the Rationalization of Hospital Work," *Health Care in America: Essays in Social History*, Susan Reverby and David Rosner, eds. (Philadelphia: Temple University Press, 1979), pp. 206–225. The quotation is on p. 218.

12. Matthew Stewart, "The Management Myth," *The Atlantic* (June 2006), pp. 80–87. The quotation is on p. 81.

13. Charles D. Wrege and Amedeo G. Perroni, "Taylor's Pig-Tale: A Historical Analysis of Frederick W. Taylor's Pig-Iron Experiment," *Academy of Management Journal* 17 (March 1974), pp. 6–27.

14. Stewart, "The Management Myth," p. 82.

15. Lepore, "Not So Fast," p. 114.

16. Frederick Taylor, "Government Efficiency," *Bulletin of the Taylor Society* 2 (December 1916), pp. 7–13. The quotation is on p. 7.

17. Stewart, "The Management Myth," p. 82.

18. Boyer, "The Road Ahead," p. 44.

19. Hindy Lauer Schachter, "Does Frederick Taylor's Ghost Still Haunt the Halls of Government? A Look at the Concept of Governmental Efficiency in Our Time," *Public Administration Review* 67 (September/October 2007), pp. 800–810.

20. Stewart, "The Management Myth," p. 82.

21. Luther Gulick and L. Urwick, eds., *Papers on the Science of Administration* (New York: Institute of Public Administration, 1937).

22. James D. Mooney and Alan C. Reiley, *The Principles of Organization* (New York: Harper & Row, 1939).

23. Henri Fayol, *General and Industrial Management* (London: Pittman, 1930).

24. Mary Parker Follett's (M.P. Follet was her *nom de plume*) most influential contribution was *Creative Experience* (New York: Longmans, Green, 1924), but her first book (one of only three that she wrote) was *The Speaker of the House of Representatives* (New York: Longmans, Green, 1896), followed by *The New State: Group Organization the Solution of Popular Government* (New York: Longmans, Green, 1920). She also contributed Chapter VIII, "The Process of Control," to Gulick and Urwick's famously influential, *Papers on the Science of Administration*. Mary Parker Follett was, without doubt, a founding "P.A. type."

25. H. Thomas Johnson, an expert on Toyota, as quoted in Cal Thomas, "Principles Come before Profits," *Savannah Morning News* (March 3, 2010).

26. NASA Engineering and Safety Center, *Technical Support to the National Highway Traffic Safety Administration (NHTSA) on the Reported Toyota Motor Corporation (TMC) Unintended Acceleration (UA) Investigation*, NESC Assessment #: TI-10-00618 (Washington, DC: U.S. Government Printing Office, 2011).

27. Alvin W. Gouldner, "Organizational Analysis," *Sociology Today*, Robert K. Merton, Leonard Broom, and Leonard S. Cottrell, Jr., eds. (New York: Basic Books, 1959), pp. 400–428.

28. Burns and Stalker, *The Management of Innovation*.

29. Fritz J. Roethlisberger and William J. Dickson, *Management and the Worker* (Cambridge: Harvard University Press, 1939).

30. Richard Herbert Franke and James D. Kaul, "The Hawthorne Experiments: First Statistical Interpretation," *American Sociological Review* 43 (October 1978), pp. 623–643.

31. Stephen R. G. Jones, "Worker Interdependence and Output: The Hawthorne Studies Reevaluated," *American Sociological Review* 55 (April 1990), pp. 176–190.

32. Abraham Maslow, *Eupsychian Management: A Journal* (Homewood, IL: Dorsey, 1965), p. 1.

33. Robert J. Vance, *Employee Engagement and Commitment: A Guide to Understanding, Measuring and Increasing Engagement in Your Organization* (Alexandria, VA: Society for Human Resource Management, 2006).

34. Frederick Herzberg, with Bernard Mausner and Barbara B. Snyderman, *The Motivation to Work* (New York: Wiley, 1959).

35. Marc Buelens and Herman Van den Broek, "An Analysis of Work Motivation between Public and Private Sector Organizations," *Public Administration Review* 67 (January/February 2007), pp. 65–72. The quotation is on p. 67.

36. U.S. Merit Systems Protection Board, *The Federal Government: A Model Employer or a Work in Progress? Perspectives from 25 Years of the Merit Principles Survey* (Washington, DC: U.S. Government Printing Office, 2008), p. 20; and U.S. Merit Protection Board, *2009 Employee Survey Results* (Washington, DC: U.S. Government Printing Office, 2010), p. 3, Question 5. Figure is for eight MSPB surveys, 1986–2009.

37. Karlyn Bowman, *Attitudes About Work and Leisure in America* (Washington, DC: American Leadership Institute, 2001), Table W-9. Data are for 1973–1994.

38. U.S. Merit Systems Protection Board, *Managing for Engagement—Communication, Connection, and Courage* (Washington, DC: U.S. Government Printing Office, 2009), p. 4.

39. Princeton Survey Research Associates and the Brookings Institution, *Health of the Public Service* (Washington, DC: Authors, 2001), http://www.brook.edu. Data are for 2001.

40. Bradley E. Wright, "Public Service and Motivation: Does Mission Matter?" *Public Administration Review* 67 (January/February 2007), pp. 54–64. The quotation is on p. 60.

41. Jessica Word and Sung Min Park, "Working across the Divide: Job Involvement in the Public and Nonprofit Sectors," *Review of Public Personnel Administration* 29 (June 2009), pp. 103–133. The quotation is on p. 103; the datum is on p. 108.

42. Brookings Institution, *Winning the Talent War: Brookings Survey Finds the Nonprofit Sector Has the Most Dedicated Workforce* (Washington, DC: Author, 2002), p. 2.

43. Mary K. Feeney and Barry Bozeman, "Staying Late: Comparing Work Hours in Public and Nonprofit Sectors," *American Review of Public Administration* 39 (September 2009), pp. 459–477. Summaries of this research are on pp. 464–465.

44. Ibid., p. 471.

45. Jeffrey L. Brudney and Deil S. Wright, "The 'Revolt in Dullsville' Revisited: Lessons for Theory, Practice, and Research from the American State Administrators Project, 1964–2008." *Public Administration Review* 70 (January/February 2010), pp. 26–37. The data are on p. 29. "Over five decades, they have averaged between 51 and 53 hours per week."

46. Jerri Killian and Enamul Choudhury, "Continuity and Change in the Role of City Managers," *Municipal Year Book, 2010* (Washington, DC: International City/County Management Association, 2010), pp. 10–18. Data (p. 15) are for 2010.

47. Charldean Newell and David M. Ammons, "Role Emphases of City Managers and Other Municipal Executives," *Public Administration Review* 47 (May/June 1987), pp. 246–253. The data are on pp. 247–248, and are for 1985.

48. Marcus Buckingham and Curt Coffman, *First, Break All the Rules: What Do the World's Greatest Managers Do Differently?* (New York: Simon and Schuster, 1999), p. 28.

49. Donald P. Moynihan and Sanjay K. Pandey, "The Ties that Bind: Social Networks, Person-Organization Value Fit, and Turnover Intention," *Journal of Public Administration Research and Theory* 18 (April 2008), pp. 205–227.

50. Craig Matheson, "The Sources of Upward Mobility within Public Sector Organizations: A Case Study," *Administration & Society* 31 (September 1999), pp. 495–324. This is a study of Australian public administrators.

51. Buckingham and Coffman, *First, Break All the Rules*, p. 28.

52. Dee W. Henderson, "Enlightened Mentoring: A Characteristic of Public Management Professionalism," *Public Administration Review* 45 (November/December 1985), pp. 857–863. The quotation is on p. 857.

53. U.S. Office of Personnel Management, *Senior Executive Service 2008 Survey Results* (Washington, DC: U.S. Government Printing Office, 2008), p. 4.

54. Doyle M. Buckwalter and Robert J. Parsons, "Local City Managers' Career Paths: Which Way to the Top?" *Municipal Year Book, 2000* (Washington, DC: International City/County Management Association, 2000), pp. 17–21.

55. Stephanie C. Payne and Ann H. Huffman, "A Longitudinal Examination of the Influence of Mentoring on Organizational Commitment and Turnover," *Academy of Management Journal* 48 (February 2005), pp. 158–168.

56. U.S. Government Accountability Office, *Mentor-Protégé Programs Have Policies that Aim to Benefit Participants but Do Not Require Postagreement Tracking,* GAO-11-548R Federal Mentor-Protégé Programs (Washington, DC: U.S. Government Printing Office, 2011). Figure is for 2011.

57. Ann S. Altmeyer, Faith Prather, and Dennis L. Thombs, "Mentoring-in-Public-Administration Scales: Construct Validation and Relationship to Level of Management," *Public Productivity & Management Review* 17 (Summer 1994), pp. 387–397.

58. Henderson, "Enlightened Mentoring," p. 862.

59. "Career Advice from Federal Employees," *Issues of Merit* (July 2009), p. 1. Figures are for 2007.

60. Danity M. Little, "Shattering the Glass Ceiling," *The Bureaucrat* 19 (Fall 1991), pp. 21–28.

61. Nick Bloom, Tobias Kretschmer, and John Van Reenen, *Work-Life Balance, Management Practices and Productivity* (London: Centre for Economic Performance, 2006).

62. Buckingham and Coffman, *First, Break All the Rules*, p. 29.

63. U.S. Merit Systems Protection Board, *The Power of Federal Employee Engagement* (Washington, DC: U.S. Government Printing Office, 2008), p. 3.

64. U.S. Merit Systems Protection Board, *Managing for Engagement*, p. 2.

65. Ethics Resource Center and Hay Group, *Ethics and Employee Engagement* (Washington, DC: Authors, 2010), p. 4.

66. Buckingham and Coffman, *First, Break All the Rules*, pp. 21–49. This purports to be "the largest study of its kind ever undertaken."

67. Payne and Huffman, "A Longitudinal Examination of the Influence of Mentoring on Organizational Commitment and Turnover."

68. As derived from data in U.S. Merit Systems Protection Board, *Prohibited Personnel Practices: Employee Perceptions* (Washington, DC: U.S. Government Printing Office, 2011), p. 37. Figure is for 2010.

69. U.S. Merit Systems Protection Board, *The Power of Federal Employee Engagement*, pp. 27–36. Data are for 2005.

70. James Gerard Caillier, "Factors Affecting Job Performance in Public Agencies," *Public*

Performance & Management Review 34 (December 2010), pp. 139–165. The quotation is on p. 139.

71. Christine L. Porath and Christine M. Pearson, "The Cost of Bad Behavior," *Organizational Dynamics* 39 (January–March 2010), pp. 63–71. The quotations are on p. 64. Figures are for 1998–2005.

72. Lilia M. Cortina, "Unseen Injustice: Incivility as Modern Discrimination in Organizations," *Academy of Management Review* 33 (January 2008), pp. 55–75.

73. Lilia M. Cortina and Vicki J. Magley, "Patterns and Profiles of Responses to Incivility in the Workplace," *Journal of Occupational Health Psychology* 14 (July 2009), pp. 272–288.

74. Porath and Pearson, "The Cost of Bad Behavior," pp. 64–66.

75. Christine M. Pearson and Christine L. Porath, "On the Nature, Consequences and Remedies of Workplace Incivility: No Time for 'Nice'? Think Again," *Academy of Management Executive* 19 (February 2005), pp. 7–18. The data are on pp. 11.

76. Porath and Pearson, "The Cost of Bad Behavior," pp. 64–66.

77. Vincent J. Roscigno, Steven H. Lopez, and Randy Hodson, "Supervisory Bullying, Status Inequalities and Organizational Context," *Social Forces* 87 (March 2009), pp. 1561–1589. This is a meta-analysis of 204 published works.

78. Russell E. Johnson, Stanley B. Silverman, Aarti Shyamsunder, *et al.*, "Acting Superior but Actually Inferior?: Correlates and Consequences of Workplace Arrogance," *Human Performance* 23 (November/December 2010), pp. 403–427.

79. Workplace Bullying Institute and Zogby International, *U.S. Workplace Bullying Survey* (Bellingham, WA, and Washington, DC: Authors, 2008), p. 1. In 2007, 7,740 American adults were surveyed.

80. Roscigno, Lopez, and Hodson, "Supervisory Bullying, Status Inequalities and Organizational Context."

81. Workplace Bullying Institute and Zogby International, *U.S. Workplace Bullying Survey*, p. 1.

82. Roscigno, Lopez, and Hodson, "Supervisory Bullying, Status Inequalities and Organizational Context."

83. Workplace Bullying Institute and Zogby International, *U.S. Workplace Bullying Survey*, p. 16. Figure is for 2007.

84. U.S. Department of Labor study, as cited Scott Shortenhaus, *Strategies for Working with Businesses and High Growth Industries* (Washington, DC: U.S. Department of Health and Human Services, Center for Faith Based and Community Initiatives, 2006).

85. Roscigno, Lopez, and Hodson, "Supervisory Bullying, Status Inequalities and Organizational Context."

86. Ethics Resource Center, *National Government Ethics Survey: An Inside View of Public Sector Ethics*, pp. 2, 20, 25, 31; *National Nonprofit Ethics Survey: An Inside View of Nonprofit Sector Ethics*, p. 15; and *National Business Ethics Survey: An Inside View of Private Sector Ethics* (Arlington, VA: Author, 2008), p. 14. Figures are for 2007.

87. Bob Woodward, "10 Take Aways From the Bush Years," *Washington Post* (January 18, 2009).

88. Richard Beckhard, *Organizational Development: Strategies and Models* (Reading, MA: Addison-Wesley, 1969), pp. 20–24.

89. Warren G. Bennis, *Organizational Development: Its Nature, Origins, and Prospects* (Reading, MA: Addison-Wesley, 1969), p. 17.

90. Bernard Burnes, "Kurt Lewin and the Harwood Studies: The Foundations of OD," *Journal of Applied Behavioral Science* 43 (June 2007), pp. 213–230.

91. Robert T. Golembiewski, Carl W. Proehl, Jr., and David Sink, "Success of OD Applications in the Public Sector: Toting Up the Score for a Decade, More or Less," *Public Administration Review* 41 (November/December 1981), pp. 679–682. The data are on p. 681. The authors counted 574 OD applications in the public sector, 1945–1980, and surveyed participants in 47 percent of them.

92. Peggy Morrison, "Evaluation in OD: A Review and an Assessment," *Group and Organization Studies* 3 (March 1978), pp. 42–70; and Jerry Porras, "The Comparative Impact of Different OD Techniques and Intervention Intensities," *Journal of Applied Behavioral Science* 15 (April 1979), pp. 156–178.

93. Peter J. Robertson and Sonal J. Seneviratne, "Outcomes of Planned Organizational Change in the Public Sector: A Meta-Analytic Comparison to the Private Sector," *Public Administration Review* 55 (November/December 1995), pp. 547–558. The quotation is on p. 554.

94. R. Wayne Boss, Benjamin B. Dunford, Alan D. Boss, *et al.*, "Sustainable Change in the Public Sector: The Longitudinal Benefits of Organization Development," *Journal of Applied Behavioral Science* 46 (December 2010), pp. 436–472. The quotations are on p. 436.

95. W. Warner Burke, "The New Agenda for Organization Development," *Organizational Dynamics* 25 (June 1997), pp. 6–20. The quotation is on p. 8.

96. Larry E. Greiner and Thomas G. Cummings, "Wanted: OD More Alive Than Dead!"*Journal of Applied Behavioral Science* 40 (Winter 2004), pp. 374–91. The quotation is on p. 374.

97. Bennis, *Organizational Development*, p. 17.

98. Simona Botti and Christopher K. Hsee, "Dazed by Choice: How the Temporal Costs of Choice Freedom Lead to Undesirable Outcomes," *Organizational Behavior and Human Decision Processes* 112 (July 2010), pp. 161–171. The quotations are on p. 161.

99. Thomas H. Fitzgerald, "The O.D. Practitioner in the Business World: Theory vs. Reality," *Organizational Dynamics* 16 (Summer 1987), pp. 20–34. The quotations are on pp. 25, 27.

100. See, for example, Chester I. Barnard, *The Functions of the Executive* (Cambridge, MA: Harvard University Press, 1938).

101. Herbert Kaufman, *Time, Chance, and Organizations: Natural Selection in a Perilous Environment* (Chatham, NJ: Chatham House, 1985), p. 67.

102. Paul R. Lawrence and Jay W. Lorsch, *Organization and Environment: Managing Differentiation and Integration* (Cambridge, MA: Harvard University Press, 1967).

103. Peter M. Blau and Richard A. Schoenherr, *The Structure of Organization* (New York: Basic Books, 1971).

104. Much of the thinking in this and the following five paragraphs is drawn from Donald Chisholm, "Organizational Response to Environmental Change," Paper presented at the Annual Meeting of the American Political Science Association (New Orleans, August 29–September 1, 1985).

105. Philip Selznick, *TVA and the Grass Roots* (Berkeley, CA: University of California Press, 1949).

106. Richard A. Couto, "Co-optation in TVA: Selznick Updated," Paper delivered at the 1981 Annual Meeting of the American Political Science Association (New York, September 3–6, 1981), abstract page.

107. Douglas McGregor, *The Theory of Human Enterprise* (New York: McGraw-Hill, 1960).

108. Peter J. Robertson, Feng Wang, and Supamas Trivisvavet, "Self- and Collective Interest in Public Organizations: An Empirical Investigation," *Public Performance & Management Review* 31 (September 2007), pp. 54–84. The quotation is on p. 54.

109. Chris Argyris, *Organization and Innovation* (Homewood, IL: Richard D. Irwin, 1965).

110. Thomas A. Wright and Barry M. Staw, "Affect and Favorable Work Outcomes: Two Longitudinal Tests of the Happy-Productive Worker Thesis," *Journal of Organizational Behavior* 20 (January 1999), pp. 1–23.

111. Allen Schick, "The Trauma of Politics: Public Administration in the Sixties," *American Public Administration: Past, Present, Future*, Frederick C. Mosher, ed. (Tuscaloosa, AL: University of Alabama Press, 1975), pp. 142–180. The quotation is on p. 170.

112. Mancur Olson, Jr., *The Logic of Collective Action: Public Goods and the Theory of Groups* (Cambridge, UK: Cambridge University Press, 1965).

113. Robert T. Golembiewski, *Behavior and Organizations* (Chicago: Rand-McNally, 1962).

114. Stewart, "The Management Myth," p. 85.

115. Eric Fromm, *The Art of Loving* (New York: Harper & Row, 1956).

116. See, for just one example of this research, Catherine Casey, " 'Come, Join Our Family': Discipline and Integration in Corporate Organizational Culture," *Human Relations* 52 (February 1999), pp. 155–178.

117. Max Weber, quoted in Elizabeth Kolbert, "Why Work? A Hundred Years of the Protestant Work Ethic," *The New Yorker* (November 29, 2004), pp. 157, 160.

118. Ralph P. Hummel, *The Bureaucratic Experience: A Critique of Life in the Modern Organization*, 4th ed. (New York: St. Martin's, 1994), p. 3.

119. Daniel Gilbert, *Stumbling on Happiness* (London: Vintage, 2007).

120. Kaufman, *Time, Chance, and Organizations*, p. 44.

121. Ibid., p. 43.

122. Rhys Andrews, "Perceived Environmental Uncertainty in Public Organizations: An

Empirical Exploration," *Public Performance & Management Review* 32 (September 2008), pp. 25–50. The quotations are on p. 41.

123. Ibid., p. 41.

124. See, for just one example, Talcott Parsons, *The Social System* (Glencoe, IL: Free Press, 1951).

125. Hal G. Rainey, *Understanding and Managing Public Organizations*, 2nd ed. (San Francisco: Jossey-Bass, 1997), p. 55.

126. Donald P. Warwick, in collaboration with Marvin Meade and Theodore Reed, *A Theory of Public Bureaucracy: Politics, Personality, and Organization in the State Department* (Cambridge, MA: Harvard University Press, 1975), p. 190.

127. As derived from data in Jeffrey Pfeffer, "Like Ships Passing in the Night: The Separate Literatures of Organization Theory and Public Management," *International Public Management Journal* 43 (4, 2006), pp. 457–465. The data are on p. 459. These types of "empirical papers" published in *Administrative Science Quarterly* declined from nearly 44 percent of all articles to less than 13 percent in the period 1985–2005.

The Fabric of Organizations: Forces

How do organizations adapt to the fury of forces that roil in them and in the society surrounding them? To answer this question, researchers weave the threads of theory into a fabric. Sometimes they weave a tapestry, other times a drop cloth.

ASSESSING ORGANIZATIONAL WORTH

Organizations use three broad "tests" to judge their own social worth.[1] Table 4-1 (see on p. 86) arrays these tests by types of organizations. (The table also shows the decision-making strategies that these organizations use, and we discuss these strategies later in the chapter.)

Testing for Efficiency

The *efficiency*, or *economic*, *test* assesses an organization's ability to fully and satisfactorily complete its tasks using the fewest resources possible. It is applicable to organizations that have "crystallized standards of desirability," and whose members believe that they fully comprehend the relationships between causes and effects.

The efficiency test is appropriately applied to for-profit companies. For example, executives in our hypothetical corporation of International Widget have a solid notion of what they want to do and how to do it: maximize profits (that is, their standards of desirability are "crystallized") and manufacture widgets as cheaply as possible (that is, there is a clear causal connection between high profits and cheap production). Thus, assessing an organization like International Widget is both objective and easy because its efficiency can be readily determined.

Testing for Effectiveness

The *effectiveness test* assesses an organization's ability to fully complete its tasks–period. Unlike the efficiency test, no judgments are made about how many resources the organization consumes (or wastes) in completing those tasks because efficiency cannot be assessed.

Effectiveness tests often are applicable to public organizations. Government agencies may have crystallized standards of desirability, but the agencies' members are uncertain about what causes what. The Department of Homeland Security, for instance, has a crystallized standard of desirability (adequate security), but its administrators cannot know whether their programs actually are assuring that security. Hence, we see Homeland Security spending as much money as it can muster as a means of maximizing its standard of desirability (that is, its untested security capacity), but International Widget spending as *little* money as possible as a means of maximizing *its* standard of desirability (that is, its profits).

Testing for Society

The *social test* assesses an organization's ability to appear relevant and useful in achieving its mission. It is applicable to those organizations that have ambiguous standards of desirability. In other words, members in such an organization are not merely uncertain about whether or not they achieving their goals; they are uncertain even about what those goals are! Such an organization might be a social service agency; often, no one in these organizations can express, except in the vaguest terms, just what it is that they do, much less the best way of doing it.

Both the effectiveness and social tests of organizational worth are the kinds of tools that societies usually use to assess their public agencies and nonprofit associations. Often, these organizations succeed because they have learned how to ace these amorphous tests by accumulating prestige—as indicated, for instance, by favorable publicity, proliferating programs, or big budgets. "External legitimacy" far outweighs changes in internal management in predicting the long-term survival of newly-founded, nonprofit social service organizations.[2] Nonprofit organizations that rely heavily on private contributions grow "at a faster rate" if they have "high status, more ties to urban elites," and are more central in networks of organizations.[3]

ORGANIZATIONAL KNOWLEDGE

Knowledge and *information* have been defined as "what changes us,"[4] or, more formally but just as accurately, "data, passed through a person's mind, that becomes meaningful." Knowledge and information are superior to *data* ("a meaningless point in time when not considered in context").[5] Organizational intelligence is less a question of unearthing and transmitting yet one more datum to complete a policy puzzle (although doing so will always remain critical) and is much more a challenge of how best to interpret data and uncertainty to solve a mystery.[6] Data we have—usually in spades. Knowledge is more elusive. There is no indication, for example, that, despite many times more data, Americans are any more knowledgeable about public affairs than they were in 1950.[7]

Information and Hierarchy

If knowledge changes us, then it is disconcerting to know that organizations change knowledge.

Absorbing Uncertainty   One of the more intriguing ways in which organizations distort knowledge is called *uncertainty absorption*,[8] whereby information that initially is regarded as uncertain and "soft" by the people who collect it becomes increasingly certain and "hard" as it is sent up through the decision-making hierarchy.

Consider, for example, the Central Intelligence Agency's (CIA) efforts to detect Iraq's weapons of mass destruction. The agency had had no spies in Iraq for five years before the invasion of 2003, and its "assessments were increasingly based on very limited information." Although the CIA's analysts expressed their reservations, those passages "tended to drop off as the reports would go up the food chain.... As a result, virtually everyone in the United States intelligence community...thought Iraq still had the illicit weapons.... And the government became a victim of its own certainty."[9]

Centralization and the Fate of Intelligence   In closed, centralized organizations, information distortion often is intertwined with personal power.

For a full year prior to the invasion of Iraq, the research director of Iraq's intelligence agency wrote "three assessments saying that the Americans would attack Iraq and that we had no chance to resist them." The director provided these reports to one General Abed, Iraqi president Saddam Hussein's most trusted aide (he was allowed, uniquely, to pack a pistol in Saddam's presence), but Abed "refused to give these [assessments] to the President.... Like everyone else, he was afraid to tell him the truth."[10]

Decentralization and the Fate of Intelligence   Even when people trust each other and are working as a team, both of which are emblematic of the open, decentralized organization, information still may fail to reach the people who need it and can act on it. In these organizations, the pathology appears to be less one of fear (although even presidents must "beg for the bad news" because subordinates "will not give it to you naturally"[11]) and more one of fumbling. Perhaps the iconic instance of how bureaucracies in democracies can falter in informing those who need to know is the shambolic failure, in 1941, of anyone to definitively alert the American troops at Pearl Harbor that they expected the Japanese to attack.[12]

Turf and Bureaucratic Jealousies An informational pathology that seems to be particularly present in public organizations, whether centralized or decentralized, concerns "*turf*," or agency rivalries that revolve around the control of areas of responsibility.

Here is an example of this pathology in a *centralized* organizational context: The notorious World War II spy "Cicero," who was the valet of the British ambassador at Ankara, sold astonishingly accurate and detailed intelligence concerning the planned D-Day invasion of Europe to one Ludwig Moyzisch, who then sent it to the Nazi foreign minister, Joachim von Ribbentrop. The foreign minister was involved in a bitter power struggle with the Reich Security Office, and he loathed Franz von Papen, the German ambassador to Turkey; Moyzich, as it happened, not only reported to the Reich Security Office but also was an attaché on Papen's staff. So Ribbentrop found it expedient to bury Cicero's information, and with it, perhaps, the Third Reich.[13]

And here is an instance of the pathology in a *decentralized* government: Even though fifty to sixty professionals in the CIA knew by March 2000 that two of the Al Qaeda hijackers involved in the terrorist attacks of September 11, 2001, were in the United States, no one informed the Federal Bureau of Investigation, which is charged with internal security, of their presence.[14]

Hierarchy, Handling, and Information Organizational structure, in short, is no panacea for curing pathologies of organizational information. We do know, however, that there is a model of *hierarchical distortion:*[15] The more hierarchical layers there are, the more organizational subunits that are charged with similar responsibilities, and the more that information is "handled" as it is passed up, down, and around the bureaucracy, the more likely it is that the information will be delayed and distorted, and the less likely that it will reach someone who can intelligently act on it.[16]

It is striking that, following 9/11, federal policymakers determinedly ignored this fact of informational life. Washington's response to that attack—a rapid and enormous expansion of the intelligence community—produced bureaucratic overlap (for instance, fifty-one agencies charged with the narrow responsibility of tracking money flows among terrorists); inefficiency (analysts publish about 50,000 intelligence reports per year, "a volume so large that many are routinely ignored"); disarray (1,271 federal organizations and 1,931 companies with terrorism duties, toiling in 10,000 locations across America); and blurred lines of authority (an estimated 854,000 professionals have top-secret clearances). These dysfunctions have, apparently, weakened the intelligence agencies' capacity to "connect the dots" and disrupt future terrorist acts.[17]

Information and Decision Making

All of us are inundated by data (Chapter 6 has the scary details), and we are unable to salvage from this flood the knowledge that we need to make optimal decisions. The economist Friedrich von Hayek famously extended this idea to large and complex organizations, and even to whole societies, arguing that no one person could ever have enough information to make rational decisions. Hayek held that market and other environmental forces provided the best information for decision making.[18]

Know-Nothing Decision Making Perhaps we should not be too surprised, therefore, that decision makers "gather information and do not use it. They ask for reports and do not read them. They act first and receive requested information later, and do not seem to be concerned about the order."[19] As much as four-fifths of organizational information may be filed away and never used,[20] and instances of information being generated that bear no discernible relationship to the decisions that they ostensibly justify are rife.[21]

Worse, the costs of collecting this unused information are horrendously high. More than seven out of ten workers say that their main job is "tracking down information,"[22] and over four out of ten managers who must search for information believe that its cost exceeds its value.[23] Because the people who gather knowledge and the decision makers who purportedly use it dwell in different organizational worlds, the expense of collecting information is largely hidden and, as a result, "individuals and organizations will consistently over invest in information."[24]

One explanation for this behavior is that organizations are not too bright. There is, however, another possibility: organizational sophistication.

Information as Symbol "The acts of seeking and using information in decisions have important symbolic value.... Since legitimacy is a necessary property of effective decisions, conspicuous consumption of information is a sensible strategy for decision makers. The strategy need not be chosen deliberately. It will characterize processes that work."[25]

The public sector seems especially adroit in its use of information as a legitimizing symbol. One investigation of management control systems in ninety-nine defense contracts found "no empirical evidence...that information was used for controlling project cost, schedule, or quality," but that "most managers still believed that collecting and reporting information led to project control." The "perceived value among managers" of information's symbolic use was the study's "most remarkable" finding.[26]

Making Decisions Faster—and Better Because decision makers implicitly recognize that information-intensive decisions are likelier to be accepted and implemented, it follows that "organizations that exhibit an elaborate information system and conspicuous consumption of information will...be more effective decision makers than those who do not."[27]

These organizations demonstrate certain behaviors that often are counterintuitive. Not only do their decision makers gather more data and counsel extensively with respected colleagues when making major decisions, but they also develop more alternatives to solve problems, and, even though these activities are time consuming, they nonetheless make their decisions more rapidly than do those who do not engage in them. These unexpected patterns of information-sensitive, advice-seeking, option-generating, yet speedy, decision making lead to "superior performance" by executives.[28]

In sum, research on how information is used in decision making implies that the process is less than rational. And, to an extraordinary extent, it is not.

DECISION MAKING IN ORGANIZATIONS

The principal reason underlying this darker side of decision making is that the people who make decisions, like all people, are less than logical.

The Bounds of Individual Rationality

Every decision maker is boxed in by mental and social bounds.

The Decision Premise All human beings make decisions on the basis of their *decision premise*, or the unique values and viewpoints held by each organizational member, and on which he or she bases every decision he or she makes regarding the organization.[29]

Sector plays a part in forming individual decision premises. "The values of profitability, competitiveness, and customer orientation," for example, "have a greater influence on business decisions; in public organizations, values such as legitimacy, lawfulness, accountability, and impartiality play a larger role."[30]

The organization also has a role. It can render its members' decision premises more reflective of the organization's values, and, when it does, it produces happier employees who stay longer with the organization.[31] Still, regardless of how much sector and organization may mold individual decision premises, people do not make more rational decisions.

Bounded Rationality and Dysrationalia This is because the human species is beset by *bounded rationality*; that is, the reasoning powers of the human mind are bound to a small and simple plot compared to the vastness and complexity of the territory spanned by the problems that human minds are expected (expected, at least, by traditional theorists in economics and management) to comprehend and solve.[32]

The psychologist, George Miller, for example, determined that the mind can distinguish a maximum of seven categories of phenomena at a time, but beyond that number loses track.[33] (This finding reputedly convinced telephone executives to give us seven-digit telephone numbers.) Emotion plays a fulsome part, and a decision seems to be an emotional, or affective, response to one's environment, which is overlain by a later, more rational response.[34] Solutions that provide quick results generally are preferred to those that result in delayed returns.[35] Decision makers often accord disproportionate weight to the first information that they receive and to recent, dramatic events; misstate the problem, thereby undermining the whole decision-making process; seek confirming evidence of their biases; and overestimate the accuracy of their forecasts.[36] Decision makers frequently use heuristic thinking (or "rules of thumb"), which is invariably flawed, and base their decisions on their perception of the *status quo*, rather than on an objective comparison of known variables.[37] Decision makers usually are overcautious, favoring stability over change,[38] and tend to prefer information that protects them against anticipated losses to information that they can use to make gains.[39] Environment generally plays a large role in how a person makes decisions.

At its worst, bounded rationality can degenerate into *dysrationalia*, or "the inability to think and behave rationally despite having adequate intelligence." President George W. Bush, in the view of at least one psychologist, was a dysrationalic decision maker,[40] as the examples provided in Chapters 1 and 9, and later in this one, suggest.

"Satisficing" Decisions Because the rationality of decision makers is so bounded by the human brain, decisions are rarely, if ever, optimal. If not optimal, then, what are they?

Herbert Simon answered this question by making up a word. He called the decisions made by people in organizations "satisficing" decisions—that is, they *satisfied* the makers of decisions and *sufficed* enough for the organization to get by, or, combined, *satisficed*.[41]

Victims of Groupthink Stress accompanies decision making, and, as a consequence, avoidance and denial are frequently the handmaidens of the decision process.[42] When decision makers are stressed, are making decisions within the context of a tightly knit in-group whose members share common values, and fail to solicit differing perspectives from outside the group, "groupthink" is the consequence. *Groupthink* is an over-conformity among decision makers that displaces critical thinking, and "is likely to result in irrational and dehumanizing actions directed against out-groups."[43]

Instances of groupthink include the American decision to invade Iraq. The basis of that decision was the "erroneous National Intelligence Estimate of October 2002,"[44] which was "the Intelligence Community's most authoritative and comprehensive judgment."[45]

How this happened, as recorded in official reports, is a primer on groupthink: "At some point" the intelligence community's "premises stopped being working hypotheses and became more or less unrebuttable conclusions; worse, the intelligence system became too willing to find confirmations of them in evidence that should have been recognized at the time to be of dubious reliability. Collectors and analysts too readily accepted any evidence that supported their theory that Iraq had stockpiles and was developing weapons programs, and they explained away or simply disregarded evidence that pointed in other directions."[46]

This destructive dynamic extended to the White House. President George W. Bush never called for a debate among his staff about whether there was a connection between Al Qaeda and Iraq, "one key reason" justifying the invasion of Iraq. More startlingly, Bush "sometimes assumed that he knew his aides' private views without asking them one-on-one. He made probably the most important decision of his presidency—whether to invade Iraq—without directly asking" the secretaries of state and defense or the director of the CIA "for their bottom-line recommendations." Nor, for that matter, did he consult his own father, who, in 1991, had led a successful invasion of Iraq.[47]

Avoiding the groupthink trap requires that public administrators aggressively mine information.

Thinking Dispositions and Good Decision Making Despite the many mental and social obstacles that inhibit good decision making, good decision makers remain. Good decision makers (and there are many) are distinctive because they employ a wide variety of "thinking dispositions" when making decisions.

Thinking dispositions are rational, psychological, decision-making touchstones that, surprisingly, do not correlate, or, at best, only weakly so, with cognitive ability. They include a capacity for thoughtful reflection; digging out information before deciding; trying to match one's degree of certainty with the strength of the evidence; examining one's biases and correcting for them; and a willingness to wait until good solutions become apparent.[48]

The Bounds of Organizational Rationality

Just as the rationality of organizational members is bounded, so is the rationality of organizations themselves.

Types of Organizational Decision Making

How an organization makes decisions depends on whether its members and stakeholders agree or disagree about what their organization should do (or its goals), and agree or disagree about what causes the attainment of those goals.[49] Table 4-1 matches these "decision issues" with decision-making strategies.

Analytical Decision Making For example, in an organization of specialists, everyone, in theory, would agree about their organization's goals (e.g., Social Security is worthwhile to society) and also agree about causality ("If you fill out the form, then you will get your Social Security checks, and society will benefit"). In such a bureaucracy, decisions would be made *analytically*, or *computationally,* that is, with little or no internal debate about values and with decisions made on the basis of shared technical perceptions (although even computational decision making still is characterized by bounded rationality).

Judgmental Decision Making In an organization in which members still agree about goals, but disagree about how to achieve them, decisions would be made *judgmentally*. The Defense Department is exemplary; its executives agree that America should be defended but disagree on how best to do it.

Compromising Decision Making When an organization's decision makers disagree about what their goals are, but agree on causation, *compromising*, or *bargaining*, *decision making* is used. The classic example is any legislature.

Inspirational and/or Authoritarian Decision Making And when decision makers disagree about *both* goals and causality, then *inspirational decision making*, or *authoritarian decision making*, or both, are favored. As we detail in Chapter 10, some organizations in the nonprofit sector seem to exemplify this combination, and their members often are unable to decide just what, exactly, their objectives are, much less how to attain them.[50]

Mismatching Organizations and Decision Making

Table 4-1 illustrates which decision-making strategy *ought* to be used by each type of organization if successful decisions are to be made. Unfortunately, in nearly six out of ten *strategic decisions*—that is, important policies with significant consequences—decision makers select a decision-making strategy that is *in*appropriate to the kinds of bounds that constrain their organization. As a result, these major policies "were much less successful" than those that were made in conjunction with the decision strategy that matched their type of organization[51] (as shown in Table 4-1).

Organized Anarchies and the Garbage Can of Decision Making

The messiest forms of decision making displayed in Table 4-1—that is, judgmental, compromising, inspirational, and authoritarian decision making—all associate with public or nonprofit organizations. More profoundly, however, these messy methods also characterize an *organized anarchy*, which is a "loose collection of ideas" in which participants do not define their preferences very precisely and do not fully understand what their organization actually does.[52]

As these characteristics imply, organized anarchies use an erratic, irrational decision-making process that is a figurative "garbage can." In making decisions, the organized anarchy "bumbles along, and discovers preferences through action more than it acts on the basis of preferences," resulting in decisions that are "a collection of choices looking for problems...solutions looking for issues to which they might be the answer, and decision makers looking for work."[53]

Decision Making in Public Organizations: A Different Dynamic

Whether the sector is public or private "creates substantive differences" in decision making.[54] Here are some.

An Attenuated Autonomy

About six out of ten Americans think that protesting against "unjust public policies" and participating in "community decision-making" are "very important...obligations" that they "owe the country."[55] In part because of

---

> ▸ **TABLE 4-1**
>
> **Societal Assessment and Organizational Decision-Making Strategies by Causation and Outcome**

		Standards of Desirability and Preferred Outcomes	
		Crystallized Standards and Agreement about Outcomes	*Ambiguous Standards and Disagreement about Outcomes*
Beliefs about cause and effect	Agreement	*Efficiency,* or *economic,* tests are used by society to assess the organization.	*Social tests* are used by society to assess the organization.
		Computational, or *analytical, decision making* is used by the organization.	*Compromise,* or *bargaining, decision making* is used by the organization.
		Example: a research lab	*Example:* Congress
	Disagreement	*Effectiveness tests* are used by society to assess the organization.	*Social tests* are used by society to assess the organization.
		Judgmental decision making is used by the organization.	*Inspirational and/or authoritarian decision making* is used by the organization.
		Example: Department of Defense	*Example:* Some nonprofit social service agencies

these views, public administrators are "monitored by everyone around them."[56]

Hence, decision making in public organizations is less autonomous than in the private sector,[57] and procedures are more constricting.[58] Overall, "the image of public organizations that emerges is one of little organizational coherence in the identification of strategic decisions. In addition, the ability of top-level managers to control the decisions and actions of their organizations is called into question."[59]

Bargaining *versus* Analyzing When making decisions, public administrators "place too great an emphasis on bargaining...but they do seem to understand the limits of analysis," in contrast to corporate managers, who "seem to place too much reliance on analytics and too little on bargaining." Public administrators believe that negotiating, in and of itself, legitimizes decisions, and thereby creates, unfortunately, "a false perception of support for a decision."[60]

A Complex Process Governments' decision makers must deal with vastly more, and more complex, decision criteria that are far broader in scope than those in business,[61] who are measurably more likely to focus on a single and straightforward datum—that of financial performance—when making decisions.[62] As we describe in Chapter 6, information technologies have proven helpful in sorting and simplifying data for public decision makers, but the unique complexity of governmental decision making persists.

Taking It Slowly and Cautiously Public executives who have business experience view governments as conservative cultures that are slow to change,[63] and research suggests that decisions are indeed made more slowly in public organizations than in private ones.[64] Slower decision making may be a product of the fact that government agencies are less likely to take risks than private companies, regardless of the organizational mission.[65]

Any organization with a cautionary culture is also likelier to have top managers who have low levels of trust in their employees; a fuzzier organizational mission (these two characteristics seem to be especially salient); ribbons of red tape; weak linkages between promotion and performance; and high involvement with elected officials[66]—features that generally are found far more in the public sector than in the other two.

Participation and Consultation Decision making in the public sector is, at least superficially, a far more participative affair than in the private one, as exemplified by agencies' growing use of "large-group interaction methods" that can involve as many as 2,000 people at one time when making decisions.[67]

"Publicness is associated with greater decision participation but not smoothness."[68] Governments' decision makers swirl sporadically through a "vortex" of intense meetings and conversations with each other and are much more likely than those in private organizations to engage in both formal and informal interaction with others when making decisions.[69]

Consulting with Whom? Public administrators network extensively with internal constituencies—"peers and underlings"—when making decisions.[70] This is a good thing: As a thorough review of the literature concludes, "our analysis of the research suggests that the greatest organizational gains from employee participation [in decision making] may come from producing *better* decisions."[71]

In marked contrast to business managers, however, when public administrators make decisions they often "discount networking" with "external constituencies," notably agency clients, citizens, and oversight bodies. This is not such a good thing. If clients and overseers were more involved in public administrators' decision making, it would "improve their chances of success."[72]

Ignoring Clients and Citizens At the client level, public managers resist the involvement of clients and other citizens when making high-stakes decisions and try to relegate them to lower-stakes issues (and so, for that matter, do private and nonprofit managers).[73]

For example, even though state agency heads routinely dismiss their "clientele groups" as having

very little actual influence in shaping "major agency policy decisions," they nonetheless "are less than satisfied" with even the marginal influence that their clients do have.[74] City and county managers perceive citizens' involvement in their "strategic decision making.... to be troublesome." Even in "communities in which citizens are ranked high in terms of placing pressure on the administration to include them in the deliberative process," citizens "are not more likely to have greater opportunities for citizen involvement."[75]

The stiff resistance among public administrators to clients and citizens participating in policymaking is regrettable for several reasons. In those communities where there are "higher degrees of citizen participation in [public] hearings and higher levels of perceived citizen impact on budgetary processes," public administrators "feel most accountable" to citizens for their programs' performance.[76] Client and citizen involvement can result in more responsive public policies and greater citizen trust in their governments,[77] conditions that can create a beneficent cycle of increasingly better governance.[78]

Ignoring Bosses and Overseers At the oversight level, public administrators are, surprisingly, less than fully communicative with the legislators or trustees to whom they report, and this lapse "has important implications. Oversight bodies have a big impact on public sector decisions. Their scrutiny can be intense, and politics is far more pervasive than in private organizations."[79]

The disinclination of public administrators to consult with their oversight bodies may have its roots in their lack of confidence in them. Executives with backgrounds in both government and business think that, compared with corporate board directors, legislators are less consistent, less informed on substantive issues, less likely to agree with administrators on organizational goals,[80] and even that government is less transparent than business.[81]

Moreover, oversight bodies question agency decisions in particularly vexing ways, and this, too, can dampen communication. Legislators and board members "derail" agency decisions "*after* a decision is made, and long after the objecting oversight body has been asked for their views.... Public organizations face fickle oversight, not the pervasive monitoring and tinkering with ideas that the literature suggests."[82]

Caution, Communication, and Unappreciated Peril Because public administrators usually have consulted and negotiated intensively (at least with peers and underlings) in making their decisions, they often are supremely confident in the quality and ultimate success of their decisions. Unfortunately, they seriously underestimate "the level of risk" that their decisions entail, which is a direct result of their poor communication with citizens and their agencies' clients and oversight bodies. Corporate decision makers, by contrast, view "the same decisions" produced by such a process "as having considerable risk," and these public/private differences hold up "no matter the cognitive makeup of the manager or the culture to which he or she was exposed."[83]

Obviously, decision makers who ignore their customers, clients, and bosses can produce decisions that "can be very dangerous" to the decision makers, especially "if an oversight body opposes" their decisions.[84] Yet this may be precisely the decision-making situation in public organizations.

The Quality Question In sum, decision making in public organizations, in contrast to its practice in private ones, seems to be a process that relies more on bargaining than analysis; is slower, sloppier, and murkier; is more intense, constrained, and complicated; is more consultative, but has elements of groupthink; is and risk averse, but unwittingly risky.

There is little research that clearly links each of these characteristics with objectively defined better or worse decisions, but what data we have do not augur well for public organizational decision making. Participative decision making is present in government agencies, and, even when confined only to agency employees, it associates with superior decisions.[85] But the negatives outnumber the positives: Limited decision-making autonomy,[86] slow decision making,[87] and a tendency toward groupthink[88] characterize decision making in public organizations, and all correlate with poorer decisions.

In one of the few attempts to match the decision-making techniques used by each sector with the quality and successful implementation of the decisions made, it was determined that government managers who relied primarily on soliciting the views of experts and used hard data made the highest quality decisions and enjoyed the highest rates of acceptance. Public administrators who relied more on studying issues or bargaining with stakeholders were less successful.[89]

Life-or-Death Decisions—Imprimatur of the Public Sector When making risky decisions, all decision makers play heavily to their own biases, distorting "their evaluations of probability and outcome information in the direction of their preferred decision alternative."[90] The riskiest of decisions are those that can result in people living or dying. This sort of decision making is largely the preserve of the public sector and appears only rarely in the other two.

A Monumental Map Mess in Georgia

We have noted that public agencies are far more influenced by factors in their external environments than are private companies and nonprofit associations. To cite just one example, the decisions made by public organizations, no matter how managerially rational, are exposed far more frequently to second-guessing and reversal by environmental forces. Here is an instance of what we mean.

The Georgia Department of Transportation had finally decided to clean up its map. The Department designs and publishes the state's official travel map, and its administrators had been fretting for at least eight years over how to make their map clearer and more useful to most travelers.

Clarifying Georgia's official map was no mean challenge. It was strewn with unincorporated communities that are so small that the U.S. Census Bureau does not recognize them. Some of these tiny towns have names so long that their monikers meandered, literally, all over the map. In Georgia, there are 519 of these boroughs, and in 2006 the Department of Transportation made the unusual, if understandable, decision to eliminate all of them from the map's 2007 edition.

Thus began "The Great DOT Map Mess." In its decision to unclutter its cartography, the Department deleted such delightful designations as Rose Dhu, Dewy Rose, and Due West; Phinizy, Funkhouser, and Flowery Tree; Pin Point and Poetry Tulip; Retreat and Roosterville; Cloudland and Kansas; Sand Hill and Sandfly; Ty Ty and Talking Rock; Hemp and Hickory Level; Jake and Juliette; Lowell and Clem; Chattoogaville and Centralhatcheee; Gum Branch and Dry Branch; Deepstep and Sharp Top; Between and Experiment; and Gay and Climax. Some counties were left with only one or two communities remaining on the official state map.

Some victimized villages had long histories, cultural significance, or really outraged residents who protested that: "This gets back to respect for rural areas"; "I was really saddened by all this"; "It's almost like disrespecting history"; "We're not country bumpkins"; "I think it's a slap in the face"; and "You know, you're just dissing here."

The Department of Transportation responded to these and other "pretty impassioned" objections with, "We're not under obligation to show every single community. While we want to, there's a balancing act. And the map was getting illegible." "It was solely an effort to produce a better product."

Still, the department quickly reinstated thirty-one "placeholders," as the Census Bureau dismissively dubs very small communities and pledged to reconsider more. The governor then wrote the department's board, asking it to "take another look" at its decision, and, fewer than twenty-four hours later (and less than a month after the department had announced its decision to simplify its map), the board reversed itself and reinstated all the vanished villages.

The Georgia Department of Transportation had met its Waterloo. Nevertheless, the fine folks in Waterloo, as well as those solid souls in Yellow Dirt, Hopeulikit, and Po Biddy Crossroads, remain vigilant. ∎

Sources: Gene Bluestein, Associated Press, "Official State Map Zaps 519 Communities," *Atlanta Journal-Constitution* (December 10, 2006) and "Georgia May Return Hundreds of Towns That Were Wiped off the Map," *Savannah Morning News* (December 15, 2006). "DOT Has Lost Its Way on Map Plan" (editorial) and Jack Wilkinson, "Folks Wiped off State Map Take Offense," both in *Atlanta Journal-Constitution* (December 15, 2006); and Ariel Hart, "Tiny Towns Go Back on Highway Map," *Atlanta Journal-Constitution* (January 4, 2007).

Life-or-death decisions can be agonizing for the public administrator making them a component that can stiflingly suppress the decision maker's emotions, then release them explosively and perilously. In these emotionally charged situations that feature "highly ego-involving issues," such as potential social disapproval, two crucial factors emerge: hope and time.[91]

If the decision maker perceives that there is some reason to hope for a problem's future solution that will be superior to the choices presently available, then he or she will adopt a decision-making strategy of coolly rational *vigilance*—that is, the decision maker assumes thinking dispositions that involve the consideration of many options; weighing their benefits, costs, and risks; actively seeking more information and expert advice; reviewing choices before selecting one; carefully planning the execution of the decision; and developing a contingency plan.

If, however, the decision maker has *no* hope for a satisfactory solution, then he or she is more likely to engage in dysrationalic *defensive avoidance*, a posture in which denial, rigidity, rationalization, procrastination, wishful thinking, and buck passing reign. Defensive avoidance "satisfies a powerful emotional need—to avoid anticipatory fear, shame, and guilt" by inducing "pseudocalm" in the decision maker.[92]

Defensive avoidance works fine, at least for the dilatory decision maker, until time runs out. Should events close in, forcing a decision, then the decision maker's defensive avoidance is shattered. His or her "thought processes are disrupted.... thinking becomes more simplistic." The decision maker snaps into *hypervigilance* mode, searching "frantically for a solution," and recklessly latching onto "a hastily contrived solution that seems to promise immediate relief."[93]

The price of this syndrome can be horrendously high. For two years, Philadelphia's otherwise able and hands-on mayor had defensively avoided dealing with a scofflaw cult that had been outrageously abusing its neighbors for more than a decade, even though the mayor had long been informed that he had the legal authority to remove the commune from its premises. When media pressure and angry residents finally brought the matter to a head, in 1985, two brief meetings were held, a planning group was appointed that was "remarkably low in rank for such a major operation," and the mayor repaired to his home before police served warrants at the cult's row house. The commune refused to be served; police unleashed water and tear gas; the cult responded with gunfire; and the police retaliated with far more firepower. Philadelphia's city manager informed the mayor that police had proposed dropping a bomb on the commune's roof, and "the mayor paused only thirty seconds before approving the idea." The result? "One of the most astounding debacles in the history of American municipal government," including an inferno that swept through three city blocks, leaving sixty-one homes in cinders, 250 people homeless, and six adults and five children dead.[94]

Decision Making in Nonprofit Organizations: More Talk, Fights, Risk

Decision making in the third sector has its own distinctiveness.

Consultative Decision Making For one, it appears to be even more interactive and consultative than it is in the public and private sectors. Decision makers in not-for-profit organizations "recycle" decisions back to earlier stages in the decision-making process and take many more "steps" than in the private sector.[95] This process works well for the third sector (but not for the other two), as bargaining in nonprofit organizations results in a greater likelihood of making better strategic decisions and implementing them successfully.[96]

Conflictual Decision Making Decision-making in independent organizations also appears to be

highly conflictual, and conflicts break out earlier in the decision-making process of not-for-profit organizations than for-profit ones. Although executives in both sectors find conflict unpleasant, corporate executives are even more averse to conflict than their nonprofit counterparts and are more likely to believe that conflict results in decisions of poorer quality. Nonprofit executives think just the opposite—that conflict defines issues more sharply and therefore produces better decisions![97]

Riskier Decision Making Third-sector administrators are especially fond of throwing the dice and have been known to radically change the very missions of their organizations if they thought it useful,[98] an option not available to public agencies and a limited one for private companies.

People who work in the independent sector are much less concerned with salaries and benefits than are either public administrators or private managers,[99] and nonprofit managers rank job security lower than do business administrators "to a statistically significant degree."[100] Both findings suggest that independent-sector executives are more willing than their colleagues in other sectors to take personal risks.

ADMINISTRATION IN ORGANIZATIONS

An important variant of decision making is administration, or strategic decision making writ small. Administration is based on *coalitions*, or informal alliances designed to advance individual goals. Coalitions appear to be basic to the human condition, and "many biologists believe that...we are a 'coalitional' species; groups compete with each other for status and influence."[101]

We note this reality because, from the perspective of organization theory, *coalition management* deftly defines the art of administration: "In the highly complex organization, power is dispersed.... [and] the central power figure is the individual who can manage the [dominant] coalition."[102] "The true basis for human action is not avarice—the lust for personal gain and comfort, but envy—the lust for primacy."[103]

The Challenges of Administering

Coalition management—that is, administering—is hard, in part because the old, easy, and authoritarian methods of administration are atrophying.

The Power of Subordinates Some seventy years ago, Simon observed that subordinates, especially "professional men," are "apt to have relatively narrow zones of acceptance" of administrative directives, "particularly in the areas of their own professional competences.... In a very real sense," the administrator "is merely a bus driver whose passengers will leave him unless he takes them in the direction they wish to go. They leave him only minor discretion."[104]

Simon's notion has merit for public administrators. *Guerrilla government* describes career bureaucrats who, quietly or brazenly, work against the wishes of their superiors, for good or ill.[105]

The evidence suggests, fortunately, that while line government workers are both dedicated to getting their jobs done and done well, they are mostly indifferent to the administrators and politicians who, presumably, manage them. A complex analysis found that, in implementing reforms, public executives and politicians are "relevant" to the "street-level bureaucrats" who must implement them, but these officials "seem to have a limited influence. More important are the understanding of the...policy by street-level bureaucrats and their knowledge of the rules."[106]

Public administrators, at least the more talented ones, seem to appreciate these administrative limitations and to work within them. They comprehend that their subordinates demand their "obedience to roles." "Cabinet officers...no less than a clerk" are "constrained to perform their roles in such a way as to demonstrate obeisance to norms.... To unseasoned actors, behaving capriciously...might seem the quintessential evidence of power. But such a strategy cannot endure in an organized setting."[107]

Widening Workers' Zones of Acceptance Is all lost for administrators? No. There are ways to render subordinates more accepting of administrators' wishes, and researchers have identified two kinds of power that facilitate their acceptance.

One sort of administrative, or leadership, power is *position power*, a category that includes four "power bases." They are: *Control*, specifically of information and the work environment; *reward power*, or the administrative leader's ability to positively recognize another; *coercive power*, or the opposite of reward power, which is the leader's capacity to punish; and *legitimate power*, or the acceptance of the administrator by others.

The other kind of power is *personal power*, and this includes three power bases: *Expert power*, which refers to the perception that the leader is knowledgeable; *referent power*, or the personal attraction that a manager holds for others; and *charisma*, or the leader's ability and will to exert great change.[108]

Public administrators have little, if any, control over some important positional power bases, notably reward power, coercive power, and legitimate power. By contrast, corporate managers enjoy a very high level of control over them. Public administrators, therefore, must depend on their personal power bases to lead and manage effectively. It is noteworthy, in this regard, that public employees perceive their administrators and executives to be far more inspirational and personally involved with them than do corporate employees.[109]

Mechanisms of Administrative Control

Once administrators have established their power bases, they can exercise greater power. They do this through six major "mechanisms of administrative control."

These mechanisms include *supervision*, or the direct observation and provision of feedback to subordinates; *input control*, or the cutting of resources to subunits; *behavior control*, or the structuring by administrators of individual and group activities; *output control*, or the evaluation of subunits' productivity; *selection-socialization control*, or the internalization of selected norms and values in subunits; and *environmental control*, or the constraints imposed by the organization's external task environment (public administrators implement environmental control by obtaining feedback from their communities).[110]

Public administrators, relative to their counterparts in the private sector, use all six mechanisms in surprisingly broad and balanced ways. Supervision is the least effective control mechanism, but the remaining five all bring desired administrative results. Public administrators must use "a more complex system of control" than business managers because they "have to supervise a workforce employing an unclear technology."[111]

The Tactics of Administration

Administrators in all sectors rely on four tactics of administration that are used with roughly equal frequency by top and middle managers to implement big, strategic decisions and policies.[112]

The Tactical Choice Our first tactic is *persuasion*, which relies on "experts" to sell a new policy, and it is used to implement nearly half, 49 percent, of decisions. Persuasion seems to be favored by public administrators, who spend an inordinate amount of their time talking with subordinates and peers; "this talk accomplishes administration."[113]

The next most favored administrative tactic is the *edict*, which simply orders that a policy be executed. Edicts are employed to implement 30 percent of decisions. Public administrators disdain the edict and rarely administer by "appealing to authority or using strong-arm tactics."[114]

Participation refers to stakeholders cooperatively implementing the decision, and it is used 13 percent of the time. Participation can range from merely "token" to (at least in theory) "comprehensive," although there is no known instance of genuine participation by all stakeholders.[115]

Finally, *intervention* involves managers justifying a need for change, establishing new performance standards, devising new means of implementation, and demonstrating the feasibility of the decision and the improvements that will result from it. It is the most aggressive tactic and the least used, accounting for only 8 percent of policies implemented. Government managers, however, appear to rely heavily on intervention, overcoming "bureaucratic obstacles" by introducing training programs (24 percent), demonstrating the benefits of new policies (23 percent), consultations with stakeholders (20 percent), and persistence (20 percent) to get their way.[116] Public administrators rely on far more kinds of "control mechanisms" and sources of information than do corporate mangers to implement decisions.[117]

Tactical Success What tactics work? Which do not?

The second most-used tactic, the edict, is the least effective, with, at best, a successful average adoption rate of 50 percent, and it associates with the lowest quality of decision: "adequate." An extensive review of related research supports this finding: "The effectiveness of formal authority in organizations," of which the edict is emblematic, "is diminishing."[118]

Persuasion, the tactic used most frequently, has an average adoption rate of 58 percent and correlates with a slightly higher-quality decision than the edict: "adequate to good." Persuasion consumes the most time of all the tactics.

Participation, the third most-used tactic, averages an adoption rate of 80 percent and associates with "good to outstanding" decisions. The broader and deeper the participation, the greater the rate of successful adoption of the policy.[119]

Intervention, "the most successful approach and the least frequently used," has a 90 percent adoption rate and correlates with decisions that are "good to outstanding." Its resource demands are modest, its implementation the fastest, and it works effectively "regardless of the situation."[120]

Effective administration, it appears, is not dictated by decree; it is done by the down and dirty. This seems to be especially the case in the public sector. "A presidential declaration doesn't make much happen." Rather, intervention "is what presidential management means—not hovering above the grimy fray, but plunging into it and getting dirty."[121]

Administration in Public Organizations: A Different Dynamic

The administrative tasks that public administrators must administer are far more "complex" than those managed by private managers,[122] rendering public administration all the more difficult, especially when it comes to setting priorities and planning.[123]

The Whirlwind Public administrators have little control over how they use their time and are more "rushed" to get things done.[124] They are far more consumed with managing crises, and devote far more time doing so, than their private-sector counterparts.[125] They spend less time alone in their offices, and, when they are by themselves, are on the telephone almost twice as long as private managers.[126]

The whirlwind of public management requires that effective public administrators be people of action. More-effective public administrators are more flexible and accord scant effort to "time management" and planning than less-effective public administrators. Quite the contrary holds true in the private sector: more-effective industrial managers plan their days, and less-effective ones do not.[127]

Public administration, it appears, is different.

The Pressures To "accomplish" their convoluted and ill-defined missions, public administrators must confront many more "conflicting environmental demands" and "external stakeholders" than business managers.[128] For example, "what appears to be more crucial" in determining a state agency's budget is not the agency's "budget aspirations," nor even its proven performance (whether low or high), but rather "political principals," such as legislators and lobbyists, who are "external to state agencies," but who can, and often do, "constrain, discipline, or even augment agency budget requests."[129] "Budget environments do influence state agency budget outcomes."[130]

These realities force public executives to interact far more frequently and formally with outside groups than their corporate counterparts.[131]

Despite these handicaps, public administrators serve the public with grace. "The 'insensitive' stereotype" of government bureaucrats "typically evokes images of public employees who are uncaring, inflexible.... and generally inept in dealing with the public." Research contradicts this stereotype: "The modal finding indicates public employees who are more sensitive than private employees. Public employees value qualities associated with sensitivity, empathy, broad mindedness, good interpersonal relations, forgiveness, politeness, helpfulness—more than or equal to private employees."[132] Ironically (and inaccurately), however, public managers are overly self-critical on this score and "tend to feel that their organizations satisfy customers less than do private organizations with their products and services."[133]

Lessons Learned Public administrators have learned some practical lessons about how to administer well. Here are the main ones:[134]

- Hire with care, and be alert to an employee's performance during the probationary period.
- Engage new employees with a welcoming first-year program that introduces them to the agency's culture.
- Communicate to build trust. Ask employees for their feedback and advice, and tell them whether you used it; meet regularly with each employee to review progress; and lead by example.
- Hold employees accountable for their performance.
- Closely link recognition, rewards, and sanctions to performance.
- Give all employees the opportunity to grow and develop.

LIMITED CHANGE: THE IMPACT OF TECHNOLOGY AND PEOPLE ON THE PUBLIC ORGANIZATON

Governments are not associated with swift-paced change. As one study put it, "high-publicness organizations...show a slow change rate" and "a low rate of change."[135] But public organizations do change.

The Likely Limited Role of Technology

Without question, the organization's *technology*, or what the organization does and how it does it, is central to what any organization is, and changing its technology causes systemic change throughout any organization.[136] However, legislatures rarely, if ever, allow government agencies to change what they do and public technology is itself resistant to change.

Executives who have served in the private and public sectors believe, accurately, that, compared to business, government is driven by processes.[137] Changing a process in any organization involves extensive convincing and coordinating, and is a much slower affair than changing a product. A study of 101 banks found that, over eleven years, "product innovations" were "adopted at a greater rate and speed than process innovations."[138] Hence, even within the same type of organization, *and even within the same organization*, processes change much more slowly than do products.

Governments produce processes, such as policies, programs, and services; rarely do they produce products, such as pickles, planes, and widgets. It follows that the public organization *necessarily* changes less rapidly than do private and nonprofit organizations, simply because of the process-intensive nature of its work.

People Changing Their Public Organization

If not technology, then what about people? As we elaborate in Chapter 5, the organization's members, though more constrained in public agencies than in corporations and independent associations, can and do cause organizational change. In fact, "managers in the civil service are as willing as their counterparts in business to engage in...reform activity."[139]

Paladins of Public Change Who is more likely to cause change in governments? Dynamic politicians, reform-minded citizens, or those stodgy old bureaucrats? The bureaucrats, hands down. "Despite controls...career public servants" at all levels of government "do innovate" and initiate innovations far more frequently than elected office holders, nonprofit public-interest groups, agency clients, and citizens.[140]

Contrary to conventional wisdom, it is not necessarily the top bureaucrats who change public organizations. "A surprising result" of a study of significant change in governments over eight years "is that the most frequent initiators of innovations were not politicians [who account for 18–36 percent of all innovations]...or even agency heads [23–36 percent, although senior public managers, while "conservative and cautious in the implementation of major organizational change," prefer implementing systemic change to tinkering[141]]... but middle managers [30–62 percent] and front-line staff" (24–29 percent).[142]

It is commonly thought, of course, that government bureaucrats resist organizational change and business executives relish it. Wrong. A study of 343 managers in public and private organizations unearthed an "unexpected" finding:

"Public managers are more change-oriented than managers in business organizations." Relative to business managers, public administrators have a much stronger "change-centered leadership style" (i.e., they generate new ideas, initiate new projects, and are future-directed and experimental); a far more "intuitive decision-making style" (i.e., they exploit possibilities, are imaginative, and ignore "practical realities"); and a much more definitive opinion about what organizational changes are the most urgently needed, an opinion that leads to the introduction of new processes, services, methods, and reorganizations. "Business managers' potential for [organizational] change is actually comparable to Swedish vicars'"—in other words, not much.[143]

Human Choice or Environmental Determinism? Organizational members count in changing their organizations. But do they count as much as the riptides of the darkling sea that drenches the organization?

All organizations' environments are growing more complex, and environmental complexity is heavy with organizational and personal peril. The sociologist Charles Perrow famously identified *normal*, or *inevitable*, *accidents* as those disasters that are born of the complexity inherent in "human-machine systems." Examples include airline crashes, blowouts of ocean-based oilrigs, and meltdowns of nuclear power plants. Interactions in these normal accidents "are not only unexpected, but are *incomprehensible* for some critical period of time."[144]

How well, or if, organizational decision makers can deal with complex environmental forces is one of the "central perspectives" constituting the "debates in organization theory,"[145] and "one of the most pervasive and central arguments" in the field.[146] That debate is *human choice* (i.e., the organization's human decision makers choose organizational destiny) *versus environmental determinism* (the environment's powerful forces determine organizational destiny).

It does not behoove us to review at length this professorial dispute.[147] In a nutshell, however, the advocates of human choice hold that leadership is significant, perhaps paramount, in achieving organizational success. Others have a more pantheistic perspective: "Even if leaders *do* appear to be as important as conventional opinions hold them to be, the quality of leadership will nevertheless prove to be randomly rather than systematically distributed among organizations, and chance will therefore remain the main factor in organizational survival."[148]

We do not subscribe to the view that the organization's people are merely the pathetic pawns of omnipotent environmental forces. We do believe, however, that the public organization's environment makes it harder for people in the public sector to change their organizations than for people in the private and independent sectors.

UNLIMITED CHANGE: THE IMPACT OF THE ENVIRONMENT ON THE PUBLIC AND NONPROFIT ORGANIZATION

The environment that surrounds and suffuses the public or nonprofit organization appears to be the primal engine of its change.

Change in Public Organizations: Politics, Pressures, and Prohibitions

Government agencies are pressured to change when specific elements in their environments change. Agencies that are dominated by professionals are pushed to adjust when outside observers (and often inside ones, too) perceive a loss of professional competence; those that are protected by patrons, such as legislators, are threatened with change when they lose their patrons; and "routinized" agencies, or those that have churned the same old unresponsive rut for many years, suffer demands for reform when expectations about what they should be doing increase in a sustained way over time.[149]

Pressure to change is no guarantee of change. Public administrators must come to grips with the forces surrounding them and make their agency more proactive. Frustratingly, even when they rise to these challenges, change *still* remains stymied unless the agency's leaders can gain "the support of oversight bodies," particularly those composed of elected officials, and then only when agencies "are *allowed* to be responsive" to environmental

demands. "Creating such arrangements is always difficult and often impossible."[150]

Ordering Agency Openness

All legislatures pass laws that change their governments' agencies. Some statutes radically open public organizations to all manner of penetration by innumerable environmental forces, and to an extent that is unheard of in the other sectors.

Burned by Sunshine An example is provided by "sunshine laws" that legislatures have imposed on federal, state, and local agencies. The federal government, all the states, and the District of Columbia have them.[151]

Under the federal Freedom of Information Act of 1966, anyone may demand information from federal agencies. Some *4 million* requests for information are made each year, and about nine out of ten are granted in full[152] (information pertaining to national security and citizen privacy is exempt). Complying with these demands is onerous: To meet a request for information, federal administrators must execute no fewer than fifteen distinct tasks, and it takes from 10 to 100 median days to do so.[153]

While there is doubtless much good that derives from sunshine laws, they clearly distract public administrators from the efficient fulfillment of their agencies' missions.

Influenced by Agency Advisory Committees Many public agencies are legislatively required to appoint advisory committees that recommend policies. In Washington alone, there are more than 900 "active federal advisory committees," with "about 65,000 members," advising fifty-two agencies,[154] meeting more than 7,000 times a year, and spending nearly $400 million annually in the process.[155]

Often, agency advisory committees are dominated by the special interests that their agencies regulate. Almost three-fourths of federal committee members themselves think that their committees have too many members whose interests are directly affected by the advice that their committees provide to their agencies.[156]

"Because of concerns that special interests had too much influence over federal agency decision makers,"[157] Congress passed the toothless Federal Advisory Committee Act of 1972, which appoints the General Services Administration and the Office of Government Ethics as loose overseers of committee appointments. The Act has not been especially effective, and, according to the Government Accountability Office, "current data on appointments indicate that some agencies may continue to inappropriately use representatives" of regulated interests.[158] There are no penalties for noncompliance with the Act.

Affected by Administrative Procedure Acts An even more agency-permeating, and more questionable, class of legislation is *administrative procedure acts* that federal, state, and local legislatures have enacted. Ostensibly, these laws pertain only to agency rulemaking, but, in this context, "rulemaking"—"the single most important function performed by agencies of government"[159]—is a euphemism for policymaking.

Administrative procedure statutes permit "notice and comment" by the public about proposed agency rules, a requirement that conventional wisdom hails as "refreshingly democratic."[160] Research indicates, however, that notices and comments are neither refreshing nor democratic.

Federal Rulemaking and Special Interest Power Federal agencies spend, on average, about four years (ranging from one year to an astonishing fourteen) to make a rule.[161] Although making rules is time consuming, agencies still retain considerable power and latitude to make rules and are not terribly constrained by procedures imposed by the president, Congress, and the courts: There is "little support for the ossification thesis" of agency rulemaking.[162]

Federal agencies are, however, constrained by special interests when they make rules. When the Forest Service considered changing a regulation about wilderness areas, it was inundated by a staggering 1.6 million comments, mostly in the form of mass e-mails and pre-printed postcards.[163]

Although researchers commonly speculate that special interests influence agency decision making indirectly, such as by working through advisory committees or Congress, federal agencies alter 49 percent of their decisions in favor of special interests purely as a result of the formal notice-and-comment process.[164] "Business interests enjoy disproportionate influence over rulemaking outputs" in federal agencies.[165]

State Rulemaking and Special Interest Power All states and the District of Columbia have administrative procedure acts.[166] In forty-seven states, administrative procedure acts require their public administrators to read the letters written by citizens about their proposed rules, and forty require that their agencies listen to citizens' opinions during agency hearings. In forty-five states, citizens may go over the agency's head and appeal to entities that review any new rules proposed (*proposed*, not enacted) by an agency.[167] It is, perhaps, small wonder that public administrators sometimes complain of tread marks left on their foreheads by citizens appealing their decisions to a higher authority.

Special interests in the states parallel federal bureaucratic power patterns. The greater the access to state agencies enabled by a state's administrative procedure act, the higher that state agency heads will rank the impact of interest groups on their agencies' rulemaking.[168] "Interest group power...is significantly influential" in an estimated 80 percent of state agency rulemaking.[169] And, in another reflection of federal patterns, business interests dominate the states' notice-and-comment process and benefit most from it relative to other groups.[170]

Even when state policymakers deliberately structure regulatory agencies in ways that protect them from special interests, agencies will actually welcome some of those interests into their rulemaking processes. "Insulating agencies via design does lead to lower reported access to regulators by interest groups, but only among those groups who supply less valuable information" to the regulators.[171]

Openness, Inundation, and Interest In sum, public agencies are required by law to respond to tsunamis of requests, advice, notices, comments, questions, and objections concerning agency actions, both real and contemplated, from citizens and special interests. This condition does not always favor agency actions that are in the public's interest: "As the interactions between...agencies and third parties increase, so too does the influence of these parties over agency policies and decisions."[172]

The Osmotic Impact of the Agency's Environment

Perhaps of greater impact on the inner workings of government agencies are not official edicts, but rather environmental forces that are not even consciously directed at influencing agencies.

Consider this: Not only do the better-financed advocacy groups get their preferred drugs approved faster than less-well-financed groups, but, if a disease is merely *mentioned* in the *Washington Post* twelve times over twelve months, then one full month, on average, is knocked off the time that it takes the Food and Drug Administration to approve a drug that purports to alleviate it. If the ailment is mentioned two-dozen times over a year, then the approval time declines by two months, and so on. This is the case regardless of the severity of the disease, its frequency, its cost, and the availability of other drugs.[173]

Or this: Not only does coverage in the *New York Times* about a disaster abroad associate with a heightened probability that the United States will send assistance to the afflicted country, but *each* story results, on average, in almost $600,000 more in additional aid. One story in the *Times* is worth more in American disaster relief than 1,500 deaths. This remains the case even after controlling for national wealth and the number of people killed or left homeless.[174]

These instances bespeak an environmental determinism of a rare order. The public organization is so attuned to nuances in its task environment—subtleties that only it, apparently, can sense—that it readily and even radically responds to them. The environment need not be comprised only of obvious and brutish forces to change the public organization; osmosis works, too.

Whether they are rough or refined, environmental forces change the accountability, structure, hierarchy, procedures, and autonomy of public organizations in ways that distinguish them from organizations in the private and nonprofit sectors.

Who's in Charge Here? A Bevy of Bosses, an Absence of Accountability

In contrast to the chief executive officers of companies and nonprofit organizations, who report to a single board of directors, the heads of government agencies typically report to dozens of their equivalents in the form of legislative oversight committees.

Consider the fate of the Department of Homeland Security. Eighty-eight congressional committees and subcommittees[175] (up from seventy-nine, seven years earlier), every Senator, and at least 412 of the 435 Representatives, or 95 percent, have some degree of responsibility for homeland security.[176] Figure 4-1 illustrates the "system" of congressional oversight for the department. It is not a diagram that one would associate with anything resembling an organization chart. It is a diagram, however, that one might associate with The Mind of God.

Why is this? Because legislative committees that oversee prominent public policies attract large numbers of legislators, who are fully aware that the resultant publicity enhances their prospects for reelection. Hence, "there has been no move toward consolidation of…. the crazy-quilt of congressional oversight" of the Department, a condition that "perpetuates the fragmentation of responsibility that led to 9/11."[177]

Because legislators require agencies to report to multiple legislative committees that oversee their conduct, responsibility for the policy meanders mindlessly around legislative corridors, tightening turf tensions that fester in both branches, undermining management of the benighted policy in question, wasting public resources, and checkmating the achievement of governments' goals.

These are serious impairments to accountability in government.

The Iron Triangle

Should we not reorganize executive branches so that policies and agencies are in greater harmony? Sure, but it rarely happens, in large part because of the political environment in which agencies operate.

The resistance to governmental restructuring is known as the *iron triangle*, or the exceptionally strong bonds that exist among the executive agency, its legislative oversight committees, and the affected special interests, all of which are threatened by any proposed rearrangement of their relationships.

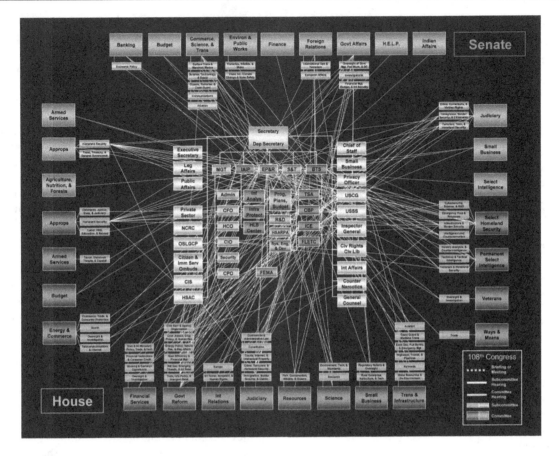

FIGURE 4-1

Congressional Oversight of the Department of Homeland Security

Source: Center for Strategic and International Studies and Business Executives for National Security, *Untangling the Web: Congressional Oversight and the Department of Homeland Security* (Washington, DC: Authors, December 10, 2004).

Washington's Iron Triangles Of the federal iron triangle's three points, the legislative one reigns supreme. "Congress must agree with any restructuring proposals submitted for consideration by the president for them to become a reality."[178]

Usually, Congress does not agree.[179] In 1938, for example, Franklin Delano Roosevelt, at the apogee of his presidential power, was roundly crushed in the House of Representatives when he attempted to reorganize his own executive branch by implementing the recommendations of the prestigious Committee on Administrative Management, noted in Chapter 2. This "defeat...was the worst that President Roosevelt would suffer in three terms as President."[180] More recently, the on-again, off-again

efforts by special interests and ideologues to dismantle the departments of Commerce, Education, and Energy have been successfully resisted for decades by countervailing special interests and ideologues.

Those few federal reorganizations that have happened (there have been only a dozen "major" ones over sixty-four years[181]) have "virtually never [been] combined to eliminate program duplication. Missions are not realigned or even rationalized. Program laps upon program. Responsibilities are not coordinated."[182]

The States' Iron Triangles In the states, the story is much the same. Although "more than half"[183] of the governors are empowered, at least in theory, to reorganize by executive order their civil services,[184] the iron triangle persists.

The states' efforts to reorganize began in the early twentieth century and took the form of five reorganizational waves.[185] Despite all this roiling, however, "by the middle of the twentieth century state bureaucracies often contained one hundred to two hundred units,"[186] all ostensibly reporting to the governor, the legislature, or an independent board, and coordinated management was hardly the rule. Between 1965 and 1990, twenty-six states reduced the number of their agencies, and, in limited ways, reorganized, mostly by introducing, for the first time, a cabinet-based executive branch.[187] These reorganizations were less than sweeping, and those few agencies that were eliminated typically "had minuscule budgets," or "their functions continue to be performed by other agencies."[188]

Attempts to reorganize state governments for greater efficiency continue to comprise a litany of failure.[189] Each state typically retains hundreds of boards and commissions, but unfilled vacancies persist, meetings are often rare, redundancy is common, many missions long have been met, and their costs are high.[190] Of course, a few states have been able to successfully consolidate some agencies, but, when the sole goal for doing so is that of saving money, rather than aligning the agencies around complementary values and missions, the result is an incomprehensible, unaccountable, lumbering Leviathan that legislatures often dismantle in order to restore services to citizens.[191]

La Bureaucratie

Governments are notoriously bureaucratic, and bureaucracies can be frustrating. A fifth of politically appointed executives in Washington cite the "bureaucratic nature of government" as an obstacle to "recruiting future political leaders"; of the more than four out of five federal career executives who have considered leaving government, 31 percent report that a main motivation is its "bureaucracy/inflexibility/slowness."[192]

The word *bureaucracy* derives from the French *bureau*, or "office," and the Greek *kratos*, or "power," which combine, in French, as *la bureaucratie*. By the early nineteenth century, the word had wended its way to Britain as the Anglicized *bureaucracy*, which then meant (in England, at least) "office," or "administrative," "tyranny."[193]

Standard dictionaries generally agree on the following: *Bureaucracy* is a combination of organizational hierarchy and red tape. *Hierarchy* refers to layers of administrative units ranked one above the other. *Red tape* is a large number of reports, forms, procedures, and, most especially, rules.

Hierarchy and red tape are symbiotic. Hierarchy produces red tape: "The larger the number of hierarchical levels, the greater the demand for explicit rules."[194] And red tape produces hierarchy: Legislative rulemaking adds to "the structural complexity of bureaucratic action" in all sectors.[195]

There is a small but "growing of set of empirical findings that suggest public organizations are not always highly bureaucratic,"[196] but, without question, governments are far more subject to unique environmental pressures that result in relatively greater bureaucratization.

Hierarchy and Government

Our first component of bureaucracy is hierarchy.

High on the Hierarchic Hog Governments live high on the hierarchic hog. Two-fifths of public employees at all ranks say that, in their agencies, there are "too many layers of supervisors and managers" between them and top management, compared to fewer than a fourth of business employees who say this.[197]

In contrast to corporate hierarchies, which are dramatically flattening,[198] the public hierarchy is heightening. The federal government's organization chart has reached ever upward as the number of different executive titles grows, nearly quadrupling over forty-four years to sixty-four titles. As a result, innovative, but odd, administrative titles are increasingly common, such as, Deputy Assistant Deputy Administrator and Principal Deputy Deputy Assistant Secretary.[199] We are not making these up.

Government's girth grows, too. Over the same forty-four years, the total number of senior title-holders in the federal government fattened by a factor of almost six, from 451 to 2,592.[200] Over a dozen years, twenty new layers of middle management and 13,000 more middle managers were added to the federal hierarchy, while, during the course of two decades, the number of lower-level federal employees plummeted by two-thirds.[201] These trends may explain why, over ten years, the proportion of supervisors and managers in the federal workforce *grew* by 7.5 percent, but the average number of subordinates whom they supervised actually *declined* by 7 percent and currently stands at fewer than eight subordinates per supervisor.[202]

Hierarchy and Effective Government   How much hierarchy is too much?

Organization theory traditionally has regarded large organizational size as a sign of skilled management, but now this is changing.[203] Anthony Downs' famous *law of hierarchy* contends that the taller and more complex the hierarchy, the more effort and expense are required for "internal" administration to the detriment of "external" achievement,[204] a theory that seems to be supported by at least some facts: Larger companies grow less competitive over time relative to smaller ones,[205] and larger state governments have more incidents of corruption than smaller ones.[206]

In the public sector, hierarchy can both undermine and improve public organizational effectiveness. For example, more hierarchy in schools correlates with lower academic performance by pupils, but also with better attendance and lower dropout rates.[207] In fact, the extent of hierarchy "is not related" to governmental failures. Instead, "the only consistent results" of empirical investigations of this issue are that public organizational failures correlate with a large number of goals and a high level of difficulty involved in achieving those goals,[208] a relationship that also is common in other sectors.

Where hierarchy contributes most to public organizational effectiveness is in those agencies that are playing defense. A "high degree of hierarchical authority" is a defining component of centralized decision making, and centralized decision making, in turn, "works best in conjunction with defending" the agency's interests against external threats. Scant hierarchy and decentralized decision making, by contrast, are most effective when the agency is continually prospecting for new opportunities in its environment.[209]

Red Tape and Government

Bureaucracy's other half is red tape.

Reams of Red Tape   Public organizations are wrapped in more ribbons of red tape than are private and nonprofit ones (red tape is lowest in the independent sector)[210] that are spooled out almost entirely by external sources, such as special interests and legislatures.[211] The greater the partisan split in Congress—the greatest split occurring when different parties control each chamber—the less discretionary authority that Congress delegates to its newly created agencies, thereby generating more red tape.[212] One analysis found that the amount of government rules more than doubles every decade because "the stock of rules expands due to a powerful internal dynamic: that is, rules breed rules."[213]

Federal bureaus must adhere to some 4,000 congressional reporting requirements that are burgeoning by about a fifth per year.[214] More than seven out of every ten laws enacted by Congress spawn rules written in agencies that are meant to "clarify the policy sketched in legislation."[215] These rules add up. The annual compilation of federal regulations, the *Federal Register*, typically prints nearly 4,000 rules on almost 80,000 pages.[216]

Smaller governments are not immune. There are sixty-four separate sources of law governing New York City's public schools, including 850 pages of state law, another 720 pages of state regulations, 15,000 formal decisions by the state commissioner of education, hundreds of pages of collective bargaining agreements, thousands of pages of federal law affecting schools, and more thousands of pages of regulations promulgated by the schools' chancellor.[217]

Rue the Rules! Perceptions of Red Tape and Their Consequences   A few years ago, a Secret Service agent dutifully registered his Glock pistol before boarding a plane. The agent then passed through airport security, which discovered that he was carrying a pen knife. Security returned to the agent his Glock, but confiscated the pen knife.[218]

It is this sort of silliness that gives red tape a bad name, particularly among public administrators. For at least a generation, and longer,[219] public employees have been far more convinced than both their independent-[220] and private-sector[221] counterparts that their organizations ensnare them in greater tangles of red tape. *Even when public managers and private consultants are working together on the same project*, "government managers perceive higher levels of organizational red tape and contracting red tape than their consultants."[222]

When public administrators sense relatively little red tape, which appears to be the case among government managers who have "broader frames of reference" and "richer career experiences,"[223] and in governments that have introduced significant personnel reforms (detailed in Chapter 9),[224] they report higher levels of motivation and commitment to constructive social change.[225] However, when public administrators perceive seriously large levels of red tape, a perception that seems to associate with managers who have narrower frames of reference[226] and highly unionized governments,[227] they are much more likely to be dissatisfied with their jobs;[228] believe that their performance is inadequately recognized;[229] and display greater alienation—red tape "is a consistently negative and statistically significant influence in all alienation models."[230]

Green Tape Rules need not be "red tape" in the sense that they foment negativity among public administrators. Rules can be "green tape," in that thoughtfully considered and well-managed rules are accepted and approved by those affected by them. Governments that use written, as opposed to oral, rules that are not overly controlling; have rules whose purposes are understood by those who must comply with, explain, and enforce them; and have rules that clearly accomplish what they are meant to accomplish are features that "significantly correlate with higher rule abidance" by public administrators. Counter-intuitively, however, consistency in applying rules seems not to matter and "is the only variable without a statistically significant influence."[231]

Red Tape and Effective Government At first glance, public executives seem wedded to the idea that red tape leads to ineffective governing. A third of top state administrators, for example, cite "less red tape" as a primary reason for privatizing their departments' programs.[232]

When government managers are pressed, however, their opinions grow more nuanced. The presence of red tape in information systems does associate negatively in their minds with the "perceived effectiveness" of those systems, but red tape is "borderline insignificant" in how human resource operations are viewed, and its perceived effects on procurement and budgeting are "not statistically significant."[233]

What do we actually *know* about red tape and efficient and effective governance? Not much: Although red tape is almost universally blamed for public administration's inefficiencies, a "purported relationship [that] is central to public management theory and practice," there is, in fact, a "dearth of research on the red tape-performance hypothesis."[234]

Red Tape and Bigger Bureaucracies Here is what we may know most definitively about red tape: It produces more bureaucrats. Legislative rulemaking in general introduces more "actors...to the [policy] implementation process."[235] When Washington imposes more regulations in the intergovernmental grants system, school districts respond by hiring more administrators.[236]

More bureaucrats, however, do not necessarily lead to less efficient bureaucracies.

Red Tape's Known Negatives Red tape has at least three negative effects on government's performance. One is direct, and two are not.

"Internal red tape," or the kind that restricts public employees but not agency clients, "surprisingly...*does* have a substantial [and deleterious] impact on equity." This type of red tape "inflicts considerable damage" on the fairness with which agency clients are treated, possibly because red tape penalizes those clients who are "less able to understand and overcome" complicated rules and procedures.[237]

Red tape also associates with a couple of indirect negatives that lurk in two areas: communication and engagement.

In agencies with "an average level of rule orientation.... task-oriented communication" increases "the likelihood of excellent performance" by a fifth. "For above-average and high rule-oriented cultures," however, such communication is "actually identified with decreased performance," and, in rule-bound agencies, task-oriented "communication is so antithetical that even excellent communication is linked to decreases in performance."[238]

Also indirect, but nonetheless important for productivity, is red tape's impact on employees' engagement. Red tape bears "the strongest" negative relationship "to the level of job involvement of managers in both the public and nonprofit sectors,"[239] and, as we described in Chapter 3, a high level of job involvement appears to be a critical variable in assuring productive people and organizations. Relative to other sectors, red tape also associates with lower job satisfaction[240] and a higher aversion to risk[241] among public employees.

Red Tape's Unproven Link with Inefficiency and Ineffectiveness When we explore the direct empirical connections between red tape and governmental efficiency and effectiveness, we find that red tape's supposedly negative impact on public performance is "somewhat weaker and less pervasive than public management theory and conventional wisdom suggest." In what may be the most detailed examination of "the red tape myth" to date, it was determined that "red tape does not have any salient effects on efficiency" and "does not seem to have any appreciable impact on customer satisfaction" with agency services.[242]

Red Tape and Longer-Term Efficiencies Where red tape may have its most positive impact is by inducing longer-term organizational efficiencies, both inside the organization and in its handling of challenges emanating from outside it.

Internally, a body of rules "radically reduces the number of decisions" that an executive "must make without sacrificing centralized coordination,"[243] a condition that almost defines efficiency.

Externally, rules help an organization to "increasingly respond to environmental challenges in a programmed way." Over time, a bureaucracy's rules expand "with decreasing increments" because a corpus of intelligent rules has boosted organizational efficiency by adapting organizational procedures to patterns of environmental pressures.[244] In these circumstances, "compliance with rules…can be an essential element of both a project's success and its accountability."[245]

There is, however, more at stake than efficiency. The "bureaucratization of the nation-state has wrought a fundamental transformation whereby rules themselves have become the primary means through which social change is accomplished."[246]

"You Can Lead a Bureaucracy to Slaughter but You Can't Make It Shrink" Can governments be made less bureaucratic? Not really: Public organizations "are *imprisoned*" by the environments that they inhabit.[247]

Their imprisonment is a consequence of their operating, by necessity and definition, in nonmarket environments, a condition that deprives them of a simple, accurate measure of their organizational success: making money. Making money, by contrast, is the universal measure of efficiency and effectiveness for all businesses (in the form of profits) and many nonprofit organizations (if not profits, then at least balancing the books).

Public agencies thus "are caught in a complex of external relationships and to cope they develop high levels of internal control."[248] These controls, of course, are hierarchy and red tape, which, in combination, clumsily and incompletely substitute for the straightforward money measure that is denied to governments. Hierarchy and red tape control spending, coordinate activities, and work to assure the fair treatment of clients and employees.

There is little that can be done to change this fact of public organizational life. "The confluence of top-down and bottom-up pressures" emanating from the public organization's environment render "simple hierarchy…the only possibility for public agencies," and their "organizational survival is increasingly based on conformity to externally imposed rules…. External agents…cannot themselves remove the conditions that favor tall hierarchies and elaborate systems of rules."[249] So, even if those "external agents," such as elected chief executives and legislators, slash the resources of public agencies, their hierarchies and red tape persist undiminished.

"You can lead a bureaucracy to slaughter but you can't make it shrink."[250]

Administrative Autonomy and the Performance of Public Organizations

Our final point about the power of the public organization's environment is that, because the environment constrains the autonomy of public organizations more than private and nonprofit ones, it weakens their performance. By contrast, when public organizations are granted greater independence, at least up to a point, they perform better.

A growing number of empirical investigations of American governments draw this conclusion.

- A study of nine citizen advisory boards in Michigan concluded that "Some of the citizen advisory boards were more effective than others in gaining their objectives and this was found to be related to the degree of independence which they attained."[251]
- "The best determinate" of some 500 schools' "effectiveness was the degree of autonomy" that a school "enjoyed from bureaucracies and other outside interference," outpacing class size, salaries, and spending per pupil.[252] "The best" public school districts out of 534 of them "are affected by far fewer forces in their environments."[253]
- "If poor performers" among two dozen nuclear power plants "are given more autonomy, this analysis suggests, their safety record is likely to improve."[254]

What this and other research by and large indicates is that, within the American context of extreme openness, some enhancement of public agencies' administrative independence and organizational autonomy likely will result in more efficient and effective government, with little or no new resources being required.[255]

The Environment and the Independent Organization

Independent, public-serving organizations, such as charities, exist in a strange environment in which organizational accountability, and even survival, defers to the whimsies of external actors.

Prospering in the Voluntary Sector Nonprofit organizations that are larger and that have larger boards of directors receive, relative to their smaller counterparts, more donations from individuals, corporations, and foundations. These donors favor those independent organizations that focus on art and culture and are statistically less enthusiastic about those with missions involving law, public advocacy, and health and human services. However, those charities that act on the principle that charity begins at home prosper: A 1 percent increase in their fund-raising budgets results in a 1.36 percent hike in contributions.[256]

Environmental Forces and Independent Death

The environmental pummeling that government agencies endure is at least equaled by the battering inflicted on independent associations. In the case of nonprofit organizations, however, these attacks are far more likely to lead to the organization's death. This is especially true if the third-sector organization is young, small, and located in an area where the population is not growing.[257]

An intriguing study of a university library that was in the process of administratively breaking down because of too many demands and not enough resources sheds some light on how independent organizations deal with increasingly harsh environments. The library ultimately summoned fourteen strategies to cope with rising levels of environmental stress, including: queuing at peak periods (e.g., keeping library patrons in waiting rooms "outside" the organization); setting priorities within the queue; eliminating the lowest priorities; expediting the most frequent requests; encouraging entrepreneurs to provide services for several libraries at lower cost; creating branch facilities; creating a mobile reserve (such as teams of personnel transferable to units as needed); developing specific performance standards; reducing those standards soon thereafter; brainstorming for a "magic formula"; promoting self-service (e.g., letting patrons into the stacks [an uncommon practice at the time—librarians themselves would retrieve requested volumes], which is a radical strategy because it represents a deliberate reduction of organizational sovereignty); "escaping" by permitting a takeover or mass resignations; limiting work to capacity as determined by rigid, ritualistic rules and characterized by the denial of error and the refusal of challenge; and, ultimately, salvaging component units. This fourteenth and final strategy is employed simply because the "dissolution of middle-sized or large institutions is seldom complete." Instead, their components are reassembled in new formats, rather like bankrupt corporations often are.[258]

The library, in a very real sense, had no choice but to play out this scenario. Unlike International Widget, it could not control environmental demands by simply hiking prices because it was not allowed to charge for its services. It had to adjust internally.

Nonprofit organizations often respond to increasing environmental stress in the way our hapless library did—that is, by becoming more negative, bureaucratic, and irrational. When small, independent colleges "moved from moderate to severe decline," decision making centralized, planning atrophied, inflexibility hardened, the "college's climate" politicized, and "special-interest group activity" accelerated.[259] This is "the cesspool syndrome." As the organization accommodates decline, "dreck" rather than "cream" rises to top, thereby furthering more decline.[260]

Environmental Forces and Independent Survival

Of course, it does not have to be like this. Many third-sector organizations are quite capable of meeting environmental challenges to their survival, and those that do are more likely to establish stable organizational hierarchies; assign explicit responsibilities for each employee; affiliate themselves with larger and similar enterprises; have "a high percentage of higher functionaries among board members"; and assure diversity among supporters and members.[261]

In addition, it is critical that the organization vigorously engage in "extroverted activities, which enhance an organization's visibility and embeddedness in the local community" and develop "broad external ties" with governments, donors, and others, to "avoid social closure and ensure access to resources." (Tactics similar to these—that is, an emphasis on external relations, but not at the expense of internal controls—also are mandatory if struggling private corporations have a chance to weather economic downturns.[262]) "The most important consideration in order to avoid organizational death" in the independent sector "is to prevent homogeneity and insulation."[263]

NOTES

1. James D. Thompson, *Organization in Action: Social Science Bases of Administrative Theory* (New York: McGraw-Hill, 1967), pp. 83–98.

2. Jitendra V. Singh, David J. Tucker, and Robert J. House, "Organizational Legitimacy and the Liability of Newness," *Administrative Science Quarterly* 31 (June 1986), pp. 171–193. This is an investigation of 389 newly-founded, nonprofit social service organizations in metropolitan Toronto.

3. Joseph Galaskiewicz, Wolfgang Bielefeld, and Myron Dowell, "Networks and Organizational Growth: A Study of Community-Based Nonprofits," *Administrative Science Quarterly* 51 (September 2006), pp. 337–380. The quotation is on p. 337. This is a study of 326 nonprofit organizations in the Minneapolis-St. Paul metropolitan region. Quite the opposite findings pertain to nonprofit organizations that are more dependent on fees or sales; these have "fewer ties to other nonprofits and local elites."

4. Stafford Beer, "Managing Modern Complexity," *The Management of Information and Knowledge. Panel on Science and Technology* (11th meeting). Proceedings before the Committee on Science and Astronautics, U.S. House of Representatives, 91st Congress, Second Session, January 27, 1970, No. 15 (Washington, DC: U.S. Government Printing Office, 1970), pp. 41–62. The quotation is on p. 43.

5. Timothy L. Cannon, "Harnessing Customer Knowledge: Merging Customer Relationship Management with Knowledge of Management," *Knowledge Management: The Catalyst for Electronic Government*, Ramón C. Barquin, Alex Bennet, and Shereen G. Remez, eds. (Vienna, VA: Management Concepts, 2001), pp. 416–417.

6. Gregory F. Trevorton, *Reshaping National Intelligence in an Age of Information* (New York: Cambridge University Press, 2003).

7. Bree Nordenson, "Overload! Journalism's Battle for Relevance in an Age of Too Much Information," *Columbia Journalism Review* (November/December 2008), http://www.cjr.org/magazine/novemberdecember08.php.

8. James G. March and Herbert A. Simon, *Organizations* (New York: John Wiley, 1958), p. 165.

9. James Risen, "Ex-Inspector Says CIA Missed Disarray in Iraqi Arms Program," *New York Times* (January 26, 2004). The chief weapons inspector, David A. Kay, is quoted.

10. Samir Khairi Tawfik, former director of the Center of the Department of Research in the Presidential Institute of Iraq, as quoted in Jon Lee Anderson, "Saddam's Ear," *The New Yorker* (May 5, 2003), p. 68.

11. Jamie Gorelick, deputy attorney general in the Clinton administration, as quoted in Joel

Achenbach, "What Does a President Really Do All Day?" *Washington Post* (April 27, 2008).

12. Perhaps the best single treatment of this fiasco is John Toland, *Infamy: Pearl Harbor and Its Aftermath* (New York: Berkley, 1982).

13. Moyzisch, however, had the last word, and his revenge, by writing after the war a book detailing the episode: L. C. Moyzich, *Operation Cicero* (New York: Coward-McCann, 1950). In 1952, his book was made into a movie, *Five Fingers*. Moyzich, somehow appropriately, was played by Peter Lorre.

14. U.S. Office of the Inspector General, Central Intelligence Agency, *OIG Report on CIA Accountability with Respect to the 9/11 Attacks* (Washington, DC: Author, June 2005), pp. xiii–xiv. A redacted version of the report was "approved for release" by the CIA in August 2007 after Congress applied pressure.

15. Gordon Tullock, *The Politics of Bureaucracy* (Washington, DC: Public Affairs Press, 1965), pp. 137–141.

16. See, for example, one of many studies supporting this finding: Harold L. Wilensky, *Organizational Intelligence: Knowledge and Policy in Government and Industry* (New York: Basic Books, 1967), pp. 43–58.

17. Dana Priest and William M. Arkin, "A Hidden World, Growing Beyond Control," *Washington Post* (July 19, 2010).

18. See, for example, Friedrich von Hayek's "Economics and Knowledge," *Economica* 4 (Fall 1937), pp. 33–54; and "The Use of Knowledge in Society," *American Economic Review* 35 (Fall 1945), pp. 519–530.

19. Martha S. Feldman and James G. March, "Information in Organizations as Signal and Symbol," Paper presented at the Western Political Science Association (San Francisco, CA, March 27–29, 1980).

20. Hemphill and Associates, as cited in "Data Data," *Inc. Magazine* (January 1999), p. 70.

21. Thomas D. Clark, Jr., and William A. Shrode, "Public Sector Decision Structures: An Empirically Based Description," *Public Administration Review* 39 (July/August 1979), pp. 343–354.

22. Pitney Bowes, *Workplace Communications in the 21st Century*, as cited in "Data Data." Seventy-one percent of workers said this.

23. Reuters Business Information Survey, as cited in ibid. Forty-four percent of managers said this.

24. Feldman and March, "Information in Organizations as Signal and Symbol," p. 23.

25. Ibid., pp. 23–24.

26. E. Sam Overman and Donna T. Lorraine, "Information for Control: Another Management Proverb?" *Public Administration Review* 54 (March/April 1994), pp. 193–195.

27. Feldman and March, "Information in Organization as Signal and Symbol," p. 25.

28. Kathleen M. Eisenhardt, "Making Fast Strategic Decisions in High-Velocity Environments," *Academy of Management Journal* 32 (September 1989), pp. 543–576.

29. Herbert A. Simon, *Administrative Behavior: A Study of Decision-Making Processes in Administration Organizations*, 3rd ed. (New York: Free Press, 1958), pp. 48–52.

30. Gjalt de Graaf and Zeger van der Wal, "On Value Differences Experienced by Sector Switchers," *Administration & Society* 40 (March 2008), pp. 79–103. The quotation is on p. 79.

31. Jennifer A. Chatman, "Matching People and Organizations: Selection and Socialization in Public Accounting Firms," *Administrative Science Quarterly* 26 (September 1991), pp. 459–484.

32. Simon, *Administrative Behavior*.

33. George Miller, "The Magic Number Seven, Plus or Minus Two," *Psychological Review* 63 (March 1956), pp. 81–97.

34. Suzanne Langer, *Mind: An Essay on Feeling* (Baltimore: Johns Hopkins University Press, 1988).

35. Robert Frank, "Shrewdly Irrational," *Sociological Forum* 2 (September 1987), pp. 21–41.

36. John S. Hammond, III, Ralph L. Keeney, and Howard Raiffa, "The Hidden Traps in Decision Making," *Harvard Business Review* 76 (September/October 1998), pp. 47–58.

37. Daniel Kahneman and Amos Tversky, "Choices, Values, Frames," *American Psychologist* 39 (June 1984), pp. 341–350.

38. Ibid.

39. James Brown and Zi-Lei Qiu, "Satisficing When Buying Information," *Organizational Behavior and Human Decision Processes* 51 (June 1992), pp. 471–482.

40. Keith E. Stanovich, *What Intelligence Tests Miss: The Psychology of Rational Thought* (New Haven, CN: Yale University Press, 2009), pp. 1–7. The quotation is on p. 2.

41. Simon, *Administrative Behavior*.
42. Irving L. Janis and Leon Mann, *Decision Making: A Psychological Analysis of Conflict, Choice, and Commitment* (New York: Free Press, 1977).
43. Irving Janis, *Victims of Groupthink* (Boston: Houghton-Mifflin, 1972), p. 13.
44. Commission on the Intelligence Capabilities of the United States Regarding Weapons of Mass Destruction, *Report to the President of the United States* (Washington, DC: U.S. Government Printing Office, 2005), p. 10.
45. Select Committee on Intelligence, United States Senate, 109th Congress, *Report on Postwar Findings About Iraq's WMD Programs and Links to Terrorism and How They Compare with Prewar Assessments, together with Additional Views* (Washington, DC: U.S. Government Printing Office, 2006), pp. 5–6.
46. Commission on the Intelligence Capabilities of the United States Regarding Weapons of Mass Destruction, *Report to the President of the United States*, p. 10.
47. Bob Woodward, "10 Take Aways From the Bush Years," *Washington Post* (January 18, 2009).
48. Robert H. Ennis, *Critical Thinking* (Upper Saddle River, NJ: Prentice-Hall, 1996).
49. James D. Thompson and Arthur Tuden, "Strategies, Structures, and Processes of Organizational Decision," *Comparative Studies in Administration*, James D. Thompson, Peter B. Hammond, Robert W. Hawkes, *et al.*, eds. (Pittsburgh: University of Pittsburgh Press, 1959), pp. 195–216.
50. Melissa M. Stone, Barbara Bigelow, and William Crittenden, "Research on Strategic Management in Nonprofit Organizations: Synthesis, Analysis, and Future Directions," *Administration & Society* 31 (July 1999), pp. 378–423.
51. Paul C. Nutt, "Making Strategic Choices," *Journal of Management Studies* 39 (January 2002), pp. 57–96. The quotation is on p. 67.
52. Michael Cohen, James G. March, and Johan Olsen, "A Garbage Can Model of Organizational Choice," *Administrative Science Quarterly* 17 (March 1972), pp. 1–25.
53. Ibid., pp. 1–2.
54. Gordon Kingsley and Pamela Norton Reed, "Decision Process Models and Organizational Context: Level and Sector Make a Difference," *Public Productivity & Management Review* 14 (Summer 1991), pp. 397–413. The quotation is on p. 409.
55. Meg Bostrom, *By, or for, the People? A Meta-analysis of Public Opinion of Government* (New York: Demos, 2006), p. 24. Figures, 61 and 59 percent, respectively, are for 1999.
56. Kent D. Peterson, "Mechanisms of Administrative Control over Managers in Educational Organizations," *Administrative Science Quarterly* 29 (December 1984), pp. 576–581. The quotation is on p. 595.
57. Marianne Antonsen and Torben Beck Jorgensen, "The 'Publicness' of Public Organizations," *Public Administration* 75 (Summer 1997), pp. 337–357.
58. Lewis C. Mainzer, *Political Bureaucracy* (Glenview, IL: Scott, Foresman, 1973).
59. Kingsley and Reed, "Decision Process Models and Organizational Context," p. 409.
60. Paul C. Nutt, "Comparing Public and Private Sector Decision-Making Practices," *Journal of Public Administration Research and Theory* 16 (April 2006), pp. 289–318. The quotation is on p. 312.
61. Antonsen and Jorgensen, "The 'Publicness' of Public Organizations."
62. Charles R. Schwenk, "Conflict in Organizational Decision-Making: An Exploratory Study of Its Effects in For-Profit and Not-for-Profit Organizations," *Management Science* 36 (January 1990), pp. 436–448. This is a study of forty private and nonprofit managers.
63. Thomas R. Davies, "The Inside Story," *Governing* (December 2003), p. 64.
64. Robert T. Golembiewski, *Humanizing Public Organizations* (Mt. Airy, MD: Lomond, 1985).
65. Myung Jae Moon, "The Pursuit of Managerial Innovation: Does Organization Matter?" *Public Administration Review* 59 (January/February 1999), pp. 31–43.
66. Barry Bozeman and Gordon Kingsley, "Risk Culture in Public and Private Organizations," *Public Administration Review* 58 (March/April 1998), pp. 109–118.
67. John M. Bryson and Sharon R. Anderson, "Applying Large-Group Interaction Methods in the Planning and Implementation of Major Change Efforts," *Public Administration Review* 60 (March/April 2000), pp. 143–162.
68. David Coursey and Barry Bozeman, "Decision Making in Public and Private Organizations:

A Test of Alternative Concepts of 'Publicness,' " *Public Administration Review* 50 (September/October 1990), p. 525.

69. David J. Hickson, Richard. J. Butler, David Cray, *et al.*, *Top Decisions: Strategic Decision Making in Organizations* (San Francisco: Jossey-Bass, 1986).

70. Nutt, "Comparing Public and Private Sector Decision-Making Practices," p. 312.

71. James L. Perry, Debra Mesch, and Laurie Paarlberg, "Motivating Employees in a New Governance Era: The Performance Paradigm Revisited," *Public Administration Review* 66 (July/August 2006), pp. 505–514. The quotation is on p. 509. Emphasis is original.

72. Nutt, "Comparing Public and Private Sector Decision-Making Practices," p. 312.

73. Kaifeng Yang and Kathe Callahan, "Citizen Involvement Efforts and Bureaucratic Responsiveness: Participatory Values, Stakeholder Pressures, and Administrative Practicality," *Public Administration Review* 67 (March/April 2007), pp. 249–264.

74. Jeffrey L. Brudney and Deil S. Wright, "The 'Revolt in Dullsville' Revisited: Lessons for Theory, Practice, and Research from the American State Administrators Project, 1964–2008," *Public Administration Review* 70 (January/February 2010), pp. 26–37. The quotations are on p. 30. Data are for 1984, 1994, and 2004.

75. Yang and Callahan, "Citizen Involvement Efforts and Bureaucratic Responsiveness," pp. 254, 257.

76. Donna Milam Handley and Michael Howell-Moroney, "Ordering Stakeholder Relationships and Citizen Participation: Evidence from the Community Development Block Grant Program," *Public Administration Review* 70 (July/August 2010), pp. 601–620. The quotations are on p. 601.

77. XiaoHu Wang and Montgomery Van Wart, "When Public Participation in Administration Leads to Trust: An Empirical Assessment of Managers' Perceptions," *Public Administration Review* 67 (March/April 2007), pp. 265–278. The quotation is on p. 186, the journal's contents page.

78. Details are in Chapter 1.

79. Nutt, "Comparing Public and Private Sector Decision-Making Practices," p. 312.

80. W. Michael Blumenthal, "Candid Reflections of a Businessman in Washington," *Fortune* (January 29, 1979), pp. 2, 6, 49; Donald Rumsfeld, "A Politician-Turned-Executive Surveys Both Worlds," *Fortune* (September 10, 1979), pp. 88, 94; and Herman L. Weiss, "Why Business and Government Exchange Executives," *Harvard Business Review* (July/August 1974), pp. 129–140.

81. Davies, "The Inside Story," p. 64.

82. Nutt, "Comparing Public and Private Sector Decision-Making Practices," p. 313. Emphasis is original.

83. Ibid., p. 312.

84. Ibid.

85. See, for example, James Surowiecki, *The Wisdom of Crowds* (New York: Little, Brown, 2004); and Eisenhardt, "Making Fast Strategic Decisions in High-Velocity Environments."

86. Marshall W. Meyer, *Bureaucratic Structure and Authority: Coordination and Control in 254 Government Agencies* (New York: Harper & Row, 1972).

87. Eisenhardt, "Making Fast Strategic Decisions in High-Velocity Environments"; and Steve Molloy and Charles R. Shwenk, "The Effects of Information Technology on Strategic Decision-Making," *Journal of Management Studies* 32 (May 1995), pp. 288–304.

88. Janis, *Victims of Groupthink*.

89. Paul C. Nutt, "Public-Private Differences and the Assessment of Alternatives for Decision Making," *Journal of Public Administration Research and Theory* 9 (April 1999), pp. 305–349. This is a study of 317 "strategic decisions" in the public, private, and nonprofit sectors.

90. Michael L. DeKay, Dalia Patino-Echeverri, and Paul S. Fischbeck, "Distortion of Probability and Outcome Information in Risky Decisions," *Organizational Behavior and Human Decision Processes* 109 (May 2009), pp. 78–92. The quotation is on p. 78.

91. Janis and Mann, *Decision Making*, p. 46.

92. Ibid., p. 85.

93. Ibid., pp. 51, 74.

94. Jack H. Nagel, "Psychological Obstacles to Administrative Responsibility: Lessons of the MOVE Disaster," *Journal of Policy Analysis and Management* 10 (Winter 1991), pp. 1–23. The quotations are on pp. 9, 1.

95. Schwenk, "Conflict in Organizational Decision Making."

96. Nutt, "Public-Private Differences and the Assessment of Alternatives for Decision Making."

97. Schwenk, "Conflict in Organizational Decision-Making."

98. See, for example, Melissa Middleton Stone, "Competing Contexts: The Evolution of a Nonprofit Organization's Governance System in Multiple Environments," *Administration & Society* 28 (May 1996), pp. 61–89.

99. Paul C. Light, "The Content of Their Character: The State of the Nonprofit Workforce," *Nonprofit Quarterly* 9 (Fall 2002), pp. 1–15; and Princeton Survey Research Associates and Brookings Institution, *Health of the Public Service* (Washington, DC: Authors, 2001), http://www.brook.edu.

100. Dennis Witmer, "Serving the People or Serving for Pay: Reward Preferences among Government, Hybrid Sector, and Business Managers," *Public Productivity & Management Review* 14 (Summer 1991), p. 379.

101. Robert Wright, "The Accidental Creationist," *The New Yorker* (December 13, 1999), p. 63.

102. Thompson, *Organization in Action*, p. 142.

103. James G. March, *A Primer on Decision Making: How Decisions Happen* (New York: Free Press, 1994), p. 119.

104. Simon, *Administrative Behavior*, pp. 131, 134.

105. Rosemary O'Leary, *The Ethics of Dissent: Managing Guerrilla Government* (Washington, DC: CQ Press, 2006).

106. Peter J. May and Soren C. Winter, "Politicians, Managers, and Street-Level Bureaucrats: Influences on Policy Implementation," *Journal of Public Administration Research and Theory* 19 (July 2009), pp. 453–476. The quotation is on p. 470. This is a study of Danish caseworkers.

107. Nicole Woolsey Biggart and Gary G. Hamilton, "The Power of Obedience," *Administrative Science Quarterly* 29 (December 1984), pp. 540–549. The quotation is on p. 548. This is a study of Ronald Reagan's and Jerry Brown's gubernatorial administrations in California.

108. John R. P. French, Jr. and Bertram Raven, "The Bases of Social Power," *Group Dynamics: Research and Theory*, Dorwin Cartwright and Alvin Zander, eds. (New York: Harper & Row,

1968), pp. 238–259; Bass, *Stodgill's Handbook of Leadership*, rev. ed.; and Gary A. Yukl, *Leadership in Organizations*, 2nd ed. (Englewood Cliffs, NJ: Prentice-Hall, 1989). French and Raven originated the five powers of reward, coercion, legitimacy, reference, and expertise. Later, Bass added charisma and Yukl added control over information and the work environment.

109. Leanne E. Atwater and Wendy J. Wright, "Power and Transformational and Transactional Leadership in Public and Private Organizations," *International Journal of Public Administration* 9 (June 1996), pp. 963–990.

110. Peterson, "Mechanisms of Administrative Control over Managers in Educational Organizations."

111. Ibid., p. 595.

112. Paul C. Nutt, "Tactics of Implementation," *Academy of Management Journal* 29 (July 1986), pp. 230–261; and "Leverage, Resistance, and the Success of Implementation Approaches," *Journal of Management Studies* 35 (March 1998), pp. 213–240. Nutt's 1986 study is of ninety-one strategic decisions, and his 1998 analysis involves 376 strategic decisions. Both analyses are of all three sectors. We are citing in the text only percentages that are drawn from the larger and more recent study (1998), but the percentages from the earlier study are largely comparable.

113. Peter C. Gronn, "Talk as Work: The Accomplishment of School Administration," *Administrative Science Quarterly* 28 (March 1983), p. 1.

114. Sandford Borins, "Loose Cannons and Rule Breakers, or Enterprising Leaders? Some Evidence about Innovative Public Managers," *Public Administration Review* 60 (November/December 2000), p. 506.

115. Nutt, "Tactics of Implementation"; and "Leverage, Resistance, and the Success of Implementation Approaches."

116. Borins, "Loose Cannons and Rule Breakers, or Enterprising Leaders?" p. 505.

117. Peterson, "Mechanisms of Administrative Control over Managers in Educational Organizations."

118. J. Bernard Keys and Thomas L. Case, "How to Become an Influential Manager," *The Executive* 4 (November 1990), pp. 38–51. The quotation is on p. 38.

119. Hickson, Butler, Cray, *et al., Top Decisions.*
120. Nutt, "Leverage, Resistance, and the Success of Implementation Approaches," pp. 222, 232.
121. Daniel Benjamin, "The Decider Who Can't Make Up His Mind," *Washington Post* (July 6, 2008). Benjamin served as director of transnational threats in the National Security Council.
122. Antonsen and Jorgensen, "The 'Publicness' of Public Organizations," p. 337. This is a study of twenty-nine "high-publicness" and twenty-four "low-publicness" government organizations in Denmark.
123. Louis C. Gawthrop, *Bureaucratic Behavior in the Executive Branch* (New York: Free Press, 1969). See also the discussion of public strategic planning in Chapter 10.
124. Lyman W. Porter and John Van Maanen, "Task Accomplishment and the Management of Time," *Managing for Accomplishment*, Bernard Bass, ed. (Lexington, MA: Lexington Books, 1970), pp. 180–192. Forty managers in city governments and forty in industry are compared.
125. Alan W. Lau, Cynthia W. Pavett, and Arthur R. Newman, "The Nature of Managerial Work: A Comparison of Public and Private Sector Jobs," *Academy of Management Proceedings* (August 1980), pp. 339–343.
126. Porter and Van Maanen, "Task Accomplishment and the Management of Time."
127. Ibid.
128. Antonsen and Jorgensen, "The 'Publicness' of Public Organizations," p. 337.
129. Jay Eungha Ryu, Cynthia J. Bowling, Chung-Lae Cho, *et al.*, "Effects of Administrators' Aspirations, Political Principals' Priorities, and Interest Groups' Influence on State Agency Budget Requests," *Public Budgeting & Finance* 27 (Summer 2007), pp. 22–49. The quotations are on pp. 43, 41, 23, 22.
130. Jay Eungha Ryu, Cynthia J. Bowling, Chung-Lae Cho, *et al.*, "Exploring Explanations of State Agency Budgets: Institutional Budget Actors or Exogenous Environment?" *Public Budgeting & Finance* 28 (Fall 2008), pp. 23–47. The quotation is on p. 23.
131. Henry Mintzberg, *The Structure of Organizations* (Englewood Cliffs, NJ: Prentice-Hall, 1979).
132. J. Norman Baldwin, "Public Versus Private Employees: Debunking Stereotypes," *Review of Public Personnel Administration* 11 (Fall 1990–Spring 1991), pp. 1–27. The quotations are on p. 9.
133. Moon, "The Pursuit of Managerial Innovation," p. 38.
134. The following list is based, with some license taken, on U.S. Merit Systems Protection Board, *Managing for Engagement: Communication, Connection, and Courage* (Washington, DC: U.S. Government Printing Office, 2009), pp. 66–74.
135. Antonsen and Jorgensen, "The 'Publicness' of Public Organizations," pp. 350–351.
136. See, for example, Thompson, *Organizations in Action,* pp. 14–82.
137. Davies, "The Inside Story," p. 64.
138. Fariborz Damanpour and Shanthi Gopalakrishnan, "The Dynamics of the Adoption of Product and Process Innovations in Organizations," *Journal of Management Studies* 38 (January 2001), pp. 45–66. The years covered were 1982–1993.
139. Lois Recascino Wise, "The Use of Innovative Practices in the Public and Private Sectors: The Role of Organization and Individual Factors," *Public Productivity & Management Review* 23 (December 1999), p. 150. The research was done in Sweden.
140. Borins, "Loose Cannons and Rule Breakers, or Enterprising Leaders?" p. 500.
141. Kuotsai Tom Liou and Ronnie Korosic, "Implementing Organizational Reform Strategies in State Governments," *Public Administration Quarterly* 33 (Fall 2009), pp. 429–452. The quotation is on p. 445.
142. Borins, "Loose Cannons and Rule Breakers, or Enterprising Leaders?" p. 500. Total figures add up to more than 100 percent because some innovations had more than one initiator.
143. Jon Aarum Andersen, "Assessing Public Managers' Change-Oriented Behavior: Are Private Managers Caught in the Doldrums?" *International Journal of Public Administration* 33 (May 2010), pp. 335–345. The quotations are on pp. 335, 337, 342, respectively; the data are on p. 341. This is a study of Swedish managers.
144. Charles Perrow, *Normal Accidents: Living with High-Risk Technologies,* 2nd ed. (Princeton, NJ: Princeton University Press, 1999), p. 9. Emphasis is original.

145. W. Graham Astley and Andrew H. Van de Ven, "Central Perspectives and Debates in Organization Theory," *Administrative Science Quarterly* 28 (June 1983), pp. 245–273. The quotation is on p. 245.

146. Lawrence G. Hrebiniak and William F. Joyce, "Organizational Adaptation: Strategic Choice and Environmental Determinism," *Administrative Science Quarterly* 30 (September 1985), pp. 336–349. The quotation is on p. 336.

147. We have changed our mind. In earlier editions of this book, we held a different view and discoursed at length on the academic disputations involving organizational determinism and choice. The reader may wish to consult the eighth edition (2001), pp. 101–105.

148. Herbert Kaufman, *Time, Chance, and Organizations: Natural Selection in a Perilous Environment* (Chatham, NJ: Chatham House, 1985), pp. 69, 150. Emphasis is original.

149. Paul C. Nutt, "Prompting the Transformation of Public Organizations," *Public Performance & Management Review* 27 (June 2004), pp. 9–33.

150. Ibid., pp. 27, 25, 30, respectively. Emphasis added.

151. As derived from data in Freedom of Information Center, University of Missouri, *State FOI Laws* (Columbia, MO: Author, 2008), http://www. nfoic.org/foi-center/state-foi-laws.html.

152. U.S. Government Accountability Office, *Information Management: Implementation of the Freedom of Information Act*, GAO-05-648T (Washington, DC: U.S. Government Printing Office, 2005), pp. 2, 13.

153. As derived from data in U.S. Government Accountability Office, *Freedom of Information Act: Processing Trends Show Importance of Improvement Plans*, GAO 07-491T (Washington, DC: U.S. Government Printing Office, 2007), pp. 6, 28.

154. U.S. Government Accountability Office, *Federal Advisory Committee Act: Issues Related to the Independence and Balance of Advisory Committees*, GAO-08-611T (Washington, DC: U.S. Government Printing Office, 2008), p. 1. Figures are for 2007, when there were 915 active federal advisory committees.

155. Jim Morris and Alejandra Fernandez Morera, *Network of 900 Advisory Panels Wields Unseen Power* (Washington, DC: Center for Public Integrity, 2007), p. 1. Figures are for 2007.

156. Thomas Cronin and Norman Thomas, "Federal Advisory Processes: Advise and Discontent," *Science* 171 (February 26, 1971), pp. 771–779.

157. U.S. Government Accountability Office, *Federal Advisory Committee Act*, Highlights page.

158. Ibid.

159. Cornelius M. Kerwin and Scott R. Furlong, *Rulemaking: How Government Agencies Write Law and Make Policy*, 4th ed. (Washington, DC: CQ Press, 2011), p. xi.

160. Michael Asimow, "On Pressing McNollgast to the Limits: The Problem of Regulatory Costs," *Law and Contemporary Problems* 57 (Winter 1994), pp. 127–137. The quotation is on p. 129.

161. U.S. Government Accountability Office, *Federal Rulemaking: Improvements Needed to Monitoring and Evaluation of Rules Development as Well as to the Transparency of OMB Regulatory Reviews*, GAO-09-205 (Washington, DC: U.S. Government Printing Office, 2009), Highlights page.

162. Jason Webb Yackee and Susan Webb Yackee, "Administrative Procedures and Bureaucratic Performance: Is Federal Agency Rule-making 'Ossified'?" *Journal of Public Administration Research and Theory* 20 (April 2010), pp. 261–282. The quotation is on p. 261.

163. Jacqueline Vaughn and Hanna J. Cortner, *George W. Bush's Healthy Forests: Reframing the Environmental Debate* (Boulder, CO: University Press of Colorado, 2005), pp. 187–188.

164. As derived from data (p. 117) in Susan Webb Yackee, "Sweet-Talking the Fourth Branch: The Influence of Interest Group Comments on Federal Agency Rulemaking," *Journal of Public Administration Research and Theory* 16 (January 2006), pp. 103–124.

165. Jason Webb Yackee and Susan Webb Yackee, "A Bias Towards Business? Assessing Interest Group Influence on the U.S. Bureaucracy," *Journal of Politics* 68 (February 2006), pp. 128–139. The quotation is on p. 129.

166. As derived from data in College of Law, Florida State University, *ABA Administrative Procedure Data Base* (Tallahassee, FL: Author, 2008), http:// www.law.fsu.edu/library/admin/admin3.html.

167. Dennis O. Grady and Kathleen M. Simon, "Political Constraints and Bureaucratic Discretion: The Case of State Government Rule Making," *Politics & Policy* 30 (December 2002), pp. 650–655. Data are for 1997.

168. Neal D. Woods, "Promoting Participation? An Examination of Rulemaking Notification and Access Procedures," *Public Administration Review* 69 (May/June 2006), pp. 518–530.

169. Paul Teske, *Regulation in the States* (Washington, DC: Brookings, 2004), p. 195. We are extrapolating somewhat liberally from Teske's findings, who notes that interest groups are "significantly influential in eight of the ten cases" that he analyzes in his book. These cases are quantitative analyses of ten policy areas in all the states.

170. Christopher Jewell and Lisa Bero, "Pubic Participation and Claimsmaking: Evidence Utilization and Divergent Policy Frames in California's Ergonomics Rulemaking," *Journal of Public Administration Research and Theory* 17 (October 2007), pp. 625–650.

171. Christopher M. Reenock and Brian J. Gerber, "Political Insulation, Information Exchange, and Interest Group Access to the Bureaucracy," *Journal of Public Administration Research and Theory* 18 (July 2008), pp. 415–440. The quotation is on p. 415.

172. Christine A. Kelleher and Susan Webb Yackee, "Who's Whispering in Your Ear? The Influence of Third Parties Over State Agency Decisions," *Political Research Quarterly* 59 (December 2006), pp. 629–643. The quotation is on p. 629. Although this is an analysis of state agencies, the conclusion also applies to federal agencies, as we detailed earlier, and we assume to local agencies as well.

173. Daniel P. Carpenter, "Groups, the Media, Agency Waiting Costs, and FDA Drug Approval," *American Journal of Political Science* 46 (July 2003), pp. 490–505. Carpenter examined the cases of 450 new drugs reviewed by the FDA, 1977–2000.

174. A. Cooper Drury, Richard Stuart Olson, and Douglas A. Van Belle, "The Politics of Humanitarian Aid: U.S. Foreign Disaster Assistance, 1964–1995," *Journal of Politics* 67 (May 2005), pp. 454–473. The authors analyzed 2,337 natural disasters.

175. Partnership for Public Service and Booz Allen Hamilton, *Securing the Future: Management Lessons of 9/11* (Washington, DC, and Herndon, VA: Authors, 2011), p. 21. Figure is for 2011.

176. Center for Strategic and International Studies and Business Executives for National Security, *Untangling the Web: Congressional Oversight and the Department of Homeland Security* (Washington, DC: Authors, 2004), p. 2. Figures are for 2004.

177. Partnership for Public Service and Booz Allen Hamilton, *Securing the Future*, p. 21.

178. U.S. General Accounting Office, *Executive Reorganization Authority: Balancing Executive and Congressional Roles in Shaping the Federal Government's Structure*, GAO-03-624T (Washington, DC: U.S. Government Printing Office, 2003), p. 7.

179. There are exceptions. The first Hoover Commission, 1947–1949, was quite successful, with 70 percent of its recommendations accepted by Congress and implemented, including twenty-six out of thirty-five proposed reorganization plans. The willingness of the Truman administration to work with Congress was instrumental in its success. See ibid., p. 9.

180. Alasdair Roberts, "Why the Brownlow Committee Failed: Neutrality and Partisanship in the Early Years of Public Administration," *Administration & Society* 28 (May 1996), pp. 3–38. The quotation is on p. 3.

181. Partnership for Public Service and Booz Allen Hamilton, *Securing the Future*, p. 4. Figure is for 1947–2011.

182. National Commission on the Public Service, *Urgent Business for America: Revitalizing the Federal Government for the 21st Century* (Washington, DC: U.S. Government Printing Office, 2003), p. 36.

183. Thad Beyle and Margaret Ferguson, "Governors and the Executive Branch," *Politics in the American States: A Comparative Analysis*, 9th ed., Virginia Gray and Russell L. Hanson, eds. (Washington, DC: CQ Press, 2008), pp. 192–228. The quotation is on p. 218.

184. Thad Beyle, "The Executive Branch," *State Constitutions for the Twenty-first Century: The Agenda of State Constitutional Reform* (Albany, NY: State University of New York Press, 2006), pp. 67–84. The reference is on p. 80.

185. Thad L. Beyle, "Enhancing Executive Leadership in the States," *State and Local Government Review* 27 (Winter 1995), pp. 18–35.

186. Richard C. Elling, "Administering State Programs: Performance and Politics," *Politics in the American States: A Comparative Analysis*,

8th ed., Virginia Gray and Russell L. Hanson, eds. (Washington, DC: CQ Press, 2004), pp. 261–289. The quotation is on p. 267.

187. James Conant, "Management Consequences of the 1960–1990 'Modernization' of State Government," *Handbook of State Government Administration*, John J. Gargan, ed. (New York: Marcel Dekker, 2000), pp. 13–32.

188. Elling, "Administering State Programs," p. 267.

189. Alan Greenblatt, "A Little Bit of Reform," *Governing* (August 2003), pp. 40–41. The author is referring to reorganization attempts undertaken since 1990.

190. Katherine Barrett and Richard Greene, "Bidding Boards Goodbye," *Governing* (August 2009), pp. 54–55.

191. Katherine Barrett and Richard Greene, "Coming Together, Breaking Apart," *Governing* (March 2009), pp. 58–59.

192. Mark A. Abramson, Steven A. Clyburn, and Elizabeth Mercier, *Results of the Government Leadership Survey: A 1999 Survey of Federal Executives* (Washington, DC: The PricewaterhouseCoopers Endowment for the Business of Government, 1999), pp. 8–9.

193. Matthew Holden, Jr., *Continuity and Disruption: Essays in Public Administration* (Pittsburgh: University of Pittsburgh Press, 1996), p. 58.

194. Donald P. Warwick, with Marvin Meade and Theodore Reed, *A Theory of Public Bureaucracy: Politics, Personality, and Organization in the State Department* (Cambridge, MA: Harvard University Press, 1975), p. 114.

195. Meier and O'Toole, *Bureaucracy in a Democratic State*, p. 62.

196. Bradley E. Wright and Sanjay K. Pandey, "Transformational Leadership in the Public Sector: Does Structure Matter?" *Journal of Public Administration Research and Theory* 20 (January 2010), pp. 75–89. The quotation is on p. 84.

197. Princeton Survey Research Associates and Brookings Institution, *Health of the Public Service*. Figures are for 2001.

198. Raghuram Rajan and Julie Wulf, *The Flattening Firm: Evidence from Panel Data on the Changing Nature of Corporate Hierarchies*, NBER Working Paper 9633 (Washington, DC: National Bureau of Economic Research, 2003). This study of more than 300 large U.S. firms found that the number of levels in the management hierarchy between division heads and CEOs had declined by a fourth 1986–2003.

199. Paul C. Light, *Fact Sheet on the Continued Thickening of Government* (Washington, DC: Brookings, 2004). The years covered are 1960–2004.

200. Ibid. The years covered are 1960–2004.

201. Paul C. Light, *Creating High Performance Government: A Once-in-a-Generation Opportunity* (New York: Robert F. Wagner School of Public Service, New York University, 2011), p. 10. Middle-level figures are for 1980–1992. Lower-level figure is for 1983–2003.

202. As derived from data in U.S. Merit Systems Protection Board, *As Supervisors Retire: An Opportunity to Reshape Organizations* (Washington, DC: U.S. Government Printing Office, 2009), p. 6. Figures are for 1998–2008.

203. For a good review of this line of thought, see Edward E. Lawler, III, "Rethinking Organization Size," *Organizational Dynamics* 26 (October 1997), pp. 24–35.

204. Anthony Downs, *Inside Bureaucracy* (Boston: Little, Brown, 1967), pp. 75–78, 262.

205. William P. Barnett and David G. McKendrick, "Why Are Some Organizations More Competitive than Others? Evidence from a Changing Global Market," *Administrative Science Quarterly* 49 (Winter 2004), pp. 535–571.

206. Rajeev K. Goel and Michael A. Nelson, "Corruption and Government Size: A Disaggregated Analysis," *Public Choice* 97 (October 1998), pp. 107–120. Data are for 1983–1987.

207. Kevin B. Smith and Christopher W. Larimer, "A Mixed Relationship: Bureaucracy and School Performance," *Public Administration Review* 64 (November/December 2004), pp. 728–736.

208. Kenneth J. Meier and John Bohte, "Not with a Bang, but a Whimper: Explaining Organizational Failures," *Administration & Society* 35 (March 2003), pp. 104–121. The quotations are on p. 104.

209. Rhys Andrews, George A. Boyne, Jennifer Law, et al., "Centralization, Organizational Strategy, and Public Service Performance," *Journal of Public Administration Research and Theory* 19 (January 2009), pp. 57–80. The quotation is on p. 57.

210. Philip H. Mirvis and Edward J. Hackett, "Work and Work Force Characteristics in the Nonprofit Sector," *Monthly Labor Review* 106 (April 1983), pp. 3–12. We cite this source because it is likely unique in that its scale is very large and it compares workers' perceptions in all three sectors.

211. Warwick, *et al.*, *A Theory of Public Bureaucracy*, pp. 72–80, 188–191.

212. Cole D. Taratoot and David C. Nixon, "With Strings Attached: Statutory Delegations of Authority to the Executive Branch," *Public Administration Review* 71 (July/August 2011), pp. 637–644. This is an analysis of agency-creating statutes, 1946–1997.

213. Arjen van Witteloostuijn and Gjalt de Jong, "Ecology of National Rule Birth: A Longitudinal Study of Dutch Higher Education Law, 1960–2004," *Journal of Public Administration Research and Theory* 20 (January 2010), pp. 187–213. The quotation is on p. 207.

214. Joint Committee on the Organization of Congress, *Organization of the Congress,* Final Report (Washington, DC: U.S. Government Printing Office, 1993), http://www.rules.house.gov/Archives/jcoc2ar.htm#a, "Legislative-Executive Relations," "Congressional Precedents and Powers," "Number of Reports." In 1992, Congress had 3,627 reporting requirements, an increase of 242 percent growth over twelve years.

215. Meier and O'Toole, *Bureaucracy in a Democratic State*, p. 60. Seventy-one percent of 137 laws "involved the subsequent development of rules."

216. Clyde Wayne Crews, Jr., *Ten Thousand Commandments 2009: An Annual Snapshot of the Federal Regulatory State* (Washington, DC: Competitive Enterprise Institute, 2009), p. 2. Figures are for 2008.

217. Diane Ravitch, "Burden of Rules, Regulations Is Eroding School Discipline," *Savannah Morning News* (January 3, 2005). In an earlier edition of this book (the tenth, 2007, pp. 89–95), we reproduced the steps that were necessary to replace a furnace in a New York City public school. We no longer do so for reasons of space; the flow chart consumed nearly seven pages.

218. Tom Brokaw witnessed and recounted this incident on "Morning Joe," CSNBC Cable Television (November 24, 2010).

219. Mirvis and Hackett, "Work and Work Force Characteristics in the Nonprofit Sector." This analysis is based on data in the University of Michigan's Quality of Employment Survey of 1977, and found that both nonprofit and private employees perceived less red tape in their organizations than public employees.

220. Mary K. Feeney and Hal G. Rainey, "Personnel Flexibility and Red Tape in Public and Nonprofit Organizations: Distinctions Due to Institutional and Political Accountability," *Journal of Public Administration Research and Theory* 20 (October 2010), pp. 801–826.

221. Moon, "The Pursuit of Managerial Innovation," p. 38.

222. Mary K. Feeney and Barry Bozeman, "Stakeholder Red Tape: Comparing Perceptions of Public Managers and Their Private Consultants," *Public Administration Review* 69 (July/August 2009), pp. 710–726. The quotation is on p. 710.

223. Branco L. Ponomariov and P. Craig Boardman, "Organizational Pathology Compared to What? Impacts of Job Characteristics and Career Trajectory on Perceptions of Organizational Red Tape," *Public Administration Review* 71 (July/August 2011), pp. 582–597. The quotations are on p. 593.

224. Feeney and Bozeman, "Stakeholder Red Tape," p. 819.

225. Patrick G. Scott and Sanjay K. Pandey, "Red Tape and Public Service Motivation: Findings from a National Survey of Managers in State Health and Human Services Agencies," *Review of Public Personnel Administration* 25 (Summer 2005), pp. 155–180.

226. Ponomariov and Boardman, "Organizational Pathology Compared to What?"

227. Feeney and Rainey, "Personnel Flexibility and Red Tape in Public and Nonprofit Organizations," p. 819.

228. Feeney and Bozeman, "Stakeholder Red Tape," p. 721.

229. Hal G. Rainey, Sanjay Pandey, and Barry Bozeman, "Research Note: Public and Private Managers' Perception of Red Tape," *Public Administration Review* 55 (November/December 1995), pp. 567–574.

230. Leisha DeHart-Davis and Sanjay K. Pandey, "Red Tape and Public Employees: Does Perceived Rule Dysfunction Alienate Managers?" *Journal*

of Public Administration Research and Theory 15 (January 2005), pp. 133–149. This is a study of managers in state health and human services agencies.

231. Leisha DeHart-Davis, "Green Tape and Public Employee Rule Abidance: Why Organizational Rule Attributes Matter," *Public Administration Review* 69 (September/October 2009), pp. 901–910. The quotations are on p. 906.

232. Keon S. Chi, Kelley A. Arnold, and Heather M. Perkins, "Privatization in State Government: Trends and Issues," *Spectrum* 76 (Fall 2003), p. 14. Figure is for 2002. "Flexibility and less red tape" ranks third out of eight possible reasons to privatize.

233. Sanjay K. Pandey, David H. Coursey, and Donald P. Moynihan, "Organizational Effectiveness and Bureaucratic Red Tape: A Multimethod Study," *Public Performance & Management Review* 30 (March 2007), pp. 398–425. The quotation is on p. 416.

234. Gene A. Brewer and Richard M. Walker, "The Impact of Red Tape on Governmental Performance: An Empirical Analysis," *Journal of Public Administration Research and Theory* 20 (January 2010), pp. 233–257. The quotation is on p. 234.

235. Meier and O'Toole, *Bureaucracy in a Democratic State*, p. 62.

236. John Meyer, W. Richard Scott, and David Strang, "Centralization, Fragmentation, and School District Complexity," *Administrative Science Quarterly* 32 (June 1987), pp. 188–201.

237. Brewer and Walker, "The Impact of Red Tape on Governmental Performance," pp. 233, 248. Emphasis is orginal.

238. James L. Garnett, Justin Marlowe, and Sanjay K. Pandey, "Penetrating the Performance Predicament: Communication as a Mediator or Moderator of Organizational Culture's Impact on Public Organizational Performance," *Public Administration Review* 68 (March/April 2008), pp. 266–281. The quotations are on p. 277.

239. Jessica Word and Sung Min Park, "Working across the Divide: Job Involvement in the Public and Nonprofit Sectors," *Review of Public Personnel Administration* 29 (June 2009), pp. 103–133. The quotation is on p. 125.

240. DeHart-Davis and Pandey, "Red Tape and Public Employees."

241. Bozeman and Kingsley, "Risk Culture in Public and Private Organizations."

242. Brewer and Walker, "The Impact of Red Tape on Governmental Performance," pp. 247–248.

243. Downs, *Inside Bureaucracy*, p. 145.

244. Martin Schulz, "Limits to Bureaucratic Growth: The Density Dependence of Organizational Rule Birth," *Administrative Science Quarterly* 43 (December 1998), pp. 845–876. The quotations are on pp. 845, 870. This is a study of an independent university's administrative and academic rules.

245. David S. Kassel, "Performance, Accountability, and the Debate over Rules," *Public Administration Review* 68 (March/April 2008), pp. 241–252. The quotation is on p. 241.

246. Marshall W. Meyer, *Change in Public Bureaucracies* (Cambridge, UK: Cambridge University Press, 1979), p. 219.

247. Antonsen and Jorgensen, "The 'Publicness' of Public Organizations," p. 350. Emphasis is original.

248. Ibid.

249. Warwick, *et al.*, *A Theory of Public Bureaucracy*, pp. 76, 192, 200, 210.

250. Ibid., p. 210.

251. David G. Houghton, "Citizen Advisory Boards: Autonomy and Effectiveness," *American Review of Public Administration* 18 (September 1988), pp. 282–295. The quotation is on p. 293.

252. Don Wycliffe, "Market System Urged as Way to Loosen Grip of School Bureaucracy," *New York Times* (June 6, 1990). Wycliffe is reviewing John E. Chubb and Terry M. Moe, *Politics, Markets, and America's Schools* (Washington, DC: Brookings, 1990).

253. Jeff Gill and Kenneth J. Meier, "Ralph's Pretty-Good Grocery versus Ralph's Super Market: Separating Excellent Agencies from the Good Ones," *Public Administration Review* 61 (January/February 2001), pp. 9–17. The quotation is on p. 14.

254. Alfred A. Marcus, "Implementing Externally Induced Innovations: A Comparison of Rule-Bound and Autonomous Approaches," *Academy of Management Journal* 31 (June 1988), pp. 235–256. The quotation is on p. 249.

255. For additional research substantiating this point, see: David M. Welborn, William Lyons, and

Larry W. Thomas, "The Federal Government in the Sunshine Act and Agency Decision Making," *Administration & Society* 20 (February 1989), pp. 480–492. To be fair, not all the research agrees that more autonomy will result in more effective public agencies. See Diane Vaughan, "Autonomy, Interdependence, and Social Control: NASA and the Space Shuttle *Challenger*," *Administrative Science Quarterly* 35 (June 1990), pp. 225–257.

256. Greg Chen, "Does Meeting Standards Affect Charitable Giving? An Empirical Study of New York Metropolitan Charities," *Nonprofit Management & Leadership* 19 (Spring 2009), pp. 349–365.

257. Dag Wollebaek, "Survival in Local Voluntary Associations," *Nonprofit Management & Leadership* 19 (Spring 2009), pp. 267–284.

258. Richard L. Meier, "Communications Overload: Proposals from the Study of a University Library," *Administrative Science Quarterly* 7 (March 1963), pp. 529–544. The strategies are on pp. 534–540, and the quotation is on p. 540.

259. John D. Sellars, "The Warning Signs of Institutional Decline," *Trusteeship* 2 (November/December 1994), p. 13.

260. Arthur G. Bedeian and Achilles A. Armenakis, "The Cesspool Syndrome: How Dreck Floats to the Top of Declining Organizations," *Academy of Management Executive* 12 (February 1998), pp. 58–67.

261. Wollebaek, "Survival in Local Voluntary Associations." The quotation is on p. 274.

262. Richard A. D'Aveni and Ian C. MacMillan, "Crisis and the Content of Managerial Communications: A Study of the Focus of Attention of the Top Managers in Surviving and Failing Firms," *Administrative Science Quarterly* 35 (October 1990), pp. 634–657.

263. Wollebaek, "Survival in Local Voluntary Associations," pp. 272, 273, 280.

The Fibres of Organizations: People

"Threads" served as our metaphor for theories of organizations. "Fabric" referred to the interwoven forces that form organizations. And "fibres"—the woof, weft, and tensile strength of organizations—describes people in organizations.

WHY WORK FOR THE PEOPLE?

What motivates people to work for government, rather than for business or the independent sector?

The Draw of the Public Sector

The reasons why people enter, or do not enter, public service are reasonably clear.

Money Does Not Make Their World Go Around

Relatively speaking, money matters little. Gaining wealth is considerably less important to those who work in government than it is to those who enter the corporate sphere.[1] Nearly two-thirds of all federal workers are satisfied with their pay (a rising proportion), including a fifth who are very satisfied.[2] Perhaps it should not surprise us that public administrators score "significantly higher" than corporate managers in their tolerance for delayed gratification.[3]

Where compensation does matter to public employees is as a way of keeping score. In an experiment, a random sample of state workers was granted full knowledge of their colleagues' salaries. Those with salaries below the median for their departments and for the same jobs reported much lower satisfaction with both their pay and their jobs, and there was a "significant increase in the likelihood of looking for a new job." Those employees earning above the median, however, reported no higher satisfaction at all and were no more inclined to stay with their employer than they had been before they knew that their pay was higher than the median.[4]

The size of their salaries seems not to matter to public workers (or, at least, to matter a lot less than to corporate workers). What matters is their salaries relative to their peers' salaries.

Making a Difference

The classic view of public administration is that of a calling, and, to a surprising degree, it still is. A study of American and Canadian zookeepers found that they "strongly identified with and found broader meaning and significance in their work.... [and] were more likely to see their work as a moral duty, to sacrifice pay, personal time, and comfort."[5]

In making the decision to work for government, doing good is far more important than doing well. About four out of ten public administrators, and seven out of ten top government executives, state that "helping the public" and "the chance to make a difference" were their major motivators for committing to careers in government.[6]

Public service motivation—that is, the desire to serve society in a secular context—is more pronounced in women, people with more education, members of professional associations,[7] and, certainly, government managers. There is, in fact, a remarkably symbiotic relationship between public service motivation and public administration: Holding a public administrative office correlates more strongly with public service motivation than any other factor, including even one's "personal characteristics,"[8] and the higher a public administrator's public service motivation, the more positive his or her perception of government.[9]

The desire to make a difference extends beyond bureaucracy's bounds. "Overall, public servants are far more active in civic affairs than are other citizens," and appear to be "catalysts" in improving society at large.[10] Public administrators are more religious,[11] compassionate, spiritual, and "transcendent"[12] than the average American. They also volunteer for charity and donate blood more frequently than their private-sector counterparts, and they match them in contributing money to charity.[13]

A Deep-Seated Need for Security There is another motivation underlying why people work for government, and it eclipses all else. It is security.

Almost six out of every ten public administrators cite "job security" as their primary reason for working in government, handily surpassing both salary (more than half cite salary) and service (fewer than two-fifths).[14] Nearly half, a plurality, of upper-level new federal hires,[15] and an astounding 97 percent of entry-level ones,[16] identify "job security" as their top reason for entering the federal service. The need for security transcends one's public career; those who choose to work in the public sector also share a uniquely strong desire for good pensions and retirement plans.[17]

The Draw of the Independent Sector

These dilemmas are not nearly as present in the independent sector. A mere 16 percent of nonprofit employees say that "their paycheck is the reason they come to work," a percentage that is half that of public workers and two-thirds lower than that of corporate employees.[18] Full-time nonprofit employees earn only 67 percent of what for-profit

employees earn in salaries and benefits, and 73 percent of what government workers earn, yet rate their pay as fair.[19]

More than six out of ten nonprofit workers state that they joined their organization "for the chance to make a difference," a proportion that is more than twice that of government employees and almost thrice that of businesspeople.[20] Those who enter the independent sector have served as volunteers more intensively and place a higher value on the organization's family-friendly policies, than either their public or private counterparts.[21]

THE BEHAVIORAL BUREAUCRAT

Organizational people are different. Very different.

"Administrative Man"

In *Models of Man*,[22] Herbert Simon contrasted *psychological*, or *Freudian*, *man*, as the model of the human condition used by psychologists to predict the behavior of individual persons who are beset by ticks, quirks, and emotional needs, with *rational*, or *economic*, *man*, which is the model used by economists to predict the behavior of the economy. Rational man thoroughly understands his or her own self-interest (i.e., acquiring money) and all the options available to fulfill it. Economic man has precisely the same goal as every other person and behaves just like every other person to achieve it.

Administrative man bridges psychological man and rational man. Administrative man has all the unique idiosyncrasies, blind spots, and limited reasoning power of psychological man, but, like economic man, also understands the mission and behavior of the organization, and knows that his or her welfare and interests and those of the organization can be somehow synchronous and complementary. (Recall, in this light, our discussion of "rational interest" in Chapter 3.)

"The Bureaucratic Personality" and "The Unbureaucratic Personality"

This freakish fusion of the Freudian and the fiscal, when combined with any organization's

obsession with minimizing uncertainty, can produce "the bureaucratic personality," a phrase that
resonates with "Veblen's concept of 'trained inca-
pacity,' Dewey's notion of 'occupational psychosis'
or Warnotte's view of 'professional deformation.'"
Rendering the bureaucracy ever more rigidly rule-
bound results in "overconformity" among its
bureaucrats, who have made inflexibility and indifference an art form.[23]

Not all bureaucrats succumb to this sad syndrome, and some American public administrators working in centralized bureaucracies that are
beribboned in reams of red tape rebel by developing an "unbureaucratic personality" that is found
in nonconformist, risk-prone public administrators who bend rules in order to provide better service.[24] Of greater importance, the syndrome itself
seems to be weak or even absent in most American
bureaucracies. As we explained in Chapter 1, the
vast majority of Americans are pleased by how
bureaucrats treat them, indicating that citizens are
dealing either with unbureaucratic rule-benders or
(we think more likely) rule-abiding bureaucrats
in agencies that are suffused with a public-service
ethic. Following well-designed regulations can, in
fact, lead to greater public organizational success
and accountability.[25]

The Energetic, Committed Bureaucrat

Public administrators seem to "hang in there"
with the same tenacity as their private-sector counterparts,[26] and studies "do not indicate a terrible
malaise in the public sector if the private sector is
used as a baseline."[27] Burnout among American
managers attains "serious proportions in both
arenas," but burnout in the public sector is "not
appreciably worse" than in the private sector.[28]
Nevertheless, it is indisputable that some types of
public employment, such as public safety, have
inherently high levels of stress. "City employees
feel more time stress than their state and federal
counterparts."[29]

Where employees in the public and private
sectors diverge is in the depth of commitment to
their jobs, and some research suggests that public
administrators may hold a passion for their work
that borders on the unhealthy. Half of federal
executives, but not much more than a third of

business executives, say that their career provides
them with the most "life satisfaction."[30]

Nonprofit employees may be the most devoted
to their jobs. They score highest in "total energy
and investment in the job," followed by government
workers and corporate employees, respectively.[31]

The Dissatisfied Bureaucrat?

Americans like their work. National polls taken
over three decades find that, in nearly every survey,
a solid majority of Americans report that they
are satisfied with their jobs.[32] Although there are
recent signs that job satisfaction may be declining
over time,[33] one review of these polls found that
four-fifths of working Americans are satisfied with
their jobs (only one out of eight is dissatisfied), and
an impressive two-thirds would take the same job
again "without hesitation."[34]

Public administrators provide some variation
on these themes, although the research on this topic
is singularly opaque. Perhaps because the field of
job satisfaction has yet to come to any clear agreement about what "job satisfaction" even means,[35]
contradictory findings on the job satisfaction of
pubic administrators are "equally abundant."[36]
There is, however, at least one commonality in this
literature: Public employees who possess *emotional
intelligence*, or the ability to comprehend, harness,
and manage moods in themselves and in others, are
more satisfied with their jobs than are those who
lack such intelligence.[37]

Job Satisfaction and Sector   There is a surprising
amount of diversity and change in the job satisfaction of public, nonprofit, and for-profit employees.

Federal Satisfaction   From the 1960s through the
1970s, the job satisfaction of federal workers was
low and falling lower.[38] For the last three decades,
however, some seven out of every ten federal
employees, a steadily rising proportion, say that, "all
in all," they are "satisfied" with their jobs.[39] Seven
out of ten of federal workers,[40] nearly a tripling from
under a fourth in the mid-1980s,[41] would recommend the federal government as a place to work.

As with most good news, there are anomalies.
Federal employees score three percentage points
lower than private-sector workers in their

satisfaction with their jobs, and they score a significant nine points lower in their satisfaction with their organizations.[42]

Grass-Roots and Third-Sector Satisfaction Although the data are less than definitive, state government administrators may be as, or possibly less, satisfied with their work than are federal and business managers.[43] Local public employees are clearly happy campers, and evidence satisfaction levels that handily surpass those of federal, state, and private-sector employees.[44]

Nonprofit workers may be the happiest of campers. Almost six out of ten say that they are "*very* satisfied" with their jobs, a rate that appears to exceed those of federal, state, and local employees, and private-sector workers as well.[45]

Gaining Recognition: The Frustrated, Hypercritical Bureaucrat

Public administrators are significantly less satisfied with how they are recognized than are their corporate counterparts.[46]

Recall that, when public employees learn that their peers are earning higher salaries than they are (and pay is a potent form of recognition), their dissatisfaction soars and the job search is on.[47] Sixty-six percent of federal employees state that "other employees in my organization did not receive awards/recognition deserved" or "received undeserved awards or recognition."[48] At 52 percent, federal employees score three percentage points lower than their private-sector colleagues in their satisfaction with the recognition that they receive for "doing a good job."[49]

The reasons underlying public administrators' frustration are enigmatic. The dissatisfaction among public employees may reflect their high commitment to their jobs, at least relative to their private-sector counterparts,[50] as "work-life" imbalance is known to induce job dissatisfaction.[51] Or it may be a consequence of uniquely high psychological needs for recognition. Or their unhappiness may be attributable to objective reality: Their frustration "could simply reflect more stringent norms or expectations among government managers" of their colleagues than are held by corporate executives.[52]

There is, in fact, some evidence that public administrators do hold their colleagues to unusually high, even harsh, standards. A review of surveys found that "Federal workers are the major purveyors of the misrepresentation that the government has too many poor performers.... Federal workers seem almost obsessed with describing the poor-performer problem."[53]

Employees in the independent sector also express some dissatisfaction over inadequate recognition for good performance; more than a fourth say that their organizations need to do better in rewarding a job well done.[54] Nonprofit employees' perceptions have some basis in reality. They are less likely to be promoted than are their counterparts in the private sector, and they are less likely to be promoted on the basis of performance.[55]

A Management Challenge

So here we have, in sum, the public and nonprofit managers' maze: Compared with business administrators, government executives are faced with employees who are hypercritical loners determined to do something of social importance, pouting prima donnas demanding unremitting recognition but who are uninterested in being bought off with monetary bonuses, and who, according to some research, have greater needs to dominate colleagues and may be wilier in getting their way than are their private-sector counterparts.[56]

Managers in the independent sector share these characteristics—with a vengeance.[57] Not only do nonprofit administrators "value work that contributes more to society" more than government managers and professionals (not to mention corporate ones), but they also "value opportunities for advancement less,"[58] and have lower needs for job security,[59] than either public- or private-sector employees.

Certainly, these are precisely the kinds of qualities that we want in our public and nonprofit administrators. But they make for a tough workforce to manage—and to be managed by.

GROWING INTO THE ORGANIZATION

The circumstances under which people are born and how they mature determine how people perceive their organization and behave in it.

Born to Conserve or Born to Rebel?

Let us consider, first, birth. The order of the person's birth relative to his or her siblings, if any, is the primary factor in determining a person's propensity to rebel—that is, to engage in revolutionary creativity.[60]

Those who are "firstborns" in a family identify with power and strength, and, when "laterborns" enter into the family picture, firstborns use their power, strength (and size), to defend their position in the family structure (and perhaps long after they have left it; adult firstborns with siblings have substantially less net worth than those without siblings[61]). Firstborns tend to be more jealous, aggressive, defensive, and confident than laterborns and are over-represented among Nobel laureates and political leaders. Winston Churchill, Ayn Rand, George Washington, and Rush Limbaugh are firstborns.

Laterborns (and firstborns who had deep conflicts with their parents), by contrast, tend to identify with fellow underdogs, question authority and the *status quo*, and to be more open, imaginative, independent, generous, and liberal than their firstborn siblings. Laterborns are disproportionately represented among explorers, rebels, and heretics. Joan of Arc, Karl Marx, Vladimir Lenin, Thomas Jefferson, Jean Jacques Rousseau, and Bill Gates are laterborns.

Why is this? The answer is biological and Darwinian: Childhood is the search for a stable niche in the family structure, just as evolution is the result of the cell's search for a stable niche in nature. Both processes pertain to Charles Darwin's "principle of divergence," which holds that diversification (whether in the family or in nature) is a tactic that helps the individual minimize competition with other individuals for scarce resources. Therefore, it "pays" firstborns to be conservers and protective of all the love and rewards that they (once) were receiving from their families on an exclusive basis, just as it "pays" laterborns to seek new ways of gaining entry to that love and those rewards.

Birth order is not an infallible method of detecting rebellious tendencies in a person. Nevertheless, birth order is the major determining factor in explaining why some people defend the establishment and other revolt against it. Firstborns are, literally, born to conserve. Laterborns are, literally, born to rebel.

Turning Points and the Organization

Birth order plays a large part in the progressive mastery of psychological tasks that determine what sort of an adult one becomes. How one approaches these tasks are known as "turning points."

Life's Turning Points Psychologists suggest that each of us confronts eight turning points in life's journey.

From birth to year one, trust or mistrust is inculcated into one's psyche as a result of his or her early experiences with others; from one to six, the turning point becomes one of developing autonomy (which "concentrates on keeping potential rivals out...most often directed against encroachments by younger siblings") *versus* shame and doubt; from six to ten, initiative (i.e., "anticipatory rivalry" directed against "those who have been there first") or guilt; from ten to fourteen, industry (the child "learns to win recognition by producing things") or inferiority; from fourteen to twenty, identity *versus* role confusion; from twenty to forty, intimacy or isolation; from forty to sixty-five, generativity (an "interest in guiding the next generation...a parental kind of responsibility") *versus* stagnation; and from sixty-five until death, ego integrity ("an emotional integration which permits participation by followership as well as acceptance of the responsibility of leadership"), as opposed to overwhelming despair.[62]

Should one take a negative path at any given turning point, all is not lost; with effort, a positive path can be taken at the next turning point.[63] Most Americans choose positive paths. Americans grow happier as they grow older. In their younger years, men and African Americans are less happy than women and whites, but these differences vanish over time.[64]

From Engagement to Settling Down—or Not
Life's turning points are reflected in organizational behavior.

"Studies have consistently found that almost all workers are engaged when they begin a job,"[65] but if these new recruits are in their twenties, and entering their first "real" jobs, then "reality shock" often can slap them in the chops, and they must cope with bottom-scraping disillusion. Just six months after joining an organization, not even two-fifths of all new employees say that they are still engaged in their employment.[66]

By their thirties, employees have overcome their reality shock and enter a period of "settling down"[67] and "career consolidation."[68] Not everyone, however, settles down. In one examination, a tenth of the sample remained "perpetual boys" and never matured, while a larger group simply stagnated;[69] in another, 45 percent of managers "had major difficulties" during their career-consolidation phase and could not create the basis for "an even moderately satisfactory mid-life."[70]

Mid-Life Crisis! Although a "mid-life transition" may occur from one's late thirties through early sixties, it is more likely to happen during one's mid-forties, and it may be experienced more by women than by men.[71] One adopts new lifestyles, spouses, and careers; or one accepts that one's life and work have gone as far as they are likely to go, and is fine with it; or one becomes embittered over one's sorry lot.[72]

It appears that if one has less egocentrism and narcissism, and more tolerance, flexibility, and openness, one improves one's chances of weathering the mid-life crisis.[73] But some administrators find this period so traumatic that they become "organizational sleepwalkers."[74]

Meaning, Identity, and Disengagement Contentment with one's life and organization typically rebounds during the late forties and fifties. This is a period of "acceptance,"[75] or "keeping the meaning" of one's life and personal principles.[76] Alternatively, however, people can become inflexible over a set of principles that may have grown hollow over time.

The roller coaster of intertwined life and career takes yet another dip in the mid-to-late fifties and continues to decline, although not as rapidly, through the early sixties as one nears retirement.[77] "As people enter mid-life, extrinsic rewards for higher levels of performance and achievement lose their lustre, as interest in affirming one's identity and concerns for protecting the self-concept increase."[78] "The longer employees work in an organization, the more engagement decreases until only 20 percent are engaged after 10 years of service."[79]

NATIONAL CULTURE AND THE ORGANIZATION

Just as birth order and aging influence how people inside organizations behave in them, so does the larger society in which they live. *National culture*, or "the collective mental programming of people in an environment,"[80] is perhaps the single greatest external determinant of organizational behavior.

Dimensions of National Culture

Certainly the most systematic and massive attempt to categorize national cultures in ways that are potentially useful to managers is by Geert Hofstede, who identified five dimensions of national culture.[81]

Power Distance One dimension is *power distance*, which refers to "the extent to which a society accepts the fact that power in institutions and organizations is distributed unequally."[82] Societies characterized by "small" power distance believe, among other things, that inequality should be minimized; superiors should be accessible; and all should have equal rights. Cultures with a "large" power distance believe that a social order rightly assures proper inequalities in society; superiors should be inaccessible; and power should have privileges.

Uncertainty Avoidance *Uncertainty avoidance* is the degree to which a culture feels threatened by ambiguity. Cultures with "weak" uncertainty avoidance have lower stress levels; believe time is free; accept dissent; are unthreatened by social deviations; more risk prone; youth oriented; and not enamored by a lot of rules. "Strong" uncertainty-avoidance cultures experience greater stress; believe time is money; promote consensus over dissent; and are security conscious, distrustful of the young, and like a lot of rules.

Individualism–Collectivism *Individualism–collectivism* refers to a continuum ranging from personal to social centeredness. In an individualist culture, society is seen as a loose grouping of people whose primary concern is caring for themselves; leadership is the ideal; and decisions are made by the individual. In a collectivist culture, society reflects a tight social framework in which in-groups are distinguished from out-groups, and the in-group is expected to take care of the individual member in exchange for his or her total allegiance to it; membership in the in-group is the ideal; and decisions are made by the group.

Masculinity–Femininity The *masculinity–femininity* dimension is a continuum ranging from a masculine pole, in which assertiveness, performance, money, independence, ambition, machismo, and indifference to others dominate, to a feminine extreme in which nurturing, quality of life, people, the environment, interdependence, service, androgyny, and caring for others are the preeminent values.

Long-Term/Short-Term Orientation Finally, *long-term/short-term orientation* refers to a cultural perspective relative to time. Nations with a long-term orientation are directed toward the future, and value thrift and persistence. Countries with a short-term orientation are more poised toward the past and present, and place premiums on respect for tradition and fulfilling social obligations.

Patterns of Geography and Language

Countries tend to group along these dimensions by geographic proximity. For example, the seven Latin American countries that Hofstede surveyed are all cultures that accept large inequalities of power relationships, strongly avoid uncertainty, and are collectivist. Asian countries are large power distance countries, collectivist, and have a long-term orientation.

Common language plays a part, too. All ten English-speaking countries, including those in Africa and Asia, are accepting of uncertainty and are masculine; and, except for those in Asia, all English-speaking countries are individualistic.

The United States is a small power distance country (i.e., its citizens value equality); is a weak uncertainty avoidance nation (in fact, it is well below average, indicating high risk-taking propensities and tolerance for dissent); is exceptionally individualistic as a society; is well above average as a masculine culture; and has a

short-term orientation. In addition, compared with Europeans, Americans are considerably more conservative, religious, patriotic,[83] and warlike.[84]

National Culture and Organizational Behavior

Researchers have found that national culture affects organizational behavior in intriguing ways.

National Culture and Managerial Authority Although the United States is a small power distance country, and equality and accessibility are valued, it does not score terribly high on this dimension, and a number of nations, such as Israel, Norway, and Sweden, have power distances that are even smaller. In these countries, organizational subordinates are much more likely to participate in decision making. In fact, in those cultures with the smallest power distances "the very idea of management prerogatives is not accepted."[85]

Indeed, management in these cultures is far more likely to be challenged. Countries that have small power distances also "have a very high proportion" of public employees, relative to those is large power distance societies, who report unethical or illegal conduct in their agencies. A majority of whistleblowers in these cultures "receive positive reactions" from peers, and most report that the conduct that led them to blow the whistle improved—also in contrast to cultures with large power distances.[86]

Nations with large power distances, such as France and Italy, show little interest in participative decision making. "This suggests that subordinates in a large Power Distance culture feel even more comfortable with superiors who are real autocrats,"[87] and they are much more accepting of bullying by bosses than are workers in small power distance societies.[88] Even so, a major study of twenty-one nations found that a high level of stress at work associates with large power distance.[89]

National Culture and the American Organization In the view of at least one distinguished European theorist, American culture is characterized by two overweening factors. One is Americans' drive to professionally specialize in their occupations.

Getting Ahead

National cultures are reflected in their bureaucracies, even when those bureaucracies administer cultures far removed from their own. From 1858 to 1947, the Civil Services of the Crown in India (composed, typically, of about 1,000 civil servants, of whom about a fifth were routinely absent due to leaves and illness) administered some 400 million Indians, Pakistanis, Bangladeshis, and Burmese. Their management was sufficiently adroit that Joseph Stalin, the Soviet dictator, grumbled in 1939 to Joachim von Ribbentrop, the Nazi foreign minister, that it was "ridiculous . . . that a few hundred Englishmen should dominate India."

How did one advance in such a civil service? Here is one way.

Sir David Barr, "a man who was bald and diffident as well as talented," was persuaded to remind Lord Curzon, viceroy of India (1899–1905), that he would be suitable for promotion to the Residency at Hyderabad. Sir David sent a telegram to the viceroy that read, in its entirety, "Psalm 132, verse 1." Lord Curzon looked up the biblical citation, which states: "Lord, remember David." Curzon, then in the hills of northern India, telegraphed back, "Psalm 75, verse 6." ("For promotion *cometh* neither from the East, nor from the West, nor from the South.") Encouraged, Sir David replied, "Psalm 121, verse 1." ("I will lift up mine eyes to the hills, from whence cometh my help.") The viceroy ended the exchange with, "II Kings, 2, verse 23," which reads, "Go up, thou bald head." Sir David had won his promotion. ■

Sources: David Gilmour, *The Ruling Caste: Imperial Lives in the Victorian Raj* (New York: Farrar, Straus and Giroux, 2005), pp. 217–218; and Indian Civil Service Association, *The Indian Civil Service Association* (Herts, UK: Author, 2001).

The other is Americans' passion for due process of law.

In American organizations, the heavy presence of professional specializations leads to the creation of turfs, which, in combination with Americans' insistence on due process, produce an abnormally high number of jurisdictional disputes inside the organization. This, in turn, creates reams of rules designed to protect each person from injustices and magnifies the role of the organization's "lawyers," or any official who is in a position to delineate organizational turf and untangle red tape. Lawyers, loosely defined, often are effective enemies of innovation in American organizations.[90]

American organizations, on the whole, tend to protect the rights of individuals more effectively, are better attuned to reality, are characterized by more cooperation and innovation, and are generally more open than European organizations. But the existence of many centers of authority in American organizations, and the difficulties that must be surmounted in coordinating them, impede change. "Willful individuals can block the intentions of whole communities for a long time . . . and generally, a large number of vicious circles will protect and reinforce local conservatism."[91] Despite these obstacles, however, a meta-analysis of 287 research articles found that small power distance and large individualism and masculinity, features that are deeply embedded in American culture, correlate, positively and strongly, with both high job satisfaction and high performance.[92]

ORGANIZATIONAL POLITICS

In 1954, Dwaine Marvick published a little-known monograph about the personality types that he discovered among federal administrators.[93] His research was prescient because, three years later, the sociologist, Alvin Gouldner, published his famous articles on "Cosmopolitans and Locals,"[94] which had an enduring academic impact, even though Marvick's investigation was far more rigorous, empirical, and sophisticated. And it certainly was more relevant to public administration, as Gouldner's findings were based on his observations of a small college's faculty and administrators.

What follows is a synopsis of the two researchers' (mainly Marvick's) explorations, with an emphasis on what they tell us about what to expect from co-workers in public agencies.

Marvick trisected public bureaucrats according to "career types"—that is, how they perceived their careers, and the ways in which they conducted themselves in their agencies—and then asked, crucially, "What must management do in order to cope with persons having different career perspectives?"[95]

What is notable about Marvick's typology is that his classifications associate with variables that can be found in any personnel file. When combined with Marvick's insights, these data provide useful personal knowledge about the organization.

Institutionalists: Loyal and Lethargic

Marvick's first career type is the *institutionalists*, who correspond to Gouldner's *locals*. Locals derive their power and sense of personal identity from internal organizational factors; are loyal to the organization as a whole; well satisfied with everything in it; suspicious of outsiders; and often oriented toward the past.

Marvick's institutionalists are all that and more. They are deeply demanding of organizational advancement and prestige. (One study found in this regard that, in contrast to nonprofit managers, who place a high value on opportunities for "increased responsibility," government managers prefer "advancement opportunities,"[96] suggesting that institutionalists may be closer to the norm in public agencies than one might find comfortable.) Institutionalists tend not to stress the task-oriented features of their jobs, but prefer to emphasize its benefits (recall that public administrators display an inordinate interest in retirement plans[97]), and are highly sociable, optimistic, complacent, and fiercely loyal to their agency and coworkers.

Institutionalists can become rule-oriented and inflexible; their sociability can degenerate into cliquishness, their loyalty into recalcitrance to change, and they resist objective performance evaluation. Yet, institutionalists stabilize the bureaucracy, and furnish the needed lubrication among interpersonal relationships.

The personnel files of institutionalists reveal that they are typically mid-level bureaucrats with long careers in government, often in the military; are encumbered by few family ties; possess relatively low educational attainments; and frequently change positions (though do not necessarily advance) within the government.

Specialists: Professional and Maladjusted

Specialists cluster at the opposite end of the spectrum. They are similar to Gouldner's *cosmopolitans*, who relate to factors external to the organization, such as their professional associations; are more loyal to a subunit of the organization than to the organization as a whole; are dissatisfied with many aspects of it; and are more highly educated, specialized, and alienated from their colleagues.

Again, as with institutionalists, Marvick's specialists are all that and more. Specialists are not particularly concerned about advancement, and have virtually no interest in organizational status. What they do want very badly, however, is to be in jobs that allow them to use their professional skills on a daily basis. They are loners and are by far the most critical of their agency's performance and of bureaucratic procedures generally; hence, they are "manifestly maladjusted" in their working relationships.[98] Although they are less likely to be involved in group decisions, specialists actually have more influence within the agency than institutionalists.

Specialists tend to displace the agency's goals because their individual projects are more important to them than the organization's welfare, and this propensity can diminish organizational performance. Moreover, their highly critical cast and lack of place commitment can cause sinking morale. Yet, when properly placed, specialists can get things done, and they are not inclined to heighten organizational tensions by competing politically with colleagues.

In terms of career histories, specialists usually have more experience in private companies and less military time than institutionalists; unlike institutionalists, who occupy generalized managerial slots, specialists are high ranking, highly educated, and, obviously, highly specialized professionals.

Hybrids: Political and Unpredictable

Gouldner found only two personality types, cosmopolitans and locals, in his campus observations. Marvick, however, uncovered a third: *hybrids*, or *politicized experts*. Hybrids, as their moniker implies, draw their characteristics from both institutionalists and specialists.

Like institutionalists, hybrids are very concerned with acquiring executive positions and moving up to higher-paying jobs (interestingly, in this light, hybrids typically have far heavier family responsibilities than either institutionalists or specialists), are not especially critical of bureaucratic paraphernalia, and are well adjusted to their jobs. Like specialists, hybrids are uninterested in organizational prestige, and become disgruntled when distracted from their work.

Hybrids bring the most dangers and benefits to the organization. Their chief peril lies in their instability. Hybrids are fair weather friends, "superficial and showy performers."[99] Their lack of both place and skill commitments renders them unpredictable. Yet, precisely because they have no sublimated needs, hybrids are the most likely to assess, accurately and holistically, the dynamics and problems of the organization. Nevertheless, hybrids must be watched, for they are prone to change the organization purely for their own self-betterment.

Hybrids' personnel files show that, in addition to supporting large families, they are highly educated professionals, occupying relatively high ranks, and have significant work experience in both the private and public spheres.

WHAT IS LEADERSHIP?

We have reviewed how several factors and forces affect how people behave in organizations. But people themselves can alter organizational behavior, and the people who are the most likely to do so are called leaders.

The Leadership Literature

Although the term "leader" surfaced in the English language around 1300, "leadership" did not appear until another half millennium had passed.[100] Given its relatively recent origin, it is surprising that no aspect of organizational behavior has had more written about it than has leadership; the number of publications about leadership appears to double from each preceding decade,[101] and there may be some 10,000 published studies on the subject.[102] The United States is the frothing fount for most of this gusher, apparently because Americans "are unabashed in their zest for leadership [and] leadership has become something of a cult concept."[103]

Not so in other countries. The French, for example, have no word that translates well as "leadership" (the French word for leader is *chef*) and are reduced, in a culture that officially bans the Anglicization of its language, to referring to *le leadership* (*Zut, alors!*). Germans, Italians, Spaniards, and some Latin Americans carry some embarrassing fascist baggage in their words for leader—"führer" in German, "duce" in Italian, and "caudillo" and "jefe" in Spanish—which may explain their current intellectual disinclination to dwell on leadership.

In light of its scholarly popularity, at least in the United States, it is passing strange that so few agree on what leadership even means. One reviewer found that more than three-fifths of the writings on leadership never defined it,[104] and another unearthed 130 different definitions of leadership among those writers who bothered to define it.[105]

Leadership "is an influence relationship among leaders and followers who intend real change that reflect their mutual purposes."[106] We like this definition because it stresses non-coercive manipulation by both leaders and followers (although leaders are, properly, granted the upper hand); the presence of multiple leaders as well as multiple followers; the purposeful attainment of substantive change; and teamwork.

Leadership or Administration?

Is leadership different from administration? Yes. Is one more important to organizational success than the other? No.

Leadership deals with change. *Administration* copes with complexity. Both are equally vital to organizational success. "Management, pure and simple, is necessary and essential to the good life...and as such it has as much going for it as leadership does.... Down with management and up with leadership is a bad idea."[107]

Both leadership and administration involve "deciding what needs to be done," creating the work and relationships to achieve it, "and then trying to insure that those people actually do the job." Leadership's way of accomplishing these three tasks is *to set a direction*—create a vision—for the organization, and then *align people, communicate,* and *inspire* to fulfill it. Administration *plans* and *budgets* for the vision, and *organizes, staffs, controls activities*, and *solves problems* to implement it.[108]

The relative importance of leadership and administration depends on the conditions of the time. In periods of slow change and a placid environment, administration is of greater significance; in times of rapid change and a turbulent environment, leadership is. "A peace time army can usually survive with good...management up and down the hierarchy.... A war time army, however, needs competent leadership at all levels. No one yet has figured out how to manage people effectively into battle; they must be led."[109]

Are Leaders Needed?

This dramatic and inspiring image of "The Leader" at the head of charging warriors persuades the less palpitating among us to ask: Are we being conned? Do we need leaders?

More precisely put, do organizations need *hierarchical leaders*, or those people who occupy high executive office? This question is even more radical than that of whether we need leaders, because chief executives do a lot more than lead. "Leadership" is only one of ten distinct roles, such as master of ceremonies, disturbance handler, and spokesperson, that an executive plays,[110] and these executive duties are common to both the public and private sectors, perhaps because "the private sector is becoming more like the public sector."[111]

The Leadership Con? At least one writer has forcefully argued that top executives actually undermine organizational productivity because they lack any organizationally useful skills, and that hierarchical leaders should be exorcized from organizations altogether![112]

Hierarchical leaders have kept their posh positions by promoting an unexamined ideology that assumes executives are needed; executives' "dramaturgical" behavior (firm handshakes, personal aloofness, unwavering gazes, winning smiles, etc.) that conveys an image of executive importance; and a "bureaupathological" enforcement of rigid rules designed to assure subordinates' subservience and loyalty.[113] One is reminded by these techniques of Mel Brooks' line in his role as the governor in the film, *Blazing Saddles*: "Gentlemen, we've got to protect our phony baloney jobs here!"

If executives are nothing more than con artists, then how do organizations get things done? The answer: Those who get things done in organizations are Marvick's specialists, such as scientists and salespeople, who have the knowledge and skills that are crucial to the achievement of organizational objectives. We do not need sociopathic leaders; we do not need sycophantic followers; we need only that leaders and their followers get out of the way so that the specialists can get on with it.

The Limits of Leadership The preceding polemic frames the question. But is it possible that organizations really do not need (or would even be better off without) chief executives and top administrators?

Well, yes, at least by inference. Although no organization is free of bosses, at least some organizations survive despite environmental limitations that constrain all leaders, whether they are talented, productive executives or slothful, clueless parasites. In the states, "there is little evidence that a governor's formal powers significantly affect policy outcomes," which "are attributable largely to the impact of economic development rather than to the governor's power."[114] At the local level, most of the variance in big-city budget allocations is attributable not to the entry of new mayors, but rather to environmentally determined characteristics of the cities themselves.[115]

Internal organizational factors also can render hierarchical leadership "not always very necessary, especially if community members do not 'need' a leader in order to be motivated to make their contribution.... In some situations, especially where the work or membership is intrinsically satisfying and work groups are cohesive, the presence of a leader is redundant."[116] But even effective teams of engaged employees are not always needed to render executives irrelevant; placidity will do. An analysis of college presidents concluded that 16 percent presided over "uneventful" campuses "running 'on automatic'...that *do not need* their presidential leaders."[117]

These external and internal organizational realities pertain to all sectors. In the nonprofit sector, the organization's "external legitimacy" far outweighs changes in internal leadership and management in predicting the long-term survival of newly-founded, social service organizations.[118]

Similarly, in the for-profit sector, the performance of large corporations correlates far more satisfactorily with the effects of time, type of industry, and traits of specific companies than with changes in their chief executive officers (CEO).[119] "Managerial succession" in professional baseball teams "has a negative effect on organizational performance."[120]

Leaders Matter In a very real sense, however, these analyses obscure a fundamental point, which is that leaders can and do have an impact on their organizations. The real question is: How much impact?

Of course, as we have discussed, a variety of conditions limit just how much a leader can do. But even when these factors are taken into account, leadership matters. "Managerial power" and ability are positively and "highly correlated with job involvement" in both the public and independent sectors, trumping even gender, age, ethnicity, and education.[121]

In public agencies, "leadership has "an enormous impact" on "follower satisfaction,"[122] and, "ultimately, the research shows that supervisory proficiency" in government "is critical to...employee motivation, engagement, and retention."[123]

We also know that public leaders correlate with effective governance. "Leadership plays an important role" in whether emergency managers view their crisis networks as effective.[124] "Mayoral quality is associated with....improved local public finance."[125] Those governments that have

superior management capacity perform better than governments with low capacity, and leadership, in turn, is central in enhancing "the impact of capacity" on public performance.[126] Able government supervisors are crucial "to individual and organizational performance."[127]

Overwhelmingly, most organizational leaders do have a significant impact, for good or ill, on their subordinates and on their organizations.

LEARNING LEADERSHIP: THE EVOLUTION OF A THEORY

The evolution of leadership theory during the last century and in this one has been characterized by ebbs, eddies, and flows. "Contrary to popular belief, none of the theories have become completely extinct. They reappear decade after decade, sometimes disguised, sometimes in another form, basically intact and flourishing."[128]

The Leader: Alone and Glorious, 1900–1930

We noted in Chapter 3 that the pioneers of management theory treated members of organizations as identical automatons who did as they were told. But when these same writers cast their eye on a particular type of organizational human being— the leader—their hearts beat aflutter. Impersonal sameness is tossed out the window, and creative, visionary, mythic heroes swagger in.

The Triumph of the Will? No longer were scholars talking about the limitless capacities of clerks to cower and laborers to labor, but of dizzying social forces that only leaders could bring to heel. A conference held in 1927 defined *leadership*, in decidedly Teutonic terminology, as "the ability to impress the will of the leader on those led and induce obedience, respect, loyalty, and cooperation."[129] This view, with some modifications, persisted decades later, when leaders remained transcendent figures endowed with a "gift of grace," who soared grandiosely at an "institutional level" over torpid, timid technicians, who toiled in the organization's innards and kept its hum drum routines running from day to day.[130]

Leadership Traits Unsurprisingly, much ado was made about leaders' "traits," or those personal qualities that made them leaders. Researchers would score and compare "leaders" (who typically were identified as leaders by nothing more than the office that they held in the organization) with "followers" on such dimensions as dominance, physical appearance, masculinity, and other characteristics that were thought to constitute leadership.

A scholar who tried to make some sense of 120 of these trait studies (essentially all of them) could discern no commonalities among leaders.[131] If not shared traits, then, what made them leaders?

The Leader in the Grip of the Group, 1930–1970

To answer this question, theorists moved away from identifying leaders' traits to learning how leaders behaved. Of greater usefulness, they tried to match which sorts of behavior associated with effective leadership. To do this, researchers observed how leaders interacted with small groups.

Leadership Behaviors By the 1940s, inspired largely by Kurt Lewin's seminal research on leadership styles,[132] researchers had identified two distinct clusters of behaviors that they believed were useful, if for different reasons, to leaders in providing leadership, and these clusters have had a lasting impact on leadership theory.

One cluster is composed of *consideration behaviors* that relate to interpersonal warmth, concern for the feelings of subordinates, and a participative/communicative style of leadership. The other cluster is *structuring, or task, behaviors*, and includes directness, obtaining task-related feedback, and achieving goals.

Investigators in this tradition find that both behavioral clusters can work well in leading groups, but *which* cluster works depends upon the nature of the group. Leadership no longer is perceived as command and control, as it was during the early twentieth century, but instead is interactive and nondirective—*leadership* becomes "personality in action under group conditions."[133]

Scholars have developed two major approaches, distinct but interrelated, to understand leaders' behaviors and their groups' responses to them.

Contingency Approaches One approach is rooted in contingency theory, which, as we explained in Chapter 3, treats the organization as an entity that is constantly forced to adapt to its surrounding environment. When applied to leadership, this approach emphasizes that leaders must deal with *contingencies*—that is, unexpected or unintended events or possibilities—that can occur as a result of any number of factors.

Fred Fiedler is perhaps the prime contributor to this line of thought.[134] Fiedler found that when a group trusts its leader implicitly, has a clear task structure, and the leader has the power to reward and punish followers, the leader has *high control* of the group. In a high-control situation, a *task-motivated leader* is the leader with the most effective set of behaviors.

When the group is distrusting or uncooperative, its task structure is ambivalent, and the leader has less power to reward and punish, the leader has *moderate control*. Task motivated leaders are less effective in a moderate control situation because they frequently became anxious and move, often inappropriately, to a quick solution; typically, they are critical and punitive toward their followers. In these moderate-control situations, a *relationship-motivated leader* is more effective.

When the group is not supportive of its leader, its task is foggy, and the leader's authority to dispense rewards and punishments is ambiguous, *low control* is the consequence. In a low-control situation, which often amounts to a crisis situation, the *task-motivated leader* once again surfaces as the most effective.

Although the contingency model has been the subject of some controversy, most empirical tests of it find it to be reflective of the real world.[135]

Transactional Approaches Still, the contingency approach has limitations. It concentrates only on the problems confronting the leader in dealing with a small group, but not the leader's subordinates and the problems confronting them. What kinds of *transactions*, or exchanges, occur between and among leaders and followers that facilitate or impair both the leader's and the group's effectiveness?

Consideration behavior by a leader is most effective when a follower's job is distasteful or boring, whereas structuring or task-oriented behavior by the leader is most effective when a subordinate's job is unstructured.[136] Group members who have a strong need for personal growth in their jobs do not like a structured, task-oriented approach under any conditions, whereas those who have low needs for personal growth, and are content with routine, even boring, work, are indifferent to a leader's consideration behaviors.[137] Subordinates who are highly dogmatic relate better to task-oriented leaders, whereas followers who are more open respond more readily to leaders who display consideration.[138]

Although, to be effective, leadership behaviors must be appropriately matched with individual tasks and personalities in the group, consideration behaviors appear to work best when leaders deal with the group as a whole. When leaders employ consideration behaviors in their decision making (i.e., when they solicit and use advice from the group), the group's "perceptions of procedural fairness" increase, and, as a result, members' "commitment to the decision, attachment to the group, and trust in its leader" also increase.[139]

Trusted Leadership and Organizational Performance

A group's trust in its leader is important. Just as popular trust in government correlates very positively with better governing (recall Chapter 1), so it is with public leaders and their employees. When public employees trust their leaders, those leaders "preside over more productive organizations" than do less trusted leaders, "and are better able to maintain and even increase organizational outcomes in agencies challenged by low level of performance and perturbations in the external environment."[140]

"Cow Psychology"

Ultimately, some scholars who studied leaders and groups got a bit carried away. As early as the 1940s, *leadership* had morphed, startlingly, into "that relationship which is characterized by love of the members for the central person."[141]

It was, perhaps, this view that gave birth to the phrase, "cow psychology," or the disparaging term applied to a literature that seemed to treat groups as herds of cows, and "cow psychology" was how leaders herded groups in the direction they wanted. This unease translated into a new phase of leadership theory, one that concentrated on the leader's relationships with not merely the group, but the organization.

Culture and Charisma: The Leader and the Organization, 1970–Present

By the 1970s, leadership researchers were finding that whereas small-group models could, in several respects, be adapted successfully to large organizations, there were some differences.[142]

Leadership Behaviors and Organizational Cultures

One difference is the presence of *organizational culture,* or the shared mores, customs, processes, and attitudes of the organization's members. Organizational "culture affects leadership as much as leadership affects culture.... there is a constant interplay between culture and leadership."[143]

The local organizational "culture matters most" in the molding of corporate leaders—far more, in fact, than the more cosmopolitan phenomenon of professionalism. Employees who work for the same company, no matter what their jobs, are 30 percent more likely to exhibit similar leadership competencies than are employees who have the identical job, but who work in different companies.[144] Culture counts.

Transformation and Charisma

Understanding the interrelationships between organizational culture, power, and leadership leads to larger notions about leaders. During the 1970s and 1980s, theorists became fascinated with *transformational leadership,* which occurs "when one or more persons engage with others in such a way that leaders and followers raise one another to higher levels of motivation and morality."[145]

The 1980s saw a movement that extended the concept of transformational leadership to, in many ways, a resurrection of Max Weber's idea of charisma. *Charismatic leaders* are those "who by force of their personal abilities are capable of having a profound and extraordinary effect on followers.... [and charisma] is usually reserved for leaders who by their influence are able to cause followers to accomplish outstanding feats."[146] A charismatic leader is an articulate, driven, elitist entrepreneur committed to radical change who possesses an "idealized vision" of the future, and, at considerable personal risk and cost, challenges the *status quo* through unconventional means.[147] Max is back.

Does Charisma Transform? Does charisma work in the public and nonprofit sectors?

Charismatic Government At the very top of government, "personality and charisma do make a difference" in presidential performance.[148] "Strong leadership from executives with strong commitment, a vision of where they would like to go, and a willingness to take risks" correlates with countries that successfully make the wrenching transformation from socialism to capitalism.[149]

When we slip a bit further down the chain of command, the evidence blurs. Among government agencies, transformational leadership is characterized by its "ineffective implementation,"[150] bears only a scant relationship to the motivation of followers, and is "not significantly related to unit performance."[151] Hierarchical authority and poor communication associate with "a lower prevalence of transformational leadership" in government, but the presence of red tape seems "to have no effect."[152]

Within groups of government workers, charisma, for those public administrators who have it, can be effective in helping them get their way.[153] Transformational leadership does associate with greater employee creativity, but only when there is also an innovative organizational climate and employees identify positively with their leader.[154]

Independent Charisma In nonprofit settings, the findings are clearer and more upbeat.

Nonprofit workers display more "positive emotions" for transformational leaders than for transactional ones. Their workplace satisfaction is higher, they exhibit greater effort, and their organizations are more effective when transformational leaders are leading.[155]

In light of their ability to energize nonprofit employees, perhaps it should not be surprising that transformational leaders in the independent sector correlate, positively and strongly, with administrative innovation, particularly when they have "higher levels of control over employees" and are relatively new to the job.[156]

Charismatic leaders also "positively affect" the "organizational accountability"—that is, fiscal responsibility, good governance, adherence to mission, and program effectiveness—of independent organizations.[157]

Transformation or Transaction? What the research suggests is that charisma works best when charisma is what the organization needs. The more critical question, however, is one of matching the leader's behaviors with the needs of the organization.

Not all (in fact, passing few) organizations are in need of transforming change, simply because they are doing a "satisficing" job already. It is in these reasonably normal situations that transactional leadership—which rests on a civilized exchange of views and arguments—has a special place. "Good leaders help change their institutions, not through transformation and the articulation of new goals or values, but through transactions that emphasize selected values already in place and move the institution toward attaining them.... Those who espouse the importance of transformational leadership should pause to consider what life would be like in an organization whose programs, procedures, and core values could be called into question by each new president."[158]

Transactional leaders do not abjure change, but, unlike transformational leaders, they do avoid draconian change because transmogrifying revolutions can be destructive to a well-functioning organization. Effective organizational leadership, whether it is transformational or transactional, is leadership that is tailored to the conditions of the organization at the time.

LEADING THE PUBLIC AND NONPROFIT ORGANIZATION

"Despite an enormous amount of discussion about leadership in public agencies, there has been relatively little broad-scale empirical analysis."[159] Still, there is some, and it indicates that organizational leadership, as with virtually all other aspects of organizations, differs by sector.

Leadership at the Top

Boards of directors, or *trustees*, are small groups that possess legal control and form the mission of, make policy for, lead, and oversee almost all organizations. Research consistently indicates that the more committed, energetic, and able board members in every sector are, the more likely that their organizations will exhibit high performance.[160]

Aside from this commonality, however, board leadership varies widely according to sector. To better understand top leaders in the public and nonprofit sectors, it is helpful to contrast them with what we know about their counterparts in the private sector.

The Private-Sector Board We should note up front that there is big and bodacious fact about private-sector boards that is rarely, if ever, present in public- and nonprofit-sector boards, and which likely explains their unique behavior—corporate board directors get paid for their part-time service. This pay is significant, and exceeds, on average, $200,000 annually. For the highest-paid boards, compensation surpasses $400,000, with some directors topping $1 million.[161]

Without question, corporate boards accord wide powers to their CEOs, who ostensibly report to those boards. Cronyism is commonplace, and many CEOs are empowered to appoint some or all of their board's members; often they appoint themselves and their own employees.[162] More than half of the CEOs of Fortune 500 companies,[163] and about four-fifths of the CEOs "at most big companies,"[164] actually chair their own boards. One of the world's wealthiest financiers asks, "How can the chairman oversee the CEO if the job is one and the same?"[165]

Corporate board directors are actively discouraged from limiting their company's CEO even when he or she misuses power excessively. When board directors push to implement any one of four actions, each of which is recommended by the Securities and Exchange Commission as useful in protecting stockholders' interests, to restrain their CEO's authority, they experience "social distancing" by their colleagues who serve with them on other boards.[166]

These patterns have consequences. Over twenty years, the ratio between the average wage of the rank-and-file worker and the average compensation of his or her CEO soared from 1-to-42 to 1-to-535 (it has since declined to a miserly 1-to-343), and CEO compensation in the top companies now averages more than $11 million.[167] Perhaps because boards with members who are "demographically similar to the firm's CEO...result in more generous CEO compensation contracts," diversity is rare among corporate directors.[168]

Analyses consistently show that when CEOs are relatively powerful, they can keep their jobs, scapegoat underlings, and raise their own compensation even as their companies' performance sags.[169] Some boards ("too many companies to list") redefine their "executives' performance incentives when the executives' performance is so abysmal that the existing incentives become worthless." Corporate boards have been known to pay retirement benefits for CEOs who do not retire (Haliburton); approve, at its CEO's request, "employment contracts that exclude, as a ground for dismissal, certain types of felony convictions" (Tyco International); and approve CEO retention bonuses while the CEO is serving time in prison (Fog Cutter Capital Group).[170]

The Public-Sector Board Nearly all public executives report directly to boards of directors or, their rough equivalents, legislative oversight committees. These officials include parole officers, university presidents, regulatory agency administrators, executive directors of special purpose governments, superintendents of education, and county, municipal, and township managers.

As we observed in Chapter 1 (and discuss further in Chapter 11), public executives often dominate the bodies to which they nominally report. But such power is much less easily acquired in an environment in which public executives have little if any control over the selection of board members. In a deep difference with corporate and nonprofit boards, government boards almost always are appointed by legislatures or elected chief executives, or are elected directly by the people.

Public-sector boards, in contrast to those in the private and nonprofit sectors, often are composed disproportionately of energetic and myopic busybodies, nearly two-fifths of whom believe that their primary duties are either both management and policymaking or just management, as opposed to just policymaking. "Board governance is a prominent part of public administration...and it is an unusually intrusive part for public administrators who report to boards."

This verity is especially the case in local governments.

City council members are far more enthusiastic about mucking about in "administrative matters" than making policy, and this tendency is accelerating over time.[171] Many city councils are increasingly micromanaging, provincial, parochial, bloated, bickering, and balkanized bodies that give them "an image of irresponsible flakiness."[172]

"County commissioners are heavily involved in administration," with counts ranging from 44 to 80 percent of commissioners, depending on the study and the administrative area, engaging in managerial activities.[173]

Boards of education spend an astonishing 54 percent of their time on administration and only 3 percent on policy and oversight.[174] Their "greatest problem...is their tendency to micro-manage and become bogged down in minutiae."[175]

In a depressing parallel with corporate CEOs, when local governments are performing poorly, their chief administrative officers (who report to councils) often blame their top team members, who then leave these organizations at more rapid rates than their chief administrators.[176]

The Third-Sector Board The directors of the boards of public-service nonprofit organizations are difficult to recruit, tend to be middle-aged and older, and, in contrast to many public-sector boards, mostly do what they are supposed to do: That is, they are "very active" in financial oversight and policymaking, and largely uninvolved in day-to-day management. Regrettably, at least from the perspectives of the employees and missions of these organizations, their directors generally spurn fund-raising.[177]

A few boards, about a sixth, devote a disproportionately large amount of time to raising funds at the expense of their service mission.

This imbalance is more likely to occur when the organization is more financially dependent on a for-profit corporation, there is "a racial mismatch between the board and agency clientele," and the board is dominated by "economic elites."[178]

As with corporate boards, there is an unseemly coziness among nonprofit board members and their CEOs. Third-sector executive directors often serve as voting board members, and, when they do, their salaries are higher than when they do not serve on the board.[179] Sometimes this lagniappe is large, such as the salary of the president of a New York foundation that, over just five years, tripled to where it was nearing $1 million, or the family foundation in Chicago that, over five years, paid two family members more than $1 million, but donated only $175,000 to charities.[180] Boards providing their executive directors and other officers with interest-free loans and mortgages amounting to millions of dollars is a growing practice.[181] Of greater significance, when the executive director serves on the board, the organization's accountability is measurably lessened, and these organizations are less likely to have outside audits and policies concerning whistle-blowing and conflicts of interest.[182]

This is unfortunate, as conflicts of interest are often apparent. Twenty-one percent of all public-serving nonprofit organizations, and 41 percent of the large ones, report that they have engaged in "financial transactions with board members."[183]

When nonprofit boards have few members who are women but many old, prestigious men, the boards are lethargic and the executive director or board chair calls most of the shots. Conversely, when third-sector boards have a relatively large number of women and younger members who have high levels of commitment to the organization's mission, the board is dynamic and its members work effectively as a team.[184]

Sector and Successful Leadership

Just as the leadership behavior of board directors differs markedly by sector, so does that of appointed chief executives. In fact, although the research is somewhat mixed, it appears that the private, public, and nonprofit sectors hold radically differing views about what leadership, especially successful leadership, even is.

Successful Private Leadership

An effective corporate leader is concerned with details; persistent; diligent; not a particularly good communicator;[185] analytic; resolute; dependable; diffident;[186] conscientious; emotionally stable; not especially flexible or open,[187] but considerate and trusting of colleagues and subordinates; wants "to have an impact" and to "exert strong positive or negative emotions in others";[188] usually lawful, but casually so; unhelpful; directive; and goal-driven.[189]

Private-sector leaders are not seen by their superiors and subordinates as being particularly successful when they monitor subordinates for legal compliance and when they provide assistance to subordinates (indeed, even *subordinates* feel that their leaders' mentoring of them does not add to their leaders' luster). When corporate leaders emphasize directing and coordinating their companies, however, their superiors and subordinates perceive them as much more effective. Leaders in the business world place great emphasis on the achievement of organizational objectives as a measure of their own effectiveness.[190] Ironically, when private-sector leaders grow more "public" through fame and recognition, they become less effective leaders as measured by their corporations' performance.[191]

Successful Public Leadership

We know less about public leaders than corporate ones.

We do know that there are some similarities: Public and private managers display virtually identical "power-motivation behavior," or the desire to make an impact and enhance one's position.[192] In this, public administrators are at a disadvantage, as administrators in *both* sectors agree that leaders in the public sector have considerably less discretion and authority to lead than their private-sector counterparts.[193]

There are additional differences as well. In contrast to the private sector, successful public leadership is more desirous of change (and, as we explained in Chapter 4, it is better than private leadership in achieving it[194]), organizational growth, and new projects; personally competitive, placing a premium on

outperforming "someone else" by surpassing "some self-imposed standard of excellence";[195] lawful; helpful; and nondirective.[196]

When government leaders stress directing and coordinating their agency, their superiors and subordinates perceive them as being much less effective.[197] Public executives, on average, "are evaluated as better transactional leaders" than transformational ones;[198] are viewed by both their superiors and subordinates as successful when they closely monitor their subordinates' work for legal compliance; and when they reach out to lend a helping hand to their fellow workers.[199]

Helping their employees is exceptionally important to public-sector leaders. Federal executives score "substantially better" in their consideration behaviors than on other measures.[200] An astounding 78 percent of city managers have a "primary leadership style" (out of four possible styles) that is "high supportive and low directed behavior."[201] Public executives are deeply committed to mentoring coworkers and giving them the freedom to grow and mature in their jobs, and their coworkers respond very favorably to this treatment.[202]

The most effective leaders in the high-stress fields of first responders, law enforcers, and social workers are "affective leaders" who are skilled in "emotional labor" that involves relationships and rapport, compassion and connectedness. "Emotional labor is inherent in effective public service."[203]

Unlike business leaders, public leaders do not perceive that there is much of a match between their leadership abilities and actually accomplishing their agency's goals.[204] This distinction may be ascribed to at least two possibilities.

One is that many agencies already are fully accomplishing their goals. For example, only a slim 6 percent of the dollars[205] that federal agencies send out in the form of more than 191 *million* checks and payments *every month*[206] are miscalculated or sent to an incorrect recipient. Even though this success rate meets any reasonable standard of mission fulfillment, Congress and the agencies are actively working to eliminate these improper payments altogether.[207]

The other is the fact that, as research long has shown, agency missions are saturated by a "pervasive vagueness" compared with crisp corporate ones.[208] Small wonder, perhaps, that top public executives are "consistently, and often dramatically, more optimistic" about their agencies' organizational successes than are lower-placed agency workers,[209] agency clients, and other outside stakeholders.[210] When organizational success itself cannot be readily understood, a condition that is common in the public sector, then leadership's success, when defined in organizational terms, is far less tenable. Thus, in the public sector, successful leadership is cast in human terms.

Successful Nonprofit Leadership Many organizations in the independent sector also have pervasively vague missions and emulate public organizations in that leadership's effectiveness can be difficult to demonstrate. Beyond that similarity, however, nonprofit organizations appear to be unique in their receptivity to transformational leaders. As we observed earlier, in third-sector settings, transactional leaders correlate with more engaged employees, greater accountability, and heightened organizational productivity.[211]

Where nonprofit leaders seem to differ with both private and public leaders is in their views of what leadership roles their boards of directors should play. In contrast to the CEOs in the private sector, and to top administrators in the public one, the chief executives of nonprofit organizations place relatively little emphasis on involving their boards in "strategy and planning," "financial oversight," "policy oversight," providing "guidance and expertise" to the organization, or even cultivating a good "relationship" between themselves and their board members. Instead, 55 percent of top nonprofit executives rank "fund development" first out of thirteen "key roles" that their boards should play; no other role gains even close to half.[212]

Public Leadership: Vision, Communication, and Dedication

The literature of organizational leadership can be reduced to a practical formula for the public administrator: Leadership equals vision, communication, and dedication.[213]

Vision as Vexation *Vision*—"the presentation of an alternative future to the status quo"[214]—is not all that easily formed in the public sector, where both the *status quo* and the agency's future are legislated. As we describe in Chapter 9, it seems of greater importance that public agencies, at least at the federal level, are increasingly likely to be headed by short-term political appointees, and rarely are such executives visionaries.

Career public administrators, by contrast, often do have a vision for their agency, but are frequently fated to be "number twos," not "number ones." "And 'number twos' do not have visions, or at least, do not go around shouting about them."[215]

Communication as Conundrum Communicating the vision can also be more difficult in the public sector than in the private one. Not only does the "number two" phenomenon impair communication, but so does much of the traditional lore of the public administrator—for instance, the need to be "neutral," to be "removed from politics" (and politics are, in essence, communication), and, to recall Louis Brownlow's famous dictum, to cultivate "a passion for anonymity."[216] These values have not enhanced the propensity of leaders of public organizations to communicate their vision of an alternative future, although many public administrators nonetheless have done so, and quite effectively.[217]

Professionalism as Passion The third component of leadership is hard work, and here many public administrators excel. Consider James Forrestal, who, when secretary of defense, "worked with his staff seven days straight. When he left his office at 10:30 p.m. on Sunday, he told them to have a nice weekend."[218]

Vision, communication, work. These are the elements of leadership, irrespective of sector. Nevertheless, in government, they seem to have their own, unique grandeur.

NOTES

1. To cite just one example of many in this research: Marc Buelens and Herman Van den Broek, "An Analysis of Work Motivation between Public and Private Sector Organizations," *Public Administration Review* 67 (January/February 2007), pp. 65–72.

2. U.S. Office of Personnel Management, *Federal Employee Viewpoint Survey, 2010* (Washington, DC: U.S. Government Printing Office, 2010), pp. 31, 40.

3. Richard W. Stackman, Patrick E. Connor, and Boris W. Becker, "Sectoral Ethos: An Investigation of the Personal Values Systems of Female and Male Managers in the Public and Private Sectors," *Journal of Public Administration Research and Theory* 16 (October 2006), pp. 577–597. The quotation is on p. 577. This is a study of 884 public- and private-sector managers.

4. David Card, Alexandre Mas, Enrico Moretti, *et al.*, *Inequality at Work: The Effect of Peer Salaries on Job Satisfaction*, NBER Working Paper No. 16396 (Cambridge, MA: National Bureau of Economic Research, 2010), p. 1. This is study of employees of the University of California.

5. J. Stuart Bunderson and Jeffery A. Thompson, "The Call of the Wild: Zookeepers, Callings, and the Double-edged Sword of Meaningful Work," *Administrative Science Quarterly* 54 (March 2009), pp. 32–57. The quotations are on p. 32.

6. Princeton Survey Research Associates and Brookings Institution, *Health of the Public Service* (Washington, DC: Authors, 2001), http://www.brook.edu, p. 4. Figures are for 2001.

7. Donald P. Moynihan and Sanjay K. Pandey, "The Role of Organizations in Fostering Public Service Motivation," *Public Administration Review* 67 (January/February 2007), pp. 40–53.

8. Leonard Bright, "Public Employees with High Levels of Public Service Motivation: Who Are They, Where Are They, and What Do They Want?" *Review of Public Personnel Administration* 25 (June 2005), pp. 138–154. This is a study of 349 responding employees in twelve major departments in a large county government in Oregon.

9. Mary K. Feeney, "Sector Perceptions among State-Level Public Managers," *Journal of Public Administration Research and Theory* 18 (July 2008), pp. 465–494. This is a study of public administrators in Georgia and Illinois.

10. Gene A. Brewer, "Building Social Capital: Attitudes and Behavior of Public Servants," *Journal of Public Administration Research and Theory* 13 (January 2003), pp. 5–20. The quotation is on p. 5.

11. David J. Houston, Patricia K. Freeman, and David L. Feldman, "How Naked Is the Public Square? Religion, Public Service, and Implications for Public Administration," *Public Administration Review* 68 (May/June 2008), pp. 428–458.

12. David J. Houston and Katherine E. Cartwright, "Spirituality and Public Service," *Public Administration Review* 67 (January/February 2007), pp. 88–102.

13. David J. Houston, "'Walking the Walk' of Public Service Motivation: Public Employees and Charitable Gifts of Time, Blood, and Money," *Journal of Public Administration Research and Theory* 16 (January 2006), pp. 67–86.

14. Princeton Survey Research Associates and the Brookings Institution, *Health of the Public Service*, p. 4. Figure is for 2001.

15. U.S. Merit Systems Protection Board, *In Search of Highly Skilled Workers: A Study on the Hiring of Upper Level Employees from Outside the Federal Government* (Washington, DC: U.S. Government Printing Office, 2008), p. 29. Figure, 47 percent, is for 2006.

16. U.S. Protection Board, *Attracting the Next Generation: A Look at Federal Entry-Level New Hires* (Washington, DC: U.S. Government Printing Office, 2008), p. 35. Figure is for 2006.

17. Young-joo Lee and Vicky M. Wilkins, "More Similarities or More Differences? Comparing Public and Nonprofit Managers' Job Motivations," *Public Administration Review* 71 (January/February 2011), pp. 45–56. This is a study of public and nonprofit managers in Georgia and Illinois.

18. Brookings Institution, *Winning the Talent War: New Brookings Survey Finds the Nonprofit Sector Has the Most Dedicated Workforce* (Washington, DC: Author, 2002), p. 2.

19. Philip H. Mirvis and Edward J. Hackett, "Work and Work Force Characteristics in the Nonprofit Sector," *Monthly Labor Review* 106 (April 1983), pp. 3–12. Data (pp. 7, 10) are for 1977.

20. Brookings Institution, *Winning the Talent War,* p. 2.

21. Houston, "'Walking the Walk' of Public Service Motivation"; and Lee and Wilkins, "More Similarities or More Differences?"

22. Herbert A. Simon, *Models of Man, Social and Rational* (New York: John Wiley and Sons, 1957).

23. Robert K. Merton, "Bureaucratic Structure and Personality," *Social Forces* 18 (May 1940), pp. 560–568. The quotations are on p. 563.

24. Leisha DeHart-Davis, "The Unbureaucratic Personality," *Public Administration Review* 67 (September/October 2007), pp. 892–903.

25. David S. Kassel, "Performance, Accountability, and the Debate over Rules," *Public Administration Review* 68 (March/April 2008), pp. 241–252.

26. Hal G. Rainey, "Public Agencies and Private Firms: Incentive Structures, Goals, and Individual Roles," *Administration & Society* 15 (August 1983), pp. 207–242,

27. Hal G. Rainey, Carol Traut, and Barry Blunt, "Reward Expectancies and Other Work-Related Attitudes in Public and Private Organizations: A Review and Extension," Paper presented at the 1985 Annual Meeting of the American Political Science Association (New Orleans, August 29–September 1, 1985), p. 9.

28. Robert T. Golembiewski, Robert A. Boudreau, Ben-Chu Sun, *et al.,* "Estimates of Burnout in Public Agencies: Worldwide, How Many Employees Have Which Degrees of Burnout, and With What Consequences?" *Public Administration Review* 58 (January/February 1998), pp. 59–64.

29. Tobin Im, "An Exploratory Study of Time Stress and Its Causes among Government Employees," *Public Administration Review* 69 (January/February 2009), pp. 104–115. The quotation is on p. 112.

30. Barry Z. Posner and Warren H. Schmidt, "The Values of Business and Federal Government Executives: More Different than Alike," *Public Personnel Management* 25 (Fall 1996), pp. 277–290. About 1,100 federal and business executives were surveyed.

31. Mirvis and Hackett, "Work and Work Force Characteristics in the Nonprofit Sector," p. 10. Data are for 1977.

32. Karlyn Brown, *Attitudes About Work and Leisure in America* (Washington, DC: American Enterprise Institute, 2001). The report covers surveys conducted 1972–2000.

33. Linda Barrington and Lynn Franco, *I Can't Get No…Job Satisfaction, That Is*, Report No. R-1459-09-RR (New York: The Conference Board, 2010). Americans' job satisfaction declined from 61 to 45 percent, 1987–2009.

34. Brown, *Attitudes About Work and Leisure in America.*

35. E. A. Locke, "The Nature and Causes of Job Satisfaction," *Handbook of Industrial and Organizational Psychology*, M. D. Dunnette, ed. (New York: Wiley, 1983), pp. 486–503. This is an analysis of about 3,500 studies.

36. Carole A. Jurkiewicz, Tom K. Massey, Jr., and Roger G. Brown, "Motivation in Public and Private Organizations: A Comparative Study," *Public Productivity & Management Review* 21 (March 1998), pp. 230–250. The quotation is on p. 325.

37. Eran Vigoda-Gadot and Galit Meisler, "Emotions in Management and the Management of Emotions: The Impact of Emotional Intelligence and Organizational Politics on Public Sector Employees," *Public Administration Review* 70 (January/February 2010), pp. 72–86. This is a study of municipal employees in two Israeli cities.

38. Frank T. Paine, Stephen J. Carroll, and Burt A. Leete, "Need Satisfactions of Managerial Personnel in a Government Agency," *Journal of Applied Psychology* 50 (June 1966), pp. 247–249.

39. U.S. Merit Systems Protection Board, *The Federal Government: A Model Employer or a Work in Progress? Perspectives from 25 Years of the Merit Principles Survey* (Washington, DC: U.S. Government Printing Office, 2008), p. 20; and U.S. Office of Personnel Management, *Federal Employee Viewpoint Survey, 2010*, p. 39. The percentages range from 67 to 75 percent, 1986–2010.

40. U.S. Office of Personnel Management, *Federal Employee Viewpoint Survey, 2010,* p. 29.

41. Warren H. Schmidt and Barry Z. Posner, "Values and Expectations of City Managers in California," *Public Administration Review* 47 (September/October 1987), pp. 404–409. The figure is on p. 408.

42. U.S. Office of Personnel Management, *Federal Employee Viewpoint Survey, 2010*, p. 41.

43. Samantha L. Durst and Victor S. DeSantis, "The Determinants of Job Satisfaction among Federal, State, and Local Government Employees," *State and Local Government Review* 29 (Winter 1997), pp. 7–16; and Hal G. Rainey, "Perceptions of Incentives in Business and Government: Implications for Civil Service Reform," *Public Administration Review* 39 (September/October 1979), pp. 440–448.

44. Durst and DeSantis, "The Determinants of Job Satisfaction among Federal, State, and Local Government Employees."

45. Brookings Institution, *Winning the Talent War*, p. 2; and Durst and DeSantis, "The Determinants of Job Satisfaction among Federal, State, and Local Government Employees," p. 12. Emphasis added.

46. Rainey, "Perceptions of Incentives in Business and Government."

47. Card, Mas, Moretti, *et al.*, *Inequality at Work.*

48. U.S. Merit Systems Protection Board, *Accomplishing Our Mission: Results of the Merit Principles Survey 2005* (Washington, DC: U.S. Government Printing Office, 2007), p. 54.

49. U.S. Office of Personnel Management, *Federal Employee Viewpoint Survey, 2010*, p. 41.

50. Posner and Schmidt, "The Values of Business and Federal Government Executives," p. 284.

51. Buelens and Van den Broeck, "An Analysis of Differences in Work of Motivation between Public and Private Sector Organizations," pp. 65–74.

52. James L. Perry and Lyman W. Porter, "Factors Affecting the Context for Motivation for Public Organizations," *Academy of Management Review* 7 (January 1982), pp. 89–98. The quotation is on p. 96.

53. U.S. Office of Personnel Management, *Poor Performers in Government: A Quest for the True Story* (Washington, DC: U.S. Government Printing Office, 1999), p. 36.

54. Light, "The Content of Their Character," p. 15.

55. Jed Devaro and Dana Brookshire, "Promotions and Incentives in Nonprofit and For-Profit Organizations," *Industrial & Labor Relations Review* 60 (April 2007), pp. 311–339.

56. James R. Rawls, Robert A. Ulrich, and Oscar T. Nelson, "A. Comparison of Managers Entering or Reentering the Profit and Nonprofit Sectors," *Academy of Management Journal* 18 (September 1975), pp. 616–622.

57. Ibid.; and Light, "The Content of Their Character."

58. Sean T. Lyons, Linda E. Duxbury, and Christopher A. Higgins, "A Comparison of the Values and Commitment of Private Sector, Public Sector, and Parapublic Sector Employees," *Public Administration Review* 66 (July/August 2006), pp. 605–618. The quotations are on p. 605. This is a study of 549 "knowledge workers" in all three sectors.

59. Dennis Wittmer, "Serving the People or Serving for Pay: Reward Preferences Among Government, Hybrid Sector, and Business Managers," *Public Productivity & Management Review* 14 (Summer 1991), pp. 369–383.

60. The following discussion is drawn from the massive research of Frank U. Sulloway, *Born to Rebel* (New York: Little, Brown, 1997).

61. Lisa A. Keister, "Sharing the Wealth: The Effects of Siblings on Adults' Wealth Ownership," *Demography* 40 (August 2003), pp. 521–542.

62. Erik H. Erikson, *Childhood and Society* (New York: Norton, 1950), pp. 219–234. The quotations are on pp. 224–226, 231, 233. Erikson, perhaps the most well known of the adult psychologists, does not segment adult development by age spans as we do in the text, but we doubt that most readers could easily identify with some of the terms that he uses instead, such as "muscular-anal" and "locomotor-genital."

63. Ibid. This extra effort often benefits, in Erikson's view, from intense psychoanalysis.

64. Yang Yang, "Social Inequalities in Happiness in the United States, 1972–2004: An Age-Period Cohort Analysis," *American Sociological Review* 73 (April 2008), pp. 204–226. This is likely the single best study on happiness.

65. U.S. Merit Systems Protection Board, *Managing for Engagement—Communication, Connection, and Courage* (Washington, DC: U.S. Government Printing Office, 2009), p. 2.

66. Ibid.

67. Daniel J. Levinson, *et al.*, *The Seasons of a Man's Life* (New York: Alfred A. Knopf, 1978), p. 79.

68. George E. Vaillant, *Adaptation to Life* (Boston: Little, Brown, 1977).

69. Ibid., p. 228.

70. Levinson, *et al.*, *The Seasons of a Man's Life*, p. 320.

71. Roger Gould, *Transformations: Growth and Change in Adult Life* (New York: Simon and Schuster, 1978), p. 294.

72. Vaillant, *Adaptation to Life,* p. 234.

73. Michael Maccoby, *The Leader* (New York: Simon & Schuster, 1981), p. 221.

74. Manfred F. R. Kets De Vries, "Organizational Sleepwalkers: Emotional Distress at Mid-Life," *Human Relations* 52 (November 1999), pp. 1377–1401.

75. Manfred F. R. Kets de Vries, Danny Miller, *et al.*, "Using the Life Cycle to Anticipate Satisfaction at Work," *Journal of Forecasting* 3 (Spring 1984), pp. 161–172.

76. Vaillant, *Adaptation to Life.*

77. Kets de Vries, Miller, *et al.*, "Using the Life Cycle to Anticipate Satisfaction at Work."

78. Ruth Kanfer and Phillip L. Ackerman, "Aging, Adult Development, and Work Motivation," *Academy of Management Review* 29 (July 2004), pp. 44–448. The quotation is on p. 450.

79. U.S. Merit Systems Protection Board, *Managing for Engagement*, p. 2.

80. Geert Hofstede, "Motivation, Leadership, and Organization: Do American Theories Apply Abroad?" *Organizational Dynamics* 9 (Summer 1980), pp. 42–63. The quotation is on p. 43.

81. The following discussion is drawn from Geert Hofstede, *Culture's Consequences: International Differences in Work-Related Values* (Beverly Hills, CA: Sage, 1980); and Geert Hofstede, "Cultural Constraints in Management Theories," *Academy of Management Executive* 7 (January 1993), pp. 21–32. There are several useful Websites devoted to "Geert Hofstede" and his research that may be quickly Googled.

82. Hofstede, "Motivation, Leadership, and Organization," p. 54.

83. Allensbach Opinion Research Institute, National Opinion Research Center, and Pew Research Center for the People and the Press, as cited in "A Nation Apart," *The Economist* (November 6, 2003), http://www.economist.

com. Data are for 2003. France, Italy, Germany, the United Kingdom, and the United States were surveyed.

84. German Marshall Fund, *Transatlantic Trends: Key Findings 2006* (Washington, DC: Author, 2006), p. 15; and German Marshall Fund survey as cited in Robert Kagan, "Staying the Course, Win or Lose," *Washington Post* (November 2, 2006). The first source reports that 24 percent of respondents in twelve European nations and 34 percent of Americans "support military force to promote democracy," and the second source states that "Europeans disagree, and by a 2 to 1 margin," that "under some conditions, war is necessary to obtain justice," but 78 percent of Americans agree with the statement.

85. Hofstede, "Motivation, Leadership, and Organization," p. 58.

86. Marit Skivenes and Sissel Trygstad, "When Whistle-Blowing Works: The Norwegian Case," *Human Relations* 63 (July 2010), pp. 1071–1097. The quotation is on p. 1071. Norway is also a feminine, risk-taking (weak uncertainty avoidance) culture, dimensions that also may correlate with more whistle blowing and better results from it.

87. Hofstede, "Motivation, Leadership, and Organization," p. 57.

88. Jennifer Loh, Simon Lloyd D. Restubog, and Thomas J. Zagenczyk, "Consequences of Workplace Bullying on Employee Identification and Satisfaction among Australians and Singaporeans," *Journal of Cross-Cultural Psychology* 41 (March 2010), pp. 236–252.

89. Mark F. Peterson, Peter B. Smith, Adebowale Akande, *et al.*, "Role Conflict, Ambiguity, and Overload: A 21-Nation Study," *Academy of Management Journal* 38 (April 1995), pp. 429–452.

90. Michael Crozier, *The Bureaucratic Phenomenon* (Chicago: University of Chicago Press, 1964).

91. Ibid., p. 236.

92. Thomas W. H. Ng, Kelly L. Sorensen, and Frederick K. K. Yim, "Does the Job Satisfaction—Job Performance Relationship Vary across Cultures?" *Journal of Cross-Cultural Psychology* 40 (September 2009), pp. 761–796.

93. Dwaine Marvick, *Career Perspectives in a Bureaucratic Setting*, University of Michigan Governmental Studies, No. 27 (Ann Arbor, MI: University of Michigan Press, 1954).

94. Alvin W. Gouldner, "Cosmopolitans and Locals: Toward an Analysis of Latent Social Roles," *Administrative Science Quarterly* 2 (December 1957 and March 1958), pp. 281–306 and 444–480, respectively.

95. Marvick, *Career Perspectives in a Bureaucratic Setting*, p. 28.

96. Lee and Wilkins, "More Similarities or More Differences?" p. 45.

97. Ibid.

98. Marvick, *Career Perspectives in a Bureaucratic Setting*, p. 134.

99. Ibid., p. 145.

100. Bernard M. Bass, *Stogdill's Handbook of Leadership*, rev. ed. (New York: Free Press, 1981), p. 7. The word "leadership" first appeared in the late nineteenth century, and then only in writings about the British parliament.

101. As derived from data in Joseph C. Rost, *Leadership for the Twenty-first Century* (New York: Praeger, 1991), p. 46. There is no sign that this literary gusher is abating.

102. Bernard M. Bass, *Stogdill's Handbook of Leadership: Theory, Research, and Managerial Applications,* 3rd ed. (New York: Free Press, 1990). Figure is an estimate. Bass counted more than 7,800 published studies of leadership as of the late 1980s, so our estimate likely is conservative.

103. "American Survey: The Leadership Thing," *The Economist* (December 9, 1995), p. 31.

104. Rost, *Leadership for the Twenty-first Century*, p. 10. Figure is for circa 1910–1990.

105. James MacGregor Burns, *Leadership* (New York: Harper and Row, 1978), p. 2.

106. Rost, *Leadership for the Twenty-first Century*, p. 102.

107. Ibid., p. 143.

108. John P. Kotter, "What Leaders Really Do," *Harvard Business Review* 68 (May/June 1990), pp. 103–111. The quotation is on p. 104.

109. Ibid., p. 104.

110. Henry Mintzberg, *The Nature of Managerial Work* (New York: Harper & Row, 1973).

111. Alan W. Lau, Arthur R. Newman, and Laurie A. Broedling, "The Nature of Managerial Work in the Public Sector," *Public Administration Review* 40 (September/October 1980), p. 519. The researchers studied 370 top-level civilian executives in the U.S. Navy.

112. Victor A. Thompson, *Modern Organizations* (New York: Knopf, 1961).

113. Ibid.

114. Thomas R. Dye, "Executive Power and Public Policy in the States," *Western Political Quarterly* 27 (December 1969), pp. 73–82. The quotation is on p. 938.

115. G. R. Salancik and Jeffrey Pfeffer, "Constraints on Administrative Discretion: The Limited Influence of Mayors on City Budgets," *Urban Affairs Quarterly* 12 (April 1977), pp. 475–498. This is an analysis of the budgets of big American cities over seventeen years.

116. Eleanor Fujita, *The Evaluation of College Presidents: Dimensions Used by Campus Leaders* (College Park, MD: National Center for Postsecondary Governance and Finance, 1990), p. 20.

117. Anna Neumann and Estela M. Bensimon, *Constructing the Presidency: College Presidents' Images of Their Leadership Roles, A Comparative Study* (College Park, MD: National Center for Postsecondary Governance and Finance, 1990), pp. 19–20. Emphasis added.

118. Jitendra V. Singh, David J. Tucker, and Robert J. House, "Organizational Legitimacy and the Liability of Newness," *Administrative Science Quarterly* 31 (June 1986), pp. 171–193. This is an investigation of 389 newly-founded, non-profit social service organizations in metropolitan Toronto.

119. Stanley Lieberson and James F. O'Connor, "Leadership and Organizational Performance: A Study of Large Corporations," *American Sociological Review* 37 (August 1972), pp. 117–130.

120. Gregory C. Hill, "Organizational Performance: A Study of Professional Baseball Managers," *Social Science Journal* 46 (September 2009), pp. 557–570. The quotation is on p. 557.

121. Jessica Word and Sung Min Park, "Working across the Divide: Job Involvement in the Public and Nonprofit Sectors," *Review of Public Personnel Administration* 29 (June 2009), pp. 103–133. The quotation is on p. 126.

122. Tracey Trottier, Montgomery Van Wart, and XiaoHu Wang, "Examining the Nature and Significance of Leadership in Government Organizations," *Public Administration Review*

68 (March/April 2008), pp. 319–333. The quotation is on p. 329. This is an analysis of 100,657 respondents to the 2002 Federal Human Capital Survey.

123. John Crum, "Improving the Performance of Federal Supervisors," *Issues of Merit* (Washington, DC: U.S. Merit Systems Protection Board, April 2010), pp. 2–3. The quotation is on p. 2.

124. Michael McGuire and Chris Silvia, "Does Leadership in Networks Matter? Examining the Effects of Leadership Behaviors on Managers' Perceptions of Network Effectiveness," *Public Performance & Management Review* 33 (September 2009), pp. 34–62. The quotation is on p. 54. This is national survey of county emergency managers.

125. Claudia N. Avellaneda, "Mayoral Quality and Local Public Finance," *Public Administration Review* 69 (May/June 2009), pp. 469–486. The quotation is on p. 469. This is an analysis of forty Colombian municipalities and their elected mayors, 2000–2004.

126. Rhys Andrews and George A. Boyne, "Capacity, Leadership, and Organizational Performance: Testing the Black Box Model of Public Management," *Public Administration Review* 70 (May/June 2010), pp. 443–453. The quotation is on p. 450. This is a study of local governments in England.

127. Crum, "Improving the Performance of Federal Supervisors," p. 2.

128. Rost, *Leadership for the Twenty-first Century*, p. 28.

129. Quoted in Ibid., p. 47.

130. Daniel Katz and Robert L. Kahn, *The Social Psychology of Organizations* (New York: Wiley, 1966).

131. Ralph M. Stodgill, "Personal Factors Associated with Leadership: A Survey of the Literature," *Journal of Psychology* 25 (June 1948), pp. 35–71.

132. Kurt Lewin, Ronald Lippitt, and Ralph K. White, "Patterns of Aggressive Behavior in Experimentally Created Social Climates," *Journal of Social Psychology* 10 (March 1939), pp. 271–299.

133. E. S. Bogardus, *Leaders and Leadership* (New York: Appleton-Century, 1934), p. 3.

134. Fred E. Fiedler, *A Theory of Leadership Effectiveness* (New York: McGraw-Hill, 1967).

135. Michael J. Strube and Joseph E. Garcia, "A Meta-Analytical Investigation of Fiedler's Contingency Model of Leadership Effectiveness," *Psychological Bulletins* 90 (September 1981), pp. 307–321.

136. Robert J. House, "A Path-Goal Theory of Leadership," *Administrative Science Quarterly* 16 (September 1971), pp. 321–338.

137. Ricky N. Griffin, "Relationships Among Individual Task Design, and Leader Behavior Variables," *Academy of Management Journal* 23 (December 1980), pp. 665–683.

138. Stanley E. Weed, Terrance R. Mitchell, and William Moffitt, "Leadership Style, Subordinate's Personality, and Task Type as Predictors of Performance and Satisfaction With Supervision," *Journal of Applied Psychology* 61 (February 1976), pp. 58–66.

139. M. Audrey Korsgaard, David M. Schweiger, and Harry J. Sapienza, "Building Commitment, Attachment, and Trust in Strategic Decision-Making Teams: The Role of Procedural Justice," *Academy of Management Journal* 38 (February 1995), pp. 60–85. The quotation is on p. 60.

140. Yoon Jik Cho and Evan J. Ringquist, "Managerial Trustworthiness and Organizational Outcomes," *Journal of Public Administration Research and Theory* 21 (January 2011), pp. 53–86. The quotation is on p. 53. This is an analysis of federal managers.

141. Fred Redl, "Group Emotion and Leadership," *Psychiatry* 5 (November 1942), pp. 574–584. The quotation is on p. 576.

142. Burns, *Leadership*.

143. Bernard M. Bass and Bruce J. Avolio, "Transformational Leadership and Organizational Culture," *Public Administration Quarterly* 17 (Spring 1993), pp. 112–122. The quotation is on p. 113.

144. Thomas Kell and Gregory T. Carrott, "Culture Matters Most," *Harvard Business Review* 83 (May 2005), pp. 22–24. This is an analysis of more than 100 corporations.

145. Burns, *Leadership*, p. 20.

146. Robert J. House, "A 1976 Theory of Charismatic Leadership," *Leadership: The Cutting Edge*, James G. Hunt and Lars Larson, eds. (Carbondale, IL: Southern Illinois University Press, 1977), pp. 189–207. The quotation is on p. 196.

147. Jay A. Conger and Rabinda N. Kanungo, "Toward a Behavioral Theory of Charismatic

Leadership in Organizational Settings," *Academy of Management Review* 12 (November 1987), pp. 637–647.

148. Robert J. House, William D. Spangler, and James Woycke, "Personality and Charisma in the U.S. Presidency: A Psychological Theory of Leader Effectiveness," *Administrative Science Quarterly* 36 (September 1991), pp. 364–396. The quotation is on p. 364. This is a study of thirty-nine presidents, from George Washington through Ronald Reagan.

149. John Williams and Stephen Haggard, "The Political Conditions for Economic Reform," *The Political Economy of Policy Reform*, John Williamson, ed. (Washington, DC: Institute for International Economics, 1993), pp. 525–599. The quotation is on p. 539. This is an analysis of thirteen, previously socialist, countries that were in the process of transforming their economies to a free-market footing.

150. Graeme Currie and Andy Lockett, "A Critique of Transformational Leadership: Moral, Professional and Contingent Dimensions of Leadership within Public Services Organizations," *Human Relations* 60 (February 2007), pp. 341–371. The quotation is on p. 341. This is an analysis of secondary schools in England.

151. Mansour Javidan and David A. Waldman, "Exploring Charismatic Leadership in the Public Sector: Measurement and Consequences," *Public Administration Review* 63 (March/April 2003), pp. 229–242. The quotation is on p. 229. This is an analysis of more than 200 middle- and upper-middle managers in the Canadian public service.

152. Bradley E. Wright and Sanjay K. Pandey, "Transformational Leadership in the Public Sector: Does Structure Matter?" *Journal of Public Administration Research and Theory* 20 (January 2010), pp. 75–89. The quotations are on p. 85. This is national a study of 1,322 responding city managers and department heads.

153. Jason L. Jensen, "Getting One's Way in Group Decision-Making: Influence Tactics Used in Group Decision-Making Settings," *Public Administration Review* 67 (March/April 2007), pp. 216–227. This is an experiment involving of fifty-one public administrators.

154. Peng Wang and Joseph Rode, "Transformational Leadership and Follower Creativity: The Moderating Effects of Identification with Leader

and Organizational Climate," *Human Relations* 63 (August 2010), pp. 1105–1128. This is a study of a "diverse sample of 212 employees and their immediate supervisors" in fifty-five organizations.

155. Anette Rohmann, "Relationships between Leadership Styles and Followers' Emotional Experience and Effectiveness in the Voluntary Sector," *Nonprofit & Voluntary Sector Quarterly* 38 (April 2009), pp. 270–286. This is a study of 288 German singers and their choir directors.

156. Kristina Jaskyte, "Predictors of Administrative and Technological Innovations in Nonprofit Organizations," *Public Administration Review* 71 (January/February 2011), pp. 77–86. The quotation is on p. 84.

157. Bobbi Watt Geer, Jill K. Maher, and Michele T. Cole, "Managing Nonprofit Organizations: The Importance of Transformational Leadership and Commitment to Operating Standards for Nonprofit Accountability," *Public Performance & Management Review* 32 (September 2008), pp. 51–75. The quotations are on p. 68. This is survey of eighty-five responding nonprofit leaders in Pennsylvania.

158. Robert Birnbaum, *How Academic Leadership Works: Understanding Success and Failure in the College Presidency* (San Francisco: Jossey-Bass, 1992), pp. 30–31

159. Trottier, Van Wart, and Wang, "Examining the Nature and Significance of Leadership in Government Organizations," p. 329.

160. There is a spate of research that supports this statement, but the following five-year study examined twenty-nine for-profit corporate boards, six nonprofit boards, and four boards of government-owned enterprises, and came to the same conclusion. See Richard Leblanc and James Gillies, *Inside the Boardroom* (Mississauga, Canada: Wiley, 2005).

161. "Directors: Feeding at the Trough," *Fortune* (January 18, 2010), p. 20. In 2008, board directors of 491 large companies were paid an average of $213,000, and the highest-paid directors in twenty-three companies earned between $400,000 and $1.6 million.

162. See, for example, M. J. Conyon and Simon L. Peck, "Board Control, Remuneration Committees and Top Management Compensation," *Academy of Management Journal* 41 (April 1998), pp. 146–157.

163. Carl C. Icahn, "Corporate Boards That Do Their Job," *Washington Post* (February 16, 2009).

164. Jonathan D. Glater and David Leonhardt, "Bill Addressing Business Fraud Is Seen As First Step," *New York Times* (July 25, 2002).

165. Icahn, "Corporate Boards That Do Their Job."

166. James D. Westphal and Poonam Khanna, "Keeping Directors in Line: Social Distancing as a Corporate Control Mechanism in the Corporate Elite," *Administrative Science Quarterly* 48 (September 2003), pp. 361–398. This is a study of more than 1,000 board directors.

167. Executive PayWatch, *Trends in CEO Pay*, http://www.aflcio.org/corporatewatch/paywatch/pay/. Figures are averages for CEOs of Standard & Poor's 500 companies. Trend figures are for 1980–2010. Current ratio is for 2010.

168. James D. Westphal and Edward J. Zajac, "Who Shall Govern? CEO/Board Power, Demographic Similarity, and New Director Selection," *Administrative Science Quarterly*, 40 (March 1995), pp. 55–71.

169. See, for example, Lucia Bebchuk and Jesse Fried, *Pay without Performance: The Unfulfilled Promise of Executive Compensation* (Cambridge, MA: Harvard University Press, 2004).

170. David Owen, "The Pay Problem," *The New Yorker* (October 12, 2009), pp. 58–63. The quotations are on p. 61.

171. James H. Svara, "The Shifting Boundaries between Elected Officials in Large Council-Manager Cities," *Public Administration Review* 59 (January/February 1999), pp. 44–53.

172. Rob Gurwit, "Are City Councils a Relic of the Past?" *Governing* (April 2003), pp. 20–24. The quotation is on p. 21.

173. James H. Svara, "Leadership and Professionalism in County Government," *The American County: Frontiers of Knowledge*, Donald C. Menzel, ed. (Tuscaloosa, AL: University of Alabama Press, 1996), pp. 109–127. The quotation is on p. 118.

174. Lynn Olson and Ann Bradley, "Boards of Contention," *Education Week Special Journal Report* (April 29, 1992), pp. 30–39. This is a five-year study of all the school boards in West Virginia.

175. Ellen Todras, *The Changing Role of School Boards*, ERIC Digest No. 84 (Eugene, OR: Eric Clearinghouse on Educational Management, May 1993), p. 1.

176. George A. Boyne, Oliver James, Peter John, et al., "Does Public Service Performance Affect Top Management Turnover?" *Journal of Public Administration Research and Theory* 20, Supplement 2 (April 2010), pp. i261–i279. This is a study of 148 English local governments conducted over four years.

177. Robert D. Herman, "Are Public Service Nonprofit Boards Meeting Their Responsibilities?" *Public Administration Review* 69 (May/June 2009), pp. 387–390. The quotations are on p. 389.

178. Kelly LeRoux, "Managing Stakeholder Demands," *Administration & Society* 41 (April 2009), pp. 158–184. The quotations are on p. 158.

179. Edward R. Dyl, Howard L. Frant, and Craig A. Stephenson, "Governance and Funds Allocation in United States Medical Research Charities," *Financial Accountability and Management* 16 (November 2000), pp. 335–352.

180. U.S. Government Accountability Office, *Tax-Exempt Sector: Governance, Transparency, and Oversight Are Critical for Maintaining Public Trust*, GAO-05-561T (Washington, DC: U.S. Government Printing Office, 2005), pp. 13–14. The GAO is citing a series of reports by the *Boston Globe* published in 2003.

181. Harry Lipman and Grant Williams, "Special Report: Borrowing the Future," *Chronicle of Philanthropy* (February 6, 2004), pp. 6–14.

182. Herman, "Are Public Service Nonprofit Boards Meeting Their Responsibilities?" p. 388.

183. Ibid. Figures are for 2006. A large organization is one that spends at least $10 million annually.

184. Vic Murray, Pat Bradshaw, and Jacob Wolpin, "Power in and Around Nonprofit Boards: A Neglected Dimension of Governance," *Nonprofit Management & Leadership* 3 (Winter 1992), pp. 165–182. This is a study of 1,200 Canadian nonprofit boards.

185. Steven N. Kaplan, Mark M. Klebanov, and Morten Sorensen, *Which CEO Characteristics and Abilities Matter?* NBER Working Paper No. 14195 (Cambridge, MA: National Bureau of Economic Research, 2008). This is a study of 316 CEOs in the private sector.

186. Jim Collins, *Good to Great* (New York: HarperBusiness, 2001). This is a five-year study of successful corporations.

187. Murray R. Barrick, Michael K. Mount, and Timothy A. Judge, "Personality and Performance

at the Beginning of the New Millennium: Where Do We Go from Here?" *International Journal of Selection and Assessment* 9 (March/June 2001), pp. 9–30. This is a review of research published throughout the twentieth century.

188. Jon Aarum Andersen, "Public versus Private Managers: How Public and Private Managers Differ in Leadership Behavior," *Public Administration Review* 70 (January/February 2010), pp. 131–141. The quotations are on p. 137. This is a study of 459 Swedish public and private managers.

189. Robert Hooijberg and Jaepil Choi, "The Impact of Organizational Characteristics on Leadership Effectiveness Models: An Examination of Leadership in Private and Public-Sector Organization," *Administration & Society* 33 (September 2001), pp. 403–431. This is a study of the leaders of a large state government agency and a Fortune 10 manufacturing firm.

190. Ibid.; and Andersen, "Public versus Private Managers."

191. Ulrike Malmendier and Geoffrey Tate, *Superstar CEOs*, NBER Working Paper No. 14140 (Cambridge, MA: National Bureau of Economic Research, 2008).

192. Andersen, "Assessing Public Managers' Change-Oriented Behavior," p. 342.

193. Hooijberg and Choi, "The Impact of Organizational Characteristics on Leadership Effectiveness Models."

194. Andersen, "Assessing Public Managers' Change-Oriented Behavior."

195. Ibid., p. 137.

196. Hooijberg and Choi, "The Impact of Organizational Characteristics on Leadership Effectiveness Models."

197. Ibid.

198. Trottier, Van Wart, and Wang, "Examining the Nature and Significance of Leadership in Government Organizations," p. 330.

199. Hooijberg and Choi, "The Impact of Organizational Characteristics on Leadership Effectiveness Models."

200. Trottier, Van Wart, and Wang, "Examining the Nature and Significance of Leadership in Government Organizations," p. 329.

201. George L. Hanbury, II, "Leadership 'Fit' and Effectiveness: Trust and Performance," Paper presented at the Annual Conference of the American Society for Public Administration (Phoenix, AZ, March 2002), p. 27. Random surveys were sent to 600 city managers, 242 of whom (40 percent) responded to questionnaires based on the Myers-Briggs Type Indicator—Form G and *Leadership Behavior Analysis II—Self*. The former is used to measure personality types, and the latter is used to measure situational leadership behavior.

202. Hooijberg and Choi, "The Impact of Organizational Characteristics on Leadership Effectiveness Models."

203. Meredith A. Newman, Mary E. Guy, and Sharon H. Mastracci, "Beyond Cognition: Affective Leadership and Emotional Labor," *Public Administration Review* 69 (January/February 2009), pp. 6–20. The quotation is on p. 17.

204. Hooijberg and Choi, "The Impact of Organizational Characteristics on Leadership Effectiveness Models."

205. U.S. Government Printing Office, *Improper Payments: Recent Efforts to Address Improper Payments and Remaining Challenges*, GAO-11-575T (Washington, DC: U.S. Government Printing Office, 2011), p. 3. Figure is for FY 2010.

206. As derived from data in Alec MacGillis, "Obama's '70 Million Checks' Per Month: Actually, It's Even More than That," *Washington Post* (July 26, 2011). Figure is for 2011 and includes payments issued by the Treasury Department and for employees, retirees, Social Security, contractors, veterans, and Defense.

207. The Improper Payments Elimination and Recovery Act of 2010 directs agencies to ultimately halt improper payments.

208. Gerald J. Miller, "Unique Public-Sector Strategies," *Public Productivity & Management Review* 13 (Winter 1989), pp. 133–144. The quotation is on p. 137.

209. M. Andrew Frazier and James E. Swiss, "Contrasting Views of Results-Based Management Tools from Different Organizational Levels," *International Public Management Journal* 11 (2, 2008), pp. 214–234. The quotation is on p. 214.

210. Rhys Andrews, George A. Boyne, Jae M. Moon, *et al.*, "Assessing Organizational Performance: Exploring Differences between Internal and External Measures," *International Public Management Journal* 13 (2, 2010), pp. 105–129.

211. Rohmann, "Relationships between Leadership Styles and Followers' Emotional Experience

and Effectiveness in the Voluntary Sector"; and Geer, Maher, and Cole, "Managing Nonprofit Organizations."

212. William A. Brown and Chao Guo, "Exploring the Key Roles for Nonprofit Boards," *Nonprofit & Voluntary Sector Quarterly* 39 (June 2010), pp. 536–546. This is a survey of 121 CEOs of community foundation executives.

213. Unless noted otherwise, this discussion is drawn from the following sources: Mark A. Abramson, "The Leadership Factor," *Public Administration Review* 49 (November/December 1989), pp. 562–565 (our primary source); Norma M. Riccucci, "'Execucrats,' Politics, and Public Policy: What Are the Ingredients for Successful Performance in the Federal Government?" *Public Administration Review* 55 (May/June 1995), pp. 219–230; N. Joseph Cayer, "Qualities of Successful Program Managers," *Managing Public Programs*, Robert E. Cleary and Nicholas Henry, eds. (San Francisco: Jossey Bass, 1989), pp. 121–142; James L. Perry, "The Effective Public Administrator," *Handbook of Public Administration*, James L. Perry, ed. (San Francisco: Jossey Bass, 1989), pp. 619–627; and Terry L. Cooper and N. Dale Wright, eds., *Exemplary Public Administrators* (San Francisco: Jossey Bass, 1992).

214. Abramson, "The Leadership Factor," p. 563.

215. Ibid., p. 564.

216. Although the famous phrase is commonly attributed to Brownlow, it makes its initial appearance in a publication written by three authors. See Louis Brownlow, Charles E. Merriam, and Luther Gulick, "Report of the President's Committee on Administrative Management," *Administrative Management in the Government of the United States, January 8, 1937* (Washington, DC: U.S. Government Printing Office, 1937), pp. 1–6. The quotation is on p. 5. Actually, the authors are referring not to career public administrators but rather to the top White House staff; the authors write that these staffers ("probably not exceeding six in number") "should be possessed of high competence, great physical vigor, and a passion for anonymity."

217. James N. Doig and Erwin C. Hargrove, eds., *Leadership and Innovation: A Biographical Perspective on Entrepreneurs in Government* (Baltimore: Johns Hopkins University Press, 1987).

218. Cecilia Stiles Cornell and Melvyn P. Leffler, "James Forrestal: The Tragic End of a Successful Entrepreneur," in ibid., Chapter 12. The quotation is on p. 374.

Public Management: Curbing Corruption, Enhancing Efficiency

Public management is the development or application of methodical and systematic techniques that are designed to analyze and make the operations of public and nonprofit organizations more efficient and effective.

In Part III, we review the public and nonprofit sectors' experiences with public management's major methods: information resources; performance measurement and program evaluation; finance and budgeting; and human capital. Each of these critical professions was initially established, in large part and occasionally in whole part, as a reaction to corrupt governance, and each still is used to curb it.

COMPREHENDING CORRUPTION

Recall that, in the introduction to Part I, we outlined the prodigious public price of corruption, but, beyond those data, what do we know about graft? Not much: "In the literature on corruption, there is much speculation on its nature, but there are hardly any empirical qualitative studies on the nature of corruption."[1] We address what there is here.

Tradition! Good Old Graft

Traditionally, *political corruption* has meant *fraud* or *graft*—that is, crooked public (and, we are learning, nonprofit) officials embezzling governments' or independent organizations' money or accepting bribes to waste it. Plundering the public and nonprofit purses can range from a single perpetrator's petty larceny to the creation of a kleptocracy.

Corruption as Sneaky-Pete Politics: Living Well in Bell Perhaps the most common kind of corruption is that which is clearly unethical, but is less clearly criminal.

Consider Bell, California, a town of 38,000 taxpayers of mostly modest means—their income per capita is a fourth less than the national average. Nevertheless, Bell's policymakers quietly found the funds to pay its city administrator a salary of $788,000 (nearly twice that of the president of the United States), replete with guaranteed annual increases of 12 percent, with comparably inflated salaries for other managers, and paying its part-time mayor and council members almost $100,000— each. Towns of comparable size pay their council members an average wage of $4,800.[2] (The mayor stoutly defended these salaries, including his, by insisting that, "our streets are cleaner." It is impossible to make this stuff up.)

Bell's officials financed their pumped-up pay through questionable means, including grossly overcharging for sewerage services; the wholesale firing of the town's minimum-wage workers; and levying a property tax that was considerably higher than that of Beverly Hills, where per capita income is almost four times larger than Bell's. Bell's debt per citizen tripled in just five years.[3] In 2010, eight Bell officials were arrested on corruption charges. In 2011, 95 percent of Bell's voters recalled four council members and elected a new mayor and an entirely new council, none of whom had ever held elective office.

Corruption as Conquest: Janitorial Joys On occasion, an otherwise-honest public agency is effectively "captured" by a corrupt sub-organization that, for all intents and purposes, is the reigning power center that really runs, or at least sufficiently intimidates, the larger organization.

An example is New York City's 8,500 school custodians, who control a half-billion dollar budget for 1,200 schools. Custodial scandals have erupted since 1924, and to this day the custodians are "systematically transforming their schools into enterprises for bribery, extortion, theft, and nepotism." Custodians give themselves, friends, and family "no-show jobs" and pay them fraudulent overtime, steal school funds to renovate their homes, and extort contractors. "Most principals" are "terrified of what they dubbed custodians' 'reigns of terror.'"[4]

Corruption as Culture: Murder and Mortification

The most ominous sort of traditional graft is that which defines the civic culture itself, and this kind of corruption can morph into one mean monster.

Consider the case of Phenix City, in Russell County, Alabama. Over the course of a century, both localities had evolved in such a way that, by the 1950s, virtually every local official had some personally-rewarding connection with racketeering; the rest of Alabama was mortified. Alabama's newly-elected attorney general, who had won on the pledge that he would clean up corruption, was assassinated shortly after the election. Alabama's governor appointed a military force to take charge of both jurisdictions, and declared martial law in Russell County. One hundred fifty-two people eventually were convicted of corruption.[5]

Fraud in the Independent Sector: Inside Jobs

Nonprofit organizations are not immune to corruption—"charity officials stole or misused at least $1.28 billion from 152 nonprofit organizations over a seven-year period"—but "very little empirical research about fraud in nonprofits exists."

Almost all fraud committed against these organizations (98 percent) is committed "solely by offenders within the organization," over a third of whom are managers. More than three-fifths are women, whereas in the other two sectors most fraudsters are men. Corruption involving collusion between employees and outsiders occurs in just 2 percent of instances of fraud, which appears to be lower than in the private and public sectors. Older employees and women account for the greatest losses.

The smaller the nonprofit organization, the likelier that it is to be a victim of fraud, "a finding counter to public-sector fraud research." Independent-sector organizations are more likely to endure significantly heavier losses to fraud when they neglect external audits, anonymous hotlines, and fiscal controls.[6]

Corruption's Causes

Corruption's causes are structural, cultural, and, of course, personal.

Structure and Corruption As we noted in Chapter 4, larger state governments suffer more incidents of corruption than smaller ones. Centralized governments also correlate with corruption,[7] but civil service structures (a term encompassing job security and reporting arrangements, among other factors) have no impact, one way or another, on public perceptions of corruption.[8]

Culture and Corruption Poverty, rural societies,[9] and low levels of social capital (e.g., politically engaged citizens)[10] associate with high rates of national corruption.

An agency's culture can encourage graft when "supervision of the corrupt official is not strong" (although heavy-handed micromanagement can ricochet, "employee misconduct is *mostly* the result of *oppressive* as well as lax controls"); "management has not promoted a clear integrity policy"; and "loyalty and solidarity" among colleagues, both inside and outside the agency, deter the reporting of corrupt activities.[11]

The Corrupt Public Official Why do public officials become corrupt? Personal enrichment is the most obvious, and leading, motivation (although, "strikingly, the corrupt official rarely receives a gift for which concrete compensation is expected"—there is "no clear quid pro quo"), but it is followed closely by the desire for "friendship or love, status, and making an impression."[12]

Who is corrupted and how? Corrupt officials often have strong, domineering personalities;

they are popular and are viewed by colleagues as effective, thereby creating for themselves "space to maneuver"; they slowly "'slide down' toward corruption" and are unlikely to view themselves as corrupt; and they "do not limit their corruption to one incident," but instead maintain "a long, institutionalized relationship" with their corruptors.[13]

Lord Acton's famous phrase, uttered in 1887, that "Power tends to corrupt, and absolute power corrupts absolutely" is largely accurate, but only up to a point. Corrupt powerful people who perceive that their power is legitimate are more corrupt and hypocritical than are corrupt powerful people who see themselves as holding power illegitimately.[14]

Corruption's Continuance

Why does corruption continue? There are several reasons.

The continuance of the same conditions that produced corrupt societies in the first place—poverty, rural societies, little social capital, and centralized governments—also ensures that corruption will persist over time.[15] The more centralized the government, the more "fused" that political power is within it, and the less access that the press has to the government, the more likely that corrupt officials will survive attempts to prosecute them.[16]

Democracies are largely free of these conditions, but there remains the depressing fact that some voters prefer corrupt democracies to honest ones. In democratic jurisdictions, graft often associates with reduced public spending. If citizens' demands for services are "relatively elastic," then this association sometimes leads to lower taxes. "Under this condition," some citizens who favor low taxes may "hold their noses and vote" for continued corruption.[17]

Corruption and Democracy

The stirring, mass revolutions—from Benghazi to Budapest, from Kiev to Cairo, from Tehran to Tunis—that began in 1974 with the Portuguese people's overthrow of their Fascist rulers invariably demand two interlocking reforms of government: curbing corruption and developing democracy.

People seem to viscerally understand that honest governance and democratic governance are symbiotic—that they reinforce each other to their mutual benefit. And they are right.

Where there is uncorrupted government, there also is vibrant democracy—that is, large numbers of citizens voting regularly in competitive elections.[18] By contrast, in democracies where there is low voter turnout and little popular participation in governance, corruption can continue for long periods.[19]

THE EVOLUTION OF AMERICAN GRAFT

The roots of Americans' concern with corruption are dense and deep and extend to the very founding of the United States itself: The word "corruption," or some variant of it, appears in *The Federalist Papers* 58 times,[20] and "administration," the main means of curtailing corruption, surfaces in these founding essays a remarkable 124 times.[21]

American perspectives on corruption, and the ways in which Americans choose to battle it, have altered over the years.

Graft Parties On, 1900–1940

During the much of the twentieth century, and earlier, America's cultural and commercial elites defined *corruption* as the political parties' systematic misuse of government and of taxpayers (i.e., those elites) who paid for the travesty. The lower, largely immigrant, classes often had a different view and welcomed corrupt political machines as their fiscal saviors, which they frequently were, and at the expense of the middle and upper classes.

The reformers of this period attacked graft by arguing for the isolation of politics from administration, discussed in Chapter 2, and using professional public administrators to free the public—or, at least, the taxpaying public—from party bosses' malevolent rule.

Graft as a Nuisance, 1940–1970

By the 1940s, the reformers had made considerable headway. A consequence was that graft was seen less as a pervasive problem, and more as a sporadic phenomenon that could be dealt with over time by applying the principles of administration (recall Chapters 2 and 3) to improve governments' organization, processes, and budgeting; these improvements would secure the public's treasure. "Out of reform, moral in its motivation, came reorganization, technical and managerial in connotation."[22]

"Fraud, Waste, and Abuse": Our New Meaning of Corruption, 1970–Present

The queerly comforting thing about good old-fashioned graft is that we can readily understand it. Beginning in the 1970s, however, corruption has been perceived as including not only traditional "fraud" but "waste" and "abuse" as well. In the presidential election of 1960, the term "fraud, waste, and abuse" was not uttered. It was spoken in subsequent contests, however, and by the 1980 election, the candidates brayed the phrase no fewer than eighty-three times; it has made strong showings ever since.[23]

Three events exploded in the 1970s and 1980s that altered, perhaps permanently, the public's perception of corruption.

Fraud as Corruption: The Fall of Washington
During the 1980s, far-reaching federal frauds reminded citizens about how governmental graft can threaten their futures.

The savings and loan scandal of the 1980s— in which $125 billion of taxpayers' treasure were used to bail out thousands of savings and loan associations that had, often fraudulently, "lost" the savings of millions of investors—was the direct result of their irresponsible deregulation by Congress. High levels of fraud in Medicare, a $460 billion health-care program for the elderly, emerged in the eighties. Washington's efforts in that decade to privatize government on an unprecedented scale resulted in billion-dollar scandals that roiled through the departments of Defense and Housing and Urban Development, and wildly corrupt contractors staged a comeback in the 2000s, following Hurricane Katrina and the reconstruction of Iraq. These events rendered the public much more sensitive to fraud's presence, and even less tolerant of it.

Waste as Corruption: The Fall of New York
New York City's fiscal crisis of 1975, in which the City narrowly averted default only because Washington bailed it out with more than $9 billion, was primarily a product of plain *waste*, or "the unnecessary costs that result from inefficient or ineffective practices, systems, or controls."[24]

The City's debacle made a deep impression on the public, which began to equate governmental waste with public corruption, a perception that has grown over time. An academic review of the literature on governmental waste identified a type of waste titled "Corruption, Fraud, Theft, and Red Tape."[25] Red tape equates with corruption, fraud, and theft? The title of a mudslinging book put it succinctly: *Government Racket: Washington Waste From A to Z.*[26] Waste is a racket?

Abuse as Corruption: The Fall of the White House
Between 1973 and 1975, a "third rate burglary" (to quote the presiding president, Richard Nixon) metamorphosed into the mother of all political scandals—"Watergate," or Nixon's efforts to cover up his aides' burglary of the offices of his opposition's party. The resulting scandal, besides forcing Nixon's resignation, also rendered the public extremely aware of how officeholders could abuse their authority.

Abuse of authority may be defined as the inappropriate, unethical, or illegal misuse of the power vested in one's public office. In Watergate, this abuse happened to be illegal, but the abuse of authority, while reprehensible, is not always criminal.

Examples of inappropriate and unethical abuses are of more recent vintage. Consider the case of the special prosecutor charged (originally) in the mid-1990s with investigating some of President Bill Clinton's personal investments when he had served as governor of Arkansas, an episode known as "Whitewater." Ultimately, the special prosecutor found no provable improprieties involving Whitewater but did expose that the president had had an affair with a White House intern.

The special prosecutor's zealous expansion of his initial mission was legal, but, in the view of most Americans, it was an abuse of authority. By contrast, Clinton's sexual exploitation of a young intern was clearly unethical (and his lying about it under oath was criminal). Both of these abuses led to the demise of the twenty-one-year-old independent prosecutor law; the impeachment, trial, and acquittal of the president by Congress; his unprecedented disbarment by the U.S. Supreme Court; and deepening of the public's perception that abuse of power, even when it is legal, nonetheless is corruption.

Incompetence as Corruption In sum, "corruption" in the popular mind now is a blurred lump composed of fraud, waste, and abuse. As a consequence, governments have added new layers of restrictions, checks, and procedures to curb not only graft but waste and abuse as well. Now incompetence can equate with criminality.

CONFRONTING CORRUPTION IN AMERICA

The United States is largely free of those structural conditions that can encourage corruption. Americans enjoy a relatively prosperous economy; live mostly in urban areas; and their governments are bombarded unrelentingly by a robust, sometimes rabid, press. In addition, Americans are governed by a decentralized and diffused public sector, a condition that discourages graft on a global scale: A large "number of administrative units in a country lowers corruption."[27] Similarly, "the finding in earlier research that federalism increases corruption is not robust,"[28] and, in fact, the illegal, tax-evading, "shadow economy is smaller in federal countries than in unitary states."[29]

Perceptions of American Corruption

The United States stacks up better than most in popular perceptions as an honest government. It ties with Belgium at the 22nd place out of 178 countries in terms of its perceived corruption— not a mortifyingly low ranking, certainly, but not one that conveys bragging rights, either (Barbados and Qatar score higher than the United States), particularly given that America's ranking has declined by a third since the mid-1990s, when the studies began.[30]

Over fifty years, the number of Americans who said that "quite a few government officials are crooked" more than doubled, from 24 to 52 percent.[31] A majority states that "corrupt political leaders" are the nation's top problem.[32]

Americans who work for governments have their own views about the extent of public corruption, and their perceptions differ from those of the public. Federal, state, and local employees report that "overtly illegal" misconduct, such as bribery and theft, in their workplaces has declined by an average of two-fifths over seven years.[33]

The Extent of Fraud

Four percent of federal workers have observed over the past year the altering of financial records in the federal government; 3 percent have noted stealing; and 2 percent are aware of bribery. These figures are bad, but not horrid. Federal employees are "the only government employees to indicate observance of misconduct at levels significantly lower than the U.S. average."[34] Less than 6 percent of federal workers have "made a formal disclosure of fraud, waste, or abuse, or unlawful behavior at work."[35]

Known financial fraud committed by federal employees against the federal government accounts for considerably less than 1 percent of the federal budget. "Nevertheless, though relatively small in terms of the percentage of the budget impacted," fraud "has proven to be extremely costly" simply because of the immensity of the federal budget.[36]

Seven percent of state workers and 6 percent of local employees have observed over the past year the altering of financial records in their governments; 8 percent of state workers and 10 percent of local ones note theft; and 4 percent each of state and local employees report bribery. The rates of each of these perceived corruptions match their U.S. averages.[37]

Corruption Controls: Striking Balances

The field has come a long way in discovering devices that can lead to cleaning up corrupt governance, but there remains "confusion in the literature on which anticorruption methods work best and most efficiently."[38]

Traditional approaches to corruption control now flourish. Standards, rules, rigidities, and investigative officers (such as inspectors general, personnel specialists, ethics officers, regulators, comptrollers, auditors, attorneys, and accountants) extend well beyond the administrative controls ever imagined in the wildest dreams of the early good-government reformers.

Do Traditional Controls Work? Have these traditional controls curtailed corruption? Yes, they have. "A strong case can be made to remain sharp in routine supervision because we now know that approximately one-third of [corruption] cases originate with institutional functions of control and investigation." No other category of exposing unethical or illegal misconduct in government— reports by public employees, citizens, contractors, and others—even approaches this level.[39]

But traditional controls work only up to a point. It is worth noting that all the recommendations (and then some!) of the early-twentieth-century reformers had long been in place in the Pentagon even as, in the late twentieth century, it was being "sold" to an unheard-of extent to corrupt private contractors. These were the years of the infamous $600 toilet seats, yet "hundreds of thousands of employees had no task other than to keep scrupulously close tabs on contractors. Seventy-nine separate offices issued voluminous acquisition regulations.... [which] equaled five times the length of Leo Tolstoy's novel *War and Peace*. The Army once promulgated fifteen pages of specifications for sugar cookies alone."[40]

Newer Methods It is undeniable that traditional corruption controls were firmly present—indeed, omnipresent, at least officially—in the Pentagon even as some of its officials were engaged in corruption of unprecedented proportions, leading some critics to conclude that these controls are outmoded. They argue that newer methods offer greater promise. For example, electronic government has had a positive impact not only in enhancing efficiency but also, surprisingly, in reducing official graft (details are in Chapter 6).

The Case for Old and New There can be no doubt that anticorruption innovations are welcome, but we should also keep in mind that "the traditional approach is not obsolete; it can never be so long

as the United States is a government of laws. But it must be adapted."[41] "The right mix of corruption controls will undoubtedly differ" from government to government, and from agency to agency within the same government, and the "optimal mix" of those controls will alter over time.[42] The key to more effective corruption controls is that they constantly be balanced and rebalanced.

Exposing Is Not Disposing We are not implying that the many methods of public management, both new and old, that have been created, at least in part, to curtail corruption can actually eliminate it. Introducing computers, measuring performance, inspecting agencies, evaluating programs, auditing the books, and reforming civil services, to list a few such controls, were never meant to crush corruption. Rather, they were designed only to discourage corruption by making its entry less easy and its discovery more likely.

Even to merely discourage graft, however, corruption controls must first be *used*. Otherwise, corruption controls are irrelevant. When anticorruption methods uncover pervasive graft, rooting it out mandates "overhauling management, eradicating special interests, and aggressively punishing misconduct."[43] Whatever the extent of the corruption, however—whether it is of the garden variety, such as purloining a pen from the office, or it is the garden itself, such as a putrescence that permeates a polity—political will is the ultimate key to its disposal.

The Prosecution Puzzle

State and local governments investigate and prosecute fraud, some quite successfully. New York City's Department of Investigation, founded in 1873, is exemplary; during the 1990s, its officers arrested on corruption charges half of the City's taxi, building, and plumbing inspectors. But there are difficulties when grass-roots governments pursue grass-roots graft. In New York's case, "It took a while to figure out how to do this—more than a hundred years"—even though the Department's "daily work consists of rounding up people whose crimes are so small, so unnecessary, and so amazingly stupid that their capture is an act of mercy."[44]

State attorneys general and district attorneys "are generally not equipped with the resources needed for a political undercover investigation"; most are elected, which can lead to their reluctance to investigate corrupt officials in their own parties; and "they often are hampered by state laws that are less expansive than federal ones."[45] As a consequence, the federal government is central to the curtailment of corruption at every governmental level, initiating "perhaps as many as 80 percent" of all prosecutions for public corruption in the United States.[46]

Even though considerably less than half (42–46 percent) of federal employees who allegedly defraud the government on their own are prosecuted (compared with 60 percent of those who collude with others to defraud), a prosecutorial rate described as "low,"[47] federal corruption prosecutions launched against federal officials nevertheless have more than tripled since 1980, and now number around 1,000 prosecutions per year. In addition, prosecutions of "others involved" (e.g., the bribers, blackmailers) in the corruption of public officials at all governmental levels have increased by 35 percent over the same period.[48]

Federal prosecutions for public corruption brought against state officials have more than doubled since 1980, and those against local officials have grown by a third.[49] In 2004, the Supreme Court further facilitated federal prosecutions of grass-roots graft by unanimously ruling that it is a federal crime to bribe a state or local official in a jurisdiction that receives federal money (which, essentially, all jurisdictions do), even though federal funds or programs are not involved.[50]

Whether these burgeoning prosecutorial levels reflect increased corruption or the increased zeal of federal prosecutors cannot be known, but there are indications that during this period Washington pushed corruption cases for partisan advantage. Consider the unprecedented dismissal of nine U.S. attorneys in 2006, allegedly because of their reluctance to politicize corruption cases, leading to the resignation in 2007 of the U.S. attorney general and other top officials in the Justice Department. Or the U.S. attorney for Maryland who "demanded that his staff bring no fewer than three 'front-page' corruption indictments by Election Day."[51]

A pernicious perplexity of corruption is that even its prosecution can be corrupted.

FROM ANTICORRUPTION TO EFFICIENCY: THE MORPHING OF PUBLIC MANAGEMENT

A cruel irony of corruption controls is that, through their time-consuming and enervating checks, rules, and red tape, they can stymie efficient and productive governing.[52] Public administrators are fully aware that balancing honest government with effective government—which is the complicated combination that improves public efficiency and productivity—requires that the many methods of curbing graft be adapted to increasingly labyrinthine social and fiscal systems.

Public administration, like any other phenomenon, is subject to W. Ross Ashby's *law of requisite variety*, which states that regulatory (or, in our case, governing) mechanisms must equal in their complexity those of the systems that they are meant to control.[53] Ashby's law pertains not only to more tangled forms of corruption, which has expanded to include waste and abuse, as well as old-fashioned fraud; it also applies equally to increasingly convoluted problems of public productivity.

In its public plumage, the law of requisite variety is expressed in the techniques of public management, and public officials, particularly elected ones, sometimes get a bit carried away with them. "These days the hip subject" among politicians "is management theory."[54] As one public administrator plaintively put it, "there is still the tendency on the part of today's elected officials and those they appoint to look at government as a business. So maybe they read something or went to a conference or went to lunch with some business people who told them about some new idea."[55] Brimming with newly burnished brainpower, these officials storm back to the office with a "revolutionary" new cure for all problems administrative—until their next lunch.

As a consequence, those public managers who toil in the bureaucracy's bowels sometimes are forced to behave like a school of fish, darting without warning first one way and then another, in a pointless effort to be "with it"—if also witless.[56]

Regrettably, the "flavor-of-the-month" approach has been employed all too often. "The level of federal reform"—in performance measurement, budgetary formats, human resources, and elsewhere—"appears to parallel the frenzy of management improvement fads in business.... Federal employees have faced one competing reform after another, leading to confusion, wasted motion, and frustration in priorities with fads and fashions that are now out of favor."[57] State and local governments are also complicit.

Personnel in these governments may harbor some self-delusion. Public organizations that "adopt fashionable management practices" are statistically more likely to be staffed by administrators who "overestimate" their organizations' service performance relative to how their clients and other external stakeholders view their performance.[58]

There doubtless is some merit to the view that "management by best seller" can do more harm than good: Time and hard work are expended by staff to establish one technique, only to see it cavalierly discarded by top management when another one cruises down the consultants' turnpike. As a consequence, managers' morale and openness to new ideas plummet, but their frustration and cynicism soar; a "wait-them-out-and-wear-them-down" mentality emerges among careerists. Because an unhappy workforce usually is an unproductive workforce, goes the argument, the new techniques are themselves counterproductive.

There is another side to this, however: A competition of new approaches can result in improved administration, *if* administrators are both confident and discerning enough to pick and choose among techniques—or even parts of techniques, old as well as new—that would improve the performance of their agencies and nonprofit organizations. It is an approach that works. Although many of the methods of public management "have ended up being castigated and even ridiculed, these methods have provided an ever-improving series of public management techniques that can, and indeed are, improving government performance."[59]

Depending on the circumstances that public and nonprofit administrators face, some or all of the notions advanced in Part III could be useful and rewarding. But to mindlessly adopt them simply because they are there likely would result in less effective management.

NOTES

1. Gjalt de Graaf and L. W. J. C. Huberts, "Portraying the Nature of Corruption Using an Exploratory Case Study Design," *Public Administration Review* 68 (July/August 2008), pp. 640–653. The quotation is on p. 650.

2. Ruben Vives, "Bell Council Seeks Resignations of 3 City Officials," *Los Angeles Times* (July 21, 2010).

3. Christopher Palmeri, "California Official's $800,000 Salary in City of 38,000 Triggers Protests," and "California City in Pay Probe Has Higher Taxes than Beverly Hills," *Bloombergnews.com* (July 20, 27, 2010, respectively). As detailed in the box in Chapter 1, the only city that pays its manager a salary known to be higher than Bell's is Vernon, which borders Bell. Perhaps there is something in the water.

4. Lydia Segal, "Roadblocks in Reforming Corrupt Agencies: The Case of the New York City School Custodians," *Public Administration Review* 62 (July/August 2002), pp. 445–460. The quotations are on pp. 445–446, 448. This reports a three-year investigation of the custodians.

5. For a good treatment of the Phenix City follies, see Alan Grady, *When Good Men Do Nothing: The Assassination of Albert Patterson* (Tuscaloosa, AL: University of Alabama Press, 2003).

6. Kristy Holtfreter, "Determinants of Fraud Losses in Nonprofit Organizations," *Nonprofit Management & Leadership* 19 (Fall 2008), pp. 45–63. The quotations are on pp. 46, 47, 52, 57, respectively. This is a study of 128 nonprofit organizations.

7. Rajeev K. Goel and Michael A. Nelson, *Causes of Corruption: History, Geography and Government*

(Helsinki, Finland: Bank of Finland Institute for Economies in Transition, 2008). This is an analysis of "about 100 nations."

8. Ellen V. Rubin and Andrew Whitford, "Effects of the Institutional Design of the Civil Service: Evidence from Corruption," *International Public Management Journal* 11 (4, 2008), pp. 404–425. This is an analysis of European civil services.

9. Goel and Nelson, *Causes of Corruption*.

10. Dong Chul Shim and Tae Ho Eom, "Anticorruption Effects of Information Communication and Technology (ICT) and Social Capital," *International Review of Administrative Sciences* 75 (March 2009), pp. 99–116.

11. De Graaf and Huberts, "Portraying the Nature of Corruption Using an Exploratory Case Study Design," pp. 645–646. Emphasis added.

12. Ibid., pp. 647, 643. This is an in-depth analysis of ten confidential criminal files involving public corruption in the Netherlands.

13. Ibid., pp. 645, 644, 649, 648, respectively.

14. Joris Lammers, Diederik A. Stapel, and Adam D. Galinsky, "Power Increases Hypocrisy: Moralizing in Reasoning, Immorality in Behavior," *Psychological Science* 21 (May 2010), pp. 737–744. This reports a set of five experiments involving Dutch students.

15. Goel and Nelson, *Causes of Corruption*; and Shim and Eom, "Anticorruption Effects of Information Communication and Technology (ICT) and Social Capital."

16. Moshe Maor, "Feeling the Heat? Anticorruption Mechanisms in Comparative Perspective," *Governance* 17 (January 2004), pp. 1–28. The author investigated five "anticorruption mechanisms" in Australia, Italy, Russia, and the United States.

17. Marco Pani, *Hold Your Nose and Vote: Why Do Some Democracies Tolerate Corruption?* IMF Working Paper No. 09/83 (Washington, DC: International Monetary Fund, 2009), p. 1.

18. Alok K. Bohara, Neil J. Mitchell, and Carl F. Mittendorff, "Compound Democracy and the Control of Corruption: A Cross-Country Investigation," *Policy Studies Journal* 32 (Winter 2004), pp. 481–499.

19. Tetsuya Fujiwara, "The Impact of Political Corruption on Voter Turnout in Industrial Democracies," Paper Presented at the Annual Meeting of the Midwest Political Science Association (Chicago, April 2005).

20. George Will, "End Run on Free Speech," *Savannah Morning News* (May 25, 2009).

21. Jerry Mitchell, *The American Experiment with Government Corporations* (Armonk, NY: Sharpe, 1998), p. 6.

22. Leonard D. White, *The Administrative Histories: The Federalists* (New York: MacMillan, 1948), p. 16.

23. Annenberg Campaign Data Base, as cited in Paul C. Light, *The True Size of Government* (Washington, DC: Brookings, 1999), p. 88.

24. Jerome B. McKinney, "Concepts and Definitions," *Fraud, Waste, and Abuse in Government: Causes, Consequences, and Cures*, Jerome B. McKinney and Michael Johnston, eds. (Philadelphia: Institute for the Study of Human Issues, 1986), pp. 1–7. The quotation is on p. 5.

25. William Stanberry and Fred Thompson, "Toward a Political Economy of Government Waste: First Step, Definitions," *Public Administration Review* 55 (September/October 1995), pp. 418–427.

26. Martin L. Gross, *Government Racket: Washington Waste from A to Z* (New York: Bantam, 1992).

27. Goel and Nelson, *Causes of Corruption*, p. 17.

28. Bohara, Mitchell, and Mittendorff, "Compound Democracy and the Control of Corruption." The quotation is on p. 481.

29. Desiree Teobaldelli, "Federalism and the Shadow Economy," *Public Choice* 146 (March 2011), pp. 269–289. The quotation is on p. 269. This is an analysis of seventy-three countries.

30. Transparency International, *Corruption Perceptions Index 2010* (Berlin: Author, 2010), p. 2. Figure is for 2010, when the U.S. was rated 7.1 on a ten-point scale, with ten being the highest rating. This is the lowest score that the U.S. has ever scored. In 1995 and 1996, the U.S. ranked fifteenth.

31. American National Election Studies, "Are Government Officials Crooked, 1958–2008," http://www.electionstudies.org/nesguide/2ndtable/t5a_4_1.htm.

32. Pew Global Attitudes Project, *Global Opinion Trends, 2002–2007* (Washington, DC: Author, 2008), pp. 35, 114, 121. Figure, 51 percent, is for 2007. Only "illegal drugs" score higher.

33. As derived from data in Ethics Resource Center, *National Government Ethics Survey: An Inside View of Public Sector Ethics* (Arlington, VA: Author, 2008), p. 3. Figure is for 2000–2007.

34. Ibid., pp. 20, 19. Figures are for 2007.

35. U.S. Merit Systems Protection Board, *Prohibited Personnel Practices: A Study Retrospective* (Washington, DC: U.S. Government Printing Office, 2010), p. 14. Figure is for 2005.

36. Sandra T. Welch, Sarah A. Holmes, and Jeffrey W. Stawser, "Fraud in the Federal Government: Part I-The Perpetrators and the Victims," *Government Accountants Journal* 46 (Spring 1997), pp. 24–27. The quotation is on p. 24.

37. Ethics Resource Center, *National Government Ethics Survey*, pp. 25, 31. Figures are for 2007.

38. De Graaf and Huberts, "Portraying the Nature of Corruption Using an Exploratory Case Study Design," p. 650.

39. Gjalt de Graaf, "A Report on Reporting: Why Peers Report Integrity and Law Violations in Public Organizations," *Public Administration Review* 70 (September/October 2010), pp. 767–779. The quotation is on p. 776.

40. Andy Pasztor, *When the Pentagon Was for Sale: Inside America's Biggest Defense Scandal* (New York: Scribner, 1995), p. 10.

41. Donald F. Kettl, *Reinventing Government? Appraising the National Performance Review* (Washington, DC: Brookings, 1994), p. 54.

42. Frank Anechiarco and James B. Jacobs, *The Pursuit of Absolute Integrity: How Corruption Control Makes Government Ineffective* (Chicago: University of Chicago Press, 1996), p. 198.

43. Segal, "Roadblocks in Reforming Corrupt Agencies," p. 445.

44. Larissa MacFarquhar, "Busted," *The New Yorker* (February 1, 2010), pp. 50–57. The quotations are on p. 53.

45. Alan Greenblatt, "The Corruption Puzzle," *Governing* (July 2008), pp. 24–30. The quotations are on p. 29.

46. Corporate Crime Reporter, *Public Corruption in the United States* (Washington, DC: Author, 2007), http://www.corporatecrimereporter.com/corrupt100807.htm.

47. Sandra T. Welch, Sarah A. Holmes, and Jeffrey W. Stawser, "Fraud in the Federal Government Part II-Characteristics of the Schemes, the Detection and Resolution of the Cases," *Government Accountants Journal* 46 (Summer 1997), pp. 38–45. The quotation is on p. 44. Figures are for the 1980s and the first half of the 1990s.

48. As derived from data in U.S. Bureau of the Census, *Statistical Abstract of the United States, 2008*, 127th ed., and *2011*, 130th ed. (Washington, DC: U.S. Government Printing Office, 2008 and 2011), Tables 328 and 335, respectively. Prosecutions refer to all persons charged, convicted, and awaiting trial. In 1980, there were federal 267 prosecutions of federal officials and 624 of others involved; in 2008, these figures were 1,093 and 841, respectively.

49. Ibid. Prosecutions refer to all persons charged, convicted, and awaiting trial. In 1980, there were 151 federal prosecutions of state officials and 497 of local officials; in 2008, these figures were 328 and 660, respectively.

50. The case is *Sabri* v. *United States*.

51. Greenblatt, "The Corruption Puzzle," pp. 30, 26. Figures are for 2002–2008.

52. Anechiarco and Jacobs, *The Pursuit of Absolute Integrity*.

53. W. Ross Ashby, *Introduction to Cybernetics* (London: Chapman and Hall, 1961).

54. "Leviathan Reengineered," *The Economist* (October 19, 1996), p. 41.

55. Terry Brock, quoted in Jonathan Walters, "Fad Mad," *Governing* (September 1996), p. 50.

56. Lex Donaldson and Frederick G. Hilmer, "Management Redeemed: The Case Against Fads that Harm Management," *Organizational Dynamics* 26 (Spring 1998), pp. 7–30.

57. Paul C. Light, "A Government Ill Executed: The Depletion of the Federal Public Service," *Public Administration Review* 68 (May/June 2008), pp. 413–419. The quotation is on p. 417.

58. Rhys Andrews, George A. Boyne, Jae M. Moon, and Richard M. Walker, "Assessing Organizational Performance: Exploring Differences between Internal and External Measures," *International Public Management Journal* 13 (2, 2010), pp. 105–129. The quotations are on p. 105.

59. Harry P. Hatry, "The Alphabet Soup Approach: You'll Love It!" *The Public Manager* 21 (Winter 1992–1993), pp. 8–12. The quotation is on p. 8.

Clarifying Complexity: The Public's Information Resource

Never before in human history have there been so many data. Two hundred and ten billion daily e-mails, more than 70 million blogs, and 150 million websites that are growing by about 10,000 *per hour* tote up to an estimated 1,000 exabytes of digital data. One *exabyte* (or 1 quintillion bytes) equals 7,400 Libraries of Congress, and digital data long ago surpassed by a factor of millions all the information in all the books ever written.[1]

The typical corporate user sends and receives an estimated 105 e-mails each day, a number that is increasing but less rapidly than in past years because of the entry of new technologies. There are, for example, nearly 2.6 billion instant messaging accounts, growing by 11 percent per year, on average, and almost 2.4 billion social networking accounts, increasing by an average of 16 percent annually.[2]

The computer has been crucial in culling useful information from the data deluge, and relevant knowledge is, in turn, critical in clarifying problems of public management. Before we can manage public programs, we first must comprehend both the problem and the program that addresses it. Cascades of data can cloud our comprehension. The computer can clarify it.

Government has led this innovative effort. A Census Bureau employee, Herman Hollerith, invented for use in the 1890 census a punch card and tabulation machine, the recognized forerunner of the computer. The federal Defense Advanced Research Projects Agency was central in creating the global positioning system, a project it began in 1959, and in 1969 the Agency invented "packet switching," which led to the Internet.

Today, Washington spends about $79 billion on information technology each year,[3] an increase of approximately four-fifths during the 2000s,[4] and federal spending for information technology is projected to grow by more than 5 percent annually.[5] No other single organization in the United States, and likely the world, spends more money on computers than does the U.S. government.[6] State and local governments spend more than $50 billion each year on information technology, an amount that is rising by about 4 percent annually.[7]

The public computer is immense, and it is integral to every person's life.

KNOWLEDGE MANAGEMENT: MANAGING THE PUBLIC'S INFORMATION RESOURCE

The public sector has problems of managing information resources that are unique to it. We call these challenges *public information resource management*, or, more simply, *knowledge management*,[8] which refers to the collection, administration, and use of social and organizational data, including the development of policies and procedures for information resources and systems, for the purpose of forming and delivering public policy.

The need to manage knowledge has given rise in all sectors to *chief information officers*

(*CIOs*), or executives charged with assuring that information systems provide useful knowledge for developing organizational tactics, strategies, and success. Herbert Simon predicted that "how to process information" will emerge as the core challenge for all executives,[9] and top public executives do indeed spend most of their time seeking and analyzing information.[10]

The Unique Complexities of Public Knowledge Management

"High-level data managers" in government deal with greater interdependence among systems, more red tape, different criteria in purchasing hardware, and more extensive "extra-organizational linkages" than do their counterparts in business.[11] These unique complexities of the public sector redound to the public's benefit, in that governments' "knowledge workers" are most attracted to their jobs by "intellectual stimulation and challenge." Those in the independent sector, by contrast, cite contributing to society; and those in business prefer the opportunities for "advancement and prestige" that their positions offer.[12]

Clarifying Public Decisions

Perhaps the single most important contribution of knowledge management is that it can produce better bureaucratic decisions by clarifying information and illuminating a decision's potential consequences.

Recall from Chapter 4 that the use of hard data, typically provided by computers, has a direct relationship with public administrators making superior decisions and with those decisions being accepted at higher rates, correlations that appear to be unique to government.[13] The adoption of information technology in county governments increases the number of participants in decision making, improves "technical decision making" (which improves further as "as more types of technology were adopted"), and has positive and "direct effect on performance."[14]

Data for Decision Makers Most of us are at least vaguely familiar with *management information*

systems, or passive technologies designed to convert data into summary information that administrators study to make more informed decisions. Less familiar, perhaps, are *decision support systems*, which are analytical, interactive computer-based technologies that work with administrators in making decisions (often by addressing "what if" scenarios) about unstructured and nonroutine problems. The evidence suggests that most agencies have decision support systems, most are pleased with them,[15] and that they can save governments money.[16]

Analytics and Enterprise Risk Management
Public administrators increasingly are trying to improve their decision making by wedding their decision support systems with analytics and enterprise risk management.

Analytics is "the extensive use of data, statistical and quantitative analysis, explanatory and predictive models, and fact-based management to drive decisions." The probability that analytics will be used in the public sector is greatly enhanced by high levels of governmental transparency and accountability.[17]

Enterprise risk management is the use of analytics to focus on potential events that accompany a decision, and then classifying them as opportunities or perils in order to exploit opportunities and mitigate hazards in the accomplishment of the organization's mission. "Risk is a fundamental condition of existence. It cannot be entirely eliminated, but taking unnecessary risks," or failing to recognize them, "can have tremendous," and adverse, "consequences." Enterprise risk management lowers the likelihood of those consequences.[18]

Geographic Information Systems An important type of decision support system is the *geographic information system* (*GIS*), which is a location-related computer program that typically combines data with maps and aerial photographs. The federal government, relying largely on the Texas GIS program, used it to recover the remains of the *Columbia* space shuttle after it crashed in 2003, scattering pieces over forty-one counties in two states.[19] State highway departments use GIS to identify where roads need improved safety. Local fire fighters use it to determine the fastest route to a fire.

Office of Management and Budget Circular A-16, issued in 1953 and revised many times since, is the basis of Washington's GIS policy. The federal government spends more than $4 billion annually on collecting and managing GIS data,[20] which account for an estimated 80–90 percent of the total price of bringing GIS online.[21]

State and local governments are thought to spend twice as much on GIS as Washington expends, or about $8 billion per year.[22] Half of all cities have a GIS in operation,[23] and counties appear to use GIS and related imagery technologies more widely than cities.[24]

Managing the Nation's Knowledge: A Far-Flung Federal Failure?

Regrettably, the federal government's experience with computers has been as maddening as computers themselves are necessary. Washington's primary knowledge-management problems are three: buying information technology, managing databases, and hiring able knowledge managers.

Purchasing Computers In 1965, Congress enacted the Brooks Act, which was passed at a time when the federal government was the computer market's biggest customer, accounting for 62 percent of all computer sales.[25] The Act's main intent was that only low bidders win federal contracts; purchasing information systems that actually worked was not really a consideration.

Times, of course, changed. Although the federal government remains the world's largest buyer of information technology, its share of the market has slipped to well under 4 percent.[26] Nevertheless, the procedures mandated by the Brooks Act remained in place, and the results were predictable.

By 1990, after spending more than $300 billion over the preceding two decades on its computers, it took the federal government forty-nine months, on average, to buy them. By contrast, comparable purchases in the private sector consumed thirteen months.[27] Senior federal managers confirmed that, as a result of the time it took to purchase information technology, they inevitably ended up "acquiring out-of-date products."[28]

In response to this crisis, Congress passed the Information Technology Management Reform Act

(also known as the Clinger–Cohen Act) of 1996, which effectively revoked the Brooks Act, streamlined purchasing, and freed procurement officers from selecting only the lowest bid when buying information systems.

Managing Records A second critical area of Washington's knowledge management is that of administering immense, complex, and decentralized databases. The federal government hosts more than 2,000 data centers, over 10,000 separate information technology systems, and 24,000 websites.[29]

The Federal Records Act of 1950 instructs agencies and the National Archives and Records Administration to manage their records in order to document all federal "policies and transactions," hardly a trivial charge, nor a small and shrinking one. The administration of George W. Bush "transferred 77 terabytes"—a *terabyte* is about 1 trillion bytes, or 1,000 gigabytes, of data, ranging from laws to e-mails—"to the Archives on leaving office, which was about 35 times the amount of data transferred by the Clinton administration," its immediate predecessor.[30]

"Records management has received low priority within the federal government," and the Government Accountability Office has been calling Congress's attention to this "remarkably persistent" lapse since 1981. Today, "almost 80 percent of agencies" are "at moderate to high risk of improper disposition of records."[31] "Many agencies do not have full-time records management personnel"; over half are not conducting "annual, formal program evaluations" of their records management and vital records operations; and there are "disturbing data about the exclusion of records management personnel from the development of new electronic systems."[32]

It is not that Congress has not been trying. In 1980, it passed the Paperwork Reduction Act, which directs the Office of Management and Budget (OMB) to develop a government-wide strategic information resources management plan, and the Information Technology Management Reform Act of 1996 required the twenty-seven largest agencies to appoint CIOs.

In 2009, President Barack Obama created two, wholly new, positions in the White House, the "federal chief information officer" and the "federal chief technology officer," who report directly to the president and work together to broadly improve federal knowledge management—a charge that includes spending, planning, and policymaking (notably, protecting personal privacy and improving governmental transparency) for information resources.

The Federal Information Resource's Human Resources

Federal CIOs have extensive past experience with information technology, and most have worked in two or more institutions—federal, state, or local government, academia, and business—before assuming their current positions as kings of the federal knowledge-management mountain. Seventy percent of them report directly to their agency heads, but seem unimpressed by their hierarchical status. The median time in office for permanently appointed CIOs is fewer than two years, with most leaving because of the "political environment" and more lucrative opportunities elsewhere.[33]

There is evidence of sincere efforts to upgrade the broader range of federal knowledge managers, but with counterproductive results. Over twenty years, the civil service hired professionals in information technology "at higher grade levels, promoted them faster, and paid them more" than it did comparably educated and experienced employees in other areas. Unfortunately, these information technology professionals perform at the same level as comparably educated and experienced professionals in other areas, and stay in the government just as long. The feds are paying more for less, or, at best, the same.[34]

Progress? Not Much

More than three decades after Congress directed the OMB to develop a government-wide information resources management plan, OMB continues to plod away on it.[35] The federal government "has compiled a record of failure that has jeopardized the nation's welfare, eroded public safety, and squandered untold billions of dollars."[36] Federal agencies, on average, use a scant 27 percent of their computers' processing power, and under 40 percent of their storage power; servers in some agencies stand idle 93 percent of the time.[37] Perhaps it should not surprise us that

Washington outsources a third of its information-resources budget to private companies.[38]

The good news is that, beginning in 2010, Washington has expended enormous energy to bring federal computer costs under control, and, in its first year of initiating these efforts, saved $3 billion.[39] In 2011, the top federal CIO announced plans to shut down, over five years, 937 of the 2,000-plus federal data centers (which had nearly quintupled in number over thirteen years), at an additional savings of more than $3 billion.[40]

The Public's Burden

Although the Paperwork Reduction Act demands that agencies lighten the public's paperwork burden, that load actually grew by 17 percent over six years, amounting to more than 8 billion, rapidly growing "burden hours" on the public.[41]

The computer-based problems of the bureaucracy go beyond burdens. Because of "software glitches," for instance, the Social Security Administration shortchanged some 700,000 retirees by $850 million in Social Security payments, including the multiple sclerosis victim who went without payments for four years, accumulated $60,000 in medical debts, and lost her house and car. So outdated are the nation's air traffic control systems that some equipment dating from the 1960s relies on vacuum tubes, and replacements must be ordered from Poland.[42]

Managing Knowledge in the States

Every state has a CIO, twenty-nine of whom report directly to the governor.[43] State CIOs stay in their jobs only twenty-six months, on average, a tenure that is not much longer than that of federal CIOs.[44]

An "overwhelming" 79 percent of state CIOs and other top knowledge managers cite "salary rates and pay grade structures" as obstacles to attracting and retaining talent.[45] Pay, however, is not a significant factor in affecting the job satisfaction of information technology employees in the states. Rather, they are much more likely to be satisfied in their jobs when there are clear communications and job descriptions; participatory management; support for career development; opportunities for advancement; and family-friendly workplace policies.[46]

The second greatest impediment in attracting and retaining able knowledge workers is the state's "civil service system," at 48 percent.[47]

Recruiting, and then keeping, talented knowledge workers is critical in bringing state knowledge systems online. Although Congress has offered funds since 1994 for states to develop information systems that detect child abusers, and forty-seven states are developing or operating such systems, the states report numerous weaknesses, including problems of inaccurate data and a median delay of two-and-half years in bringing their systems online.[48] Thirteen years after Washington had provided funding for these systems, sixteen states were still in the development stage.[49] Nearly two dozen years went by before all the states were in compliance with the requirement, in the Family Support Act of 1988, that state information systems for enforcing child support payments be operational.[50]

In light of these difficulties, it is somewhat surprising that a third, a plurality, of the states report a decrease over five years in contracting out their knowledge-management positions, up marginally from 30 percent four years earlier when a plurality of nearly two-fifths reported an *increase* in privatization.[51] And the states also display some innovative knowledge management. Maryland has adopted StateStat, an information system that coordinates policy knowledge across the state. Fifteen states use CourTools, software that incorporates ten basic metrics of judicial administration in an effort to improve their courts' efficiency.[52]

Managing Knowledge in Local Governments

Local governments are the nation's information resource leaders, accounting for some 9,000 different applications, or four times the number of federal digital applications, and three times that of state applications.[53] City managers rank the "use of new technologies" in the top tier (out of four tiers) of their priorities.[54] Larger cities with higher voter registration levels are likelier to adopt new electronic services for citizens.[55]

Cities that invest in information systems make major, long-term gains in the areas of fiscal control, cost avoidance, and improved relations with citizens,[56] but rapid, short-term gains are present, too. After New York City's Police Department pioneered, in 1994, Compstat, a computer program that weekly analyzes performance in each of its precincts, the city's murder rate dropped by two-thirds in just five years. In 2000, Baltimore, expanded Compstat to CitiStat, including not only law enforcement but other areas as well, and in only two years almost halved the blood lead levels in children.[57] Twenty-eight percent of cities and counties, mostly large ones, use "stat systems" that include "formal CitiSTAT-type processes," but which also "have added a focus on improvement and linking operations to outcomes."[58]

Unsurprisingly, local administrators feel good about computers. Ninety-two percent of municipal finance directors report that "computers have improved their government's efficiency and productivity."[59]

There are inevitable challenges in managing local information systems, and most involve relations between administrators who provide computer services and those who use them,[60] and the difficulties of hiring and training competent technical staff.[61] Nevertheless, local governments appear to be improving their knowledge management over time. In 1982, 22 percent of cities and counties contracted out their "data processing" to private companies,[62] a proportion that has been halved to 11 percent today.[63] Relative to the federal and many state governments, some local governments have become the "employer of choice" for professionals in information technology, "in spite of public sector constraints."[64]

A Pessimistic (but Realistic) Perspective on Public Knowledge Management

One should keep in mind that the public sector's problems of knowledge management are hardly unique to it. "The majority of information systems developments," regardless of sector, "are unsuccessful." Experts estimate that 20–30 percent are "total failures" (i.e., the project is abandoned), and around 30–60 percent are "partial failures," involving "time or cost overruns or other problems."[65] The *average* cost overrun for all information systems developments is almost 200 percent.[66]

The larger the project, the less likely that it will be successful. Governments, of course, require big, often the biggest, information systems, and their success rate, or lack thereof, reflects their enormous size and ambition. Eighteen percent of all governments' information technology projects are successful; the success rates in the manufacturing, financial, and retail sectors range from double to triple that of the public sector.[67]

Fifty-three percent of the federal government's information technology projects are "poorly planned, poorly performing, or both."[68] It is, therefore, good news that, beginning in 2010, the feds were at last making "the tough management decisions to terminate, halt or turn around failing projects.... The era of the grand design" in Washington's information-resource ambitions "finally might by drawing to a quiet close."[69]

Best Practices for Knowledge Management

There is "an extremely limited body of knowledge" about managing information resources in the public sector,[70] but what little there is[71] we have reduced to six guidelines that we believe have a particular salience. They are:

- *Strong, skilled leadership is essential.* Clear communication of changing needs and the unambiguous assignment of responsibility are critical. Public employees in particular must be pushed to "get with the program," as they tend to hunker down until this fad, too, shall pass.
- *The goals of new information systems must clearly align with legislative and agency goals, and be comprehensively integrated throughout the organization.* The clearer this alignment, the likelier that legislative support will continue. A formal strategic process that uses both radical and incremental strategies, and which continuously monitors progress, is mandatory.
- *Organizational processes, not software or hardware, should be the focus in introducing and managing information resources.* Once the administrative processes are right, then the software can be rewritten to accommodate them.

- *Develop strong skills among information resource managers, strong relationships between these managers and the rest of the organization, and rigorous performance measures.*
- *Minimize risks.* Politics contribute to agencies' risks, because competitive agencies or subunits will protect their traditional turfs, which new data systems can threaten; hence, wringing agreements about project specifications from department heads is both vital and tough. Unbundling projects into separate modules also reduces risk because failures are isolated, and the whole system is less likely to crash.
- *Remember to be a pessimistic, "recalcitrant, suspicious, and skeptical adopter" of information technology.*[72] Most information system projects fail.

PRIVACY *VERSUS* POLICY: THE PARTICULAR PROBLEM OF THE PUBLIC COMPUTER

As the public information resource grows ever more pervasive, a duo of devilish dilemmas has grown ever more ominous. At what point does the collection, storage, retrieval, and sharing of personal information for purposes of making better public policy become an invasion of a citizen's privacy? Where lies the delicate balance between protecting the people and protecting the person?

The Meaning of Privacy *versus* Policy

Here is an example of what we mean. The Internal Revenue Service (IRS) is the only federal agency that maintains a database of all federal taxpayers. Congress requires the IRS to keep its database confidential, and a consequence of this policy is that other government agencies cannot know which supposed taxpayers are really tax cheaters.

The sorry result is that federal agencies funnel, through contracts, payments, loans, and grants, nearly $13 billion in tax revenue each year to 189,000 organizations and individuals who have not paid their taxes. These are incomplete figures. Federal officials know, but are unable to document, that there are far more scofflaws who receive many more billions. Criminal acts abound in all these instances.[73]

This is the problem of privacy *versus* policy. On the one hand, the confidentiality of individual citizens' private information is protected, shielding them from personal embarrassment, identity theft, and financial loss. On the other hand, that same protection deprives every citizen of uncounted government benefits because it drains revenue from all public policies by transferring tax dollars to tax cheats. Personal privacy is preserved at the expense of efficient and effective public policy.

What Does Government Know?

Governments' store of personal information is exceptionally diverse and broadly distributed. Although all governments have enormous databases about their individual residents, the federal government clearly has the most.

Washington Wants to Know   Federal agencies collect information not only about the citizen in question but also match it with data about his or her spouse, children, dependents, and parents. They record one's legal name, maiden name, aliases, the dates of one's marriages and divorces, educational level, occupation, height, eye color, driver's license number, phone numbers, e-mail addresses, salary, investments, net worth, credit history, child support payments, bankruptcies, litigation, and

criminal and drug convictions.[74] This is just a sampling; there is much more.

Your federal government knows an awfully lot about you. And it shares.

Washington Wants Others to Know   *Computer matching* (the trendier term is "mashup") is the electronic comparison of two or more sets of data. Many of these mashups are of personal data, a practice encouraged by Congress. There are at least five major laws enacted since 1980 that match files to find fraudsters, debtors, tax evaders, and terrorists.

Federal agencies share their files about citizens with far more entities than merely their fellow feds. Twenty-seven states, 64,000 law enforcement agencies, and over a million officers participate in the Federal Bureau of Investigation's (FBI) National Crime Information Center, which stores more than 15 million individual arrest histories and the fingerprints of 55 million people.[75] Congress has enacted legislation that links federal, state, and local databases, and even foreign ones, to deal with welfare abusers, terrorists, and other criminals.

Without question, governments' practice of matching files brings benefits. Federal agencies estimate that they save "at least" $900 million each year through their "data sharing initiatives."[76] The box in this chapter provides a disturbing example of how public policy, and the public, can be harmed when agencies do *not* match personal information.

But there is a downside: The threat to personal privacy.

A Case of Unmatched Failure

Although the practice of mixing and matching government databases is a serious issue of privacy, distressing breakdowns of public policy can be a consequence when governments fail to mix and match their data. Here is one example.

Dean Arthur Schwartzmiller may hold the world record as a serial child predator. In 2005, police discovered seven notebooks containing 36,000 separate

entries by Schwartzmiller listing the names and other details of children whom, Schwartzmiller wrote, he had molested. Schwartzmiller had been arrested for child molestation in five states over the course of thirty-five years, and had spent twelve years in prison, but the stunning extent of his self-described molestations had been unknown to authorities.

(continued)

(continued)

How did this apparent failure of public policy happen? In large part, it happened because silos of public information were not matched.

All fifty states maintain databases that list and track sex offenders, and convicted child molesters such as Schwartzmiller are required to record in these databases where they live and work. (In 2003, the Supreme Court ruled that these registration requirements may be imposed even on offenders whose crimes took place before states had enacted such laws.) Schwartzmiller, however, simply did not register—not anywhere, not anytime. Indeed, the whereabouts of an estimated one-fourth of all convicted sex offenders is unknown because they fail to register. Because there was no national database (the U.S. Justice Department initiated such a database a month after the news about Schwartzmiller broke), or any system for the states to share not only their sex offender registrations but also their arrest and conviction records for sexual crimes, Schwartzmiller, and likely other child molesters, was never tracked. This failure enabled Schwartzmiller, presumably, to continue his molestation with far greater abandon for more than three decades. ■

Sources: Caroline Marshall, "Child Molester Is Suspected of Hundreds of Cases," *New York Times* (June 17, 2005); Kevin Johnson, "National Online Registry of Sex Offenders Launched," *USA Today* (July 20, 2005); and Donna Horowitz and Eric Malnic, "Child Advocate Calls for National Web Site for Tracking Molesters," *Los Angeles Times* (June 18, 2005).

Stealing You: Identity Theft

Perhaps the invasion of privacy that Americans fear most is *identity theft*, or the stealing of personal information for fraudulent use, typically for economic gain. Nearly 5 percent of the adult population are victims of identity theft, with reported losses amounting to more than $50 billion every year.[77]

Over a fourth of data breaches that lead to identity theft occur in government databases,[78] perhaps because government officials may not be well attuned to the sensitivity of private data. About 200 million personal records are exposed on the Internet per year, many by public officials who "viewed the new technology as a natural extension of the public domain and rushed to put information online," including deeds, divorces, bankruptcies, and occasionally Social Security and telephone numbers.[79]

Simple theft plays a part, too. In 2006, an employee of the U.S. Department of Veterans Affairs, in violation of standing, but laxly enforced, regulations, took home a departmental computer for work-related use. That evening, the computer was stolen, and, with it, the names, Social Security numbers, and other personal information of more than 26 million veterans. Fortunately, the computer eventually was returned (anonymously), with no apparent lifting of the data in it.

Although it was the largest theft of personal data from a government in history, it pales by comparison to its counterparts in the private sector, such as the 40 million personal identities of credit cardholders stolen by hackers in 2005, or the 130 million identities looted in 2009 from private companies. Small wonder, perhaps, that twice as many Americans "worry most" that companies, rather than governments, might infringe their privacy.[80]

Protecting Privacy: Federal Efforts

In light of these developments, it is not surprising that from 80 to 90 percent of Americans consistently state that they are concerned over problems of personal privacy,[81] a dramatic increase from only 35 percent in 1970.[82] As Americans' worries have deepened, each of the three branches of the federal government has grown more involved in the issue.

The Judiciary's Zone of Privacy In 1977, in *Whalen* v. *Roe*, the Supreme Court recognized for the first time a constitutionally protected "zone of privacy" that entitles each person to have his or her personal information kept private.

The courts since have developed a three-pronged test, based on the Constitution's Fourth

Amendment (the Unwarrantable Search and Seizure Clause), that should be used in balancing an employee's right to privacy with an employer's need to know. These tests are: *Reasonableness*—any intrusion by management into the personal life of an employee must involve the notification and consent of the employee; *compelling interest*—a serious issue must be present, such as the life-and-death responsibilities of air traffic controllers; and *job relatedness*—the intrusion cannot exceed the scope of business necessity.[83]

Congress, Privacy, and Policy Congress has enacted two principal laws that reconcile personal privacy with federal procedures. The *Privacy Act* of 1974 assures individual access to personal federal records. The *Electronic Government Act* of 2002 directs agencies to provide "privacy impact assessments" when purchasing new information technologies or initiating new collections of personal information. Congress has passed at least four additional laws that protect people's financial and other personal records from snooping by federal agencies, and another five statutes that shield these records from the view of colleges and corporations. The *Intelligence Reform and Terrorism Prevention Act* of 2004 created the Privacy and Civil Liberties Oversight Board, which reports to the president about these privacy issues.

In 2001, following the terrorist attacks of September 11th, Congress tilted more toward policy at the expense of privacy. The *USA Patriot Act* of 2001 expands Washington's authority to monitor citizens' electronic communications, and the *Real ID Act* of 2005 creates an immense database that centralizes the information collected by the states' departments of motor vehicles and can distribute it among federal, state, local, Canadian, and Mexican agencies.

Protecting Privacy in the Executive Branch Federal agencies have "generally complied with key requirements and guidance pertaining to… privacy,"[84] and compliance with the Privacy Act is "generally high," with 71 percent of agencies enforcing "the requirement that personal information should be complete, accurate, relevant, and timely before it is disclosed to a nonfederal organization."[85] In addition, OMB has issued at least a half-dozen memoranda that protect against identity theft, a crime over which seven federal agencies have some jurisdiction.[86]

Federal officials take these directives seriously. Over five years, 1,300 IRS employees were investigated for snooping in personal income tax returns, and 420 were found guilty.[87]

An accelerating trend is the appointment of agency executives charged with protecting personal privacy. The IRS in 1993 appointed the federal government's first "privacy advocate," and Congress soon began requiring, through legislation, "chief privacy officers" in selected agencies. In 2007, Congress passed the Implementing Recommendations of the 9/11 Commission Act, which extricated Congress from this thorny thicket by authorizing the Privacy and Civil Liberties Oversight Board to require any agencies that it chose to appoint privacy and civil liberties officers.

Protecting Privacy at the Grass Roots

Congress requires state and local agencies to shield personal data. Three laws enacted since 1990 bar all governments from releasing Social Security numbers, disclosing personal information by state departments of motor vehicles, and electronically transmitting personal health information.

Forty-six states have enacted privacy laws, but only 18 percent have a chief privacy officer, compared with 77 percent of financial services companies that have one. Forty-two percent of the states have no "privacy program" in place (a sizable 16 percent do not know if they have one, suggesting that they probably do not), and privacy programs are "just starting" in 18 percent.[88] All in all, it appears that more state and local records of personal data are exposed annually than are comparable federal records.[89]

There is some good news. Forty-seven states have enacted "security freeze laws" that block unauthorized persons from obtaining private credit information,[90] and forty-five require that citizens be notified of data breaches that affect them.[91] "More than 20 states" have redacted "personal information," notably Social Security numbers, from their records, amounting to "a major shift in public records laws."[92]

CYBERCRIME AND CYBERSECURITY

Citizens, as we have seen, fear how governments and companies will misuse information about them. But the opposite pertains, too: Governments and companies fear how citizens will the misuse *their* information. In a word, *hacking*, or the illegal access to computer databases by unauthorized persons.

We use the word loosely. Technically, hackers are one of nine "sources of cybersecurity threats" identified by the federal government, including nations, terrorists, "insiders," and "phishers," that penetrate data systems using a dozen forms of sabotage, ranging from "war driving" to "worms."[93] There are "at least fifty-thousand computer viruses" in the World Wide Web, and "any fool can enter, alter, and destroy even the most seemingly impregnable Web sites."[94]

Hacking: Harrowing and Humiliating

From $67 billion[95] to possibly $100 billion[96] is lost each year to computer crime. Approximately seven out of every ten organizations in all sectors are hacked every year.[97]

In the public sector, the major cybercrime is the simple theft of computers themselves, accounting for 44 percent of all data breaches in the public sector, compared with 20 percent in the private one. Seventeen percent of governments' data breaches are attributable to "outside hackers" (13 percent) and "insider malfeasance" (5 percent),[98] such as the Army private who, in 2010, was incarcerated because he allegedly had provided WikiLeaks, a website dedicated to outing federal secrets, with hundreds of thousands of secret military and diplomatic documents, the release of which inarguably harmed the national interest.

The federal government offers the richest public source for hackers. Despite the presence of an estimated 135,000 cybersecurity personnel,[99] all federal agencies report more than 50,000 security incidents each year, an astounding increase of more than 650 percent in just five years. Some of these incidents are very grave, such as the loss, in 2011, of 24,000 sensitive Pentagon files to a foreign government's single intrusion of a contractor's databank.[100]

The leading type of incident is the insertion of "malicious code," or software that infects operating systems.[101] More than half of federal agencies experience a "cybersecurity incident" on a weekly (23 percent) or daily (31 percent) basis.[102] Incidents involving the introduction of malicious software into federal computers tripled over just two years.[103]

"Accidental" breaches are handily the primary cause of all "internal" breaches in state agencies. Regrettably, it is followed by "malicious software," such as computer viruses, inserted by insiders. Malicious software introduced by outsiders is the leading reason for all "external" data breaches in the states.[104]

Attacking Hacking

Governments, with varying degrees of success, have built defenses against hackers.

Information Security Measures "Experts and leading organizations" identify "four key attributes of successful" information security measures. They should be "quantifiable, meaningful (i.e., have targets for tracking progress, be clearly defined, and be linked to organizational priorities), repeatable and consistent, and actionable."

To determine whether information security measures are indeed successful, they should be evaluated according to three criteria that are common to all sectors. They are the measure's *compliance* with standards, policies, and laws; the *effectiveness* of information security controls; and the overall *impact* of the information security program.[105]

Federal Cybersecurity The terrorist attacks of September 11, 2001, "changed the way federal agencies approach" cybersecurity,[106] and nowhere was this change more pronounced than in funding it. In the four years following 9/11, federal expenditures for computer security quadrupled[107] and have since leveled off to about $6 billion annually, with a 4 percent annual growth rate.[108]

Congress and Cybersecurity Congress has passed several laws to protect federal databases, but the main ones include the *USA Patriot Act* of 2001, which directed the Secret Service to establish a national network of electronic crime task forces; the *Homeland Security Act* of 2002, which charged the Department of Homeland Security that it created with protecting the nation's information infrastructure; and the *Federal Information Security Management Act* of 2002, which provides a comprehensive framework for assuring information security that is implemented through a preexisting certification process managed by the National Institute of Standards and Technology.

The President and Cybersecurity The beginning of the executive branch's interest in cybersecurity is marked by OMB Circular A-130, issued in 1985, which established the security certification system just noted. In 1997, the Government Accountability Office declared federal information security to be a "high-risk area" that required careful attention, and it remains one today. In 1998, President Bill Clinton issued Presidential Decision Directives 62, a secret directive that pertains to terrorist cybercrimes, and 63, directing agencies to reduce the vulnerability of their computer systems, and appointed the first cabinet-level officer for cybersecurity. President George W. Bush retained the position, but eliminated its cabinet status.

In 2003, Homeland Security Presidential Directive 7 expanded the Department of Homeland Security's cybersecurity role, and the U.S. Computer Emergency Readiness Team, a public-private partnership designed to coordinate responses to cyberattacks, was launched. In 2009, the president appointed a special assistant to the president and cybersecurity coordinator, and the Department of Homeland Security opened its National Cybersecurity and Communications Integration Center, charged with coordinating the private sector's and the federal, state, and local governments' counterattacks.

Progress and Problems In securing information, federal agencies tend to rely on compliance measures at the expense of more effective impact measures. Key attributes of, and best practices for, successful cybersecurity measures are "not always exhibited" by agencies,[109] and, despite "hundreds of recommendations" from federal inspectors, all of the twenty-four major federal agencies "continue to be afflicted by persistent information security control weaknesses."[110]

Although the Federal Information Security Management Act is "game-changing" legislation that has improved data security[111] (up to a point—recall that it was an Army *private* who reportedly passed massive loads of secret documents to WikiLeaks), it also has resulted in "unsustainable" snarls of red tape because it fails to distinguish between high- and low-level risk,[112] and "wastes" as much as $500 million a year because of its "outdated manual reporting requirement."[113]

Cybersecurity in the States Forty-five states have a chief information security officer, three-quarters of whom report to their states' CIO.[114] The states' CIOs have, notably, placed "security" as the top skill set that they want when recruiting and retaining employees.[115] Four years earlier, security ranked second.[116]

Nearly half (47 percent) of state chief information security officers have tiny staffs ranging from one to five professionals, a disturbingly low number when compared with financial services organizations of "similar size to that of an average state" in the private sector, where more than 100 full-time professionals, on average, report to the chief information security officer. Unsurprisingly, perhaps, a modest 35 percent of state cybersecurity officers are "very" or "extremely confident" in their organization's ability to protect its information assets from external threats, and just 13 percent say the same for internal threats.[117]

Almost nine out of ten state information security officers consider their often shrinking budgets to be the "major barrier" facing their agencies in protecting its information systems (no other obstacle comes even remotely close to this one), a less than startling opinion given that half of the states' cybersecurity budgets constitute from just 1 to 3 percent of the states' overall information technology budgets.[118]

E-GOV: LEAN, SEEN, AND CLEAN GOVERNMENT

The often gloomy caverns of public knowledge management do have at least one bright and shining light: E-gov. *Electronic government, e-government, e-gov,* or *digital government* is the introduction of governmental websites and portals (*portals* are integrated websites for targeted services) that furnish information to, and facilitate services for, users. All federal agencies and most state and local agencies have websites, and two-thirds of all Internet users have visited at least one.[119]

Overall, e-gov is gradually moving away from a technology that primarily provides information, and to the *transaction* stage, or the interactive provision of public services to citizens. A remarkable 89 percent of federal and state websites (up from 22 percent in 2000),[120] and 40 percent of local ones (up from 13 percent in 2000),[121] offer services that can be fully executed online.

Federal.gov

Paper and print are costly. Washington spends about $1.5 billion for printing and reproduction each year, and electronic government offers the surest way to significantly lower these costs.[122]

The Government Paperwork Elimination Act of 1998, which directs agencies to make as much information as possible available electronically to other agencies and the public, provides the basis of federal e-gov. The Electronic Government Act of 2002 added impetus to these objectives, and rapid progress ensued.

More than four-fifths of all federal benefits programs use at least one electronic benefits payment method, and most of these programs provide benefits electronically to most of their beneficiaries.[123] More than three-quarters of all citizens who receive federal benefits acquire them electronically.[124] The savings are significant. It costs the federal government a dollar to issue a paper check, but just a dime to do so electronically.[125]

Seventy-nine percent of all federal individual tax returns are filed electronically, up from 52 percent in just six years.[126] It costs the IRS just 19 cents to process an e-filed return, compared with a whopping $3.29 to process a paper one,[127] and the IRS estimates that for every 2.4 million taxpayers who e-file, enough funding is freed to hire 2,200 new agents.[128] "E-rulemaking" by regulatory agencies could save $94 million over three years.[129]

State.gov

As a result of mandates in the federal Personal Responsibility and Work Opportunity Reconciliation Act of 1996, all states now use *electronic benefit transfer systems,* or bankcards to deliver some federal and state welfare benefits. Purchasing transaction costs have been slashed by more than 90 percent as states move from paper to computers.[130]

States that are the most likely to adopt "e-government innovation" have larger economies; better educated and more homogeneous populations; and Republican-controlled legislatures that are highly professional, with committees dedicated to e-gov in each chamber. It is the variables that do *not* associate with the states' use of e-gov, however, that are intriguing, and these factors include the presence of an information technology department in the executive branch; governments that have higher per-capita revenues; higher urbanization; greater racial diversity; higher voter turnout; more competitive parties; and "greater policy liberalism" among citizens.[131]

Local.gov

Local governments have adopted e-gov with breathtaking speed,[132] moving from around half of cities and counties on the Internet to nearly all in just five years.[133] Local progress is all the more impressive because, to expand web-based services, local governments must surmount privacy concerns, confidentiality laws,[134] and financial obstacles, and smaller governments often must overcome limited expertise as well.[135] It follows, perhaps, that a fourth of local governments contract out the operation of their websites to the private sector.[136]

In Love with E-Gov

Everybody loves e-gov.

Governments Love E-Gov More than eight out of ten senior employees in the federal, state, and local governments believe that digital government will have a positive impact on government, and "not a single public official" states that e-gov affects government operations negatively.[137]

The Governed Love E-Gov Similar enthusiasm is present outside of government. Although there is some evidence that most citizens rate governmental portals lower than their commercial counterparts,[138] two-thirds of e-gov users think that it has made it more convenient for them to conduct transactions with the government, and three-fourths credit it for making it easier to stay informed about public services.[139]

A Surfeit of Satisfying Surprises Digital government has brought benefits that have startled even its most ardent advocates. Here are some.

E-Gov Improves Governments Benchmarking performance (reviewed in Chapter 7), a useful but difficult method for raising public productivity, is eased by e-gov.[140]

The use of e-gov within agencies also "is associated with reduction in red tape,"[141] a reduction that may lead to improved customer service; well over half of local administrators think that e-gov has done so.[142]

Almost seven out of ten local managers think that e-gov has improved their communication with the public.[143]

Governments' transparency and financial accountability are improved by e-gov, if somewhat passively so.[144]

More broadly, e-gov "leads to radical and structural...political and administrative reforms" that strengthen governments' overall accountability.[145]

E-Gov Curtails Corruption Even more surprisingly, e-gov is reducing corruption on a global scale. When corrupt officials are denied face-to-face contact with citizens and their transactions with them are automatically recorded—conditions that are greatly advanced by e-gov—the possibility of bribery dramatically diminishes. "Statistical analysis reveals that e-government has a consistently positive impact on reducing corruption" that matches those of "traditional anti-corruption factors," such as bureaucratic professionalism and law enforcement.[146] Other global research also has found that "information communication and technology....is an effective tool for reducing corruption."[147]

E-Gov Promotes Civic Engagement E-gov appears to play a part in promoting proactive citizenship. People who have greater access to the Internet, and who use it more frequently (including access to, and use of, government portals), "are more likely to be civically engaged," ranging from voting to volunteering, "than non-users."[148]

E-Gov Restores Trust in Government E-gov may be restoring Americans' faith in government. More than six out of ten of Americans believe that e-gov can make governments more accountable.[149] The more that citizens use governmental websites, the more satisfied they are with e-gov, and "e-government satisfaction is positively associated with trust in government."[150]

E-gov, in sum, "could raise public confidence in government."[151]

A Caveat

Although, as we have seen, e-gov robustly correlates with curbing corruption among public officials, it also associates equally vibrantly with high rates of fraud perpetrated on government by crooked citizens.

Public health care programs, where fraud is estimated to cost the federal government at least $60 billion every year,[152] are graft's poster boys in this regard, but they are hardly unique; Washington's contract reimbursements, welfare payments, and economic stimulus programs, among others, are also highly vulnerable. In fact, over seventy federal programs in twenty agencies improperly pay claimants (not all of whom, it should be said, are fraudsters) to the tune of more than $125 billion, accounting for nearly 6 percent of all federal outlays.[153] Medicare and Medicaid alone are responsible for about half of these payments.[154]

The common thread in this privately perpetrated fraud is e-gov, or, more specifically, the practice of governments automatically sending electronic payments to vast numbers of claimants. "Most [of these] claims are adjudicated by computers using rule-based systems, with no human intervention at all. Fraud perpetrators have only to learn the rules; then they can submit thousands of claims electronically and with relative impunity," such as the Los Angeles pastor and his wife who fraudulently claimed from Medicare more than $14 million, much of it successfully.[155] "Medicare fraud has grown so lucrative and so easy that drug dealers and organized crime rings are tapping into it."[156]

Congress, in an effort to end these misguided payments, enacted the Improper Payments Elimination and Recovery Act of 2010. With just ten programs accounting for 94 percent of all improper federal payments,[157] there seems to be a reasonable chance that Congress will succeed.

THE INFORMATION RESOURCE AND THE FUTURE OF GOVERNING

It is difficult to overstate the computer's impact. Galileo and Copernicus showed us that human beings are not at the center of the universe, "attended by sun and stars"; Darwin demonstrated that humanity is not "the species created and specially endowed by God with soul and reason"; with Freud, humankind "ceased to be the species whose behavior was—potentially—governable by rational mind"; and the computer is teaching us that the human race is not uniquely capable of intelligently manipulating its environment.[158]

Bye-Bye Bureaucracy?

Under these circumstances, it should not shock us that information technology has transformed much of government, and bodes to transmogrify all of it.

"State governments with high scores on information technology development also reported high scores on…eliminating layers" of bureaucracy.[159] A third of local officials state that e-gov has "changed the role of staff"; more than a fourth say that it has "reengineered business processes"; and a few report that e-gov has reduced the number of staff.[160]

"System-level bureaucracies," in which public administrators routinely communicate with citizens via computers, are replacing "street-level bureaucracies," in which bureaucrat-to-citizen interaction was face-to-face, thereby shriveling administrative discretion.[161] This may not be a bad thing, as

research indicates that, when automation replaces face-to-face interaction between citizens and street-level bureaucrats, biased bureaucratic discretion is reduced and citizens are more likely to receive the benefits to which they are entitled.[162]

Ultimately, "infocrats" displace bureaucrats. This displacement threatens to downgrade bureaucratic positions;[163] a study of the private sector found, in this regard, that the introduction of "e-business…threatened" some employees' "professional identities."[164] Of greater significance, however, because infocrats are far more cognizant of the uses of information resources than are elected officeholders, these "non-elected public officials have a free playing field," and "know better than the people's representatives" the conditions and opinions of these representatives' own constituencies; thus, power at the top of the bureaucracy slides from politicians to infocrats.[165]

Blue Skies? The Coming Cloud

Over a half century, computers evolved from monstrous mainframes to pocket-sized pods and pads and now are entering a new paradigm that has significant implications for government and all of society.

Cloud computing, an emerging and far-from-definitively-defined concept, is a knowledge-management model that enables cheap, quick, and easy access to a shared pool of computing resources that are elastic, require minimal management, and are location- and device-independent. In other words, due to additional network bandwidth and storage capacity, one can inexpensively, or even at no cost, access information at any time, from anywhere, and with anything. Information becomes as conveniently and reliably accessible as electrical power, which is why cloud computing is also called *on-demand, utility,* or *grid,* computing. It is anticipated that state and local governments will adopt it initially (23 percent of these governments have implemented cloud computing, and 29 percent have plans to adopt it),[166] although Washington seems committed to it as well.

Not everyone is enamored with it; Oracle's chief executive officer rants that cloud computing is "complete gibberish. It's insane. When is this idiocy going to stop?"[167] But most of those who have some understanding of "The Cloud" herald it as transformative. Los Angeles County, for example, used cloud computing to open its congressional redistricting process, a process that historically has been a plaything of politicians and special interests, to its 4.5 million registered voters.[168]

The computer is not merely mutating governing. It is transfiguring democracy.

NOTES

1. As derived from data in Bree Nordenson, "Overload! Journalism's Battle for Relevance in an Age of Too Much Information," *Columbia Journalism Review* (November/December 2008), http://www.cjr.org/magazine/november-december08.php. Nordenson writes that 988 exabytes were projected for 2010.

2. Sara Radicati and Quoc Hoang, *Email Statistics Report, 2011–2015* (Palo Alto, CA: The Radicati Group, Inc., 2011), pp. 3–4. Figures are global and are for 2011. Growth figures are projected, 2011–2015.

3. U.S. Government Accountability Office, *Information Technology: Investment Oversight and Management Have Improved but Continued Attention Is Needed*, GAO-11-454T (Washington, DC: U.S. Government Printing Office, 2011), Highlights page. Figure is for 2011.

4. Michael Hardy, "The $79.4B Buzz Killer," *Federal Computer Week* (February 8, 2010), p. 3. Figure is for 2001–2010.

5. WinGov, *Federal Information Technology Market, 2010–2015* (Washington, DC: Deltek, 2011).

6. Brian Deagon, "The Government Looks at Why Huge Technology Efforts Often Fail," *Investor's Business Daily* (July 12, 1994).

7. "Government Slideshow: IT Spending Priorities in Local Government," *CIOInsight* (June 10, 2010), http://www.cioinsight.com/c/a/Government/IT-Spending-Priorities-in-Local-Government-255107/. Figures are for 2010–2011.

8. The notion of "knowledge management" first appeared in Nicholas Henry, "Knowledge Management: A New Concern for Public Administration," *Public Administration Review* 34 (May/June 1974), pp. 189–196. In 2006, Oxford University Press issued a catalogue, titled *Knowledge Management & Information Technology*, touting more than fifty books and journals in the area.

9. Herbert A. Simon, *Administrative Behavior: A Study of Decision-Making Processes in Administrative Organizations*, 3rd ed. (New York: Free Press, 1976), p. 292.

10. See, for example, David N. Ammons and Charldean Newell, *City Executives: Leadership Roles, Work Characteristics, and Time Management* (Albany: State University of New York Press, 1989); and Herbert A. Kaufman, *The Administrative Behavior of Federal Bureau Chiefs* (Washington, DC: Johns Hopkins, 1981).

11. Stuart Bretschneider, "Management Information Systems in Public and Private Organizations: An Empirical Test," *Public Administration Review* 50 (September/October 1990), pp. 536–545. This is a study of more than 1,000 "high-level data managers" in state governments and the private sector.

12. Sean T. Lyons, Linda E. Duxbury, and Christopher A. Higgins, "A Comparison of the Values of Commitment of Private Sector, Public Sector, and Parapublic Sector Employees," *Public Administration Review* 66 (July/August 2006), pp. 605–618. This is a study of 549 Canadian "knowledge workers" in all three sectors.

13. Paul C. Nutt, "Public-Private Differences and the Assessment of Alternatives for Decision Making," *Journal of Public Administration Research and Theory* 9 (April 1999), pp. 305–349.

14. Theresa Heintz and Stuart Bretschneider, "Information Technology and Restructuring in Public Organizations: Does Adoption of Information Technology Affect Organizational Structures, Communications, and Decision Making?" *Journal of Public Administration Research and Theory* 10 (October 2000), pp. 801–828.

15. Robert P. McGowan and Gary A. Lombardo, "Decision Support Systems in State Government: Promises and Pitfalls," *Public Administration Review*, Special Issue 46 (November 1986), pp. 581–582.

16. C. E. Teasley, III and Susan W. Harrell, "A Real Garbage Can Model: Measuring the Costs of Politics with Computer Assisted Decision Support Software (DSS) Programs," *Public Administration Quarterly* 19 (Winter 1996), pp. 479–492.

17. Tom Davenport, as quoted in Michael J. Keegan, "Introduction—Analytics and Risk Management: Tools for Making Better Decisions," *The Business of Government* (Spring 2010), pp. 41–42. The quotation is on p. 41.

18. Ibid., pp. 41–42.

19. U.S. General Accounting Office, *Geographic Information Systems: Challenges to Effective Data Sharing*, GAO-03-874T (Washington, DC: U.S. Government Printing Office, 2003), p. 4.

20. Ibid., p. 5.

21. Ibid.; and Rhonda Mitschele, "Share and Share Alike: Creating a Cost Effective GIS," *American City and County* 111 (March 1996), pp. 25–33.

22. U.S. General Accounting Office, *Geographic Information Systems: Challenges to Effective Data Sharing*, p. 6.

23. Public Technologies, Inc., as cited in Terry F. Buss and F. Stevens Redburn, "Information Technology and Governance," *Modernizing Democracy: Innovations in Citizen Participation*, Terry F. Buss, F. Stevens Redburn, and Kristina Guo, eds. (Armonk, NY: M. E. Sharpe, 2006), pp. 170–202. The figures are on p. 173. Figure is for 2003.

24. Timothy Haithcoat, Lisa Warnecke, and Zorica Nedovic-Budic, "Geographic Information Technology in Local Government: Experience and Issues," *Municipal Year Book, 2001* (Washington, DC: International City/County Management Association, 2001), pp. 47–57.

25. Ralph Vartabedian, "Federal Computers: A System Gone Haywire?" *Los Angeles Times* (December 8, 1996).

26. Ibid.

27. Al Gore, *From Red Tape to Results: Creating a Government That Works Better and Costs Less, Reinventing Federal Procurement* (Washington, DC: U.S. Government Printing Office, 1993), p. 28.

28. Information Technology Association of America, *Key Issues in Federal Information Technology* (Arlington, VA: Author, 1992), p. 4.

29. Geoff Colvin, "Uncle Sam's First CIO," *Fortune* (July 25, 2011), pp. 56–61. Figures are for 2011.

30. U.S. Government Accountability Office, *Information Management: The Challenges of Managing Electronic Records*, GAO-10-838T

(Washington, DC: U.S. Government Printing Office, 2010), p. 11.

31. Ibid., pp. 5, 7. Figure is for 2009.

32. U.S. National Archives and Records Administration, *2010 Records Management Self-Assessment Report: An Assessment of Records Management Programs in the Federal Government* (Washington, DC: U.S. Government Printing Office, 2011), p. 46.

33. U.S. Government Accountability Office, *Federal Chief Information Officers: Responsibilities, Reporting Relationships, Tenure, and Challenges*, GAO-04-823 (Washington, DC: U.S. Government Printing Office, 2004), Highlights page and pp. 20, 22. The quotation is on p. 20. Federal CIOs average twenty-three months in office.

34. Gregory B. Lewis and Zhenhua Hu, "Information Technology Workers in the Federal Service: More Than a Quiet Crisis?" *Review of Public Personnel Administration* 25 (September 2005), pp. 207–224. The quotations are on pp. 207, 222. Data are for 1976–2003.

35. U.S. General Accounting Office, *Paperwork Reduction Act: Record Increase in Agencies' Burden Estimates*, GAO-03-691T (Washington, DC: U.S. Government Printing Office, 2003), p. 2. As noted earlier in the text, the Paperwork Reduction Act of 1980 requires OMB to write a government-wide information resources plan.

36. Vartabedian, "Federal Computers."

37. Colvin, "Uncle Sam's First CIO," pp. 59, 56. Figures are for 2011.

38. As derived from data in U.S. General Accounting Office, *Contracting for Information Technology Services*, GAO-03-384R Contracting for IT Services (Washington, DC: U.S. Government Printing Office, 2003), p. 2; and Colleen O'Hara, Diane Frank, and Dan Caterinicchia, "Budget Hawks Watch IT Projects," *Federal Computer Week* (August 2001), pp. 28–30.

39. U.S. Government Accountability Office, *Information Technology: Investment Oversight and Management Have Improved but Continued Attention Is Needed*, pp. 10–11. Figure is for 2010.

40. Colvin, "Uncle Sam's First CIO," p. 56, 59. Data center growth figure is for 1998–2011.

41. U.S. General Accounting Office, *Paperwork Reduction Act*, pp. 4–12. Figures are for 1995–2001.

42. Vartabedian, "Federal Computers."

43. Jack Gallt, Chris Dixon, and Mary Gay Whitmer, "Trends in State Information and Technology Management," *Book of the States*, (Lexington, KY: Council of State Governments, 2004), pp. 439–442. The data are on p. 440. Figure is for 2003.

44. Ellen Perlman, "Topside Turnover," *Governing* (April 2007), p. 40. Figure is for 2007.

45. National Association of State Chief Information Officers, *State IT Workforce: Under Pressure* (Lexington, KY: Author, 2011), pp. 3, 14.

46. Soonhee Kim, "IT Employee Job Satisfaction in the Public Sector," *International Journal of Public Administration* 32 (October 2009), pp. 1070–1097. This is a national survey of state IT employees.

47. National Association of State Chief Information Officers, *State IT Workforce: Under Pressure*, p. 13.

48. U.S. General Accounting Office, *Child Welfare: States Face Challenges in Developing Information Systems and Reporting Reliable Child Welfare Data*, GAO-04-267T (Washington, DC: U.S. Government Printing Office, 2003). Figure is for 2003.

49. U.S. Department of Health and Human Services, as cited in Ellen Perlman, "A Very Long Haul," *Governing* (October 2006), p. 64. Figure is for 2006.

50. "S.C. Child Support System Almost Operational," *Savannah Morning News* (March 27, 2010).

51. National Association of State Chief Information Officers, *State IT Workforce: Under Pressure*, p. 19, for the 2011 figure; and National Association of State Chief Information Officers, *State IT Workforce: Here Today, Gone Tomorrow?* p. 19, for the 2007 figure.

52. Katherine Barrett and Richard Greene, "Swift Justice," *Governing* (August 2011), pp. 50–51.

53. Forester Research, Inc., as cited in "e-Gov Momentum," *Governing* (August 2001), p. 46. These figures are projections. In 2000, local governments had roughly 1,500 e-gov applications, and the federal and state governments about 1,000 each. It was projected that, by 2006, local applications would hit 9,000, federal applications 2,000, and state applications 3,000.

54. Jerri Killian and Enamul Choudhury, "Continuity and Change in the Role of City Managers," *Municipal Year Book, 2010* (Washington, DC: International City/County Management Association, 2010), pp. 10–18. The datum (p. 14) is for 2010.

55. Christopher Weare, Juliet A. Musso, and Matthew L. Hale, "Electronic Democracy and the Diffusion of Municipal Web Pages in California," *Administration & Society* 31 (March 1999), pp. 3–27.

56. Alana Northrop, Kenneth L. Kraemer, Debora Dunkle, *et al.*, "Payoffs from Computerization: Lessons Over Time," *Public Administration Review* 50 (September/October 1990), pp. 505–514.

57. Mark A. Abramson, Jonathan D. Gould, and John M. Kamensky, *Four Trends Transforming Government* (Washington, DC: IBM Center for the Business of Government, 2003), p. 10.

58. Anne Spray Kinney and John Ruggini, "Measuring for a Purpose: Trends in Public-Sector Measurement and Management Practices," *Government Finance Review* 24 (August 2008), pp. 14–23. Figures are for 2006. The quotation is on pp. 19.

59. Glen Hahn Cope, "Budgeting for Performance in Local Government," *Municipal Year Book, 1995* (Washington, DC: International City/County Management Association, 1995), pp. 42–52. The quotation is on p. 51.

60. James N. Danziger, Kenneth L. Kraemer, Debora E. Dunkle, *et al.*, "Enhancing the Quality of Computer Service: Technology, Structure, and People," *Public Administration Review* 53 (March/April 1993), pp. 161–169.

61. Evelina R. Moulder, "E-Government: Trends, Opportunities, and Challenges," *Municipal Year Book, 2003* (Washington, DC: International City/County Management Association, 2003), pp. 39–45.

62. Harry P. Hatry and Carl F. Valente, "Alternative Delivery Approaches Involving Increased Use of the Private Sector," *Municipal Year Book, 1983* (Washington, DC: International City Management Association, 1983), pp. 199–217. Figure is on p. 200.

63. Mildred Warner and Amir Hefetz, "Cooperative Competition: Alternative Service Delivery, 2002–2007," *Municipal Year Book, 2009* (Washington, DC: International City/County Management Association, 2009), pp. 11–20. Figure (p. 14) is for 2007.

64. G. Zhiyong Lan, Lera Riley, and N. Joseph Cayer, "How Can Local Government

Become an Employer of Choice for Technical Professionals? Lessons and Experiences from the City of Phoenix," *Review of Public Personnel Administration* 25 (Fall 2005), pp. 225–242. The Quotations are on p. 225.

65. Shaun Goldfinch, "Pessimism, Failure, and Information Systems Development in the Public Sector," *Public Administration Review* 67 (September/October 2007), pp. 917–929. The quotations are on p. 917.

66. Standish Group, *Extreme Chaos* (West Yarmouth, MA: Author, 2001), http://www.standishgroup.com/sample_research/PDFpages/extreme_chaos.pdf.

67. Ibid.

68. As derived from data in U.S. Government Accountability Office, *Information Technology: OMB and Agencies Need to Improve Planning, Management, and Oversight of Projects Totaling Billions of Dollars*, GAO-08-1051T (Washington, DC: U.S. Government Printing Office, 2008), p. 2. Figure is for 2008.

69. "Say Goodbye to the Era of Grand Design," *Federal Computer Week* (September 27, 2010), p. 3.

70. Stephen J. Bajjaly, "Managing Emerging Information Systems in the Public Sector," *Public Productivity & Management Review* 23 (September 1999), pp. 40–47. The quotation is on p. 46.

71. We have relied largely on Sharon S. Dawes, Anthony M. Cresswell, and Theresa A. Pardo, "From 'Need to Know' to 'Need to Share': Tangled Problems of Information Boundaries, and the Building of Public Sector Knowledge Networks," *Public Administration Review* 69 (May/June 2009), pp. 392–402; Bajjaly, "Managing Emerging Information Systems in the Public Sector"; U.S. General Accounting Office, *Improving Mission Performance Through Strategic Information Management and Technology*; and National Association of State Information Resource Executives, *Best Practices in the Use of Information Technology in State Government* (Lexington, KY: Author, 2000).

72. Goldfinch, "Pessimism, Computer Failure, and Information Systems Development in the Public Sector," p. 917.

73. Chapter 11 has details and sources for federal contracts with for-profit recipients and Medicare payments. Chapter 12 has details and sources for federal contracts, loans, and grants to nonprofit recipients.

74. U.S. General Accounting Office, *Information Management: Selected Agencies' Handling of Personal Information*, GAO-02-1058 (Washington, DC: U.S. Government Printing Office, 2002), p. 1.

75. Anne R. Field, " 'Big Brother, Inc.' May Be Closer than You Thought," *Business Week* (February 9, 1987), pp. 27–28; and Christopher Swope, "Sherlock Online," *Governing* (September 2000), pp. 80–84.

76. U.S. Government Accountability Office, *Taxpayer Information: Options Exist to Enable Data Sharing between IRS and USCIS but Each Presents Challenges*, GAO-06-100 (Washington, DC: U.S. Government Printing Office, 2005), p. 1. Figure is for 2000.

77. U.S. Government Accountability Office, *Identity Theft: Governments Have Acted to Protect Personally Identifiable Information, but Vulnerabilities Remain*, GAO-09-759T (Washington, DC: U.S. Government Printing Office, 2009), Highlights page.

78. Symantic, as cited in Elizabeth Daigneau, "Defending Cyberspace," *Governing* (March 2009), p. 59. Figure, 26 percent, is for "the first half of 2007."

79. John Pulley, "Sorting the Personal from the Public," *Federal Computer Week* (October 29, 2007), http://fcw.com. Figure is for 2007 and is provided by Identity Truth.

80. Meg Bostrom, *By, or for, the People? A Meta-analysis of Public Opinion of Government* (New York: Demos, 2006), p. 41. In 2002, 57 percent "worried most about banks and credit cards," and 29 percent about the feds.

81. Electronic Privacy Information Center, Graphic, Verification, and Usability Center, Georgia Institute of Technology, *Public Opinion on Privacy* (Atlanta: Author, 2007). This is a review of fairly recent, major polls on the topic.

82. Harris polls, as cited in Robert S. Boyd, "An Eagle's Eye," *Savannah Morning News* (July 22, 1990).

83. Don E. Cozzetto and Theodore B. Pedeliski, "Privacy and the Workplace: Future Implications for Managers," *Review of Public Personnel Administration* 16 (Spring 1996), pp. 21–31.

84. U.S. General Accounting Office, *Information Management: Selected Agencies' Handling of Personal Information*, p. 1.

85. U.S. General Accounting Office, *Privacy Act: OMB Leadership Needed to Improve Agency Compliance*, Highlights page. Twenty-five agencies were surveyed.

86. U.S. Government Accountability Office, *Identity Theft: Governments Have Acted to Protect Personally Identifiable Information, but Vulnerabilities Remain*, pp. 17–18. OMB figure is for 2005–2009.

87. Kristin Davis, "Your Life Is Just a Stroke Away," *Baltimore Sun* (July 21, 1996). The testimony cited was given in 1994.

88. Deloitte and National Association of State Information Officers, *State Governments at Risk: A Call to Secure Citizen Data and Inspire Public Trust* (Washington, DC; Lexington, KY: Authors, 2010), pp. 16–17. Figures are for 2010. Forty-nine states responded.

89. William Jackson, "Data Breaches at State, Local Agencies Expose Data about Millions," *Government Computer News* (October 20, 2008), p. 18.

90. U.S. Government Accountability Office, *Identity Theft: Governments Have Acted to Protect Personally Identifiable Information, but Vulnerabilities Remain*, pp. 7–8. Figure is for 2009.

91. As derived from data in Defend Your Dollars. org, *States with Notice of Security Breach Laws*, http://www.defendyourdollars.org/2005/02/ states_with_not.html. Figure is for 2009.

92. Kay Stimson, "Secretaries of State: Focused on Redacting Social Security Numbers from Public Records in the Digital Age," *Book of the States, 2008* (Lexington, KY: Council of State Governments, 2008), pp. 218–222. The quotations are on p. 218. Figure is for 2008.

93. U.S. Government Accountability Office, *Cyberspace: United States Faces Challenges in Addressing Global Cybersecurity and Governance*, GAO-10-606 (Washington, DC: U.S. Government Printing Office, 2010), pp. 4–5.

94. Michael Specter, "The Doomsday Click," *The New Yorker* (May 28, 2001), pp. 101–102.

95. FBI study as cited in U.S. Government Accountability Office, *Cybercrime: Public and Private Entities Face Challenges in Addressing Cyber Threats*, GAO-07-705 (Washington, DC: U.S. Government Printing Office, 2007), p. 2. Figure is for 2005.

96. Michael McConnell, director, U.S. Office of National Intelligence, as cited in Lawrence Wright, "The Spymaster," *The New Yorker* (January 21, 2008), pp. 51–52.

97. Computer Emergency Response Team, Carnegie Mellon University, *Cert/CC Statistics 1988–2005* (Philadelphia: Author, 2005), http://www. cert.org.

98. Beth Rosenberg, *Chronology of Data Breaches 2006: Analysis* (Privacy Rights Clearinghouse, 2007), http://www.privacyrights.org/ar/ DataBreaches2006-Analysis.htm. Data are for 2006 and include the military.

99. Booz Allen Hamilton and Partnership for Public Service, *Cyber In-Security: Strengthening the Federal Cybersecurity Workforce* (Washington, DC: Authors, 2009), p. 7. Data are for 2009 and exclude the intelligence agencies.

100. Tom Shanker and Elisabeth Bumiller, "Hackers Gained Access to Sensitive Military Files," *New York Times* (July 14, 2011).

101. U.S. Government Accountability Office, *Cybersecurity: Continued Attention Needed to Protect Our Nation's Critical Infrastructure and Federal Information Systems*, GAO-11-463T (Washington, DC: U.S. Government Printing Office, 2011), p. 4.

102. Stephen Weigend, "Agencies Identify Biggest Threats to Cybersecurity," *Federal Computer Week* (January 25, 2010), p. 33. Figures are for 2009.

103. U.S. Government Accountability Office, *Cybersecurity: Continued Attention Needed to Protect Our Nation's Critical Infrastructure*, GAO-11-865T (Washington, DC: U.S. Government Printing Office, 2011), p. 6. Figure is for 2009–2010.

104. Deloitte and National Association of State Information Officers, *State Governments at Risk*, pp. 18–19. Figures are for 2010.

105. U.S. Government Accountability Office, *Information Security: Concerted Effort Needed to Improve Federal Performance Measures*, GAO-09-617 (Washington, DC: U.S. Government Printing Office, 2009), Highlights page.

106. Florence Olsen, "Input: Security Spending to Rise," *Federal Computer Week* (March 17, 2005), http://www.fcw.com.

107. Florence Olsen, "Input: IT Security Spending to Catch Its Breath," *Federal Computer Week* (July 14, 2005), http://www.fcw.com.

108. Olsen, "Input: Security Spending to Rise"; and Olsen, "Input: Security Spending to Catch Its Breath."

109. U.S. Government Accountability Office, *Information Security: Concerted Effort Needed to Improve Federal Performance Measures*, Highlights page.

110. U.S. Government Accountability Office, *Cybersecurity: Continued Attention Needed to Protect Our Nation's Critical Infrastructure and Information Systems*, pp. 10, 9. Datum is for 2010.

111. William Jackson, "Update: The Case for FISMA Reform," *Government Computer News* (April 5, 2010), p. 7.

112. Jamil Farshchi and Ahmad Douglas, "How to Move Past the FISMA Mindset," *Federal Computer Week* (September 13, 2010), p. 20.

113. Wyatt Kash, "A Cyber Bill Worth Enacting," *Government Computer News* 29 (June 21, 2010), p. 4.

114. Deloitte and National Association of State Chief Information Officers, *State Governments at Risk*, p. 6. Figures are for 2010.

115. National Association of State Chief Information Officers, *State IT Workforce: Under Pressure*, p. 15. Security was the only skill chosen by a majority, 52 percent, of CIOs in 2011, followed by project management, at 50 percent.

116. National Association of State Chief Information Officers, *State IT Workforce: Here Today, Gone Tomorrow?* p. 18. Project management was chosen by 63 percent of CIOs in 2007, followed by security, at 59 percent.

117. Deloitte and National Association of State Chief Information Officers, *State Governments at Risk*, pp. 6–7, 18. Data are for 2010.

118. Ibid., p. 14. Figures are for 2010.

119. U.S. Bureau of the Census, *Statistical Abstract of the United States, 2011*, 130th ed. (Washington, DC: U.S. Government Printing Office, 2011), Table 1158. Figure is for 2010.

120. Darrell M. West, *State and Federal Electronic Government in the United States, 2008* (Washington, DC: Brookings, 2008), p. 2. Current figure is for 2008.

121. Darrell M. West, *Urban E-Government, 2004* (Providence, RI: Center for Public Policy, Brown University, 2004), p. 3. Current figure is for 2004.

122. Nicole Blake Johnson, "Agencies Move to Eliminate Paper Use, Boost Electronic Business," *Federal Times* (April 1, 2011), FederalTimes.com. These costs totaled $1.4 billion in 2010.

123. U.S. Government Accountability Office, *Electronic Payments: Many Programs Electronically Disburse Federal Benefits, and More Outreach Could Increase Use*, GAO-08-645 (Washington, DC: U.S. Government Printing Office, 2008), Highlights page. Figures are for 2008.

124. U.S. General Accounting Office, *Electronic Transfers: Use by Federal Payment Recipients Has Increased but Obstacles to Greater Participation Remain*, GAO-02-913 (Washington, DC: U.S. Government Printing Office, 2002). Figure is for 2002. The Debt Collection Improvement Act of 1996 directed agencies to make all federal payments, except tax refund payments, via electronic fund transfers. Congress added Food Stamps as an electronically delivered benefit in 2000.

125. Johnson, "Agencies Move to Eliminate Paper Use, Boost Electronic Business."

126. U.S. Government Accountability Office, *E-Filing Tax Returns: Penalty Authority and Digitizing More Paper Return Data Could Increase Benefits*, GAO-12-33 (Washington, DC: U.S. Government Printing Office, 2011), Highlights page. Figure is for FY 2011.

127. U.S. Government Accountability Office, *2010 Tax Filing Season: IRS's Performance Improved in Some Key Areas, but Efficiency Gains Are Possible in Others*, GAO-11-111 (Washington, DC: U.S. Government Printing Office, 2010), p. 6. Growth figures are for 2005–2010. Cost figures are for 2009.

128. Buss and Redburn, "Information Technology and Governance," p. 184.

129. U.S. Government Accountability Office, *Electronic Rulemaking: Progress Made in Developing Centralized E-Rulemaking System*, GAO-05-777 (Washington, DC: U.S. Government Printing Office, 2005).

130. "Slowdown Ahead for Financing E-Procurement," *Governing* (July 2001), p. 70.

131. Caroline J. Tolbert, Karen Mossberger, and Ramona McNeal, "Institutions, Policy Innovation, and E-Government in the American States," *Public Administration Review* 68 (May/June 2008), pp. 549–563. The quotation is on p. 554.

132. Donald F. Norris and M. Jae Moon, "Advancing E-Government at the Grassroots: Tortoise or Hare?" *Public Administration Review* 65 (January/February 2005), pp. 64–73.

133. John O'Looney, "Use of the Internet for Citizen Participation and Service Delivery," *Municipal Year Book, 2001* (Washington, DC: International City/County Management Association, 2001), p. 28. In 2000, 96 percent of all cities and counties had websites.

134. Civic Resource Group, *Cities on the Internet, 2001: E-Government Applied* (Santa Monica, CA: Author, 2001). Figures are for 2001.

135. David Coursey, "E-Government: Trends, Benefits, and Challenges," *Municipal Year Book, 2005* (Washington, DC: International City/County Management Association, 2005), pp. 14–21.

136. Moulder, "E-Government," p. 43. Figure is for 2002.

137. Council for Excellence in Government, *The New E-Government Equation: Ease, Engagement, Privacy and Protection* (Washington, DC: Author, 2003), p. 24. Figures are for 2003.

138. Forrest V. Morgeson, III, and Sunil Mithas, "Does E-Government Measure Up to E-Business? Comparing End User Perceptions of U.S. Federal Government of U.S. Federal Government and E-Business Web Sites," *Public Administration Review* 69 (July/August 2009), pp. 740–752.

139. Council for Excellence in Government, *The New E-Government Equation*, pp. 2, 5. Figures are for 2003.

140. Vicente Pina, Lourdes Torres, and Sonia Royo, "Is E-Government Leading to More Accountable and Transparent Local Governments? An Overall View," *Financial Accountability & Management* 26 (February 2010), pp. 3–20. This is a study of local governments in the European Union.

141. Eric W. Welch and Sanjay K. Pandey, "E-Government and Bureaucracy: Toward a Better Understanding of Intranet Implementation and Its Effect on Red Tape," *Journal of Public Administration Research and Theory* 17 (October 2007), pp. 379–404. The quotation is on p. 379.

142. Coursey, "E-Government," p. 17. Figure is for 2004.

143. Ibid. Figure is for 2004.

144. Pina, Torres, and Royo, "Is E-Government Leading to More Accountable and Transparent Local Governments?"

145. Ibid.; and Hiroko Kudo, "Does E-Government Guarantee Accountability in Public Sector? Experiences in Italy and Japan," *Public Administration Quarterly* 32 (April 2008), pp. 93–120. The quotations are on p. 93.

146. Dong Chul Shim and Tae Ho Eom, "E-Government and Anti-Corruption: Empirical Analysis of International Data," *International Journal of Public Administration* 31 (3, 2008), pp. 298–316. The quotation is on p. 298.

147. Dong Chul Shim and Tae Ho Eom, "Anticorruption Effects of Information Communication and Technology (ICT) and Social Capital," *International Review of Administrative Sciences* 75 (March 2009), pp. 99–116.

148. Corporation for National and Community Service and National Conference on Citizenship, *Civic Life in America: Key Findings on the Civic Health of the Nation, Issue Brief* (Washington, DC: Authors, 2010), pp. 11, 22–23.

149. Council for Excellence in Government, *E-Government: To Connect, Protect, and Serve Us* (Washington, DC: Author, 2002), pp. 19–20. Figures are for 2001.

150. Eric C. Welch, "Linking Citizen Satisfaction with E- Government and Trust in Government," *Journal of Public Administration Research and Theory* 15 (Summer 2005), pp. 371–392. The quotation is on p. 371. See also Caroline J. Tolbert and Karen Mossberger, "The Effects of E-Government on Trust and Confidence in Government," *Public Administration Review* 66 (May/June 2006), pp. 324–369.

151. Peter Hart, as quoted in Joshua Dean, "E-Gov Efforts Could Raise Public Trust, Poll Shows,"

Government Executive (September 29, 2000), p. 24.

152. Jane Zhang, "Lawmakers Target Medicare and Medicaid Fraud," *Wall Street Journal* (October 29, 2009).

153. U.S. Government Printing Office, *Improper Payments: Recent Efforts to Address Improper Payments and Remaining Challenges*, GAO-11-575T (Washington, DC: U.S. Government Printing Office, 2011), p. 3. Figures are for FY 2010.

154. U.S. Government Accounting Office, *Improper Payments: Progress Made but Challenges Remain in Estimating and Reducing Improper Payments*, GAO-09-628T (Washington, DC: U.S. Government Printing Office, 2009), Highlights page. Figure is for FY 2008.

155. Malcolm Sparrow, Associated Press, "An E-Ripoff of U.S. Health Care," *Savannah Morning News* (August 24, 2011).

156. Kelli Kennedy, Associated Press, "Medicare Yanks Licenses, Returns Them," *Savannah Morning News* (October 17, 2011).

157. U.S. Government Printing Office, *Improper Payments: Recent Efforts to Address Improper Payments and Remaining Challenges*, p. 3. Figure is for FY 2010.

158. Herbert A. Simon, *The Shape of Automation for Men and Management* (New York: Harper & Row, 1965), p. 52.

159. Kuotsai Tom Liou and Ronnie Korosec, "Implementing Organizational Reform Strategies in State Government," *Public Administration Quarterly* 33 (Fall 2009), pp. 429–452. The quotation is on p. 447.

160. Coursey, "E Government," p. 17. Figures are for 2004; 2 percent of local officials reported employee reductions attributable to computers.

161. Mark Bovens and Stavros Zouridis, "From Street-Level to System-Level Bureaucracies: How Information and Communication Technology Is Transforming Administrative Discretion and Control," *Public Administration Review* 62 (March/April 2002), pp. 174–184.

162. Jeffrey B. Wenger and Vicky M. Wilkins, "At the Discretion of Rogue Agents: How Automation Improves Women's Outcomes in Unemployment Insurance," *Journal of Public Administration Research and Theory* 19 (April 2009), pp. 313–333. In this case, the technology in question was the telephone.

163. Ignace Snellen, "Electronic Governance: Implications for Citizens, Politicians and Public Servants," *International Review of Administrative Sciences* 65 (June 2002), pp. 190–194. The quotation is on p.194.

164. Ulla Eriksson-Zetterquist, Kajsa Lindberg, and Alexander Styhre, "When the Good Times Are Over: Professionals Encountering New Technology," *Human Relations* 62 (August 2009), pp. 1145–1170. The quotations are on p. 1145.

165. Snellen, "Electronic Governance."

166. Russell Nichols, "Blue Skies?" *Governing* (July 2011), pp. 44–47. Figures are for 2011.

167. Larry Ellison, as quoted in David C. Wyld, *Moving to the Cloud: An Introduction to Cloud Computing in Government* (Washington, DC: IBM Center for the Business of Government, 2010), p. 11. This discussion is based on this source.

168. Robert L. Mitchell, "Redistricting for the Masses," *Computerworld* (May 23, 2011), pp. 21–23. Of course, the redistricting plan still required the approval of the county's elected board of supervisors.

The Constant Quest: Efficient and Effective Governance

All governments have issues of efficiency and effectiveness. A probably apocryphal example: Following World War II, a British commission charged with modernizing government discovered that "the civil service was paying a full-time worker to light bonfires along the Dover cliffs if a Spanish Armada was sighted," a fleet last spotted in 1588.[1]

Although our example might seem to belie it, more productive public administration is colossally consequential. If the federal government, for instance, "could achieve the 15 percent or more productivity improvement we typically expect from a major private-sector change program," the savings would tally to "more than $445 per citizen."[2] Multiply that figure by more than 300 million people, and suddenly we are talking about real money.

Efficient and effective public administration has lain leadenly on the minds of American public officials even before there was a United States of America. Consider some complaints about the lack of productive public administration made by some distinguished Americans who served in Congress under the Articles of Confederation, that odd interregnum when the government had no executive branch, thereby forcing legislators to also be administrators:[3]

- Thomas Burke: Because members of Congress "cannot reject any [administrative] business addressed to them...much time is spent on unimportant business."
- Robert Morris: "No man living can attend the daily deliberations of Congress and do executive parts of business at the same time."
- Thomas Jefferson: "Nothing is so embarrassing nor so mischievous in a great assembly as the details of execution. The smallest trifle of that kind occupies [legislators' time] as long as the most important act of legislation, and takes [the] place of everything else."

These frustrations over inefficient government led James Madison, in particular, to use "an efficiency argument" for creating, as a vital part of the nation's new Constitution, a separate executive branch authorized to implement congressional legislation. "We have been taught that the separation of powers was meant to provide mutual checks, with consequent inefficiency in operation," a consequence often hailed by political scientists as the reasonable price of protecting citizens from despotic governmental efficiency. But the founders' "primary need was to *achieve* efficiency.... The modern cult of checks as the primary virtue of the Constitution was not shared by its framers." Indeed not. The term "check" appears a mere five times in *The Federalist Papers*, and then only when referring to "governmental machinery," and the word is nowhere to be found in the Constitution.[4]

UNDERSTANDING PUBLIC PRODUCTIVITY

Planted in a lush landscape of large political change and reared in reformist roots, the public productivity movement sprouted into the Saguaro cactus of public management: tall, tough, prickly, and dry. Nevertheless, public productivity also constitutes a proactive environment of optimism about the prospects of improving governmental efficiency and effectiveness, but its sunny nature must be tempered by reality if it is to succeed.

Productive Definitions

The Chinese have a saying that, translated very roughly, means, "First, we must name things what they are." Nowhere is this sentence more salient than in the subtle and sometimes confusing world of public productivity.

Efficiency is the full accomplishment of a job using the fewest resources possible, or "the biggest bang for the buck." *Effectiveness* is the full production of the intended result.

We remind ourselves of these basic definitions because the terms are not as universal as one might expect. There is, for example, no word in Russian for efficiency, although there is one for effectiveness.[5] Those who ever faced the fearsome might of the Red Army can appreciate that the Russians understand effectiveness.

Public productivity is government's improvement of efficiency and effectiveness in delivering its services, programs, and policies. A more formal definition of *public productivity* is "a ratio between inputs and outputs. Productivity is improved when increases of output are achieved per unit of input."[6] *Inputs* are the resources used by a program, such as money, people, or time. *Outputs* are the final products of a program, such as garbage collected or Social Security checks sent.

Outcomes, or *impacts*, are the social or economic changes produced by a program's outputs. For instance, the *output* of tons of garbage collected results in the *outcomes* of fewer rats, fewer plagues, and improved public health.

Ghettos of Public Productivity

One should be fully aware that these definitions, while straightforward and clear, are the basis of a field that is convoluted and murky. "The amazing thing about public productivity research is different clusters of researchers investigate the same problems in different ways...the majority of researchers in one cluster are not aware, let alone familiar with, the studies of the other clusters...all these differences put researchers into intellectual ghettos."[7]

The confusing ghettos of public productivity are not merely intellectual ones but practical ones, too: To achieve substantially greater public efficiencies requires actions that are beyond the ken of "public productivity" as we normally understand that term. Hence, we address in this or other chapters (or ghettos of our own making) the primary proposals for more efficient governing.

These proposals include: eliminating improper payments; consolidating agency services and information resources, streamlining procurement and hiring; reducing the number of public administrative personnel, including political appointees, and, if possible, managerial layers; strengthening administrative oversight by expanding professional workforces in purchasing, inspections, auditing, accounting, and knowledge management, and aligning legislative oversight with executive functions; pursuing tax delinquents more aggressively; cutting back on excessive outsourcing; improving the accuracy of performance measures; investing more in job training;[8] discarding (when legislatures permit it) redundant or unneeded programs;[9] ensuring that top leadership and dedicated implementation teams drive the transformation of public agencies into more efficient organizations; setting implementation goals for that transformation; involving employees in the transformation so that they gain ownership of it; targeting short-term as well as long-term efficiency initiatives; and building an agency capacity for improving efficiency by creating a department that shares best practices, standardizes training, and solicits advice from experts.[10]

There is, obviously, no lack of proven ways to improve public productivity. In this chapter, and throughout this book, we explore, or have explored earlier, these and other methods for improving governments' efficiency and effectiveness, including a few that are widely thought to enhance public productivity but which seem to have an opposite effect.

Public Productivity: Some Unexpected Correlations

There are some common conditions in governments that can limit or enable their productivity. Those conditions, however, are not necessarily what one might expect.

Discretion and Engagement Employee attitudes is one. In those agencies where the legislature has delegated greater administrative discretion, employees "who like their work more than their pay use their discretion to enhance productivity, while employees who like their pay more than their work use their discretion to reduce productivity."[11]

Personnel Policies Public policies for public employees can shape their attitudes in ways that can, in turn, indirectly raise or lower productivity. For example, in governments that assure a high level of job security, there is "a positive impact on employee productivity."[12]

Federalism Finally, there is a positive global correlation between federal governmental structures, such as the United States has (and unlike those in nations with unitary governments), and more productive, efficient governance. A study of seventy-three countries found that "the mobility of individuals among competing jurisdictions leads policy makers to adopt policies that are more efficient in terms of taxation and public good provision."[13]

Why Can't Governments Be More Efficient?

An astonishing 98 percent of Americans think that government wastes "a lot" (72 percent) or "some" (26 percent) tax money,[14] and "for years surveys have shown that the public believes close to half

of tax dollars are wasted."[15] A third of federal managers say that their own government "misuses tax dollars."[16] These perceptions flourish, in part, because there are so few facts that counter—or confirm—them.

Nevertheless, governments, as we shall see in this chapter, can be made more efficient. For example, when President Barack Obama directed, in 2009, that his cabinet departments reduce their administrative spending by $100 million, they lowered it instead by $243 million.[17]

For four fundamental reasons, governments remain inherently unable to attain the same level of productivity found in the private sector.

Constrained American Governments As we reviewed in Chapter 1 and Part II, American governments (but not private and nonprofit organizations) function in a culture that is uniquely constraining; thus, they find it very hard to change, even for reasons of gaining greater efficiency.

Global Governmental Bureaucratization As we discussed in Chapter 4, no government (not just American ones) can be streamlined—that is, reduced in its hierarchy and red tape—to the extent that a company or nonprofit organization can be.

Environmental Turbulence When the external environment of public organizations becomes more turbulent—a condition that arguably is amplifying over time—that turbulence has a measurably "negative effect" on the performance of government agencies.[18]

Parsing Policy Execution Perhaps this turbulence's single most negative impact on governmental efficiency is that of legislatures creating a single public policy, and then scattering, like seeds to the wind, slices of that policy among passels of public agencies, with (of course) the stern legislative mandate that the agencies somehow manage the policy efficiently.

Redundancy Royale The problem of program overlap permeates the states and larger local governments, but it seems most pronounced at the federal level. Eighty-five percent of "new or substantially revised programs" enacted by Congress call for the involvement of two or more entities, "rather than a single administrative unit," to implement them.[19] Most federal agencies execute three or more of the fifteen federal "budget functions"—that is, Washington's biggest, and wholly different, public policies, such as "National Defense." The Department of Agriculture, for instance, spends only about two-fifths of its appropriated funds on agriculture; another two-fifths goes to income security programs.[20]

Consider some other instances of this legislative parsing of policy implementation.[21]

- Thirteen of the fourteen cabinet departments administer 342 economic development programs.
- Twenty-nine agencies execute 541 clean air, water, and waste programs.
- More than fifty federal agencies are charged with planning and executing drug control strategies.

Redundancy, Taxpayers, Clients, and Inefficiency This redundancy of policy execution invariably leads to gross governmental inefficiency, and this inefficiency can produce public hardships, whether the public is defined as taxpayers or as recipients of public services.

Let us consider, first, taxpayers. Here is an example that links programmatic duplication to needlessly high costs that must be borne by taxpayers: The federal government's forty job training programs (fourteen of which serve fewer than 4,000 trainees each, and one of these serves just 318) are administered by seven agencies at an annual cost of nearly $12 billion, including administrative costs that range from an eyebrow-raising 7 percent of all expenditures to an eye-popping 20 percent.[22]

Now let us consider clients. Here is an example (specifically, federal human services programs) that links programmatic redundancy to poorly served Americans.

Six federal agencies...state and local agencies, as well as for-profit and nonprofit agencies directly provide services.... This array of programs [is] too fragmented and overly complex—for clients to navigate, [and] for program operators to administer effectively....Individuals often must visit multiple offices to apply for aid and provide the same information and documentation each time.... The complexity and variation in eligibility rules and other requirements among programs contribute to time-consuming and duplicative administrative processes that add to overall costs. Some programs provide similar services through separate programs, resulting in additional inefficiencies.[23]

The same sorts of programmatic proliferation and duplication, and its resultant human hardship, saturate all other policy areas, too. It would appear that no public program, no matter that it is identical to a slew of others, is so redundant that legislators will not only protect it, but often add more redundancy.

Why Can't the Independent Sector, as well as the Public Sector, Be More Efficient?

There are two additional reasons why governments cannot be as efficient as for-profit companies. Uniquely, these reasons also apply to the independent sector.

Process Change Equals Glacial Change

It is an inescapable and stubborn fact that the core activity of all governments, and essentially of all nonprofit public serving organizations, is providing services. Providing services, of course, is a process, and processes, as we explained in Chapter 4, are far more difficult to change than are products, which are produced almost exclusively by the private sector. Thus, to attain greater efficiencies in the public and nonprofit sectors requires disproportionately that processes be changed, and this is a far larger challenge than in the private sector.

Technology, Productivity, and Service Quality

Finally, the public and independent sectors are unable to exploit new technologies to boost productivity to the extent that the private sector can.

In the product-intensive private sector—specifically, in manufacturing and agriculture—investments can be made in technologies that increase productivity by replacing labor. But in the service-intensive public and nonprofit sectors, technologies cannot replace labor because their workers are direct, hands-on producers of services, and quality is a defining component of service efficiency and effectiveness. Hence, it is extremely difficult to make teachers more productive by increasing their class sizes, to make social workers more productive by expanding their caseloads, to make police and firefighters more productive by decreasing their numbers, or to make nonprofit program managers more productive by cutting their funding. In these instances, the quality of service inevitably suffers.[24] "The same might be said for playing a string quartet with two instruments: More productive, perhaps, but it's not the same thing."[25]

As with all generalizations, there are exceptions. One is technologies that achieve greater energy efficiency. Energy savings boost productivity in all sectors, including the public and nonprofit ones.

The other exception is that of information technology, which also has improved productivity in all sectors. Certainly this is true for governments, where computers have displaced labor. An example: In 1983, clerical workers accounted for 20 percent of federal civilian employees; today, they account for 6 percent.[26] As a former federal secretary observed, "The stuff I did 15 or 16 years ago is no longer necessary. Now we all need some level of computer literacy."[27]

THE EVOLUTION OF PUBLIC PRODUCTIVITY

Aside from the creation of the Constitution itself and, with it, an executive branch, governments' attempts to improve their own productivity can be traced back to at least 1816, when the House of Representatives established a standing committee to examine the operations of the War Department.[28]

Efficiency for Good Government, 1900–1939

In the modern era, Washington first demonstrated that it was concerned with federal productivity when President Robert A. Taft appointed, in 1910, the Commission on Economy and Efficiency. In 1937, the president's Committee on Administrative Management, detailed in Chapter 2, published its impressive report and minced no words about the centrality of efficiency to good government: "Efficiency is thus axiom number one in the value scale of administration. This brings administration into apparent conflict with the value scale of politics."[29]

The states did not evidence much interest in improving governmental efficiency until well into the twentieth century, but this was far from the case in local governments, where most governing was done. At the beginning of the twentieth century, aside from the national defense and diplomacy budgets, nearly three-fourths of all public expenditures were expended by local governments.[30] Moreover, because the functions of local governments at that time were (and still are) mostly to provide routine, repetitive services, such as garbage collection, local governmental tasks often were receptive to improved efficiency.

The New York Bureau of Municipal Research, founded in 1906, and its proliferous progeny (noted in Chapter 2) were pioneers in the development of public performance measures;[31] many of these "bureaus of efficiency" actually featured the word "efficiency" in their titles.[32] The National Committee on Municipal Standards, formed in 1928, largely by the Government (then Municipal) Finance Officers Association, also devised some of the nation's early performance measures in the public sector. What is now the International City/County Management Association emerged in the 1930s as an ardent advocate of these metrics, publishing, in 1938, Clarence Ridley's and Herbert Simon's classic *Measuring Municipal Activities*.[33]

Controlling Costs, 1940–1970

With the 1940s, interest in performance measurement and program evaluation took a seat well to the rear of public administrators' concerns with costs, budgeting, and organization. Nevertheless, the early pioneers of organization development, reviewed in Chapter 3, devised in the 1940s some of the basic theoretical precepts of program evaluation, and the "Great Society" programs of the 1960s encouraged social scientists to evaluate the impact of public programs in poverty, education, and related issues.

Managing for Efficiency and Effectiveness, 1970–1980

The 1970s were an important decade for measuring, assessing, and improving public productivity.

Federal Forward—Fitfully In 1970, scholars observed that "the whole federal machinery for making policy and budget decisions suffers from a crucial weakness; it lacks a comprehensive system for measuring program effectiveness,"[34] and a powerful Senator alerted the Government Accountability Office that it was "distressing that we have no real measures of the efficiency of the federal sector."[35]

Despite these critiques, efforts by the executive branch to measure and improve its efficiency during this period were feeble at best. Congress, however, was more aggressive, and in 1978 passed the Inspector General Act, which created offices of inspectors general (IG), now emplaced in 69 federal bureaus, employing more than 12,600 professionals.[36]

IGs are public administrators, found at all governmental levels, who are charged with improving agency performance; exposing waste, fraud, and abuse; and helping administrators eliminate these problems. The Inspector General Reform Act of 2008 made it more difficult to remove or transfer IGs and enhanced their power in related ways.

Federal IGs save the government $44 billion annually via audit recommendations and recoveries, and this amount increases each year. They conduct nearly 6,000 criminal investigations, file more than 6,000 indictments, and resolve over 1,000 civil actions each year; these numbers are declining over time.[37]

Despite this commendable record, political backing for the IGs ranges from "Congressional indifference to inspectors general recommendations,"[38] to outright hostility, as

evidenced by politicians' treatment of the Office of Special Inspector General for Iraq Reconstruction. Created by Congress in 2003, a politically-embarrassed Congress and a conniving White House secretly terminated it, in 2006, after it uncovered billions of dollars lost to mismanagement and theft; only after the press exposed these machinations was the office reinstated.

In addition, IGs do not help themselves with their fellow bureaucrats when they relish the role of a "gotcha gang" in unearthing administrative inefficiencies, such as the IG who was quoted in the *Washington Post* as stating (he denied it) that his own agency had "a crime rate higher than downtown Detroit."[39] Regrettably, there remains only a tepid propensity of IGs to work with line managers in writing their final recommendations, and there is no measurable increase in their inclination to do so over time.[40]

Perhaps for these reason, IGs themselves recognize that they are at a "vulnerable junction" with regard to their resources and their independence and respect from Congress and the executive branch.[41] Nevertheless, "It is safe to say that the federal government is a lot better off today because of the IG's efforts."[42]

State and Local Governments: Learning and Leading The 1970s marked the first real commitment by the states to assessing their programs. Between 1970 and 1980, the number of states in which most major agencies were conducting productivity analyses doubled, from one-fifth to two-fifths.[43]

The 1970s also were a decade for local governments to rediscover productivity, often as a consequence of renewed professional interest in the area. In 1971 fewer than two-fifths of these governments had some form of program evaluation unit in even one agency, a proportion that had burgeoned to nearly two-thirds only five years later.[44]

A Mixed Passel of Productivity, 1981–1990

During the 1980s, federal bureaucrats advanced productivity despite presidential indifference; state governments' efforts flattened; and local governments achieved remarkable gains.

A Committed Federal Bureaucracy Despite the White House's Herculean efforts during the 1980s to substitute public productivity with privatization, the federal bureaucracy made some significant advances. Remarkably, even though there was a significant decline during the 1980s in federal resources for evaluation research, the number of program evaluations produced by federal agencies remained about the same as in earlier years, "suggesting continued executive branch interest in obtaining evaluation information."[45]

State Stabilization and Local Leadership By the mid-1980s, legislatures in thirty-five states had expanded existing agencies or had created new ones charged with the state-wide evaluation of program effectiveness and efficiency,[46] but the number of states in which most major agencies conducted productivity analyses was only nominally more than it had been at the close of the 1970s.[47]

Local governments more than retained their position of leadership. By the end of the 1980s, an astounding four-fifths of municipal governments were conducting program evaluations.[48]

A New Public Management, 1991–Present

By the final decade of the twentieth century, public managers were so frustrated over being chained (they believed) to antiquated practices that prohibited them from governing well that the term "liberation management"[49] was coined to express their felt need for greater flexibility, and, by the mid-1990s, just 10 percent of federal, state, and local agencies had "no experience" with the bundle of techniques that we associate with "the new public management."[50]

Notable Notions of the New Pubic Management The *new public management* is a proactive commitment to entrepreneurial and accountable innovation in governance for the purpose of raising governmental performance. It may be reduced to the following features:

- *Efficiency and Effectiveness.* Citizens and public managers alike expect their systems of governance to provide more cost-effective services to more people.
- *Independence and Accountability.* Granting public administrators greater flexibility in managing their governments doubtless would add to their productivity, but enhanced freedom cannot be attained at the expense of their accountability to the law, professional values, and the public interest.
- *Competition and Collaboration.* Governments compete and collaborate with other governments, companies, and nonprofit organizations to enhance public performance and citizen participation in governance.
- *High Performance Public Agencies.* The characteristics of high performance public agencies include agility, adaptability, alertness in anticipating and solving problems, and the aggressive use of information.[51]

These ideas lead to a much greater emphasis on certain kinds of public management that have been stressed only intermittently in the past, notably intersectoral and intergovernmental administration, performance measurement and feedback, program evaluation, strategic planning, training, decentralization, and streamlining and innovating the processes of procurement, budgeting, and human resources.

Katrina, Crisis, and Collapse

A bit more of the new public management, with its emphasis on alertness, agility, and adaptability, would have been welcomed by the people of the Gulf Coast when Hurricane Katrina slammed into Alabama, Louisiana, and Mississippi on August 29, 2005, leaving in its wake 1,836 confirmed dead, 705 missing and assumed dead, and hundreds of thousands homeless. New Orleans was especially hard hit. Were governments alert, agile, and adaptable in responding to that city's plight?

(continued)

(continued)

Katrina, then a tropical storm, was first observed over the Central Bahamas on August 24th, five days before it struck the Gulf Coast, and a hurricane warning was issued that day.

Washington's response was limp. It sent serious assistance to the region only after: Nine days had elapsed *after* Katrina was spotted; eight days *after* it glanced off Florida, causing at least two deaths; seven days *after* Hurricane Katrina had attained Category 3 dimensions and was projected to hit Gulfport and New Orleans, and Louisiana declared a state of emergency; six days *after* Mississippi and New Orleans declared states of emergency; five days *after* Katrina registered as a Category 5 hurricane, the most destructive storm possible, Alabama declared a state of emergency, and a mandatory evacuation was ordered by the mayor of New Orleans; four days *after* Katrina made landfall as a Category 3 hurricane, and New Orleans began to flood; three days *after* 80 percent of New Orleans was flooded and widespread looting had erupted; two days *after* the evacuation of 25,000 people trapped in New Orleans' Superdome began; and one day *after* some rescue efforts in New Orleans were suspended because of sniper fire. Only on the next day, September 2nd, did significant federal aid arrive, in the form of 26,000 National Guard troops.

The president was at his ranch in Texas when the hurricane hit and evidently was not seriously engaged in the crisis until days after landfall, perhaps because most of the top officials in the Federal Emergency Management Agency (FEMA), the main federal bureau responsible for responding to disasters, held their offices more by dint of experience in party politics than in emergency management (details are in the box in Chapter 9).

FEMA declined assistance from states and other federal agencies. New Orleans' levees were breached on the very night that Katrina struck, but, days later, both the director of FEMA and the secretary of Homeland Security were publicly contending that they were unaware that anything was seriously awry on the Gulf Coast, despite unremitting media coverage that sent a quite contrary message.

The president was proud of FEMA's performance, praising his FEMA director with a phrase that may long endure in the discourse of disconnectedness: "Brownie, you're doin' a heckuva job." The director resigned two months after Katrina hit, following intense national criticism.

Numerous nations offered a total of $845 million in in oil and cash to help Katrina's victims. Washington demurred. "Most of the aid went uncollected.... [and] of the $126 million in cash that has been received, most" had not been used nearly two years following Katrina's landfall. Federal agencies "declined 54 of 77 recorded aid offers from three of it is staunchest allies: Canada, Britain, and Israel" (Solomon and Hsu).

Louisiana's governor refused to declare martial law and declined the White House's proposal to place her National Guard under federal control. Despite adequate warning given fifty-six hours before Katrina made landfall, the governor ordered no evacuation of New Orleans.

New Orleans' mayor ordered an evacuation just nineteen hours before the hurricane struck, when highways already were jammed with evacuees, but failed to mobilize the city's busses to transport those 100,000 citizens who did not own cars. More than 70,000 people were trapped in floodwaters reaching twenty feet and higher, awaiting rescue. They were stranded many days.

New Orleans' government collapsed. About 15 percent (figures vary, but this seems to be the approximate midpoint) of New Orleans' finest, its police officers, failed to report for duty after the hurricane made landfall. The Police Department "as an institution...disintegrated with the first drop of water" in dealing with its impact (Select Bipartisan Committee, p. 246).

Fraud flourished in Katrina's aftermath. Within the first six months following landfall, 16 percent of federal emergency funds were lost to fraud, such as the $10 million for displaced residents that went to people who were not displaced, including 1,170 prison inmates. FEMA made "improper payments" and "overpayments" toting up to some $1.3 billion, including "at least $3 million to more than 500 ineligible foreign students" (U.S. Government Accountability Office, 2007, Highlights page). More than a year following the disaster, 70 percent of $11 billion in federal contracts to relief providers were "plagued by waste, fraud, abuse, or mismanagement" (Committee on Government Reform, Summary page).

"Hurricane Katrina revealed a national emergency management system in disarray" (Waugh and Streib, p. 131), and Katrina's victims understandably focused their ire on their public administrators. A local elected official expressed the situation straightforwardly: "The bureaucracy has murdered people in the greater New Orleans area" (Schneider, p. 515). ∎

Sources: Select Bipartisan Committee to Investigate the Preparation for and Response to Hurricane Katrina, U.S. House of Representatives, 109th Congress, Second Session, *A Failure of Initiative: Final Report* (Washington, DC: U.S. Government Printing Office, 2006); Brookings Institution, *Hurricane Katrina Timeline* (Washington, DC: Author, 2005); John Solomon and Spencer S. Hsu, "Most Katrina Aid from Overseas Went Unclaimed," *Washington Post* (April 29, 2007); Committee on Government Reform—Minority Staff Special Investigations Division, U.S. House of Representatives, *Waste, Fraud, and Abuse in Hurricane Katrina Contracts* (Washington, DC: U.S. Government Printing Office, 2006); U.S. Government Accountability Office, *Hurricanes Katrina & Rita Disaster Relief: Continued Findings of Fraud, Waste, and Abuse,* GAO-07-300 (Washington, DC: U.S. Government Printing Office, 2007); Eric Lipton, "Interior Dept. Report Describes FEMA's Scant Use of Its Help," *New York Times* (January 30, 2006); William L. Waugh, Jr. and Gregory Streib, "Collaboration and Leadership for Effective Emergency Management," *Public Administration Review,* Supplement to Vol. 66 (December 2006), pp. 131–140; and Saundra K. Schneider, "Special Report: Administrative Breakdowns in the Governmental Response to Hurricane Katrina," *Public Administration Review* 65 (September/October 2005), pp. 515–516.

The New Federal Management Within three months after being sworn into office in 1993, President Bill Clinton created the National Performance Review, composed of some 250 experienced federal employees, declaring that, "Our goal is to make the entire federal government both less expensive and more efficient."[52]

The National Performance Review reported that, by 1996, almost two-thirds of its 1,200 recommendations[53] had been enacted (but almost none after that year), resulting in savings of more than $136 billion. By 2000, the federal government had published over 4,000 new customer service standards, scrapped some 640,000 pages of internal agency rules, and eliminated 250 programs and agencies, 2,000 field offices, and 426,200 federal jobs.[54] Historically, the federal civilian workforce, which comprised about 1 percent of the population from 1960 to 1990,[55] was cut by 11 percent during the 1990s,[56] and federal civilian employees have accounted for two-thirds of 1 percent of the population since 2000.[57]

The National Performance Review was "the longest-running reform in the history of the Federal Government,"[58] and it was a relatively successful one; a "report card" graded it at a "B," noting that "no such effort has ever received such lasting high-

level support."[59] The new federal management has since evolved into a concern with performance measurement and program evaluation, explained later in this chapter.

The New State Management From over a fifth to more than four-fifths of state governments are seriously engaged in *public quality management,*[60] or the continuous betterment of government programs.

The evidence suggests that the new public management is making a positive impact in state governance. An analysis of nearly 300 state agencies concluded that "taking risks, being innovative, and being proactive [which was "the most influential factor of the three"] contribute positively to organizational performance" by state agencies.[61]

A massive survey of state employees found that a remarkable 72 percent of them believe that the new public management's "harder" techniques, notably, strategic planning, performance measurement, and process improvements, plus the "softer" factor of performance feedback, have a significantly greater impact on improving agency performance than do customer service, empowerment, teamwork, training, employee awards, and recognition programs.[62]

The New Local Management Local interest in the new public management can be traced to the introduction in the early 1980s of *Quality Circles*, which is a technique that gathers small groups of employees to analyze problems and develop solutions. A third of municipalities use Quality Circles.[63]

Today, city managers support "reinvention" by better than nine to one.[64] "Nearly all" city managers "believe that taxpayers should be treated as customers, that third-party contracting and competition in service delivery are acceptable, that government should be mission-driven and entrepreneurial, and that nontax revenue sources should be developed."[65] More than half of all city and county services are delivered, in whole or in part, by organizations other than the governments that are paying for them;[66] over half of cities and counties conduct surveys that plumb their citizens' satisfaction with their services;[67] and better than seven out of ten municipalities have initiated programs to improve services to their "customers."[68]

There is evidence that these techniques are beneficial at the local level, as there is a positive empirical correlation between innovative entrepreneurialism and enhanced local governmental performance.[69] When local governments adopt a "market orientation" in their governing, "consumer satisfaction" becomes "quite strong," particularly when local officials view themselves as competing with other service providers and conscientiously coordinate their own service provision.[70] Accordingly, perhaps, "city councils are very agreeable to proposals to reinvent government," adopting 70 percent of eight reforms that associate with the new public management when they are recommended by their city managers.[71]

MEASURING PUBLIC AND NONPROFIT PERFORMANCE

A foundation of the public sector's effort to improve its efficiency and effectiveness is *performance measurement*, or "the ongoing monitoring and reporting of program accomplishments, particularly progress towards pre-established goals."[72]

Measuring performance has grown immeasurably as a dominating concern of both the public and public administrators. Seventy percent of Americans "favor creating a system of evaluating government agencies by the [objective] results they produce rather than by the programs they initiate or the money they spend."[73] The single most important "operational issue," by far, to senior public executives in five developed countries, including the United States, is "improved quality of service," identified by a remarkable 84 percent, followed by "improved productivity," at 75 percent.[74]

In the nonprofit sector, performance measurement remains an "emerging issue" that is relegated "primarily, and almost exclusively, to monitor and assess the use of funds." The more significant challenge of using measures to actually improve organizational performance receives only "limited attention."[75]

Performance Measurement: Benefits and Limitations

There are some obvious (and less obvious) benefits of measuring performance, and some inevitable limitations as well.

Some Benefits of Performance Measurement
Improving the public and independent sectors' efficiency and effectiveness remains the undisputed potential benefit of using performance measures, but there are other advantages, too.

In the Public Sector One is pride. More than eight out of ten federal employees who believe that they work in high-performing agencies (a belief that, presumably, derives from their agencies' performance scores) report that they are satisfied with their jobs, compared to six out of ten government-wide.[76]

Other benefits include improving programs and their accountability, enhancing collaboration with other agencies, and maintaining continuity during leadership transitions.[77]

A not so subtle, but also not so well known, benefit of performance measurement is that it is effective in ridding governments of probably inept officials. Voters do not reward incumbent candidates seeking reelection when they learn from published comprehensive performance scores that the candidates' governments are performing well, or withdraw their support even when they are performing "weakly," but voters do punish them when their agencies are performing poorly: Incumbents in governments with the poorest published performance scores suffer, on average, a 6 percent loss in voter support.[78]

There is a similar impact on upper-level public administrators: "Local governments that saw a 10-percentage point reduction in citizen satisfaction" resulting from published performance scores "(not an uncommon occurrence...) on average had a five percentage point higher senior management turnover rate." A ten-point decrease in the scores for core services "increases the senior management turnover rate by three percentage points."[79]

Perhaps, however, performance measurement's most lasting contribution may be its strengthening of government's legitimacy in society. Performance measurement "is being embraced with equal fervor by conservatives and liberals. Conservatives see it as a way of bringing accountability to government; liberals see it as a way to illustrate that government *is* worth paying for—and may even be worth paying *more* for."[80]

In the Third Sector   Those relatively few nonprofit organizations that use performance measures also find that they pay dividends. Employing a broad range of performance measures correlates positively with more effective strategic decision making in nonprofit organizations.[81] Not only does using performance measures associate with "substantial improvement" in these organizations' performance, but, "somewhat surprisingly," independent organizations that used "common performance measures" received "large increases in funding" from the state legislature. Those that used measures that were unique to them, by contrast, "were cut dramatically."[82]

Some Limitations of Performance Measurement

Some public agencies (and most nonprofit organizations) find performance measures far more useful and easier to use than others. Highway safety departments, for instance, with their straightforward, measurable mission, have found performance measures to be rewardingly productive, but child welfare programs, with a necessarily more subjective, judgmental mission, have not.[83]

Variables other than mission come into play, too. One exhaustive review of the literature identified no fewer than thirty-seven barriers to improving governmental performance, ranging from the lack of political appeal inherent in the productivity techniques themselves to various "performance myths" held about these techniques.[84]

Of these barriers, culture, both organizational and social, seems to count most. A densely careful and comprehensive study of implementing performance-based management systems, involving thousands of high-level practitioners, concluded that cultural factors have a greater impact (whether positive or negative) than technical, rational, and even political factors on the use of performance information in governments and universities.[85]

In light of these challenges, the literature of integrating performance measures with agency management reminds one of mobilizing for war: "Transforming a public bureaucracy into a results-based organization is not for the faint of heart. It requires bold and sustained leadership" to win "the hearts and minds of both managers and employees deep in the organization."[86]

Measuring Federal Performance

In 1991, not even a tenth of federal agencies were measuring their performance in useable ways. In part because the federal government "came late to this revolution," the feds' ability to measure agency performance ranked "on a scale of 10 about at a 2."[87]

But Washington displayed an early determination to raise this ranking. The National Performance Review, created in 1993, and the Government Performance and Results Act of 1993 (also known as the Results Act) point by their titles alone to this conclusion. The Results Act, uniquely, marked the first time that Congress, rather than the executive branch, required measurable program performance, and this requirement's "base in law ensures both congressional and executive branch involvement and makes it harder for its sponsors to retreat."[88]

Progress in the Second Millennium By 2004, almost nine out of ten agencies had performance measures in place,[89] and, by 2007, roughly half of agency administrators were using information obtained from performance measurement to a "great or very great extent."[90] Although federal officials' use of performance measures has flattened, even as their number has grown,[91] they are finding that using performance measurement is becoming easier over time.[92] More than three-fifths, up from about half ten years earlier, of federal managers use "performance information" to reward "government employees I manage or supervise."[93]

In 2009, President Barack Obama appointed the federal government's first "chief performance officer," who reports directly to the president, and in 2010 he signed into law the Government Performance and Results Act Modernization Act.

Perhaps the act's most significant new requirement is that OMB and certain congressional committees develop a handful of long-range, "cross-agency," government-wide priority goals every two years, although there is also, without doubt, some significance in the law's provision that, if an agency fails to meet its performance targets in three years, Congress will consider revising or terminating the programs in question. The legislation also aligns the agencies' strategic plans with presidential terms; links annual performance goals with strategic plans; mandates more performance reporting; and legislates agency-based chief operating officers and program improvement officers (a position that had been created three years earlier by executive order).

"If effectively implemented," the act could lead to greater efficiencies and accountability, rectify "weaknesses in major management functions," and assure that "performance information is both useful and used."[94] Or, as a Senator put it, "This is the biggest little bill that nobody ever heard of."[95]

Problems in the Second Millennium These are all good auguries for federal performance measurement, but some systemic problems remain.

In measuring their own performance, agencies often omit some basic measures of efficiency. In nearly seven out of ten applications, input measures are not used, and in over a fourth, both input and output measures are absent, causing one to wonder how, in these instances, performance could be even remotely assessed. This situation is less the result of inept administrators, who express frustration in trying to develop meaningful measures, and is much more a reflection of the unique difficulties inherent in measuring public performance.[96]

In addition to these structural problems, agency-based performance improvement officers cite inadequate authority to raise performance and a lack of top-level support in building a performance-sensitive culture (and culture, recall, trumps every other factor, including politics, in its impact on public performance systems[97]), which they think is already weak. They have so many additional responsibilities that they spend less than half of their time, on average, on performance management.[98]

Measuring State Performance

As with Washington, the state capitals are making significant gains in measuring their performance.

Measurable State Strides All states mandate a budget process that demands from agencies data that measure their programs' outputs,[99] and "every state uses some form of performance management built into the oversight and evaluation of its programs; however the sophistication, breadth and quality of those programs vary significantly."[100]

More than seven out of ten state departmental administrators say that the efficiency and effectiveness of their agency has been enhanced because of performance measures,[101] and improved communication and service quality correlate with their use by state agencies.[102]

Somewhat surprisingly, state legislatures that are peopled by part-time citizen legislators "are associated with better administrative practices" in "the managerial use of performance measures...than professional legislatures."[103] To keep using performance measures over time, states must have a lot of people, as large populations seems to the single variable that associates with their long-term use.[104]

A Time to Trust? State agencies, like their federal and local counterparts, typically self-report their own performance to their legislatures. Unique to the states, however, is the troubling reality that legislators do not trust those reports. In fact, self-reported agency performance information is less trusted by legislators than information coming from any other source. Other than legislators' own personal experiences with the agency, outside audits of agency performance are legislators' most trusted source of information.[105]

Measuring Local Performance

"Stat fever" is raging in local governments,[106] and a major symptom is performance measurement, which is used by six out of ten cities and counties. Two-fifths of those governments with performance measures use them government-wide.[107] More populous cities and those with a city manager are the most likely to adopt performance measures.[108]

Three-fifths of the thirty largest cities and almost three-fifths of the thirty largest counties track performance targets over time and report whether these targets are hit or missed. Twenty-seven percent of smaller cities and about 5 percent of smaller counties (i.e., those with populations of between 10,000 and 500,000) do so.[109]

From two-thirds to four-fifths of city managers cite the improvement of managerial and budgetary decisions and the assurance of greater accountability as their top reasons for adopting performance measures.[110]

Almost two-fifths of top city administrators rate performance measures as "very effective," and nearly three-fifths rate them as "somewhat effective" in improving efficiency.[111]

Those local governments that are most successful in using performance measures have a participative management style; high levels of privatization; an emphasis on economic development; a comparatively low reliance on state and federal sources of revenue;[112] and extensive civil service reforms.[113]

PERMUTATIONS AND PRACTICES OF PERFORMANCE MEASUREMENT

Measuring public performance is complicated, clarifying, and constrained.

Permutations of Performance Measurement

Governments use five, generally recognized, kinds of performance measures. All levels of government employ these indicators, and Washington's use of each of them grew at "statistically significant" rates over a decade.[114]

Workload, or *output*, *measures* calculate the amount of work performed or service provided. An example is tons of trash collected. These indicators are used most extensively by the federal, state, and local governments.[115]

Unit cost, or *efficiency*, *measures* assess the monetary expense per unit of output or workload. An example is the cost of trash collected per residence.

Efficiency measures are used least by the federal, state, and local governments.[116] This is unfortunate, because "the likelihood that performance data will be used to influence operations is enhanced by the collection of and reliance on higher-order measures, especially efficiency measures, rather than simply workload or output measures."[117]

The extent of governments' use of the remaining three indicators falls at levels between those of workload and efficiency measures.

Outcome, or *effectiveness*, *measures*, quantify the extent to which goals are attained, needs are met, and desired effects are produced. An example is counting the number of renovated homes in a neighborhood that is undergoing renewal.

Service quality measures are value-based assessments of management's responsiveness to clients' needs or expectations. Often, these measures focus on timeliness, accuracy, and courtesy. Although responsiveness sometimes can be objectively measured (e.g., the time that it takes for an ambulance to arrive at an accident), determining whether or not the response is of adequate quality is often a subjective judgment. (Does an average arrival time of thirty minutes amount to adequate service quality, or should it be five minutes?)

A final sort of major performance measure is the *citizen satisfaction measure*, which assesses the extent to which citizens feel that their needs have been met by a program.

The Measurement Mire

At least eight issues of performance measurement have been identified that public administrators should be cognizant of before they employ them.[118]

Measuring the Wrong Thing

Imprecision in defining what one wants to measure can result in measuring something else entirely. For instance, in determining how much government should invest in health, safety, and related programs, it was decided that government must know how much a human life was worth. But the real question is less the worth of a human life and more one of people's willingness to pay, through taxes, for their own health, and this determination can be made through analyzing opinion polls or prices in markets where risk is a factor.[119]

Using Meaningless Measures

Consider this: "During my more than 30 years as a cop, I produced and sometimes created crime statistics.... No official order was ever given to underreport or not report crimes...[but the] mayor didn't like high crime stats with no arrests....Consequently, it was a bad idea for a rookie to report a robbery with no arrests."[120]

Or, at its worst, this: When the District of Columbia launched in its public schools a tough new regimen that linked student test scores with big bonuses for, and punitive firings of, teachers and principals (nearly 45 percent of teachers and principals were replaced), scores in some schools soared by more than 40 percent. It later turned out that "the high-performing D.C. schools had alarmingly high instances of wrong-to-right erasure rates on test answers.... before the sheets were machine-graded." When performance measurement and reporting degenerates into "management-by-fear," or even merely management-by-greed, cheating happens.[121]

These instances illustrate a serious problem in the data that administrators sometimes must use in measuring performance: unreliability. Unreliable data pop up more frequently when resources are scarce, demands are extreme, the daily activities of administrators are not closely monitored, and performance is linked to incentives.[122]

Differing Interpretations of the "Same" Concept

Different officials sometimes define what they want to measure differently, and some officials choose definitions that benefit their agencies (e.g., agency "clients" are defined as anyone who occasionally phones in, thereby expanding their client base and their resultant budget as well), but not their clients (clients are defined only as those whom the agency serves intensely, a much smaller base).

Displacing Goals

"In Poland under communism, the performance of furniture factories was measured in the tonnes of furniture shipped. As a result, Poland now has the heaviest furniture on the planet."[123] Weight displaced furniture as Poland's furniture-production goal because of the performance measure used. However, had the Polish communists instead stipulated free-standing items of furniture, rather than tonnage, as their measure of performance, Poland might now have the lightest—and the tiniest—furniture on the planet.

Shifting Costs Instead of Saving Costs

Because agency programs are often measured in isolation, program managers can claim that they are saving public funds when in reality they are merely shifting costs to other programs. For example, a hospital allegedly shipped its dying patients to nursing homes shortly before they expired—a practice that not only shifted costs, but also resulted in splendidly declining mortality rates for the hospital.[124] Welfare agencies typically use "exits" as a measure of their success, but "few systemic attempts...are made to discover why people leave welfare, for how long, and where they go."[125]

Disguising Subgroup Differences with Aggregate Indicators

By concentrating on "the big picture," performance measures can hide critical (and perhaps, embarrassing) information. For instance, even though the U.S. Census Bureau once reported an annual rise in all Americans' average income of 1.2 percent, it neglected to note that the wealthiest fifth of the population saw its income rise by 2.2 percent, but the poorest fifth witnessed its income fall by 1.8 percent. The aggregate indicator of rising average income (the good news) obscured a widening income gap between the richest and poorest Americans (the bad news).[126]

Ignoring the Limitations of Objective Measures
Even when properly done, measuring performance can take us only so far. For years, the Internal Revenue Service (IRS) measured the performance of its agents on the basis of a single indicator: collection rates. The result was some ruthless agents, dubious practices, anguished taxpayers, and an overhauled, reorganized, and redirected IRS when Congress responded to rising public anger in 1998 by passing the IRS Restructuring and Reform Act.

Failing to Address How and Why Questions
When performance measures are used in isolation, and do not consider relevant how-and-why questions, such as poor management or over-funding, they can be useless or even counterproductive. What if, for instance, the sole employer in a town closed down? Performance measures of the town's employment agency would tell us only that the agency was failing to find jobs for unemployed townspeople. They would not tell us, however, that there were no jobs in town.

Benchmarking Performance
Benchmarking performance is an extension of measuring performance that tries to raise a program's performance by comparing it with comparable programs.

From Measurement to Comparison
Most governments track their performance over time. Fifty-six percent apiece of the thirty most populous cities and the thirty largest counties track and report performance over time, compared with 30 percent of smaller cities and 5 percent of smaller counties (those with 10,000–500,000 people).[127]

The reason why governments track their performance is that doing so shows whether the productivity of a program is going up or down. Benchmarking, however, does this and more: It asks, are we doing this particular job *as well as* other organizations like ours in similar circumstances? Or are we doing it better? Or worse?

Benchmarking Benchmarking
Benchmarking is making some, if slow, progress in American governments. The federal government has established a Federal Benchmarking Consortium and an Inter-Agency Benchmarking and Best Practices Council.

Almost three-fourths of state agencies compare their agencies' performance data with data from other government agencies, at least sometimes;[128] a half-dozen states have actually enacted legislation that specifically requires their governments to benchmark.[129] Thirty-one percent of cities and counties cooperatively coordinate formal benchmarking systems.[130]

Benchmarking's Benefits and Limitations
Benchmarking may be as close as the public and nonprofit sectors can get to an equivalent of competition in the free market, and this could result in greater efficiency. Public administrators report that benchmarking provides some "substantial benefits," notably the identification of unusually high programmatic costs,[131] and its use enhances the probability that performance measures will influence governmental operations.[132]

Accounting for Public Performance
It is not commonly known, but the federal government has had a huge impact on the public presence of the accountancy profession, a profession that is growing mightily in the measurement of public performance.

Washington Accounts for Performance
In 1972, as a result of interest displayed by the Government Accountability Office, the nonprofit Financial Accounting Foundation (FAF) was chartered with the mission of improving pubic financial accountability. In the following year, the GAO also was instrumental in the founding of the nonprofit Financial Accounting Standards Board, which honed in on federal accounting; it is overseen by the FAF.

More than a decade later, Washington turned its accountancy attentions to the grass roots. In 1984, Congress enacted the Single Audit Act, which forces state and local governments receiving federal grants to submit to government-wide audits, rather than relying on grant-by-grant audits, and, again with the enthusiastic encouragement of the GAO, the Governmental Accounting

Standards Board (GASB) was created as a nonprofit organization. GASB is the sole body recognized by the American Institute of Certified Public Accountants as possessing the authority to set Generally Accepted Accounting Principles for state and local governments.

Accountancy and Performance From its origins, the GASB has tried to move "beyond the realm of monetary accounting...and into the realm of performance measurement" of state and local public programs.[133] In 1994, it issued an official "Concepts Statement" about accountants' reporting of governmental "Service Efforts and Accomplishments," and in 1999 the GASB followed up with its innocuously titled, "Statement 34," which calls for comprehensive "performance reporting" by state and local governments.

Statement 34 united most of the major associations of grass-roots governments in opposition to the Board's foray, resulting in a "new and higher level of strain in the already-tense relationship between GASB and state and local officials."[134]

Performance Accounting and the Price of Governing Why are governments so threatened? Because municipal bond ratings are determined by outside accountants, bond ratings, in turn, determine the cost to governments of borrowing money; and the cost of borrowing money significantly determines the cost of governing. Just the mere existence of the GASB's "reporting framework...is likely to influence state and local governments throughout the country."[135]

All the states audit performance,[136] as do at least 70 percent of large American cities.[137] In 2005, Washington State's voters passed Initiative 900, which dedicates a significant stream of tax revenue to funding performance audits in all state and local agencies.

Performance audits are taken seriously. An analysis of 3,788 potentially embarrassing performance audits conducted in federal, state, and local agencies found that only twenty-six were ignored by managers.[138]

When it comes to measuring governmental performance, never underestimate those quiet powerhouses who sport green eyeshades.

Reporting Performance

Central to measuring performance is reporting it so that citizens and decision makers can use it to improve performance.

Washington Measures Up Measures of outcomes in performance reporting associate with reporting of high quality, and it is heartening to learn that outcome measures account for an impressive four-fifths of the indicators that appear in federal performance reports. "Nearly all of the indicators" in these reports meet the five standard criteria for quality reporting in that they are specific, measurable, achievable, relevant, and mandate sensible, deadlines. "The United States stands out" in the high quality of its measures and in its extensive use of baseline data and performance targets surpassing the governments of Australia, Canada, and Ireland.[139]

Grass-Roots' Performance Reporting State and local performance reports do not fare as well as their federal counterparts.

A national analysis of the performance reports released by 200 state agencies found low overall quality, and a slender 1 percent were rated as high quality.[140] A study of 121 cities, using the same methods as the state analysis just cited, concluded that their performance reports exhibited "substantial progress made in quality and quantity over the past 10 years.... [but] the number of high-quality reports" remained "very low overall.... [and] is virtually identical with our study of state agencies."[141]

Strategic Measurement for Strategic Management

Perhaps the main weakness in governments' performance reports is that they often swamp their readers with data.

Many, Many Measures Federal performance reports typically contain quite a lot of measures—from thirty to forty of them. Surprisingly, however, this is "a relatively small number" when compared with performance reports issued by the governments of Australia (where more than a hundred measures flood each report), Canada, and

Ireland,[142] and with American grass-roots governments as well.

Oregon became so enamored with performance measurement that it ended up with 259 statewide measures (plus hundreds of agency and local ones), including numeric targets for reducing tooth decay, raising aerobic exercise, traveling in cities, and entertaining foreign visitors. A state official conceded that Oregon's performance measures were "a little out of control."[143]

"Many city and county governments use between 150 and 1500 indicators,"[144] and there may be, on average, more than thirty performance measures for each municipal service.[145]

From Data to Dashboards

Using "a multitude of measures" to assess agency performance is counterproductive because doing so "is daunting for most officials and for the public."[146] Enter *strategic measurement, total organizational performance systems,* or *outcome-oriented performance management systems,* all of which refer to the winnowing and simplifying of performance measures and integrating them with large-scale goals.

This winnowing has brought us *key performance indicators,* which provide executives with a "dashboard" that quickly informs them of progress toward larger goals.[147] These indicators are being used increasingly to help link public strategic planning with managing and budgeting, linkages that are crucial in attaining broader objectives.

Toward a Federal Dashboard Federal interest in developing these approaches began with the Reports Consolidation Act of 2000, which helped to "force agencies to build self-discipline" in performance reporting.[148] Congress proposed a "key national indicator system" in 2008, and, in 2010, the Patient Protection and Affordable Care Act set up the Commission on Key National Indicators, charged with implementing such a system.

The basis of the yet-to-be-developed federal dashboard is more than seventy agencies that currently collect statistics about their programs, each of which "was established separately in response to different needs," but, together, amount to a "federal statistical system" that is coordinated by ten "principal federal statistical agencies."[149]

Creating a single, government-wide, federal dashboard is a massive undertaking.

Grass-Roots' Dashboards An impressive 47 percent of cities and counties link performance measures to goals stated in their strategic plans, and 17 percent use a dashboard-like "balanced scorecard" of measures to gain a holistic perspective on performance.[150]

Simplicity Equals Payoff

Strategic approaches to performance measurement pay off.

Federal efforts to consolidate and simplify their performance reports have improved agencies' transparency and accountability.[151]

Those states that establish comprehensive systems for managing results are more likely to integrate goals throughout their agencies; provide strong "strategic guidance"; balance bottom-up and top-down approaches; and display significantly superior accountability and performance in their public administration.[152]

Local governments that incorporate performance measures in "key management systems" are likelier to use those measures in day-to-day managing.[153]

Lessons Learned: Minimizing the Pitfalls of Performance Measurement

In sum, here is what we have learned about successfully measuring public and nonprofit performance:[154]

Lessons Learned About Measures

A large chunk of avoidable pitfalls concerns the measures themselves.

- *Be realistic about the political and organizational context in which the measures will be used—or not be used.* As the physicians say, do no harm.
- *Try to include quantifiable impact measures, as well as input and output measures.*
- *Keep the number of measures used to the barest minimum possible.*
- *Always test measurements in advance.*
- *Assure that executive and legislative staffers agree on what "key results measures" will*

appear in budget documents "that legislators will see."[155]

■ *Recognize that the broader the phenomenon being measured, the less control that the agency will have over outcomes.* This is not necessarily a bad thing.

Lessons Learned About Process We also have learned a lot about how best to manage performance measurement programs.

■ *Identify the organization's key failure*—its most consequential performance deficit.

■ *Assure the presence of performance goals that are specific, measurable, relevant, and achievable, and which have sensible deadlines attached.* These are the internationally recognized standards for performance management of high quality.[156]

■ *Set a specific, and, if possible, quantifiable, performance target.* "The extent of performance improvement is influenced positively by the presence of a target,"[157] and there is "no evidence of any of the dysfunctional effects" of performance targets, such as managers ignoring untargeted programs, "that have been hypothesized" in the literature.[158] "Goal clarity" associates positively with "more extensive results-oriented reform efforts" and stakeholders' "normative commitment" to the agency.[159]

■ *Be timely.* Measures that can be acted upon are more important than plans. State and local administrators are finding that "performance-tracking software," which integrates budgetary and performance data, to be extremely useful in this regard, causing some governments to abandon annual, and inevitably dated, management reports, "long considered akin to the Bible among public-sector managers."[160]

■ *Review, revise, and update measures frequently.*

■ *Check for distortions by ensuring that the mission is actually being accomplished.*

■ *Communicate clearly.* Adopt a plain language policy; present data around desired outcomes; show trends, as well as the percentages of

targets met; let the data to speak for themselves; and exploit the Web and other media.

■ *Learn to make modifications in order to ratchet up performance again.*

■ *To assure that performance measurement continues, secure its own home in the bureaucracy.* Get it on the organization chart.

Lessons Learned About People Our final set of lessons learned deals with the people who do, are affected by, and involved with, the measuring.

■ *Do not introduce performance measurement unless vital political support is guaranteed.* "Managerial perceptions of [solid] political support have a direct [and positive] influence on the implementation of results-oriented reforms."[161]

■ *Actively involve stakeholders.* Their involvement in developing and reviewing program measures assures that they can earn a sense of accomplishment from the process. Including in the process not only agency personnel but also "external professionals," especially those in the central budget office, "improves the perception of measurement quality" among stakeholders, notably legislators and agency employees.[162]

■ *Recognize that running a successful measurement program does not require a large staff, but that selecting enthusiastic and adaptable people to manage it is essential.*

■ *Be sensitive to the needs of front-line supervisors.* These supervisors "play an important role" in improving government's "organizational performance and effectiveness,"[163] a finding that is supported by some 1,500 additional investigations, which conclude that "the most effective way to improve organizational performance is to improve first-level supervisors."[164]

■ *Anticipate the emergence transformational leaders.* "In direct contradiction with expectations," a public organization's use of performance measures positively associates "with significant increases in a chief administrative officer's use of transformational leadership behaviors."[165] Who knew?

EVALUATING PUBLIC AND NONPROFIT PROGRAMS

Public program evaluation is our second pillar of governmental and nonprofit productivity.

The Purposes of Public and Nonprofit Program Evaluation

Public and nonprofit program evaluation, or *evaluation research*, is the "individual systematic studies conducted periodically or on an ad hoc basis to assess how well a program is working."[166]

Program evaluation differs from performance measurement on two dimensions: focus and use.

Performance measurement focuses on whether a program has achieved its measurable goals, whereas a program evaluation examines a greater range of information in a larger environment.

In terms of use, performance measurement is used mostly as an early warning system to managers should a program falter, and as a method for improving governmental accountability to the public; a program evaluation, by contrast, is a deeper inquiry into a program's performance and context, and seeks to develop a comprehensive assessment of how it might be improved.[167]

Public and nonprofit program evaluation is more than a bureaucrat lethargically asking, "How're we doin'?" Because a program evaluation "is always undertaken in a context of decisions about the use of resources," it "accordingly, has implications for the acquisition, distribution, and loss of... power. Sometimes evaluation is undertaken to justify or endorse an ongoing program and sometimes to investigate or audit the program in order to lay blame for failure, abolish it, change its leadership, or curtail its activities."[168]

Although a program evaluation can be threatening, especially to those who manage the program being evaluated, its threat can be overstated. Not even 1 percent of the evaluations of some 600 municipal programs "led to termination of the evaluated activities," but 78 percent of these evaluations "led to adjustments of program activities."[169] Despite the aura of paranoia that sometimes seems to suffuse program evaluation, it draws far short of a slash-and-burn attack on public or nonprofit management; it can result, however, in improving the productivity of public programs.

Evaluating Federal Programs

With performance measurement gaining federal ground, successful program evaluation soon followed.

The single most significant development in this regard is the Government Performance and Results Act of 1993 which moves federal administrators away from the tradition of reporting on their compliance with procedures and toward reporting on their achievement of measurable results. In addition, Congress has enacted the Government Performance and Results Act Modernization Act of 2010, described earlier, and more than fifty other laws since 1993 that contain their own, unique performance measures and agency reporting requirements for specific policies.[170]

There are also eleven broad statutes that deal with information and financial management. Of these, perhaps the most important is the Chief Financial Officers Act of 1990, which has been described as "the most comprehensive financial management reform legislation in 40 years," resulting in "a clear cultural change."[171]

"Implemented together" these statutes "provide a powerful framework.... [which] should promote a more results-oriented management and decision making process within both Congress and the executive branch;" and could save taxpayers "billions" previously lost to "waste, fraud, and mismanagement."[172] A "monumental" achievement resulting from this legislation appeared in 1998: the federal government's first-ever government-wide audited financial statements, which "provided a perspective for assessing the federal financial condition that was not previously available."[173]

Evaluating State and Local Programs

The grass-roots governments have made significant gains in evaluating their programs.

All states use some method of managing for results,[174] and budget offices in forty-five states conduct program evaluations.[175] The proportion of states in which most major agencies conduct productivity analyses more than doubled over three decades, from a fifth to more than half.[176]

Three-quarters of cities long have been using program evaluations, a level that experts generally believe to be the maximum that is reasonably possible for the adoption of any innovative technique of public management. Thirty-six percent of municipal administrators rate program evaluations as "very effective" in managing and decision making.[177]

Evaluating Nonprofit, Public-Serving Programs

The programs conducted by nonprofit, public-serving organizations also are evaluated. But who evaluates them makes a big difference in their fundraising.

When charities, on their own, "position themselves as cost efficient"—that is, when they self-report that they have low administrative expenses relative to their total expenditures—the more "efficient appearing" charities fare "no better over time than less efficient appearing organizations" in terms of donations from individuals, corporations, and foundations.[178] Yet, when a respected and well-known *external* evaluator evaluates, rates, and publicizes the cost-effectiveness of these organizations, those with the top ratings rake in large increases in their contributions.

Perhaps the best-known external evaluator of nonprofit programs is the Better Business Bureau, which assesses these programs against standards of best governance and management practices. Meeting all these standards "could lead to an increase in public support [i.e., donations from individuals, corporations, and foundations] of 30 percent, compared to those that do not meet all the standards, other key nonprofit organization characteristics being equal.... Meeting one extra standard is associated with an increase in public support of more than 7 percent."[179]

These are impressive figures, but they have limits. When an independent-sector organization receives from the Better Business Bureau a "pass" rating for its accountability, it receives "statistically significant" more contributions. When, however, a charity receives a ranking of "did not pass," the effect on donations is "nonsignificant."[180]

Donors give to causes that they like, regardless of the competency (and, perhaps, honesty) with which those causes are managed. Donors, however, give quite a bit more to well-managed—and well-evaluated—causes.

Permutations of Public and Nonprofit Program Evaluation

A diversity of forms of program evaluation has flourished, and the many overlapping categories of program evaluations likely exceed 100.[181] For our purposes, we have reduced the major taxonomies to six types of evaluation research,[182] and they comprise its "everyday repertoire," representing "widespread agreement in the field with regard to common practice in program evaluation."[183] They are not particularly neat categories, and we present them, roughly, in the order that they are appropriate to use as the program is conducted over time.

Front-End Analyses A *front-end analysis* is a program evaluation that estimates how feasible a proposed new program might be and its possible effects. It is integral to planning and can provide a rational basis for a later, more thorough, evaluation. An example is the GAO's study of teenage pregnancy that was provided to Congress before legislation was introduced proposing service programs for pregnant teenagers.[184]

Evaluability Assessments An *evaluability assessment* judges the reasonableness of the original assumptions justifying a program. It usually is conducted early in the course of a public program, focuses on its implementation and management, and amounts to something of a first-pass evaluation that is meant to determine the practicality of undertaking a later, full-scale evaluation of the program's effectiveness. An example is the assessment of whether the federal Senior Executive Service has met its goals.[185]

Program and Problem Monitoring *Program and problem monitoring* provides ongoing information on how the issue that the program addresses may be changing; whether the program is continuing to comply with the law; how service delivery methods may have altered; and related developments. Its unique value is that, through such methods as time-series analysis and the periodic completion of standard forms by program managers, it enables administrators to follow the evolution of problems and the program's affect on them continuously over time. An example is the GAO's study of the Comprehensive Employment and Training Act, which tracked changing program costs, characteristics of the participants, and the effectiveness of its services in placing participants in jobs.[186]

Process, or Implementation, Evaluations

The *process*, or *implementation*, *evaluation* assesses the extent to which a program is operating as intended. It does this by evaluating the procedures of discrete program activities, such as management and conformance to legal requirements. It can be very helpful in determining the effects of a program on its clientele group, and, when used in tandem with an effectiveness evaluation (discussed next), in answering questions of accountability. Examples of a process evaluation are those studies that focus on how innovations in the public sector are circulated and become routine among governments.[187]

Effectiveness, Outcome, or Impact Evaluations

An *effectiveness*, *outcome*, or *impact evaluation* assesses the extent to which a program achieves its objectives and identifies unintended outcomes.

An important aspect of these evaluations is that of estimating whether a program's outcomes would have occurred anyway—that is, without the program. "This, of course, is the quintessential accountability question,"[188] and most of these evaluations address this critical question.

A well-known effectiveness evaluation is the Kansas City Police Department's study about the effectiveness of police patrols in preventing crime. It found that there were no statistically significant differences in crime rates, citizen attitudes, the reported number of crimes, citizen behavior, or even in the rate of traffic accidents among areas where no police patrols were sent out, and police responded only to specific calls for help; patrols were maintained at previous levels; and patrols were doubled or tripled in size.[189]

Meta-Evaluations, or Evaluation Syntheses A *meta-evaluation*, or an *evaluation synthesis*, re-analyzes findings from a number of previous evaluations (but occasionally from just one) to find out what has been learned about a public program. A meta-evaluation is the most comprehensive, retrospective, and flexible form of evaluation research. An example is the GAO's study of drinking-age laws and their effects on highway safety.[190]

PUBLIC AND NONPROFIT PROGRAM EVALUATION IN PRACTICE

Practicing public program evaluation can be reduced to three fundamental steps: choosing the evaluators, defining the problem, and designing the evaluation.

Step 1: Selecting the Evaluators

Who should evaluate an agency's program?

Insiders, Outsiders, and Program Managers Program evaluators can be drawn from inside the agency running the program, or from outside of it and invited in.

Inside evaluators bring benefits to the evaluation that outside evaluators cannot, such as a more detailed knowledge of the organization and the greater likelihood that they will be able to conduct a continuing evaluation over time. Outsiders are more likely than insiders to devote their time more fully to the research, and may be more effective mediators because of their objectivity.

For several reasons, program managers may find themselves engaged in more kerfuffles with outside evaluators than inside ones. Managers want to solve immediate problems and resist potentially disruptive, but productive, change. Outsiders are more interested in long-term problem solving, often have views that differ from those of managers, question the basic premises of the organization, and sometimes push for wholesale change.[191]

Ironically, managers are probably more likely to accept and implement the recommendations made by outside evaluators whom they have hired than to follow the suggestions made by inside evaluators. This is because administrators pay a surcharge for evaluations made by outsiders, but not by insiders. Researchers have found that "people use paid advice significantly more than free advice."[192]

Games Evaluators Play Whether they are insiders or outsiders, program evaluators play many roles that affect the ways they discharge their responsibilities. A study of federal policy analysts identified the *entrepreneur*, who has excellent analytical and political skills; the *politician*, who has reasonable political skills but who is less impressive in intellectual analysis; the *technician*, who has good analytical skills but is apolitical; and the *pretender*, who is weak both analytically and politically.[193] Some evaluators go off on odd tangents, dreamily speculating "on the role of performance measurement as it relates to democracy and efficiency," or endlessly "developing hypotheses, defining terms."[194]

Program evaluators can range from the brainless and pompous, to the self-serving and dishonest, to the intelligent and skilled. *Caveat emptor.*

Step 2: What Is Your Problem?

To determine a decision maker's needs, we must ask what the decision maker's perceptions of the problem are.

Defining the Problem All the evaluation's participants, from evaluators to agency decision makers, must fully comprehend the history and goals of the program and why it is being evaluated. To achieve this, write it down. Not only should this document list the program's intended benefits, but it should also include how many of those benefits are expected to be attained and when; any important qualitative features; possible recipients of unintended benefits or adverse consequences; and any objectives that may conflict with each other or, conversely, be in support of one another. "The importance of taking such a comprehensive view of objectives cannot be overstated."[195]

Critical to defining the problem is, oddly, defining success. That is, how do we know, and when do we know, that our program is successful? When program managers have clear understandings of what programmatic success means, they can upgrade their definition of success, and their productivity, over time.[196]

Is Evaluating the Problem Worthwhile? Once the agency's problem is defined, then another question arises: Is the agency's problem worth the expense and energy involved in evaluating it?

To answer this, five questions must be addressed:

- *Validity.* How much confidence can agency administrators have in the evaluation's findings and conclusions?
- *Relevance.* Will its results be useful to the agency?
- *Significance.* Will the research provide the program's administrators with substantially more insights than they can glean from their own observations?
- *Efficiency.* Will the value of research exceed its cost?
- *Timeliness.* Will the study be completed in time to meet agency schedules?

If the responses to these questions are affirmative, then the evaluation is worth undertaking.

Step 3: Designing the Evaluation

Designing a program evaluation is a tricky business because evaluation research differs from basic research.[197] Although both types are concerned with theory and experimental design, evaluation research is a form of applied or "action research"; that is, it contributes to social action. Its chief purpose is to evaluate comprehensively a particular activity, and to meet an agency's deadline in the process.

Moreover, with evaluation research "there is often a tradeoff between the breadth of a study and the precision of results" that does not plague basic research.[198] With breadth comes fuzziness, and with clarity, narrowness.

The Study Plan Preparing a detailed study plan is the initial step in designing an evaluation. A study plan should include the following components:

- A clear statement of the problem.
- The objectives of the research.

- A careful listing of the assumptions and constraints to be used in addressing the problem.
- The resources to be committed.
- The methods to be employed.
- Measures of the evaluation's attainment of its objectives.
- Lines of communication.
- Specific procedures for amending the study plan.
- A schedule for completing major components of the evaluation, including a final deadline.
- Specific procedures for using the results of the evaluation.

The Attenuations of Action Research: Technical Challenges

Once the study plan is completed, the core design issues must be faced.

First, "it is difficult to refuse service to those who seek it and provide service to those who resist it."[199] When a *control group* (i.e., clients who are excluded from receiving the benefits of a particular program) is set aside for purposes of comparing it with an *experimental group* (clients who do receive the benefits), there is often a great deal of pressure to provide the benefits of that program to both groups. Should benefits be extended to the control group, the evaluation would be ruined.

Second, accurately evaluating a program's impact can suffer from hidden motives on the part of evaluators. Often these motives involve money, a potential problem when outside evaluators are used. Outside, paid evaluators have been known over promise and under deliver.[200]

The Attenuations of Action Research: Ethical Challenges

In designing their research, evaluators also should be cognizant of some ethical issues.

Privacy, Confidentiality, and Informed Consent *Privacy* refers to the state of the person. It hinges on the degree to which the evaluator's questions, in and of themselves, are perceived by the respondent to be prying or embarrassing. The test of an invasion of privacy is to ask if the respondent will voluntarily furnish answers under conditions that appropriately restrict the use of those answers.

Confidentiality refers to a state of information. The legal fact of the matter is that social science research records, such as those obtained by evaluators, are not protected under statutory law as a privileged communication, as are the records of lawyers and physicians.

Informed consent refers to whether or not a respondent understands what he or she is agreeing to. Lawyers have questioned the legality of randomly assigning participants to control groups or to experimental groups, and the grounds of their "questioning include the issues of informed consent."[201]

You Got a Problem with That? When ethical issues arise in conducting program evaluations, what do the evaluators do? More often than not, they disagree on whether or not an ethical question is even present. "The bad news is that one voice" among evaluators "does not exist" when ethics are involved, and evaluators who are private consultants are "less likely than those in other settings," such as universities, to think that a situation in a program evaluation is unethical.[202]

Once it is determined that ethics have been violated, more than nine out of ten researchers report it, but to whom they report it depends on how close they are to the research. Three-fourths of research administrators will report unethical practices to "externally accountable individuals," whereas 58 percent of hands-on researchers are more likely to report such incidents to colleagues on their own research teams and to no one else. This propensity among researchers raises the question of whether their "behavior constitutes professional self-regulation or cover-up."[203]

USING PUBLIC AND NONPROFIT PROGRAM EVALUATIONS

Are evaluators accountable for the evaluation being used, or, once they have completed the evaluation, should they instead leave it to the tender mercies of the program's administrator?

Passive or Active Evaluation?

These questions lie at the heart of a consuming debate in evaluation circles. One wing argues that, because public and nonprofit administrators must deal with many kinds of information, of which the evaluation is just one part, it is appropriate for the evaluator to withdraw once the evaluation is done; the responsibility of the evaluator does not exceed that of providing adequate and accurate knowledge.[204]

The other wing of the debate contends that the evaluator has the responsibility to assume an active role in promoting the evaluation's use.[205] "There is a pervasive sense" among program evaluators "that most research studies bounce off the policy process without making much of a dent in the course of events."[206]

This is, of course, frustrating. The evaluation community appears to favor an activist role for evaluators, going so far as to propose tactics designed to overcome bureaucratic resistance to program evaluations.[207]

One such tactic is *consensual cooperation*, or *collaborative modes of evaluation*, which means that evaluators work closely with administrators in evaluating those administrators' programs. The peril, of course, is one of "misutilization," which is how evaluators describe those "serious questions about the evaluator's ability to maintain a sufficiently bias-free stance due to pressures emanating mainly" from the administrators whose programs are being evaluated.[208] Among nonprofit organizations, for example, there are empirical indications that the collaborative model can corrupt objective evaluations: "The more political power or influence stakeholder groups hold over" such factors as funding and data access, "the more evaluators were willing to modify their [evaluation] design choices to accommodate perceived stakeholder concerns."[209]

Does Public Program Evaluation Matter?

We rather favor the more passive model of how to use an evaluation—that is, less collaboration between evaluators and administrators. We favor it not only because it is safer from contamination by those with interests in assuring that certain findings appear in the evaluation but for two additional reasons as well.

Evaluations Are Used One is that policymakers use program evaluations more extensively and immediately than evaluators may realize. Recall that almost four-fifths of local evaluations lead to adjustments in the evaluated programs.[210] The actions taken by public decision makers reflect the influence of "all types of information" gleaned from evaluation data, and, comfortingly, "large-scale and case study data are more influential relative to anecdotal accounts."[211]

There is reason to believe that program evaluations will be used even more in the future, as some federal agencies have "given evaluation more clout" by requiring local governments seeking federal grants to implement only those policies that have been professionally evaluated as being effective.[212]

Evaluations Are Enlightening Second, evaluation has longer-term effects that are both important and under recognized by evaluators. This is "the enlightenment function" of evaluation research.[213]

In this view, program evaluation sensitizes policymakers, opening new options that, over time, policymakers are more likely to adopt because of the data provided in an earlier evaluation. Evaluation research may not be used as immediately and radically as the evaluation researcher might wish, but in the long run program evaluations are employed by policymakers, and perhaps on a broader plane than evaluation researchers realize.

Evaluation—and enlightenment—count.

NOTES

1. Al Gore, *From Red Tape to Results: Creating a Government that Works Better & Costs Less*, Report of the National Performance Review (Washington, DC: U.S. Government Printing Office, 1993), p. 94.
2. Francois Bouvard, Thomas Dohrmann, and Nick Lovegrove, "The Case for Government Reform Now," *McKinsey Quarterly* (June 2009), pp. 1–13. The quotation is on p. 2. Figure is for FY 2010.
3. The following quotations are in Garry Wills, *A Necessary Evil: A History of American Distrust of Government* (New York: Simon & Schuster, 1999), pp. 72–73.

4. Ibid., pp. 73, 75. Emphasis is original.
5. Susan E. Knapp, "Budget Reform in Kazakstan," *IPA Report* (Summer 1998), p. 1.
6. Robert Birnbaum, *Leadership and Campus Productivity* (College Park, MD: National Center for Post Secondary Governance and Finance, 1990), p. 1.
7. Geert Bouckaert, "The History of the Productivity Movement," *Public Productivity & Management Review* 14 (Fall 1990), pp. 53–89. The quotation is on p. 83.
8. Paul C. Light, *Creating High Performance Government: A Once-in-a-Generation Opportunity* (New York: Robert F. Wagner School of Public Policy, New York University, 2011), pp. 5–7.
9. U.S. Government Accountability Office, *Human Services Programs: Opportunities to Reduce Inefficiencies*, GAO-11-531T (Washington, DC: U.S. Government Printing Office, 2011).
10. U.S. Government Accountability Office, *Streamlining Government: Key Practices from Select Efficiency Initiatives Should Be Shared Governmentwide*, GA0-11-908 (Washington, DC: U.S. Government Printing Office, 2011), Highlights page. This is a study of four cabinet-level federal departments and five state governments.
11. Laura Langbein, "Controlling Federal Agencies: The Contingent Impact of External Controls on Worker Discretion and Productivity," *International Public Management Journal* 12 (1, 2009), pp. 82–115. The quotation is on p. 82.
12. R. Paul Battaglio, Jr., "Public Service Reform and Motivation: Evidence from an Employment At-Will Environment," *Review of Public Personnel Administration* 30 (September 2010), pp. 341–363. The quotation is on p. 355, which also cites eight other studies supporting this finding.
13. Desiree Teobaldelli, "Federalism and the Shadow Economy," *Public Choice* 146 (March 2011), pp. 269–289. The quotation is on p. 269.
14. Center for Political Studies, *American National Election Studies* (Ann Arbor, MI: Author, 2010), http://www.electionstudies.org. Figures are for 2008.
15. Meg Bostrom, *By, or for, the People? A Meta-analysis of Public Opinion of Government* (New York: Demos, 2006), p. 35.
16. Primavera Systems and O'Keeffe & Co. survey of 382 federal managers, as cited in Alyssa Rosenberg, "Federal Managers Pessimistic about Government Performance," *Government Executive* (September 23, 2008), http://www.govexec.com. Figure is for 2008.
17. U.S. Government Accountability Office, *Streamlining Government: Key Practices from Select Efficiency Initiatives Should Be Shared Governmentwide*, p. 6.
18. George Boyne and Kenneth Meier, "Environmental Turbulence, Organizational Stability, and Public Service Performance," *Administration & Society* 40 (January 2009), pp. 799–824. The quotation is on p. 799. This is a study of Texan school districts.
19. Kenneth J. Meier and Laurence J. O'Toole, Jr., *Bureaucracy in a Democratic State: A Governance Perspective* (Baltimore, MD: Johns Hopkins University Press, 2006), p. 56.
20. U.S. General Accounting Office, *Federal Budget: Agency Obligations by Budget Function and Object Classification for Fiscal Year 2003*, GAO-04-834 (Washington, DC: U.S. Government Printing Office, 2004), Highlights page. Figures are for 2003.
21. The following examples are drawn from National Commission on the Public Service, *Urgent Business for America: Revitalizing the Federal Government for the 21st Century* (Washington, DC: U.S. Government Printing Office, 2003), pp. 15–16, 36–37.
22. Light, *Creating High Performance Government*, p. 21.
23. U.S. Government Accountability Office, *Human Services Programs: Opportunities to Reduce Inefficiencies*, Highlights page.
24. The intellect underlying this thesis is that of William Baumol. See his *Welfare Economics and the Theory of the State* (Cambridge, MA: Harvard University Press, 1965), to cite just one example.
25. John E. Petersen, "Productivity Pinch," *Governing* (September 2003), p. 62.
26. U.S. Merit Systems Protection Board, *The Federal Government: A Model Employer or a Work in Progress? Perspectives from 25 Years of the Merit Principles Survey* (Washington, DC: U.S. Government Printing Office, 2008), p. 9. Current figure is for 2007.
27. Susie M. Grant, as quoted in Michael A. Fletcher, "A Sea Change in the Secretarial Pool," *Washington Post* (May 11, 2000).
28. U.S. Office of Personnel Management, *Investing in Federal Productivity and Quality*

(Washington, DC: U.S. Government Printing Office, 1992).

29. Luther Gulick, "Science, Values, and Public Administration," *Papers on the Science of Administration*, Luther Gulick and L. Urwick, eds. (New York: Institute of Public Administration, 1937), pp. 189–195. The quotation is on p. 192.

30. Frederick C. Mosher and Orville F. Poland, *The Costs of American Governments: Facts, Trends, Myths* (New York: Dodd, Mead, 1964), pp. 12–15.

31. Daniel W. Williams, "Measuring Government in the Early Twentieth Century," *Public Administration Review* 63 (November/December 2003), pp. 643–659.

32. Mordecai Lee, *Bureaus of Efficiency: Reforming Local Government in the Progressive Era* (Milwaukee, WI: Marquette University Press, 2008).

33. Clarence E. Ridley and Herbert A. Simon, *Measuring Municipal Activities: A Survey of Suggested Criteria and Reporting Forms for Appraising Administration* (Chicago: International City Managers Association, 1938).

34. Joseph S. Wholey, John W. Scanlon, Hugh G. Duffy, *et al.*, *Federal Evaluation Policy: Analyzing the Effects of Public Programs* (Washington, DC: Urban Institute, 1970), p. 23.

35. Senator William Proxmire, quoted in Thomas D. Morris, William H. Corbett, and Brian L. Usilaner, "Productivity Measures in the Federal Government," *Public Administration Review* 32 (November/December 1972), pp. 753–763. The quotation is on p. 754.

36. Council of the Inspectors General on Integrity and Efficiency, *A Progress Report to the President, Fiscal Year 2009* (Washington, DC: U.S. Government Printing Office, 2010), Foreword.

37. Ibid., Tables 3, 5–9. Current figures are for FY 2009. Trends are for FY 2005–FY 2009.

38. Kathryn E. Newcomer, "The Changing Nature of Accountability: The Role of the Inspector General in Federal Agencies," *Public Administration Review* 58 (March/April 1998), pp. 129–136. The quotation is on p. 135.

39. Quoted in Tom Shoop, "The IG Enigma," *Government Executive* (January 1992), p. 39. The bureau in question was the Agency for International Development.

40. As derived from data in Kathryn E. Newcomer, "Opportunities and Incentives for Improving Program Quality: Auditing and Evaluating," *Public Administration Review* 54 (March/April 1994), pp. 147–154 (the data are on p. 153.), and Newcomer, "The Changing Nature of Accountability," p. 134. Data are for 1992–1996.

41. Newcomer, "The Changing Nature of Accountability," p. 135.

42. U.S. General Accounting Office, *Inspectors General: Enhancing Federal Accountability*, GAO-04-117T (Washington, DC: U.S. Government Printing Office, 2003), p. 1.

43. Robert C. Burns and Robert D. Lee, Jr., "The Ups and Downs of State Budget Process Reform: Experience of Three Decades," *Public Budgeting & Finance* 24 (Fall 2004), pp. 1–19. Figures (p. 10) are for 1970–2000.

44. Richard E. Winnie, "Local Government Budgeting, Program Planning, and Evaluation," *Urban Data Services Report* 4 (May 1972), and as derived from data in Rackham S. Fukuhara, "Productivity Improvement in Cities," *Municipal Year Book, 1977* (Washington, DC: International City Management Association, 1977), pp. 193–200. Figures are for 1971–1976.

45. U.S. General Accounting Office, *Federal Evaluation: Fewer Units, Reduced Resources, Different Studies From 1980*, GAO/PEMD-87-9 (Washington, DC: U.S. Government Printing Office, 1987), p. 1.

46. Judith R. Brown, "Legislative Program Evaluation: Refining a Legislative Service and a Profession," *Public Administration Review* 44 (May/June 1984), pp. 258–260.

47. Burns and Lee, "The Ups and Downs of State Budget Process Reform," p. 10. In 1990, 44 percent of agencies conducted productivity analyses, compared with 41 percent in 1980.

48. Theodore H. Poister and and Gregory Streib, "Management Tools in Municipal Government: Trends over the Past Decade," *Public Administration Review* 49 (May/June 1989), pp. 240–248. Figure is for 1987.

49. B. Guy Peters, *The Future of Governing: Four Emerging Models* (Lawrence, KS: University Press of Kansas, 1996).

50. Samantha L. Durst and Charldean Newell, "Better, Faster, Stronger: Government Reinvention in the 1990s," *American Review of Public Administration* 29 (March 1999), pp. 61–76. The quotation is on p. 63. Figure is for 1996.

51. Paul C. Light, *The Four Pillars of High Performance: How Robust Organizations Achieve Extraordinary Results* (Washington, DC: Brookings, 2005).

52. Cited in Al Gore, *From Red Tape to Results: Creating a Government That Works Better and Costs Less*, Report of the National Performance Review (Washington, DC: U.S. Superintendent of Documents, 1993), p. 1. In 1998, the National Performance Review was retitled the National Partnership for Reinventing Government, and in 2001 it was terminated.

53. Al Gore, *Creating a Government That Works Better and Costs Less: Status Report of the National Performance Review* (Washington, DC: U.S. Government Printing Office, 1994).

54. National Partnership for Reinventing Government, "Accomplishments, 1993–2000: A Summary," *History of the National Partnership for Reinventing Government* (Washington, DC: Author, 2001), pp. 1–2. The GAO contends that the NPR's claims concerning the number of its reforms implemented and their resultant savings should be lowered. See U.S. General Accounting Office, *Management Reform: Completion Status of Agency Actions Under the National Performance Review*, GAO/GGD-96-94 (Washington, DC: U.S. Government Printing Office, 1996); and U.S. General Accounting Office, *NPR's Savings: Claimed Agency Savings Cannot All Be Attributed to NPR*, GAO/GGD-99-120 (Washington, DC: U.S. Government Printing Office, 1999).

55. Max Stier, as cited in Fred Hiatt, "600,000 Bad Hires?" *Washington Post* (April 27, 2009).

56. As derived from data in U.S. Bureau of Census, *Statistical Abstract of the United States, 2006*, 125th ed. (Washington, DC: U.S. Government Printing Office, 2006), Table 481. In 1993 there were 3,043,000 federal civilian employees, and in 2001 there were 2,704,000.

57. Max Stier, as cited in Hiatt, "600,000 Bad Hires?"

58. National Partnership for Reinventing Government, "Accomplishments, 1993–2000," p. 1.

59. Donald F. Kettl, *Reinventing Government: A Fifth Year Report Card* (Washington, DC: Brookings, 1998), p. 8.

60. Keon Chi, Drew Leathersby, Cindy Jasper, et al., *Managing for Success: A Profile of State Governments for the 21st Century* (Lexington, KY: Council of State Governments, 1997); Donald E. Rosenhoover and Harold W. Kuhn, Jr., "Total Quality Management and the Public Sector," *Public Administration Quarterly* 19 (Winter 1996), pp. 434–455; and Jeffrey L. Brudney, F. Ted Hebert, and Deil S. Wright, "Reinventing Government in the American States: Measuring and Explaining Administrative Reform," *Public Administration Review* 59 (January/February 1999), pp. 19–30.

61. Younhee Kim, "Improving Performance in U.S. State Governments: Risk-Taking, Innovativeness, and Proactiveness Practices," *Public Performance & Management Review* 34 (September 2010), pp. 104–129. The quotation is on p. 104.

62. Andy Frazier, "The Significance of the Hard Framework on Agency Performance," *Public Performance & Management Review* 32 (September 2008), pp. 76–102. The quotations are on p. 76. This is an analysis of 4,186 responding employees in eight state revenue agencies.

63. Theodore H. Poister and Gregory Streib, "Municipal Management Tools from 1976 to 1993: An Overview and Update," *Public Productivity & Management Review* 18 (Winter 1994), pp. 115–125. Figure (p. 122) is for 1993.

64. Barry M. Feldman, "Reinventing Local Government: Beyond Rhetoric to Action," *Municipal Year Book, 1999* (Washington, DC: International City/County Management Association, 1999), pp. 20–24. Data (pp. 23–24) are for 1998.

65. Richard C. Kearney, Barry M. Feldman, and Carmine P. F. Scavo, "Reinventing Government: City Manager Attitudes and Actions," *Public Administration Review* 60 (November/December 2000), pp. 535–548. Data (p. 544) are for 1997.

66. Mildred E. Warner and Amir Hefetz, "Cooperative Competition: Alternative Service Delivery, 2002–2007," *Municipal Year Book, 2009* (Washington, DC: International City/County Management Association, 2009), pp. 11–20.

67. Evelina R. Moulder, "Citizen Engagement: An Evolving Process," *Municipal Year Book, 2010* (Washington, DC: International City/County Management Association, 2010), pp. 28–32. Figure, 51 percent (p. 31), is for 2009.

68. Richard C. Kearney, "Reinventing Government and Battling Budget Crises: Manager and Municipal Government Actions in 2003," *Municipal Year*

Book, 2005 (Washington, DC: International City/County Management Association, 2005), pp. 27–32. Figure (p. 31) is for 2003.

69. Rhys Andrews, George A. Boyne, and Richard M. Walker, "Strategy Content and Organizational Performance: An Empirical Analysis," *Public Administration Review* 66 (January/February 2006), pp. 52–63. This is a study of 119 local governments in England.

70. Richard M. Walker, Gene A. Brewer, George A. Boyne, *et al.*, "Market Orientation and Public Service Performance: New Public Management Gone Mad?" *Public Administration Review* 71 (September/October 2011), pp. 707–717. The quotations are on p. 714. This is a study of English local governments.

71. Timothy B. Krebs and John P. Peliserro, "What Influences City Council Adoption and Support for Reinventing Government? Environmental or Institutional Factors?" *Public Administration Review* 70 (March/April 2010), pp. 258–267. Figure is for 1997. The quotation is on p. 260.

72. U.S. General Accounting Office, *Performance Measurement and Evaluation: Definitions and Relationships*, GAO/GGD-98-26 (Washington, DC: U.S. Government Printing Office, 1998), p. 3.

73. Americans Talk Issues Foundation, as cited in Kevin Merida, "Americans Want a Direct Say in Decision-Making, Pollsters Find," *Washington Post* (April 17, 1994). Figure is for 1994.

74. KPMG International, *Performance Agenda: An International Government Survey* (Toronto, ON: Author, 2007), p. 8. Figures are for 2007.

75. Claire Moxham, "Help or Hindrance? Examining the Role of Performance Measurement in UK Nonprofit Organizations," *Public Performance & Management Review* 33 (March 2010), pp. 342–354. The quotations are on p. 342.

76. U.S. Office of Personnel Management, *Working for the Government: What Federal Employees Think, 1999 Employee Survey*, http://www.employeesurvey.gov.

77. U.S. General Accounting Office, *Managing for Results: Emerging Benefits from Selected Agencies' Use of Performance Agreements*, GAO-01-115 (Washington, DC: U.S. Government Printing Office, 2000).

78. Oliver James and Peter John, "Public Management at the Ballot Box: Performance Information and Electoral Support for Incumbent English Local Governments," *Journal of Public Administration Research and Theory* 17 (October 2007), pp. 567–580. The data are on p. 574. This is a study of the introduction of Comprehensive Performance Assessments scores.

79. George A. Boyne, Oliver James, Peter John, *et al.*, "Does Public Service Performance Affect Top Management Turnover?" *Journal of Public Administration Research and Theory* 20, Supplement 2 (April 2010), pp. i261–i279. The quotations are on pp. i272, i271. This is a study of 148 English local governments conducted over four years.

80. Jonathan Walters, "The Benchmarking Craze," *Governing* (April 1994), p. 37. Emphases are original.

81. Kelly LeRoux and Nathaniel S. Wright, "Does Performance Measurement Improve Strategic Decision Making? Findings from a National Survey of Nonprofit Social Service Agencies," *Nonprofit Leadership & Voluntary Sector Quarterly* 39 (August 2010), pp. 571–587.

82. Janet Carlson, Alison S. Kelley, and Ken Smith, "Government Performance Reforms and Nonprofit Human Services: 20 Years in Oregon," *Nonprofit Leadership & Voluntary Sector Quarterly* 39 (March 2010), pp. 630–652. The quotations are on p. 652.

83. Jane Lynch, "Skewed Results," *Governing* (December 2004), pp. 42–45.

84. David N. Ammons, "Common Barriers to Productivity Improvement in Local Government," *Public Productivity Review* 9 (Winter 1985), pp. 293–310.

85. Patria de Lancer Julnes, *Performance-Based Management Systems: Effective Implementation and Maintenance* (Boca Raton, FL: CRC Press, 2008).

86. Frank Hodsoll, quoted in Charles F. Bingham, "Installing the M-Team," *Government Executive* (January 1992), p. 25. Hodsoll was deputy director of management at OMB.

87. M. Bryna Sanger, "Getting to the Roots of Change: Performance Management and Organizational Culture," *Public Performance & Management Review* 31 (June 2008), pp. 621–653. The quotation is on p. 641.

88. Donald F. Kettl, *Reinventing Government? Appraising the National Performance Review* (Washington, DC: Brookings, 1994), p. 43.

89. U.S. Government Accountability Office, *Managing for Results: Enhancing Agency Use*

of Performance Information for Manage-ment Decision Making, GAO-05-927 (Washington, DC: U.S. Government Printing Office, 2005), Highlights page. In 2004, 89 percent of federal agencies had performance measures.

90. U.S. Government Accountability Office, *Government Performance: Lessons Learned for the Next Administration on Using Performance Information to Improve Results*, GAO-08-1026T (Washington, DC: U.S. Government Printing Office, 2008), p. 8.

91. U.S. Government Accountability Office, *Managing for Results: Enhancing Agency Use of Performance Information for Management Decision Making*. Trend is for 1997–2003.

92. U.S. General Accounting Office, *Results-Oriented Government: GPRA Has Established a Solid Foundation for Achieving Greater Results*, GAO-04-38 (Washington, DC: U.S. Government Printing Office, 2004), p. 38.

93. U.S. Government Accountability Office, *Government Performance: Lessons Learned for the Next Administration on Using Performance Information to Improve Results*, p. 6. Figures are for 1997–2007.

94. U.S. Government Accountability Office, *Government Performance: GPRA Modernization Act Provides Opportunities to Help Address Fiscal, Performance, and Management Challenges*, GAO-11-466T (Washington, DC: U.S. Government Printing Office, 2011), Highlights page.

95. Senator Mark Warner, quoted in John M. Kamensky, "Congress Overhauls Results Act, Wants Results," *PA Times* (March/April 2011), p. 8.

96. U.S. Government Accountability Office, *Streamlining Government: Opportunities Exist to Strengthen OMB's Approach to Improving Efficiency*, GAO-10-394 (Washington, DC: U.S. Government Printing Office, 2010). Data are for 2008–2010.

97. Julnes, *Performance-Based Management Systems*.

98. Partnership for Public Service and Grant Thornton, *A Critical Role at a Critical Time: A Survey of Performance Improvement Officers* (Washington, DC, and Alexandria, VA, 2011), p. 1. Twenty-three officers at twenty-three of the twenty-four largest agencies were surveyed in 2010.

99. Julie Melkers and Katherine Willoughby, *Staying the Course: The Use of Performance Measurements in State Governments* (Washington, DC: IBM Center for the Business of Government, 2004).

100. Jennifer Burnett, "Statewide Performance Measurement Initiatives," *Book of the States, 2010* (Lexington, KY: Council of State Governments, 2010), http://knowledgecenter. csg.org/drupal/content/statewide-performance-measurement-initiatives.

101. Julia E. Melklers, Katherine G. Willoughby, Brian James, *et al. Performance Measurement at the State and Local Levels: A Summary of Results* Washington, DC: Governmental Accounting Standards Board, 2002), p. 12.

102. Katherine G. Willoughby, "Performance Measurement and Budget Balancing: State Government Perspectives," *Public Budgeting & Finance* 24 (June 2004), pp. 21–39. Data are for 2003.

103. Carolyn Bourdeaux and Grace Chikoto, "Legislative Influence on Performance Management Reform," *Public Administration Review* 68 (March/April 2008), pp. 253–265. The quotation is on p. 253.

104. Robert D. Lee, Jr. and Robert C. Burns, "Performance Measurement in State Budgeting: Advancement and Backsliding from 1990 to 1995," *Public Budgeting & Finance* 20 (March 2000), pp. 50–51.

105. Carolyn Bourdeaux, "Integrating Performance Information into Legislative Budget Processes," *Public Performance & Management Review* 31 (June 2008), pp. 547–569. "Agency self-reported performance information" ranked eleventh out of eleven possible information sources among Georgia state legislators.

106. Ellen Perlman, "'Stat' Fever," *Governing* (January 2007), pp. 48–50.

107. Anne Spray Kinney and John Ruggini, "Measuring for a Purpose: Trends in Public-Sector Measurement and Management Practices," *Government Finance Review* 24 (August 2008), pp. 14–23. Figures (p. 16) are for 2006.

108. Theodore H. Poister and Gregory Streib, "Performance Measurement in Municipal Government: Assessing the State of the Practice," *Public Administration Review* 59 (July/August 1999), pp. 325–335.

109. Alfred Tat-Kei Ho, "PBB in American Local Governments: It's More than a Management

Tool," *Public Administration Review* 71 (May/ June 2011), pp. 391–401. Figures (p. 392) are for 2011.

110. David H. Folz, Reem Abdelrazek, and Yeonsoo Chung, "The Adoption, Use, and Impacts of Performance Measures in Medium-Size Cities: Progress Toward Performance Management," *Public Performance & Management Review* 33 (September 2009), pp. 63–87. Data (p. 70) are for 2004.

111. Gregory Streib and Theodore H. Poister, "Performance Measurement in Municipal Governments," *Municipal Year Book, 1998* (Washington, DC: International City/County Management Association, 1998), pp. 9–15. Figures (p. 11) are for 1997.

112. David H. Foly and William Lyons, "The Measurement of Municipal Service Quality and Productivity," *Public Productivity Review* 10 (Winter 1986), pp. 21–33.

113. Jonathan P. West, "City Government Productivity and Civil Service Reforms," *Public Productivity Review* 10 (Fall 1986), pp. 45–59.

114. U.S. Government Accountability Office, *Government Performance: Lessons Learned for the Next Administration on Using Performance Information to Improve Results*, p. 4. "Decade" refers to 1997–2007.

115. As derived from data in ibid., Figure 1, p. 4; Governmental Accounting Standards Board, *Performance Measurement at the State and Local Levels*, pp. 5–6; and Poister and Streib, "Performance Measurement in Municipal Government," p. 329. Federal data are for 2007; state data are for 2001; and municipal data are for 1997.

116. As derived from data in ibid. (all three citations).

117. David N. Ammons and William C. Rivenbark, "Factors Influencing the Use of Performance Data to Improve Municipal Services: Evidence from the North Carolina Benchmarking Project," *Public Administration Review* 68 (March/April 2008), pp. 304–318. The quotation is on p. 315.

118. This discussion is based (with some modifications) mostly on: Burt Perrin, "Effective Use and Misuse of Performance Measurement," *American Journal of Evaluation* 19 (Fall 1998), pp. 367–379.

119. Maureen L. Cropper and George L. Van Houtven, *When Is A Life Too Costly to Save?* (Washington, DC: Resources for the Future, 1994).

120. Joseph T. McNamara, "Crime Statistics—Only Game in Town," *Savannah Morning News* (February 5, 2002).

121. Ken Miller, "Ditching the Carrot & Stick," *Governing* (June 2011), pp. 50–53. The quotations are on p. 52.

122. John Bohte and Kenneth J. Meier, "Goal Displacement: Assessing the Motivation for Organizational Cheating," *Public Administration Review* 60 (March/April 2000), pp. 173–182.

123. "Report on Business," *Toronto Globe and Mail,* "about 1996," as quoted in Perrin, "Effective Use and Misuse of Performance Evaluation," p. 367.

124. Katherine Barrett and Richard Greene, "Poisoned Measures," *Governing* (May 1998), p. 60.

125. Perrin, "Effective Use and Misuse of Performance Measurement," p. 375.

126. Cited in ibid., p. 376. Figures are for 1996.

127. Ho, "PBB in American Local Governments," p. 392. Figures are for 2011.

128. Governmental Accounting Standards Board, *Performance Measurement at the State and Local Levels*, p. 12. Figure is for 2001.

129. Julia Melkers and Katherine Willoughby, "The State of the States: Performance-Based Budgeting in 47 out of 50," *Public Administration Review* 88 (January/February 1998), pp. 66–73. The datum is on p. 69.

130. Kinney and Ruggini, "Measuring for a Purpose," p. 18. Figure is for 2006.

131. David N. Ammons, Charles Coe, and Michael Lombardo, "Performance-Comparison Projects in Local Government: Participants' Perspectives," *Public Administration Review* 61 (January/February 2001), pp. 100–110. The quotation is on p. 106.

132. Ammons and Rivenbark, "Factors Influencing the Use of Performance Data to Improve Municipal Services."

133. Paul D. Epstein, "Redeeming the Promise of Performance Measurement: Issues and Obstacles for Governments in the United States," *Organizational Performance and Measurement in the Public Sector: Toward Service, Effort, and Accomplishment Reporting*, Arie Halachmi and Geert Bouckaert, eds. (Westport, CN: Quorum Books, 1996), pp. 51–76. The quotation is on p. 62.

134. Penelope Lemov, "Rough SEAs," *Governing* (February 2007), p. 53.

135. Epstein, "Redeeming the Promise of Performance Measurement," p. 62.

136. Council of State Governments, *Book of the States, 2004* (Lexington, KY: Author, 2004), Table 4.29. "Performance audits include economy and efficiency audits and program audits."

137. John D. Heaton, Linda J. Savage, and Judith K. Welch, "Performance Auditing in Municipal Governments," *Government Accountants Journal* 42 (Summer 1993), pp. 51–60. Figure is for 1992.

138. Peter Babachicos, Daniel Kyle, Karen McKenzie, *et al.*, "Why Performance Audits Preceding Scandals Were Ignored," *Government Accountants Journal* 45 (Spring 1996), pp. 10–18.

139. Richard Boyle, *Performance Reporting: Insights from International Practice* (Washington, DC: IBM Center for the Business of Government, 2009), pp. 11, 13–14.

140. Ken A. Smith, Rita Hartung Cheng, Ola M. Smith, *et al.*, "Performance Reporting by State Agencies: Bridging the Gap between Current Practices and GASB Suggested Criteria," *Journal of Government Financial Reporting* 57 (Summer 2008), pp. 42–47.

141. Kenneth A. Smith and Lee Schiffel, "Improvements in City Government Performance Reporting," *Journal of Government Financial Management* 58 (Summer 2009), pp. 36–42. The quotations are on pp. 37, 39. The ten-year data are for 1997–2007.

142. Boyle, *Performance Reporting*, p. 11.

143. Dana Milbank, "It's in the Cards that Oregon Will Get Even Better by 2010," *Wall Street Journal* (December 9, 1996).

144. Ronald C. Nyhan and Herbert Marlowe, "Performance Measurement in the Public Sector: Challenges and Opportunities," *Public Productivity & Management Review* 18 (Summer 1995), pp. 333–348. The quotation is on p. 336.

145. Alfred Tat-Kei Ho and Anna Ya Ni, "Have Cities Shifted to Outcome-Oriented Performance Reporting?—A Content Analysis of City Budgets," *Public Budgeting & Finance* 25 (Summer 2005), pp. 61–83. Figure (p. 72) is for 2002.

146. Nyhan and Marlowe, "Performance Measurement in the Public Sector," p. 336.

147. David Edwards and John Clayton Thomas, "Developing a Municipal Performance-Measurement System: Reflections on the Atlanta Dashboard," *Public Administration Review* 65 (May/June 2005), pp. 369–376.

148. Valerie J. Richardson, *Increasing Transparency and Accountability in Federal Performance Reporting: Lessons from the OMB Pilot Program* (Washington, DC: IBM Center for the Business of Government, 2009), p. 6.

149. U.S. Government Accountability Office, *Key Indicator Systems: Experiences of Other National and Subnational Systems Offer Insights for the United States*, GAO-11-396 (Washington, DC: U.S. Government Printing Office, 2011), p. 10.

150. Kinney and Ruggini, "Measuring for a Purpose," pp. 18–19. Figures are for 2006.

151. Richardson, *Increasing Transparency and Accountability in Federal Performance Reporting*.

152. Donald P. Moynihan and Patricia W. Ingraham, "Look for the Silver Lining: When Performance-Based Accountability Systems Work," *Journal of Public Administration Research and Theory* 13 (Fall 2003), pp. 469–562.

153. Ammons and Rivenbark, "Factors Influencing the Use of Performance Data to Improve Municipal Services," p. 315.

154. In addition to works cited in the following bullets, this discussion is based on Perrin, "Effective Use and Misuse of Performance Evaluation"; Robert D. Behn, *Performance Leadership: 11 Better Practices That Can Ratchet Up Performance*, 2nd ed. (Washington, DC: IBM Center for the Business of Government, 2006); and Kathe Callahan and Kathryn Kloby, *Moving toward Outcome-Oriented Performance Measurement Systems* (Washington, DC: IBM Center for the Business of Government, 2009).

155. Judy Zelio, *Five Actions to Enhance State Legislative Use of Performance Information* (Washington, DC: IBM Center for the Business of Government, 2008), p. 3.

156. Boyle, *Performance Reporting*, p. 13.

157. George A. Boyne and Alex A. Chen, "Performance Targets and Public Service Improvement," *Journal of Public Administration Research and Theory* 17 (October 2007), pp. 455–477. The quotation is on p. 455. This is an analysis of pupils' test results in 147 local education authorities in England, 1998–2003.

158. Steven Kelman and John N. Friedman, "Performance Improvement and Performance Dysfunction: An Empirical Examination of Distortionary Impacts of the Emergency Room Wait-Time Target in the English National Health Service," *Journal of Public Administration Research and Theory* 19 (October 2009), pp. 917–946. The quotation is on p. 917.

159. Kaifeng Yang and Sanjay K. Pandey, "How Do Perceived Political Environment and Administrative Reform Affect Employee Commitment?" *Journal of Public Administration Research and Theory* 19 (April 2009), pp. 335–360. The quotations are on p. 335. This is a national survey of state human services managers.

160. Jonathan Walters, "Computing Performance," *Governing* (June 2010), pp. 48–49.

161. Yang and Pandey, "How Do Perceived Political Environment and Administrative Reform Affect Employee Commitment?" p. 335.

162. Yi Lu, "Improving the Design of Performance Measures: The Role of Agencies," *Public Performance & Management Review* 32 (September 2008), pp. 7–24. The quotations are on p. 21. This is an analysis of state agency heads and budgetary officers in Georgia.

163. Gene A. Brewer, "In the Eye of the Storm: Front-Line Supervisors and Federal Agency Performance," *Journal of Public Administration Research and Theory* 15 (October 2005), pp. 505–523. The quotation is on p. 505.

164. U.S. Merit Systems Protection Board, *A Call to Action: Improving First-Level Supervision of Federal Employees* (Washington, DC: U.S. Government Printing Office, 2010), p. 1.

165. Bradley E. Wright and Sanjay K. Pandey, "Tranformational Leadership in the Public Sector: Does Structure Matter?" *Journal of Public Administration Research and Theory* 20 (January 2010), pp. 75–89. The quotations are on p. 85. This is national a study of 1,322 responding city managers and department heads.

166. U.S. General Accounting Office, *Performance Measurement and Evaluation: Definitions and Relationships,* p. 3.

167. Ibid.

168. Henry W. Riecken, "Principal Components of the Evaluation Process," *Professional Psychology* 8 (November 1977), pp. 392–410. The quotation is on p. 405.

169. Peter Dahler-Larsen, "Surviving the Routinization of Evaluation: The Administrative Use of Evaluations in Danish Municipalities," *Administration & Society* 32 (March 2000), pp. 79–92. The quotation is on p. 70.

170. Kathryn E. Newcomer, "How Does Program Performance Assessment Affect Program Management in the Federal Government?" *Public Performance & Management Review* 30 (March 2007), pp. 332–350. The datum is on p. 334. An example is the No Child Left Behind Act.

171. U.S. Government Accountability Office, *CFO Act of 1990: Driving the Transformation of Federal Financial Management*, GAO-06-242T (Washington, DC: U.S. Government Printing Office, 2005), Highlights page.

172. U.S. General Accounting Office, *Managing for Results: The Statutory Framework for Performance-Based Management and Accountability*, GAO/GGD/AIMD-98-52 (Washington, DC: U.S. Government Printing Office, 1998), pp. 1, 3.

173. Ronald Longo and Harold I. Steinberg, "The Federal Government's First Audited Governmentwide Financial Statements," *Government Accountants Journal* 42 (Summer 1998), pp. 16–25. The quotations are on p. 16.

174. Moynihan and Ingraham, "Look for the Silver Lining," p. 469.

175. National Association of State Budget Officers, *Budget Processes in the States* (Washington, DC: Author, 2008), p. 10. Figure is for 2008.

176. Burns and Lee, "The Ups and Downs of State Budget Process Reform," p. 10. Figures are for 1970–2000.

177. Poister and Streib, "Municipal Management Tools from 1976 to 1993," p. 122. Figures are for 1993.

178. Peter Frumkin and Mark T. Kim, "Strategic Positioning and the Financing of Nonprofit Organizations: Is Efficiency Rewarded in the Contributions Marketplace?" *Public Administration Review* 61 (May/June 2001), pp. 266–275. The quotations are on p. 266.

179. Greg Chen, "Does Meeting Standards Affect Charitable Giving? An Empirical Study of New York Metropolitan Charities," *Nonprofit Management & Leadership* 19 (Spring 2009), pp. 349–365. The quotations are on p. 363. This

is an analysis of the Better Business Bureau's Charity Review program.

180. Margaret F. Sloan, "The Effects of Nonprofit Accountability Ratings on Donor Behavior," *Nonprofit Management & Voluntary Quarterly* 38 (April 2009), pp. 220–236. The quotations are on p. 220. This is an analysis of the Better Business Bureau's Wise Giving Alliance.

181. For examples, see the seventh edition (1998) of this book, pp. 213–217.

182. We have collapsed the Evaluation Research Society's six types of program evaluation and the GAO's four into six types. See Evaluation Research Society Standards Committee, "Evaluation Research Society Standards for Program Evaluation," *Standards for Evaluation Practice*, P. H. Rossi, ed. (San Francisco: Jossey-Bass, 1982); and U.S. General Accounting Office, *Performance Measurement and Evaluation: Definitions and Relationships*.

183. Eleanor Chelinsky, "Evaluating Public Programs," *Handbook of Public Administration*, James L. Perry, ed. (San Francisco: Jossey-Bass, 1989), pp. 259–274. The quotation is on p. 269. The writer is citing the Evaluation Research Society's six types of evaluation.

184. U.S. General Accounting *Teenage Pregnancy: 500,000 Births a Year But Few Tested Programs*, GAO/PEMD-86-16BR (Washington, DC: Author, 1986).

185. Bruce B. Buchanan, III, "The Senior Executive Service: How Can We Tell If It Works?" *Public Administration Review* 41 (May/June 1981), pp. 349–358.

186. U.S. General Accounting Office, *CETA Programs for Disadvantaged Adults—What Do We Know About Their Enrollees, Services, and Effectiveness?* GAO/IPE-82-2 (Washington, DC: Author, 1982).

187. Robert K. Yin, "Life Histories of Innovations: How New Practices Become Routinized," *Public Administration Review* 41 (January/February 1981), pp. 21–28.

188. Chelinsky, "Evaluating Public Programs," p. 268.

189. George L. Kelling, Tony Pate, Duane Dieckman, et al., *The Kansas City Preventive Patrol Experiment: Summary Report* (Washington, DC: The Police Foundation, 1974).

190. U.S. General Accounting Office, *Drinking-Age Laws: An Evaluation Synthesis of Their Impact on Highway Safety*, GAO/PEMD-87-10 (Washington, DC: U.S. General Accounting Office, 1987).

191. Francis G. Caro, "Evaluation Research: An Overview," *Readings in Evaluation Research*, Francis G. Caro, ed. (New York: Russell Sage Foundation, 1971), pp. 17, 13–15.

192. Francesca Gino, "Do We Listen to Advice Just Because We Paid for It? The Impact of Advice Cost on Its Use," *Organizational Behavior and Human Decision Processes* 107 (November 2008), pp. 234–245. The quotation is on p. 234.

193. Arnold J. Meltsner, *Policy Analysis in the Bureaucracy* (Berkeley, CA: University of California Press, 1976), Chapter 2.

194. William D. Coplin, Astrid E. Merget, and Carolyn Bourdeaux, "The Professional Researcher as Change Agent in the Government-Performance Movement," *Public Administration Review* 62 (November/December 2002), pp. 699–711. The quotations are drawn from pp. 701–702.

195. U.S. General Accounting Office, *Evaluation and Analysis to Support Decision-Making*, p. 14.

196. Mary E. Poulin, Phillip R. Harris, and Peter R. Jones, "The Significance of Definitions of Success in Program Evaluation," *Evaluation Review* 24 (October 2000), pp. 516–536.

197. Much of this discussion on evaluation design is drawn from U.S. General Accounting Office, *Evaluation and Analysis to Support Decision-Making*, especially pp. 11–41; Caro, "Evaluation Research," especially pp. 23–27; and U.S. General Accounting Office, *Designing Evaluations*, GAO/PEMD-10.1.4 (Washington, DC: Author, 1991).

198. U.S. General Accounting Office, *Evaluation and Analysis to Support Decision-Making*, p. 13.

199. Caro, "Evaluation Research," p. 24.

200. For a horrific example, see H. Donald Messer, "Drug Abuse Treatment: An Evaluation That Wasn't," *Program Evaluation at HEW: Research Versus Reality: Part 1: Health*, James G. Abert, ed. (New York: Marcel Dekker, 1979), pp. 113–168.

201. Riecken, "Principal Components of the Evaluation Process," p. 408.

202. Michael Morris and Lynette R. Jacobs, "You Got a Problem with That? Exploring Evaluators' Disagreements about Ethics," *Evaluation*

Review 24 (August 2000), pp. 384–406. The quotations are on pp. 384 and 403.

203. Neil S. Wenger, Stanley G. Kornman, Richard Berk, *et al.*, "Reporting Unethical Research Behavior," *Evaluation Review* 23 (October 1999), pp. 553–570. The quotation is on p. 553.

204. See, for example, Carol H. Weiss, "Evaluation for Decisions: Is Anybody There? Does Anybody Care?" *Evaluation Practice* 9 (Spring 1988), pp. 5–19.

205. See, for example, M. O. Patton, "The Evaluator's Responsibility for Utilization," *Evaluation Research* 9 (Summer 1988), pp. 5–24.

206. Carol H. Weiss, "Research for Policy's Sake: The Enlightenment Function of Social Research," *Policy Analysis* 3 (Fall 1977), pp. 531–545. The quotation is on p. 532.

207. Thomas V. Bonoma, "Overcoming Resistance to Change Recommended for Operating Programs," *Professional Psychology* 8 (November 1977), pp. 451–463.

208. Lynn M. Shulha and J. Bradley Cousins, "Evaluation Use: Theory, Research, and Practice Since 1986," *Evaluation Practice* 18 (Fall 1997), pp. 195–208. The quotation is on p. 200.

209. Tarek Azzam, "Evaluator Responsiveness to Stakeholders," *American Journal of Evaluation* 31 (March 2010), pp. 45–65. The quotation is on p. 65. This is a report on a simulation.

210. Dahler-Larsen, "Surviving the Routinization of Evaluation," p. 70.

211. Christina A. Christie, "Reported Influence of Evaluation Data on Decision Makers' Actions," *American Journal of Evaluation* 28 (March 2007), pp. 8–25. The quotations are on p. 8.

212. Carol H. Weiss, Erin Murphy-Graham, Anthony Petrosino, *et al.*, "The Fairy Godmother—and Her Warts," *American Journal of Evaluation* 29 (March 2008), pp. 29–47. The quotation is on p. 29.

213. Weiss, "Research for Policy's Sake," pp. 535, 544.

The Public Trough: Financing and Budgeting Governments

In government, money is blood. Currency courses through the body politic, carrying with it civic health or public pestilence, depending upon how governments derive and disburse their dollars.

Liberals may froth that government should have more money, and conservatives may fume that government should have less, but in fact there are limits on the price that Americans are willing to pay for their governments. Americans do not mindlessly demand lower taxes and less government, but they do insist that government deliver more and at a relatively fixed price.

There are understandable reasons for Americans' insistence. Since 1972, the portion of personal income allocated by families to basic needs, notably food, clothing, transportation, and savings, has fallen to accommodate the rising costs of two other necessities—health care, the cost of which doubled, and "other services," particularly financial services, that increased by some 50 percent over thirty years.[1]

Because of these trends in home economics, the price that Americans pay for government has remained fairly constant. Over thirty years, Americans have paid from 35 to 37 percent of their personal incomes for all governments. The federal government's share ranges from 20 to 22 percent, although, since 2001, the federal share of personal income has fallen below 20 percent as a result of unprecedented federal tax cuts. State governments account for 7.3–8.3 percent of personal income, and local governments take from 6 to 6.6 percent.[2]

These trends are occurring in an atmosphere of occlusion. "At least 85 percent" of Americans agree "overwhelmingly...across all levels of government" that "government officials should be accountable to citizens about financial management and...provide transparent financial information." Yet, although the figures are improving, 51 percent of Americans are dissatisfied with the federal government on these scores (so, for that matter, are federal administrators[3]), 49 percent are less than satisfied with state governments, and 40 percent with local governments.[4]

When citizens are relatively knowledgeable about governments' money, good things happen. A unique analysis of forty national budget components in forty-one countries found "a positive relationship" between budget transparency and balanced budgets. "The more information the budget discloses, the less the politicians can use fiscal deficits to achieve opportunistic goals."[5]

Some good news: Beginning in 2009, Washington, by creating new websites, opened its budgetary books to unprecedented levels of transparency and, through legislation and regulation, by that same year had "tipped the balance" in the states as well, pushing them "to the point of no return" in increasing their own fiscal transparencies.[6]

PUBLIC FINANCE: PAYING FOR PUBLIC POLICY

The basis for governments' budgets is *public finance,* or the raising by governments of revenues that are then expended to fund public policies. *Fiscal policy* is government's effort to fund public programs through its taxing, spending, and borrowing decisions.

General revenue, or *general purpose revenue,* is money that the government collects and may spend for any purpose. A *general tax* is the major method of generating general revenue. A *general fund* is that part of the public budget which is composed of general revenue. *General fund expenditures,* or *discretionary spending,* is the allocation of general revenue to fund any purpose.

A *special fund* is composed of those revenues that may be expended only for a specific, preestablished purpose, or what is known as *nondiscretionary spending.* The principal justification for this arrangement is that some special funds underwrite public policies that are so vital that they must be protected by law from the political tides and their accompanying opportunists.

FINANCING THE FEDERAL GOVERNMENT

Federal finance is fraught with foment.

Federal General Revenue

General revenue accounts for 62 percent of total federal revenue, down by nearly a third from 89 percent in 1950.[7] Because essentially all federal general revenue is provided by taxes, "general revenue" and "tax revenue" typically are treated in federal circles as one and the same. This, as we shall see, is not the case in state and local governments, where tax revenue accounts for only about half of the states' general revenue, and for even less—some two-fifths—in local governments.

The Personal Income Tax The primary source of federal general revenue is the *personal,* or *individual, income tax,* which is a general tax on the annual income of each person. It began (aside from a few intermittent and brief appearances in the 1800s) with the ratification, in 1913, of the Constitution's Sixteenth Amendment, which permits the federal government to tax all incomes. The personal income tax accounts for a whopping 76 percent of Washington's general revenue, up by almost a third from 46 percent in 1950.[8]

The Corporate Income Tax The *corporate,* or *corporation, income tax* is a general tax on the annual profits of businesses. The first federal corporate income tax was enacted in 1909. It contributes 16 percent of general revenue, down by almost half from 30 percent in 1950.[9]

The Excise Tax The *excise tax* is a general tax on specific items that usually is paid by their manufacturer. The main excise taxes are placed on companies that make gasoline, alcoholic beverages, telephone systems, and tobacco products. Congress relied principally on excise taxes to fund the Revolution, and it remained the most productive federal tax through the early twentieth century. Excise taxes account for 6 percent of general revenue, falling by almost three-quarters from 22 percent in 1950.[10]

Gift and Estate Taxes The *gift tax* is a general tax on the transfer of property by one person to another, and the person making the transfer receives nothing, or less than full value, in return. The *estate tax* is a general tax on a person's right to transfer his or her property when he or she dies. Together, gift and estate taxes account for less than 2 percent of general revenue, matching their take in 1950.[11]

Social Insurance and Retirement Receipts

Social insurance and retirement receipts are not general revenue and cannot be used for discretionary expenditures. They account for 42 percent of total federal revenue, nearly quadrupling from 11 percent in 1950.[12]

The five special funds that comprise social insurance and retirement receipts are Old-Age and

Survivors Insurance (or Social Security); Disability Insurance (nine major programs, targeted, for the most part, at people aged fifty to sixty-four); Hospital Insurance (or Medicare); Unemployment Insurance; and relatively small sums paid toward the retirement funds of federal and railroad employees.

Social Security and Medicare, which are retirement and health insurance programs for people aged sixty-five (more or less) and older, account for more than four-fifths of all social insurance and retirement receipts.[13] These two massive programs (which are primarily responsible for the fact that Washington spends seven times more, per capita, on the elderly than it spends on children[14]) are funded with what are called, with unfortunate coyness, "insurance contributions." *Insurance contributions* are actually a compulsory payroll tax, and they derive their name from the Federal Insurance Contributions Act (FICA) of 1935, which underwrites Social Security and Medicare exclusively. Employers and employees pay this tax in equal shares, and their combined tax rate has quintupled from about 3 percent of payrolls in 1950 to over 15 percent in 2010.[15] (In 2011, Washington temporarily cut the combined rate to more than 8 percent in an effort to energize the economy.) The payroll taxes collected through FICA account for 33 percent of total federal revenue, nearly a septupling from 5 percent in 1950.[16]

Federal Expenditures

In general, federal spending since 1950 gradually has lessened for the military and enlarged for social programs.

Spending on What? The federal government spends nearly three-fifths of its money on *payments for individuals*, which are federal grants to individual persons. Almost three out of ten Americans receive some kind of cash benefit from the federal government, a proportion equaled by those who live in households that receive from Washington a benefit in a form other than cash. Nineteen percent of federal dollars is allocated to national defense, and nearly 5 percent pays the interest on the national debt.[17]

Nondiscretionary *versus* Discretionary Expenditures Another way of understanding federal expenditures is to separate them into nondiscretionary and discretionary spending.

Federal nondiscretionary spending is conducted through twenty-six major *mandatory and related programs*, a category that includes interest on the national debt and sixteen large entitlement programs, such as Social Security and Medicare, that are funded by formulas.

In 1962, only 32 percent of all federal expenditures had to be spent on mandatory and related programs, and a comfortable 68 percent was reserved for discretionary purposes. Nearly a half-century later, these proportions had almost reversed: 61 percent of spending is for nondiscretionary programs and 39 percent for discretionary ones.[18]

GRASS-ROOTS' REVENUES

When we leave the world of Washington and consider the financing of state and local governments, new kinds, categories, and complexities of revenue emerge.

General Revenue

In these governments, general revenue officially[19] is composed not only of general tax revenue, as is the case with federal general revenue, but also of intergovernmental revenue, fees collected from users of special public services, and miscellaneous general sources.

Intergovernmental Revenue *Intergovernmental revenue* is money that state and local governments receive from other governments. Although intergovernmental revenue is an official component of these governments' general revenue, which, in theory, can be spent for anything, it is problematic because, in reality, it typically arrives in state and local coffers in the form of grants that narrowly specify how they may be spent.

Service Charges A *service charge*, or a *fee for services*, is a particular type of user fee that is charged for providing a special service, such as hospitals and public housing. A *user fee* is "in general related to some voluntary transaction or request for government goods or services" that are "above and beyond what is normally available to the public."[20]

Service charges, but not other sorts of user fees (specifically, public employee contributions to insurance trusts and customer payments to publicly owned utilities and liquor stores, described later), officially are counted as part of a state or local government's general revenue.

Like intergovernmental revenue, service charges flout the philosophic foundation of general revenue because they may not be spent for any purpose that the government chooses. Instead, they are paid to, and kept by, the agency providing the service.

Why Is This? Why is it that the public finance community includes intergovernmental revenue and service charges, neither one of which truly allows discretionary spending, as components of state-and-local general revenue? The reasoning is that discretionary spending (of a sort) occurs when state and local governments, of their own volition, (1) apply for and accept intergovernmental grants and spend the intergovernmental revenue in them, and (2) when they choose to offer and spend for nonbasic, special services. No one mandated that they undertake either activity; they did so at their discretion.

Real Discretionary Spending The hanging question is, How much revenue do state and local governments actually have available to spend at their discretion?

When general revenue is officially defined, 73 percent of all state revenue, and 87 percent of total local revenue, may, at least in theory, be spent as general purpose expenditures. When we cull intergovernmental revenue and service charges from official general revenue, ostensibly discretionary state funds sink by two-fifths to 44 percent of total state revenue, and local general revenue declines by nearly half to 46 percent of all local revenue. In reality, state legislatures have 39 percent less money available for discretionary spending than official definitions of "general revenue" imply, and local councils have 54 percent less.[21]

Earmarking General Revenue Complicating further the role of general revenue at the grass roots is the propensity of some governments to convert general purpose revenue into special purpose revenue by earmarking general tax revenue for particular uses. California is a conspicuous example. Some 500 amendments bind California's constitution, rendering it, after India's, the longest and most convoluted in the world, containing "so many set-asides and mandates that the legislature can control only about seven per cent of the budget."[22] The remaining 93 percent of general revenue effectively has been reserved for special purposes, ranging from prisons to schools.

Own Source Revenue

Due to the presence of intergovernmental revenue, state and local governments must identify their *own source revenue*, or income that these governments garner from within their own jurisdictions. (This category is absent in federal finance because all federal revenue derives from the government's own sources.) Most own source revenue is the product of state or local taxes, but user fees, interest earnings, and property sales, among other own sources, also contribute.

There are two types of own source revenue.

General Revenue From Own Sources One type is *general revenue from own sources*, which is all general revenue, other than intergovernmental revenue, collected by state or local governments—specifically, general taxes, service charges, and miscellaneous general revenue.

Other Than General Revenue The other type is *other than general revenue*, which is own source revenue that cannot be used for discretionary expenditures. There are two official sources of other than general revenue, each of which relies on its own type of user fee to support itself.

Insurance Trusts One is *insurance trusts* that are funded by government employees' *contributions* to three special funds that are dedicated to their workers' compensation fund for work-related injuries, unemployment insurance, and retirement.

Utilities and Liquor Stores The other is government-owned and -operated *utilities* and *liquor stores* that collect customer *payments* for publicly provided goods. Utilities are electric and gas power plants, water and sewer works, and public transit. Most utilities are owned by local governments. Most liquor stores are owned by the states.

FINANCING STATE GOVERNMENTS

We shall treat state finance (and, later, local finance, too) in terms of their general revenue, followed by other than general revenue and expenditures, and conclude with a review of tax and expenditure limitations.

State General Revenue

As noted earlier, the states' general revenue amounts to almost three-quarters of their total revenue and is composed of intergovernmental revenue and three sorts of general revenue that are drawn from the states' own sources: general taxes, service charges, and miscellaneous general revenue.

State Intergovernmental Revenue Intergovernmental revenue contributes 29 percent of state general revenue; 95 percent of the states' intergovernmental revenue arrives as direct federal grants, and the rest as payments from their local governments. Intergovernmental revenue's share of the states' general revenue has grown by nearly a fourth since 1950, when it accounted for 22 percent.[23]

The remaining 71 percent of state general revenue comes from the states' own sources.

State General Tax Revenue State general taxes contribute 52 percent of all general revenue, having shrunk by a fourth since 1950, when their share stood at an impressive 70 percent. Taxes' portion of own source general revenue, however, has narrowed by only 6 percent, from 74 percent in 1950.[24]

The State Sales Tax The most important tax for the states is the *sales tax*, which is a general tax on the selling price of goods and services that usually is paid at the point-of-sale, such as a retail store. West Virginia levied the first state sales tax in 1921, when states relied heavily on property taxes, and today forty-five states impose it.[25] The sales tax accounts for 46 percent of all state tax revenue, down by about a third from almost three-fifths in 1950.[26]

State Income Taxes The decline in sales tax revenue is attributable to the rise of the state income tax. Wisconsin was the first state to impose an income tax, both personal and corporate, in 1911.

Forty-three states levy the personal income tax, including two, New Hampshire and Tennessee, which limit this tax to dividends and interest income.[27] The individual income tax generates 35 percent of state tax revenue, nearly a quadrupling of its 9 percent share in 1950.[28]

Forty-seven states use the corporate income tax,[29] which accounts for 7 percent of all state tax revenue,[30] exactly its share in 1950.[31] The stasis of the state corporate income tax over seven decades has been attributed to shrewd tax planning by corporations[32] that occurs in tandem with a cutthroat competition among state governments that are frantically lowering their corporate income taxes to lure companies to relocate to their states.[33]

State Service Charges and Miscellany Charges for services, led by education, account for 10 percent of all general revenue and 14 percent of general revenue that is derived from the states' own sources. The remaining sources of state general revenue are miscellaneous ones (e.g., special assessments, property sales), led by interest earnings.[34]

Combined, service charges and miscellaneous general revenue account for 19 percent of all general revenue (more than doubling from 8 percent in 1950) and 27 percent of own source general revenue (a tripling from 9 percent).[35] These two sources, plus the less dramatic rise in intergovernmental revenue, largely explain why taxes are declining as contributors to the states' general funds.

State Other-Than-General Revenue

Other-than-general revenue (i.e., insurance trusts, utilities, and liquor stores) makes up 27 percent of total state revenue (an increase of more than a third since the mid-twentieth century, when its share was 20 percent) and 36 percent of state own source revenue (increasing by half, from 24 percent). Insurance trusts, with a share of 96 percent, dominate this category.[36]

State Expenditures

The states' largest single expenditure, at 36 percent of total direct expenditures (i.e., spending money that is drawn from general revenue and other-than-general revenue funds), is for social services and income maintenance; four-fifths of this spending is for public welfare. Nineteen percent is devoted to education, four-fifths of which is channeled to higher education. Sixteen percent of all direct expenditures is spent by insurance trusts. Transportation accounts for 8 percent, almost all of it for highways. Six percent is spent for public safety. Governmental administration and interest on the general debt each account for 4 percent. Environment and housing amounts to 3 percent, and utilities spend 2 percent, of all direct expenditures.[37]

State Tax and Expenditure Limitations

The states do not like to tax, or even spend, and thirty states have imposed on themselves at least one tax or expenditure limitation.[38]

Seven state legislatures have legislated revenue limits on their governments, including three that also limit expenditures. In addition, since Arkansas originated the practice, in 1934, sixteen states now require legislative "supermajorities," ranging from 60 to 75 percent of legislators' votes in both chambers, to raise some or all taxes, including three states that *also* require voter approval; one, Colorado, requires only voter approval to raise taxes.[39]

Twenty-six states cap expenditures, including three that also limit taxes.[40] The fiscal impact of these limits is small. Even the most effective tax-and-spend-tamping policies (most notably,

legislative supermajorities and popular referenda) result in only 2–3 percent less spending, and, in the wealthier states, caps actually correlate with *more* spending![41]

FINANCING LOCAL GOVERNMENTS

Finance consumes local governments. "Fiscal management" has been "*the* dominant priority of city managers" ever since the first study of the issue was conducted more than thirty years ago.[42]

Because the nation's 89,476 local governments are incredibly diverse, with special-purpose governments accounting for well over half of them, average figures about the revenues that they collect and spend are less meaningful than they are for the federal and state governments. Nevertheless, we paint here some broad brushstrokes about the financing of all local governments, both general and special purpose.

Local General Revenue

As we noted earlier, general revenue accounts for nearly nine out of ten dollars of all local revenue and, just as it is in the states, is composed of intergovernmental revenue and three sorts of own source general revenue: general taxes, service charges, and miscellaneous general revenue.

Local Intergovernmental Revenue More than any other level of government, local governments depend on other governments to keep them going. Intergovernmental revenue contributes 38 percent of local general revenue, an increase of almost a fifth since 1950, when it contributed 32 percent.[43]

On paper, at least, 89 percent of local intergovernmental revenue is provided by state governments and 11 percent as direct federal grants.[44] However, an estimated one-third of the intergovernmental revenue that local governments receive from their states has actually been furnished by Washington in the form of pass-through grants.[45] *Pass-through grants* are funds granted by the federal government to the states with the stipulation that the states pass on these funds to a "sub-recipient," typically their local governments, for use in specific programs that have been earmarked by Washington.

If we count these pass-through grants as intergovernmental revenue that localities receive from Washington, rather than from the states, then the money that Washington provides increases its share of local intergovernmental revenue, rising from 11 percent (in direct federal grants only) to an estimated 14 percent (direct grants plus pass-through grants). Washington's contribution to local general revenue more than triples from 4 percent to an estimated 14 percent.[46]

Although the states have always sent the most substantial subsidies to local governments, Washington also is a large, and largely hidden, source of their revenue. Figure 8-1 illustrates these intergovernmental fiscal flows in terms of their effects on state and local general revenue and total revenue (i.e., general revenue and other than general revenue).

The remaining 62 percent of local general revenue comes from local governments' own sources.

Local General Tax Revenue The proportion of localities' general revenue that is generated by their general taxes barely exceeds, at 39 percent, the share provided by intergovernmental revenue, and their portion has shrunk by nearly a fifth since 1950, when they accounted for 68 percent. Still, taxes contribute an impressive 62 percent of the general revenue that local governments collect from their own sources, a modest decline of less than a tenth, from 69 percent in 1950.[47]

The Local Property Tax The principal tax for local governments is the *property tax*, an ancient form of taxation that is a general tax on personal wealth.

To determine a property's value, governments (counties usually are responsible for the administration of the property tax) hire and train professional assessors, who employ one or more of the

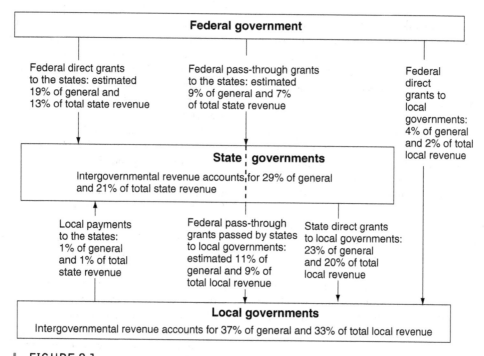

FIGURE 8-1

Intergovernmental Revenues as Percentages of State and Local Governments' General Revenue and Total Revenue, 2006–2007

following assessment methods: base the property's value on how much the property last sold for (a method sometimes dubbed, with leaden irony, "welcome stranger"); estimate the price that it currently would fetch in the open market; estimate how much it would cost to replace it; or estimate how much sustainable net income it will produce. Once the assessment is made, the property tax is levied on a predetermined fraction (say, 60 percent) of the property's assessed value.

All states permit their local governments to levy property taxes, which generate more than seven out of every ten local tax dollars. In 1950, and even into the 1960s, they accounted for nearly nine out of ten dollars of local tax revenue, a share that has since slipped by almost a fifth.[48]

Bucking, but not reversing, this trend is the fact that local governments will, among other revenue-raising responses, raise the property tax when the states cut their intergovernmental aid. Cities and towns offset these cuts by raising the property tax by an average of nine cents for each state dollar cut,[49] and school districts raise it by twenty-three cents per dollar cut.[50]

In part, the shrinking of the property tax is attributable to state legislatures allowing their local governments to introduce competing sales and income taxes. Forty-three states authorize their local governments to levy, if they so choose, taxes on sales, personal income, or both.[51]

The Local Sales Tax In 1950, just one state permitted at least some of its local governments to collect sales taxes,[52] and today thirty-eight do.[53] The sales tax accounts for 17 percent of all local tax dollars, nearly tripling from 6 percent in 1950.[54]

The Local Personal Income Tax The first local tax on personal income was introduced in 1938 by Philadelphia, and currently eighteen states permit at least some types of their local governments to impose a tax on individual incomes or payrolls.[55] Local personal income taxes, almost all of which are levied by municipalities, account for 5 percent of all local tax revenue, up from a fraction of 1 percent in 1950.[56]

Local Service Charges and Miscellany Charges for local services, led by education, contribute

16 percent of all local general revenue and 25 percent of the general revenue that local governments draw from their own sources. The remaining sources of local general revenue are miscellaneous ones, led by interest earnings.[57]

Combined, service charges and miscellaneous general revenue account for 21 percent of all local general revenue (almost doubling, from 11 percent, in 1950) and 38 percent of own source general revenue (more than doubling, from 17 percent).[58]

Local Other-Than-General Revenue

Other-than-general revenue accounts for 13 percent of total local revenue and 19 percent of own source revenue, percentages that have not changed much since the mid-twentieth century. More than three-fifths of other-than-general revenue is generated by local utilities, followed by insurance trusts at nearly two-fifths.[59]

Local Expenditures

Education accounts for 38 percent of total direct expenditures (i.e., spending general revenue and other than general revenue funds) by all local governments. More than four-fifths of education funds are disbursed by school districts, and almost all the rest is spent by counties, municipalities, and townships.

Eleven percent of all direct local expenditures is allocated to social services and income maintenance (counties spend six out of every ten of these dollars), most of it for public welfare, followed by hospitals. Utilities account for another 11 percent. Ten percent is spent on environment and housing, led by sewerage.

Nine percent of total spending by all local governments is channeled to public safety, although, at 15 percent, this category leads all others as a percentage of general expenditures by counties, cities, and towns. Interest on the general debt, governmental administration, and transportation each account for 5 percent of spending by all local governments, with highways consuming 70 percent of local transportation spending. Insurance trust expenditures make up 2 percent and miscellaneous expenditures fill in the rest.[60]

Local Tax and Expenditure Limitations

Tax and expenditure limitations are not confined to the states. Local governments have them, too.

State-Imposed Limitations

Forty-six states have imposed some form of tax or expenditure limitation on their local governments. Four of these states, however, require only that their local governments fully disclose their finances, a wholly reasonable limit.[61]

Four states limit their local governments' general revenue growth, and eight limit local general expenditure growth.[62]

The states' most favored form of local tax limitation, by far, however, focuses on their local governments' primary source of tax revenue, the property tax. As early as the 1880s, when the states began granting home rule to their communities, legislatures were restraining their local governments' use of the property tax,[63] and today thirty-three states limit property tax rates in their municipalities, counties, or school districts, including twenty-three that impose this limit on all three types of local government. A dozen states limit how much a property may be assessed. Twenty-eight combine caps on both rates and assessments, a policy known as a *property tax levy limit*, which constrains the growth of overall property tax revenue.[64]

Voter-Imposed Limitations

Limitations on local taxation and spending are mandated not only by state legislatures but also by local voters. Voters in 13 percent of cities have enacted tax and expenditure limitations on their municipal governments that are "distinct from (and more stringent than) any fiscal restriction imposed by their state government." Of these cities, 42 percent constrain property tax rates, 15 percent limit property tax levies, and 7 percent cap assessments. Nine percent of these cities impose limits on local sales taxes (no state legislature has done this[65]), and 6 percent limit their own general revenue or expenditures. Voters in cities with home rule charters, who are in metropolitan areas which have few municipalities, and who have rapidly changing populations are the most likely to adopt these limits.[66]

Do Limitations Reflect Local Preferences?

The irony in local tax and expenditure limitations, whether they are mandated by the states or (in a small minority of municipalities) local voters, is that most local residents display a firm willingness to pay for local services. It is not at all clear that these limitations actually are what people want.

A survey of more than 1,400 households in politically and fiscally conservative Phoenix, Arizona, found that from more than half to nearly four-fifths of all respondents were willing to pay for twenty-three (or 82 percent) out of twenty-eight local services, ranging from wastewater plants to libraries. "These findings buttress previous reports that residents will pay for local public services and are willing to be reasonable when confronted with matters of local public finance."[67] Stunningly, the poor are "overwhelmingly" more willing to pay for local services than are the wealthy.[68]

The Effects of Limitations

Tax and expenditure limitations seem to affect local governments more severely than the states, and their impact appears to be deepening over time.[69] Although a plurality, two-fifths, of cities report that these limits have had "no clear effect" on their operations, a fifth say that they have "reduced service provision" because of limitations, and 13 percent have turned to "new revenue sources."[70]

Charges over Taxes

What are these new revenue sources? Principally, they are new or increased charges for local services, a trend that, in part, is reflective of citizens' willingness to pay for those services.

Hiking fees for services is clearly the preferred option for local governments. "Nearly three-quarters" of city and town managers accord raising service charges their "highest" preference (out of nine possible responses) for dealing with stressed budgets.[71] Their attraction to service charges is understandable. Unlike raising unpopular local taxes, which only state legislatures can do, "all cities have the discretion to impose charges and user fees for services."[72] In addition, service charges also enable local (and, indeed, all) governments to draw revenue from sources that are tax exempt, such as charitable organizations.

The result of these realities is that fees for services are "by far the fastest growing significant category of city revenues."[73] Just prior to the tax revolt that was presaged, in 1978, by the passage of California's Proposition 13 (described in Chapter 1), which slashed local property taxes, service charges accounted for a modest 11 percent of all municipal general revenue and 18 percent of cities' general revenue that came from their own sources.[74] Some three decades later, service charges had more than doubled their shares, accounting for 28 percent of all municipal general revenue and 39 percent of own source general revenue.[75] Municipal service charges, which, over twenty-four years, rose by 110 percent per capita in 162 big cities, more than compensated for the flattening revenue rates generated by the property tax, which inched upward by less than 4 percent per capita.[76]

Cities are not alone in this trend. An analysis of nearly 2,700 counties over thirty years concluded that tax and expenditure limitations led to increases in the counties' service charges.[77]

Public administrators and citizens, in short, do not like taxes. So how can taxes be made more tolerable?

TAXING TIMES: DETERMINING TOLERABLE TAXES

In 1938, when taxes imposed by all governments relieved Americans, on average, of 17 percent of their income, "nearly half" of the citizenry thought that they paid too much in taxes relative to what they got in return. Today, a "remarkably similar" 46 percent think this, even though the average tax bite has nearly doubled.[78]

That Americans' views of taxes remain fairly constant over time, even as their taxes rise, may reflect tax systems that might be improving with age.

All tax systems share five features that determine their tolerability to taxpayers. They are as follows:[79]

- *Transparency:* A tax's structure that taxpayers are able to understand.
- *Administerability:* Government can collect the tax easily and cost-effectively.

- *Simplicity:* Low costs to taxpayers in complying with tax policy.
- *Efficiency Costs:* The price of creating and collecting the tax.
- *Equity:* The fairness of the tax.

Adjusting any one of these elements invariably alters each of the remaining four.

Understanding the Income Tax

The income tax is the single most consequential and productive tax in public finance.

Issues with Income Taxes Together, personal and corporate income taxes account for a third of all tax dollars collected by *all* governments, including those governments that do not levy income taxes.[80]

Income taxes may be progressive, proportional, or regressive. A *progressive income tax* taxes higher incomes at a higher rate than it taxes lower incomes. A *proportional income tax*, or *flat tax*, taxes all incomes, high and low alike, at the same rate. A *regressive income tax* taxes higher incomes at a lower rate than it taxes lower incomes.

Although pollsters find that majorities of Americans "have not heard the term 'progressive taxes,' philosophically it is the approach they prefer."[81] Accordingly, most governments, including the federal one, that levy a personal income tax try, at least nominally, to apply a moderately progressive tax rate; seven of the forty-three states with this tax, however, levy flat tax rates on personal income.[82] Although the federal corporate income tax is progressive, thirty-two of the forty-seven states with this tax employ a flat rate.[83]

The Federal Experience Income taxes are vital to federal finance. Washington's taxes on personal and corporate incomes amount to half of all federal revenue, and the federal government rakes in nearly four-fifths of all income-tax dollars collected by all governments combined.[84]

The downside of federal income taxes is that they fail, in the view of many, to fulfill the five criteria of a tolerable tax.

Transparency Is Tarnished "Numerous tax provisions have made it more difficult for taxpayers to understand how their tax liabilities are calculated, the logic behind the tax laws, and what other taxpayers are required to pay."[85] Witness, for example, the massive confusion among taxpayers concerning tax policies: Each year, the Internal Revenue Service (IRS) receives 299 million website visits, 277 million website searches, and 77 million telephone calls, and all concern taxpayers' tax questions.[86]

Administerability Is Occluded Administerability is not merely the responsibility of the IRS, which consumes a budget of about $12 billion[87] to process 139 million individual income tax returns annually[88] but is also a duty of taxpayers, employers, tax professionals, and a teeming host of others. Estimates of their administrative costs range from $100 billion to $200 billion per year,[89] so administerability is as important as the word itself is awful.

Simplicity Is Scarce The United States Tax Code is nearing 4 million words. The instruction booklet accompanying Form 1040, the individual itemized income tax form, has grown from 2 pages in 1935 to 179 pages today. Individual income taxpayers, 90 percent of whom hire accountants or buy software to help them prepare their tax returns at an average cost of $250 per taxpayer, devote nineteen hours, on average, to tax preparation.[90] There are no comprehensive estimates of the cost to taxpayers of complying with the federal tax system, but the broader studies suggest a magnitude of 2–5 percent of the gross domestic product (GDP).[91]

Efficiency Is Impaired Though difficult to measure, partial estimates "suggest that the overall efficiency costs imposed by the tax system are large—on the order of several percentage points" of GDP.[92] Taxpayers' voluntary compliance with tax policy is central to a tax system's efficiency, and it is heartening that relatively few Americans deliberately evade taxes. The untaxed underground economy in the United States is estimated to be 8 percent of GDP, compared with, say, Greece's, at 30 percent.[93] The shadow economy of the European continent is pegged at 20 percent.[94] Nevertheless, because of "persistent levels of noncompliance" by American taxpayers,[95] about 15 percent of federal taxes owed go uncollected

each year, despite "powerful tools" at the IRS's disposal to collect these taxes.[96]

Just by collecting the taxes owed it, Washington could have eliminated almost all of the preceding federal deficits.

Equity Issues Endure Inequities are found not only in the income tax but also in that important variant of it, the compulsory payroll tax (or FICA, described earlier) that funds Social Security and Medicare.

Federal personal and corporate income taxes feature 173 exemptions.[97] Their number more than doubled over thirty years, the tax revenue lost because of them tripled,[98] and they now cost federal coffers more than $1 trillion annually.[99] These exemptions allow 45 percent of American households to pay no federal income tax at all.[100] The top 400 income earners, whose average annual income is almost $345 million and who should pay the topmost tax bracket of 35 percent, pay instead an average of not quite 17 percent in federal income taxes, down by more than a third over fifteen years.[101] Not only are these exemptions unfair to those taxpayers who do not qualify for them, but they are costly, too, amounting to an estimated, and alarming, 7.5 percent of GDP.[102]

A different sort of inequity pervades the payroll tax. Its Social Security portion, which accounts for more than four-fifths of the payroll tax, is quite regressive. After an employee has been paid a set amount ($106,800 in 2011) for the year, the Social Security tax stops, and then restarts at the beginning of the next calendar year. (If an employee were paid $213,600 in 2011, then the contribution to Social Security would disappear from his or her paycheck after June, and reappear in January of 2012.) If an employee's annual pay does not exceed the preestablished payroll limit, then the tax never stops, and this is the case for the vast majority of Americans: An astonishing 86 percent of all households with wage earners, and about two-thirds of *all* taxpayers (including retirees, who pay no payroll tax), pay *more* in regressive payroll taxes than they pay in progressive federal personal income taxes.[103]

The remaining fifth of the payroll tax, Medicare, differs from Social Security in that it has no payroll cap and is a proportional tax. Nevertheless, the "average effective tax rate" of the payroll tax, both Social Security and Medicare combined, is clearly regressive, with the richest fifth of payroll taxpayers taxed at a rate that is more than two-fifths lower than the average rate paid by each of the remaining four fifths.[104]

Understanding the Sales Tax

The sales tax is the purview of the states. It is the states' mainstay tax, accounting for 18 percent of their (and 6 percent of local governments') total revenue.[105]

A Regressive Tax   The sales tax is inherently regressive because it is, at root, a tax on consumption. Although the sales tax taxes all consumers at the same rate, its burden inevitably falls on those consumers who are poor. Because the poor must spend a greater proportion of their money on essentials, such as medicine and food, the indigent effectively are taxed at a higher rate than are the wealthy.

States have attempted to alleviate the more regressive elements of the sales tax by exempting basic necessities. Forty-four of the forty-five states with a sales tax exempt prescription drugs, and ten exempt off-the-shelf drugs; the sole remaining state, Illinois, reduces its sales tax rate for both categories of medicines. Thirty-one states exempt groceries; five states lower their sales tax rates for foodstuffs; and five tax them but offer poor people a rebate or income tax credit.[106]

These sorts of measures relieve, but cannot eliminate, the sales tax's structurally regressive nature.

Issues of Inequity, Intricacy, and Obscurantism   In addition, the sales tax seems to be uncommonly buffeted by the political winds of the day. Powerful (or at least stealthy) legislators have been known to exempt favored constituents from the sales tax with no apparent economic or philosophic rationale for doing so.

Florida's legislature, for example, has exempted some 440 transactions from its sales tax, thereby exempting more than two-fifths of all purchases and slashing sales tax revenue by more than three out of every ten sales-tax dollars.[107]

Charges for charter fishing trips in Florida's waters are exempt, but not charges for fishing rods; food for racehorses is exempt, but not food for cats and dogs.[108] One state senator confessed that he had voted unwittingly for many of these exemptions because they had been "sneaked through."[109]

Florida is by no means the exception. Thirty state legislatures have exempted the sale of custom computer programs; thirteen states exempt repairers; eight exempt hotel rooms; seven exempt telecommunications services; and three states exempt contractors.[110] The logic justifying these and other exemptions is not obvious.

Understanding the Property Tax

The property tax, as the principal tax for local governments, accounts for 24 percent of their (and 6 percent of state governments') total revenue.[111]

Another Regressive Tax   As with the sales tax, the property tax has some regressive elements.

As a practical matter, the property tax concentrates on people's homes as its major source of revenue. Middle-class homeowners have a relatively large portion of their wealth tied up in their residences. By contrast, the wealthy, who often salt away their wealth in other ways, have proportionately less of their wealth parked in their homes. Hence, the property tax collects a greater proportion of the middle class's wealth than it collects from the rich. It also collects relatively more money from the poor. The poor rent their homes more frequently than the better-off classes, and their landlords pass on the cost of their property taxes to their tenants.

Relieving Regressivity   State governments have attempted to ameliorate the regressivity of the local property tax through two main mechanisms.

One is the *circuit breaker*, which automatically "trips" when the property tax overloads a property owner's preestablished income level. The owner is not required to pay above that level. Thirty-five states have circuit breaker programs, and two-thirds of these states offer circuit breakers to renters as well as to homeowners. One state, Oregon, offers a circuit breaker program to renters only.[112] Because circuit breakers often are poorly publicized and application procedures can be onerous, however, it appears that perhaps less than half of eligible property owners take advantage of circuit breakers.[113]

The other mechanism is assessing or taxing residential property less than commercial property. Four-fifths of the states protect homeowners through *homestead exemptions*, which exempt, or at least shield, from property taxes some portion of the value of everyone's home.[114] Half the states either assess residential property at lower levels (eighteen) or tax residential property at lower rates (seven) than commercial property.[115]

While helpful, these attempts to ameliorate the property tax cannot render it progressive because, as with the sales tax, it is structurally regressive.

America's Most Disliked Tax The property tax is the most disliked tax among Americans.[116] Not only does it penalize property taxpayers with fixed incomes, but it also has severe problems of administerability because it relies on the varying consistency of government assessors who determine the value of individual properties—a "lack of uniformity" that is its "greatest problem."[117]

RETHINKING FEDERAL TAXES

Proposals for federal tax reform range from the incremental to the radical.

Reforming Federal Income Taxes

Proposed reforms of the income tax focus on exemptions, simplification, and the rich.

Tackling Tax Exemptions Eliminating or narrowing tax exemptions not only would render Washington's income taxes more equitable but also more efficient, simple, transparent, and administerable.[118]

Simplifying Taxes Simplifying income reporting by integrating the personal and corporate income taxes, or by replacing their progressive rates with flat ones, would improve the system's efficiency, simplicity, and administerability, but perhaps not its equity and transparency.[119]

Bracketing the Top Adding more progressive tax brackets is a proposed reform that garners "overwhelming support" among taxpayers, both conservative as well as liberal.[120] The likely reason for this support is Americans' growing concern over the widening gap between rich and poor; about three-fifths of Americans agree or strongly agree that "differences in income in America is too large," a figure that has remained in this numerical ballpark since the late 1980s.[121]

Americans' belief is founded on fact. Since 1979, the top 1 percent of income earners more than doubled their share of the nation's inflation-adjusted, after-tax income, rising from 8 percent to 17 percent. For the most affluent fifth, income increased by 10 percent; for the three-fifths of the population in the middle, it declined by 2–3 percent, and, for the bottom fifth, income slid by 18 percent. The top 1 percent of income earners account for nearly 24 percent of America's total income, a figure that has not been seen since 1928.[122] America's income gap is not only far wider than Europe's and Japan's, but it is even wider than India's, Iran's, and Uganda's, among others.[123]

This concentrating, after-tax income at the top has been abetted by federal income tax policies that, over three decades, increasingly have favored the rich[124]—but especially the very rich. The top tax bracket taxes incomes of about $375,000 and higher at 35 percent. But the top 400 earners rake in, on average, nearly a thousand times that amount, or almost $345 million annually.[125] "A few extra brackets at the top could…bring in tens of billions of dollars in additional revenue."[126] Moreover, those new brackets would address constructively all five dimensions of tolerable taxes.

A Federal Tax on Consumption?

Some reformers focus not on income but on outgo and urge that Congress eliminate, or at least radically reduce, the income tax and make up the loss with some sort of consumption tax. Consumption taxes, while rife with equity issues, can generate immense revenue.

One such proposal is the imposition of a *national retail sales tax*. Less than a fourth of

Americans think that a federal sales tax is a "good idea," and nearly two-fifths believe that it is a bad one.[127]

Another consumption tax is the *value-added tax*, or *VAT*, which taxes the difference between a firm's sales and its purchases of goods and services, the logic being that each sale marks a value added to the product purchased. The VAT also has been defined, less charitably, as "an embedded sales tax that hides all those nickels and dimes along the production chain."[128] Introduced in 1954 by France, the VAT is now used by 136 countries, every one of which also has an income tax. There is some evidence that a VAT may be "less expensive to administer than an income tax," although it is complex and compliance burdens are weighty.[129]

OF DEFICITS AND DEBT: WASHINGTON'S GIFTS

Much of the fiscal turmoil that is battering all governments can be laid at Washington's door.

Understanding Federal Deficits

A *deficit* occurs when a government's annual spending exceeds its annual income. To make up the difference, the government borrows money.

Federal Deficits and the Economy In general, small or no federal deficits and little or no federal borrowing are good for the economy because they lower long-term interest rates and check inflation. (Inflation, though widely feared, has not been a major factor in the American economy; there have been only two extended inflationary periods—that is, three straight years of double-digit inflation—since 1900.[130]) Under certain circumstances, such as a recession, even very high—but *brief*—deficit spending can actually help restore the economy's health.

Keeping in mind the caveat that economics is a field distinctive for its disputatiousness (as a distinguished economist once remarked, "Ask five economists and you'll get five different answers—six if one went to Harvard"[131]), economists generally agree that as long as annual deficit spending

does not surpass annual economic growth, thereby enlarging the federal debt's share of GDP, deficits cause little economic harm. Many economists peg a relatively safe rate of deficit spending at around 2 percent of GDP or lower, and a perilous rate at 5 percent or higher.[132]

The Awful Eighties The federal budget has never balanced (i.e., income equaled outlays), and, in only four years since 1950, have there been surpluses. Historically, deficits have not been large as a percentage of GDP, but, beginning in the 1980s, this tradition was abandoned. In just three years, deficits doubled from 3 percent of GDP, in 1980, to an astonishing 6 percent, in 1983, and, by 1992, deficit spending had increased fivefold. Observers attribute this quintupling to the "watershed" Omnibus Budget Reconciliation Act of 1981, which cut individual income taxes by about a fourth but ignored spending.[133]

Before 1980, conservatives had routinely accused Washington of "tax-and-spend" profligacy; after 1980, this profligacy was better described as "borrow and spend"—or, as some wags would have it, "spend and spend."

Congress' Quixotic Quest: Decreasing Deficits, 1985–2001

Americans understand the gravity of the big and unremitting deficits of the last four decades. "A sweeping majority," 70 percent, worry about the size of the federal deficit "some" or "a lot."[134].

Congress listened, and launched a long, and quixotic, quest to lower deficit spending.

Failure: The Balanced Budget and Emergency Deficit Control Acts of 1985 and 1987 Initially, Congress enacted two laws designed to bring the deficit under control: the Balanced Budget and Emergency Deficit Control Acts of 1985 and 1987. The 1985 Act was designed to achieve a balanced budget by 1990, which the 1987 Act extended to 1993, through *sequestration*, or a series of automatic, across-the-board spending cuts (interest payments and most entitlement programs were exempt) that would come into play if the federal budget did not fall within $10 billion of targeted deficit reductions. Congress avoided the unpleasantness of sequestration by adopting overly optimistic economic forecasts in its budget making, and the acts never lived up to expectations.

Success: The Budget Enforcement Act of 1990
Congress got relatively tough in 1990 and passed the Budget Enforcement Act. The legislation required that new discretionary spending, new tax cuts, and congressional expansion of entitlement programs (but, significantly, not budgetary expansions that were already built into the design of these programs) must be offset with new, or reallocated, revenue. This requirement was known as "PAYGO," an acronym for "pay as you go." PAYGO's spending caps were set in the legislation to expire automatically in 2002.

Sense and Sensibility: The Omnibus Budget Reconciliation Act of 1993
The Omnibus Budget Reconciliation Act of 1993, which passed the Senate by one vote (the vice president's), raised taxes by some $250 billion and cut programs by a similar amount, over five years. Beginning in 1993, federal deficits steadily declined for the next eight years.

Frustration: The Line-Item Veto Act of 1996
In 1996, still frustrated by the deficit, Congress committed an act of extraordinary rarity: It increased the budget-making power of the president. It did this by passing the Line-Item Veto Act, which granted the president the *line-item veto*, or *rescission*, which is the power of the chief elected executive to delete parts of a bill passed by the legislature, but still sign the remaining bill into law. Forty-three governors have this authority.

In 1998, the Supreme Court ruled that the Act was unconstitutional because it allowed the president to "cancel" a budget item, rather than "decline to spend" it.[135]

It seems clear that rescission would have lowered deficits. If presidents had had the line-item veto, they would have trimmed federal spending by an average of nearly 7 percent annually over five years.[136]

Dysfunctionality: The Balanced Budget Act of 1997
Even though deficits were declining, Congress and the White House engaged in unusually bitter wrangling over their continuance. In 1997, a complicated compromise was achieved in the form of the Balanced Budget Act, which promised to eliminate federal deficits in 2002 by introducing stringent spending caps (which Congress quickly ignored), but it also included a counterintuitive tax cut of $152 billion that added to future deficits.

Nirvana Attained? The Budget Surpluses
In 1999 (Fiscal Year 1998), the federal government not only had no deficit but also produced an impressive surplus of $70 billion. In 2000, the surplus hit $127 billion, and in 2001, $236 billion. The Budget Enforcement Act of 1990 and the Omnibus Budget Reconciliation Act of 1993 were critical in attaining these surpluses.

Though welcome, these budgetary surpluses were not wholly deserving of full-throated cheering. Federal surpluses include the surplus generated by Social Security taxes and a relatively tiny surplus provided by the Postal Service. Social Security and the Postal Service are classified as the government's only two *off-budget entities*; that is, the revenues that they generate do not appear in the federal budget. These sources contribute a surplus that has ranged over ten years from $77 billion to $186 billion annually.[137] If these off-budget surpluses were *not* counted against the budget deficits, then they would have converted the 1999 and 2000 budget surpluses into deficits and eradicated most of the 2001 surplus.

Federal Fiscal Follies, 2001–2008
Regrettably, federal surpluses, much less balanced budgets, are no longer with us. No surprise, perhaps, in light of the unprecedented tax slashing and profligate spending that Washington indulged in with unblushing abandon during the 2000s.

Radically Reducing Revenue
In 2001, Congress passed, at the president's urging, the Economic Growth and Tax Relief Reconciliation Act, which cut federal taxes by a record $1.35 trillion over ten years. The Act stipulated that its tax rate reduc-

tions would automatically expire in 2011 unless Congress extended them, which Congress dutifully did by extending them through 2012. In addition, Congress added, expanded, accelerated, or deepened these and other tax cuts in each and every year after 2001.

By 2010, as a result of these cuts and a historically severe recession, federal revenue as a percentage of GDP had shrunk to a level so low that it had not been neared since 1949.[138] By 2011, the tax slashing that had begun in 2001 had cost the federal government an estimated $2.8 trillion in lost revenue. To place this sum in perspective, the wars in Afghanistan (started in 2001) and Iraq (2003), *combined*, had, by 2011, cost the federal treasury a total of $1.26 trillion. The revenue lost to tax cuts could have financed both wars, and Washington still would have had more than enough money left to pay for two more wars of comparable size and duration.[139]

Enormously Expanding Expenditures Between 1992 and 2000, federal spending as a percentage of GDP declined steadily by about 1 percent per year.[140] But change was afoot. And it was not responsible change.

Bedazzled by the budget surplus of 1999, the first surplus in twenty-nine years, Congress indulged in a spending frenzy that vitiated the pay-as-you-go principle mandated by the Budget Enforcement Act. When Congress wanted to spend more than the act allowed, it often simply increased spending cap limits, or, less visibly, circumvented those limits by using advance appropriations, payment delays, and, most creatively, "emergency" funding, which was exempt under the act.[141] Average annual emergency funding in 1999–2002 was five times more than in 1991–1998.[142] "Emergencies" included funding the decennial census, an item that has been in the Constitution for four centuries.

The impetus motivating Congress to engage in these subterfuges was removed in 2002, when the Budget Enforcement Act's spending caps automatically terminated. (In 2010, at the president's urging, Congress passed the Statutory Pay-As-You-Go Act, which reinstated PAYGO in law, a status that "can help prevent further

deterioration" of federal finances but will not balance budgets.[143]) After 2002, Congress openly and enthusiastically passed *supplemental appropriations*, which are budget allocations for unforeseen needs, such as, of course, emergencies, which accounted for 99 percent of all supplemental appropriations.[144] During the 2000s, just as in the 1990s, "nonemergency items were slipped into the emergency supplemental."[145] Supplemental appropriations exploded from not even 1 percent of the total federal budget, and 3 percent of new discretionary spending throughout most of the 1990s, to 6 percent of total budget authority, and 14 percent of discretionary spending, by the mid-2000s.[146]

Congress's fiscal irresponsibility and the president's equally irresponsible refusal to veto virtually any spending bill that Congress sent him were soon felt. After eight years in which federal spending as a percentage of GDP had declined steadily, federal spending as a percentage of GDP actually grew, even though federal revenue was shriveling.[147]

They're Ba-a-ack

Needless to say, these foolhardy fiscal policies affected federal deficits, which, like a bad penny, returned in 2002.

Then the roof caved in. In the final quarter of 2007, the United States spiraled into economic free-fall and sank into the deepest recession since the Great Depression of the 1930s.

In response, Washington applied Keynesian measures. In 2008, Congress enacted the Emergency Economic Stability Act, which reserved $700 billion in its Troubled Asset Relief Program to bail out the financial system. In 2009, Congress passed the American Recovery and Reinvestment Act, which lowered a number of tax rates and allocated $747 billion for an ailing economy; the act saved or created up to 3.6 million jobs, and lowered unemployment by as much as nearly two percentage points over four fiscal years.[148] In 2010, Congress approved the Tax Relief, Unemployment Insurance Reauthorization, and Job Creation Act, which, with a tab of $352 billion, postponed until the end of 2012 the automatic sunset of the tax cuts that began in 2001, reduced the FICA and estate taxes, and extended unemployment benefits.

The slashing of tax rates, the resultant radical reduction in revenue, and enormous increases in expenditures had predictable but still startling effects on federal deficits. In 2008, the deficit hit a record $459 billion, or over 3 percent of GDP. In 2009, because of the Great Recession and the reactive economic-stimulus legislation just noted, the deficit tripled to a staggering $1.4 trillion, equaling 9.9 percent of the economy, and in 2010 it surpassed $1.5 trillion, or 10.6 percent of GDP.[149] Only eight *nations* had GDPs that were larger than each one of America's trillion-dollar-plus deficits.[150] Times have been worse. The World War II years saw deficits ranging from 14 to 30 percent of GDP.[151]

Understanding Federal Debt

Big deficits bring big debt. Congress incurred the nation's first debt in 1790 ($75 million to finance the Revolution), and the only year in which the United States had no debt was in Fiscal Year 1834 (1834–1835).

As with deficits, the larger the debt as a proportion of GDP, the likelier that the economy will suffer. Historically, a humongous federal debt has been an aberration. From the nation's first fiscal year of 1797, the federal debt as a percentage of the economy "rose substantially *only* as the result of wars and recessions."[152] After 1980, however, this pattern changed radically, even though the times were mostly peaceful and prosperous.

Public, or National, Debt The traditional type of federal debt is *public*, or *national, debt*, which is composed largely of the federal government's debts owed to foreign countries and to holders of its bonds, such as U.S. Savings Bonds.

In 1980, public debt accounted for 26 percent of the GDP. By the fall of 2007, just prior to the advent of the Great Recession, it had swollen by a third to 36 percent. Just three years later, following an immense influx of economic stimulus funds,

the national debt had more than doubled its 1980 share of GDP, attaining 62 percent.[153]

In 2011, the Government Accountability Office projected, depending on which assumptions are used about expenditures for Social Security and health care, that the national debt would account for, or be awfully close to, 200 percent of GDP by 2030 or 2050, either one of which would be "unsustainable."[154] In that same year, the Congressional Budget Office forecast that the national debt would be larger than GDP in ten years and would be twice as big as the economy on or before 2036.[155]

Gross, or Total, Debt The other sort of federal debt is relatively new and is known as *gross*, or *total, debt*, or public debt plus *intragovernmental debt*, which is composed mostly of debts owed to trust funds, notably the Social Security and Medicare trust funds.

Between 1980 and the fall of 2007, the gross federal debt's share of GDP nearly doubled, from 33 to 64 percent. Three years later, the total debt's proportion of GDP had risen by 180 percent from its 1980 share and accounted for 93 percent of GDP. It was expected to surpass 100 percent of GDP in the following year, and to continue enlarging over time. (The gross debt's all-time record in this regard was achieved in 1946, when it accounted for 122 percent of the economy.)[156]

Among those developed countries with the highest total-debt-to-GDP ratios, the United States ranks seventh. (Japan tops the list.) Almost 31 percent of the gross federal debt is owed to foreign countries, led by China, which is owed less than 8 percent, followed closely by Japan.[157]

Big Debt, Big Worry Whether the debt is public or gross, big debt warrants big worry. A study of debt in forty-four countries, including the United States, concluded that economic growth rates in nations with large national debts are less than half of those in countries with small debts. "Over the past two centuries, [public] debt in excess of 90 percent [of GDP] has typically been associated with mean growth of 1.7 percent versus 3.7 percent when debt is low (under 30 percent of GDP)."[158]

There are other downsides. In addition to stunting economic growth, a large debt requires higher interest payments on it, thereby mandating higher taxes or reduced services; reduces "policymakers' ability to use tax and spending policies to respond to unexpected challenges"; and heightens "the probability of a sudden fiscal crisis."[159]

A FORLORN FISCAL FUTURE?

The early 2010s witnessed federal fiscal foolishness of fantastic dimensions.

The Perfect Storm

By 2011, Washington was borrowing forty-one cents out of every dollar that it spent, and, in January of that year, the biggest freshman class (ninety-three of them) in more than sixty years entered the House of Representatives. It was a perfect storm.

When the deadline for raising the debt ceiling came up for renewal in 2011, many of these new Representatives (who were more passionate about smaller government than balanced budgets) insisted that they would vote not to extend it unless the extension was accompanied by spending cuts and no new taxes. And they had the votes to block it.

The political establishment was shocked. Raising the debt ceiling had been done routinely since 1917, when Congress first established the ceiling by passing the Second Liberty Bond Act. The business establishment was even more shaken, and understandably so. If the ceiling were not extended, then the nation would, for the first time in its history, default on its debts. Default would assure long-term economic catastrophe.

Calamity was barely averted when, with just a few hours remaining before the United States would be forced to stiff its creditors, Congress and the president raised the debt ceiling. The price was high: No new revenues but significant spending cuts—$917 billion over ten years.[160]

Americans were not pleased with what they viewed as an irresponsible political circus in Washington that rattled their, and the globe's, confidence in their nation's fiscal accountability. "Nearly three-quarters" of Americans polled "offered a negative word" about the budget negotiations, led by "ridiculous," "disgusting," and "stupid"; "just 2 percent had anything nice to say."[161] A clear majority favored, and still favors, what virtually every economist and fiscal analyst believe is a necessity: a balanced approach to a balanced budget, one that includes new revenue as well as spending cuts.[162]

Not One, but Two, Gorillas in the Room

Washington's self-inflicted fiscal and political wounds of 2011 fell far short of restoring federal fiscal discipline, largely because they failed to address the two gorillas in the room: Social Security and health care, most especially Medicare, which are the almost-exclusive drivers of growing federal spending.[163]

Under current policies, Social Security's trust fund will be "exhausted" by 2037, although, thanks to continuing payroll tax revenue, Social Security should be able to pay for about three-quarters of its promised benefits over the next forty or fifty years.[164]

Health care presents even graver problems. Federal obligations for Medicare "alone exceed the unfunded obligations for Social Security."[165]

America's governments account for more than half of all spending for health care in the United States,[166] and health care alone is expected to account for 80 percent of the growth in federal spending over twenty-five years.[167] Even after the enactment of the Patient Protection and Affordable Care Act of 2010, which, in part, was an effort to contain health care costs, Medicare's trust fund still will remain solvent only until 2029, after which it will experience shortfalls ranging from about a tenth to nearly a fourth.[168]

Dealing with these issues will not be easy. Just 3 percent of Americans would cut Social Security, and only 4 percent would cut Medicare, as their "first step" in balancing the federal budget.[169]

Federal Finances: Bleak, Imprudent, and Unsustainable

At the height of debt-ceiling furor, one of the three principal credit rating firms lowered its rating of long-term U.S. Treasury bonds from AAA, the highest possible rating, to AA+, the next highest, because the firm's analysts were concerned about the size of the U.S. debt and Washington's apparent inability to deal with it. These bonds had been universally rated AAA ever since rating them began, nearly a century ago. It is unclear what other economic effects, if any, of the downgrade might be, although the interest rate that Washington pays on its debt (some $250 billion annually) could increase.

The historic downgrade was, in the view of many, a wake-up call to right flummoxed federal finances. They were hardly the first. Consider some earlier, and highly authoritative, wake-up calls. The "long-term fiscal outlook" of the United States is "bleak," "imprudent," and "unsustainable."[170] "Absent reform, the nation will ultimately have to choose between persistent, escalating federal deficits, significant tax increases, and/or dramatic budget cuts of unprecedented magnitude."[171]

These realities hurt people. "Over the long-term, the costs of federal borrowing will be borne by tomorrow's workers and taxpayers" and will "*inevitably* result in declining GDP and future living standards." Averting even some federal borrowing, by contrast, will be quite beneficial for Americans. A permanent deficit reduction of only 1 percent as a share of GDP would, after fifty years, amount to nearly $2,000 in real higher income for every man, woman, and child in the United States.[172]

Subnational Sorrows

State and local governments suffer even more fiscal sorrows than the federal government. Yet, with some exceptions, they have been more fiscally responsible than has Washington.

An impressive forty-eight state legislatures require their state governments to balance their budgets each year,[173] and all states closely restrict the finances of their local governments.[174] These governments long have taken "harsh austerity measures" to balance their budgets "that would face far more resistance in Washington."[175]

Linked Perversely, Washington has been the cause of many subnational sorrows. "The fundamental fiscal problems of the federal government" and those of state and local governments "are similar and are linked."[176]

Linked, indeed. Federal "negative impacts" on grass-roots finances are accelerating and have reduced Washington's "positive impacts" by fully one-third. Examples of these negative impacts include the shifting of expenses in some programs from Washington to the states; federal tax changes that cause these governments to lose revenue; and "the failure of the federal government to solve problems in state finances that only it can solve," such as the inability of subnational governments to tax international tax shelters and electronic commerce.[177]

The Crushing Cost of Health Care Nowhere is this linkage more damaging than in health care. "The projected rise in health-related costs is the root of the fiscal difficulties" for state and local governments.[178] Over three decades, health care spending nearly doubled, from 12 percent of the grass-roots governments' overall expenditures to 20 percent.[179]

Much of this expansion is attributable to Medicaid, a federal health care program for the poor, the costs of which are shared between the federal and state governments. "Medicaid has become a budgetary Death Star, gobbling up ever more scarce dollars," yet the Patient Protection and Affordable Care Act of 2010 is projected to increase, by nearly 16 million, the population served by Medicaid by the end of the decade, at an annual additional cost to the states of $21 billion.[180] Even before the act's passage, however, state and local expenditures for health care were "projected to more than double by 2050." Because of this doubling, "*all* their other spending will shrink by 27 percent."[181]

The next highest subnational health-related cost after Medicaid is health insurance for state and local governments' employees—and retirees.[182]

Pensions and Public Penury Those retirees present a special fiscal problem for their former employers.

The Worrisome Size of Public Pensions The "unfunded liability" of state pension plans (including health care) is the equivalent of more than three full years of the states' total general revenue, an equivalency that is "almost exactly the same" for city and county plans.[183] Miami's pension fund obligations, for example, consume 25 percent of the city's budget.[184] The states and their participating localities fall 30 percent short (a "conservative" figure) of what they need to meet their retirement obligations—not an insurmountable challenge, one might think, until we realize that that 30 percent totes up to at least a $1 *trillion* shortfall.[185]

Big, and financially draining, pension payouts can last for many years and can result in fewer teachers, police, firefighters, and garbage collectors, and, increasingly, lower-than-promised, or even terminated, pensions for retirees.

Pension Politics As we discuss in Chapters 9 and 11, public-sector unions and governments long have tussled over compensation, collective bargaining rights, and the outsourcing of government jobs. These negotiations differ in an important respect from bargaining over public-employee pensions: Their impact on public finances is known, immediate, and transparent. The effects of pensions on public finances, by contrast, cannot possibly be known to public employees, public officials, and taxpayers because their fiscal effects are long term. Over the longer haul, of course, economies, and, hence, government revenues, can turn up or down.

Here is an example: In 1999, when California's economy was booming, the state's legislature enacted Senate Bill 400, which allowed many police officers and fire fighters to retire at the age of fifty with up to 90 percent of their salaries and lowered the retirement age for some public employees by five years (one beneficiary of these upgrades was the lifeguard who retired at fifty-seven with a six-figure pension[186]), among a bevy of other benefits that hiked state and local pension obligations, on average, by more than 25 percent.[187] There was not much debate in either chamber; the senate passed the bill after forty-five seconds of discussion and with no dissenting votes.[188]

Within a decade, these decisions were haunting the state like Marley's ghost, placing California's finances in even graver peril than they already were. A board member of the state's huge public pension system (it covers more than 1.6 million public employees), which had recommended the package to the legislature, admitted that, "This was probably the worst public policy decision in the state's history.... We had no idea what we were doing."[189]

Precisely. Politically astute and powerful public unions exploit this universal ignorance of governments' fiscal futures for their members' ends. In California, for instance, the board of directors of the state's enormous retirement system is effectively in organized labor's pocket: Of its thirteen members, all of whom are elected, six were voted in by government retirees or workers (as required by state law), one is a union official, and two were elected as the result of union endorsements and campaign contributions (we discuss public unions' savvy electoral infighting in Chapter 9).[190]

Unions' political clout is a heady draw for some elected officials (the more cynical and rapacious ones), who are certain in their knowledge that any future fiscal problems generated by catastrophically costly retirement benefits that they negotiate will never be problems for them. It perhaps is no accident that, on average, state and local governments contribute more than twice as much revenue to public pension funds as do state and local employees.[191]

Is Revenue Running Out? Health care and pension costs, not to mention declining tax revenue, have been burgeoning budgetary banes for decades. Over thirty years, expenditures by state and local governments "grew faster than own-source revenues in almost all states." Budgets balanced because of the growth in federal grants and also because, during the final dozen of those years, states and localities increasingly borrowed money, rather than spend tax and other revenues, to fund capital projects; this borrowing freed up revenue to pay for the cost of providing their services.[192]

This is not a sustainable situation. "Since most state and local governments are required to balance their operating budgets, the declining fiscal conditions ... suggest that these governments would need to make substantial policy changes to avoid growing fiscal imbalances." "Substantial" seems a milquetoast description. Closing the anticipated fiscal gap for subnational jurisdictions will require them to cut their expenditures, or increase revenue, by nearly 13 percent each and every year until at least 2060![193]

Grass-Roots Borrowing: The Mysterious Municipal Bond

State and local governments' unprecedented levels of borrowing are executed through a device that is unique to them: the municipal bond.

A *municipal bond* is a certificate of ownership of a specified portion of a debt due to be paid by a state agency or local government to an individual holder and usually bearing a fixed rate of interest. All state and local governments issue municipal bonds and sell them in the nearly $3 trillion bond market.[194] They spend most of this borrowed money on capital projects, such as roads and schools.[195]

Of Obligations and Money Makers There are two major kinds of municipal bonds.

General obligation bonds have the full faith and backing of the government issuing them, a backing that includes raising taxes, if need be, to cover their obligations. Two-thirds of cities and towns, which are among the primary issuers of these bonds, require that all local bond measures be approved by voters.[196]

Revenue bonds fund projects, such as college dormitories, that generate revenue and are by far the most common bond issued by public authorities. In contrast to general obligation bonds, revenue bonds are "nonguaranteed" and lack the full faith and credit of the governments that issue them, but compensate for this deficiency by paying higher interest to their buyers.

Revenue bonds are now governments' bond of choice. In 1950, they accounted for a slender 17 percent of all municipal bond sales;[197] they doubled this percentage in just twenty years; peaked in the mid-1980s at 80 percent,[198] and have since slipped to a still respectable 62 percent.[199]

Both general obligation bonds and revenue bonds are sturdy, stable investments. Although defaults on all bond issues rose during the Great Recession of the late 2000s, historically, far fewer than 1 percent fail.[200]

Whoopee! Tax Free! (Mostly) Municipal bonds typically sell quickly, and individual investors are their biggest buyers—a startling two-thirds of all municipal bonds are owned by individual investors.[201]

Why is this? Individual purchasers strongly favor these bonds largely because the interest income generated by almost all of them is exempt from the federal, and most states', taxes on personal income.

Congress has exempted from the federal personal income tax the income gained from the interest derived from municipal bonds for as long as there has been such a tax (the Revenue Act of 1913 initiated this policy), even though the exemption costs the federal government about $37 billion in lost revenue each year.[202] Although there are a few exceptions that are subject to taxation they do not amount to much: From 94 to 95 percent of all municipal bonds are exempt from the income tax.[203]

Thirty-eight of the forty-three states that levy an individual income tax exempt the interest income produced by the bonds that they or their local governments issue, and two, Florida and Indiana (plus the District of Columbia), apply this exemption to bonds issued in every other state as well.[204] These practices were upheld by the Supreme Court in 2008.[205]

Borrowing's Backlash: State and Local Debt

Municipal bonds are how state and local debts are made. State and local governments always have carried debt, but, unlike the federal government's debt, which is akin to a happy-go-lucky teenager's credit card debt, the grassroots governments' debt historically has resembled a responsible homeowner's fixed mortgage, in that it is largely a product of loans used to fund needed capital projects.

Now this is changing, and not for the better. Even though forty-eight of the fifty states prohibit themselves from spending in deficit,[206] and even though forty-eight states impose debt ceilings on their cities, and forty on their counties,[207] state and local debt nearly tripled over just seventeen years to more than $3 trillion, and now accounts for 17 percent of GDP.[208] Some analysts think that these governments' debt is actually quite a bit higher.[209]

Still, "states and cities carry much less debt relative to the size of their economies than do troubled national governments like those of Greece or Spain (or the United States, for that matter),"[210] devoting from 5 to 8 percent of their revenue to paying interest on their debt, "which is considered a reasonable level."[211] In the view of many analysts, "state and local governments really don't have a crushing *debt* problem."[212] What they do have, of course, is a crushing *revenue* problem.

The Blessing of Bankruptcy?   There is a possible hatch through which local governments could escape their fiscal woes: They could default on their debts and declare bankruptcy under Chapter 9 of the United States Code. (A *default* refers to a debtor's refusal to pay a debt that the debtor is legally required to pay. A *bankruptcy* is a legal finding that imposes a court-supervised restructuring of a debtor's finances.) Localities have had this option since 1934, when Congress amended the Bankruptcy Act to include them.

Only about 600 local governments have filed for bankruptcy since the first one, in 1937,[213] and they have averaged slightly more than eight per year since 1980. Less than a fifth of these bankrupt governments were general purpose local governments; the vast majority was special districts and public authorities.[214]

The law prohibits federal judges, who must rule on the appropriateness of such bankruptcies, from mandating tax hikes as a means of relieving fiscal stress, but it does allow local governments to not only stiff their creditors but to also renege on their contractual obligations, such as those with their employees and pensioners. Typically, however, states rescue, or simply take over, their fiscally faltering localities, thereby averting default or bankruptcy. Rescue, however, is by no means assured. When Orange County, in 1994, and the City of Vallejo, in 2008, declared bankruptcy, California was nowhere to be seen; nor was Idaho, when Boise County went belly up in 2011.

In "about half" of the states, municipalities, and counties can declare bankruptcy only with the permission of their state legislatures.[215] Or, states can simply order their localities to not declare themselves bankrupt, an order often motivated by a desire to prevent a lowering of their own credit ratings; Connecticut so ordered Bridgeport in 1991, and Michigan did the same

with Hamtramck in 2010. Georgia bans local bankruptcies.[216]

Congress does not allow state governments to go bankrupt. When facing financial ruin, states must slash services, raise taxes and fees, or secure federal bailouts to pay their debts and honor their contracts. These grim prospects loom in several states—including some of the biggest—that are undergoing levels of fiscal duress not experienced since the 1930s.

When all is said and done, however, declaring bankruptcy is no panacea for governments' fiscal failures. "The fantasy of using bankruptcy to suspend government runs up against a hard truth: even in bankruptcy, cities and states don't disappear—nor do their obligations."[217] Almost always, even bankrupt governments ultimately pay off their debts.

A Dismal Science: Deficits, Debt, and Democracy

Economists share a dismal doubt about democracy. It is: Democracies are unable to avoid burying future generations in debt due to the need of elected policymakers to be elected and reelected. Elected office holders assure their reelection by giving voters bigger benefits, lower taxes, and larger deficits. Eventually, these accrued deficits create a public debt so humongous that it crushes some future generation to the point that it overthrows democracy as its form of government. The nation's first secretary of the treasury understood this doubt well, as the box in this chapter indicates.

The federal government is America's least financially responsible government because the core issue is one of a national fiscal policy. "It is not that the size of the [federal] debt itself is the problem…Instead, it is the recent trend that is ominous. For that trend results not from a deliberate political decision to spend in deficit [a decision often made, for example, when a nation goes to war], but rather from nothing more than the sum of myriad decisions regarding taxing and spending that, collectively, now substitutes for fiscal policy. In a very real sense, the federal government *has* no fiscal policy, for the tail of political expediency has long wagged the dog of prudent policy in Washington."[218]

A Founder on Debt

In 1984, President Ronald Reagan quipped that he was "not worried about the deficit. It is big enough to take care of itself," thereby establishing a lasting Washington tradition of dismissing deficits; in 2002, Vice President Dick Cheney reportedly stated, "deficits don't matter."

Both officials differed with Alexander Hamilton, the first treasury secretary, who fully understood that deficits matter. "To extinguish a Debt which exists and to avoid contracting more," Hamilton wrote, are "almost always favored" by the public, "but to pay Taxes," which is "the only means of avoiding the evil, is almost always more or less unpopular. These contradictions are in human nature." Hence, elected policymakers will decry the public debt "as an abstract thesis," but will be "vehement against any plan of taxation" to pay down that debt, a vehemence motivated by their desire to boost "their own popularity or to make other sinister account." Read on.

The consequence is, that the Public Debt swells, 'till its magnitude becomes enormous, and the Burthens of the people gradually increase 'till their weight becomes intolerable. Of such a state of things great disorders in the whole political economy, convulsions & revolutions of Government are a Natural offspring.

[My previous report] suggests the idea of "*incorporating as a fundamental maxim* in the SYSTEM of PUBLIC CREDIT of the United States, *that the creation of Debt should always be accompanied with the means of extinguishment—* that this is the true secret for rendering public credit immortal, and that it is difficult to conceive a situation in which there may not be an adherence to the Maxim" and it expresses an unfeigned solicitude that this may be attempted by the United States. ■

Sources: http://en.wikiquote.org/wiki/Ronald_Reagan; Jonathan Weisman, "Reagan Policies Gave Green Light to Red Ink," *Washington Post* (June 9, 2004); and Alexander Hamilton, "Report on a Plan for the Further Support of Public Credit" (January 16, 1795), as published in *The Papers of Alexander Hamilton*, Vol. 18, Harold C. Syrett, ed. (New York: Columbia University Press, 1973), p. 80.

PUBLIC BUDGETING: SPENDING FOR PUBLIC POLICY

A *budget* is "a series of goals with price tags attached."[219]

Budgets are beyond dollars. They are choices, policies, and philosophies. We trace how these fiscal philosophies, or budgetary formats, have altered over time. The time frames associated with these budget forms refer to when the federal government favored them, but each format has been adopted by state and local governments, too.[220] More to the point, while budget systems may fade, they do not fade away. Like vampires, budgetary formats often metamorphose into forms that differ from their initial incarnations, or, like Frankenstein, parts of them are stitched together in ways that create new forms. Budget systems always live beyond their nominal life spans, lurking in the sunless recesses of budgetary bureaucracies.

LINE-ITEM BUDGETING, 1921–1949

During the early twentieth century, the budget expanded from a tool that kept track of expenses (often inadequately) into a system for assuring governmental honesty.

Reform! Introducing the Public Budget

The Progressive Movement expressed these dynamics, and they ultimately resulted in historic budgetary change.

The Consolidated Executive Budget During the early twentieth century, Progressives pushed two reforms: Fiscal reform, which advocated such novelties as auditing governments' books, and the "administrative integration movement," which promoted strengthening the power of the executive branch by consolidating agencies.

Both of these interrelated efforts pushed governments to adopt a *consolidated executive budget*, which is a comprehensive plan of expenditures for the whole of government, formulated by the elected chief executive, and subject to approval by the legislature. The first consolidated executive budget was adopted, via constitutional amendment, by Maryland in 1916, largely because the state had grossly overspent its revenues.

The Budget and Accounting Act of 1921

In 1912, the President's Commission on Economy and Efficiency proposed a consolidated executive budget for the federal government (or, as the Commission accurately put it, simply "a national budget," unconsciously indicating just how primitive early public financial management was),[221] a suggestion fulfilled nearly a decade later with the passage of the Budget and Accounting Act of 1921. The Act created the Bureau of the Budget (BOB), reporting to the treasury secretary, and established the General Accounting Office (re-titled in 2004 to the Government Accountability Office), which reports to Congress, as the congressional check on federal money management.

The Budget and Accounting Act was historic legislation that radically improved federal efficiency and finance. In its first year of operation, the Budget Bureau cut federal expenditures by an astonishing 35 percent and raked in a record surplus.[222]

What Is Line-Item Budgeting?

The consolidated executive budgets, a major governmental innovation when introduced, nonetheless assumed a very traditional form: the Line-Item Budget.

A Line-Item Budget is what most of us visualize when we think about budgets. Each line on a sheet of paper has an item, or object (e.g., pencils, 112), on the left side followed by a cost ($75.00) on the right side. Hence, the first public budgets acquired their descriptive title of *Line-Item*, or *Objects-of-Expenditure*, *Budget* which is the allocation of resources according to the cost of each item, from pencils to personnel, used by a government agency.

Honesty, Efficiency, and Inflexibility

The Line-Item Budget rapidly became associated with governmental honesty, efficiency, and less propitiously, inflexibility. In 1923, Charles G. Dawes, as first director of the Budget Bureau, wrote: "The Bureau of the Budget is concerned only with the humbler and routine business of government.... it is concerned with no question of policy, save that of economy and efficiency."[223]

Inputs and the Budgetary Treatment of Paperclips and Parks

The Line-Item Budget covers *inputs* only, meaning that it deals only with what it takes to make a project continue. Consider two examples: paperclips and parks. Under a Line-Item Budget, the only policy-related questions that a public administrator would be channeled into asking are the following: How many paperclips do we need and what will they cost? Or how many parks do we need and what will it cost to build and maintain them?

The Legacies of Line-Item Budgeting

The Line-Item Budget fulfills a vital financial function: It shows in detail what public administrators are spending their money on. Consequently, four-fifth of all cities and counties still use Line-Item Budgeting, often "in conjunction with another type of budget format."[224] But its scope is limited, and when it is used at broader organizational levels, it can result in micro-management at the top.

PROGRAM/PERFORMANCE BUDGETING, 1950–1964

Although lone voices were heard throughout the 1920s and 1930s advocating a budget attuned to identifying broader programs and government performance, the shift to this kind of thinking came with President Franklin D. Roosevelt's New Deal.

The New Deal and the Need for a New Budget

Roosevelt assumed the presidency in 1932 and immediately focused federal power on wrenching the economy out of the Great Depression. Between 1932 and 1940, federal expenditures more than doubled, and the Budget Bureau faced up to this challenge by expanding its staff by a factor of ten and relying increasingly on public administrators, rather than accountants, to manage federal spending. In 1939, Executive Order 8248 formalized BOB's new managerial emphasis by transferring it from the Treasury Department to the newly founded Executive Office of the President.

Clarifying Programs and Performance

The broadening of budgeting into management illustrated with increasing clarity two growing problems of federal administration.

The Programs Problem The Line-Item Budget has no capacity to show policymakers what programs public money is being spent for, and was never meant to. The federal Line-Item Budget of 1949 dumped on its readers some one-and-a-half million words printed on 1,625 pages. The first Hoover Commission questioned the Line-Item Budget's utility as a document that facilitated more effective public management and advocated organizing the budget by "programs."[225]

The Performance Problem The second issue involved the gnawing question of whether the money being budgeted for public policies was actually doing any good. In the 1940s, the Budget Bureau introduced "Functional Budgeting," or "Activity Budgeting," which involved the development of performance measures and standards and their linkage to an agency's budget. The first Hoover Commission strongly encouraged BOB's initiative and gave it one of the names by which we know it: "Performance Budgeting."

The Emergence of Program/Performance Budgeting The Hoover Commission's 1949 report brought swift results. In that same year, Congress passed amendments to the National Security Act of 1947, which established Program/Performance Budgeting in the Defense Department, and in 1950, Congress enacted the Budgeting and Accounting Procedures Act, which emplaced it in

the remaining agencies. A new budgetary age was at hand.

What Is Program/Performance Budgeting?

We call it *Program/Performance Budgeting,* but this kind of budget more commonly is known as either a *Program Budget,* emphasizing its budgeting of discrete governmental operations, or a *Performance Budget,* stressing its focus on agency efficiency and effectiveness and their measurement. In reality, when it was introduced to the nation in the mid-twentieth century, it did both, so we call it *Program/Performance Budgeting* and define it as a system of resource allocation that organizes the budget document by operations and links the productivity of those operations with specific budget amounts.

Inputs and Outputs Program/Performance Budgeting considers *outputs,* as well as *inputs.* The Budget Bureau's role evolved from a fiduciary one to that of clarifying what policies the budget was paying for and assuring efficiency in program delivery.

Of Paperclips and Parks What did this new role of the budget signify for our examples of paperclips and parks? In terms of programs, the Program/Performance Budget asks these: To what programs do paperclips and parks pertain? Do we have a paperclips program? Do we have a parks program? In terms of performance, the Program/Performance Budget asks these: How many papers will be clipped? How many people will be served by the parks?

The Legacies of Program/Performance Budgeting

The most lasting and pervasive impact of Program/Performance Budgeting was its organization of the budget by programs. It hauled public administrators out of the micro-mire of the Line-Item Budget and revealed the much bigger picture of the programmatic purposes of the public budget.

The other pillar of Program/Performance Budgeting—its focus on measuring results and linking those results with agency budgets—was less successful, but merely its introduction expanded the vision of budgeters from one of controlling costs to viewing the budget as a means of fulfilling public purposes.

PLANNING-PROGRAMMING-BUDGETING, 1965–1971

Program/Performance Budgeting swept through governments, but, once its sweep was complete, its limitations grew increasingly aggravating.

An Emerging New Standard for Budgetary Theory

Those limitations revolved around questions of performance and policy.

The Performance Problem (Again) Half of Program/Performance Budgeting, the performance half, was not working well. As the second Hoover Commission's report of 1955 circumspectly noted with exquisite tact, "the installation of performance budgeting...has met with varying degrees of success."[226]

The Policy Problem Although Program/Performance Budgeting rewards efficiency in implementing public policy, or tries to, it cannot enlighten us if those policies are worth having in the first place. As a New York legislator exclaimed after looking over his state's Program/Performance Budget, "Who the hell cares how much a pound of laundry costs?"[227] The more important question is, Why is there a policy that requires the state to wash laundry?

The Emergence of Planning-Programming-Budgeting These concerns eventually led to an interest in Planning-Programming-Budgeting (PPB), a budgeting system that was birthed in the auto industry; variants of it had been used as early as 1924 by General Motors Corporation. Elements of PPB first emerged in federal circles during World War II, but it was in 1961, when Robert McNamara, the chief executive officer of Ford Motor Company, became secretary of defense, that PPB made its major impact.

The defense establishment that McNamara entered was beset by almost cutthroat competition among the services. McNamara and his "whiz kids" (a not entirely affectionate appellation given the McNamara team by the military) shook up the services by reestablishing central control through the imposition of PPB. PPB remains the Pentagon's budgeting system to this day.

President Lyndon B. Johnson was sufficiently impressed that in 1965 he ordered PPB to be adopted throughout the federal government.

What Is Planning-Programming-Budgeting?

Planning-Programming-Budgeting, also known as *Planning-Programming-Budgeting System*, or *PPBS*, is a system of resource allocation designed to improve government efficiency and effectiveness by establishing long-range planning goals, analyzing the costs and benefits of alternative programs that would meet these goals, and articulating programs as budgetary and legislative proposals and long-term projections.[228]

Inputs, Outputs, Outcomes, and Alternatives PPB is concerned not only with *inputs* and *outputs* but also with *outcomes* (defined in Chapter 7—in other words, impacts or effects) and *alternatives*. The budget agency is seen more than ever before as a centralized, systemic, planning, and policymaking body—a far cry from Dawes' statement of 1923 about budgeting being concerned with the "humbler and routine business of government."

Of Paperclips and Parks In terms of paperclips and parks, PPB expands our queries to include their outcomes and alternatives.

To determine the outcomes, or effects, of paperclips, we must ask these questions: What impact do clipped papers have on the agency's mission-related outcomes? We then must ask about alternatives. Should we use staples instead?

When we ask about the outcomes of parks, we inevitably must ask, What are parks really meant to do? Parks provide recreation, or an opportunity for their visitors to "re-create." But how do we determine this? Counting outputs, such as the number of park visitors, no longer is adequate. Finding alternatives to parks is even tougher and requires that we consider the whole recreational system, and even beyond. After all, those who visit parks in the wee hours may be exclusively muggers and their victims, lending an entirely new meaning to "re-creating."

The Legacies of Programming-Planning-Budgeting

PPB is, perhaps, the single most comprehensively "rational" budgeting system ever perpetrated in American governments.

Successes of PPB
Washington's experience with PPB suggests that PBB brings benefits. Few federal administrators ever "argued against the goals of PPBS," and it "is credited with instituting improvement in federal program management," including better information, more systems analysis, and "a long-standing legacy of increases in the amount and quality of program evaluation."[229]

When PPB's two dominant features, rigorous rationality and systems analysis, are present in a government's budgetary format, then budget making "reduces expenditures in aggregate."[230] This is, of course, precisely what public budgeting is meant to do.

Limitations of PPB
PPB's complexity, rigidity, and obsession with details and uniformity are its overriding weaknesses and make it very difficult to adopt and use. It did not help that, at least in Washington, PPB also was clumsily introduced. President Johnson gave his administrators all of six months to have PPB up and running, but the sole department to implement it successfully and permanently, Defense, consumed no fewer than *ten years* to phase it in.[231]

Understandably, perhaps, PPB overwhelmed most federal agencies. The secretary of agriculture, whose department had been identified by the Budget Bureau as one of only five that had made substantial progress in adopting PPB,[232] phoned the director of BOB and began the conversation

with, "Elmer, I have a stack of PPBS papers on my desk about four feet high. What am I supposed to do with them?"[233] So traumatized were most federal administrators by their experience with PPB, that, for the remaining third of the twentieth century, *every* successive budgetary format had, as defining features, high levels of plasticity and an outstanding ease of adoption.

It is doubtful that PPB's limitations can be overcome. When a federal agency brought back PPB in 2002, it found, seven years later, that the same "difficulties that led to the abandonment" of PPB "by the civilian bureaucracy almost 40 years ago" were still front and center.[234]

BUDGETING-BY-OBJECTIVES, 1972–1977

With Richard Nixon's election as president in 1968, the federal government moved steadily away from the policy-planning mission of PPB, and toward a managerial and political one.

The clearest and earliest indicator of this shift was the reorienting and renaming in 1970 of the Bureau of the Budget to the Office of Management and Budget (OMB). Its new title reflected Nixon's effort to politicize federal management,[235] and OMB soon became known in Washington as the "Office of Meddling and Bumbling,"[236] a moniker that, thankfully, OMB has long since shed.

In 1971, OMB dispatched a memorandum to all federal agencies that, "with remarkably little comment,"[237] officially terminated PPB, rendering it "an unthing."[238]

Policymakers quickly turned to a new thing: Budgeting-by-Objectives (BBO). In 1973, Nixon formally initiated BBO with a memorandum to twenty-one agencies, and in 1975, OMB issued Circular A-11, effectively extending BBO to all agencies.

What Is Budgeting-by-Objectives?

Budgeting-by-Objectives has its roots in a technique of project management called Management-by-Objectives (MBO), which got its start in the private sector.[239] When used as a budgeting system, MBO morphs into *Budgeting-by-Objectives*, which may be defined as "a process whereby organizational goals...are set through the participation of organizational members in terms of results expected,"[240] and resources are allocated according to the extent to which those goals are achieved.

Inputs, Outputs, and Outcomes   BBO is concerned with *inputs*, *outputs*, and *outcomes*, but not with alternatives. It deals primarily with the effectiveness of governmental programs, but when it comes to pushing policymakers to ask what else might government do to accomplish a particular social mission, BBO is at somewhat of a loss. Goals are set centrally but only after extensive consultation.

Of Paperclips and Parks   In relating BBO to our ongoing examples of paperclips and parks, we ask these questions: How much does it cost to keep us in paperclips and parks? What do paperclips and parks actually do? How effective are paperclips in achieving the agency's mission? We do not ask, however, what alternatives there are to paperclips or to parks.

The Legacies of Budgeting and Managing by Objectives

We have scant statistical data about BBO's linkage with governments' efficiency, but BBO's foundation and stalking horse, Management-by-Objectives, clearly correlates with significant increases in public productivity—gains of 58 percent, on average, and it matches those of the private sector.[241]

Although the federal government's brief interlude with BBO left little legacy, "to some extent, the basic concepts of MBO—negotiating goals and holding subordinates accountable for achieving them—have survived in federal management practices."[242] MBO has proven itself to be quite "versatile" in local governments, especially in the areas of "quality enhancement, cost control, productivity improvement, and special problem solving."[243]

ZERO BASE BUDGETING, 1977–1980

A new face in the White House brought with it a new budgeting concept. That new face was Jimmy Carter's, who, as governor of Georgia, was the first elected executive to introduce Zero Base Budgeting (ZBB) to government.

ZBB was not entirely unknown in federal circles prior to Carter's arrival; the Department of Agriculture had been using it since the early 1960s.[244] Nevertheless, in 1977, Carter broadened ZBB to the whole of government through OMB Bulletin No. 77-9. In contrast to PPB, ZBB made rapid headway. One seasoned bureaucrat noted, "Never has any management fad so completely taken over this town."[245]

What Is Zero Base Budgeting?

Zero Base Budgeting is the allocation of resources to agencies on the basis of those agencies periodically reevaluating through intense consultation the need for all of the programs for which the agency is responsible and justifying the continuance or termination of each program in the agency's budget proposal. In other words, an agency reassesses what it is doing from top to bottom from a hypothetical "zero base."

ZBB is by no means as radical as its name implies; programs virtually never are cut to zero. Typically, agencies submit their Zero Base Budgets at levels ranging from 75 to 90 percent of last year's budgets.[246]

Alternatives   The odd aspect about ZBB is that it really does not pay much attention to inputs, outputs, and outcomes. Rather, it fixates on *alternatives*. Although ZBB does ask some vague questions about the outputs and outcomes of existing policies, its core query remains: What should we do instead?

Of Paperclips and Parks   So what impact would ZBB have on an agency's use of paperclips or a city's parks program? At the agency level, the head of the Office of Paper Fastening Technologies would be deciding between purchasing more paperclips, staples, tape, or glue, but at the top level, the chief executive might be choosing between purchasing more paperclips or closing more parks. Ultimately, paperclips and parks would be rank-ordered in terms of their relative usefulness to the government's overall mission.

The Legacies of ZBB

Does ZBB work? Yes, but within narrow limits and under certain circumstances.

Successes of ZBB Program managers clearly feel that they participate more in the budgetary process, and communication among all levels of the governmental bureaucracy is enhanced when ZBB is introduced. These seem to be the most conclusive findings of the research.[247]

At the heart of ZBB is the prioritization of programs, and this feature may be its most lasting benefit, particularly in the states. In 1975, just prior to ZBB's adoption by Washington, not even three out of ten state budgets prioritized programs, but today more than eight out of ten rank them.[248]

At the local level, most administrators believe ZBB to be quite useful in holding down costs.[249]

Limitations of ZBB In contrast to the local experience, however, ZBB does not seem to reduce spending by the federal and state governments.[250]

A chronic condition of ZBB is paperwork. Federal paperwork exploded by 229 percent, on average, during ZBB's first year of implementation,[251] and ZBB is thought to outstrip even PPB in producing paper.[252]

And, despite its radical-sounding title, ZBB is far from revolutionary. "ZBB was initially intended to get away from 'incrementalism' but ended up by being, perhaps, the most incremental of any budgeting approach."[253]

TARGET BASE BUDGETING, 1981–PRESENT

In 1981, newly-elected President Ronald Reagan abandoned the long-standing presidential tradition of theatrically introducing a new budgetary format, and instead quietly slipped in Target Base Budgeting (TBB) by directing OMB only to officially terminate its predecessor, ZBB. (Elements of ZBB nevertheless persisted in federal budgeting until 1994.[254]) Even though TBB was not entirely new to Washington (some agencies had been using it by other names since the 1940s[255]), Reagan's embrace of it was revolutionary, and today it continues to work in tandem with its budgetary successors at all governmental levels.

What Is Target Base Budgeting?

Target Base Budgeting, also known as *Target Budgeting, Fixed-Ceiling Budgeting*, and *Top-Down Budgeting*, is a method of allocating resources to agencies in which agency spending limits (and, often, agency goals, too), or "targets," are set by the elected chief executive.

The radical thing about Top-Down Budgeting is that it reverses the traditional budgetary process, which is "bottom-up": Instead of departments sending their budget requests up the hierarchy, the chief-elected executive sends down to them the budget that they may request, and then leaves the achievement of departmental goals to the departments' devices.

Inputs, Outputs, and Outcomes The most salient feature of TBB is that it focuses on the chief executive's sole mission (Reagan's mission was, with the exception of the armed forces, a smaller government), and the mission is achieved by redirecting resources (i.e., *inputs*) to that mission to assure the *outputs* and *outcomes* desired. *Alternatives* are irrelevant; the government is not interested in them.

Of Paperclips and Parks In terms of how TBB would deal with paperclips and parks, it might push us into choosing either paperclips or parks to the exclusion of all other programs. Let us say that we, as the government's top policymaker, chose paperclips. Parks would wither, as would all other public programs, to the extent that we could politically defend and advance our paperclip mission by prising every penny from other programs.

Cutback Management: TBB's Administrative Adjunct

TBB is based on revenue, and when revenue declines, the grass-roots governments—which are, of course, almost always mandated by law to balance the books—must cut costs.

Cutting governments' spending is fraught with self-defeating snares: Budget cutters can cut sub-budgets that cost the overall budget more than they save. "One of the easiest places to cut," for example, "are analysis shops," which, when cut, often undermine future planning for cost savings. Cutting inspections and permitting units can stall construction, thereby weakening economies and reducing public revenue.[256] Cutting tax auditors ("auditors pay for themselves many times over") and revenue departments (in Montana, each one dollar cut from the revenue department led to three dollars lost in revenue) is so obviously self-defeating that it remains a wonder that some governments do it. Cutting self-funding or profit-making units, such as departments of motor vehicles or liquor stores, is equally short-sighted. Cutting round-the-clock agencies and those with high volumes of work, which must pay overtime when furloughs are handed out, reduce overall revenue, even in strong economies.[257]

"All cuts, clearly, do not save money. Some actually wind up costing money," but, regrettably, "real specifics about how much every dollar in budgetary cuts actually cost are few and far between."[258]

Enter *cutback management*, an administrative extension of TBB, which is the bundle of managerial techniques that lower costs when governments are confronted by fiscal constraints.[259] State, but particularly local, governments developed these techniques.

The techniques of cutback management include short-term and long-term approaches.

Cutting Back for the Short Term

Examples of short-term cutbacks include reducing temporary employees, deferring maintenance, and postponing equipment purchases.

Short-term cutback management does little more than buy time; its cuts are inherently transitory, and often harbor hidden long-term costs, but appear to be the most commonly used.

Eighty to 90 percent of state agencies rely on short-term methods, and they are handily their most favored approach.[260]

Two short-term techniques are especially common and illuminate the deficiencies of the approach.

Freezing Hiring One is the *hiring freeze*, which means that no one is hired. It relies on a process of natural attrition (i.e., employees retiring or finding jobs outside the agency) to effect cost savings. Hiring freezes can disadvantage some units of government more than others if, for whatever reason, some agencies lose more employees to attrition than do others but still are not allowed to hire replacements.

Across-the-Board Budget Cuts Undifferentiated, or *across-the-board*, *budget cuts* reduce the budgets of all agencies by the same percentage. What is undifferentiated in these cuts is agency missions and needs; typically, these cuts harm those agencies that have a high proportion of skilled workers providing sophisticated services, such as those "analysis shops," mentioned earlier, whereas they do not have a major impact on agencies which deliver a routine service, such as mowing highway medians, that easily can be slowed down to accommodate a budget cut.

Cutting Back for the Long Term

Reducing expenditures permanently requires longer-term approaches.

An all-too-common, but misguided, proposal in this regard is that of reorganizing government agencies so that they can manage policy areas more efficiently. As we explained in Chapter 4, reorganizing public organizations is difficult and often futile, and this futility includes cutting costs. Reorganizations of the federal government "virtually never" realize greater cost savings;[261] state reorganizations bring no new "economies into bureaucracy";[262] and analyses of restructuring in local governments arrive at comparable conclusions.[263]

There are four primary techniques of cutback management that are geared to the longer haul.

Improving Productivity As we detailed in Chapter 7, all levels of government are deeply engaged in improving productivity in the forms of performance measures and other methods. Sixty to 70 percent of state agencies manage cutbacks by introducing productivity improvements.[264]

Using Alternative Delivery Systems   At root, *alternative methods of service delivery* are those means of providing public services that rely, in whole or part, on people who are not employees of the government sponsoring the program. From 40 to 60 percent of state agencies cut back by using these approaches.[265] We review the major methods of alternative service delivery in Chapter 11.

Rearranging Intergovernmental Relations   Governments often can achieve economies of scale and simplify processes by entering into intergovernmental service agreements, annexing adjacent territory by local governments, and undertaking regional approaches to governing. From two- to three-fifths of state agencies reduce fiscal stress by simply shifting their programs to local governments.[266] We explain these phenomena in Chapter 12.

Prioritizing Programs   Our final long-term approach to cutback management is prioritizing programs, and then cutting the lowest-ranked programs, a method favored by roughly two-thirds of state agencies.[267] Practicing public administrators agree that the following steps should be taken when faced with cutbacks:[268]

- Be sure that all interested parties are informed of the need for cutbacks, and solicit their views on those cutbacks. Share information.
- Determine the criteria for how priorities should be set. Ideally, these priorities should be established well before the advent of a budget crisis, as it is this step that can identify programs that, if cut, could cost more money than they save. While these criteria should be determined by the chief executive, the views of other employees in the agency should be carefully considered, and if possible, implemented. Use teams in planning cuts.
- Establish a preliminary and tentative priority list based on the explicit criteria that have been developed for priority setting.

- Attempt to build some public consensus through various meetings to develop a final priority list.
- Ensure that elected officials and other pertinent decision makers approve of the priority list.
- Understand that there will never be complete agreement in the priority setting process, but keep explaining to the public at large and to agency employees why the priorities have been set in the manner that they have.
- Preserve core organizational competencies by "carefully managing the reduction of organized complexity," a process that includes the finding of a new identity for the downsized agency; identifying and integrating its "key strategic components"; taking care of those employees being let go before assimilating those who remain; and "dramatically" slowing the pace of cutbacks by "strategically waiting."[269]
- Public executives faced with cutting public programs should be accessible, and remain honest, open, professional, and unflappable in the painful process of prioritization. Cutback management is, above all, a process of conflict reduction.

The Legacies of TBB

In addition to cutback management, TBB has left several legacies of consequence, all of them positive.

Budgetary Realism   TBB is an unusually realistic budgeting system because it is driven by revenue. Agency budgets have a greater likelihood of reflecting available revenue because the chief executive is setting their targets.

Seeing the Big Picture Through a Common Language of the Budget   TBB also has greatly smoothed communication between public administrators and legislators by providing them with a common budget vocabulary. This, in turn, has enhanced the ability of top executives to understand, through a budgetary lens, the "big picture" of how the whole of government spends its funds—all its funds.[270]

Enhancing Executive Control TBB's top-down target setting accords the elected chief executive much more budgetary control over the agencies. Prior to the adoption of TBB, elected chief executives relied on their agency heads to identify where their budgets could be cut. "How does one convince administrators to collect information that might help others, but can only harm them?"[271] The answer, of course, is that one cannot. TBB resolves this dilemma by capping or cutting agency budgets and then letting agency administrators deal with it.

PERFORMANCE-BASED BUDGETING, 1993–PRESENT

A new budgeting phase is now with us, and it re-invokes, for at least the third time in the evolution of the budget, the vexing problem of paying for measurable performance, rather than shelling out public money to government agencies simply because the agencies are there. Welcome to Performance-Based Budgeting (PPB).

What Is Performance-Based Budgeting?

Performance-Based Budgeting, also known as *Budgeting for Results*, *Results Budgeting*, *Mission Budgeting*, *Entrepreneurial Budgeting*, *Performance Budgeting*, and *Performance-Informed Budgeting*, is a system of resource allocation that "links the performance levels" of programs with "specific budget amounts."[272]

PBB is, most definitely, a return to the traditions of Program/Performance Budgeting, or at least to the Performance half of it. It is also a partial return to the complexities of Programming-Planning-Budgeting; three-fourths of state budgeters think that Performance-Based Budgeting has "increased my workload."[273]

Inputs and Outputs Like PPB, PBB is essentially limited to *inputs* and *outputs*, and perhaps emphasizes the quality of outputs more than PPB. PBB addresses alternatives, kind of, but only alternative policy-implementation mechanisms, and not alternative policies.

Of Paperclips and Parks PBB asks essentially the same questions about paperclips and parks that PPB asks: How many papers are being clipped? How many people are being served by the parks?

Budgeting for Federal Performance

"The federal government has been pursuing performance-informed budget reforms for more than 50 years"[274] (at least), but, by 1990, the idea of linking budgetary allocations with programs' results enjoyed "far broader and more enthusiastic support throughout the bureaucracy than earlier efforts."[275] This bureaucratic enthusiasm culminated in 1993 with the passage of the Government Performance and Results Act (also known as the Results Act), directing agencies to link budget inputs with performance outcomes.

The early auguries are cautiously promising. Federal fiscal and budgetary management improved during the 1990s. During the following decade, agencies' performance scores affected agency budget allocations in "statistically significant"[276] and "limited yet important"[277] ways. And, in the 2010s, these trends strengthened, despite the facts that a lurching economy and an ideologically fractured Congress are known to undermine the full potential of federal PBB.[278]

Budgeting for State Performance

All the states now have laws or executive orders that include the routine collection and reporting of performance data for budgetary purposes.[279] All but one of these requirements were enacted after 1990,[280] so the states' interest in PBB is recent, renewed, and real.

PBB has made some headway. In 1993, it had not gained enough statewide credibility to influence legislative budget-allocation decisions in the five states that were leaders in its adoption,[281] but a dozen years later "performance information" in the five leading states "influenced legislative budgeting deliberations."[282]

A deep analysis of all the states' use of PBB over fifteen years determined that the states emulate, in several ways, federal practices. PBB "is only selectively applied by legislators in most states, whereas top executive policy makers, middle managers, and staff embrace and utilize PBB systems more extensively." It "functions more effectively for executive management than for legislative purposes." States rely far more on PBB when their economies are thriving, but its use can "sputter a bit" when times are tough.[283]

There Oughtta Be a Law   Thirty-nine states have legislated PBB, and all ten states that are ranked as "strong users of performance information for budgetary decision making" have adopted PBB via legislation; only eight of these states (21 percent) are classified as "weak." By contrast, none of the eleven states without a law (they rely instead on administrative mandates) rank as strong users, and seven (64 percent) are categorized as weak in their use of PBB.[284]

There also oughtta be a better law. The states that use PBB most effectively have laws that include many of the following features: They link their states' budgets, performance measures, and their states' and agencies' strategic plans; they provide incentives and sanctions for high and low performance; they specify benchmarks, outcome measures, a role for citizens, and the frequency of performance data reports; and they identify who is responsible for strategic planning, measuring, evaluating, and checking.[285]

Benefits of Budgeting for State Performance   Three-quarters of state budget officers think that PBB has made their states "better off," and almost two-fifths report that "some changes in appropriations are directly attributable" to PBB.[286]

These changes bring benefits. "Those states that have begun to make policy decisions based on" PBB "have saved impressive amounts of money—some in very short periods of time," and have laid a "foundation for a leaner, more effective government" in the future.[287] One analysis found that PBB has "a statistically significant and positive effect on budget outcomes" in those states that have implemented it, and the citizens of these states benefit from it: States that use PBB spend $332 more per capita annually than those states that do not.[288]

Budgeting for Local Performance

Forty-seven percent of cities and counties "use performance measures to justify departmental budget requests,"[289] up from a quarter that used at least one performance measure in even one department some four decades earlier.[290] "About 70 percent" of the thirty largest cities and the thirty largest counties use performance measures in their budgets, but "only 37 percent of smaller cities and 8 percent of smaller counties (those with populations of 10,000–500,000) have adopted the practice."[291]

Almost three out of ten city managers have recommended to their councils that they change their "budget format to fund outcomes instead of inputs"[292] and report that this was among the most difficult, but worthwhile, innovations that they undertook.[293]

Their efforts are not wasted: More than nine out of ten of cities that use performance measures city-wide report that budgetary reallocations have resulted from using performance-measurement data, including 11 percent where reallocations were substantial.[294] Twelve percent of *all* cities reward their departments for meeting their performance targets by granting them additional budget allocations.[295] In the context of traditional, incremental, public budgeting, these are significant shifts.

All in all, PBB, when "strong executive leadership" is present, "can improve local budgeting despite severe political constraints.... Even though the budget amount appropriated to a department may remain relatively stable and may seem to have little linkage with performance indicators, performance measurement can be used by managers at the program (operational) level to restructure activity planning and reallocate resources."[296]

The Possible Legacy of PBB

If—and it is a big if—governments can, with at least some accuracy, determine programmatic performance; reward good performance with larger budgets; and sanction poor performance with lesser budgets, then governments that are more efficient, effective, and valued by the citizenry should emerge. Governments have tried this before and typically have been disappointed. PBB is based on measuring agencies' performance, and, as we explained in

Chapter 7, performance measurement is fraught with difficult, and sometimes insurmountable, problems. But the clear determination of governments in the twenty-first century to methodically and meticulously marry money with measurable results may be unprecedented. If PBB fulfills the investment being placed in it, then it will leave a legacy of lasting magnitude.

ACQUIRING BUDGETS: ADMINISTRATORS AND ARGUMENTS

Budgetary notions change, but how a bureaucrat gets a budget does not. "What really counts in helping an agency get the appropriations it desires? As several informants put it in almost identical words, 'It's not what's in your estimates but how good a politician you are that matters.' "[297]

To be a good budgetary politician requires the use of standing strategies and opportunistic tactics.[298]

Standing Strategies for Securing Budgets

Standing strategies are used on a continuing basis by an agency. There are at least three variants.

Find, Serve, and Use a Clientele for the Services You Perform
An agency, when threatened, mobilizes its clients. Public safety and parks departments, for example, often have solid bases of citizen defenders, and they are not above deploying them in budgetary battles.

Establish Confidence in the Mind of the Reviewer That You Can Carry Out the Complicated Program (Which He or She Seldom Understands) Efficiently and Effectively
If those who allocate budgets believe in an agency's abilities, big budgets are almost certain. A prime example is the Department of Defense, at least when the Republican Party is in power.

Capitalize on the Fragmentary Budgetary Review Process
The Pentagon has successfully argued that the development of new weapons systems cannot be held to a rigid schedule. When combined with Congress's fragmentary budget review process, defense projects are extended, often reluctantly, year after year on the logic that there is little choice if the research is to pay off.

Opportunistic Tactics for Securing Budgets

Opportunistic tactics are designed to capitalize on unusual opportunities that might defend or expand the agency's budgetary base. There are three variations.

Guard Against Cuts in Old Programs
There are several ways that an agency can defend its programs, but a favored one is to eliminate its most popular ones. When the National Institutes of Health decided to start a dental research program, Congress directed that it be funded by drawing money from other programs. The Institutes obliged, cutting their programs in heart disease, cancer, and mental health. Congress, not only restored these funds, but also boosted the budget for dental research.

Inch Ahead with Old Programs
The National Institutes of Health traditionally have inched ahead with old programs by reducing the number of research grants ("Look! We're economizing!"), but increasing the total dollars in them (thus inching ahead).

Add New Programs
When an agency wants to add new programs, a truckload of tactics is at its disposal. Because the new and novel often are distrusted by those who allocate budgets, agencies may present new programs as old and dull ones; as only temporary; as money-savers; as ways to reduce backlogs; as so trivial they warrant no examination; or as merely logical continuations of old programs.

Selling new programs can deteriorate into "the sort of haggling more likely to be found at a car dealership than a Senate conference room." For example, "Air Force officials assured cost-conscious lawmakers that they had swung a deal to get...Raptor fighter jets for the bargain-basement price of $110 million each. Of course, if they wanted a few extras that could lump another $40 million to $60 million onto the sticker price. Only when pressed did they acknowledge that one of the extras happens to be the engine." As one Representative ruefully noted, "I've learned that you've got to ask exactly the right question at exactly the right time."[299]

The Budget-Minimizing Bureaucrat

If the foregoing review of budget-acquiring strategies and tactics sounds cynical, it is. To be cynical, however, is not necessarily to be scrofulous.

Overall, government employees, relative to private-sector workers, generally support policies that lead to larger governments,[300] but, when we ascend a bit higher up the public hierarchy, government executives "are no more likely than the average citizen to favor bigger government budgets."[301] Although there are indications that some agency chiefs behave as "budget-maximizing bureaucrats" who will always try to fatten their budgets,[302] most public executives are actually "budget-minimizing bureaucrats." Senior federal administrators "are more frugal and less inclined to favor increased government spending than the general public....even on issues that fall within their own departments' jurisdictions."[303] An example: Defense Secretary Robert Gates famously argued, in 2010, that, to strengthen national security, his department's budget should be cut and the State Department's enlarged.

A similar executive bias is found in the states. "To a substantial extent," surveys of state agency heads conducted over five decades have "debunked" theories of budgetary "bureaucratic maximizing" and find instead a "substantial component of conservers."[304]

LEGISLATING BUDGETS: POLITICIANS AND POWER

Just as getting a budget is a political process, so is granting one.

Legislating Federal Budgets

The federal government's budget allocation process is characterized by endless conflict and near collapse.

The Congressional Budget and Impoundment Control Act of 1974
By the 1950s, congressional budget making had become an impenetrable insiders' game that was undermining responsible fiscal policy. In 1974, Congress decided to gain a comprehensive grip on the budgetary process, and enacted the Congressional Budget and Impoundment Control Act, also known as the Congressional Budget Act.[305]

Comprehensive Budget Committees The Congressional Budget Act established in each chamber a budget committee responsible for reviewing the president's annual budget proposals as a whole and determining their potential effects on the economy.

Concurrent Budget Resolutions The Act requires that, on two prescribed dates every year, Congress must vote explicitly on the budget as an entire package and on budget priorities. In 1982, Congress abandoned the first of these votes, which set budgetary targets, but retained the second vote on the "binding concurrent budget resolution," which remains "the only time Congress votes on total spending, revenues, budget priorities, and the size of the deficit."[306]

Reconciliation The key in forcing Congress to vote as a body on budgets is "reconciliation," which was "almost an afterthought in 1974, [but] has in many ways become the most important part of the process."[307] Reconciliation empowers the budget committees in each chamber to require, if need be, other committees to bring their policies' costs within overall spending limits.

A Budget-Making Timetable The Act established a logical sequence of steps in the budgetary process. Congress is not allowed to adjourn until it has ironed out all differences on budgetary matters.

Improved Spending Controls Patterns of "backdoor" spending had developed that were not subject to the regular appropriations process, and President

Nixon had grown increasingly enamored of *impounding* (i.e., not spending) funds appropriated by Congress. The Act brought backdoor spending under greater congressional control, and the impoundment of funds was stringently limited.

The Congressional Budget Office Finally, the Act established a Congressional Budget Office (CBO) as a budgetary "counter bureaucracy" to offset the power of the OMB in the executive branch, improve Congress's analytical base, and make fiscal projections.

Congress Gets into the Act The Congressional Budget and Impoundment Control Act of 1974 has been described as "the most important change in the budget process since the Budget and Accounting Act of 1921."[308] It encouraged the "further centralization of appropriations and budget power" within Congress, without diminishing the president's role in the budget process.[309]

Nevertheless, the Act has proven controversial, and "hardly anything favorable has been said" about the process that it set up.[310] Many of the criticisms leveled against it, however, are not only inaccurate but also irrelevant in that they miss the Act's point. That point is supremely simple: To assure that Congress adopts budgets by a majority vote, explicitly and openly, and enforces its own policy on tax and spending measures.

The Ruination of Resolution and Reconciliation Has the Congressional Budget Act accomplished this? It did, at least for a while. For two dozen years, Congress could not "avoid voting on the totals and on the deficit, as it could before 1974, nor [could] it allocate funds that exceed total spending approved in the budget resolution."[311]

Since 1998, however, "both the budget process and budget discipline have greatly eroded."[312] In Fiscal Years 1999, 2003, 2005, 2007, and 2011 Congress failed to pass binding concurrent budget resolutions, the Act's key provision.[313] Instead, one or both chambers enacted *deeming resolutions*, an unofficial device that gives, or "deems," new spending caps for each appropriation, even though the total budget has not been agreed upon.

A Tardy and Terrible Timetable Congress has passed all its appropriations bills on time in only six years since 1974, when the Congressional Budget Act was enacted.[314] "The last time Congress passed all of its spending bills by the Oct. 1 deadline, *Seinfeld* was on television and people were dancing the Macarena," or Fiscal Year 1998.[315] When time runs out, Congress passes a *continuing spending resolution*, or a *continuing resolution*, which is a temporary appropriations act that typically permits an agency to spend what it was allocated the previous year, but does not actually grant it the money to do so. Continuing resolutions last, on average, three months, and their duration is lengthening over time.[316]

Because agency administrators are uncertain about their budgets, they may hoard funds and postpone contracting and purchasing; worried contractors and vendors, consequently, raise prices. Hiring is frozen. "You're almost guaranteeing that there will be incompetence, because the agencies don't have the resources to do the job."[317]

From Incrementalism to Revenue Forecasting The Congressional Budget Act requires that each year the CBO make economic projections on which revenue forecasts can be based, and the accuracy of its forecasts have "varied wildly from year to year."[318]

Why is this? For one, economic forecasts are based on a welter of changing variables, such as pretax corporate profits, the GDP deflater, and the yield on ten-year Treasury Notes, among many others. "Each of these things is the product of multiple factors, and each of those depends on multiple factors, and so on, with the whole thing becoming an ever-branching Tree of Uncertainty."[319]

For another, infinitesimal changes in economic assumptions can yield immense differences in predicted federal revenue. The prospect of rosy scenarios can tempt, and has tempted, budget makers into tweaking economic assumptions in ways that ease, but greatly distort, their revenue estimates and thus their budget making.

Budget Brawls Originally, revenue estimates were meant to guide policy, but, in the words of a Washington lobbyist, "revenue estimating has *become* policy."[320]

The CBO typically uses one set of assumptions in developing its revenue projections, while the OMB uses its own. Ultimately, these differences cause conflict, and budgetary battles have accounted for seventeen department-wide or broader shutdowns in the federal government since the Congressional Budget Act went into effect.[321]

The two most notorious of these shutdowns occurred in the winter of 1995–1996, and their genesis was differing revenue forecasts posited by a Republican Congress and a Democratic president. The difference between CBO's and OMB's economic-growth projections over seven years was a microscopic nine one-hundredths of 1 percent, but the resulting difference in how much budgets would need to be cut over the ensuing seven years was vast: $475 billion.[322]

This fractional distinction led to a political stand-off between Congress and the president that resulted in a meltdown of the government: The first shutdown lasted five days and furloughed 800,000 workers. The second, which began twenty-six days after the first, was the longest in history at twenty-one days, and furloughed 284,000 employees and deferred paying salaries to an additional 475,000. In both, parks and museums were closed, at a loss of 9 million visitors,[323] and 170,000 veterans did not receive their benefits for two months, among many other crashes of federal services. The two shutdowns were so costly that they likely added $2 billion to the federal deficit![324]

The Emergence of OMB The collapse of congressional discipline in forming budgets was fortuitous for OMB. "The first Reagan year [1981] witnessed the striking and sudden emergence of OMB to the posture of principal executive leader, short of the president himself, in policymaking and politics."[325] Reagan transferred from the agency heads to OMB the long-standing responsibility for shepherding through Congress the president's proposed budgets, and this greatly strengthened OMB's budgetary—and policymaking—hand.[326]

Today, the four public administrators in OMB who hold "the unheralded title of associate director for programs...a name worthy of a dutiful bean counter," wield "power that outstrips that of most Cabinet secretaries.... They are arguably the most powerful people on the civilian side of the government."[327]

Legislating State Budgets

Few of Washington's bizarre budgetary ways are found in state capitals, but there are two similarities: All states have budget offices in their legislative branches as well as in their executive ones, and all states forecast revenue, a practice that has become central in budgeting at all governmental levels.

Revenue Forecasting in the States All governors' budget proposals contain revenue estimates, which, in forty states, are made by budget offices.[328] The accuracy of these estimates is critical. In New York, for instance, a 1 percent error in forecasting what the general fund's revenue will be amounts to nearly half of what the state spends annually on public assistance.[329]

From 1975 through 1992, state forecasters' revenue estimates were, on average, 2.1 percent lower per year than the revenues that the states actually collected. These forecasting errors were largely deliberate. When times were prosperous, forecasters "routinely underforecast revenues," resulting in revenue surpluses. Why? Because, in the words of one state budgeter, "I am a hero when there is more money than I predicted and a villain when there is less. Let me tell you, it is much better to be a hero than a villain." When times were tough, by contrast, "the average forecast error...was near zero."[330]

Since then, state revenue forecasting has grown befogged. From 1987 to 2009, the median error rate has averaged 3.5 percent per year, and revenue estimates have "worsened progressively" over time. In sixteen of those twenty-three years, forecasters overestimated revenues (thereby maintaining past traditions), and in seven they underestimated them. Forecasting errors grow in size and frequency with each recession.[331]

The primary reason underlying this deterioration is not the states' forecasting methods, but lies instead in factors beyond the forecasters' control. The forty-three states that have a personal income tax have grown intensely dependent on it for revenue, but the unpredictable impact of capital gains on individual incomes renders revenue gained from that tax also unpredictable.[332]

Not all errors can be attributed to external variables. "A large fraction of forecast errors can be explained by political pressures on budget forecasters." In election years, governors who are up for reelection sometimes persuade forecasters to adopt overly-optimistic economic assumptions so that their proposed budgets will, as required by law in forty-eight states, balance. Because of these election-year rosy scenarios, the resultant state budget deficits are, on average, twenty-seven dollars more per capita in election years than in non-election years.[333]

When the governor has the primary authority to estimate revenue, he or she, rather than the legislature, is more influential in shaping the overall budget.[334] Fortunately for executive authority, governors dominate the process. In two dozen states, these estimates are prepared solely in the governor's office. In no state does the legislature have the exclusive power to estimate revenue, and in only eight does it share this authority with the governor's office.[335]

When budget officers in both branches work together, their governments gain more accurate revenue forecasts than when they work separately. These superior joint forecasts actually add small, but still "significant dollar amounts," to state budgets.[336]

A Withering of the Governors' Budget Making Powers?

Governors achieved the apex of their budgetary powers by the middle of the twentieth century, when the introduction of the executive budget in the states was largely completed. But times change.

Despite the governors' mastery of the critical budgetary function of revenue forecasting, in only 36 percent of the states do state budget officials in both the legislative and executive branches agree that their governors are their states' primary budget formulator.[337] This proportion represents a drop of nearly two-fifths over just a dozen years.[338]

In addition, the process of legislative budget making itself erodes gubernatorial authority in most states. As the budget is being formulated, legislatures in twenty-nine states split their governors' proposed executive budget into "pieces" (i.e., spending bills, often hundreds of them), a practice that "increases the chance that pieces of the budget

will be isolated and captured by special interest groups...weakening executive authority."[339]

"It is not so much that the governors have lost [budget-forming] power in recent years as that the legislatures have gained power."[340]

Tensions, but No Meltdowns Over time, state budget offices in the executive and legislative branches have grown "more competitive in terms of their organizational and technological capacities....[and] there will continue to be a struggle for dominance" between the branches "in the budget development process,"[341] but these struggles have yet to result in a federal-style meltdown in any state government.

The Rise of State Budget Offices Budget analysts and similar professionals in state budget offices have increased by a fifth since 1975,[342] and their professionalism has deepened. Almost three-fifths of the "professional personnel" in these offices have at least a master's degree,[343] compared to not even a sixth thirty years earlier,[344] and fully eight out of ten were working in their state governments prior to their appointment.[345]

These trends have empowered the budgeters. The proportion of state budget offices that control the expenditure of legislatively appropriated funds by line agencies has grown over three decades from about three-quarters to "virtually all budget offices."[346] Budgeters are now policymakers, wielding "significant influence in state policymaking."[347]

Legislating Local Budgets

With the rapid introduction of chief administrative officers into local governments during the twentieth century and in this one, local budgeting significantly improved in terms of its usefulness and accountability.

Revenue Forecasting in Local Governments All cities and counties monitor financial trends and forecast their revenues and expenses. In contrast to the federal and state governments, revenue-estimating tensions between executives and legislators are largely absent because budget professionals in the executive offices dominate local revenue forecasting. City and county councils appear "to play only an informal, indirect role" in the process.[348]

Local revenue forecasters routinely underforecast revenue—in their case, by 1–7 percent. Part of the reason why is a desire by local forecasters to hedge their bets (thereby reflecting state forecasters' preferences), but, "unlike other levels of government, local finance officials receive limited political or bureaucratic scrutiny that might induce more accurate forecasts."[349]

Making and Managing Local Budgets City managers are extremely serious about their budgets: 92 percent of them report that "budgetary constraints" are "very influential in their decision making," and they rank those constraints at the very top of twenty-six possible "influences" when making decisions.[350] Typically, the city or county manager recommends a budget to the local council or board, which approves the proposed budget with few, if any, alterations of consequence.

Better financial management in local governments associates with outsiders. Top local finance managers who are more innovative and attentive to their governments' financial viability are more likely to have been hired from outside their government rather than having been promoted from within,[351] and appointing financial-oversight committees appears to be "an effective tool" in improving local fiscal accountability.[352]

Enter the State Budgeting in local governments differs markedly from budgeting in the federal and state governments because the states stipulate, often in miasmic detail, how their local governments may budget. Forty-three states set the fiscal year for their local governments. Laws in thirty-one states specify the budget form that their cities must use, and thirty-two states do so for counties. The clear trend is one of additional states adopting these and other restrictions.[353]

State involvement in the budgetary and fiscal affairs of their local governments is sometimes needed, but it is not without problems. Because they are often part of state constitutions, state budgetary regulations are usually rigid, across-the-board, and quickly become dated; thus, they cause

unnecessary inefficiencies in local administration. More gravely, they sometimes favor special interests over the general interest, thereby "creating budget processes" that override local priorities and minimize services.[354]

"BUDGETEERS": HUMBLE NEVERMORE

Almost 26,000 budget analysts work in American governments, accounting for an impressive 44 percent of all budgeters in the country.[355] They are an ill-understood lot.

We quoted earlier the first budget director of the United States to the effect that his office was concerned only with the "humbler," humdrum, housekeeping ticky-tack of government, and *never*, heavens forefend, with any "question of policy."[356]

This obsequious and misleading, but influential, claim suggests not only that budgeting is humble but that budgeters are, too. (The ponderous irony here is that the budgeter who made this claim was himself far from humble; he served as ambassador to Britain, vice president, and, for good measure, won the Nobel Peace Prize.) Some empathetic academics think that our benighted budgeters could benefit from a bit of cheerleading, and the word "budgeteer" is increasingly common in the literature—a sign of an apparent effort to boost the presumably low self-esteem of bottom-lining budgeters by identifying them with more raffish company: buccaneers, privateers, profiteers, musketeers, and mutineers.

We suspect that few, if any, budget officers need a literary artifice to bolster their allegedly anemic egos. Indeed, public budgeters seem quite comfortable in their own skins: As one of only two public administrative professions commanding salaries that are roughly comparable to those of their corporate counterparts,[357] budgeters are recognized as highly valued contributors to good governance, and they are happily immersing themselves in the "humbler and routine business of government,"[358] knowing full well that those routines, in reality, often do involve determining major questions of public policy.

NOTES

1. David Osborne and Peter Hutchinson, *The Price of Government: Getting the Results We Need in an Age of Permanent Fiscal Crisis* (New York: Basic Books, 2004), p. 45. Figures are for 1972–2002.

2. Ibid., pp. 44–47. Figures are for 1972–2002.

3. U.S. Government Accountability Office, *Fiscal Year 2010 U.S. Government Financial Statements: Federal Government Continues to Face Financial Management and Long-Term Fiscal Challenges*, GAO-11-363T (Washington, DC: U.S. Government Printing Office, 2011).

4. Association of Government Accountants, *Public Attitudes Toward Government Accountability and Transparency 2010* (Alexandria, VA: Author, 2010), pp. 2–3. Figures are for 2009.

5. Bernardino Benito and Francisco Bastida, "Budget Transparency, Fiscal Performance, and Political Turnout: An International Approach," *Public Administration Review* 69 (May/June 2009), pp. 403–417. The quotation is on p. 403.

6. "Utah budget executive," as quoted in John Kamensky, "Transparency: New Frontier for Performance Management," *The Business of Government* (June 2009), pp. 16–18. The quotations are on p. 18.

7. As derived from data in U.S. Office of Management and Budget, "Historical Tables," *The President's Budget for Fiscal Year 2012* (Washington, DC: U.S. Government Printing Office, 2011), Tables 1.1, 2.1, 2.5. Current figure is for 2010. For purposes of this discussion, federal "general revenue" is the sum of revenues provided by personal and corporate income taxes, excise taxes, and gift and estate taxes.

8. As derived from data in ibid. Current figure is for 2010.

9. Ibid.

10. Ibid.

11. Ibid., Tables 1.1, 2.5.

12. Ibid., Table 2.2.

13. Ibid., Table 2.4. Figure (62 percent for Social Security and 21 percent for Medicare) is for 2010.

14. Julia B. Isaacs, *Public Spending on Children and the Elderly from a Life-Cycle Perspective* (Washington, DC: Brookings, 2009), p. 2.

15. C. Eugene Steuerle, *Contemporary U.S. Tax Policy* (Washington, DC: Urban Institute, 2004), p. 38.

16. As derived from data in U.S. Office of Management and Budget, "Historical Tables," Tables 1.1, 2.4. Figure (25 percent for Social Security and 8 percent for Medicare) is for 2010.

17. As derived from data in U.S. Bureau of the Census, *Statistical Abstract United States, 2011*, 130th ed. (Washington, DC: U.S. Government Printing Office, 2011), Tables 469, 540, 541. Figures for payments for individuals (59 percent), defense, and interest are for 2009. Figures for cash (28 percent) and noncash (29 percent) benefits are for 2008.

18. As derived from data in U.S. Office of Management and Budget, "Historical Tables," Tables 1.1, 8.5. Data are for 2010.

19. By "officially," we refer to how the U.S. Census Bureau and the public finance community categorizes state and local revenues. See John L. Mikesell, *Fiscal Administration: Analysis and Applications for the Public Sector* (Homewood, IL: Dorsey, 1982), p. 415.

20. U.S. Government Accountability Office, *Federal User Fees: A Design Guide*, GAO-08-386SP (Washington, DC: U.S. Government Printing Office, 2008), p. 4.

21. As derived from data in U.S. Bureau of the Census, "Table 1. Summary of State and Local Finances by Level of Government: 2006–07," *Census of Governments, 2007* (Washington, DC: U.S. Government Printing Office, 2009), http://www2.census.gov/govs/estimate/0700ussl_1.txt. Figures are for 2006–2007.

22. Hendrik Hertzberg, "The States We're In," *The New Yorker* (August 24, 2009), pp. 19–20. The quotation is on p. 20.

23. As derived from data in U.S. Bureau of the Census, "Table 1"; and American Council on Intergovernmental Relations, *Significant Features of Fiscal Federalism, 1995*, Vol. 2 (Washington, DC: Author, 1998), p. 73. Current figures are for 2006–2007.

24. As derived from data in ibid. (both citations, but p. 75 for the latter citation). Current figures are for 2006–2007.

25. As derived from data in Federation of Tax Administrators, *State Sales Tax Rates and*

Food & Drug Exemptions (Washington, DC: Author, 2011). Figure is for 2011.

26. As derived from data in U.S. Bureau of the Census, "Table 1"; and U.S. Advisory Commission on Intergovernmental Relations, *Significant Features of Fiscal Federalism, 1980–81*, M-132 (Washington, DC: U.S. Government Printing Office, 1981), p. 40. Current figure is for 2006–2007.

27. As derived from data in Federation of Tax Administrators, *State Individual Income Taxes* (Washington, DC: Author, 2011). Figure is for 2011.

28. As derived from data in U.S. Bureau of the Census, "Table 1"; and U.S. Advisory Commission on Intergovernmental Relations, *Significant Features of Fiscal Federalism, 1980–81*, p. 41. Current figure is for 2006–2007.

29. As derived from data in Federation of Tax Administrators, *Range of State Corporate Income Tax Rates* (Washington, DC: Author, 2011). Figure is for 2011.

30. As derived from data in U.S. Bureau of the Census, "Table 1." Figures are for 2006–2007.

31. As derived from data in U.S. Advisory Commission on Intergovernmental Relations, *Significant Features of Fiscal Federalism, 1980–81*, p. 41.

32. Gary Cornia, Kelly D. Edmiston, David L. Sjoquist, *et al.*, "The Disappearing State Corporate Income Tax," *National Tax Journal* 58 (March 2005), pp. 115–139.

33. Robert Tannenwald, *Are State and Local Revenue Systems Becoming Obsolete?* (Washington, DC: National League of Cities, 2004).

34. As derived from data in U.S. Bureau of the Census, "Table 1." Figures are for 2006–2007.

35. As derived from data in ibid. and American Council on Intergovernmental Relations, *Significant Features of Fiscal Federalism, 1995*, Vol. 2, pp. 72–73. Current figures are for 2006–2007.

36. As derived from data in ibid. (both citations, but pp. 52, 72 for the latter citation). Current data are for 2006–2007. Mid-century figures are for 1952.

37. As derived from data in U.S. Bureau of the Census, "Table 1." Figures are for 2006–2007. Education data exclude libraries.

38. Tax Policy Center, *The Tax Policy Briefing Book* (Washington, DC: Author, 2010), Entry 3. Figure is for 2008.

39. Bert Waisanen, *State Tax and Expenditure Limits—2008* (Denver, CO: National Conference of State Legislatures, 2010). Figures are for 2008.

40. Ibid. Figures are for 2008.

41. Matthew Mitchell, *T.E.L. It Like It Is: Do State Tax and Expenditure Limits Actually Limit Spending?* Working Paper No. 10-71 (Fairfax, VA: Mercatus Center, George Mason University, 2010).

42. Jerri Killian and Enamul Choudhury, "Continuity and Change in the Role of City Managers," *Municipal Year Book, 2010* (Washington, DC: International City/County Management Association, 2010), pp. 10–18. The quotation is on p. 14. Emphasis added. The initial study of this topic is Paul E. Peterson, *City Limits* (Chicago, IL: University of Chicago Press, 1981).

43. As derived from data in U.S. Bureau of the Census, "Table 1"; and American Council on Intergovernmental Relations, *Significant Features of Fiscal Federalism, 1995*, Vol. 2, p. 75. Current figure is for 2006–2007.

44. As derived from data in U.S. Bureau of the Census, "Table 1." Figures are for 2006–2007.

45. David B. Walker, *The Rebirth of Federalism: Slouching toward Washington*, 2nd ed. (New York: Chatham House, 2000), p. 227. Figure is the average for seven selected years, 1957–1990.

46. As derived from data in U.S. Bureau of the Census, "Table 1." Figures are for 2006–2007. We have assumed that one-third of federal aid to the states continues to be pass-through grants to local governments.

47. As derived from data in ibid.; and American Council on Intergovernmental Relations, *Significant Features of Fiscal Federalism, 1995*, Vol. 2, p. 75. Figures are for 2006–2007.

48. As derived from data in U.S. Bureau of the Census, "Table 1"; and U.S. Advisory Commission on Intergovernmental Relations, *Significant Features of Fiscal Federalism, 1980–81*, p. 40. Property taxes, which accounted for 71 percent of local general tax revenue in 2006–2007, accounted for 88 percent in 1950 and 86 percent in 1963.

49. Yongshong Wu, "How Municipal Property Tax Responded to State Aid Cuts: The Case of Massachusetts Municipalities in the Post-2001

Fiscal Crisis," *Public Budgeting & Finance* 29 (December 2009), pp. 74–89.

50. Richard F. Dye and Andrew Reschovsky, "Property Tax Response to State Aid Cuts in the Recent Fiscal Crisis," *Public Budgeting & Finance* 28 (June 2008), pp. 87–111.

51. National Conference of State Legislatures, *Local Option Taxes* (Denver, CO: Author, 2011). Figure is for 2011.

52. Scott Mackey, *Critical Issues in State-Local Fiscal Policy, Part 2: A Guide to Local Option Taxes* (Denver, CO: National Conference of State Legislatures, 1997).

53. National Conference of State Legislatures, *Local Option Taxes*. Figure is for 2011.

54. As derived from data in U.S. Bureau of the Census, "Table 1"; and U.S. Advisory Commission on Intergovernmental Relations, *Significant Features of Fiscal Federalism, 1980–81*, p. 40. Current figure is for 2006–2007.

55. National Conference of State Legislatures, *Local Option Taxes*. Figure is for 2006 and includes local payroll taxes.

56. As derived from data in U.S. Bureau of the Census, "Table 1"; and U.S. Advisory Commission on Intergovernmental Relations, *Significant Features of Fiscal Federalism, 1980–81*, p. 40. Current figure is for 2006–2007.

57. As derived from data in U.S. Bureau of the Census, "Table 1." Figures are for 2006–2007.

58. As derived from data in Ibid.; and American Council on Intergovernmental Relations, *Significant Features of Fiscal Federalism, 1995*, Vol. 2, pp. 74, 75. Current figures are for 2006–2007.

59. As derived from data in U.S. Bureau of the Census, "Table 1"; and American Council on Intergovernmental Relations, *Significant Features of Fiscal Federalism, 1995*, Vol. 2, pp. 52, 74. Current data are for 2006–2007. Mid-century figures, 14 and 17 percent, respectively, are for 1952.

60. As derived from data in U.S. Bureau of the Census, "Table 1" and "Table 2." Figures are for 2006–2007. Education data exclude libraries.

61. Daniel R. Mullins and Bruce A. Wallin, "Tax and Expenditure Limitations: Introduction and Overview," *Public Budgeting & Finance* 24 (December 2004), pp. 2–15. Figures (pp. 7, 4–5) are for 2002.

62. Ibid., p. 7. Figures are for 2002.

63. U.S. Advisory Commission on Intergovernmental Relations, *Tax and Expenditure Limits on Local Governments*, M-194 (Washington, DC: U.S. Government Printing Office, 1995), p. 1.

64. Mullins and Wallin, "Tax and Expenditure Limitations," p. 7. Figures are for 2002.

65. Ibid. Datum is for 2002.

66. Leah Brooks and Justin Phillips, "Municipally Imposed Tax and Expenditure Limits," *Land Lines* 21 (April 2009), pp. 8–13. The quotation is on p. 9. Data (pp. 10–12) are for 2007.

67. Nicholas O. Alozie and Catherine McNamara, "Gender Differences in Willingness to Pay for Urban Public Services," *Urban Affairs Review* 45 (January 2010), pp. 377–390. The quotation is on p. 381.

68. Nicholas O. Alozie and Catherine McNamara, "Poverty Status and Willingness to Pay for Local Public Services," *Public Administration Quarterly* 33 (Winter 2009), pp. 520–531. The quotation is on p. 520.

69. Mullins and Wallin, "Tax and Expenditure Limitations," p. 15.

70. Brooks and Phillips, "Municipally Imposed Tax and Expenditure Limits," p. 12. Figures are for 2007.

71. Richard C. Kearney, "Reinventing Government and Battling Budget Crises: Manager and Municipal Government Actions in 2003," *Municipal Year Book, 2005* (Washington, DC: International City/County Management Association, 2005), pp. 27–32. The quotations are on p. 30. Figure is for 2003.

72. Bruce A. Wallin, *Budgeting for Basics: The Changing Landscape of City Finances* (Washington, DC: Brookings, 2005), p. 6.

73. Ibid.

74. As derived from data in U.S. Bureau of the Census, *Statistical Abstract of the United States, 1986*, 106th ed. (Washington, DC: U.S. Government Printing Office, 1986), Table 475. Figures are for 1975.

75. As derived from data in Ibid. and U.S. Bureau of the Census, "Table 2. Summary of State and Local Finances by Level of Government: 2006–07," *Census of Governments, 2007* (Washington, DC: U.S. Government Printing Office, 2009), http://www2.census.gov/govs/estimate/0700ussl_2.txt. Figures are for 1975–2006–2007.

76. Wallin, *Budgeting for Basics*, p. 6. Figures are for 1977–2000.

77. Changhoon Jung and Suho Bae, "Changing Revenue and Expenditure Structure and the Reliance on User Charges and Fees in American Counties, 1972–2002," *American Review of Public Administration* 41 (January 2011), pp. 92–110.

78. Nina Easton, "How Obama Plans to Pay for His Agenda: A Little Tax Here. A Little Tax There. And Soon You're Talking Real Money," *Fortune* (May 24, 2010), p. 52. Current figures are for 2009, when taxes accounted for an average of 30 percent of income.

79. Much of the following discussion is drawn from U.S. Government Accountability Office, *Understanding the Tax Reform Debate: Background, Criteria, and Questions*, GAO-05-1009SP (Washington, DC: U.S. Government Printing Office, 2005).

80. As derived from data in U.S. Bureau of the Census, *Statistical Abstract the United States, 2011*, Tables 428, 473. Figure is for 2009.

81. Meg Bostrom, *By, or for, the People? A Meta-analysis of Public Opinion of Government* (New York: Demos, 2006), p. 18. Data are for 2003.

82. Federation of Tax Administrators, *State Individual Income Taxes*. Figure is for 2008.

83. As derived from Federation of Tax Administrators, *Range of State Corporate Income Tax Rates*. Figure is for 2008.

84. As derived from data in U.S. Bureau of the Census, *Statistical Abstract the United States, 2011*, Tables 473, 428. Figures (50 and 78 percent, respectively) are for 2009.

85. U.S. Government Accountability Office, *Understanding the Tax Reform Debate*, p. 49.

86. U.S. Government Accountability Office, *Tax Administration: Information on Selected Foreign Practices That May Provide Useful Insights*, GAO-11-439 (Washington, DC: U.S. Government Printing Office, 2011), p. 4. Figures are for FY 2010.

87. U.S. Government Accountability Office, *Tax Administration: Review of the Fiscal Year 2010 Budget Request*, GAO-09-754 (Washington, DC: U.S. Government Printing Office, 2009), Highlights page. Figure is for 2009.

88. U.S. Government Accountability Office, *2009 Tax Filing Season: IRS Met Many 2009 Goals, but Telephone Access Remained Low, and Taxpayer Service and Enforcement Could Be Improved*, GAO-10-225 (Washington, DC: U.S. Government Printing Office, 2009), Highlights page. Figure is for 2009.

89. U.S. Government Accountability Office, *Understanding the Tax Reform Debate*, p. 51.

90. David Keating, *A Taxing Trend: The Rise in Complexity, Forms, and Paperwork Burdens*, NTU Policy Paper 128 (Alexandria, VA: National Taxpayers Union, 2011). Figures are for 2010. Average cost and preparation figures pertain to both "non business" and business taxpayers.

91. U.S. Government Accountability Office, *Tax Policy: Summary of Estimates of the Cost of the Federal Tax System*, GAO-05-878 (Washington, DC: U.S. Government Printing Office, 2005).

92. U.S. Government Accountability Office, *Understanding the Tax Reform Debate*, p. 40.

93. John E. Peterson, "Sacramento's Socratic Moment," *Governing* (July 2010), p. 50.

94. Richard W. Rahn, "New Underground Economy," *Washington Times* (December 9, 2009).

95. U.S. Government Accountability Office, *Tax Gap: Multiple Strategies, Better Compliance Data, and Long-term Goals Are Needed to Improve Taxpayer Compliance*, GAO-06-208T (Washington, DC: U.S. Government Printing Office, 2005), Highlights page.

96. U.S. Government Accountability Office, *Tax Compliance: Businesses Owe Billions in Federal Payroll Taxes*, GAO-08-617 (Washington, DC: U.S. Government Printing Office, 2008), Highlights page. The quotation pertains to payroll taxes, but likely could extend to most, if not all, federal taxes.

97. U.S. Government Accountability Office, *Tax Administration: Information on Selected Foreign Practices That May Provide Useful Insights*, p. 5. Figure is for FY 2010.

98. U.S. Government Accountability Office, *Government Performance and Accountability: Tax Expenditures Represent a Substantial Federal Commitment and Need to Be Reexamined*, GAO-05-690 (U.S. Government Printing Office, 2005). Figures are for 1974–2004. There were 146 tax exemptions in 2004.

99. U.S. Government Accountability Office, *Tax Administration: Information on Selected Foreign Practices That May Provide Useful Insights*, p. 5. Figure is for FY 2010.

100. Eric Toder and Rachel Johnson, "Held Harmless by Higher Income Tax Rates?" *Tax Notes* (Washington, DC: Tax Policy Center, March 1, 2010), p. 1115. Figure is for 2010.

101. As derived from data in U.S. Internal Revenue Service, *The 400 Individual Income Tax Returns Reporting the Highest Adjusted Gross Incomes Each Year, 1992–2007* (Washington, DC: U.S. Government Printing Office, 2011), Table 1, columns 7, 178. Average annual income figure is for 2007. Decline figure, 35 percent, is for 1992–2007.

102. U.S. Government Accountability Office, *Government Performance and Accountability: Tax Expenditures Represent a Substantial Federal Commitment and Need to Be Reexamined.* Figure is for 2004.

103. Leonard E. Burman and Greg Leiserson, *Two-Thirds of Tax Units Pay More Payroll Than Income Tax* (Washington, DC: Tax Policy Center, 2007), p. 1. Figures are for 2006.

104. As derived from data in Rachel M. Johnson and Jeffrey Rohaly, *The Distribution of Federal Taxes, 2009–12* (Washington, DC: Tax Policy Center, 2009), pp. 5, 8, 13, 20. Data are for 2009–2012 and include Medicare and the employee and employer portions of the Social Security tax.

105. As derived from data in U.S. Bureau of the Census, "Table 1." Figures are for 2006–2007.

106. As derived from data in Federation of Tax Administrators, *State Sales Tax Rates and Food & Drug Exemptions.* Figures are for 2011.

107. George F. Will, "A Taxing Challenge," *Washington Post* (February 6, 2005).

108. Ibid.; and Michael Sandler, "State Sales Tax 'Not in Synch,'" *St. Petersburg Times* (August 7, 2003).

109. Quoted in Sandler, "State Sales Tax 'Not in Synch.'"

110. U.S. Advisory Commission on Intergovernmental Relations, *Significant Features of Fiscal Federalism, 1995*, Vol. 1, M-197 (Washington, DC: U.S. Government Printing Office, 1995), pp. 89–90. Figures are for 1994.

111. As derived from data in U.S. Bureau of the Census, "Table 1." Figure is for 2006–2007.

112. David Baer, *State Programs and Practices for Reducing Residential Property Taxes* (Washington, DC: AARP Public Policy Institute, American Association of Retired Persons, 2003), p. ii. Figures are for 2003.

113. Andrew Reschovsky, *The State Role in Providing Property Tax Relief* (Madison, WI: Department of Political Science, University of Wisconsin, no date), http://www.leg.state.nv.us.

114. Baer, *State Programs and Practices for Reducing Residential Property Taxes*, p. ii. Figure is for 2003.

115. Ibid., p. iii. Figures are for 2000.

116. U.S. Advisory Commission on Intergovernmental Relations, *Changing Public Attitudes on Governments and Taxes*, Reports S-1 through S-23 (Washington, DC: U.S. Government Printing Office, 1972–1994).

117. Mikesell, *Fiscal Administration*, p. 230.

118. President's Advisory Panel on Federal Tax Reform, *Simple, Fair, & Pro-Growth: Proposals to Fix America's Tax System* (Washington, DC: U.S. Government Printing Office, 2005).

119. U.S. Government Accountability Office, *Understanding the Tax Reform Debate*, p. 22.

120. Quinnipiac poll of 2010, as cited in James Surewiecki, "Soak the Very, Very Rich," *The New Yorker* (August 16 & 23, 2011), p. 33.

121. "Repeated surveys by the National Opinion Research Center since 1987," as cited in Peter Whoriskey, "With Executive Pay, Rich Pull Away from the Rest of America," *Washington Post* (June 18, 2011).

122. U.S. Congressional Budget Office, *Trends in the Distribution of Household Income between 1979 and 2007* (Washington, DC: U.S. Government Printing Office, 2011). Figures are for 1979–2007.

123. U.S. Central Intelligence Agency, "Distribution of Family Income—Gini Index," *World Factbook* (Washington, DC: U.S. Government Printing Office, 2011), https://www.cia.gov/library/publications/the-world-factbook/rankon.

124. U.S. Congressional Budget Office, *Trends in the Distribution of Household Income between 1979 and 2007.* Datum is for 1979–2007.

125. David Cay Johnson, *Tax Rates for Top 400 Earners Fall as Income Soars*, Tax Analysts Doc 2010-3372 (Washington, DC: Tax Analysts, 2010). Figure is for 2007.

126. Surewiecki, "Soak the Very, Very Rich," p. 33. Figure is for 2007 and includes capital gains.

127. Bostrom, *By, or for, the People?* p. 18. Figures, 24 and 38 percent, respectively, are for 2003.

128. Easton, "How Obama Plans to Pay for His Agenda."

129. U.S. Government Accountability Office, *Value-Added Taxes: Lessons Learned from Other Countries on Compliance Risks, Administrative Costs, Compliance Burden, and Transition*, GAO-08-566 (Washington, DC: U.S. Government Printing Office, 2008). The quotation is on p. 4.

130. Barry Bernard Bannister, Jr., *War, Legacy Debt, and Social Costs as Catalysts for a U.S. Inflation Cycle* (Baltimore, MD: Legg Mason Wood Walker, 2003), p. 2. The two extended inflationary periods were 1917–1920 and 1979–1981.

131. Edgar R. Fiedler, as quoted in: http://view.atdmt.com.

132. Louis Uchitelle, "Politicians May Be Up in Arms about Government Deficits, but Economists Aren't," *New York Times* (November 8, 1996); John Cassidy, "Ace in the Hole," *The New Yorker* (June 10, 1996), pp. 36–43; John M. Berry, "The Deficit Is (a) Still Really Big, or (b) No Big Deal," *Washington Post* (March 24, 1994); and Louis Uchitelle, "The Pitfalls of a Balanced Budget," *New York Times* (February 21, 1995).

133. Philip G. Joyce, "Congressional Budget Reform: The Unanticipated Implications of Federal Policymaking," *Public Administration Review* 56 (July/August 1996), pp. 317–327. The quotation is on p. 317.

134. Associated Press/Ipsos survey, as cited in Robert Tanner, Associated Press, "Headed for a Crash?" *Savannah Morning News* (September 4, 2005). Figure is for 2005.

135. The case is *Clinton v. City of New York.*

136. U.S. General Accounting Office, *Line-Item Veto: Estimating Potential Savings*, AFMD-92-7 (Washington, DC: U.S. Government Printing Office, 1992). Figure is for 1984–1989.

137. U.S. Office of Management and Budget, "Historical Tables," Table 1.1. Figures are for 2000–2010. The low figure is for 2010, and is something of an anomaly. The Post Office's share of off-budget revenue is about 3 percent, and Social Security contributes the rest.

138. As derived from data in ibid., Table 1.2. Current figure, 14.9 percent, refers to total receipts in 2010.

139. Glenn Kessler, "The Fact Checker: Revisiting the Cost of the Bush Tax Cuts," *Washington Post* (May 10, 2011).

140. As derived from data in U.S. Office of Management and Budget, "Historical Tables," Table 1.2.

141. Philip G. Joyce and Roy T. Meyers, "Budgeting During the Clinton Presidency," *Public Budgeting & Finance Review* 21 (March 2001), p. 8.

142. U.S. Congressional Budget Office, *The Budget and Economic Outlook: Fiscal Years 2004–2013* (Washington, DC: U.S. Government Printing Office, 2003), Appendix A. Emergency spending averaged about $8 billion annually, 1991–1998, and close to $39 billion annually, 1999–2002.

143. U.S. Government Accountability Office, *Budget Process: Enforcing Fiscal Choices*, GAO-11-626T (Washington, DC: U.S. Government Printing Office, 2011), p. 8.

144. As derived from data in Veronique de Rugy, *Mercatus on Policy: What's the Emergency?* No. 19 (Arlington, VA: Mercatus Center, George Mason University, 2008), p. 2. Figure is for 2007, and does not include "emergency-designated spending in regular appropriations."

145. Irene Rubin, "Budgeting during the Bush Administration," *Public Budgeting & Finance* 29 (September 2009), pp. 1–14. The quotations are on pp. 5–6.

146. Thomas L. Hungerford, *Supplemental Appropriations: Trends and Budgetary Impacts Since 1981*, CRS Report Number RL33134 (Washington, DC: Congressional Research Service, 2005), p. 2, for total budget authority figures (current figure is for 2005); and de Rugy, *Mercatus on Policy*, pp. 2–3, for discretionary spending figures (current figure is for 2007).

147. U.S. Office of Management and Budget, "Historical Tables," Table 1.2. Federal spending increased from 18.2 to 23.8 percent of GDP, 2001–2010.

148. As derived from data in U.S. Congressional Budget Office, *Estimated Impact of the American Recovery and Reinvestment Act on Employment and Economic Output from January 2011 Through March 2011* (Washington, DC: Author, 2011), p. 3. Figures are for FY 2009–FY 2012.

149. Ibid., Table 1.3. Figures are in current dollars.

150. As derived from data in International Monetary Fund, *Report for Selected Countries and Subjects* (New York: Author, 2010), Table 5. Data are for 2009.

151. U.S. Office of Management and Budget, "Historical Tables," Table 1.3. Figures are for 1942–1945.

152. U.S. Government Accountability Office, *Federal Debt: Answers to Frequently Asked Questions, An Update*, GAO-04-485SP Federal Debt (Washington, DC: U.S. Government Printing Office, 2004), p. 17. Emphasis added.

153. U.S. Office of Management and Budget, "Historical Tables," Table 7.1. Current figure is for 2010.

154. U.S. Government Accountability Office, *The Federal Government's Long-Term Fiscal Outlook, January 2011 Update*, GAO-11-451SP (Washington, DC: U.S. Government Printing Office, 2011), p. 2. Figures incorporate the health care legislation enacted in 2010.

155. U.S. Congressional Budget Office, *CBO's 2011 Long-Term Budget Outlook* (Washington, DC: U.S. Government Printing Office, 2011). Figures incorporate the health care legislation enacted in 2010.

156. U.S. Office of Management and Budget, "Historical Tables," Table 7.1. Current figure is for 2010.

157. As derived from data in Brian Dumaine, "Who's Most in Debt?" *Fortune* (August 15, 2011), p. 22. Figures are for 2011.

158. Carmen M. Reinhart and Kenneth S. Rogoff, "Growth in a Time of Debt," Paper Presented at the National Conference of the American Economic Association (Washington, DC, January 4, 2010), pp. 5, 11. This is a study of national debts. (Gross debts did not exist 200 years ago.)

159. U.S. Congressional Budget Office, *CBO's 2011 Long-Term Budget Outlook*, pp. 3–4.

160. Douglas W. Elmendorf, Director, Congressional Budget Office, Letter of August 1, 2011, to the Speaker of the House and the Majority Leader of the Senate.

161. *Washington Post* and Pew Research Center survey, as cited in Jon Cohen, "Budget Talks in a Word: 'Ridiculous,' 'Disgusting' and 'Stupid' Top Poll," *Washington Post* (August 1, 2011).

162. CNN, *Washington Post*-ABC, and Pew Research Center surveys, as cited in Peyton M. Crayhill, "Polls: Did the Public Get What It Wanted in Debt Deal?" *Washington Post* (August 1, 2011).

163. U.S. Congressional Budget Office, *CBO's 2011 Long-Term Budget Outlook*.

164. U.S. Government Accountability Office, *A Citizen's Guide to the 2010 Financial Report of the United States Government* (Washington,

DC: U.S. Government Printing Office, 2010), p. viii *n*. Data are for 2037–2084.

165. U.S. Government Accountability Office, *The Nation's Long-Term Fiscal Outlook, August 2007 Update: Despite Improvement in the Annual Deficit, Federal Fiscal Policy Remains Unsustainable*, GAO-07-1261R (Washington, DC: U.S. Government Printing Office, 2007), p. 2. The reference to Medicare refers to Part D only.

166. Christopher J. Truffer, Sean Keehan, Sheila Smith, *et al.*, "Health Spending Projections Through 2019: The Recession's Impact Continues," *Health Affairs* (February 4, 2010), http://content.healthaffairs.org/cgi/content/abstract/hlthaff.2009.1074. Figure is a projection for 2012.

167. U.S. Congressional Budget Office, *CBO's 2011 Long-Term Budget Outlook*.

168. U.S. Government Accountability Office, *A Citizen's Guide to the 2010 Financial Report of the United States Government*, p. viii *n*. Figures are for 2029–2084.

169. 60 Minutes and Vanity Fair, *60 Minutes/Vanity Fair Poll: January Edition*, http://www.vanityfair.com/ads/newad.html. Figures are for 2011.

170. U.S. Government Accountability Office, *The Nation's Long-Term Fiscal Outlook, April 2008 Update*, GAO-08-783R (Washington, DC: U.S. Government Printing Office, 2008), p. 2.

171. U.S. General Accounting Office, *Social Security Reform: Analysis of a Trust Fund Exhaustion Scenario Illustrates the Difficult Choices and the Need for Early Action*, GAO-03-1038T (Washington, DC: U.S. Government Printing Office, 2003), p. 1.

172. U.S. Government Accountability Office, *Federal Debt*, pp. 39, 41–42. Emphasis added. Figure is for 2003–2054.

173. U.S. General Accounting Office, *Balanced Budget Requirements: State Experiences and Implications for the Federal Government*, GAO/FMD-93-58BR (Washington, DC: U.S. Government Printing Office, 1993), p. 3. The two exceptions are Vermont and Wyoming.

174. U.S. Advisory Commission on Intergovernmental Relations, *State Laws Governing Local Government Structure and Administration*, M-186 (Washington, DC: U.S. Government Printing Office, 1993), pp. 41–47.

175. Dan Morgan, "How States Handle Debt May Not Work for Nation," *Washington Post* (February 28, 1995).

176. U.S. Government Accountability Office, *State and Local Governments: Persistent Fiscal Challenges Will Likely Emerge within the Next Decade*, GAO-07-1080SP (Washington, DC: U.S. Government Printing Office, 2007), pp. 2, 4.

177. Iris J. Lav, "Piling on Problems: How Federal Policies Affect State Fiscal Conditions," *National Tax Journal* 56 (September 2003), pp. 535–554. The quotation is on p. 538.

178. U.S. Government Accountability Office, *State and Local Governments: Persistent Fiscal Challenges Will Likely Emerge within the Next Decade*, p. 2.

179. U.S. Government Accountability Office, *State and Local Governments: Fiscal Pressures Could Have Implications for Future Delivery of Intergovernmental Programs*, GAO-10-899 (Washington, DC: U.S. Government Printing Office, 2010), Highlight page. Figures are for 1977–2007.

180. Henry J. Kaiser Family Foundation study, as cited in Donald F. Kettl, "Vegetarian Federalism," *Governing* (February 2011), pp. 14–15. The quotation is on p. 14. Figures are for 2019.

181. U.S. Government Accountability Office, *State and Local Governments: Persistent Fiscal Challenges Will Likely Emerge within the Next Decade*, p. 4. Emphasis added.

182. U.S. Government Accountability Office, *State and Local Governments' Fiscal Outlook: April 2011 Update*, GAO-11-495SP (Washington, DC: U.S. Government Printing Office, 2011), p. 3

183. Robert Novy-Marx and Joshua Rauh, "The Crisis in Local Government Pensions in the United States," Paper Presented at the Brookings–Nomura–Wharton Research Conference on Growing Old: Paying for Retirement and Institutional Money Management after the Financial Crisis, Washington, DC, October 15, 2010, p. 4. Figure, 3.2 years, is for 2006.

184. Roger Lowenstein, "Broke Town, U.S.A.," *New York Times* (March 3, 2011).

185. Pew Center on the States, *The Trillion Dollar Gap: Underfunded State Retirement Systems and the Road to Reform* (Washington, DC: Author, 2011), p. 1. Figure is for FY 2008.

186. Charles Duhigg, "Public Unions Take On Boss to Win Big Pensions," *New York Times* (June 21, 2011).

187. Tad Friend, "Contract City," *The New Yorker* (September 5, 2011), pp. 34–40. The data are on p. 38.

188. Duhigg, "Public Unions Take On Boss to Win Big Pensions."

189. Ibid.

190. Ibid. Data are for 2011.

191. Iris J. Lav and Elizabeth McNichol, *Misunderstandings Regarding State Debt, Pensions, and Retiree Health Costs Create Unnecessary Alarm* (Washington, DC: Center on Budget and Policy Priorities, 2011), p. 14. Public employees contributed 13 percent of public pension revenues, employers 27 percent, and investment earnings 60 percent, 1982–2009.

192. U.S. Government Accountability Office, *State and Local Governments: Fiscal Pressures Could Have Implications for Future Delivery of Intergovernmental Programs*. The quotation is on the Highlights page. Thirty-year data are for 1977–2007. Balanced-budget data are for 1995–2007.

193. U.S. Government Accountability Office, *State and Local Governments' Fiscal Outlook: April 2011 Update*, pp. 1–2.

194. Lowenstein, "Broke Town, U.S.A."

195. U.S. Government Accountability Office, *State and Local Governments: Fiscal Pressures Could Have Implications for Future Delivery of Intergovernmental Programs*.

196. Evelina R. Moulder, "Municipal Form of Government: Trends in Structure, Responsibility, and Composition," *Municipal Year Book, 2008* (Washington, DC: International City/County Management Association, 2008), pp. 3–8. Figure (p. 6) is for 2006.

197. As derived from data in U.S. Bureau of the Census, *Statistical Abstract of the United States, 1951*, 72nd ed. (Washington, DC: U.S. Government Printing Office, 1951), Table 406. Refers to nonguaranteed debt as a percentage of long-term debt.

198. As derived from data in U.S. Bureau of the Census, *Statistical Abstract of the United States, 1992*, 112th ed. (Washington, DC: U.S. Government Printing Office, 1992), Table 458.

199. As derived from data in U.S. Bureau of the Census, *Statistical Abstract of the United States, 2011*, Table 438. Figure is for 2009.

200. Lowenstein, "Broke Town, U.S.A."

201. Ibid. Figure is for 2011 and includes direct and indirect (e.g., via mutual funds) owners.

202. U.S. Government Accountability Office, *Tax Policy: Tax-Exempt Status of Certain Bonds Merits Reconsideration, and Apparent Noncompliance with Issuance Cost Limitations Should Be Addressed*, GAO-08-364 (Washington, DC: U.S. Government Printing Office, 2008), pp. 16–17. Figure is an average, and applies, with some annual variation, to 2000–2012 (projected).

203. Alicia H. Munnell, Jean-Pierre Aubry, and Laura Quinby, *Issue Brief: The Impact of Pensions on State Borrowing Costs* (Washington, DC: Center for State & Local Government Excellence, 2011), p. 4. Figures are for 2005–2008. In 2009 and 2010, 81 and 73 percent, respectively, of municipal bonds were tax exempt as a result of a federal tax rebate provision in the American Recovery and Reinvestment Act of 2009 that was designed to help state and local governments weather the Great Recession. The program, Build America Bonds, automatically terminated on the final day of 2010.

204. As derived from data in Securities Industry and Financial Markets Association (SIFMA), *State Taxation of Municipal Bonds for Individuals*, http://www.investinginbonds.com. Data are for 2010.

205. The case is *Department of Revenue of Kentucky v. Davis*.

206. U.S. General Accounting Office, *Balanced Budget Requirements Joinie Experiences for the Federal Government*, p. 3.

207. U.S. Advisory Commission on Intergovernmental Relations, *Tax and Expenditure Limits on Local Governments*, pp. 3, 5–10. Figures are for 1994.

208. As derived from data in U.S. Bureau of the Census, *Statistical Abstract of the United States, 2011*, Tables 433, 666. Growth figure is for 1990–2007. Current figures are for 2007.

209. John E. Petersen, "Deeper and Deeper in Debt," *Governing* (January 2010), p. 51.

210. Lowenstein, "Broke Town, U.S.A."

211. Ryan Holeywell, "How Bad Is It?" *Governing* (May 2011), pp. 26–30. The quotation is on p. 28.

212. Lowenstein, "Broke Town, U.S.A." Robert Kurtter, a managing director at Moody's, is quoted. Emphasis is original.

213. Monica Davey, "Michigan Town Is Left Pleading for Bankruptcy," *New York Times* (December 27, 2010).

214. As derived from data in Holeywell, "How Bad Is It?" p. 30. Of the 250 local bankruptcies, 1980–2010, forty-six were of general purpose governments.

215. Ibid., p. 29.

216. Davey, "Michigan Town Is Left Pleading for Bankruptcy."

217. Lowenstein, "Broke Town, U.S.A."

218. John Steele Gordon, *Hamilton's Blessing: The Extraordinary Life and Times of our National Debt* (New York: Walker, 1997), p. 5. Emphasis is original.

219. Aaron Wildavsky, *The Politics of the Budgetary Process*, 2nd ed. (Boston, MA: Little, Brown, 1974), p. 4.

220. Much of the following discussion, at least as it pertains through the 1960s, is based on: Bertram M. Gross, "The New Systems Budgeting," *Public administration review* 29 (March/April 1969), pp. 113–137, and Allen Schick, "The Road to PBB: The Stages of Budget Reform," *Public Adminstration review* 26 (December 1966), pp. 243–258.

221. President's Commission on Economy and Efficiency, *The Need for a National Budget* (Washington, DC: Author, 1912).

222. "The Nobel Prize for Peace 1925," Nobelprize.com, http://nobelprize.org/, and as derived from data in U.S. Office of Management and Budget, "Historical Tables," Table 1.1. Data are for FY 1921–FY 1922.

223. Charles G. Dawes, *The First Year of the Budget of the United States* (Washington, DC: U.S. Government Printing Office, 1923), p. ii.

224. Glen Hahn Cope, "Budgeting for Performance in Local Government," *Municipal Year Book, 1995* (Washington, DC: International City/County Management Association, 1995), pp. 42–52. The quotation is on p. 42.

225. Commission on Organization of the Executive Branch of Government, *Budgeting and Accounting* (Washington, DC: U.S. Government Printing Office, 1949), p. 8.

226. Quoted in U.S. General Accounting Office, *Performance Budgeting: Past Initiatives Offer Insights for GPRA Implementation*, GAO/AIMD-97-46 (Washington, DC: U.S. Government Printing Office, 1997), p. 34.

227. Quoted in Allen Schick, *Budget Innovation in the States* (Washington, DC: Brookings, 1971), p. 127.

228. This definition is based on one contained in U.S. General Accounting Office, *Performance Budgeting: Past Initiatives Offer Insights for GPRA Implementation*, p. 35.

229. Ibid., p. 40.

230. Christopher G. Reddick, "Testing Rival Theories of Budgetary Decision-Making in the U.S. States," *Financial Accountability and Management* 19 (Winter 2004), pp. 315–335. The quotation is on p. 315.

231. U.S. General Accounting Office, *Performance Budgeting: Past Initiatives Offer Insights for GPRA Implementation*, pp. 35–41

232. Edwin L. Harper, Fred A. Kramer, and Andrew M. Rouse, *Implementation and Use of PPB in Sixteen Federal Agencies* (Washington, DC: U.S. Bureau of the Budget, 1969).

233. Orville Freeman, quoted in Verne B. Lewis, "Reflections on Budget Systems," *Public Budgeting & Finance* 8 (March 1988), pp. 4–19. The quotaton is on p. 11.

234. William F. West, Eric Lindquist, and Katrina N. Mosher-Howe, "NOAA's Resurrection of Program Budgeting: Déjà Vu All Over Again?" *Public Administration Review* 69 (May/June 2009), pp. 435–447. The quotation is on p. 435.

235. Richard P. Nathan, *The Plot That Failed: Nixon and the Administrative Presidency* (New York: John Wiley and Sons, 1975).

236. Larry Berman, "OMB and the Hazards of Presidential Staff Work," *Public Administration Review* 38 (November/December 1978), pp. 520–524.

237. U.S. General Accounting Office, *Performance Budgeting: Past Initiatives Offer Insights for GPRA Implementation*, p. 39.

238. Allen Schick, "A Death in the Bureaucracy: The Demise of Federal PPB," *Public Administration Review* 33 (March/April 1973), pp. 146–156. The quotation is on p. 146.

239. The first major expression of MBO is generally credited to Peter Drucker, *The Practice of Management* (New York: Harper & Row, 1954).

240. Jong S. Jun, "Management by Objectives and the Public Sector, Introduction," *Public Administration Review* 26 (January/February 1976), pp. 1–4. The quotation is on p. 3.

241. Robert Rodgers and John E. Hunter, "A Foundation of Good Management Practice in Government: Management by Objectives," *Public Administration Review* 52 (January/February 1992), pp. 27–39.

242. U.S. General Accounting Office, *Performance Budgeting: Past Initiatives Offer Insights for GPRA Implementation*, p. 45.

243. Theodore H. Poister and Gregory Streib, "MBO in Municipal Government: Variations on the Traditional Management Tool," *Public Administration Review* 55 (January/February 1995), pp. 48–56. The quotation is on p. 55.

244. Aaron Wildavsky and Arthur Hammond, "Comprehensive Versus Incremental Budgeting in the Department of Agriculture," *Administrative Science Quarterly* 10 (December 1965), pp. 321–346.

245. Quoted in Donald F. Haider, "Zero Base: Federal Style," *Public Administration Review* 37 (July/August 1977), pp. 400–406. The quotation is on p. 401.

246. Frank D. Draper and Bernard T. Pitsvada, "ZBB—Looking Back After Ten Years," *Public Administration Review* 41 (January/February 1981), pp. 76–83.

247. Ibid.; and Thomas H. Hammond and Jack H. Knott, *A Zero-Based Look at Zero-Base Budgeting* (New Brunswick, NJ: Transaction, 1980).

248. Robert C. Burns and Robert D. Lee, Jr., "The Ups and Downs of State Budget Process Reform: Experience of Three Decades," *Public Budgeting & Finance* 24 (September 2004), pp. 1–19. Figures (p. 4) are for 1975–2000, and include the District of Columbia.

249. Perry Moore, "Zero-Base Budgeting in American Cities," *Public Administration Review* 40 (May/June 1980), pp. 253–258.

250. U.S. General Accounting Office, *Streamlining Zero-Base Budgeting Will Benefit Decision-Making*, PAD 79-74 (Washington, DC: U.S. Government Printing Office, 1979); and Allen Schick, *Zero-Base 80: The Status of Zero-Base Budgeting in the States* (Washington, DC: National Association of State Budget Officers and The Urban Institute, 1979).

251. U.S. General Accounting Office, *Performance Budgeting: Past Initiatives Offer Insights for GPRA Implementation*, p. 49.

252. Harry P. Hatry, "The Alphabet Soup Approach: You'll Love It!" *Public Manager* 21 (Winter 1992–1993), pp. 8–12.

253. Ibid., p. 9.

254. U.S. General Accounting Office, *Performance Budgeting: Past Initiatives Offer Insight for GPRA Implementation*, p. 49.

255. Lewis, "Reflections on Budget Systems," p. 15.

256. Katherine Barrett and Richard Greene, *The Costs of Cuts: A Column by Barrett and Greene* (Washington, DC: IBM Center for The Business of Government, 2011), http://www.businessof government.org/lesson/cost-cuts.

257. Katherine Barrett and Richard Greene, "Fit for Few," *Governing* (July 2011), pp. 58–59.

258. Barrett and Greene, *The Costs of Cuts*.

259. Much of the following discussion is based on the chapter by Frank Sackton, "Financing Public Programs Under Fiscal Constraints," *Managing Public Programs: Balancing Politics, Administration, and Public Needs*, Robert E. Cleary and Nicholas Henry, eds. (San Francisco, CA: Jossey Bass, 1989), pp. 147–166.

260. Jeffrey L. Brudney, Cynthia J. Bowling, and Deil S. Wright, *Continuity and Change in Public Administration Across the 50 States: Linking Practice, Theory, and Research through the American State Administrators Project, 1964–2008* (Auburn, AL: Center for Governmental Services, Auburn University, 2010), p. 21. Figures are for 1981–1984 and 2001–2004, when states had to cut budgets by about 5 percent per annum.

261. National Commission on the Public Service, *Urgent Business for America: Revitalizing the Federal Government for the 21st Century*, Report of the National Commission on the Public Service (Washington, DC: U.S. Government Printing Office, 2003), p. 36.

262. Kenneth J. Meier, "Executive Reorganization of Government: Impact on Employment and Expenditures," *American Journal of Political Science* 24 (August 1980), pp. 396–412. The quotation is on p. 410. This is a comparison of sixteen reorganized states with sixteen states that did not reorganize.

263. Katherine Barrett and Richard Greene, "Coming Together, Breaking Apart," *Governing* (March 2009), pp. 58–59.

264. Brudney, Bowling, and Wright, *Continuity and Change in Public Administration Across the 50 States*, p. 21.

265. Ibid.

266. Ibid. "Shifting programs" includes intergovernmental agreements.

267. Ibid.; and 60–70 percent of state agencies use prioritization.

268. The sources for the following list are Sackton, "Financing Public Programs Under Fiscal Constraints"; and Paul C. Nutt and Michael F. Hogan, "Downsizing Guidelines Found in a Success Story," *Public Performance & Management Review* 32 (September 2008), pp. 103–131.

269. Nutt and Hogan, "Downsizing Guidelines Found in a Success Story," p. 122.

270. David G. Mathiasen, "The Evolution of the Office of Management and Budget Under President Reagan," *Public Budgeting & Finance* 8 (Autumn 1988), pp. 3–14.

271. Aaron Wildavsky, *Speaking Truth to Power* (Boston, MA: Little Brown, 1979), p. 212.

272. U.S. General Accounting Office, *Performance Budgeting: State Experiences and Implications for the Federal Government*, GAO/AFMD-93-41 (Washington, DC: U.S. Government Printing Office, 1993), p. 1.

273. Julia E. Melkers and Katherine G. Willoughby, "Budgeters' Views of State Performance-Budgeting Systems: Distinctions across Branches," *Public Administration Review* 61 (January/February 2001), pp. 54–64. The quotation is on p. 61. Figure is for 1997.

274. Philip G. Joyce, "The Obama Administration and PBB: Building on the Legacy of Federal Performance-Informed Budgeting?" *Public Administration Review* 71 (May/June 2011), pp. 356–367. The quotation is on p. 53.

275. Donald F. Kettl, *Reinventing Government? Appraising the National Performance Review* (Washington, DC: Brookings, 1994), p. 43.

276. John B. Gilmour and David E. Lewis, "Assessing Performance Budgeting at OMB: The Influence of Politics, Performance, and Program Size," *Journal of Public Administration Research and Theory* 16 (April 2006), pp. 169–186. The quotation is on p. 169.

277. John B. Gilmour and David E. Lewis, "Does Performance Budgeting Work? An Examination of the Office of Management and Budget's PART Scores," *Public Administration Review* 66 (September/October 2006), pp. 742–752. The quotation is on p. 750.

278. Joyce, "The Obama Administration and PBB."

279. Julia C. Melkers and Katherine G. Willoughby, *Staying the Course: The Use of Performance*

Measurement in State Governments (Washington, DC: IBM Center for the Business of Government, 2004).

280. Julia C. Melkers and Katherine G. Willoughby, "The State of the States: Performance-Based Budgeting Requirements in 47 out of 50," *Public Administration Review* 58 (January/February 1998), pp. 66–75. The datum is on p. 68. Hawaii's Executive Budget Act dates to 1970.

281. U.S. General Accounting Office, *Performance Budgeting: State Experiences and Implications for the Federal Government.*

282. U.S. Government Accountability Office, *Performance Budgeting: States' Experiences Can Inform Federal Efforts*, GAO-05-215 (Washington, DC: U.S. Government Printing Office, 2005), p. 9.

283. Yilin Hou, Robin S. Lunsford, Katy C. Sides, *et al.*, "State Performance-Based Budgeting in Boom and Bust Years: An Analytical Framework and Survey of the States," *Public Administration Review* 71 (May/June 2011), pp. 370–388. The quotations are on pp. 370, 377.

284. Yi Lu, Katherine Willoughby, and Sarah Arnett, "Legislating Results: Examining the Legal Systems of PPB Systems in the States," *Public Performance & Management Review* 33 (December 2009), pp. 266–287. Data (p. 275) are for 2008.

285. Ibid., p. 277.

286. Melkers and Willoughby, "Budgeters' Views of State Performance-Budgeting Systems," p. 61. Figures are for 1997.

287. Center on the States, Pew Charitable Trusts, *Trade-off Time: How Four States Continue to Deliver* (Washington, DC: Author, 2009), p. 2.

288. Kenneth A. Kiase and Michael J. Dougherty, "The Impact of Performance Budgeting on State Budget Outcomes," *Journal of Public Budgeting, Accounting, & Financial Management* 20 (Fall 2008), pp. 277–298. The quotation is on p. 295.

289. Anne Spray Kinney and John Ruggini, "Measuring for a Purpose: Trends in Public-Sector Measurement and Management Practices," *Government Finance Review* 24 (August 2008), pp. 14–23. The quotation is on p. 18. Figure is for 2006.

290. Harry P. Hatry, "The Status of Productivity Measurement in the Public Sector," *Public Administration Review* 38 (January/February 1978), pp. 28–33. Figure is for 1977.

291. Alfred Tat-Kei Ho, "PBB in American Local Governments: It's More than a Management Tool," *Public Administration Review* 71 (May/June 2011), pp. 391–401. The quotations are on p. 392. Figures are for 2011.

292. Kearney, "Reinventing Government and Battling Budget Crises." Figure, 29 percent (p. 28), is for 2003.

293. Richard C. Kearney, Barry M. Feldman, and Carmine P. F. Scavo, "Reinventing Government: City Manager Attitudes and Actions," *Public Administration Review* 60 (November/December 2000), pp. 541–542.

294. Theodore H. Poister and Gregory Streib, "Performance Measurement in Municipal Government: Assessing the State of the Practice," *Public Administration Review* 59 (July/August 1999), pp. 325–335.

295. Julia Melkers and Katherine Willoughby, "Models of Performance-Measurements Used in Local Governments: Understanding Budgeting, Communication, and Lasting Effects," *Public Administration Review* 65 (March/April 2005), pp. 180–190. Figure (p. 184) is for 2000.

296. Ho, "PBB in American Local Governments," pp. 391, 399.

297. Wildavsky, *The Politics of the Budgetary Process*, p. 64.

298. The following discussion of budgetary strategy is drawn from ibid. pp. 63–127. Wildavsky calls these "ubiquitous" and "contingent strategies." We think that our terms are clearer.

299. Jeffrey McMurray, Associated Press, "Tight Budgets Heighten Scrutiny of F/A-22 Raptor," *Savannah Morning News* (April 4, 2004). Representative John Murtha is quoted.

300. James C. Garand, Katherine T. Parkhurst, and Rusanne Jourdan Seoud, "Bureaucrats, Policy Attitudes, and Political Behavior: Extension of the Bureau Voting Model of Government Growth," and "Testing the Bureau Voting Model: A Research Note on Federal and State-Local Employees," *Journal of Public Administration Research and Theory* 1 (April 1991), pp. 177–212 and 229–233, respectively.

301. Gregory B. Lewis, "In Search of Machiavellian Milquetoasts: Comparing Attitudes of Bureaucrats and Ordinary People," *Public Administration Review* 50 (March/April 1990), pp. 220–227. The quotation is on p. 222.

302. William A. Niskanen, *Bureaucracy and Representative Government* (Chicago, IL: Aldine Atherton, 1971).

303. Julie Dolan, "The Budget-Minimizing Bureaucrat? Empirical Evidence from the Senior Executive Service," *Public Administration Review* 62 (January/February 2002), pp. 42–50. The quotations are on pp. 45, 42.

304. Jeffrey L. Brudney and Deil S. Wright, "The 'Revolt in Dullsville' Revisited: Lessons for Theory, Practice, and Research from the American State Administrators Project," *Public Administration Review* 70 (January/February 2010), pp. 26–37. The quotations are on p. 31. Data are for 1964–2008.

305. Most of the following discussion of the Congressional Budget Act is drawn from Committee for Economic Development, *The New Congressional Budget Process and the Economy* (New York: Author, 1975).

306. James A. Thurber, "Twenty Years of Congressional Budget Reform," *Public Manager* 25 (Summer 1996), pp. 6–10. The quotation is on p. 6.

307. Joyce, "Congressional Budget Reform," p. 319.

308. Allen Schick, "The Majority Rules: Don't Look Now, but the Congressional Budget Process Is Working," *Brookings Review* 14 (Winter 1996), pp. 42–55. The quotation is on p. 43.

309. James A. Thurber, "Congressional Budget Reform: Impact on the Appropriations Committees," *Public Budgeting & Finance* 17 (September 1997), pp. 62–73. The quotation is on p. 70.

310. Ibid., p. 70.

311. Joyce, "Congressional Budget Reform," pp. 317–325. The quotation is on p. 317. Much of the following discussion is based on this article and Thurber, "Twenty Years of Budget Reform."

312. Roy T. Meyers and Philip G. Joyce, "Congressional Budgeting at Age 30: Is It Worth Saving?" *Public Budgeting & Finance* 25 (December 2005), pp. 68–82. The quotation is on p. 68.

313. Megan Suzanne Lynch, *The "Deeming Resolution": A Budget Enforcement Tool* (Washington, DC: Congressional Research Service, 2011), p. 3.

314. Bill Heniff, Jr., *The Congressional Budget Process Timetable* (Washington, DC:

Congressional Research Service, 2008), p. CRS-2, for 1974–2008 count. Continuing resolutions continued in FY 2009–FY 2012.

315. Gregory Korte, "Congress Examines Budget Process," *USA Today* (October 4, 2011).

316. U.S. Government Accountability Office, *Continuing Resolutions: Uncertainty Limited Management Options and Increased Workload in Selected Agencies*, GAO-09-879 (Washington, DC: U.S. Government Printing Office, 2009). Period analyzed is 1999–2009.

317. Leon Panetta, as quoted in David Ignatius, "Life in Budget Limbo," *Washington Post* (November 1, 2007).

318. U.S. Office of Management and Budget, *Budget of the United States Government: Fiscal Year 2003* (Washington, DC: U.S. Government Printing Office, 2002), p. 6.

319. Joel Achenbach, "Pick a Number, Any Number," *Washington Post* (November 20, 1995).

320. Mark Bloomfield, quoted in Albert B. Crenshaw, "Putting Their Best Guess Forward," *Washington Post* (May 23, 1993). Emphasis is original.

321. As derived from data in Clinton T. Brass, *Shutdown of the Federal Government: Causes, Processes, and Effects*, RL34680 (Washington, DC: U.S. Congressional Research Service, 2011), p. 2. Figure is for FY 1977–FY 2010.

322. James Gerstenzang, "Tiny Gap in Projections Become a Big Issue," *Los Angeles Times* (November 20, 1995).

323. Brass, *Shutdown of the Federal Government*, pp. 6–8.

324. "The Cost of Gridlock," *Newsweek* (January 15, 1996), p. 28.

325. Frederick C. Mosher and Max O. Stephenson, Jr., "The Office of Management and Budget in a Changing Scene," *Public Budgeting & Finance* 2 (December 1982), pp. 23–41. The quotation is on p. 28.

326. Hugh Heclo, "Executive Budget Making," *Federal Budget Policy in the 1980s*, Gregory B. Mills and John L. Palmer, eds. (Washington, DC: Urban Institute, 1984), pp. 255–294.

327. Steven Mufson, "PADs' Wise to Ways of Power," *Washington Post* (April 25, 1990).

328. National Association of State Budget Officers, *Budget Processes in the States* (Washington, DC: Author, 2008), pp. 22, 9. Figures are for 2008.

329. Nelson A. Rockefeller Institute of Government and Pew Center on the States, *States' Revenue Estimating: Cracks in the Crystal Ball* (Albany, NY and Washington, DC: Authors, 2011).

330. Robert Rodgers and Philip Joyce, "The Effect of Underforecasting on the Accuracy of Revenue Forecasts by State Governments," *Public Administration Review* 56 (January/February 1996), pp. 48–56. The quotations are on pp. 48–49. This is an analysis of 336 state revenue forecast errors in all the states, 1975–1992.

331. Nelson A. Rockefeller, Institute of Government and Pew Center on the States, *States' Revenue Estimating*, p. 3.

332. Ibid.

333. Richard T. Boylan, "Political Distortions in State Forecasts," *Public Choice* 136 (September 2008), pp. 411–427. The quotation is on p. 426.

334. Glenn Abney and Thomas P. Lauth, "The End of Executive Dominance in State Appropriations," *Public Administration Review* 58 (September/October 1998), pp. 388–394.

335. As derived from data in National Association of State Budget Officers, *Budget Processes in the States*, pp. 3, 22. Figures are for 2008.

336. William R. Voorhees, "More Is Better: Conceptual Forecasting and State Revenue Forecast Error," *International Journal of Public Administration* 27 (November 2004), pp. 651–671. The quotation is on p. 651.

337. Abney and Lauth, "The End of Executive Dominance in State Appropriations." In 1994, 32 percent of ninety-nine budget officials in both branches said the legislature was dominant, and 31 percent said their influence was about equal.

338. As derived from data in ibid. and Glenn Abney and Thomas P. Lauth, "Perceptions of the Impact of Governors and Legislatures in the Appropriations Process," *Western Political Quarterly* 40 (Fall 1987), pp. 335–342. Figure is for 1982–1994.

339. National Commission on the State and Local Public Service, *Hard Truths/Tough Choices: An Agenda for State and Local Government Reform*, First Report (Albany, NY: Nelson A. Rockefeller Institute of Government, State University of New York, 1993), p. 20.

340. Irene S. Rubin, *The Politics of Public Budgeting: Getting and Spending, Borrowing and Balancing*, 6th ed. (Washington, DC: CQ Press, 2010), p. 129.

341. Katherine G. Willoughby and Mary A. Finn, "Organizational Professionalism and Technological Sophistication: Budget Offices in the South," *Public Productivity & Management Review* 18 (Fall 1994), pp. 19–35. The quotation is on p. 33.

342. Robert D. Lee. Jr., "Educational Characteristics of Budget Office Personnel and State Budgetary Processes," *Public Budgeting & Finance* 11 (September 1991), pp. 69–79 (the data are on pp. 70, 72), and as derived from data in National Association of State Budget Officers, *Budget Processes in the States*, p. 15.

343. Robert D. Lee, Jr., Ronald W. Johnson, and Philip G. Joyce, *Public Budgeting Systems*, 8th ed. (Boston, MA: Jones and Bartlett, 2008), p. 55.

344. Burns and Lee, "The Ups and Downs of State Budget Process Reform," p. 14. Figures include the District of Columbia.

345. Robert D. Lee, Jr. and Robert C. Burns, "U.S. State Budget Directors: Characteristics, Experience, and Attitudes," *Public Budgeting & Finance* 23 (June 2003), pp. 39–52. Figure (p. 42) is for 2000 and includes the District of Columbia.

346. Burns and Lee, "The Ups and Downs of State Budget Process Reform," p. 13. Figures are for 1970–2000 and include the District of Columbia.

347. James J. Gosling, "The State Budget Office and Policy Making," *Public Budgeting & Finance* 7 (March 1987), pp. 51–65.

348. Ronald W. Schack, "Local Government Revenue Estimation Practices," *Municipal Year Book, 2000* (Washington, DC: International City/County Management Association, 2000), pp. 3–7. The quotation is on p. 3.

349. Howard A. Frank and Yongfeng Zhao, "Determinants of Local Government Revenue Forecasting Practice: Empirical Evidence from Florida," *Journal of Public Budgeting, Accounting, & Financial Management* 21 (Spring 2009), pp. 17–35. The quotation is on p. 17.

350. Killian and Choudhury, "Continuity and Change in the Role of City Managers," p. 13. Figures are for 2010.

351. W. Bartley Hildreth, Samuel J. Yeager, Gerald R. Miller, *et al.*, "Implications of Successful Career Paths of Top Local Government Finance Managers," *Public Budgeting & Finance* 30 (December 2010), pp. 82–97.

352. David S. T. Matkin, "Before There Was Enron, There Was Orange County: A Study of Local Government Financial-Oversight Committees," *Public Budgeting & Finance* 30 (September 2010), pp. 27–50. The quotation is on p. 27.

353. U.S. Advisory Commission on Intergovernmental Relations, *State Laws Governing Local Government Structure and Administration*, pp. 41–47. Data are for 1990.

354. Rubin, *The Politics of Public Budgeting*, pp. 130–138. The quotation is on p. 133.

355. As derived from data in U.S. Bureau of Labor Statistics, *Occupational Employment Statistics* (Washington, DC: U.S. Government Printing Office, 2011), http://stats.bls.gov/oes/current/oes. Figures are for 2010.

356. Dawes, *The First Year of the Budget of the United States*, p. ii.

357. Michael A. Miller, "The Public/Private Pay Debate: What Do the Data Show?" *Monthly Labor Review* 119 (May 1996), pp. 18–29. Refers to state and local budget analysts only. The other profession is personnel specialists.

358. Dawes, *The First Year of the Budget of the United States*, p. ii.

Managing Human Capital in the Public and Nonprofit Sectors

Sixty-six percent of all Americans have jobs, and nearly 15 percent of this labor force, or almost 22.5 million workers, are employed by governments.[1] Managing them is a challenge of no modest dimensions.

Public personnel administration, or *public personnel management*, is the planning and policymaking for, and managing of, governmental employees and often is limited to "traditional internal processes," such as recruitment and compensation.[2] During the 1980s, a more modish moniker emerged: *public human resource* (or *resources*) *management*, a "people-focused" form of governmental personnel system dedicated to developing "the kind of workforce needed in government" through such "external" means as performance appraisals and professional development.[3] Currently, *public human capital management* is in fashion, which is the administration of public employees as governmental "assets whose value can be enhanced through investment," and the alignment of public personnel policies with the fulfillment of an agency's mission.[4]

Personnelists, or professionals and specialists in the field, often use these terms interchangeably, as do we, but they do have differences: Each successive title represents a broader concept that places an increasing emphasis on the worth of public employees.

WHO WANTS TO WORK FOR GOVERNMENT? AND WHO DOES?

Although the pool of talented and committed people who want to work for government may be shrinking, governments nonetheless are hiring well.

Who Wants to Work for Government?

For every American who would like to work in government (a group in which veterans, minorities, and Democrats are overrepresented), three would rather work in business.[5]

Young People and Public Service Young adults also display a significant interest in government service, with almost all surveys taken over a dozen years indicating that from a third to two-fifths find it appealing,[6] perhaps because they are receiving increasing encouragement to enter it. Over thirteen years, the proportion of Americans who would recommend government to young people starting their careers doubled, from two-fifths[7] to four-fifths.[8]

On a more intimate plane, however, only 11 percent of parents rank government as the *most* desirable career choice.[9] This is disturbing, as 33 percent, a plurality, of young adults would give "a great deal of consideration" to a parental request to enter government service.[10]

Teachers and professors, at 24 percent, are more than twice as positive than parents about government as the best career for young people,[11] 27 percent of whom would give a great deal of consideration to their recommendation.[12]

Able but Uninterested Talent counts. A classic analysis found that a superior manager or professional produced 48 percent more output than an average one.[13]

So, if public agencies are to be more productive, they must attract talented applicants.

Are most people with talent interested in working for government? The evidence suggests, not really.

Young Adults More highly educated young Americans seem less attracted to government employment than do young people in general. Although undergraduates' leading choice out of an impressive forty-six possible "industries" in which they "ideally" would want to work following graduation is "government/public service," only a modest 17 percent of undergraduates actually choose it.[14] Worse, only a slender 5 percent of top undergraduates rank government as their "most preferred employer," compared with seven times more (34 percent) who prefer large corporations.[15]

Of course, there are many young adults who want work that will help better society, but, as we noted in Chapter 2, the independent sector stakes a much greater claim on these youthful ambitions than does the public one. Thirty-five percent, a plurality, of young adults are "extremely or very interested" in working for a community service organization, compared with just 23 percent who say the same about working for the federal government, and an even lower 19 percent who say this about local government.[16]

Other Able Cohorts Other well-qualified cohorts also evidence little enthusiasm for the civil service. An astonishing 56 percent of corporate and nonprofit managers are not (21 percent), or "not at all" (35 percent), interested in working for the federal government, and only 17 percent express any interest in doing so. These managers (as well as young adults and professionals in fields that are particularly relevant to federal agencies) rank Washington "lowest" in its "ability to provide a competitive environment, innovation and creativity, and attracting the best and brightest, in comparison with the private and nonprofit sectors."[17]

Who Works for Government?

In light of these depressing trends, have governments hired and kept people of competency and commitment?

Acquiring Public Talent Although, as we discuss later, government employees are frustrated by what they consider to be applicant pools that offer minimal talent and problematic hiring procedures, it appears that, in general, governments are hiring fairly well.

Some Good News The proportion of federal workers who think that their agencies are "able to recruit people with the right skills" has held constant at about 45 percent, a plurality, over the years (28 percent believe otherwise).[18] The number of federal executives and top professionals who are hired from outside the federal government who think that the quality of federal supervisors is better than in their last place of employment surpasses by almost three-to-one those who think that it is worse, and more than twice as many of them think that the quality of their federal co-workers is better than in their former workplace than think it is worse.[19]

The bulk of objective evidence suggests that the federal workforce remains one of high quality. Almost half of all entering federal employees have college degrees in specifically relevant fields.[20] There is "little difference in the education levels and grade point averages" among applicants who accept offers of federal employment and those who decline them in favor of other options, indicating that Washington competes successfully with other employers in hiring.[21] The major reason for the proportional expansion over sixteen years of employees who occupy higher positions in the federal hierarchy is the rise in the quality of its administrators.[22]

A Caveat Even though, as we noted earlier, private-sector managers express some contempt for federal employment, a solid majority of upper-level new federal hires (59 percent)[23] and a dominating plurality of entry-level ones (40 percent)[24] are drawn directly from the private sector. State administrators and professionals who were hired directly from corporations typically supervised few corporate subordinates, and their switch often entailed a public-sector promotion.[25] Overwhelmingly, these sector switchers cite "job security" as their leading motivation for making the switch.[26]

Do these patterns imply that the public sector has a special attraction for managers whose corporate careers are stuttering, or even stuck, and only then does government become their belated second choice? It is an all-the-more intriguing question when we realize that only 3 percent of upper-level new federal hires,[27] and 4 percent of entry-level ones,[28] are drawn from the independent sector—the sector that, as we noted in Chapter 4, far surpasses the other two in terms of its employees' disdain for job security and their strong need for socially meaningful work.

Keeping Public Talent Have governments been able to retain their more capable employees, or are they departing for other sectors? The patterns are mixed.

Although about 1 percent of federal employees claim that they plan to leave the government within the year,[29] few actually do so, and those who do depart may not be the best and brightest. There is "no evidence to support the conclusion that the federal government is losing its most capable employees," a finding "consistent with previous research on the exit quality of federal employees."[30]

Regrettably, the same cannot be said for state and local governments, where there is a brain drain. States are losing high-quality male employees and managers, and local governments are losing high-quality minority and female employees and clerical workers.[31]

THE EVOLUTION OF PUBLIC HUMAN CAPITAL MANAGEMENT

The evolution of public human resources management in the United States can be roughly divided into six phases.

Government by Gentlemen, 1789–1829

The United States' first half-dozen presidents favored "government by gentlemen,"[32] or those who were reputed to be persons of character and competence, qualities that were defined largely by a respected family background and a high degree of formal education. Being a member of the establishment counted for a lot: During the country's first forty years, almost two-thirds of the, eighty to a hundred or so, top appointees were drawn from the landed gentry, merchant, and professional classes.[33]

Government by Spoilers, 1829–1883

Even as they were being governed by gentlemen, however, Americans were growing less gentlemanly in their politics. When independence was declared in 1776, over four-fifths of the states required that, to vote, men must own land or have paid taxes (often the two were one and the same), but by 1830, only half of the states retained these stipulations. As a result, far more men could vote, and many could not be described as gentlemen. When combined with a populist candidate—in the form of Andrew Jackson in the election of 1828—voting turnout more than tripled from the previous election and surpassed half of all eligible voters for the first time.[34]

These fundamental political changes meant only one thing: spoils. If presidents were to emerge, like Jackson, from the class that earned its own living, then politics had to be made to pay.

Contrary to conventional wisdom, however, Jackson maintained past establishmentarian patterns, dismissing about the same share of political appointees as had his gentlemanly predecessors.[35] John Tyler (1841–1845) was the first president who implemented a comprehensive spoils system, a practice that reached its apex with the presidency of Abraham Lincoln (1861–1865), whose "sweep of people from office was the most extensive in United States history,"[36] but spoils continued to mar government for the next several decades.

It is difficult for those of us reared in an environment of largely honest government to appreciate the extent—and the brazenness—of the spoils system. After an election, newspaper advertising typically swelled with such announcements as, "WANTED—A GOVERNMENT CLERKSHIP at a salary of not less that $1000 per annum. Will give $100 to anyone securing me such a position." Following the election of 1880, newly elected President James A. Garfield, according to a government archive, found "hungry office-seekers lying in wait for him like vultures for a wounded bison."[37]

Government by the Good, 1883–1906

The corrupt excesses of the spoils system eventually resulted in a reform movement, beginning in1865, determined to rid government of those bureaucrats who owed their office to nothing more than party hackwork. The assassination of President Garfield by a deranged office seeker in 1881 effectively assured national civil service reform.

A Very American Reform: The Civil Service Act of 1883

Just two years following Garfield's assassination, Congress passed the Civil Service Act, which created a bipartisan Civil Service Commission charged with creating a nonpartisan federal service.

Although the Civil Service Act of 1883 had been influenced by the British system of public service, the Senate inserted some major provisos that were uniquely American.

One such clause was that civil service examinations must be "practical in character," a requisite that would provide the basis for a future system of position classification.

The Senate also omitted the British requirement that an applicant could enter the federal service only at the lowest grade, thereby paving the way for "in-and-outers," who could enjoy "lateral entry" into high offices in an "open" civil service.

Again in contrast to Britain and Western Europe, no tracks were laid between the public service and the universities. A major effort to upgrade the educational level of the federal service began, eventually, in the 1930s.

Finally, the act set up no special "administrative class" of "permanent undersecretaries." Political neutrality was not upheld at the potential expense of social responsiveness—nor, regrettably, experienced professionalism. Instead, the top bureaucratic echelons were occupied by political executives appointed by the president.

Long-Lasting Legacies

"Government by the good"[38] led, in 1907, to President Theodore Roosevelt's Civil Service Rule I, which prohibited almost seven out of ten federal workers from participating in political campaigns (a prohibition lifted in 1993[39]) and barred the solicitation of political contributions from federal employees. These reforms were strengthened and broadened by the Political Activities Act, also known as the Hatch Act, of 1939.

In 1940, the Hatch Act was amended to extend its coverage to state and local workers whose salaries are paid primarily with federal funds and to prohibit these employees from running for public office if their salaries are even partially paid with federal funds.

All the states have enacted their own legislation that restricts in various ways their public employees' political activities, including thirty-six states that have passed "little Hatch Acts" that reflect the federal version.[40]

Over time, civil service commissions, and the personnel departments that they spawned, became associated "with morality, with a connotation of 'goodness' vs. 'badness,' quite apart from the purposes for which people were employed."[41] To put it crassly but clearly: The bureaucrats responsible for keeping government moral and apolitical, and the bureaucrats responsible for getting a job done, became increasingly distinct entities.

Government by Scientific Managers, 1906–1937

Despite government by the good, good government remained elusive. In 1912, an analyst decried the "snail like pace" of government employees, alleging that they wasted from 40 to 70 percent of their work time.[42]

The influential New York Bureau of Municipal Research (detailed in Chapter 2), a privately supported think tank founded in 1906, agreed with this assessment, and its first forays focused on getting public "workers to do the work they were hired to do," a focus that quickly incorporated a "strong link between the bureau and scientific management."[43] "Science" thus entered the world of public personnel administration. Scientific principles of public administration were part of an inconsistent but soothing amalgam of civil-service beliefs that packed merit, morality, neutrality, and efficiency into one conceptual lump.

It was, nonetheless, a likable lump, and it left legacies. A major one is the position classification system, first adopted by Chicago in 1912, and which has been described as "the ascendancy of scientific management."[44] The council-manager form of local government emerged as a direct outgrowth of the period's precepts; the first government to adopt a council-manager plan was Sumter, South Carolina, in 1912, and by 1930, 418 local governments had adopted it.[45]

Certainly government by scientific managers served to extend the reach and power of the Civil Service System. Between 1900 and 1930: the proportion of federal civilian employees administered by the Civil Service Commission shot from 46 to 80 percent;[46] the number of states that had merit systems expanded from two to nine;[47] and cities with civil service commissions nearly quadrupled from 65 to 250.[48]

Government by Policymaking Administrators, 1937–1955

In 1937, the report of the president's Committee on Administrative Management was published, and "administration" was introduced to the public service.

In the Service of Public Administrators

"Administration" implied that personnel managers should use their skills to help line administrators administer more effectively.

In 1938, President Franklin D. Roosevelt issued Executive Order 7916, which required the establishment of professionally staffed personnel offices in each major agency. The first Hoover Commission was appointed in 1949, and "little Hoover commissions" in many states soon followed, all of which promoted, usually successfully, the emplacement in each agency of personnel directors who reported to its top administrator.

Acknowledging Power There was more. "Administration" also expressed the long-denied reality that public administrators make public policy.

Although Roosevelt's Committee on Administrative Management bowed briefly to the belief, still widely held, that politics and administration were separate entities, it also concentrated on those administrative "positions which are actually policy-determining" (consistency, evidently, was dismissed as the hobgoblin of small minds).[49]

When, in 1953, Dwight D. Eisenhower, a Republican, assumed the presidency after two decades of Democratic government, he "laid bare with shocking results the problems of political transition."[50] Ike discovered, maddeningly, a huge civilian bureaucracy that had more than quadrupled in size since the last Republican administration,[51]

and which was run by entrenched Democratic policymakers, who, perversely, were protected by civil service regulations that were based on the premise that politics should not intrude on administration. Although academia during this period was just beginning to recognize that bureaucrats made public policy, elected policymakers clearly understood that they did.

Government by Professionals, 1955–Present

By mid-century, another value was entering the milieu of public personnel administration: professionalism.

The professional period encompasses two distinct systems of public human resource management. One is *Specialized Public Professional Systems*, or those public personnel systems that are geared to the career needs of highly educated specialists. The other is the *Professional Public Administration System*, which reflects the idea that human resource systems should encourage the effective and efficient management by competent generalist administrators. They are two of five systems of public human capital management, each with its own values and mission, that we review next.

THE CIVIL SERVICE SYSTEM: THE MEANING OF MERIT

The civil service has been the historic heart of public administration. The general *Civil Service System*, or *merit system* (a phrase that emphasizes the values of public service, in contrast to its bureaucratic structure), is career personnel who have tenure and who are administered according to "traditional merit practices."[52]

The Meaning of Merit

Just what are these practices?

The Position Most centrally, the overriding practice of the merit system is its emphasis on the position. The Civil Service System assumes that government positions can be objectively and correctly classified.

Fairness as Classification Public personnel managers hold dear one value that eclipses all others: "Equity."[53] *Equity* is defined as equal work for equal pay—in other words, the job classification system. Line agency administrators, by contrast, value productivity. Ultimately, preserving equity and boosting productivity are at odds.

Hiring and Promoting by Score Entry into, and promotion in, the civil service is determined by the "merit" of applicants, and merit, traditionally, is determined by the score that one earns on competitive examinations. Gender, race, religion, family, politics, connections, and other nonmeritorious factors are not merely irrelevant but are actively suppressed. Egalitarianism and political neutrality reign.

A Sovereign Civil Service The "merit principle," as it often is called, also demands that human capital management be sovereign and separate from the rest of government, and that the staffing decisions made by personnel administrators must be unilateral and final. If the civil service were not independent and powerful, this logic holds, a more partisan and corrupt government would be the unacceptable consequence.

Personnel Administrators Rule! Sounds good, but there were problems. Most notably, a sovereign civil service grew obsessed with writing and imposing rules on every other agency. By the 1990s, the federal government's chief human resources bureau, the Office of Personnel Management (OPM), had filled a staggering 10,000 pages with its regulations, a practice emulated by personnel offices in state and local governments as well.[54] These swamps of civil service rules reflected the disturbing reality that "compliance with regulations" had become "the central focus of the personnel system."[55]

The Murkiness of Merit These essentially ethical and faith-based (faith, that is, in science, not religion) values underlie the Civil Service System. As we shall see throughout this chapter, however, "developments since World War II have befogged the meaning of merit principles and confused the content of merit systems."[56]

The Profession of Public Human Capital Management

There are 95,600 human capital managers and professionals who work in government, comprising 12 percent of all personnel employees.[57]

Over two-fifths of these civil service administrators and professionals are women, more than nine out of ten are college graduates, and they have long career histories in their field and in government.[58] Public personnel employees appear to have a high job satisfaction (and with some reason—they are one of only two categories of public professionals whose salaries are comparable with those of their corporate counterparts[59]), and most perceive their jobs as being a long-term career.[60]

What do governments' human capital managers do? Their major duties, listed in the order of the most time that they devote to them, are recruiting and hiring; benefits administration; pay administration; developing human resources policy; position classification; training and development; processing grievances; and performance appraisals, among other activities.[61]

Recruiting Bureaucrats

Recruiting new talent into the public sector could stand some improvement. Three-fifths of young adults report that no one, including government, has ever asked them if they would consider working in government.[62]

Federal Recruiting As much as a third of all federal job openings are never publicly announced;[63] more than half of those that are announced appear for only two weeks or less;[64] 44 percent of the announcements for supervisory positions provide "no substantive information about the nature of the position's supervisory responsibilities";[65] and the feds themselves rate only 2 percent of their job announcements as "good" in terms of quality (53 percent are ranked as "poor").[66] "Consequently, many announcements can actually discourage potential applicants from applying for Federal jobs."[67]

State Recruiting The states are introducing major reforms designed to decentralize and simplify recruiting. A plurality of states, twenty-two, have decentralized recruitment to the agencies, and another eighteen share this responsibility with the central personnel bureau.[68] Nevertheless, nearly four out of ten state agency heads think that the complexity of personnel procedures is their most serious impediment for recruiting.[69]

Local Recruiting Local governments have focused on proactive recruitment. Six out of ten cities and counties post job vacancies on their web sites.[70] Most local governments use internships as a recruiting tool.[71]

Hiring Bureaucrats

Hiring well is one of the public sector's more vexing issues.

Applicant Pools The hiring challenge starts with who is available for hire. Almost two-fifths of federal managers cite a "shortage of qualified applicants" as their "primary obstacle in hiring employees"; no other obstacle to hiring comes remotely close to this one.[72]

The situation may be much the same for state governments. Twenty-two percent of new hires in state governments are not retained during the probationary period, suggesting a possible problem in hiring public personnel of high quality that begins with the applicant pool.[73]

Federal Hiring Seventy-four percent of Americans rate the ability of federal agencies to attract "the best employees" as just fair to poor (only 15 percent rank them as good to excellent),[74] and a startling 21 percent of federal workers think that the process by which they themselves were hired was "unfair"—these are the people who were *hired*, not rejected—a percentage that is at least three times greater than those in businesses and nonprofit organizations.[75]

Systemic problems have bedeviled federal recruitment and hiring for decades. The main ones follow.

Federal Fragmentation The federal government has no standard job application form, and nearly two-fifths of college students do not understand those forms that it does have.[76] These forms must be submitted to one of more than 200 *hiring*, or *appointment*, *authorities*, each of which has its own hiring procedures.[77] In one agency, the hiring process had 110 steps involving 45 people.[78]

Confused Applicants Unsurprisingly, 57 percent of federal employees found their hiring process to be "confusing," about double the percentages in the nonprofit and private sectors.[79] Even when Washington does find "outstanding candidates, the complexity of the hiring process often drives all but the most dedicated away."[80]

A Glacial Process Nearly four-fifths of federal employees describe their hiring process as "slow," a proportion that is significantly higher than those of corporate and nonprofit workers who say this.[81] Nearly a third of entry-level new hires cite "the length of the process" as the "greatest obstacle" in their federal job search, far outdistancing any other hurdle.[82]

Sickly Screening When government uses robust selection procedures (and, for that matter, business, too[83]), the productivity of its managers and professionals increases by an impressive 17 percent.[84] Regrettably, federal screening is more mealy than meaningful.

There is no uniform process for assessing candidates' qualifications, but most federal agencies rely on the *unassembled examination*,[85] which ranks applicants based on their self-reported education and experience. It is "the least effective available predictor of job performance."[86]

Federal "surveys suggest that agency… screening practices may be harming…the quality of applicant pools."[87] An astonishing 44 percent of the supervisors who supervise new federal hires had no say in hiring them! Unsurprisingly, only 71 percent of these supervisors are "very satisfied" with their new hires, compared with 80 percent who were involved in the hiring decision.[88] Senior federal executives appear to be hired with even more laxity: "18-year old military recruits undergo more rigorous behavioral and leadership testing than those who will manage huge budgets."[89]

Young People Need Not Apply   Two decades ago, the chief federal personnel administrator characterized the finding of an entry-level federal administrative position as "intellectually confusing, procedurally nightmarish, inaccessible to students and very difficult to explain."[90] It still is.

Although President Barack Obama pledged to young Americans that he wanted "to make Government cool again,"[91] it is not at all clear that federal recruiters yearn to reach beyond their own bureaucracies for new, young public administrators. When federal managers have vacant positions, more than seven out of every ten do not hire external candidates, but instead select federal employees to fill them.[92]

The two major federal student employment programs, which average some 60,000 participants per year, have "squandered" this human capital and send just 7 percent of them to permanent federal jobs; by contrast, 50 percent of private-sector interns are hired as permanent employees.[93] Fewer than a fourth of all new federal hires are hired for entry-level professional and administrative positions, less than a quarter of whom enter federal service immediately after graduation from college, and their average age is a mature thirty-three.[94]

As a consequence, the proportion of federal civilian workers who are twenty-nine or younger has been nearly halved, from 15 to 8 percent, in just twenty-five years.[95] By contrast, 12 percent of local government employees, 15 percent of state workers, and 24 percent of private-sector employees are under thirty years of age. "The federal government workforce is older, on average, than any other sector of employees in the United States."[96]

A Less Irrational Federal Future?   There may be some reason to hope that federal hiring is becoming less irrational. In 2000, Executive Order 13162 created the Federal Career Intern Program, and it has become the channel of choice for new bureaucratic blood. Since 2007, it has accounted for fully half of all entry-level new hires,[97] with the remainder entering federal service through appointment authorities whose percentages are "each in the single digits."[98]

In 2010, President Obama directed all agencies to dramatically shorten hiring schedules; simplify résumé-format requirements; and reach out to campuses for recruits.[99] It is, perhaps, a start.

Hiring in the States   For every applicant that state governments hire, an average of twenty-three apply,[100] indicating a reasonably competitive selection process.

"Agencies in almost all states [forty-seven] have complete authority to select a candidate for an open position."[101] Despite these efforts to decentralize hiring to the agencies, almost three out of ten state agency heads consider complicated procedures to be the greatest obstacle in hiring well.[102]

Classifying Bureaucrats

Once hired, bureaucrats are classified. Position classification is a core tenet of the Civil Service System. Indeed, employees in the civil service are also known as "classified" employees.

Washington's General Schedule   Until 1923, when the Classification Act was enacted, federal supervisors had unlimited autonomy to determine the pay of workers, and federal employees were growing increasingly angry about their lack of rigor and, often, fairness. The Classification Act authorized the Civil Service Commission to group public positions into rational classes, and pay the occupants of these classifications accordingly.

A more comprehensive Classification Act was enacted in 1949. It established the dominant classification and pay system for the federal government, the General Schedule. The General Schedule is composed of fifteen grades for white-collar workers, and within these grades there are more than 450 job categories called "series." At the very top are the 8,000 members of the Senior Executive and Senior Foreign services, each with their own classification systems. Blue-collar and Postal Service employees, and about twenty agencies, also have their own systems.

Classifying at the Grass Roots   All state governments have position classification systems. Eight states have decentralized the responsibility for classifying positions from their central personnel office to the agencies, and another eight distribute this duty between their human capital and line agencies.[103]

A dozen states require their cities to adopt classification plans,[104] although almost all local governments of any size have them.

Paying Bureaucrats

The classification of bureaucrats by position is the foundation for determining their pay. The appendix has detailed information on governmental salaries at all levels.

Perhaps the most significant issue of public pay is its comparability with private-sector pay. (Comparable public pay is much less an issue with the independent sector, where, as we detailed in Chapter 5, compensation averages more than a fourth less than in government.[105]) One must enter prudently this thorny thicket. A review of the literature of comparable pay revealed that its "conclusions may be more closely linked to methodology and ideology than is desirable."[106] Nevertheless, some conclusions seem unambiguous, and we discuss them here.

The Federal Experience By the 1980s, federal salaries were falling well behind those in business, and large numbers of federal executives were leaving for the private sector because of it.[107] In 1990, Congress addressed these problems by enacting the Federal Employees Pay Comparability Act, which set federal pay by a position's comparability with the private sector and by locality (85 percent of federal employees work in places other than the District of Columbia[108]).

Although two-thirds of federal employees report that they are satisfied with their pay,[109] an increase of nearly three-fifths from just prior to the passage of the Federal Employees Pay Comparability Act,[110] this trend has little to do with the act. In the words of a normally sober-sided analyst, "the unwillingness of any recent administration to comply with the provisions and intent" of this "anemic" law is "egregious." The act "has not been fully implemented and, consequently, is a farce."[111]

In fact, the compensation of federal executives is not even "on a par...with counterpart positions in state or local government."[112] Consider just two examples: The salaries of state university presidents and city managers, other than in the smallest

colleges and towns, commonly exceed those of federal cabinet secretaries.

The State and Local Experience On a general plane, public workers at the grass roots are paid well. The total compensation costs (i.e., pay plus benefits) for state and local government employees are 51 percent higher than those of private-sector workers; salaries and wages are 43 percent higher, and benefits are 73 percent higher. These disparities are attributable to the public sector's greater proportion of jobs that require higher levels of education or physical risk, and heavier unionization.[113]

When we compare state and local employees with private employees *who are working in the same jobs*, however, then the grass-roots workers fare far less well. State employees are paid, on average, 11 percent less than their private-sector counterparts who are working in the same positions, and their total compensation is nearly 7 percent less. Local government workers are paid, on average, 12 percent less than their corporate colleagues with the same jobs, and their overall compensation is more than 7 percent less.[114]

As in Washington, the higher that one ascends the grass-roots hierarchy, the wider this gap grows. A massive analysis found that "the differences in pay between the two sectors were most pronounced in the higher paid professional and administrative jobs." Indeed, in 95 percent of these positions, public pay was lower than private pay, and, in the remaining 5 percent, government's pay merely "approached" the private sector's pay for the same positions.[115]

In another unfortunate parallel with the federal experience, the compensation of state and local government employees, especially administrators and professionals, has, since the late 1980s, been steadily declining relative to their counterparts in the private sector.[116]

Training Bureaucrats

Training workers to improve their workplace skills is closely and clearly linked with organizational productivity,[117] and the more productive organizations devote significant resources to training. "The most effective private firms" spend from 3 to 5 percent of their budgets on training.[118] The Australian government—often cited as a model of efficient and effective public administration—spends an impressive 5 percent of its budget on employee training, and Australians cite upgraded training as being the "most useful" of their government's innovations.[119]

Training heightens state and local government employees' job satisfaction and organizational commitment and lowers their inclination to consider quitting their jobs[120]—not a surprising correlation in light of the fact that, as government training expenditures rise, so do promotion rates, and significantly so.[121] Sixty percent of local government employees who receive training benefits report that they "like their jobs very much," compared with only 48 percent who do not receive such benefits.[122]

Training Feds Most federal in-service training emerged when the Government Employees Training Act was enacted in 1958, and today there are Management Development Centers and a Federal Executive Institute dedicated to training federal administrators. Washington spends a modest 1.3 percent of its "personnel budget" on training,[123] and, worse, federal administrators are prone to focus on agency training programs when they need to cut budgets, and to cut them back more than other programs.[124]

The proportion of federal workers who say that they need more training to do their jobs rose from less than a third in the early nineties to almost half by the end of the decade and has been stuck at that level ever since.[125] More than a third of new supervisors receive no formal training at all, and, of the 64 percent who are trained, almost half are trained for just a week or less.[126]

Somewhat more than half of federal workers consistently express satisfaction with their training, a proportion that falls short of the two-thirds of private-sector employees who are satisfied with their training.[127]

Training at the Grass Roots State governments devote, on average, "more than 1.3 percent" of their annual payrolls to training, a conservative calculation, with some states spending "upwards of 5 percent." Average state training expenditures per employee nearly doubled over just three years.[128]

State administrators spend an average of twenty-five hours a year in "formal classroom training."[129] Although the states seem serious about training, determining training needs and whether the training was effective need strengthening.[130] "Unfortunately, many states" copy a questionable federal tradition and "report that the training budget is the first thing eliminated in spending freezes or budget cuts."[131]

Forty-six states impose training requirements on municipal employees, and forty-five do so for county employees. Most require training only for police and firefighters; only seven states impose training requirements for "other" city employees, and thirteen for county employees other than police officers.[132]

Some training programs for state and local administrators are conducted in-house or by professional societies and private consultants, but many (likely most) are done by universities.[133] About four-fifths of state and local officials report that they have used university-based institutes for a variety of services and rank them as comparable to services furnished by the private sector, but they accord their very highest marks to university-based training programs.[134]

Bolstering Bureaucrats' Bravery

Whistle-blowers, who are found in all sectors, are a courageous (some would say crazy) class of employee who "blow the whistle" on their organizations for engaging in shoddy or corrupt practices.

Does Whistle-Blowing Work? Whistle-blowing works. Although it is less effective when corruption is deeply rooted,[135] more than half of all whistle-blowing, regardless of sector, results in an external investigation. More than three-fifths of whistle-blowers see evidence of positive change within their organizations after they blew the whistle.[136] Washington has collected an impressive $27 billion as the direct result of blown whistles.[137]

Encouraging Whistle-Blowing In light of these billions in recovered dollars, the federal, state, and local governments have enacted laws that encourage whistle-blowing.

Federal Encouragement The most significant legislation that Congress has passed is the *1986 amendments to the False Claims Act* of 1863. They permit the federal government to award whistle-blowers from 15 to 30 percent of any money recovered from fraudulent practices, with the exception of tax fraud, that they report in any federally funded contract or program.

These amendments have been quite effective. Prior to their passage, only three out of every ten federal workers who observed an illegal or wasteful activity reported it, but, following their enactment, fully half did so.[138] A decade after their enactment, more than 1,100 companies were exposed by whistle-blowers for defrauding the government, compared with just twenty during the previous decade.[139]

The *Tax Relief and Health Care Act* of 2006 extends the False Claims Act's policies to whistle-blowers who report tax fraud involving at least $2 million. Each year, the Internal Revenue Service (IRS) receives nearly 500 tips on more than 1,900 alleged tax cheaters that meet this threshold,[140] but "about 66 percent" of all claims that had been submitted three to four years earlier "were still in process."[141] The IRS states that its lack of follow-through is the result of its extending greater appeals rights to those accused,[142] but critics charge that enforcement "has been hampered by excessive secrecy and continuing animosity within the agency's old guard."[143]

The *Fraud Enforcement and Recovery Act* of 2009 expands the scope of the False Claims Act by allowing the feds to share pertinent information with whistle-blowers and state agencies, thereby raising incentives and lowering barriers for prospective whistle-blowing.

Grass-Roots' Encouragement State and local legislatures also promote whistle-blowing. Twenty-seven states (eight of which limit themselves to Medicaid fraud), the District of Columbia, and the cities of Chicago and New York, have enacted laws that reward whistle-blowers.[144]

The Whistle-Blowers The typical whistle-blower is a well-educated family man in his late forties who has been in his organization about seven years[145] and has a strong belief in "universal moral standards."[146]

Most whistle-blowers in American governments have a stronger public service motivation

(described in Chapter 5), higher pay, and higher levels of education than those who do not blow whistles.[147] There are not many of them. Whistle-blowers account for only a "tiny" 9 percent of all the initial reports exposing unethical or illegal conduct in public agencies, far fewer than those exposures that result from routine inspections and audits.[148]

The Retaliators No one enjoys hearing the shrill screech of whistles being blown on them. What sorts of persons and organizations retaliate against whistle-blowers?

People exposed by whistle-blowers are more likely to retaliate when they perceive the whistle-blowers to be "strong threats" to their egos or to "a prosperous system," and possess high levels of "Machiavellianism," among other factors.[149]

If the organization itself has "high levels of group cohesiveness," a "highly unethical climate," or there exists a shared perception that unethical behavior is legitimate, then the probability of retaliation also grows.[150] The more entrenched the organizational corruption, the more vicious the vengeance leveled against those who expose it.[151]

Shielding Whistle-Blowers Because whistle-blowing can be rough, tough, and perilous, Congress and state legislatures have taken steps to shield whistle-blowers from reprisals. Doing so is critically important because the more that potential whistle-blowers fear retaliation (which is the single greatest damper in reporting misconduct[152]), the more that misconduct flourishes in the organization.[153]

Shielding Federal Whistle-Blowers There are several laws designed to protect federal whistle-blowers. The first was the *Civil Service Reform Act* of 1978, which created, for the first time, "specific statutory provisions that directly addressed the issue of retaliation against Federal employees who blow the whistle." Because not one case was made to protect whistle-blowers after 1979, a disgusted Congress passed the stronger *Whistleblower Protection Act* in 1989. More recent legislation that protects whistle-blowers includes the *Notification and Federal Employee Antidiscrimination and Retaliation (No FEAR) Act* of 2002, which requires agencies to be more accountable for violations of whistle-blower protection laws. The *American Recovery and Reinvestment Act* of 2009 shields nonfederal employees from retaliation when they expose wasteful, dangerous, or illegal acts in the use of economic recovery funds.

Shielding Whistle-Blowers at the Grass Roots Thirty-seven states also have passed an odd mishmash of laws that protect whistle-blowers. Twenty-one apply these laws to both public- and private-sector whistle-blowers; eight state governments and the District of Columbia protect only their own employees; seven cover whistle-blowers who work in any government, but none who are privately employed; and one, North Dakota, shields only private-sector employees.[154]

Have Legal Protections Helped? Consider the sad lot of whistle-blowers before laws that successfully protected them were enacted. A survey of more whistle-blowers than in "any previous survey" in all sectors (74 percent of whom worked in governments and 5 percent in the independent sector), which was conducted just prior to the passage of the Whistleblower Protection Act, found that after whistle-blowers blew the whistle 95 percent of them in all sectors reported some form of retaliation; more than three-fifths lost their jobs; over half became mired in personally-costly proceedings for two years; nearly a third sought psychiatric counseling; and almost a fifth were harassed or transferred.[155]

Subsequent legislation seems to have substantially alleviated this suffering. During the first year in which the Whistleblower Protection Act went into effect, there were more allegations of reprisals made by whistle-blowers that were upheld by administrative law judges than were upheld in the *ten* years before the act was passed![156] In 1989, the year that the act was passed, nearly 7 percent of whistle-blowers who had disclosed "health/safety danger or unlawful behavior" in their agencies felt that they were retaliated against.[157] That figure has since been more than halved, and today just 3 percent of federal whistle-blowers perceive reprisals stemming from their "whistle blowing activity,"[158] an inarguably low proportion when compared with the private sector, where 15 percent (a rising percentage)

of workers believe that they were retaliated against because they had reported misconduct.[159]

What Happens to Whistle-Blowers? Here is how an unusually courageous federal whistle-blower succinctly described his experience after he blew the whistle: "They shrivel you up."[160]

If whistle-blowing causes personal pain, however, it also can bring personal gain. One such boon is emotional. Over four-fifths of all whistle-blowers, only 5 percent of whom reported "no retaliation," say that they would do it again.[161] As a government whistle-blower put it, "Finding honesty within myself was more powerful than I expected."[162]

Another is economic. Washington alone has awarded more than $2 billion to whistle-blowers; the average award is $1.5 million, with the largest awards topping $100 million.[163]

Securing Bureaucrats' Jobs

The popular image of the Civil Service System is one of a job for life. Do, in fact, government employees actually have more secure jobs than private-sector employees?

You bet they do.

The median job tenure for workers in all governments is "about 80 percent higher" than that of employees in companies, and this striking difference is widening. Over the course of a quarter century, the median job tenure of public-sector workers grew from six years to seven, but that of private-sector employees remained stuck at fewer than four years.[164]

THE SLIPPAGE OF THE CIVIL SERVICE SYSTEM

It is manifestly apparent that, after decades of dominance, the Civil Service System is in trouble.

The Civil Service System is predicated on the merit principle, and the long-standing definition of *merit system* is "a personnel system in which comparative merit or achievement governs each individual's selection and progress."[165]

The meaning of merit has been wrenchingly twisted in practice.

So sheepish are public administrators about the disconnect between the meaning of "merit" and its practice that they now refrain from even uttering the term "merit pay."[166] The implications of this linguistic lapse are worrisome, and hint that the merit principle itself has morphed into a culture of leech-like entitlement that saturates the public bureaucracy.

Without putting too fine a point on it, the practice of merit no longer reflects its commonly accepted meaning. One is reminded of "newspeak," the sinister and perverted language demanded of the populace by the thought police in George Orwell's *1984*: War is peace; freedom is slavery; ignorance is strength.[167] To which we might add, merit is sinecure.

Does the Civil Service System Impair Public Administration?

Here is a depressing noncorrelation: Human capital bureaus seem not to be terribly useful, or even relevant, in developing organizational talent. In other words, the connection between even a strong personnel office and able general administrators is, at best, obscure.[168]

Opinions among public executives reflect this finding. One out of three federal administrators complains that their government's central human resources office accords them little or no help in recruiting, developing, or utilizing employees.[169] In state governments, "the general picture that emerges is one of administrators trapped by rigid, slow, and cumbersome systems that are incapable of meeting government's human resources needs."[170]

After reviewing this research, Catbert comes to mind. Catbert is one of the more memorable characters in the popular comic strip *Dilbert* and he invariably is identified as the perennially "evil director of human resources." In the opinion of many public administrators, it seems, Catbert rules.

In light of these difficulties, should we be surprised that the Civil Service System is being diminished in most governments, and dismantled in some?

A Faltering Federal Civil Service

When the Civil Service Act was passed in 1883, it covered a fraction more than one out of every ten federal civilian employees,[171] but at its apex, a hundred years later, almost all federal civil servants were managed under its auspices.[172]

A Slippage of Centralized Control Then, in the 1990s, came change. In 1994, OPM shocked traditionalists by slashing the revered *Federal Personnel Manual*, which had been federal civil service policy for half a century, to a tenth of its former self.[173] In 1996, OPM radically decentralized hiring by creating in the agencies nearly 700 "delegated examining units" that have "the authority to perform all hiring-related tasks."[174] During the 1990s OPM eliminated nearly half of its employees, "a far greater reduction than that of any other Federal agency,"[175] and, from 1991 to 1998, personnel professionals in all federal agencies were cut by a fifth.[176]

In 2002, Congress further decentralized personnel duties. The Chief Human Capital Officers Act mandated the appointment of chief human capital officers in all major agencies.

The act also authorized OPM to grant *direct-hire authority* to agencies, which allows them, in cases of shortages of qualified applicants, to hire applicants without regard to standing civil service regulations. Agencies tripled their use of direct-hire authority in just four years following its introduction,[177] a spike reflecting the enthusiasm that their chief human capital officers have for it: Nearly three-quarters find it useful, almost half of whom accord it the highest rating possible, and its popularity is growing.[178]

The agencies themselves also are decentralizing their human capital management. A survey of representative federal agencies found that, by the mid-2000s, all of them were transferring responsibility for at least some of their "human capital activities" to other entities, usually to private businesses.[179]

By the close of the decade, it was clear that Washington's central personnel bureau, the OPM, had lost its historic grip on human resources. That iconic symbol of its power, the General Schedule, which covered 98 percent of federal civilian employees in 1983, and 94 percent as late as 1995, applies to 78 percent today.[180] About half of all civilian workers are exempt from at least some of the traditional regulations, such as those pertaining to classification and pay, that associate with the

Civil Service System,[181] and these exemptions correlate with reduced job satisfaction among federal employees.[182]

Dissed and Destroyed? Barely half, the lowest ranking out of eight possible options, of "seasoned political appointees" think that managing their relationships with OPM is important.[183] Little wonder that, among the twenty-four major federal agencies, the morale of OPM's employees ranks eighteenth.[184]

Just as agency directors evidence little regard for OPM, they show scant respect for human resources management in general. Although a respectable 46 percent of human resource executives think that their "agency leadership" views, "to a great or very great extent," personnel officers as trusted advisors, rather than as clerical paper shufflers, this proportion had shrunk by a third over just three years. Small wonder, perhaps, that only two-fifths of these administrators think that their "staff has the competencies it needs to succeed in the future...to a great or very great extent."[185]

The federal Civil Service System "is broken. It cannot repaired."[186] More than half of chief human capital officers "volunteered" in interviews that "bold reform of our civil service system is necessary."[187]

The evisceration of the federal Civil Service System has been so sudden, so swift, and so severe that "fragmentation within the civil service" is now the rule: "The federal government is quickly approaching the point where 'standard governmentwide' human capital policies and processes are neither standard nor governmentwide."[188]

Civil Service Slippage at the Grass Roots

By the 1980s, the peak of popularity for the Civil Service System, about three-fourths of the states had comprehensive merit systems,[189] and 60 percent of all state employees worked in them.[190] Eighty-eight percent of cities with populations of more than 50,000 had merit systems,[191] and an estimated 95 percent of all municipal employees worked in them.[192] During the 1990s and beyond, however, hundreds of personnel reforms were in the offing in the grass roots, and many were less than auspicious for the Civil Service System.[193]

Civil Service Reform in the States: Radical and Revolutionary The most sweeping reforms are occurring in the states and bode ill for the historic power of the civil service. In 1983, the heads of state personnel agencies in thirty-nine states reported directly to the governor;[194] two decades later, this held true in only twenty states.[195]

As in Washington, states are decentralizing their personnel functions from civil service bureaus to line agencies. As we noted earlier, more than four-fifths of the states have decentralized recruitment and hiring from personnel bureaus to the agencies.[196] Sixteen states have contracted out at least some of their personnel services to the private sector.[197]

There has been a discernible decline in state-employee job security in thirty-one states, twenty-eight of which have adopted, in whole or part, *at-will employment*—that is, employees serve at the sufferance of their supervisors sans protection by the merit system.[198] Florida, Georgia, and Texas have, for all intents and purposes, eliminated their civil services, dramatically increasing their line agencies' responsibility for human resource management.[199] Of the three, Georgia enacted the "most dramatic reforms,"[200] which, in an indirect but telling blow to the Civil Service System, were hailed by prestigious professionals as "likely the best in the country."[201]

States most likely to implement these reforms tend to have relatively weak public unions, Republican-controlled governments, high administrative[202] and legislative professionalism, low unemployment, and plentiful resources.[203]

Civil Service Reform in Communities: Moderate but Meaningful Civil service reform is at the heart of local governmental reform; perhaps 70 percent of all local reforms relate to personnel policies.[204] Nearly 8 percent of cities and counties contract out their personnel services to companies, nonprofit organizations, or other governments.[205]

The Impact of Civil Service Reform

The impact of civil service reforms is mixed, but there are some unambiguous benefits.

On a general level, the more that governments decentralize human resource activities, the more that "positive relationships" develop between "senior line managers" and human capital executives, and these relationships increase human resources' influence and performance.[206]

In the states, where civil service reform sometimes amounts to civil service revolution, "patronage hiring appears to proceed along typical levels" after reforms are introduced,[207] and civil service reform has "not produced widespread concerns about politicization of an independent public service" among those senior state administrators who are charged with preventing its politicization.[208]

In addition, hiring, promoting, reassigning, and firing have been streamlined,[209] and, although at-will state employees are dismissed more expeditiously than are employees who are protected by traditional civil service regulations, at-will employment does not associate with greater numbers of employees being fired.[210] State employees who serve at will are "significantly less negative about the full range" of civil service reforms than are their co-workers who are in the civil service.[211]

A Modest Proposal

In an effort to strengthen public management, many traditional duties of the Civil Service System are being withdrawn from personnel bureaus. For precisely the same reason, however, some responsibilities should be retained by human capital offices on the grounds that they can be handled more effectively by a central agency. These include labor relations, research, and the administration of wages, salaries, benefits, services, and, most especially, employee development and training.

The Civil Service System does have a future. Nevertheless, it is a future that will require some adaptation.

THE COLLECTIVE SYSTEM: BLUE-COLLAR BUREAUCRATS

Our second public human capital system is the *Collective System*, and it refers primarily to blue-collar workers whose jobs are administered via agreements between management and organized

workers. The core value of the Collective System is worker solidarity; in a word, *unions*.

Efforts to organize public employees first surfaced in the 1830s, and with reason: Wages and working conditions typically were abysmal. In 1907, New York City's fire fighters worked twenty-one hours *a day* and had only one day off in eight.[212]

Distinctive Values, Unique Leverage

The Collective System has some characteristics that are exclusive to it, notably its values and its potential power over its members' employers.

Merit *versus* Solidarity   At root, there are two philosophic differences between the Civil Service and Collective systems.

One such value is *sovereignty*. The Civil Service System contends that the state is sovereign and that a public position is a privilege that obliges its occupant to uphold the public trust granted by the people through their government. (The Seventh Circuit Court of Appeals undermined this position by ruling, in 1968, that regulations prohibiting public employees from organizing are unconstitutional.[213]) The Collective System holds that public employees have a right to use their collective power to improve their conditions of employment, a position that the Civil Service System sees as a threat to the sovereignty of the state.

The second difference is that of *individualism*. The Civil Service System holds dear that the individual worker be judged on the basis of his or her unique merits for fulfilling the duties of a specific position. The Collective System argues that the identity of the individual should be absorbed in a collective effort to better the conditions of all workers.

Among the conflicts that result from these fundamental differences are these: disputes over employee participation and rights (equal treatment *versus* union shop); recruitment (competitive tests *versus* union membership); position classification and pay (objective analysis *versus* negotiation); working conditions (determination by legislatures and management *versus* settlement by negotiations); and grievances (determination by civil service commissioners *versus* union representation to third-party arbitrators).

Merit and solidarity are starkly different.

Want to Fire Your Boss? Public unionism's distinctive values correlate with a unique employee–employer relationship that is found only in government, or, more to the point, with a unique union member–elected official relationship.

Union members are bargaining for benefits with bosses whose jobs they can threaten, or effectively fire, through elections. In no other sector do employees have this leverage, and public unions have made the most of it. As a long-serving state legislator put it, "You learned pretty quickly that you don't want to upset these guys."[214]

At the local level, some estimates have it that local government employees out-vote other voters in local elections by ratios ranging from two-to-one to six-to-one.[215] Moreover, local government employee unions can mount highly effective voter mobilization campaigns that "significantly affect the turnout levels" of likely sympathetic voters in local elections.[216]

The Scope of Organized Labor

With the passage in 1935 of the National Labor Relations Act (the Wagner Act), which guaranteed private-sector workers the rights to unionize, bargain collectively, and strike, unions surged forward. At its height, in 1953, organized labor included almost a third of all nonagricultural employees in the nation. Thirty-six percent of private-sector employees, and 12 percent of public-sector workers, were organized.[217]

Since then, organized labor has regressed to levels last seen during the Great Depression,[218] when the hope of millions of jobless Americans was to just find work, not to find justice at work. Total union membership has shrunk to a third of its former self, accounting for less than 12 percent of all workers, and private-sector union membership has shriveled to under a fourth of its apex in 1953 and stands at less than 7 percent of private-sector employees.[219]

Public Employees: Labor's Life-Blood Union membership would be far lower were it not for the public sector, where membership is almost five times that of the private sector. The number of government employees in unions has tripled since 1953 and account for over 36 percent, or 7.6 million, of all public workers. Government employees, whose share of all employees is a modest 17 percent, now are the life-blood of organized labor, accounting for 42 percent of all union members.[220]

Still, the glory days of unionized government workers have been waning since the early 1980s. By the mid-1990s, it was apparent that "public sector unionism…has topped out, both in membership and market share," with declines evident in both.[221]

The Federal Collective System In 1912, with the passage of the Lloyd-La Follette Act, federal employees secured the right to organize and to petition Congress to redress their grievances. In 1978, Congress made an exception in the form of Public Law 95-610, which bans unionization of the armed forces. Twenty-seven percent of all federal civilian employees[222] belong to about 125 unions or similar organizations in roughly 2,200 bargaining units, figures that have remained fairly constant over the years.[223]

The Grass-Roots Collective System Thirty-one percent of state employees and 42 percent of local workers are members of unions.[224] Fire fighters have long led the list as the most heavily organized of public employees, followed by teachers and police. These and other grass-roots employees are represented by nearly 34,000 bargaining units.[225]

Representation Versus Membership All public unions represent slightly more workers than those who actually are members of them. Unions represent 40 percent of all public employees—31 percent of federal workers, 35 percent of state employees, and 46 percent of local workers. Employees who are represented by unions, but who do not pay dues to them, are nonetheless included in any benefits that the unions may have negotiated with management. Overall, however, members of public unions earn somewhat more than do employees represented by unions; a marginal exception is the federal government, where the reverse is true.[226]

Bargaining with Governments

Collective bargaining, or *collective negotiations*, is the main method that unions and governments use to resolve issues, and it permits decisions to be made jointly between employee and employer representatives. Collective bargaining is used far less extensively in the public sector, where 66 percent of all workers have collective negotiating rights, than in the private one, where 78 percent do.[227]

Federal Bargaining Washington bitterly battled bargaining with unions for the better part of the twentieth century, but, in 1962, President John F. Kennedy's Executive Order 10988 declared peace by stating that certain conditions of employment could be bargained for collectively. The Federal Service Labor-Management Relations Reform Statute of 1978, which, for the first time, cast into law the right of federal employees to negotiate, effectively extracted collective bargaining from presidential whim.

In 1993, President Bill Clinton issued Executive Order 12871, which significantly expanded the scope of issues that unions could negotiate. Eight years later, President George W. Bush released Executive Order 13203, decentralizing to the agencies the authority to adopt a labor-relations strategy best suited to their own needs. Overall, the first decade of the new millennium witnessed a federal tilt in labor-management relations that pushed "the balance of power even further in favor of management."[228]

Grass-Roots Bargaining Although Congress long ago addressed collective negotiations for private-sector and federal workers, it has never done so for the grass-roots governments, leaving them to their own devices. In 1958, New York City became the first major local government to legalize collective bargaining with unions. In 1959, Wisconsin passed the first state law allowing public employees (specifically, its municipal workers) to bargain collectively. (Ironically, Wisconsin, in 2011, pioneered a radical reduction in the number and types of public workers who could negotiate collectively, withdrawing collective-bargaining rights from essentially all its state and local employees, save those in public safety positions.)

Thirty-four states and the District of Columbia require collective bargaining for some or all public employees. In eleven states, collective bargaining is permitted, and in five it is prohibited,[229] three of which stipulate that meet-and-confer negotiations be used instead.[230] *Meet-and-confer negotiations* occur when both sides must talk with each other, but management has the final decision. Ninety-four percent of all cities engage in collective bargaining with their employees,[231] and twenty-eight states authorize their counties to bargain collectively.[232]

Mediation, Conciliation, and Arbitration Should labor and management reach an impasse, *mediation*, or the voluntary use of an impartial third party to resolve differences and suggest compromises, can be introduced. *Conciliation* is an option, too, and it differs from mediation in that the third party may not suggest solutions to problems. The Federal Mediation and Conciliation Service and state governments provide mediators and conciliators in these disputes.

Should mediation and conciliation fail, arbitration may be brought in, especially if some essential public service is involved. *Arbitration* is a formal process of hearings and fact finding, and it may be *voluntary*, in which both sides agree beforehand to accept the arbitrator's decision, or *compulsory*, also known as *binding*, in which both sides must, under law, accept as final the arbitrator's decision. In 2001, the Supreme Court ruled that employers may compel their workers to take job-related disputes to arbitration.[233]

Arbitration, both voluntary and compulsory, is favored among public employees. Nearly a fourth of all grievances filed against public employers result in a demand for an arbitration hearing.[234] Public unions consistently win more arbitrations than private-sector unions.[235]

Twenty-one states and the District of Columbia have compulsory arbitration requirements,[236] and they bring a singular benefit: They are "the policy choice most likely" to minimize strikes, surpassing in their effectiveness prohibitions of, and penalties for, strikes.[237]

Striking Government

The emotional issue of public employees' right to strike runs deep. Some argue that a strike by public employees amounts to an act of insurrection; others contend that the right of government workers to strike is a basic freedom. The courts have held that there is no constitutional right of public workers to strike, but neither has the judiciary prohibited the enactment of laws permitting government employees to strike.

Striking Washington The Taft-Hartley Act of 1947 was the first legislation to prohibit strikes by federal employees. In 1970, more than 210,000 postal workers violated the law by staging an unprecedented walkout; the Labor Department met almost all their demands, and the strike was over in just two weeks. A nonplussed Congress soon divested itself of its postal problem by passing the Postal Reorganization Act of 1970, which transformed the Post Office Department, a federal agency, into the Postal Service, a federal corporation. More broadly, Congress reasserted its anti-strike policy with the Civil Service Reform Act of 1978, which forbids strikes and slowdowns by federal employees.

In 1981, however, 95 percent of the 13,000 members of the Professional Association of Air Traffic Controllers, possibly justifiably, probably arrogantly, and certainly foolishly, struck. Washington promptly *decertified* the Association— that is, no longer recognized the union as the official representative of its members—and dismissed more than 11,000 air traffic controllers, breaking their union in the process. President Ronald Reagan's decertification and mass dismissals were historic actions that likely strengthened the hand of public administrators in all governments when dealing with unions.

Striking the Grass Roots Thirteen states directly protect their public employees' right to strike, although each of these states places clear restrictions (most commonly, prohibiting strikes by public safety workers) on that right. One, Rhode Island, extends the right to strike to only state employees, but the remaining dozen include both state and local workers.[238]

During the 1960s and 1970s, strikes by state and local workers surged. When asked where the money for higher pensions for his members would be coming from, a union officer replied, revealingly, "That's the government's problem. Just because

there is a pinch for money, it's no excuse to make the employees do without."[239]

Labor's arrogance attenuated in 1979, when New Orleans' police struck just prior to Mardi Gras, effectively canceling the holiday and costing the city millions. This stunning gaffe focused the public's perception of organized labor's irresponsible gluttony and contributed to a dramatic shriveling of public unions' power. Strikes and work stoppages by government workers toppled from their all-time national record in that year— when there were 583 of them[240]—and never recovered. The number of strikes and stoppages by state and local employees, which averaged 340 per year during the 1970s,[241] has averaged six a year since the early 1980s. In the 2000s, they averaged fewer than five per year.[242]

Pay and Public Unions

Public unions long have devoted full-time staffs to analyzing governments' budgets with an eye toward winkling out more public money for their members, and with some success.[243] As we discussed in Chapter 8, public labor's greatest gains are in winning more generous pensions, but their effectiveness in raising wages and salaries is more mixed.

Overall, unionized public employees earn 17 percent more pay than workers who are not union members. The heavily white-collar federal government is an exception, where unionized employees earn 7 percent *less*, on average, than nonunion employees.[244]

Among state government workers, however, "state employee union density" is "the most consistent and important determinant of compensation,"[245] and those in unions are paid 17 percent more, on average, than those who are not. Organized labor brings home the bacon for local government workers, where union members average 24 percent more in wages and salaries than nonunion workers.[246]

The wage increases negotiated by public-sector unions generally have less of a financial impact on their governments than the wage increases negotiated by private-sector unions have on their companies,[247] which may explain why, out of twenty-six policy priorities, city managers rank "staff unions" a lowly twenty-third.[248]Out of eleven "spending areas" in 162 large cities, spending for salaries and wages as a share of general expenditures withered over twenty-four years, declining from an average of 50 to 43 percent. The cities' spending per capita on salaries and wages increased by only a fifth, whereas average spending across the board grew by almost twice that rate; employee pay statistically tied with the long-benighted budgets of public libraries for the lowest rate of growth.[249]

THE POLITICAL EXECUTIVE SYSTEM: POLITICS IN ADMINISTRATION

Political executives are those public officials appointed to an office without tenure, and who have significant policymaking powers. They have been called "the true nexus between politics and administration."[250] The Political Executive System fixates on *policy*—that is, developing and implementing a policy agenda for the elected chief executive.

Political Executives in Washington

Federal executives who are nominated or appointed by the president have ballooned by more than eleven-fold since 1960,[251] and now number about 3,500,[252] or thirty-five times more than those who work for the chief elected executives of Britain, France, and Germany, where they must make do with roughly 100 apiece.[253]

Baroquely Burdensome: The Appointment Process The baroque presidential appointment process—which has tripled in length from two-and-a-half months in the 1960s to more than eight months today—stands as a looming impediment to appointing top executives to federal offices.[254] "At least half of the delays" in this slower-than-molasses process "appear to involve bureaucratic red tape and duplication of effort," and a fourth involve inappropriate senatorial interference. The Senate in 2004 rejected reforms proposed by the House, and a consequence is some 2,500 "at will" presidential appointees who serve without Senate confirmation.[255]

Almost a fourth of presidential appointees describe the appointments process, which demands that candidates answer nearly 250 questions[256] that test "for almost everything but a candidate's qualifications for service,"[257] as "embarrassing," and a fifth find it "confusing."[258] More senior executives think that their own "application process discourages high quality candidates from applying" (36 percent) than not (30 percent).[259] "The senior executive hiring process," in short, "is broken."[260]

It is not only new college graduates who find the federal hiring process daunting, but seasoned executives are as well, and this has consequences: "The cascade of failures that have beset the federal government" is "rooted, *first and foremost*, in the appointments process and the vacancies it so often produces."[261]

The Rise of the White House Loyalty Test In the early 1960s, the appointment of political executives was "a highly centralized and personalized process revolving around the respective department and agency heads," and when a rare difference of opinion arose between the secretary and the White House staff over a candidate, "the secretary generally won."[262]

Beginning in the 1970s, however, the White House grew increasingly intrusive. As a result, "the views of politically appointed officials more and more closely resembled the…party and ideology…of the administration they were serving."[263]

No one can reasonably dispute the desirability of a democratically elected chief executive establishing his or her control over the executive branch, and appointing loyalists can be an important means of establishing that control. But appointing loyalists, let alone competent loyalists, is far more challenging than often is realized. A former presidential personnel assistant, who was notorious for his obsession with presidential control of the civil service, admitted, "It's an awfully difficult job just to handle the *presidential* appointees….if you try to do too much, you may be diluted to the point where you're not as effective."[264]

What have been the results of a lumbering, shambolic appointments process that, for roughly fifty years (the following studies cover, altogether, 1964–2009), tilted toward loyalty and politicization at the expense of experience and professionalism?

An Uncaring Elite? One result was the entry of political executives who evidenced little interest in achievement. Over some fifty years, the average percentages of presidential appointees who thought that "accomplishing important public objectives" brought them the most satisfaction plummeted by more than three-fifths and bottomed out at a remarkably modest 15 percent.[265]

It is of singular note in this regard that out of seventeen factors affecting political executives' length of tenure, "the least important…is resources," suggesting that actually achieving important goals rests in peace at the bottom of their ambitions. In fact, "a *very* large increase in the budget would be required to have only a *moderate* impact on [extending] appointee service duration."[266]

An Avaricious Elite? Another is that growing numbers of federal political executives seem to be more interested in making money than in improving the citizens' lot.

During the 1980s and 1990s, fully 30 percent of presidential appointees said that, once appointed, they earned "a lot more" money, and only 6 percent earned "a lot less." The legally dubious practice of political executives "burrowing in" to protected civil service positions after their appointive terms are completed more than tripled over nearly five decades, suggesting that these officials recognize a lucrative sinecure when they see one. Over the same period, the average percentages of presidential appointees who said that enhancing their "long-term career opportunities" was the "most satisfying part of the job" burgeoned by four-fifths.[267]

When better-paid positions outside of government are offered, these appointees snap them up: "*The* primary determinants of the [brief] duration of appointee service are related to the costs of public service."[268]

An Inept Elite? In light of these numbers, should we be surprised that just 11 percent of federal political executives *themselves* think that their colleagues "represent the best and the brightest that America has to offer"?[269] Only 18 percent of the Senior Executive Service's retired careerists believe that political appointees have "good leadership qualities," and just 15 percent think that they have "good management skills."[270]

Sixty-three percent of these executives who had been supervised by "noncareer" political appointees cite the "politicization" of their agencies as their "reason for leaving," compared with just 37 percent of those who reported to careerist, *non*political appointees; half of the former group say that they left because of their immediate supervisors' "incompetence" *versus* a third of the latter; and 46 percent of those who reported to political appointees attribute their departure to their "ethical concerns about practices at higher agency levels," compared with 30 percent of those who reported to careerists.[271]

Quantitative data support the proposition that too many federal political executives are in over their heads. After more lucrative job offers, the main motivation of political appointees to leave government is "the difficulty of public administration"—in other words, they find managing government to be just too, too hard.[272]

A Failed Elite? Despite monumental presidential efforts to hire loyalists who will unwaveringly implement their agendas, political executives are not much good at it. The "primary result" of a thoroughgoing analysis of federal political executives is that "ideological allies rarely make optimal appointees."[273] The reasons why political executives fulfill presidential programs relate not to loyalty but instead to opportunities for change available in the agency that the appointee heads, and the appointee's own managerial abilities, personality, and plan for attaining his or her goals.[274]

Fulfilling presidential agendas, in sum, is done by public administrators, not by partisan hacks.

The Costs of Incompetent Political Executives
Presidents' preferences for politicized loyalists over much of the past five decades have harmed the federal government's management capacity in surprisingly systemic ways.

The Cost to Careerists   Federal career executives have become hermitic, clerical, and rule bound, growing less communicative with "other sectors of government or with other actors in the political system.... less likely to see themselves in the role of advocates and facilitators and more likely to see themselves responding to technical and legal criteria."[275]

These limiting self-perceptions are reinforced by the hiring, training, and assessment practices for top federal careerists, which emphasize technical skills at the expense of their strategic leadership capacities. They result in their promotion to senior positions "even if they do not have executive ability."[276] Consequently, only a third of senior federal executives report that they spend from 36 percent to at least 55 percent of their time advising "top management," and another third devote that same amount of their time to tasks of "a technical/professional nature."[277]

The Cost to Governing   This is not leadership. It is barely bureaucratic. Worse, these executive patterns of politicization, isolation, and technical creep seep downward—with predictably ill effects.

The federal workforce's "decline in morale is sharpest where politicization has been most intense."[278] Although there has been some gradual improvement over time, it is nonetheless notable that just 56 percent of federal civilian employees have "a high level of respect for my organization's senior leaders," and only 45 percent are "satisfied with the policies and practices" of these leaders.[279]

The connection between employee morale and political executives has predictably deleterious effects on governing. The more political executives there are in an agency, the lower employee productivity: "Each additional political appointee reduces individual employee performance by .002" on an eleven-point scale.[280]

It has not always been like this. The federal service historically has boasted smart, visionary, tenacious, and tough public executives, who, against enormous odds, accomplished great things. Those federal administrative heroes (the noun is no exaggeration) chronicled in Ken Burns' documentary "America's Best Idea," who created the world's first national parks system and who often sacrificed their health and wealth in the effort, exemplify the federal service at its best.

Is this selfless, courageous class of federal executives still with us?

A Question of Competence:

▶ FEDERAL POLITICAL EXECUTIVES, 1969–2009

Many analysts trace the origins of the politicization of contemporary federal governance to President Richard M. Nixon's administration (1969–1974), and there has remained a constant and immutable tension between political loyalty and professional competence ever since.

To choose one at the expense of the other appears to be equally damaging for presidential agendas. As we detailed in Chapter 1, Ronald Reagan (1981–1989), who is generally thought to have been a transformative president, understood that if his ideas were to be implemented as policies, it was vital to appoint administrators who were both loyal and able. Other presidents, however, have ignored his insight.

Jimmy Carter (1977–1981), for example, emphasized competence and serenely assumed, often erroneously, loyalty. This proved to be costly. As one of Carter's assistant secretaries observed, some of his colleagues "are in business for themselves. Officially, when they testify on the Hill, they say the right thing in respect to the President's budget and legislative programs, but privately, they tell committee staff members, 'I don't really think that'" (Bonafede). Such disloyal undermining, even by able administrators, derails executive agendas, and Carter's legacy is largely one of little accomplished, despite the fact that he likely ranks as one of history's hardest working presidents.

George W. Bush (2001–2009) took an opposite tack and radically politicized the bureaucracy with scant, if any, regard for

(continued)

(continued)

assuring its capability. From 2000 to 2007, federal employees' perception that they had "experienced coercion related to political activity in the preceding 2 years" nearly doubled, an unprecedented spurt in its growth rate (it returned to its 2000 level in 2010) (U.S. Merit Systems Protection Board, p. 29). In Bush's White House, "substantive policy discussions were rare, and were routinely trumped by political considerations" (Moynihan and Roberts, p. 574). A former insider averred that, "There is no precedent in any modern White House for what is going on in this one.... Everything, and I mean everything, [is] being run by the political arm. It's the reign of the Mayberry Machiavellis" ("Ex-Aide Insists White House Puts Politics Ahead of Policy").

Bush's demand for political loyalty resulted in a record of administrative ineptitude that blocked or mangled almost all of his policy initiatives. Over time, politicization "was applied for its own sake," having "slipped from strategy to dogma"; Bush's bias for "Bushies" ultimately "constituted a direct challenge to the possibility of competence" ever encroaching into his administration (Moynihan and Roberts, p. 575; emphasis is original).

Two case studies follow that demonstrate how politicizing the bureaucracy dismantles effective governing. The first occurred over thirty of the fifty or so years that, in general, were decades of relatively politicized governance in Washington. The second unfolded during the George W. Bush administration, which set the modern standard for relying on loyalists to govern.

DECADES OF DEBACLES

The Federal Emergency Management Agency (FEMA) is a sad little bureau with big responsibilities: Its 2,600 employees are charged with providing rescue and related services to areas hit by disasters.

Since its creation in 1979, FEMA has had seven permanent (and ten acting) directors. At least one served with distinction, but most have been incompetent cronies, political hacks, or simply weird, such as Louis Giuffrida (1981–1985), a retired colonel who insisted on being addressed as "General," always wore a sidearm, and, at enormous cost to FEMA's mission, converted FEMA into "black-budget agency" that became a "paranoid harbinger of World War III" (Cooper and Block, p. 52). The General resigned after it became public that he had used FEMA funds to build a luxurious home for himself.

Most directors, however, have been less colorful but equally inept. There was, for instance, Wallace

Stickney (1990–1993), a former neighbor of the president's chief of staff, who had no experience in disaster management, but who longed to return to federal service in order to, in his words, "put a nice retirement package together." During this period, FEMA was "lumbering and lethargic...a caricature of Washington bureaucracy" (Cooper and Block, p. 56), as demonstrated by the answer that a FEMA official gave the mayor of Charleston, South Carolina, after the mayor asked what he should do as he was watching Hurricane Hugo shred his city: "You need to make sure you're accounting for all your expenses."

Or consider Joe Allbaugh (2001–2003), one of the president's top three campaign managers. He also was devoid of experience in emergency management, but was attracted to the directorship because, in his words, "you are in the limelight [and] it's for all the marbles." Allbaugh routinely referred to local emergency managers, who are crucial responders, as "goobers," and left what had been a resurgent and widely admired FEMA politicized and demoralized.

And, of course, there was the infamous Michael Brown (2003–2005), a college roommate of Allbaugh's, whom Allbaugh brought to FEMA from his previous post as commissioner of the International Arabian Horse Association. When Hurricane Katrina struck in 2005, five of the eight highest executives in FEMA, including its director, had come "to their posts with virtually no experience in handling disasters" (Hsu), but did have significant partisan backgrounds. Three of FEMA's five chiefs for natural disasters, and nine of its ten regional directors, were in acting positions because FEMA's seasoned professionals had been forced out or had quit in disgust. FEMA's pathetic incompetence in responding to Katrina, detailed in the box in Chapter 7, was a direct outcome of its buffoonish administrators.

Even in Katrina's catastrophic wake, President George W. Bush remained determined to assure a politicized FEMA. In signing the Post-Katrina Emergency Management Reform Act of 2006, which required that future FEMA directors be professionally qualified, Bush issued a "signing statement" in which he insisted that he was not legally bound to appoint qualified directors.

Why destroy an agency whose singular mission is to save lives that are in imminent danger? "Why," asked a former presidential chief of staff, "politicize FEMA when you've got Commerce?"

A WRECK IN IRAQ

Following the invasion of Iraq in 2003, Washington created the Coalition Provisional Authority (CPA) to administer the country until its governance could be handed back to the Iraqis. The CPA needed civilian administrators quickly, and one James O'Beirne, husband of a conservative pundit and White House liaison to the Pentagon, took charge.

A loophole enabled O'Beirne to bypass regulations requiring the hiring of competent administrators, and he was free to select them according to their ideological fealty. Officers in the CPA's Washington office reported that, "I watched résumés of immensely talented individuals...and senior civil servants...thrown in the trash." "The criterion for sending people over there was that they had to have the right political credentials."

Ultimately, these appointees numbered an estimated 1,500 (no one had ever actually counted them). Most had never worked outside the United States, and more than half were thought to have obtained their very first passport just to travel to Iraq. Their most telling traits were their supreme loyalty to the "Cult of Bush"—as one put it, "I'm not here for the Iraqis. I'm here for George Bush"—and their searing incompetence: "An Iraqi woman at the Embassy who had seen many Americans come and go—and revered a few of them—declared that seventy per cent were 'useless, crippled,' avoiding debt back home or escaping a bad marriage" (Packer, p. 62). The deputy director of the CPA's Washington office admitted, "We didn't send the A-team."

Six youthful applicants, who had been selected by O'Beirne to be "gofers," soon were assigned, despite their zero familiarity with finance, to manage Iraq's $13 billion budget. L. Paul Bremer III, head of the CPA, distanced himself from the CPA's few respected administrators, and created an inner circle consisting of three young (one was twenty-four) political

operatives who had no prior experience in the Arab world and did not speak Arabic. Why did Bremer "surround himself with such unseasoned advisers? Like the president, Bremer valued loyalty above all else" (Chandrasekaran, p. 196).

When Bremer returned sovereignty to Iraq in 2004, electricity generation in Baghdad was one-third less and trained Iraqi soldiers (Bremer had demobilized Iraq's army) were two-thirds less than he had promised; a mere 15,000 Iraqis were working on reconstruction projects, a trifle shy of the 250,000 promised; at least $9 billion of the $12 billion in U.S. currency that had been airlifted to Iraq had gone missing; and the Iraqi insurgency was off and rolling.

The Coalition Provisional Authority's *opera buffa* had, according to a "senior American general...'cost us one very valuable year'" (Chandrasekaran, p. 289).

INEPT ADMINISTRATION EQUALS IMPOTENT POLITICS

It is disturbing, as the politicization and ruination of FEMA and the CPA reveal, that some federal deciders are deeply contemptuous of professionally competent, and even exceptionally able, public administrators. It is beyond puzzling, however, that these same deciders cannot comprehend that their contempt brings with it political and policy woes.

It is arguably the case that FEMA's fumbled response to Hurricane Andrew in 1992 cost President George H. W. Bush his reelection that year. The CPA's bumfuzzled botchery in Iraq and FEMA's failure following Hurricane Katrina, which "crystallized negative perceptions" about a "bungling administration" that were "far from fully realized before Katrina hit" (Balz), will forever blight George W. Bush's legacy . In the year following Katrina, a Pew survey found that "the term most frequently associated with the president was 'incompetent,'" and, by the close of Bush's presidency, public approval of his performance was "the lowest in the Gallup Poll's history" (Moynihan and Roberts, p. 578).

Competent public administration can be, and usually is, astute politics. Incompetent public

(*continued*)

(continued)

administration, however, wreaks destruction far beyond political missteps. Not only did Bush's blind insistence on madly loyal underlings lay waste to his own policy initiatives, but, despite his obsession with rebuilding the institution of the presidency relative to Congress, Bush's dogmatism deeply eroded the office's legitimacy as well. "By 2007, public confidence in the presidency as an institution was at its lowest point since Gallup began measurement in 1992" (Moynihan and Roberts, p. 578).

Competence counts. ∎

Notes: John J. DiIulio, Jr., is the Bush insider quoted in the introduction. To be fair, Giuffrida was a general in the California National Guard, if only for the day before he retired. The comment concerning FEMA and Commerce is Leon Panetta's.

Sources: Dom Bonafede, "Carter Sounds Retreat from 'Cabinet' Government," *National Journal* (November 18, 1978), p. 1852; U.S. Merit Systems Protection Board, *Prohibited Personnel Practices: Employee Perceptions* (Washington, DC: U.S. Government Printing Office, 2011); Donald P. Moynihan and Alasdair S. Roberts, "The Triumph of Loyalty over Competence: The Bush Administration and the Exhaustion of the Politicized Presidency," *Public Administration Review* 70 (July/August 2010), pp. 572–581; "Ex-Aide Insists White House Puts Politics Ahead of Policy," *New York Times* (December 2, 2002); Christopher Cooper and Robert Block, *Disaster: Hurricane Katrina and the Failure of Homeland Security* (New York: Times Books, 2006); Spencer S. Hsu, "Leaders Lacking in Disaster Experience: 'Brain Drain' at Agency Cited," *Washington Post* (September 9, 2005); Rajiv Chandrasekaran, *Imperial Life in the Emerald City: Inside Iraq's Green Zone* (New York: Knopf, 2007); George Packer, "Betrayal," *The New Yorker* (March 26, 2007), pp. 52–73; Donald L. Bartlett and James B. Steele, "Billions over Baghdad," *Vanity Fair* (October 2007), pp. 336–339; and Dan Balz, "Bush's Hurricane Damage," *Washington Post* (August 28, 2007).

Political Executives at the Grass Roots

In contrast to developments at the federal level, in the political executive systems of state and local governments, political patronage is down and public professionalism is up.

The Departure of Patronage The Supreme Court has been involving itself in the area of patronage-based political appointments since 1976, and the clear drift of judicial opinion is one of reducing the power of patronage in state and local governments.[281]

In State Governments Perhaps the most important anti-patronage decision is the Supreme Court's 1990 ruling in *Rutan* v. *Illinois Republican Party*, in which the Court banned party affiliation as a factor in the hiring, promoting, or transferring of most of Illinois' 60,000 gubernatorial appointees. (As this large number suggests, few gubernatorial appointees are political executives; most are of humbler station.) The governor of Illinois was shocked, saying the decision "turns politics on its head."[282]

States that traditionally have had a lot of political appointees—Illinois, Indiana, Massachusetts, New York, North Carolina, Pennsylvania, and West Virginia—have taken steps to reduce the power of partisan politics in their personnel systems as a direct consequence of *Rutan*. "Nobody wants to be sued. They tend to pay attention to a major decision like this."[283]

In Local Governments What is true for the states is even more in evidence among local governments. Although partisan elections are still used by most counties, nearly four-fifths of municipalities and essentially all school districts elect their legislators using ballots that do not identify candidates' political affiliations.[284] The number of mayors who hold the exclusive power to develop municipal budgets sank by 35 percent over fifteen years, and today just 11 percent retain this authority.[285] Mayors who possess the sole power to appoint department heads declined by 37 percent over ten years, and only 17 percent still have this capability.[286]

The Entry of Professionalism As patronage passes from the grass-roots governments, professionalism enters.

In State Governments In the states, interest in developing a cadre of professional public executives bloomed in the 1960s as part of administratively inspired reorganizations that swept most state governments for three decades.[287] Four states had executive personnel systems in place before the federal government founded its Senior Executive Service in 1978, and fourteen states now have them, typically encompassing an elite 1 percent of these states' employees.[288]

Analyses consistently show that the quality and professionalism of top state administrators are steadily rising.[289] In 1964, fewer than two-thirds of state agency heads (who usually are gubernatorial appointees) had a bachelor's degree (by contrast, nine-tenths of their federal equivalents had completed college[290]), including two-fifths who had taken some graduate courses or held a graduate degree. Just twenty years later, more than nine out of ten of these executives had completed college, lifting them to educational parity with their federal counterparts, and today 95 percent are university graduates, including three-fourths of all state agency heads who have some graduate study or advanced degrees.[291]

Another criterion of professionalism is commitment to a career, and this they have. State agency heads have worked in their governments for a median eighteen years and thirteen years in their agencies. Their years in service have grown by a third over fifty or so years.[292]

Like their federal counterparts, senior state administrators worry over the quality of their political executives. A minute 4 percent of these officials agree that "increased numbers of political appointees enhance [state] government effectiveness," and an overwhelming 80 percent disagree (24 percent "strongly" so) that they do.[293]

In Local Governments Local governmental interest in developing a deep pool of executive talent associates with the dramatically accelerating adoption, beginning immediately after World War II, by local jurisdictions of the council-manager plan and similarly professional forms of government.[294]

Eighty-five percent of cities and towns,[295] and 56 percent of counties,[296] are managed by nonpartisan chief administrative officers, and these figures are growing over time. These officers are called *city,* or *town, managers,* or *county administrators* or *managers.* Most of them have powers that any political appointee would envy.

In 65 percent of all cities and towns (including those without city managers), the city manager has exclusive responsibility for developing the budget and in another 8 percent the city manager and the mayor develop the budget together; in 10 percent of all municipalities, the budget is developed solely by another bureaucrat, the chief financial officer.[297] In 37 percent of all cities and towns, the city manager has sole authority to appoint department heads, and in 11 percent the manager shares this power with the mayor.[298] In 56 percent of all counties (including those without county administrators), these officials have the authority to develop the budget, and, in 22 percent, they may both form the budget and hire and fire department heads.[299]

Top local administrators are well educated and experienced. Only 2 percent of city managers lack a bachelor's degree; a fifth have only a bachelor's degree; and nearly four-fifths have that plus an advanced degree. Most, 51 percent, hold a master's of public administration, their "most frequently earned degree." Like state agency heads, top local executives are in it for the longer haul and have a mean tenure of more than fifteen years as chief administrative officers.[300]

Experience and Sector: Our New Understanding of Executive Quality

The federal government offers a unique insight into an age-old argument about who makes the best public executives: political appointees or career bureaucrats.

There are two reasons for this uniqueness. First, the federal government has a far greater population of political appointees who are "in-and-outers," or those political executives who have more experience in sectors (academia, business, etc.) other than in the public one than do either state or local governments. Second, the federal government has a single system in which each of its agencies (and, by association, their directors) is graded for its comparative performance against all other agencies.

The Less Experienced Political Executive

"Roughly one-fourth" of federal political executives "depart by the end of the first year. Almost half are gone by the end of their second year, and only about a third serve past the end of their third year."[301] The average tenure of top political appointees in their positions is roughly eighteen months,[302] compared with twice that time—more than three years—for their careerist counterparts.[303]

When we consider the totality of their governmental experience, the differences between appointees and careerists are even more dramatic. Presidentially appointed executives, on average, have more than nine, usually discontinuous, years of experience in a variety of federal positions, whereas career executives, who average an impressive twenty-six continuous years of federal service, have nearly three times the federal experience of political appointees.[304]

Turnover and Time Matter These starkly contrasting tenures should give us pause. "Among upper-tier private sector managers, such attrition rates would undoubtedly lead to ailing profits, and stockholder calls for higher salaries and better selection decisions,"[305] conditions that have their own analogies in the public sector. Merely the fact that federal political executives remain so briefly in office undermines agency achievement: high rates of turnover are "negatively related" to public organizations' performance.[306]

When more ambitious missions are undertaken, brief executive tenures almost guarantee their derailment. "The experiences of successful major change management initiatives in large private and public sector organizations suggest that it can often take at least 5 to 7 years before the initiatives are fully implemented and the related cultures are transformed in a sustainable manner."[307]

It takes many years for leaders to make a lasting difference. Eighteen months on the job will not cut it.

Sector and Experience Matter A hoary myth, at least in Washington, is that political executives, with their lifetimes of cosmopolitan administrative experiences in a rich variety of settings, administer better than career federal executives who have devoted their professional lives to government and to only government. Do they?

No. A seminal analysis of 242 federal bureau chiefs found that politically appointed chiefs got "systematically lower management grades than bureau chiefs drawn from the civil service." Why?

The career bureau chiefs had twice as much federal experience, and this is "significantly related to management performance."[308]

Other evidence buttresses the finding that not just experience, but *experience in the public sector*, matters more than experience in many sectors. The more years that big-city American mayors serve in office, for instance, the more physically developed their cities and the more effective their law enforcement and social services.[309] The longer the tenure of municipal budget officers, the more smoothly, efficiently, and effectively they manage public funds.[310]

Administrative experience in government trumps even that other major measure of professional capability, education. More than half of federal political executives hold advanced degrees,[311] a proportion that places them, on average, on a higher educational plane than their careerist counterparts, yet these less educated but far more governmentally experienced careerists manage more productive agencies.[312] The same relationship applies to administratively involved mayors; years of mayoral experience associate more positively with more productive local governments than do years of education.[313]

The American founders, as usual, were way ahead of us and understood that "a government of strangers"[314]—or, more to the point, ignoramuses in the ways of public administration, who do not serve in government long enough to learn about their jobs or each other—is unlikely to be skilled. If public executives were to stay only briefly in office, Alexander Hamilton wrote, it would "occasion a disgraceful and ruinous mutability in the administration of government."[315]

"Amateur government" is, at best, mediocre government.[316]

SPECIALIZED PUBLIC PROFESSIONAL SYSTEMS: THE PERSON OVER THE POSITION

A *profession* is an easily identifiable and specialized occupation, normally requiring at least four years of college education, which offers a lifetime career to the persons in it. The emergence of numerous specialized professions—such as criminal justice and public health—in governments began in the mid-twentieth century and brought to public human capital management a new value: the *person* and the management of his or her career.

The Scope of Specialized Public Professional Systems

Beginning in 1955, the proportion of specialized professionals (other than public administrators) working in the public sector grew dramatically.[317]

Twenty-eight percent of the federal civilian workforce are specialized "professionals," a term that excludes "officials," "managers," "administrators," "administrative support positions," and "technicians"—categories that arguably are also professional ones.[318] Both the percentages of federally employed professionals and federal employees who have baccalaureate degrees are expanding their share of the federal workforce over time.[319]

State and local governments also host a huge proportion of specialized professionals—26 percent.[320] This figure does not include educators—more than 11 million of them—who constitute 56 percent of the total grass-roots workforce.[321] When combined with professionals who are not in education, professionals add up, roughly, to a stunning four-fifths of all employees in state and local governments.

How do these numbers compare with the total civilian labor force? They shunt it well into the shade: A comparatively tiny 11 percent of the civilian labor force is working in professions.[322]

The Public Implications of Specialized Public Professionalism

Professions embody expertise, prestige, autonomy, dignity, and formal learning, values that often are incompatible with politics. The historic struggles of public professions to purge themselves of politics—for example, the city manager *versus* party hacks; the librarian *versus* ignorant censors; the environmental scientist *versus* political ideologues—all reflect this resistance.

Nor do professionals like bureaucracy, which they often view as an impediment to the free exercise of their specializations. Federal employees in some professions, such as science, express much less satisfaction with their work than do federal executives,[323] and, as we described in Chapter 5, professional "specialists" are "manifestly maladjusted" in their government workplaces.[324] Put bluntly, professionals who choose the public service often must overcome their antipathy for its two major features: politics and administration.

To make matters worse, professionals with different specializations sometimes engage in infighting that undermines public productivity. This is a common condition among city managers and city attorneys, whose "personal and professional relations...have often been marked by suspicions and competition," leading to "significant [and negative] consequences for municipal government effectiveness."[325]

The more established that a profession is in society, and the scarcer the professionals available to a particular agency for hire, the greater the likelihood that the professional elite in question will exercise effective control over the agency's entire personnel system, irrespective of the *de jure* control over personnel practices supposedly exercised by the Civil Service System.[326] In the federal government, OPM has "excepted virtually all of the established and general professional fields, [and] a great many emergent professions" from its official purview.[327]

THE PROFESSIONAL PUBLIC ADMINISTRATION SYSTEM: EMBRACING THE PROFESSIONS OF POLITICS AND MANAGEMENT

In stark contrast to Specialized Public Professional Systems, the Professional Public Administration System not only tolerates politics (as in *public*) and bureaucracy (as in *administration*) but also embraces them. Its central value is *high-performance public and nonprofit organizations*. Professional management reigns.

The Roots of the Professional Public Administration System

The Professional Public Administration System is the result of a trio of developments that emerged in the 1970s.

The Model Public Personnel Administration Law of 1970 In 1970, the now-defunct National Civil Service League released its sixth and last Model Public Personnel Administration Law, reflecting "a sea change in the views of the cognoscenti about what the public service should be and how it should be governed." Rather than emphasizing the protection of the civil service against partisan patronage and similar transgressions, as the League's previous model laws had done, the 1970 version incorporated the values of the President's Committee on Administrative Management of 1937: "Personnel administration must be regarded as a part of management, not a protector against it."[328]

Only eight years following the model law's release, the federal government enacted the first major reform of its human capital management policies in nearly a century, the Civil Service Reform Act. By the mid-1970s, close to two-thirds of all state and local civil services reported that they were greatly influenced by the model law in reformulating their personnel policies, and over half had taken steps to make their personnel directors more responsive to executive leadership.[329]

Watergate and the Muffled Mouthpiece for "Merit" "Watergate," perhaps the most searing political scandal of the twentieth century, erupted in 1973. For two years, the president's criminality and that of his public administrators were paraded before the nation.

"However justified or unjustified they may have been, the effects of Watergate unquestionably were to tarnish the reputation of the public service in general....And the U.S. Civil Service Commission, which had been set up in part as a watchdog of the integrity of the civil service system, did not attack, or growl, or even bark until the affair had ridden most of its course....Watergate generated doubts in the nation as a whole...about the public service as a whole, both career and noncareer."[330]

The Civil Service Reform Act of 1978 If federal human resource managers were notably weak-kneed when it came to protecting the merit principle from presidential corruption, they seemed positively untamed in using it to harass federal managers. Fierce frustration festered among federal administrators over inadequate authority to

hire and promote their own employees, and they attributed at least some of their impotence to the indifference of federal personnel managers.

Management at Last Frustration generates change. In his 1978 State of the Union address, President Jimmy Carter said that reform of the civil service was "absolutely vital."[331]

As a consequence of these initiatives, there ensued a hugely ambitious study of federal personnel administration involving more than 1,500 personnelists. Ultimately the Civil Service Reform Act of 1978 was enacted, thus replacing the Civil Service Act, which, for ninety-five years, had been the human capital policy of the United States. "The main thrust of the Carter reforms, repeated in virtually all the speeches and arguments of their supporters, was management....Here was the culminating event of 'government by managers,' espoused four decades earlier" by the Committee on Administrative Management.[332]

The Bureaucracy of Reform The act created three new bureaus for federal human capital management. Their directors and deputy directors, or board members, are nominated by the president, confirmed by the Senate, and serve at the president's pleasure.

The OPM replaced the Civil Service Commission. OPM advises the president on policy and coordinates the government's personnel programs. OPM also manages another of the act's creations, the Senior Executive Service, a topmost professional administrative class in the European tradition. Senior executives may be assigned, reassigned, or removed on the basis of their ability or performance.

A bipartisan Merit Systems Protection Board, composed of three members, adjudicates employee appeals, investigates allegations that federal personnel laws have been violated and may order agency compliance with its rulings.

Finally, the Act created the Federal Labor Relations Authority, noted earlier, which is charged with developing and enforcing federal policy for unions.

Roots, Reforms, and Results The consequence of these developments has been the gradual emergence of new thinking about people in the public service, and this thinking is expressed in the Professional Public Administration System. Most particularly, it focuses on loosening rigid position classification protocols and managing employee performance.

Reforming Classification: Broadbanding

Broadbanding, paybanding, or *salary banding* refer to the reduction of position classifications into broad bands of job "families." Broadbanding job classifications is generally thought to facilitate more effective recruiting and to be a necessary first step before additional managerial reforms can be installed.[333]

At the federal level, some 250,000 employees are in broadbanding systems.[334] Still, authorities think that more needs to be done and have recommended that the fifteen grades in the General Schedule be roughly halved in number.[335] Only 14 percent of federal chief human capital officers think that the General Schedule's classification system should be retained.[336]

Personnelists also have proposed that the thousands of position classifications in the grassroots governments be slashed to a few dozen,[337] and these governments have responded.

Beginning in the mid-1990s, five times as many states were cutting their position classifications than were adding them.[338] Today, a dozen states use "a full-scale broadbanding system"; four use it on "a limited scale"[339] "About 12 percent of the states" have adopted broadbanding for at least three-fourths of their employees. The average number of "active job titles" in these states (370) is just a fourth of those in states that have paybanded less extensively (1,536).[340]

In those states that have salary banded to a significant extent, the numbers of employees who are eligible for inclusion in a half-dozen innovative "pay strategies" outpace by two to six times those in states that have not broadbanded, and transfer rates within these governments are about two-thirds lower, suggesting greater contentment among public employees in paybanded agencies.[341]

More than half of cities have consolidated some position classifications.[342]

Managing Public Administrators' Performance

Increasingly, the Professional Public Administration System is defined in terms of *performance management*, or clearly expressing what is expected of an employee, and then reasonably demonstrating whether he or she has fulfilled expectations.[343] When performance management is done well, employees are more satisfied, turnover declines, and productivity increases.[344] Managing for federal performance correlates positively with greater job satisfaction,[345] and "a decrease in the likelihood that federal employees will leave their agencies."[346]

There are, however, three deeply problematic challenges of public performance management. They are the difficulties of rating the performance of public employees; dealing with employees who perform poorly; and linking employees' performance with incentives.

Performance Management Challenge 1: Appraising Employees' Performance

Performance appraisal, also known as *performance assessment* or *performance rating,* is the evaluation of an employee's actual achievements and productivity in his or her job. Although appraisals of public personnel have a long history (Congress first ordered assessments of federal workers in 1842[347]), they never really addressed the idea that public administrators should produce results. When governments were adopting the merit system, civil service reformers were more than satisfied that it did nothing more than inhibit public administrators from routinely plundering the public till. Hence, for many decades, a productive public administrator was, as a practical matter, one who simply did not commit criminal acts and followed the rules. Not a particularly high standard, perhaps, but one that was needed, certainly, during most of the nineteenth century and well into the twentieth.

Over time, this modest objective was replaced by efforts to assess individual productivity and professionalism. The federal government, forty-nine states[348] (nearly nine out of ten state classified employees, on average, are appraised at least annually[349]), and over four-fifths of cities and counties[350] now use performance assessments.

The Pit of Public Performance Assessment Dissatisfaction with performance rating is much more pronounced in government than it is in business.[351]

Why is this? Rater bias, inadequate documentation and communication, process errors, and little or no training (fewer than three out of ten new federal supervisors receive any training in documenting their employees' performance, and only two out of ten are trained in "helping all employees improve their performance"[352]) are a few of the factors that reduce both the reliability and the reputation of public-sector performance rating.[353]

The most intransigent problem in the pit of public performance appraisal is that the performance of some public administrators is far less subject to assessment than others. Service to clients, for instance, can be measured by how many calls an administrator answers per hour, and how often his or her answers satisfy callers. But how does one quantify the performance of the international staff of the U.S. Treasury, which is supposed to monitor developments in the international economy, coordinate with other governments, and push for certain policies?[354]

Successful Performance Assessment To successfully assess individual performance requires both personal and systemic approaches,[355] and this is increasingly the mode favored by state and local governments.

At the one-on-one, supervisor-to-subordinate level, assessors must be adequately trained in leading, managing, and communicating, including, certainly, setting clearly expressed performance measures that communicate precisely what is expected.[356] To mitigate against personal favoritism in the rating process, establish "independent reasonableness reviews" by outside agencies, such as human resource offices, and transparency and accountability mechanisms.[357]

To be effective, performance assessments should be embedded in a coherent system, based on consensual values and goals,[358] that focuses on improving not only individual performance but organizational performance as well. Individual and organizational objectives should be closely aligned, and individual competencies, as well as performance, should be assessed.[359]

The Prospects for Performance Appraisal There is a flickering glimmer of hope on this human capital horizon. Although a few governments "still approach performance appraisals as discrete events," in keeping with best practices "most have implemented systems that encompass sets of activities to assess, develop, and reward employees."[360]

The number of federal workers who think that their performance assessments are "appropriate" or "fair" has risen from 55 percent in 1986[361] to 68 percent currently.[362]

When Washington State in 1998 replaced a traditional performance assessment system that had registered a disapproval rate of 93 percent among the state's employees with a new system that emphasized communication and collaboration, and eliminated rating scales, employee satisfaction shot to 97 percent, "a staggering figure, considering the typical employee attitude toward performance appraisal."[363]

During the 2000s, Georgia initiated a carefully planned and sophisticated "ePerformance" system that links pay with performance and provides immediate performance feedback to employees, administrators, and human capital specialists. It incorporates radically reduced job descriptions (from 3,500 to 750) and explicit core competencies for not only employees but also for those who assess employees' performance.[364]

Performance Management Challenge 2: Coping with Incompetents

The dark side of performance appraisal is that it sometimes fails to identify "poor performers," or "nonperformers," as incompetent government employees are officially described. Even a few poor performers can have a disproportionately negative impact on the productivity of the entire public workplace,[365] leading to increased turnover and absenteeism.[366] Dealing with a poor performer can cost up to three times the poor performer's salary.[367]

There can be little question that correcting poor performance is a tough challenge, principally because incompetent employees are sublimely unaware that they are incompetent. "A lack of skill leaves individuals both performing poorly and

unable to recognize their poor performances....
[Poor performers] show dramatic overconfidence
on tasks about which they have likely received
substantial feedback in the past ... [and possess] little
insight into the depth of their deficiencies relative to
their peers.... Poor performers overestimate their
performances even when given strong incentives
for accuracy." Top performers, by contrast, tend "to
underestimate their performances."[368]

Dealing with Federal Incompetents

"The
exact number of poor performers in the federal
government is unknown."[369] Federal employees,
however, report that up to a fourth of their
coworkers "are not up to par," a figure that is
matched by employees in the private sector,[370] but
federal supervisors deem not even 4 percent of their
employees to be "poor performers."[371]

Whatever their number, poor performers are
deeply entrenched in their jobs, and average an
astonishing fourteen years in the federal employ![372]
A fraction of 1 percent of federal employees are
fired outright or leave voluntarily for reasons of
poor performance or misconduct, and another
1,400 or so are demoted or denied automatic salary increases because of poor performance. As the
civil service itself notes, "removing or demoting
inadequate performers still remains relatively rare
in the civil service."[373]

A Pernicious Personnel Problem "Relatively rare"?
Consider some "inadequate performers" whom
the federal civil service kept. The postal worker
who was reinstated and awarded back pay after
being fired for shooting a colleague in the workplace.[374] The part-timer who broke a secretary's
jaw when she complained about filing delays;
the part-timer received a transfer, a permanent
job, and a nearly $4,000 raise. Or the biologist
who was let go because it took him four months
to do what his supervisors could do in two days;
he was reinstated because no one had explained
what "too slow" meant. Or the secretary who was
fired for incompetence, but who was reinstated
and transferred because coping with incompetent
bosses had "induced a mental handicap that had
to be tolerated."[375]

Why Do Incompetent Federal Employees Hang On? The
reasons underlying the retention of poor federal
performers are several.

A Little-Used Probationary Period One is that federal managers rarely use the single best opportunity
that they have to rid themselves of poor performers—
that is, new employees' year-long probationary
periods—a problem that federal reports have called
attention to since 2005.[376] Supervisors let go less
than 2 percent of probationary employees.[377]
Managers remove less than one-half of 1 percent of
probationary supervisors.[378]

An Awful Appeals Process Another reason is the
presence of a tangled appeals process involving no
fewer than five federal agencies, each of which vary
in their authority, procedures, and body of case
law. Any given case may be brought before one *or
more* of these agencies, which, of course, further
extends and confuses the appellate process.[379]

And the process is lengthy. Most employee
complaints take nearly a year to process, a period
that almost doubles if the aggrieved worker appeals
a decision.[380] One appeal of the firing of an
$8,000-a-year federal employee, who was a con-
sistent no-show and offered no valid reasons for
the absences, consumed twenty-one months.[381] In
another case, an agency driver was suspended. His
appeal involved at least three agencies over the course
of more than four years. He was denied pay for three
of those years, and, in the remaining year, he was
paid for doing nothing. He won his job back.[382]

Why the appeals process is so convoluted is a
mystery because federal employees have no greater
legal protections than do workers in any other
sector, or even in state and local governments.[383]

Taking Unsatisfactory Action Almost six out of
ten federal supervisors state that they have encountered problems of performance or conduct in their
employees over the preceding two years.[384] Nearly
nine out of ten federal supervisors counsel a poorly
performing employee (and spend a remarkable five
hours a working week, on average, doing so,[385] a
time commitment that matches that of the private
sector[386]); over a fourth take formal action against
the employee; and a third give the employee "a less

than satisfactory performance rating"[387] (although not even a third of 1 percent of all federal employees receive an "unacceptable" rating[388]).

The results of these actions are less than gratifying. More than half of supervisors think that counseling failed to improve the performance of nonperformers, and nearly two-thirds report that taking formal action also failed.[389] These unsatisfactory results may be a partial result of a lack of preparedness among federal managers when coping with poor performers. Two-fifths say that their ignorance of relevant statutes is a "difficulty" in disciplining them, and a fifth cite their dislike of confrontation.[390] Regrettably, they are getting scant help in overcoming their timidity: Only about a fifth of new federal supervisors receive training in "managing poor performers" and "conflict management."[391]

A Supine System For more than thirty years, federal employees have rated their government's handling of poor performers as one of its greatest failures, and often as its single greatest failure.[392] Only 31 percent of federal employees agree that, "In my work unit, steps are taken to deal with a poor performer who cannot or will not improve" (compared with 52 percent each of private- and nonprofit-sector workers[393]), and 42 percent disagree.[394] Forty-two percent of upper-level federal executives and professionals who were hired from outside the federal government state that that their agencies are "worse" than their pervious employer in "dealing effectively with poor performers," and just 7 percent say that their agencies handle them "better."[395]

More top federal executives think that their agencies fail to deal "effectively with executives who perform poorly" (31 percent) than those who think that they do (26 percent).[396] Keep in mind that these self-abnegating administrators are the same people who are running the agencies!

Unsurprisingly, these perceptions lower morale among supervisors. The less support that federal supervisors feel that they receive from upper management in dealing with incompetent employees, the more likely that those supervisors will stop trying to rectify the problem, and the greater the possibility that they will leave the agency.[397]

Dealing with State Incompetents State administrators seem to be doing a better job of dealing with incompetent employees than their federal counterparts, and the rate at which state employees are dismissed, while still low at less than 2 percent,[398] significantly surpasses the federal government's less than one-third of 1 percent who are separated for poor performance.[399] And, as we observed earlier, more than a fifth of new hires in state governments are not retained during the probationary period, a rate that is more than ten times that of the federal one.[400]

Whereas two-thirds of federal administrators report that their agencies fail in disciplining poor performers,[401] only a third of state agency heads think that personnel rules and procedures make it difficult to discipline or discharge poorly performing employees.[402] In contrast to federal administrators, who, as we have noted, can spend years in processing workers' complaints, state administrators spend a speedy twenty-nine days, on average, in terminating a classified employee for "performance issues," and an even briefer eighteen for "behavioral issues."[403] Even in highly unionized state governments, not even 5 percent of state administrators report that agreements reached with state workers through collective bargaining is a "serious impediment" to their managerial authority.[404]

Dealing with Local Incompetents Local managers have taken some care in laying a groundwork to deal with nonperforming employees. Of the more than nine out of ten cities that have collective bargaining agreements, 91 percent insert a management rights clause in at least one of their contracts. About four-fifths of these clauses specifically give management the right to take disciplinary action.[405]

In addition, employee appeals of these actions seem to be handled with considerable dispatch. The average length of time that it takes to resolve grievances in more than nine out of ten cities is fewer than three months.[406]

Performance Management Challenge 3: Performance and Pay

Our third and final component of performance management is that of developing and implementing incentives that encourage higher performance by employees. *Performance pay, incentive pay, performance-related pay, performance-based pay, pay for performance, pay for contribution,* or *pay for competence* links pay and other rewards, in whole or in part, to individual, group, and/or organizational performance.[407] Research suggests that, in the typical workgroup, only 15–20 percent of workers are judged by their coworkers to be really productive.[408]

The prospect of performance pay could be a central factor in reinvigorating the civil service: A majority of Americans say that they would be "most interested in exploring a job in government" because of "opportunities for growth and advancement based on performance."[409]

Despite popular enthusiasm for rewarding public administrators for good performance, however, almost all governments still retain a pair of public-pay pillars, neither one of which is on speaking terms with performance. One is the *cost-of-living adjustment,* which is an automatic annual addition to (and, in theory but not in practice, deduction from) the salaries of employees that reflect changes in their purchasing power. The other pillar is the *step increase,* or a salary raise that is granted as a public employee automatically (performance need be only satisfactory) ascends each "step" within each pay grade.

Paying Performers in Washington Although, as we noted earlier, most federal employees are satisfied with their pay, they are far from content with the fairness of that pay.

Over a fourth say that ensuring that employees received equal pay for equal work is a major problem—a perception shared at "every level of the pay scale."[410] Paying them for their performance should, at least in theory, mitigate federal workers' worries over how fairly they are paid.

Washington has addressed performance pay from several angles.

Presidents have intermittently tried, with varying degrees of success, to cap yearly cost-of-living adjustments (although, in 2010, President Obama successfully imposed a two-year freeze on them). Step increases, however, flourish. There are ten steps in each of the fifteen grades in the General

Schedule, and employees who are in it (or nearly four-fifths of all federal civilian workers) must wait at each step for a minimum of one to three years (the higher the grade, the longer the required wait) before advancing to a higher step and, with it, to higher pay.

Congress also has involved itself with performance pay, in part because the Civil Service Reform Act, which requires that federal administrators be paid for performance, fails to specify how this requirement should be implemented. This situation grew so frustrating that, by the late 1990s, all major federal offices were cutting back on their use of monetary incentives.[411] After nearly three decades of federal floundering, involving a dozen demonstration projects, fewer than 43,000 employees were covered by pay-for-performance systems,[412] and seven out of every ten of the top 8,000 federal executives were earning precisely identical salaries.[413]

With the inauguration of President George W. Bush, performance pay was reenergized. Congress in 2002 and 2004 required that the departments of Homeland Security and Defense establish performance pay systems, and, in 2003, Congress authorized up to $500 million to be appropriated annually to a new Human Capital Performance Fund to be used by OPM for special increases for top performers.

These initiatives fizzled. So controversial were the performance pay systems in Defense and Homeland Security that, in 2009, Congress and the president abandoned them. Congress in 2004 appropriated a disappointing $1 million for the Human Capital Performance Fund, and none since.

Washington has not deserted performance pay: More than three-fifths of federal managers, up from about half ten years earlier, use "performance information" to reward "government employees I manage or supervise."[414]

In 2009, the Senate Budget Committee appointed a Task Force on Government Performance that has performance pay high on its agenda. In the same year, Washington terminated its arbitrary "time-in-grade" rule, first imposed in 1952, that required employees to spend at least one year in a grade before they could be promoted, a policy that seemed at odds with promoting (and paying) for performance. OPM is working on a performance pay plan that could replace the General Schedule. Notably, Congress has kept pay-for-performance programs in agencies (if small ones) where they seem to work.[415]

Paying Performers at the Grass Roots The grass-roots governments also are entering the complex world of performance pay.

In the states, there is some, if mixed, progress. Although the proportion of state employees who are eligible for cost-of-living adjustments increased from 48 to 70 percent in just three years, those who are eligible for step increases declined from a fourth to a fifth over the same period.[416] "Pay-for-performance salary increases" expanded their share of pay systems, however, and "are now the second most available compensation strategy" in the states, exceeded only by cost-of-living adjustments.[417]

Seven out of every ten local governments have pay-for-performance plans.[418] Close to half of the largest counties pay for performance "very often" (36 percent) or "often" (11 percent); only a fourth never use performance pay.[419]

Skeptical Public Personnel Public employees exhibit little fondness for performance pay.

The proportion of federal workers who think that "recognition and rewards are based on performance in my work unit," though nearly tripling over two dozen years,[420] has yet to attain even half of all employees, and only about a fourth agree that "pay raises depend on how well employees perform their jobs."[421]

Surveys of state employees typically reveal significant dissatisfaction with statewide performance pay systems.[422] The leading hindrance in improving state agency performance is that of "adequately rewarding outstanding employees"; more than half of state agency managers identify it as a "serious problem."[423]

Should It Be Done? Most analyses of paying-for-performance in the public sector conclude that it "consistently fails to deliver on its promise" of improving individual performance and public productivity,[424] and "almost always produces hidden costs."[425]

That may not be the half of it: There is evidence suggesting that public-sector performance

pay correlates with *less* performance. One of the "most interesting findings" from an empirical study of the subject "is that the ability to reward a good manager...consistently lowers governmental performance. The reasons for this finding are not altogether clear, but it appears that differential pay for public managers (and possibly other employees) creates dissension and takes a heavy toll on governmental performance—a finding that is consistent with the public management literatures on public service motivation and pay for performance but which runs counter to conventional wisdom and management practice."[426]

It is a singular irony that those few government employees who favor pay-for-performance may not be the ones who are the higher performers. Public workers who are disengaged from their jobs and are "extrinsically motivated" by such motivators as salary bonuses evidence greater receptivity to performance pay than do those probably-already-higher-performing workers who are engaged with their jobs and are "intrinsically motivated" (recall Chapter 3) by such factors as doing a job well—not a good sign if performance pay is to be linked to productivity.[427] Supporting this unfortunate augury is the positive relationship between high public service motivation and higher performing civil servants.[428]

When public performance pay falters, inept administrators are often blamed. But the more culpable causes may well be stubborn, perhaps immutable, institutional and cultural constraints that are unique to the public sector. These include squeezed public budgets; greater transparency in government (where, for example, salaries are public knowledge); and stiff public resistance to big bonuses for bureaucrats.[429]

Despite these concerns, most knowledgeable observers contend, perhaps out of desperation, that paying for performance "would be a huge improvement over the current system, which fails at virtually every task it undertakes."[430]

It's All Relative Let us place this bleak outlook into some perspective.

It is well worth keeping in mind that the private sector wins no prizes in matching performance with pay. A meta-analysis of 137 empirical publications and manuscripts found that more than 40 percent of the performance pay rewarded to corporate chief executive officers (CEO) is the result of their company's size (the bigger the company, the bigger the percentage), "while firm performance accounts for less than 5%" of their presumed "performance" pay.[431]

The only sector where there is a clear and consistent correlation between individual performance and pay is the third one. A unique, four-year study of 2,439 professional fundraisers "currently employed across all subsectors of the nonprofit field" concluded that there is "a significant and positive relationship between money raised and compensation."[432]

Conditions for Successful Public Performance Pay

Pubic-sector incentive pay seems to be relatively successful when the following conditions are present: there is a "clear separation of interests," such as separate career paths, "between politicians and senior civil servants";[433] there is a strong collaboration with unions; staff are involved in establishing and reviewing the pay system; objectives are communicated clearly; individual and organizational goals are linked; the performance-pay system has its own budget; rewards are high and well-differentiated; there is the possibility that the system can be reviewed both internally and externally; pay is combined with other incentives, such as promotion; the job itself is satisfying; the organization and its managers are flexible;[434] there are high levels of trust and professionalism in the agency; performance appraisals are effective; and when performance appraisals are used at lower organizational levels, where job responsibilities are often clearer and more quantifiable."[435]

"The shift to pay for performance," to quote one understated assessment, "is going to be difficult."[436]

The Prospects for Performance Management

Among the literature's "most consistent findings" is that the "absence of good performance management practices" constitutes a "critical flaw."[437] Fortunately, there are some signs of improvement, such as the fact that more than nine out of ten top federal personnel executives think that their agencies do "a good job

of aligning organizational goals to individual performance" to a "moderate" (36 percent) or "great or very great extent" (56 percent).[438]

There are, happily, additional reasons to hope.

Far-Reaching Rulings One such reason is the stance of the Supreme Court under Chief Justice John Roberts, beginning with his appointment in 2005. A review of the Roberts Court's decisions in government worker cases concluded that they "more narrowly define the constitutional rights of public employees," and that, apparently, the chief justice "has the votes" to continue the "deconstitutionalization of public personnel management" for the foreseeable future.[439]

Perhaps the most radical ruling in this "deconstitutionalization" is the Court's decision, rendered in 2008, that greatly enhances the power of all public administrators to improve their performance management. In *Engquist* v. *Oregon Department of Agriculture*, the Court held that, provided discrimination played no part in an employee's dismissal, the Constitution's Fourteenth Amendment (the Equal Protection Clause) does not prohibit a state employee from being fired, even for "arbitrary, vindictive, and malicious reasons." The government needs "broad discretion" to make "subjective" judgments about its workforce that rest "on a wide variety of factors that are difficult to articulate and quantify."

With *Engquist*, public administrators now have that broad discretion, and no longer are expected, apparently, to legally justify their dismissal of employees, both good as well as bad ones.

Practical Performance Management A second reason to be hopeful about the prospects for performance management is that public executives have developed some practical approaches to its improvement. They include the following[440]:

- *Involve employees in building a high performance organization.*
- *Select supervisors who will effectively manage performance.*
- *Hold every supervisor accountable for effective performance management.*
- *Provide supervisors with the training, resources, and managerial support they need to improve their employees' performance.*

There is some distance to travel in this regard; for example, a fifth of federal managers state that they are inadequately trained in performance management,[441] and we documented earlier the tepid managerial support that these administrators receive when disciplining poor performers.

■ *Evaluate the effectiveness of the agency's current performance appraisal system.*

Between the potentially revolutionary ruling by the Supreme Court in *Engquist* and the slow but steady learning curve about how to manage performance, the prospects for improving public employees' performance seem at least possible, and even cautiously encouraging.

RACE, SEX, AGE, DISABILITY, AND JOBS: THE CHALLENGE OF AFFIRMATIVE ACTION

Although it is in decline, prejudice is still present in America, and it is working against women, people of color, the disabled, and older citizens.[442] In the context of employment, we find such phenomena as "sticky floors" (or jobs with limited potential for promotion), "glass ceilings" (organization-wide limitations on advancement for certain groups), and "glass walls" (fields that employ few people from disadvantaged groups).[443]

To counter such biases, government originated the policy of *affirmative action*, which argues for the hiring and promoting of members of disadvantaged groups on the grounds that jobs should be open to as many qualified people as possible.

The Federal Impact: A Tortuous Evolution

What is "conspicuously evident" about the evolution of affirmative action is that its "various laws and rules grew without a strong governmental or legal theory binding them coherently together. Therefore, some of the laws are conflicting and contradictory and exceedingly difficult to interpret, and thus weakening their effectiveness and giving the courts unclear directions in interpreting them."[444]

Roots The roots of this difficult legal history can be traced to 1941, when President Franklin D. Roosevelt issued Executive Order 8802, which barred discrimination by race, religion, or national origin in industries with federal contracts. After a hiatus of two decades, President John F. Kennedy followed with his Executive Order 10925 of 1961, which encouraged the employment of minorities but had no enforcement procedures attached to it.

LBJ: Archangel of Affirmative Action The archangel of affirmative action, however, was President Lyndon Baines Johnson. It was Johnson who, largely by sheer force of personality, pushed through the Civil Rights Act of 1964, Titles VI and VII of which prohibit all forms of discrimination in public- and private-sector hiring. The act included, for the first time, women, Hispanic-Americans, Native Americans, and Asian-Americans, as well as African Americans, as groups whose rights are protected by federal law.

LBJ followed this historic legislation with Executive Order 11246 of 1965, which directed all companies and organizations that had federal contracts to take "affirmative action"—that is, aggressive, proactive execution— to provide equality of opportunity, irrespective of race, religion, or national origin. Executive Order 11246 has been described, properly, as "the most important affirmative action document in the government."[445]

In 1967, Johnson issued Executive Order 11375, which added women, for the first time, to the ranks of those who are specifically protected by affirmative action.

Age Discrimination In 1967, Congress passed the Age Discrimination in Employment Act. The act, as amended in 1974 and 1981, prohibits compulsory retirement in most jobs for reasons of age and protects all workers from age discrimination who are forty years old or older. The act covers some 75 million Americans, or about half of the nation's labor pool.

Vietnam Era Veterans In 1974, Congress enacted the Vietnam Era Veterans' Readjustment Assistance Act, which requires federal contractors to apply affirmative action in the hiring and advancement of more than 8 million veterans of the Vietnam War.

Setting Aside for Minorities and Women

In 1977, Congress passed the Public Works Employment Act, which initiated *set-side programs*, or policies that require governments to reserve (or "set aside") a portion of their contracts for businesses owned by minorities or women. These companies typically account for about a tenth of all federal contract dollars,[446] and uncounted slices of state and local contracts.

In *Fullilove* v. *Klutznick*, the Supreme Court in 1980 ruled that set-asides were constitutional, but later partially backtracked. In *Adarand Constructors, Inc.* v. *Peña* (1996), which pertained to federal set-asides, and *City of Richmond* v. *Croson* (1989), which applied to state and local governments, the Court ruled that set-asides were subject to "strict scrutiny" by the judiciary, and, unless there was a "compelling" public interest in imposing set-asides that were "narrowly tailored" to a alleviating discrimination, set-side programs were unconstitutional.

In response to *Adarand*, the president suspended those set-asides that set numerical goals for awarding contracts to minority- and women-owned businesses, affecting at least $1 billion in set-aside contracts.[447] These actions may have had consequences. A decade following *Adarand*, applications to a large federal fund submitted by white-owned community development organizations were three times more successful, and were awarded almost four times more dollars, than were their minority-owned counterparts.[448]

The grass-roots governments responded to these judicial developments quite differently from Washington. *Croson* forced state and local governments to undertake *disparity studies*, or analyses that demonstrate whether or not set-asides are needed to counter discrimination. "In nearly all of the disparity studies" in one large sample, "there was little serious evaluation" and virtually all these jurisdictions blithely were continuing their set-aside programs.[449] In supposedly complying with *Croson*, state and local governments happily talked the talk, but discreetly declined to walk the walk.

Disabled Americans

In 1990, Congress enacted the Americans with Disabilities Act, which prohibits discrimination against the mentally and physically disabled in employment and accommodations, and affects about 15 percent of the population. The act is "one of the most sweeping nondiscrimination pieces of legislation since the Civil Rights Act of 1964,"[450] although employers have won more than nine out of ten of the suits brought under the act's auspices.[451]

Sexual Orientation

Less than 1 percent of the employees of each type of government and of independent organizations are gay, lesbian, or bisexual. Five percent of gay men and 7 percent of lesbian women with college degrees work in the federal government; 8 percent of each group is employed by state governments; and 7 percent work in local governments. Nearly 16 percent of degreed gay men and 22 percent of lesbians with degrees are nonprofit employees.[452]

There is no federal law that shields federal civilian employees from discrimination on the basis of their sexual orientation, but, in 1998, President Bill Clinton issued Executive Order 13087, which implemented this protection. Extraordinarily few federal employees—about 1 percent, the lowest rate of any discrimination category—allege that they were victims of discrimination because of their sexual orientation.[453]

In contrast to 90 percent of Fortune 500 companies,[454] just thirty-seven states and the District of Columbia prohibit discrimination in employment on the basis of sexual orientation,[455] and, unlike the federal government, twenty-one states and the District of Columbia do so by statute.[456] "Surprisingly," in those states that have banned discrimination by law, rather than by executive order, gay and lesbian representation in state and local governments is "significantly higher."[457] As in the federal government, "relatively few" formal sexual-orientation charges of discrimination have followed the introduction of these policies in the states.[458]

More than 200 local governments have barred discrimination on the basis of sexual orientation.[459]

Affirmative Action for Almost Everyone

Together, these *protected classes*,[460] as they are

called, constitute an impressively large chunk of the American population: More than nine out of ten American adults are protected by federal affirmative action policies.[461]

Federal Enforcement of Affirmative Action

All three branches of the federal government have affirmatively enforced affirmative action.

Congressional Enforcement The critical law in the enforcement of affirmative action is the Equal Employment Opportunity Act of 1972. The act established the Equal Employment Opportunity Commission, which investigates charges of employment discrimination from around the nation and may fine employers in all sectors if it finds discrimination.

Judicial Enforcement Perhaps the judiciary's most notable innovation in enforcement is that of "disparate impact," a doctrine first enunciated by the Supreme Court in 1971, in *Griggs* v. *Duke Power Company*; overturned in 1989 by the Court's five-to-four decision in *Ward's Cove Packing Co.* v. *Antonio*; and reinstated by Congress in the Civil Rights Act of 1991.

Disparate, or *adverse*, *impact* holds that employees who allege discrimination in the workplace do not have to prove that their employer deliberately tried to discriminate against them, but only that they have been disproportionately harmed by workplace policies. Hence, employers can be fined and required to change workplace policies, even though they have not intentionally discriminated.

Over the years, the Supreme Court, citing Title VII of the Civil Rights Act of 1964, has applied adverse impact in cases involving discrimination on the basis of sex, religion, race, or national origin. In 2005, the Court, citing the Age Discrimination in Employment Act, extended adverse impact to age discrimination.[462] These rulings accord a specially protected status to these groups.

In 2009, the Court added a new rule that is central to disparate impact. No African Americans had passed a firefighters' promotion test, although

seventeen whites, including one who was disabled by dyslexia, and a Latino had passed it. Citing adverse impact, the City of New Haven decided to promote no one. In *Ricci* v. *Destefano*, the Court overruled the city and held that a government may not dismiss valid test results and disqualify employees from being promoted simply because of "fear of litigation alone." It is possible that *Ricci* "will make it much more difficult for public employers to fine-tune" their tests in an effort to minimize their adverse impact.[463]

Executive Enforcement The Equal Employment Opportunity Commission is the executive branch's chief enforcer of affirmative action in businesses, governments, and nonprofit organizations, but executive orders and other agencies also are involved.

LBJ's Executive Orders 11246 and 11375 cover some 160,000 government contractors.[464] They are enforced by the Department of Labor's Order Number 4 of 1971 (now Revised Order Number 4, issued in 1978), which requires organizations with federal contracts to establish plans and timetables for achieving specific affirmative-action goals.

Other agencies enforce affirmative action for those employers that do not have federal contracts. The Federal Reserve Board, the Comptroller of the Currency, and the Department of Housing and Urban Development, among others, enforce affirmative action among the nation's banks, mortgage companies, and insurance companies. The Federal Communications Commission is the enforcer for the nation's 5,000 radio stations and 1,500 television stations. In 1990, the Supreme Court upheld that the Commission may take race into account in distributing broadcast licenses.[465]

Retaliation Enforcement Besides investigating discrimination complaints, the Equal Employment Opportunity Commission also investigates charges of retaliation against those employees who charged discrimination. Complaints of retaliation have doubled since 1993, perhaps because "it is often easier for employees to demonstrate that they were retaliated against than that they were victims of discrimination in the first place."[466]

In 2008, the Supreme Court supported the Commission's practice of sanctioning retaliation by ruling in two cases that employees must be protected from reprisal when they complain about racial[467] or age[468] discrimination.

Affirmative Action and the Grass-Roots Governments

State and local governments, where nearly 20 million jobs reside, were initially resistant to federal affirmative action policies when they were introduced in the 1960s,[469] but local public administrators led a change in grass-roots attitudes. By the 1970s, more than four-fifths of all affirmative action plans in municipal governments had been initiated by city managers, about half of whom had developed these plans with no support whatsoever from their own city councils. City managers were "*far and away* the principal initiators of affirmative action in their governments."[470]

The early and visionary initiative that city managers exerted on behalf of affirmative action has held and broadened throughout urban bureaucracies: By the late 1980s, over two-thirds of cities and counties had government-wide affirmative action policies, up from about half fifteen years earlier.[471]

"Reverse Discrimination" and the Quota Question

How is success measured in affirmative action? Can an employer succeed by merely promising (earnestly, of course) to review the job applications of a few more people in the protected classes? Or does success mandate the dismissal of all mentally and physically fit white men under forty years of age, and their replacement by people from those same classes?

These queries bring us quickly to the question of *quotas*, or the hiring and promoting of specific numbers of applicants from protected classes. Usually, these numbers reflect each protected class's percentage in the general population or labor force. The rub, of course, is that qualified applicants who are not from protected classes might not be hired. When this occurs, the charge of "reverse discrimination" is occasionally leveled.

Two Defining Decisions The Supreme Court first addressed reverse discrimination in 1978, in the famous case of *Regents of the University of California* v. *Bakke*, in which Allan Bakke, a white male, was denied admission to the University of California's medical school because it had set aside a portion of each entering class for "approved minorities." The Court ruled five-to-four that the Civil Rights Act required that Bakke be admitted, but all nine justices also held that affirmative action programs *per se* were neither unconstitutional nor illegal, and that being from a minority group could "be deemed a 'plus' in a particular applicant's file."

In 1979, the Supreme Court heard the "blue-collar *Bakke*" case, *Weber* v. *Kaiser Aluminum and Steel Corporation and United Steel Workers Union*. Brian Weber, a white lab technician, charged discrimination against whites in a training program that mandated that half of its available positions be filled by blacks. The Court held that employers could consider race as one of many factors not only in training policies, but in hiring and promotion policies as well.

Both decisions ostensibly outlawed quotas, but left some leeway for colleges and employers to improve the odds for minority applicants and employees.

Two Definitive Decisions For the next quarter-century, the judiciary hemmed and hawed, churning out a series of largely ambivalent rulings that wobbled either for diversity or ignored it.

In 2003, the Supreme Court decided a pair of cases, both brought by the University of Michigan, that clarified its views. In *Gratz* v. *Bollinger*, the Court stated that the University's undergraduate admissions policy, which amounted to a point system designed in part to increase diversity, was ill conceived and unconstitutional. In *Grutter* v. *Bollinger*, the Court held that the University's law school's admissions policy, which also took race into account, did so more pliably than the University's undergraduate admissions policy, and this flexibility rendered it constitutional.

In both decisions, the Court ruled that attaining diversity is a constitutionally defensible goal, but, to pass constitutional muster, the diversity-relevant components of personnel policies should be largely free of numbers, characterized by vaguely-expressed goals, and imbued with human judgment.

The "Quota Bill" of 1991 We cannot leave the subject of quotas without noting that imposing them can sometimes be perversely counterproductive. In 1991, Congress passed a Civil Rights Act that made it much more difficult—and costly—for employers to fire workers in the protected classes. Opponents derided the act as a "quota bill."

Employers soon circumvented the act by abandoning their standard practice of firing an unsatisfactory employee outright "for cause" (a procedure that accounts for about a fifth of all workers who are let go), and relying instead on laying off groups of workers when business was down. These layoffs included protected employees who employers actually wanted to fire for cause, thereby making discrimination very hard to prove.

African American men are now fired for cause much less frequently, but this reduction has been cancelled out by their far more frequent layoffs; for white men, the ratio of firings to layoffs has stayed the same.[472] The Civil Rights Act of 1991 has helped end "a decades-long trend" of gains that minorities and women had made in "historically unwelcoming sectors."[473]

Tests: The Validation Vexation

A dimension of affirmative action that is closely related to reverse discrimination is that of testing applicants for hire or promotion.

Validating Tests In 1971, the Supreme Court ruled in the landmark case, *Griggs* v. *Duke Power Co.*, that to hire people on the basis of qualifications that could not be shown to be relevant to the knowledge and skills that are actually needed to do the job in question is discriminatory under the Civil Rights Act of 1964.

In a word, the Court held that such tests must be valid. *Test validity* is the level of confidence that employers can reasonably have in the power of an examination to predict how well, or how badly, an applicant will fare in a specific job. Cognitive-ability tests have the greatest validity and utility and the lowest costs.[474]

African Americans and Hispanic Americans usually score lower than whites on cognitive-ability tests,[475] and women score slightly lower than men.[476] Local public administrators consistently identify "test results" as the single greatest disqualifier of minorities seeking employment.[477]

Why is this? Researchers and justices attribute these disparities to *cultural bias*, or the tendency of test writers to unwittingly slant their tests' questions in ways that reflect the majority culture, and thereby handicap those test takers who were reared in minority cultures. The Supreme Court has ruled not only that culturally biased tests are illegal, even when the employer is not discriminating intentionally,[478] but that, even when no discrimination is present, the use of culturally biased tests is *still* illegal![479]

Human capital managers in all sectors, but particularly those in the public one, face an exquisite dilemma. They may choose the simplest, cheapest, and probably best predictor of job performance, the cognitive-ability test, to hire and promote, but risk incurring a judicial ruling of adverse impact if they do. Or they may choose "other, less effective predictors and potentially increasing minority representation in the workforce."[480]

Federal Fecklessness The federal government responded to this dilemma by largely abandoning written tests altogether. Washington first introduced a "universal" test (i.e., a single test for entry to all agencies) in 1955, and, from 1960 to 1980, from half to three-fifths of the federal government's nearly 2 million applicants took it or other written tests.[481] Because the examination had a disparate impact on minorities, the judiciary forbade its use in 1981. The OPM found no replacement until 1990, and then only because the courts demanded it. So few agencies used it, however, that, only four years later, OPM radically reduced its applicability, and it has not been replaced.[482] The Chief Human Capital Officers Act of 2002 allows agencies to ignore applicants' test scores in favor of their own ranking system and to hire candidates directly. Competitive examinations are now used to hire fewer than three out of ten federal new hires, and their use is in decline.[483]

Grass-Roots Problem Solving In contrast to feckless federal personnel administrators, their state and local counterparts not only are using written tests extensively—95 percent of large cities use them in hiring, and their use is growing[484]—but they also have dealt with the dilemma of testing with greater creativity—and effectiveness.

Race Norming and Banding In 1979, the Supreme Court declared *veterans' preference*, or the policy of adding points to veterans' test scores, to be constitutional.[485] It quickly and understandably occurred to state and local personnel administrators: Why not do the same for minorities? Hence, in the early 1980s, some governments introduced *race norming*, or adding points to a test score if the test taker is from a minority group.

The Civil Rights Act of 1991 bans race norming, but still requires preferential treatment of applicants from protected classes. In 2001, the Seventh Circuit Court of Appeals attempted to reconcile the act's conflicting positions, and ruled that race norming was not the same as *banding*, which is the simplification and consolidation of test scores. The court held that race norming is illegal, but banding, which amounts to back-door race norming and front-door preferential treatment, is acceptable.[486]

Following the Rules. It Works! A far more straightforward tack is to follow the rules, and, when governments do, they are surprisingly successful in melding cognitive ability with equal opportunity.

During the 1970s, following the Supreme Court's *Griggs* decision, the proportion of state and local personnel offices that validated their tests burgeoned from 54 percent[487] to 87 percent[488] in only five years. The courts have supported these efforts, and have held, quite consistently, that if a public agency uses a cognitive-ability test that has been developed and validated, preferably by experts using professional standards, and if the cutoff scores are properly set, then the test is legal.[489]

Women's Work?

Women hoe a rocky row in the public workplace. A national survey of 1,600 of these employees "from different levels of the public sector" found that women are more likely than men to be single or divorced, have fewer or no children, and have more onerous household responsibilities.[490]

Women who work in government also are paid less than their male colleagues. Although, as we explain later, the *gender pay gap*, in which men are paid, on average, more than women, is much narrower in the public sector than in the private and nonprofit sectors and is narrowing further, government's gap nevertheless persists. Its persistence appears to be related to the fact that "gender affects the amount of authority that is delegated to an employee [and women are granted less authority than men], which, in turn, affects the variance in pay between men and women."[491]

The deprivations do not end there but actually continue into retirement. "A primary factor" in those government pension plans that are among the most "significantly" underfunded (recall Chapter 8) is the presence of "more female active participants in the plan, suggesting another risk to women's retirement income."[492]

As a consequence of these and other inequities, most of which occur both in and out of government, three policies have emerged that are designed to curb sexual discrimination in employment, including public employment. Each has a special relevance for women, although none of them is the sole preserve of women.

The *Bona Fide* Occupational Qualification Until the 1970s, there were numerous state *protective labor laws* that prohibited women from entering jobs that were deemed to be too strenuous for them.

Congress eventually intervened. The Equal Pay Act of 1963 banned several artificial job qualifications, and Title VII of the Civil Rights Act of 1964 required that employers specify only a "bona fide occupational qualification reasonably necessary."

Both laws were quickly challenged in the courts, but to little avail. The Supreme Court ruled in 1968 that protective labor laws could not be used to deny women jobs or promotions,[493] and the Fifth Circuit Court of Appeals held in 1969 that, in judging the validity of a job qualification, the burden of proof lies with the employer.[494]

The Curious Question of Comparable Worth

Comparable worth means that employees in one position classification should be paid the same as employees performing tasks in another classification that involve comparable levels of importance, knowledge, stress, skills, and responsibilities, even though the tasks themselves may be quite different. As a practical matter, comparable worth works to raise the salaries of employees in position classifications dominated by women.

Comparable worth assumes that the social value of occupations can be assessed and compared, and this can be a tricky business. Are, for instance, the musicians in a city's symphony orchestra worth "more" to society than the plumbers in the municipal waterworks? The major case on comparable worth to date is *American Federation of State, County, and Municipal Employees (AFSCME) v. State of Washington*, in which the Ninth Circuit Court of Appeals held in 1985 that Washington State was not obliged to award back pay to 15,500 state employees in position classifications dominated by women. Ultimately, the case was settled out of court, and the state agreed to set new pay levels for some 60,000 state employees in an effort to bring women's salaries in line with those of men.

Perhaps because popular opinion favors comparable worth by as much as three to one,[495] governments have been responsive. Twenty states have raised pay for women, eight states have enacted laws establishing the principle of comparable worth for all state employees, and only five states have failed to undertake some sort of comparable-worth activity.[496]

Ten percent of cities and 12 percent of counties have enacted comparable worth policies.[497]

Implementing comparable worth is, paradoxically, both economical and difficult. In the eight states that passed comparable worth laws, the aggregate gender pay gap ranged from 14 to 31 percent in state agencies, but closing these gaps required relatively modest expenditures that ranged from 1 to 4 percent of total state payrolls. Downsides, however, were evident: pay compression intensified; state salaries declined relative to private-sector salaries; men left their state jobs at greater rates;[498] and, in all states, male state employees suffered an "average wage penalty" relative to the private sector. Nevertheless, comparable worth has achieved its ends, and female state workers in all states now enjoy an "average wage premium" relative to the private sector.[499]

The New Meaning of Sex at Work

Sexual harassment is a comment or act by a co-worker in the workplace, or a workplace environment, that is interpreted by a worker to have sexual overtones and causes discomfort in, or is offensive to, the worker. About 1 percent of American adults say that they have been sexually harassed.[500]

Most private firms, the federal government, at least two-thirds of the states (only eight states clearly fail to address this issue),[501] and almost nine out of ten local governments[502] have policies prohibiting sexual harassment. Not quite 12,000 sexual harassment charges are filed each year, and constitute less than 12 percent of all discrimination charges received by the Equal Employment Opportunity Commission.[503]

There is some good news, however. Even as all forms of discrimination charges in all sectors rose by 24 percent over thirteen years, sexual harassment charges declined by 26 percent over the same period.[504] More public employees than ever— more than nine out of ten federal male employees, up from less than a third fourteen years earlier— understand what sexual harassment is.[505]

Who Harasses and Where? More than two-fifths of women and nearly a fifth of men who work in federal agencies report incidents of "unwanted sexual attention" that occurred over the preceding two years.[506] Perspective, of course, is pertinent, and it appears that sexual harassment in government does not attain its levels in the private sector. Twenty-two percent of those federal workers who have worked outside the government believe that there is more sexual harassment in these workplaces, compared to 7 percent who think there is less.[507] Nearly two-thirds of women executives in private industry report that they have been sexually harassed—a third more than in government.[508]

The Court Weighs In In 1986, the Supreme Court heard its first sexual harassment case and decided that Title VII of the Civil Rights Act of 1964 covered sexual harassment, in effect declaring sexual harassment to be a form of discrimination.[509]

Victims of such discrimination, the Court ruled in 1992, could sue their harassers for damages.[510]

In the following year, the justices agreed unanimously that women are different from men. The Court held that sexual remarks that may not be offensive to men could offend a "reasonable woman," thereby creating a "hostile environment" in the workplace. Such a woman could sue for relief "before the harassing conduct leads to a nervous breakdown."[511]

In 1998, the Court decided three cases that did much to clarify the legalities of sexual harassment. One was *Oncale* v. *Sundowner Offshore Services*, in which the justices unanimously found that harassment could occur in same-sex situations.

In *Fanagher* v. *City of Boca Raton* and *Burlington Industries, Inc.* v. *Ellerth*, the Court held that, even if an employer was unaware of a supervisor harassing a subordinate, the employer was still liable for damages if the subordinate had suffered a "tangible adverse action," such as a demotion. If, however, there were anti-harassment policies and complaint procedures in place that displayed "reasonable care" by the employer in preventing and correcting harassment, and if harassed employees chose to ignore these policies and procedures, then they could expect little if any protection from the judiciary.

What a Strange Trip It's Been: The Unique Experiences of Minority and Women Public Administrators

The experiences of minority and female public administrators differ from those of majority and male public administrators.

Public Administrators of Color: Mixed Perceptions, Mixed Evidence The proportion of all federal workers who think that they have experienced racial discrimination in their workplace has declined by a factor of almost three over nearly two decades, and now stands at a slim 5 percent.[512] Of greater importance, federal minority employees think that their lot is improving. The percentage of federal African American workers who perceive that "they had been denied a job, promotion or pay increase" because of their race declined by

three-fourths over fifteen years and fell by three-fifths for Hispanic employees over the same period; currently, 9 percent of each group perceives discrimination.[513] In the states, views may differ. African American public administrators report "that they experience career-impeding supervisory behaviors at a greater rate than their white colleagues."[514]

The evidence supporting these perceptions is mixed. Federal administrators and professionals of color, for instance, have lower pay grades, "even after controlling for education, experience, and other advancement-related factors," and "receive, on average, lower performance ratings"; yet they still have "generally comparable" promotion rates.[515] An examination of more than 248,000 performance appraisals of state employees found "no support" for the charge that management's use of detailed performance-rating instruments resulted in an adverse impact on minority and women employees.[516]

Why Perceptions Matter Regardless of how accurate their concerns may be, however, when people believe that they are being discriminated against, or simply treated unfairly, in the workplace, their organization's performance falters. Workers who think that they have endured discrimination exhibit declining "organizational citizenship," commitment, satisfaction, and productivity, and rising rates of absenteeism, grievances, and turnover.[517]

Public employees "who feel that they are treated unfairly are more likely" appeal more decisions, file more discrimination and safety complaints, and take more sick leave than do workers who think that they are treated fairly.[518]

The stronger the perception of "procedural justice" in the Defense Department (which, as a *very* closed-model organization, logically should be indifferent to fairness), the higher the rates of employee satisfaction and trust in management, and the less that they consider leaving the Pentagon for another job; managers actually exhibit these patterns more strongly than other employees.[519]

In sum, it is in the best interest of any organization to not only eliminate discrimination and unfairness but to eliminate perceptions of them, too. Regrettably, this is easier said than done. Even when minority and white employees have comparable levels of understanding about the politics of their workplaces, minority anxiety does not lower, nor does job satisfaction rise; by contrast, anxiety lessens and satisfaction increases among white employees when they better understand their workplace dynamics.[520]

Women Public Administrators: Comparable and Confident

The proportion of all federal workers who think that they have experienced gender discrimination in their workplace has fallen by a factor of more than three over nearly two decades, and now stands at a less than 4 percent.[521] Thirteen percent of federal women employees presently perceive that "they had been denied a job, promotion or pay increase" because of their gender, a decline of more than two-fifths over fifteen years.[522] Even though women in government are sexually harassed more than twice as much as men,[523] women are only marginally more likely than men to think that they were denied a job benefit due to their gender.[524]

So women public administrators are not cowed. Nor is there reason for them to be. Women who work in government: Have personal values, as "numerous studies" suggest, that share "a significant similarity" with those of men;[525] are as committed to the public service as men;[526] "have almost identical responsibilities" as men;[527] prioritize tasks the same as men;[528] have political and professional characteristics that are "indistinguishable" from men's;[529] and are "as confident as men in their ability to supervise their workforce."[530]

Women Public Administrators: Capacities and Competencies

Beyond these comparable values and views, women and men differ in their administrative strengths and weaknesses.

On a general plane, a high level of testosterone "does not predict" a person's "status within the group,"[531] and women as a gender remember better than men,[532] obviously an important advantage in any administrative work.

When we focus on government, women public administrators surpass men in listening, communicating,[533] compassion, and their attraction to policymaking.[534] They are less experienced professionally (they are also younger)[535] and spend less time on "internal management" than men.[536] These

factors may account for women being less effective than men in networking "the external environment" of their agencies,[537] an activity that produces more positive organizational outcomes for men than for women. By contrast, "networking with peers is more beneficial for women" than for men.[538]

Of greater significance than varying managerial capacities, women public administrators deliver. Women workers are more likely than men to report problems that higher management should know about.[539] The more women who work directly with citizens in an agency, the higher the agency's performance.[540] Federal female administrators "typically" receive higher performance ratings than men in the same grades and in the same agencies.[541] Women public administrators "consistently get better performance" than men from the boards and councils to which they report,[542] and women seem to understand why: "most interestingly, women executives" in government "rate themselves as relatively more influential than do their male colleagues."[543]

Backlash!

Americans, regardless of ethnicity, are growing more accepting of one another.[544]

Public Opinions on Affirmative Action

These demographics likely have brought Americans closer together on a number of broad racial issues.[545] White support for affirmative action has grown significantly since the mid-1990s,[546] an ironic trend in light of a burgeoning belief among African Americans that they no longer need government's help to get ahead. In 1970, four-fifths of blacks agreed that "Washington should make every effort to improve the social and economic position of blacks," a proportion that, by 1992, had declined by about half to approximately two-fifths and has remained there ever since.[547]

Still, there is controversy. Eleven percent of Americans say that they have been hurt, and only 4 percent say that they have been helped, by affirmative action.[548] White men have long harbored the deepest reservations about affirmative action. (Researchers have found that white males protect their "self-esteem [and] sense of self-competence" by choosing to believe that "affirmative action is a quota-based policy."[549]) Although a solid majority of white men currently support affirmative action,[550] 17 percent (compared with 9 percent of white women) say that they have been hurt by the policy. On this question, political ideology plays little, if any, part, and the responses of conservative and liberal white people are virtually identical.[551]

Affirmative Action's Odder Outcomes No doubt, some odd interpretations, at least by traditional criteria, of what a person's civil rights ought to be have fueled a growing disaffection with affirmative action among whites and minorities alike. Examples include the apparently unpleasant couple who sued their local chapter of Mothers Against Drunk Driving on the grounds that they had been barred from joining due to the chapter's "personality bias." Or the lawyer who won in court the right of "nerds" to gain entry to a nightclub.[552] The nasty and nerdy are protected classes? Pasadena grants preferences to Armenian Americans seeking city contracts; Cincinnati favors citizens of "Appalachian regional origin"; and Massachusetts protects Portuguese Americans.[553]

White cynicism also plays a part, as exemplified by Los Angeles, which established "ethnic review committees" that investigated "ethnic discrepancies" among teachers.[554] Shades of the Third Reich, which also investigated ethnic discrepancies.

Affirmative Action as Stigma? More than a fourth of the public thinks that affirmative action stigmatizes minorities, and far more African Americans than whites believe this to be true.[555]

Two extensive experiments support this view. People were given specially created files that showed identical performance levels among women managers and were asked to rank them and award salary increases. When certain managers were identified as "affirmative action hires," they were ranked as less competent and granted smaller increases. Remarkably, even when a second set of files demonstrated clearly superior performance by "affirmative action hires," they still received lower rankings.[556]

A Grass-Roots Rebellion? In a few states, this perspective is becoming public policy. In 1995, the Board of Regents of the 220,000-student University of California banned the use of affirmative action in its ten campuses' admissions policies, a decision copied by Colorado's and Florida's state universities.

In 1996, 54 percent of California's voters approved Proposition 209, which prohibits the state's government from granting race- and gender-based preferences in hiring, promoting, contracting, and college admissions. In 1998, 59 percent of Washington State's voters enacted Initiative 200; in 2006, 58 percent of Michigan's electorate passed Proposal 2; and in 2008, 58 percent of Nebraska's voters enacted Initiative 424, but 51 percent of Colorado's electorate narrowly defeated Amendment 46. All were virtual clones of California's Proposition 209.

These referenda have consequences. "Employment among women and minorities dropped sharply" following Proposition 209's passage, suggesting "that affirmative action programs in California either had been inefficient...or had been effective while in place but had failed to create lasting change in employers' prejudicial attitudes."[557] With the marginal exception of the hair's-breadth defeat of Colorado's Amendment 46, there is an even larger point being made by these referenda: Affirmative action no longer is an acceptable public policy to many citizens.

Is Affirmative Action a Defensible Policy?

As the backlash indicates, affirmative action is a controversial policy. Why?

An Un-American Policy? Affirmative action is sometimes accused of violating the American tradition of equality of opportunity by singling out certain groups for special treatment. But granting advantages to selected groups wars in no fashion against American tradition. Need-based scholarships; veterans' preference in governmental hiring; and small business set-asides, enacted by Congress twenty-four years before it enacted minority business set-asides, are examples of policies that favor certain groups precisely because those groups are disadvantaged. Affirmative action simply continues this tradition among groups with strong cases that they are disadvantaged in education and income and by social prejudice. Whether affirmative action is a good or bad policy, it is, nonetheless, a wholly American one.

Is Diversity Desirable? A cornerstone of affirmative action, and a gigantic judicial justification of it, is that it promotes diversity on campuses and in workplaces. But is diversity so desirable that it warrants the billions of dollars spent through affirmative action policies to achieve it?

Yes, probably. A massive and unique analysis concludes that, "Ability matters. But—here's the catch—so does diversity." In fact, collective diversity consistently "trumps" individual ability. In every sector, the more diverse organizations make more accurate predictions and solve problems better.[558] In the private sector, with its uniquely clear metrics of organizational performance, the more racially and gender-diverse businesses have significantly, even dramatically, more market share, customers, sales, and profits.[559] In the public sector, "contrary to expectations, racial diversity is associated with less division" and conflict among school board members.[560]

Among the benefits that diversity produces are personal ones. The more diverse the university, the more likely that there will be "widespread beneficial effects," including superior retention rates, grades, and self-confidence among students, "irrespective of race."[561] "On the whole, studies show" that greater diversity in governments "leads to... policy outcomes that benefit represented groups," whether female, male, black, brown, or white.[562]

Diversity Management: The Crucial Component

Groups and governments, schools and cities, companies and countries, all perform measurably better when they are more diverse, but only when certain, specific conditions are present. Diversity improves collective performance: Only when "identity diversity," such as gender or ethnicity, is "linked with cognitive diversity," which is a product of experience and training; only when diversity is "relevant" ("we cannot expect that adding a poet to a medical research team would enable them to find a cure for the common cold"); and only when the people in diverse groups "get along" (if they do not, then "the cognitive differences between them may be little more than disconnected silos of ideas"). "Well-managed identity diversity does produce benefits."[563]

American governments seem to manage diversity reasonably well. Federal employees' complaints of discrimination have declined over time, even as complaints from all other employment categories, on average, have risen substantially.[564] An analysis of a "very large sample of federal employees" in sixty-seven agencies found that those workers in agencies with high levels of racial diversity perceived "lower organizational effectiveness" in their agencies. "But strikingly, where they perceive that *diversity is effectively managed*," they also think that their agencies' "effectiveness is higher," even in those agencies with greater racial diversity.[565] Somewhat surprisingly, older public administrators manage diversity more effectively than younger ones.[566]

The People *versus* Person Problem Perhaps the deepest critique of affirmative action is that it perpetrates its own injustices. Specifically, affirmative action can grant advantages to already-advantaged individuals in disadvantaged groups, and deny advantages to disadvantaged persons who are not in disadvantaged groups. There can be little doubt that, because affirmative action concerns itself with groups rather than individual persons, it can create individual injustices. The question, however, is this: Would its elimination result in greater justice?

Our answer is no; indeed, quite the opposite. The contention that, because some undeserving people may benefit from affirmative action, we should close it down is a classic expression of the odd rationale that, because a good policy is not perfect, we should discard that policy because it is merely good. It is a case of throwing out babies with bath water.

Worse, the argument also assumes that we have a perfect method for fairly assessing and ranking the relative merit of every single person in society. No society has that ability, and never will. Justice and life cannot be reasonably separated, and the people-*versus*-person argument contends that they can. "The black person who moves up the line thanks to affirmative action may not logically 'deserve' the place he gets. But, for the same reason, the white person who loses that place doesn't 'deserve' it either...The point is that a pure, discrimination-free society is not merely a hopeless ideal; it is a logical mirage."[567]

The Effects of the Efforts

What has affirmative action, a public policy for nearly a half-century, achieved?

"The majority of the empirical research demonstrates the positive impact" of affirmative action "on educational policies and employment opportunities for minorities and women." Affirmative action "is decidedly less significant when it comes to other major goals such as hiring, equal pay, and the elimination of discrimination once minorities and women are hired."[568]

Its impact has been especially salubrious in government.

The Federal Record   Washington has made significant progress in providing equal opportunity to its employees.

Federal Employees of Color   People of color comprise 34 percent of the American population and nearly 33 percent of federal employees in white-collar jobs. Seventeen percent of these civilian workers are African American (whose proportion of the total American resident population

is less than 14 percent); almost 8 percent are Hispanic Americans (who number 15 percent of the population); and nearly 8 percent are American Indians, Alaska Natives, Asian Americans, and Pacific Islanders (who account for 5 percent).[569]

For the most part, these are encouraging figures. African Americans, Native Americans, Alaska Natives, and Pacific Islanders "have greatly benefited from the federal government's affirmative action programs....Asians have also benefited...but not as extensively," but "Hispanics are considerably underemployed in almost every category of federal occupations in relation to their availability in the labor force."[570]

As Table 9-1 indicates, over twenty-seven years, minority progress in the federal government has been steady. Twenty percent of the top federal executives are African American, Hispanic American, or are from other minority groups.[571]

TABLE 9-1

Percentages of Federal Full-Time Civilian Black, Hispanic, and Women Employees, by General Schedule and Related Grades, 1980 and 2007

Grade Range	1980			2007		
	Black	Hispanic	Women*	Black	Hispanic	Women*
Total Executive/Senior Pay Levels ($$$$$)	5%	Fewer than 50	4%	6%	4%	31%
Grades 13–15 ($$$$)	5	2	8	12	5	35
Grades 9–12 ($$$)	9	3	19	17	8	46
Grades 5–8 ($$)	20	4	46	25	9	63
Grades 1–4 ($)	24	5	74	24	9	64
Totals, All Employees	15	4	45	17	8	48

Notes: Percentages have been rounded and are expressed as a percentage of all federal employees in each grade range. Covers executive branch, General Schedule and related employees, and Executive/Senior Pay Levels only. Excludes employees in the Postal Service, Wage Pay System, and other pay systems.

*Data for women in all grade ranges for "2007" are actually for 2006, with the exception of the grade range, "Total Executive/Senior Pay Levels," which is for 2009. (Women comprised 27 percent of this range in 2006.) For women only, this top grade range covers only the Senior Executive Service, or about a third of the larger range. Some grade ranges for women varied slightly in 1980 from those in 2006. For women only, Grades 9–12 in the table were actually Grades 11–12 for women in 1980; Grades 5–8 were Grades 7–10 in 1980; and Grades 1–4 were Grades 1–6 in 1980. Grades 13–15 were the same for women in 1980 and 2006.

Sources: As derived from data in U.S. Bureau of the Census, *Statistical Abstract of the United States, 2011*, 130th ed. (Washington, DC: U.S. Government Printing Office, 2011), Table 499; U.S. Office of Personnel Management, *Federal Civilian Workforce Statistics: The Fact Book, 2007 edition* (Washington, DC: U.S. Government Printing Office, 2010), pp. 28, 48, 50, 52, 73; and U.S. Merit Systems Protection Board, *Women in the Federal Government: Ambitions and Achievements* (Washington, DC: U.S. Government Printing Office, 2011), p. 6.

Federal Women Employees A similar configuration is evident for women in the federal employ. Women comprise 51 percent of the American population, and 48 percent of the full-time civilian employees who work in federal white-collar jobs.[572] As Table 9-1 shows, women have made substantial progress, with 31 percent of top posts occupied by women.

The level of education held by federal women administrators has increased. Forty-six percent have a bachelor's degree or higher, compared with 38 percent eighteen years earlier. Male federal administrators with a four-year degree actually slipped over the same period, from 56 to 54 percent.[573]

These educational trends, among other factors, are reflected in more equitable pay. Over two decades, the federal government's overall gender pay gap "declined significantly"—by nearly a third—from 28 to 19 percent,[574] and it is 14 percent narrower than that of the national workforce.[575] The narrowing gender pay gap has been especially salubrious for federal female administrators and professionals. Over a period of thirty-three years, these women moved from earning just 79 percent of what their male counterparts earned, to 93 percent, and most of this narrowing has been relatively recent.[576]

With fairer salaries has come greater respect; over sixteen years, the proportion of women federal employees who agreed that "women and men are respected equally" at work grew by a fourth, and now stands at two-fifths.[577]

The Grass-Roots' Record Like the federal government, state and local jurisdictions have, with some exceptions, made substantial advances in developing fairer places to work.

State and Local Employees of Color A full third of all full-time state and local employees (excluding educators) are from minority groups.[578] As Table 9-2 indicates, African Americans have made steady progress in all occupational categories over two dozen years, and Hispanic Americans have doubled, at a minimum, their representation in every category.

African Americans "are overrepresented in many" state governments, although "Latinos are typically underrepresented."[579] In 1964, 2 percent of state agency heads were minorities, evenly divided between African and Asian Americans. Today, 10 percent are, with blacks occupying nearly 6 percent of top positions, and Hispanics and Asian Americans at almost 2 percent apiece.[580] At the local

---

▎**TABLE 9-2**

Percentages of Full-Time Black, Hispanic, and Women Employees in State and Local Governments (Excluding Educators), by Occupational Category, 1980 and 2007

Occupational Category	1980			2007		
	Black	Hispanic	Women	Black	Hispanic	Women
Officials/Administrators ($$$$)	6%	2%	23%	12%	6%	39%
Professionals ($$$)	9	3	44	15	8	57
Technicians ($$)	12	4	39	15	11	42
Blue Collar/Clerical ($)	19	5	40	21	12	42
Totals, All Employees	16	4	41	18	11	46

Notes: Percentages have been rounded and are expressed as a percentage of all state and local employees in each occupational category. The occupational category, "Blue Collar/Clerical," includes Protective Services, Paraprofessionals, Administrative Support, Skilled Craft, and Service Maintenance.

Sources: As derived from data in U.S. Bureau of the Census, *Statistical Abstract of the United States, 2011,* 130th ed. (Washington, DC: U.S. Government Printing Office, 2011), Table 462, and U.S. Bureau of the Census, *Statistical Abstract of the United States, 1982–1983,* 103rd ed. (Washington, DC: U.S. Government Printing Office, 1982), Table 504.

level, there is less progress. Only 5 percent of the highest appointed local executives, city managers, are minorities. This proportion is unchanged from ten years earlier, but is an improvement from twenty years ago, when just 1 percent were minorities.[581]

State and Local Women Employees   Table 9-2 shows that that 46 percent of all full-time state and local employees (again excluding educators) are women, and relatively large numbers of women are found in the upper rungs of the grass-roots occupational ladders.[582]

"Women are generally overrepresented in state government employment" relative to the civilian labor force within their states.[583] and, as we noted earlier, are paid more, on average, than are their private-sector counterparts.[584]

Twenty-nine percent of state department heads are women, up from just 2 percent in 1964,[585] and women state executives command salaries that are "similar" to those of men.[586]

Eleven percent of city managers are women, a slight decline from a decade earlier, but an elevenfold increase from more than thirty-five years ago.[587]

Why the Lag in Local Governments?   The chief appointed executives of general purpose local governments are, obviously, at least twice as white and male as are their counterparts in the federal and state governments. This is much less the case with special purpose local governments; more than two decades ago, a fourth of the executive directors of public authorities were women,[588] and their representation is likely higher today.

The sad situation in cities and counties seems to be less a function of curmudgeonly top executives (who, recall, were early and underappreciated champions of affirmative action) and more a reflection of those who appoint them. City and county managers do not appoint city and county managers. City and county councils do.

The Third Sector Record   In terms of providing fair workplaces, the independent sector is best described as an oddly mixed bag.

Independent Employees of Color   Twenty-three percent of all public-serving nonprofit, full-time employees

are people of color, not quite doubling from twenty-five years earlier. Thirteen percent of their board members (a tripling over the same period) and 6 percent of their CEOs (an increase of three-and-a-half times over a quarter-century) are from minority groups.[589] At the 400 largest philanthropies (i.e., those that raise the most money), 6 percent of their CEOs are minorities, the same percentage as for all public-serving nonprofit organizations.[590]

Nonprofit CEOs view fundraising as crucial to their organizations' success (and, often, survival),[591] so it is heartening to learn that "race is generally not significant (either black or other)" as a variable in determining the compensation of professional fundraisers.[592]

Although it has made progress, the independent sector in general has not extended workplace opportunities to people of color to the degree that the public sector has.

Independent Women Employees   Over the same quarter-century, "the entire foundation field became overwhelmingly 'female.' " Seventy-six percent of all public-serving nonprofit, full-time employees are women, an increase of 15 percent over twenty-five years. Fifty-two percent of their CEOs are white women (a growth of 30 percent over sixteen years), as are 31 percent of their board members (up by 15 percent over the same period).[593] In the 400 largest nonprofit organizations, however, 19 percent of CEOs are women, nearly two-thirds lower than the overall figure.[594] Women are more likely to be CEOs and board chairs when the association has a smaller budget, is relatively new, is in some city other than Washington, DC, and has a relatively large percentage of women serving on its board.[595]

Despite their takeover of the independent sector, issues for women persist. A national study of professional fundraising found "a gender-pay gap, even after controlling for all factors traditionally associated with pay differentials between males and females," notably organizational size and location, and professional experience and education. Chief development officers, staffers, and even consultants who were women had "significantly" lower compensation than their male counterparts.[596] On average, female fundraisers earn salaries that are a fourth lower than male fundraisers and hold a larger number of lower-paying jobs than men. Moreover, the gender–wage gap for these employees almost doubled over seventeen years.[597]

In sum, the third sector seems to be on a rough par with the public one in terms of advancing women up the executive ladder (with the very large exception of city and county governments, which fall well behind nonprofit organizations), but it seriously lags in closing the gender wage gap.

A Palpably Progressive Sector Minorities and women fare far better in public sector than in the private one.

A review of analyses of the pay gap in federal, state, and local governments found a "consensus" among them to the effect that "the wage gap between white males and both minorities and women persists, although it is lower in the public sector than in the private sector."[598]

Women who work in governments are "decreasing their levels of occupational segregation in civil service employment and moving toward achieving a representative bureaucracy.... Women appear to be most successful, both financially and career-wise, in historically male-dominated fields."[599]

"Federal agencies are on a par, or even ahead, of their corporate counterparts in the initiation of new recruitment, training, and development" of members of disadvantaged groups.[600]

"In the aggregate, state and local governments are doing considerably better than the private sector in living up the challenge of attaining sexual and racial-ethnic employment equity," establishing a record that is "quite impressive."[601]

These advances stand in stark contrast to the private sector. The proportion of CEOs of the Fortune 500 companies who are minorities or women does not exceed a fraction of 1 percent,[602] far below—and, in some instances, radically below—their proportions in the public (and third) sector.

To a statistically significant degree, female corporate managers "are viewed with suspicion and...their commitment and competence are over-tested" when decisions on advancements are being made.[603] Even though women managers in the private sector are more aggressive in pursuing

promotions and have higher performance scores than males, men nevertheless are offered more promotions per years of service than are women.[604]

Women seem to have gotten the message. Women who work in companies, in an apparent contrast to women in governments, are less confrontational than men and prefer avoidance to argument.[605] "Competitive workplaces" in the private sector "can in fact significantly decrease the propensity of women to apply for a job compared to that of men."[606]

Compared with the private sector, then, minorities and women in the public sector not only are doing good but doing well.

A Demographic Solution?

Is affirmative action responsible for the increased diversity in colleges and companies, nonprofit organizations and governments? Possibly not. "Only a small fraction of the public"—a modest 16 percent—"reports having been directly affected by affirmative action programs," whether for good or ill.[607] Demographic trends may be more responsible than affirmative action for diversity, although it seems irrefutable that affirmative action has helped make these trends felt in organizations.

In 1950, white men comprised 70 percent of the civilian workforce.[608] Since then, their share has slipped by nearly a fourth to 53 percent, and likely will slide further, to 43 percent, by 2018.[609] The drainage of white males from the labor pool reflects America's dwindling supply of young white men.[610]

Increasingly, minorities and women are taking the place of white men. Between 1980 and 2009, the proportion of workers in the civilian labor force who were not white expanded by 46 percent, from 13 percent to nearly 19 percent, and minority workers are projected to comprise 21 percent of all workers by 2018.[611] The largest increases likely will be among Asians and Hispanics.[612]

In 1950, women constituted 30 percent of the civilian labor force.[613] Since then, the number of women in the workforce almost tripled, while men increased by a modest 30 percent.[614] Today, women constitute 47 percent of the labor force, a proportion that is expected to remain steady for the ensuing decade.[615]

These demographic trends foretell organizations that will be far more diverse than they are now. When we combine demographics with what appears to be a propensity among both minorities and women to enter the public sector at a more rapid rate than the private sector,[616] and their apparently greater satisfaction with government work than whites and men,[617] then we may anticipate governments leading by example in the diversification of America.

NOTES

1. As derived from data in U.S. Bureau of the Census, *Statistical Abstract of the United States, 2011*, 130th ed. (Washington, DC: U.S. Government Printing Office, 2011), Tables 459 and 584. Figures are for 2008 and include postal workers but not military personnel.
2. Evan M. Berman, James S. Bowman, Jonathan P. West, *et al.*, *Human Resource Management in Public Service: Paradoxes, Processes, and Problems* (Thousand Oaks, CA: Sage, 2001), p. 7.
3. Ibid.
4. U.S. General Accounting Office, *Human Capital: A Self-Assessment Checklist for Agency Leaders, Version 1*, GAO/OCG-00-14G (Washington, DC: U.S. Government Printing Office, 2000), pp. 1–2.
5. Gregory B. Lewis and Sue A. Frank, "Who Wants to Work for the Government?" *Public Administration Review* 62 (July/August 2002), pp. 395–344. Figures are for 1998.
6. William C. Adams and Donna Lind Infeld, "Surprising Majority of Americans Endorse Careers in Government," *PA Times* (August 2009), pp. 1–2. For earlier surveys, see the eleventh edition (2010) of this book, p. 244, Note 7.
7. Pew Research Center, as cited in Partnership for Public Service, *Public Opinion on Public Service*, Poll Watch PPS-05-3 (Washington, DC: Author, 2005), p. 4. Figure, 40 percent, is for 1998.
8. Adams and Infeld, "Surprising Majority of Americans Endorse Careers in Government," p. 2. Figure, 79 percent, is for 2009.
9. Harris Poll, as cited in Paul C. Light, "To Restore and Renew: Now Is the Time to Rebuild the Federal Government Public Service," *Government Executive* (November 2001), http://www.brook.edu. Figure is for 2000.
10. Council for Excellence in Government, Gallup, and Accenture, *The Appeal of Public Service: Who...What...and How?* (Washington, DC: Authors, 2008), p. 4. Figure is for 2008.
11. Harris Poll, as cited in Light, "To Restore and Renew." Figure is for 2000.
12. Council for Excellence in Government, Gallup, and Accenture, *The Appeal of Public Service*, p. 4. Figure is for 2008.
13. H. C. Taylor and J. T. Russell, "The Relationship of Validity Coefficients to the Practical Effectiveness of Tests in Selection: Discussion and Tables," *Journal of Applied Psychology* 23 (October 1939), pp. 565–578.
14. Partnership for Public Service and Universum, *Great Expectations: What Students Want in an Employer and How Federal Agencies Can Deliver It* (Washington, DC, and Philadelphia: Authors, 2009), p. i. Figure is for 2008.
15. National Commission on the Public Service, *Leadership for America: Rebuilding the Public Service* (Washington, DC: Author, 1989). Figures refer to students admitted to campus honor societies.
16. Council for Excellence in Government and Peter D. Hart Research, *Calling Young People to Government Service: From "Ask Not..." to "Not Asked"* (Washington, DC: Authors, 2004), pp. 3–4. Figures are for 2004.
17. Council for Excellence in Government and Gallup Organization, *Within Reach...But Out of Synch: The Possibilities and Challenges of Shaping Tomorrow's Government Workforce* (Washington, DC: Authors, 2007), pp. 6, 8. Data are for 2006.
18. U.S. Office of Personnel Management, *Federal Employee Viewpoint Survey, 2010* (Washington, DC: U.S. Government Printing Office, 2010), pp. 37, 28. Positive figure is for 2006–2010; negative one is for 2010.
19. U.S. Merit Systems Protection Board, *In Search of Highly Skilled Workers: A Study on the Hiring of Upper Level Employees from Outside the Federal Government* (Washington, DC: U.S. Government Printing Office, 2008), p. 33. Figures are for 2006, and pertain to

those hired for grades 12–15 in the General Schedule.

20. Larry M. Lane and James E. Wolf, *The Human Resource Crisis in the Public Sector: Rebuilding the Capacity to Govern* (New York: Quorum Books, 1990).

21. U.S. General Accounting Office, *Federal Recruiting: Comparison of Applicants Who Accepted or Declined Federal Job Offers*, GAO/GGD-92-61BR (Washington, DC: U.S. Government Printing Office, 1993), p. 3.

22. Gregory B. Lewis, "Grade Creep in the Federal Service?" *American Review of Public Administration* 27 (March 1997), pp. 4–21. The years covered are 1977–1993.

23. As derived from data in U.S. Merit Systems Protection Board, *In Search of Highly Skilled Workers*, p. 13. Figure is for 2006.

24. As derived from data in U.S. Merit Systems Protection Board, *Attracting the Next Generation: A Look at Federal Entry-Level New Hires* (Washington, DC: U.S. Government Printing Office, 2008), p. 20. Figure is for 2006.

25. Xuhong Su and Barry Bozeman, "Dynamics of Sector Switching: Hazard Models Predicting Changes from Private Sector Jobs to Public and Nonprofit Sector Jobs," *Public Administration Review* 69 (November/December 2009), pp. 1106–1114.

26. As derived from data in U.S. Merit Systems Protection Board, *In Search of Highly Skilled Workers*, p. 29, and *Attracting the Next Generation*, p. 35. In 2006, 47 percent, a plurality, of upper-level federal new hires and 97 percent of entry-level ones cited job security as their leading reason for joining the federal service.

27. U.S. Merit Systems Protection Board, *In Search of Highly Skilled Workers*, p. 13. Figure is for 2006.

28. U.S. Merit Systems Protection Board, *Attracting the Next Generation*, p. 20. Figure is for 2006.

29. U.S. Office of Personnel Management, *Ensuring the Federal Government Has an Effective Civilian Workforce: 2008 Employee Survey Results* (Washington, DC: U.S Government Printing Office, 2009), Question 84. Figure is for 2008, but is quite steady over time.

30. Phillip C. Crewson, "Are the Best and the Brightest Fleeing Public Sector Employment? Evidence from the National Longitudinal Study of Youth," *Public Productivity & Management Review* 20 (June 1997), pp. 363–371. The quotation is on p. 368.

31. Ibid.

32. Frederick C. Mosher, *Democracy and the Public Service*, 2nd ed. (New York: Oxford University Press, 1982), p. 57.

33. Sidney H. Aronson, *Status and Kinship in the Higher Civil Service* (Cambridge, MA: Harvard University Press, 1964), p. 61.

34. Erik W. Austin, *Political Facts of the United States Since 1789* (New York: Oxford University Press, 1986), pp. 370–376, 328. In 1824, voter turn-out was 16 percent; in 1828, it hit 52 percent.

35. Mosher, *Democracy and the Public Service*, pp. 66–72; and Aronson, *Status and Kinship in the Higher Civil Service*, p. 61.

36. N. Joseph Cayer, *Public Personnel Administration in the United States*, 2nd ed. (New York: St. Martin's, 1986), p. 22.

37. The quotations are cited in Ann Gerhart, "A New Deal," *Washington Post* (March 28, 2005).

38. Mosher, *Democracy and the Public Service*, p. 66.

39. The Hatch Act Reform Amendments of 1993 allowed federal employees to participate in political campaigns, but they still may not be candidates in partisan elections or engage in political activity while on duty.

40. James S. Bowman and Jonathan P. West, "State Government 'Little Hatch Acts' in an Era of Civil Service Reform," *Review of Public Personnel Administration* 29 (March 2009), pp. 20–40. Figure (p. 22) is for 2007.

41. Mosher, *Democracy and the Public Service*, p. 68.

42. Benjamin F. Welton, "The Problems of Securing Efficiency in Municipal Labor," *Annals of the American Academy of Political and Social Science* XLI (May 1912), pp. 103–114. The quotation is on p. 103.

43. Daniel W. Williams, "Measuring Government in the Early Twentieth Century," *Public Administration Review* 63 (November/December 2003), pp. 643–659. The quotations are on p. 649.

44. Norma M. Riccucci and Katherine C. Naff, *Personnel Management in Government: Politics and Processes*, 6th ed. (Boca Raton, FL: CRC Press, 2008), p. 175.

45. "Inside the Year Book," *Municipal Year Book, 2006* (Washington, DC: International City/County Management Association, 2006), p. x.

46. O. Glenn Stahl, *Public Personnel Administration,* 8th ed. (New York: Harper & Row, 1983), p. 42.

47. Anirudh V. S. Ruhil and Pedro J. Camoes, "What Lies beneath: The Political Roots of State Merit Systems," *Journal of Public Administration Research and Theory* 13 (January 2003), pp. 27–42. The figures are on p. 30.

48. Riccucci and Naff, *Personnel Management in Government,* p. 34.

49. Committee on Administrative Management, *Personnel Administration in the Federal Service* (Washington, DC: U.S. Government Printing Office, 1937). The quotation is on pp. 7–8.

50. Mosher, *Democracy and the Public Service,* p. 89.

51. As derived from data in U.S. Bureau of the Census, *Statistical Abstract of the United States, 1933,* 55th ed., and *1953,* 74th ed. (Washington, DC: U.S. Government Printing Office, 1933 and 1953), Tables 155 and 405, respectively. "Bureaucracy" refers to civilian employees.

52. This definition is based on one found in Mosher, *Democracy and the Public Service,* p. 145.

53. Steven W. Hays and Richard C. Kearney, "Anticipated Changes in Human Resource Management: Views from the Field," *Public Administration Review* 61 (September/October 2001), pp. 585–597. The datum is on p. 592.

54. Gary S. Marshall, "Whither (or Wither) OPM?" *Public Administration Review* 58 (May/June 1998), p. 21.

55. Colleen A. Woodard, "Merit by Any Other Name—Reframing the Civil Service First Principle," *Public Administration Review* 65 (January/February 2005), pp. 100–118. The quotation is on p. 110.

56. Mosher, *Democracy and the Public Service,* pp. 217–218. The foregoing discussion is based loosely on pp. 217–221.

57. As derived from data in U.S. Bureau of Labor Statistics, *Occupational Employment Statistics* (Washington, DC: U.S. Government Printing Office, 2011), Tables 11-3111, 11-3121, 11-3131, and 13-1078. Figures are for 2010 and cover human capital managers and specialists in training, development, labor relations, compensation, benefits, or job analysis.

58. Hays and Kearney, "Anticipated Changes in Human Resource Management."

59. Michael A. Miller, "The Public/Private Pay Debate: What Do the Data Show?" *Monthly Labor Review* 119 (May 1996), pp. 18–29. Refers to state and local personnel specialists only. The other profession is budgeters.

60. Myron D. Fottler and Norman A. Townsend, "Characteristics of Public and Private Personnel Directors," *Public Personnel Management* 6 (July 1977), pp. 250–258; and American Society of Personnel Administrators, *The Personnel Executive's Job* (Englewood Cliffs, NJ: Prentice-Hall, 1977).

61. Hays and Kearney, "Anticipated Changes in Human Resource Management," p. 593. Data are for 1998.

62. Council for Excellence in Government, Gallup, and Accenture, *The Appeal of Public Service,* p. 4. Figure is for 2008, and is reasonably consistent over time. See Council for Excellence in Government and Peter D. Hart Research, *Calling Young People to Government Service,* p. 7.

63. U.S. Office of Personnel Management, as cited in Light, "To Restore and Renew." Figure is for 1999.

64. U.S. Merit Systems Protection Board, *Help Wanted: A Review of Federal Vacancy Announcements* (Washington, DC: U.S. Government Printing Office, 2003), p. 7. Figure, 52 percent, is for 2002.

65. U.S. Merit Systems Protection Board, "Supervisory Job Announcements: Truth in Advertising," *Issues of Merit* (April 2010), pp. 1, 7. The quotation is on p. 1. Figure is for 2009.

66. U.S. Merit Systems Protection Board, *Help Wanted,* p. 9. Figures are for 2002.

67. U.S. Merit Systems Protection Board, "Taking Aim at Federal Hiring," *Issues of Merit* (July 2008), p. 3.

68. Sally Coleman Selden, Patricia Wallace Ingraham, and Willow Jacobson, "Human Resource Practices in State Government: Findings from a National Survey," *Public Administration Review* 61 (September/October 2001), pp. 598–607. The figures are on pp. 600–601, and are for 1998.

69. Richard C. Elling, Lyke Thompson, and Valerie Monet, "The Problematic World of State Management: The More Things Change the More They Remain the Same," Paper Presented at the Annual Meeting of the Midwest Political Science Association (Chicago, 2003). Figure is for 2000–2001.

70. David Coursey, "E-Government: Trends, Benefits, and Challenges," *Municipal Year Book, 2005* (Washington, DC: International City/County Management Association, 2005), p. 17. Figures are for 2004.

71. Siegrun Fox Freyss, "Continuity and Change in Local Personnel Policies and Practices," *Municipal Year Book, 1996* (Washington, DC: International City/County Management Association, 1996), pp. 11–17.

72. U.S. Merit Systems Protection Board, *Accomplishing Our Mission: Results of the Merit Principles Survey 2005* (Washington, DC: U.S. Government Printing Office, 2007), p. 14. Figure, 38 percent, is for 2005.

73. Sally Coleman Selden, *Human Capital: Tools and Strategies for the Public Sector* (Washington, DC: CQ Press, 2009), p. 51. Figure is for 2007.

74. Partnership for Public Service and Gallup Consulting, *In the Public We Trust: Renewing the Connection between the Federal Government and the Public* (Washington, DC, and New York: Authors, 2008), p. 5. Figure is for 2008.

75. Princeton Survey Research Associates, *Final Topline Report: Health of the Nonprofit, For-Profit, and Public Service Sectors* (Princeton, NJ: Author, 2002), p. 13. Figures are for 2000–2001.

76. Marilyn Mackes, National Association of Colleges and Employers, "Keys to Finding Quality Entry-Level Employees," Paper Presented to the National Academy of Public Administration (Washington, DC, 2001). Figure, 37 percent, is for 2001.

77. U.S. Merit Systems Protection Board, *Federal Appointment Authorities: Cutting through the Confusion* (Washington, DC: U.S. Government Printing Office, 2008), p. 4. Data are for 2005.

78. "The Memo That Roared," *Washington Post* (June 19, 2009). The agency is the Federal Student Aid program.

79. Princeton Survey Research Associates, *Final Topline Report*, p. 13. Figures are for 2000–2001.

80. National Commission on the Public Service, *Leadership for America*, p. 28.

81. Princeton Survey Research Associates, *Final Topline Report*, p. 13. Seventy-nine percent of federal workers, 50 percent of nonprofit employees, and 42 percent of private-sector workers so reported. Figures are for 2000–2001.

82. U.S. Merit Systems Protection Board, *Attracting the Next Generation*, p. 49. Figure is for 2005. Slow hiring handily tops seven possible responses. Federal entry-level new hires are those entering General and Related Grades 5, 7, and 9.

83. David E. Terpstra and Elizabeth J. Roxell, "The Relationship of Staffing Practices to Organizational Level Measures of Performance," *Personnel Psychology* 46 (Spring 1993), pp. 27–48.

84. Frank L. Schmidt, John E. Hunter, Alice N. Outerbridge, *et al.*, "The Economic Impact of Job Selection Methods on Size, Productivity and Payroll Costs of the Federal Work Force: An Empirically Based Demonstration," *Personnel Psychology* 39 (Spring 1986), pp. 1–30.

85. U.S. Merit Systems Protection Board, *The Role of Delegated Examining Units: Hiring New Employees in a Decentralized Civil Service* (Washington, DC: U.S. Government Printing Office, 1999), p. 5.

86. Partnership for Public Service, *Asking the Wrong Questions: A Look at How the Federal Government Assesses and Selects Its Workforce* (Washington, DC: Author, 2004), p. 1.

87. U.S. Merit Systems Protection Board, *Fair and Equitable Treatment: Progress Made and Challenges Remaining* (Washington, DC: U.S. Government Printing Office, 2009), p. 11.

88. U.S. Merit Systems Protection Board, *Federal Appointment Authorities*, p. 29. Figures are for 2005.

89. Partnership for Public Service and Booz Allen Hamilton, *Unrealized Vision: Reimagining the Senior Executive Service* (Washington, DC, and Herndon, VA: Authors, 2009), p. 14.

90. Constance Horner, director, OPM, as quoted in Judith Havemann, "New Federal Job Exams Set for June," *Washington Post* (April 22, 1990).

91. Barack Obama, quoted as a presidential candidate, September 11, 2008, Columbia University, New York, in U.S. Merit Systems Protection Board, *Job Simulations: Trying Out for a Federal Job* (Washington, DC: U.S. Government Printing Office, 2009), p. 1.

92. U.S. Merit Systems Protection Board, "Who Gets Selected for Federal Jobs?" *Issues of Merit* (August 2001), pp. 1–3. Figure is for 1998–2001.

93. Partnership for Public Service, *Leaving Talent on the Table: The Need to Capitalize on High*

Performing Student Interns (Washington, DC: Author, 2009), Executive Summary page. Figures are for 2007.

94. U.S. Merit Systems Protection Board, *Attracting the Next Generation*, pp. 6, 8, 17, 20. Figures are for 2005.

95. U.S. Merit Systems Protection Board, *The Federal Government: A Model Employer or a Work in Progress? Perspectives from 25 years of the Merit Principles Survey* (Washington, DC: U.S. Government Printing Office, 2008), p. 9. Figures are for 1983–2007.

96. As derived from data in Partnership for Public Service and Booz Allen Hamilton, *Unrealized Vision*, p. 7. Figures are for 2009.

97. U.S. Merit Systems Protection Board, "Fast Fact: The FCIP Continues to Grow," *Issues of Merit* (February 2010), p. 3. Figure, 50 percent, is for 2007 and 2008, and refers to "new hires in professional and administrative positions" at grades 5, 7, and 9.

98. U.S. Merit Systems Protection Board, *Attracting the Next Generation*, p. 13.

99. Barack Obama, *Memorandum for the Heads of Executive Departments and Agencies, Subject: Improving the Federal Recruitment and Hiring Process* (Washington, DC: The White House, May 11, 2010).

100. Pew Center on the States, *People Forward: Human Capital Trends and Innovations* (Washington, DC: Author, 2009), p. 13. Figure is for thirty responding states in 2007.

101. Selden, Ingraham, and Jacobson, "Human Resource Practices in State Government," p. 603. Figure is for 1998.

102. Elling, Thompson, and Monet, "The Problematic World of State Management." Figure is for 2000–2001.

103. Selden, Ingraham, and Jacobson, "Human Resource Practices in State Government," p. 600. Figures are for 1998.

104. U.S. Advisory Commission on Intergovernmental Relations, *State Laws Governing Local Government Structure and Administration*, M-186 (Washington, DC: U.S. Government Printing Office, 1993), p. 49. Figure is for 1990.

105. Philip H. Mirvis and Edward J. Hackett, "Work and Work Force Characteristics in the Nonprofit Sector," *Monthly Labor Review* 106 (April 1983), pp. 3–12. Figure is for 1977.

106. Miller, "The Public/Private Pay Debate," p. 19.

107. U.S. Merit Systems Protection Board, *Why Are Employees Leaving the Federal Government? Results of an Exit Survey* (Washington, DC: U.S. Government Printing Office, 1990).

108. U.S. Bureau of Labor Statistics, "Federal Government," *Career Guide to Industries, 2010–2011 Edition*, http://www.bls.gov/oco/cg/cgs041.htm. Figure is for 2010.

109. U.S. Office of Personnel Management, *Federal Employee Viewpoint Survey, 2010*, p. 16. Figure, 66 percent, is for 2010.

110. U.S. Merit Systems Protection Board, *The Changing Federal Workplace: Employee Perspectives* (Washington, DC: U.S. Government Printing Office, 1998), p. 28. In 1989, 28 percent of federal workers were satisfied with their salaries.

111. Kenneth L. Yoder, "Federal Employee Pay Comparability," *Armed Forces Comptroller* (March 22, 2002), http://www.allbusiness.com.

112. National Commission on the Public Service, *Urgent Business for America: Revitalizing the Federal Government for the 21st Century* (Washington, DC: U.S. Government Printing Office, 1993), pp. 23–24.

113. Ken McDonnell, "Benefit Cost Comparisons between State and Local Governments and Private-Sector Employers," *EBRI Notes* 29 (June 2008), pp. 2–6. Figures are for 2007.

114. Keith A. Bender and John S. Heywood, *Out of Balance? Comparing Public and Private Sector Compensation over 20 Years* (Washington, DC: Center for State & Local Government Excellence and National Institute on Retirement Security, 2010), p. 16. Data are for 2008.

115. As derived from data in Miller, "The Public/Private Pay Debate," pp. 23, 22. Forty-three positions were examined, two of which, personnel specialist and budget analyst, had comparable pay in both sectors.

116. Bender and Heywood, *Out of Balance?* pp. 9–14.

117. Patrick L. Owens, Jr., "One More Reason Not to Cut Your Training Budget: The Relationship between Training and Organizational Outcomes," *Public Personnel Management* 35 (Summer 2006), pp. 163–172.

118. National Commission on the Public Service, *Leadership for America*, p. 43.

119. Donald F. Kettl, *Reinventing Government? Appraising the National Performance Review* (Washington, DC: Brookings, 1994), p. 20.

120. Owens, "One More Reason Not to Cut Your Training Budget."

121. As derived from data in Selden, *Human Capital*, p. 89. State training spending rose by 56 percent, and the percentage of classified workforce promoted increased by 27 percent, FY 2003–FY 2006.

122. Victor S. De Santis and Samantha L. Durst, "Job Satisfaction Among Local Government Employees Lessons for Public Managers," *Municipal Year Book, 1997* (Washington DC: International City/County Management Association, 1997), p. 10.

123. Kettl, *Reinventing Government?* p. 20. Figure is for 1992.

124. U.S. General Accounting Office, *Training Budgets: Agency Budget Reductions in Response to the Balanced Budget Act*, GAO-GGD-86-98BR (Washington, DC: U.S. Government Printing Office, 1986), p. 2.

125. U.S. Merit Systems Protection Board, *Accomplishing Our Mission*, p. 16. Figures are for 1992–2005. Forty-eight percent say they need more training, 1998–2005.

126. U.S. Merit Systems Protection Board, *A Call to Action: Improving First-Level Supervision of Federal Employees* (Washington, DC: U.S Government Printing Office, 2010), p. 34. Figure, 48 percent, is for 2009.

127. U.S. Office of Personnel Management, *Federal Employee Viewpoint Survey, 2010*, pp. 39, 41. Federal figure, 54–56 percent, is for 2006–2010. Private sector figure, 66 percent, is for 2010.

128. Selden, *Human Capital*, pp. 85, 89. Expenditure is for 2007. Average spending per employee rose from $217 to $421, FY 2003–FY 2006.

129. Pew Center on the States, *People Forward*, p. 3. Figure is for 2007.

130. George R. Gray, McKenzie E. Hall, Marianne Miller, *et al.*, "Training Practices in State Government Agencies," *Public Personnel Management* 26 (Summer 1997), pp. 187–202.

131. Pew Center on the States, *People Forward*, p. 23.

132. U.S. Advisory Commission on Intergovernmental Relations, *State Laws Governing Local Government Structure and Administration*, p. 49. Figures are for 1990.

133. Charles J. Spindler, "University-Based Public Sector Management Development and Training," *Public Productivity & Management Review* 15 (Summer 1992), pp. 439–448.

134. Joseph W. Whorton, Jr., Frank K. Gibson, and Delmer D. Dunn, "The Culture of University Public Service: A National Survey of the Perspectives of Users and Providers," *Public Administration Review* 46 (January/February 1986), pp. 39–40.

135. Marcia P. Meceli and Janet P. Near, "What Makes Whistle-Blowers Effective? Three Field Studies," *Human Relations* 55 (April 2002), pp. 455–479.

136. Philip H. Jos, Mark E. Tompkins, and Steven W. Hays, "In Praise of Difficult People: A Portrait of the Committed Whistleblower," *Public Administration Review* 49 (November/December 1989), pp. 552–561. The datum is on p. 555.

137. PR Newswire, United Business Media, *Justice Department Recovers $2.4 Billion in False Claims Cases in Fiscal Year 2009; More than $24 Billion Since 1986* (November 19, 2009), http://www.prnewswire.com/; and Taxpayers against Fraud, *FY 2010 False Claims Act Settlements*, http://www.taf.org/total2010.htm. Figure is for FY 1986–FY 2010 and refers to funds collected under the False Claims Act's 1986 amendments.

138. U.S. Merit Systems Protection Board, *Whistleblowing in the Federal Government: An Update* (Washington, DC: U.S. Government Printing Office, 1993), p. ii. Figures are for 1983 and 1992.

139. Bloomberg Business News, "Some Criticize Whistleblowers as Bounty Hunters," *Baltimore Sun* (June 16, 1996).

140. U.S. Internal Revenue Service, Whistleblower Office, *Annual Report to Congress on the Use of Section 7623* (Washington, DC: Author, 2010). Figures are for FY 2009.

141. U.S. Government Accountability Office, *Tax Whistleblowers: Incomplete Data Hinders IRS's Ability to Manage Claim Processing Time and Enhance External Communication*, GAO-11-683 (Washington, DC: U.S. Government Printing Office, 2011), Highlights page. Data are for 2007–2008 and 2011.

142. U.S. Internal Revenue Service, Whistleblower Office, *Annual Report to Congress on the Use of Section 7623*.

143. Michael Hudson, "IRS Red Tape, Old Guard Slow Whistleblowing on Corporate Tax Cheats," *i watch* (June 22, 2011), http://www.iwatchnews.org.

144. As derived from data in False Claims Act Legal Center, Taxpayers against Fraud Education Fund, http://www.taf.org/. Data are for 2010.

145. Unpublished study by Karen L. Soeken and Donald L. Soeken, "A Survey of Whistleblowers: Their Stressors and Coping Strategies," 1987, as reported in Clyde H. Farnsworth, "Survey of Whistle Blowers Finds Retaliation but Few Regrets," *New York Times* (February 27, 1987).

146. Jos, Tompkins, and Hays, "In Praise of Difficult People," p. 557.

147. Janet P. Near and Marcia P. Miceli, "Wrongdoing, Whistle-Blowing, and Retaliation in the U.S. Government: What Have Researchers Learned from the Merit Systems Protection Board (MSPB) Survey Results?" *Review of Public Personnel Administration* 28 (September 2008), pp. 263–281. The data are on pp. 271–272.

148. Gjalt de Graaf, "A Report on Reporting: Why Peers Report Integrity and Law Violations in Public Organizations," *Public Administration Review* 70 (September/October 2010), pp. 767–779. The quotation is on p. 772.

149. John J. Sumanth, David M. Mayer, and Virginia S. Kay, "Why Good Guys Finish Last: The Role of Justification Motives, Cognition, and Emotions in Predicting Retaliation against Whistleblowers," *Organizational Psychology Review* (1, 2011), pp. 165–184. This is a meta-analysis of the global literature.

150. Ibid., pp. 176–178.

151. Meceli and Near, "What Makes Whistle-Blowers Effective?"

152. Ethics Resource Center, *Retaliation: The Cost to Your Company and Its Employees* (Arlington, VA: Author, 2010), p. 1.

153. Michael Griffin and Tracy Davis, *Sourcing Competitive Advantage from Organizational Integrity: The Hidden Cost of Misconduct* (Arlington, VA: Corporate Executive Board, 2007), https://gcr.executiveboard.com/public/documents/gcr_researchalert.html.

154. As derived from data in National Conference of State Legislatures, *State Whistleblower Laws* (Washington, DC: Author, 2009), http://www.ncsl.org/default.aspx?tabid=13390. Data are for 2009.

155. Jos, Tompkins, and Hays, "In Praise of Difficult People," pp. 553–554. This survey (response rate: 56 percent) was completed in 1987 and 1988 by 161 whistleblowers.

156. Philip H. Jos, "The Nature and Limits of the Whistleblower's Contribution to Administrative Responsibility," *American Review of Public Administration* 21 (June 1991), pp. 105–118. The data are on p. 106.

157. As derived from data in U.S. Merit Systems Protection Board, *Prohibited Personnel Practices: A Study Retrospective* (Washington, DC: U.S. Government Printing Office, 2010), p. 15.

158. U.S. Merit Systems Protection Board, *Prohibited Personnel Practices: Employee Perceptions* (Washington, DC: U.S. Government Printing Office, 2011), p. 33. Current figure is for 2010.

159. Ethics Resource Center, *Retaliation*, p. 5. Figure is for 2009. In 2007 it was 12 percent.

160. Ernest Fitzgerald, quoted in Mary McGrory, "The Whistleblower's Lament," *Washington Post* (September 22, 1996).

161. Jos, Tompkins, and Hays, "In Praise of Difficult People," p. 555.

162. Quoted in Farnsworth, "Survey of Whistle Blowers Finds Retaliation but Few Regrets."

163. Reuters, "Whistleblower Rewards Top $2 Billion" (January 2, 2008), http://www.reuters.com. Figures are for 1986–2008.

164. Craig Copeland, "Employee Tenure, 2008," *EBRI.org Notes* 31 (January 2010), pp. 2–12. The quotation is on p. 2. Trend figures are for 1983–2008.

165. Stahl, *Public Personnel Administration*, p. 35.

166. Howard Risher, *Pay for Performance: A Guide for Federal Managers* (Washington, DC: IBM Center for the Business of Government, 2004), pp. 4, 7.

167. George Orwell, *1984* (London: Secker and Warburg, 1949).

168. Ed Michaels, Helen Hatfield-Jones, and Beth Axelrod, *The War for Talent* (Cambridge, MA: Harvard Business School Press, 2001); and Baruch Lev, *Intangibles: Management, Measurement, and Reporting* (Washington, DC: Brookings, 2001).

169. U.S. Merit Systems Protection Board, *Civil Service Evaluation: The Evolving Role of the U.S. Office of Personnel Management* (Washington, DC: U.S. Government Printing Office, 1999), p. 24. Figure is for 1997, and was the highest negative response in the survey.

170. Jerrell D. Coggburn, "Personnel Deregulation: Exploring Differences in the American States,"

Journal of Public Administration Research and Theory 11 (April 2001), pp. 223–244. The quotation is on p. 227.

171. Stahl, *Public Personnel Administration*, p. 42.

172. U.S. Merit Systems Protection Board, *The Federal Government: A Model Employer or a Work in Progress?* p. 9.

173. Marshall, "Whither (or Wither) OPM?" p. 21.

174. U.S. Merit Systems Protection Board, *The Role of the Delegated Examining Units: Hiring New Employees in a Decentralized Civil Service* (Washington, DC: U.S. Government Printing Office, 1999), pp. vi, viii. Delegated examining units still must follow traditional civil service regulations and procedures.

175. U.S. Office of Personnel Management, *Federal Human Resources Management for the 21st Century* (Washington, DC: U.S. Government Printing Office, 1997), p. 8.

176. John Crum, "Lessons Learned: Making Strategic Hiring Decisions," *Issues of Merit* (September 2011), pp. 2–3.

177. U.S. Merit Systems Protection Board, "Exploring the Use of Direct-Hire Authority," *Issues of Merit* (July 2008), p. 5.

178. As derived from data in Partnership for Public Service and Grant Thornton, *Closing the Gap*, p. 6. Figures, 74 and 46 percent, respectively, are for 2010.

179. U.S. General Accounting Office, *Human Capital: Selected Agencies' Use of Alternative Service Delivery Options for Human Capital Activities*, GAO-04-679 (Washington, DC: U.S. Government Printing Office, 2004). Eight federal agencies were surveyed in 2003–2004.

180. U.S. Merit Systems Protection Board, *The Federal Government: A Model Employer or a Work in Progress?* p. 9. Current figure is for 2007.

181. U.S. General Accounting Office, *Human Capital: OPM Can Better Assist Agencies in Using Personnel Flexibilities*, GAO-03-428 (Washington, DC: U.S. Government Printing Office, 2003), p. 7. Figure is for 2003.

182. Kaifeng Yang and Anthony Kassekert, "Linking Management Reform with Employee Job Satisfaction: Evidence from Federal Agencies," *Journal of Public Administration Research and Theory* 20 (April 2010), pp. 413–436.

183. G. Edward DeSeve, *Speeding Up the Learning Curve: Observations from a Survey of Seasoned Political Appointees* (Washington, DC: IBM Center for the Business of Government, 2009), p. 6. Figure, 52 percent, is for 2008.

184. U.S. Merit Systems Protection Board, *The Power of Federal Employee Engagement* (Washington, DC: U.S. Government Printing Office, 2008), p. 24. Figure is for 2005.

185. Partnership for Public Service and Grant Thornton, *Closing the Gap*, p. 17. Figure is for 2010. In 2007, 68 percent thought this. The term, "paper shufflers," is ours; the study uses instead, "transaction managers."

186. Howard Risher, "How Much Should Federal Employees Be Paid? The Problems with Using a Market Philosophy in a Broadband System," *Public Personnel Management* 34 (Summer 2005), pp. 121–140. The quotation is on p. 121.

187. Partnership for Public Service and Grant Thornton, *Elevating Our Federal Workforce: Chief Human Capital Officers Offer Advice to President Obama* (Washington, DC, and Alexandria, VA: Authors, 2009), p. ii. Figure is for 2008.

188. U.S. Government Accountability Office, *Human Capital: Selected Agencies' Statutory Authorities Could Offer Options in Developing a Framework for Governmentwide Reform*, GAO-05-398R Human Capital Authorities (Washington, DC: U.S. Government Printing Office, 2005), p. 1.

189. Stahl, *Public Personnel Administration*, p. 41.

190. Riccucci and Naff, *Personnel Management in Government*, p. 34.

191. Ibid. Figure is for the mid-1980s.

192. Andrew W. Boessel, "Local Personnel Management," *Municipal Year Book, 1974* (Washington, DC: International City Management Association, 1974), pp. 92–93. Figure is for 1974, and excludes education.

193. Steven W. Hays, "Trends and Best Practices in State and Local Human Resource Management," *Review of Public Personnel Administration* 24 (October 2004), pp. 256–275.

194. Keon S. Chi, "Trends in State Civil Service Systems: Personnel Agencies, Reform Efforts, Classifications and Workforce Planning," *Book of the States* (Lexington, KY: Council of State Governments, 2004), pp. 405–412. The data are on p. 406.

195. As derived from data in "Chapter Eight: State Management and Administration," *Book of the States, 2004*, pp. 399–482. Table 8.1. Figure is for 2003.

196. Selden, Ingraham, and Jacobson, "Human Resource Practices in State Government," pp. 603, 600. Figures are for 1998.

197. As derived from data in Keon S. Chi, Kelley A. Arnold, and Heather M. Perkins, "Privatization in Government: Trends and Issues," *Spectrum* 76 (Fall 2003), pp. 12–21. The datum is on p. 16. Figure is for 2002.

198. Steven W. Hays and Jessica E. Sowa, "A Broader Look at the 'Accountability' Movement: Some Grim Realities in State Civil Service Systems," *Review of Public Personnel Administration* 26 (June 2006), pp. 102–117.

199. Jonathan Walters, *Life after Civil Service Reform: The Texas, Georgia, and Florida Experiences*, Human Capital Series (Washington, DC: IBM Endowment for the Business of Government, 2002), pp. 5, 12.

200. Robert M. Sanders, "GeorgiaGain or GeorgiaLoss? The Great Experiment in State Civil Service Reform," *Public Personnel Management* 33 (Summer 2004), pp. 151–164. The quotation is on p. 151.

201. "Georgia: Grading the States, 2005," *Governing* (February 2005), p. 49. The Government Performance Project accorded Georgia an "A" for its management of human resources.

202. Coggburn, "Personnel Deregulation," p. 241.

203. J. Edward Kellough and Sally Coleman Selden, "The Reinvention of Public Personnel Administration: An Analysis of the Diffusion of Personnel Management Reforms in the States," *Public Administration Review* 63 (March/April 2003), pp. 165–176.

204. Sally Coleman Selden, "Human Resource Management in American Counties, 2002," *Public Personnel Management* 34 (Spring 2005), p. 61. Figure is for 2002.

205. As derived from data in Mildred Warner and Amir Hefetz, "Cooperative Competition: Alternative Service Delivery in Local Government, 2002–2007," *Municipal Year Book, 2009* (Washington, DC: International City/County Management Association, 2009), pp. 11–20. Figure (p. 14) is for 2007.

206. Stephen T. T. Teo and John J. Rodwell, "To Be Strategic in the New Public Sector, HR Must Remember Its Operational Activities," *Human Resource Management* 46 (Summer 2007), pp. 265–284.

207. Walters, *Life after Civil Service Reform*, pp. 5, 12.

208. Bowman and West, "State Government 'Little Hatch Acts' in an Era of Civil Service Reform," p. 35.

209. Walters, *Life after Civil Service Reform*, pp. 5, 12.

210. Sally Coleman Selden, "The Impact of Discipline on the Use and Rapidity of Dismissal in State Governments," *Review of Public Personnel Administration* 26 (June 2006), pp. 335–355.

211. J. Edward Kellough and Lloyd G. Nigro, "Dramatic Reform in the Public Service: At-Will Employment and the Creation of a New Public Workforce," *Journal of Public Administration Research and Theory* 16 (July 2006), pp. 447–466. The quotation is on p. 447.

212. Hugh O'Neill, "The Growth of Municipal Employee Unions," *Unionization of Municipal Employees*, Robert H. Connery and William V. Farr, eds., *Proceedings of the Academy of Political Science* (New York: Academy of Political Science, December 1970), pp. 1–13. The quotation is on p. 4.

213. The case is *McLaughlin* v. *Tilendis*.

214. Joe Nation, former California legislator, as quoted in Charles Duhigg, "Public Unions Take on Bosses to Win Big Pensions," *New York Times* (June 21, 2011).

215. Unidentified studies cited by Paul E. Peterson, "The New Politics of Federalism," *Spectrum* 78 (Spring 2005), p. 7.

216. J. Ryan Lamare, "Union Influence on Voter Turnout: Results from Three Los Angeles County Elections," *Industrial and Labor Relations Review* 63 (April 2010), pp. 454–470. The quotation is on p. 454.

217. Seymour Martin Lipset and Ivan Katchanovski, "The Future of Public Sector Unions in the U.S.," *Journal of Labor Research* 22 (Spring 2001), pp. 229–244. The data are on p. 230.

218. Joel Cutcher-Gershenfeld and Thomas Kochan, "Taking Stock: Collective Bargaining at the Turn of the Century," *Industrial and Labor Relations Review* 58 (October 2004), pp. 3–21. The reference is on p. 3

219. U.S. Bureau of Labor Statistics, *Union Members—2010* (Washington, DC: Author, 2011), Table 3. Figures are for 2010.

220. Ibid. Figures are for 2010.

221. Leo Troy, "Has Public Sector Unionism Topped Out? What Is the Clinton Administration Doing about It?" *Government Union Review* 17 (Spring 1996), pp. 1–40. The quotations are on p. 1.

222. U.S. Bureau of Labor Statistics, *Union Members—2010*, Table 3. Figure is for 2010.

223. U.S. Office of Personnel Management, *Union Recognition and Agreements in the Federal Government* (Washington, DC: U.S. Government Printing Office, 1991), pp. 6–7.

224. U.S. Bureau of Labor Statistics, *Union Members—2010*, Table 3. Figures are for 2010.

225. U.S. Bureau of the Census, *Statistical Abstract of the United States, 1986*, 106th ed. (Washington, DC: U.S. Government Printing Office, 1986), Table 714. Figure is for 1982.

226. U.S. Bureau of Labor Statistics, *Union Members—2010*, Tables 3 and 4. Data are for 2010.

227. U.S. General Accounting Office, *Collective Bargaining Rights: Information on the Number of Workers with and without Collective Bargaining Rights*, GAO-02-835 (Washington, DC: U.S. Government Printing Office, 2002), p. 6.

228. James R. Thompson, "Federal Labor-Management Relations Reforms Under Bush: Enlightened Management or..." *Review of Public Personnel Administration* 27 (June 2007), pp. 105–124. The quotation is on p. 105.

229. As derived from data in James Joyner, "Collective Bargaining Rights by State," *Outside the Beltway* (Washington, DC: Outside the Beltway, 2011). Data are for February 2011.

230. David A. Dilts, William J. Walsh, and Constanza Hagmann, "State Labor-Management Relations Legislation: Adaptive Modeling," *Journal of Collective Negotiations in the Public Sector* 22 (1, 1993), p. 79–86. Alabama, Kansas, and West Virginia have meet-and-confer requirements.

231. Robert Hebdon, "Labor-Management Relations in the United States, 1999," *Municipal Year Book, 2000* (Washington, DC: International City/County Management Association, 2000), p. 22–27.

232. U.S. Advisory Commission on Intergovernmental Relations, *State Laws Governing Local Government and Administration*, M-186 (Washington, DC: U.S. Government Printing Office, 1993), p. 49. Figure is for 1990.

233. The case was *Circuit City Stores, Inc.* v. *Adams*.

234. G. W. Bohlander, "Public Sector Grievance Arbitration: Structure and Administration," *Journal of Collective Negotiations in the Public Sector* 21 (2, 1992), pp. 271–286.

235. Debra J. Mesch and Olga Shamayera, "Arbitration in Practice: A Profile of Public Sector Arbitration Cases," *Public Personnel Management* 25 (Spring 1996), pp. 119–136; and D. A. Dilts and E. C. Leonard, Jr., "Win-Loss Rates in Public Sector Grievance Arbitration Cases: Implications for the Selection of Arbitrators," *Journal of Collective Negotiations in the Public Sector* 18 (3, 1989), pp. 337–334.

236. U.S. General Accounting Office, *Collective Bargaining Rights: Information on the Number of Workers with and without Collective Bargaining Rights*, p. 10 *n*.

237. Dane M. Partridge, "Teacher Strikes and Public Policy: Does the Law Matter?" *Journal of Collective Negotiations in the Public Sector* 25 (1, 1996), pp. 3–21. The quotation is on p. 3.

238. Riccucci and Naff, *Personnel Management in Government*, p. 509. Figures are for 2000.

239. The "pension specialist" of the AFSCME, quoted in Sterling Spero and John M. Capozzola, *The Urban Community and Its Unionized Bureaucracy* (New York: Dunellen, 1973), p. 218.

240. U.S. Bureau of the Census, *Statistical Abstract of the United States, 1984*, 104th ed. (Washington, DC: U.S. Government Printing Office, 1984), Table 731.

241. Ibid. and U.S. Bureau of the Census, *Statistical Abstract of the United States, 1974*, 95th ed., *1977*, 98th ed., and *1980*, 101st ed. (Washington, DC: U.S. Government Printing Office, 1974, 1977, 1980), Tables 596, 684, and 721, respectively. Figure is for 1970–1979.

242. As derived from data in Michael H. Cimini, "1982–1997 State and Local Government Work Stoppages and Their Legal Background," *Compensation and Working Conditions* 30 (Fall 1998), pp. 32–38, Table 5; and U.S. Bureau of Labor Statistics, *Major Work Stoppages*, http://www.bls.gov/schedule/archives/all_nr.htm. "Six" figure is for 1982–2007. "Fewer than five" figure (4.7) is for 2000–2010.

243. Llewellyn M. Toulmin, "The Treasure Hunt: Budget Search Behavior by Public Employee Unions," *Public Administration Review* 48 (March/April 1988), pp. 620–630.

244. As derived from data in U.S. Bureau of Labor Statistics, *Union Members—2010*, Table 4. Figure is for 2010.

245. Richard C. Kearney, "The Determinants of State Employee Compensation," *Review of Public Personnel Administration* 23 (December 2003), pp. 305–322. The quotation is on p. 305.

246. As derived from data in U.S. Bureau of Labor Statistics, *Union Members—2010*, Table 4. Figures are for 2010.

247. Richard C. Kearney, with David G. Carnevale, *Labor Relations in the Public Sector*, 3rd ed. (New York: Marcel Dekker, 2001).

248. As derived from data in Jerri Killian and Enamul Choudhury, "Continuity and Change in the Role of City Managers," *Municipal Year Book, 2010* (Washington, DC: International City/County Management Association, 2010), pp. 10–18. Figure (p. 14) is for 2010.

249. Bruce A. Wallin, *Budgeting for Basics: The Changing Landscape of City Finances* (Washington, DC: Brookings, 2005), pp. 8–9. Figures are for 1977–2000.

250. Frederick C. Mosher, *Democracy and the Public Service* (New York: Oxford University Press, 1968), p. 166. This is the first edition of this book. Unless noted otherwise, all references to this work are of the second (1982) edition.

251. National Commission on the Public Service, *Urgent Business for America*, p. 18. In 1960, there were 286 political executive positions.

252. Joseph A. Ferrara and Lynn C. Ross, *Getting to Know You: Rules of Engagement for Political Appointees and Career Executives* (Arlington, VA: IBM Center for the Business of Government, 2005), p. 9. Figure is for 2003.

253. James P. Pfiffner, "Political Appointees and Career Executives: The Democracy-Bureaucracy Nexus in the Third Century," *Public Administration Review* 47 (January/February 1987), pp. 57–65. The figure is on p. 57.

254. National Commission on the Public Service, *Urgent Business for America*, p. 19.

255. Paul C. Light, "Nominate and Wait," *New York Times* (March 24, 2009). Data are for 2009.

256. Paul C. Light, "Nuclear Option for the Recruiter-in-Chief," *Washington Post* (May 27, 2010).

257. Paul C. Light, "Recommendations Forestalled or Forgotten? The National Commission on the Public Service and Presidential Appointments," *Public Administration Review* 67 (May/June 2007), pp. 404–417. The quotation is on p. 408.

258. Paul C. Light and Virginia L. Thomas, *The Merit and Reputation of an Administration: Presidential Appointments on the Appointments Process* (Washington, DC: Brookings and Heritage Foundation, 2000), p. 10. Figures are averages for 1984–1999.

259. U.S. Office of Personnel Management, *Senior Executive Service 2008 Survey Results* (Washington, DC: U.S. Government Printing Office, 2008), p. 4.

260. Partnership for Public Service and Booz Allen Hamilton, *Unrealized Vision*, p. ii.

261. Light, "Recommendations Forestalled or Forgotten?" p. 414. Emphasis is original.

262. Dean E. Mann and Jameson W. Doig, *The Assistant Secretaries: Problems and Processes of Appointment* (Washington, DC: Brookings, 1965), pp. 99, 165.

263. Joel D. Aberbach and Bert A. Rockman, "The Past and Future of Political-Administrative Relations: Research from Bureaucrats and Politicians to In the Web of Politics—and Beyond," *International Journal of Public Administration* 29 (12, 2006), pp. 977–995. The quotation is on p. 988.

264. Fred Malek, presidential personnel assistant in the Nixon Administration, as quoted in Pfiffner, "Political Appointees and Career Executives," pp. 63–64. Emphasis is original.

265. Light and Thomas, *The Merit and Reputation of an Administration*, p. 5. Presidential appointees who cited accomplishing public goals sank from 39 to 15 percent, on average, 1964–1989 to 1984–1999.

266. B. Dan Wood and Miner P. Marchbanks, III, "What Determines How Long Political Appointees Serve?" *Journal of Public Administration Research and Theory* 18 (July 2008), pp. 375–396. The quotations are on pp. 391, 393. Emphases are original. Political executives serving 1982–2003 were analyzed.

267. Light and Thomas, *The Merit and Reputation of an Administration*, pp. 6, 35, 5. "Money" figure

is an average for 1984–1999. "Burrowing" figures are averages for 1964–1989, when 4 percent burrowed in, and 1984–1999 (13 percent). The practice continued at high rates in the 2000s. See Gregg Carlstrom, "Bush Appointees 'Burrow In,'" *Federal Times.com* (November 30, 2008), http://www.federaltimes. com. Presidential appointees who cited enhanced career opportunities rose from 2 to 10 percent, on average, 1964–1989 to 1984–1999.

268. Wood and Marchbanks, "What Determines How Long Political Appointees Serve?" p. 390. Emphasis added.

269. Light and Thomas, *The Merit and Reputation of an Administration*, p. 9. Figure is an average for 1984–1999.

270. U.S. Merit Systems Protection Board, *The Senior Executive Service: Views of Former Federal Executives* (Washington, DC: U.S. Government Printing Office, 1989), pp. 20–21. Data are for 1989.

271. Ibid. Data are for 1989.

272. Wood and Marchbanks, "What Determines How Long Political Appointees Serve?" p. 390.

273. Anthony Bertelli and Sven E. Feldmann, "Strategic Appointments," *Journal of Public Administration Research and Theory* 17 (January 2007), pp. 19–38. The quotation is on p. 36.

274. Laurence E. Lynn, Jr., "The Reagan Administration and the Renitent Bureaucracy," *The Reagan Presidency and the Governing of America*, Lester M. Salamon and Michael S. Lund, eds. (Washington, DC: Urban Institute, 1985), pp. 339–374.

275. Aberbach and Rockman, "The Past and Future of Political-Administrative Relations," The quotations are on pp. 987–988.

276. Partnership for Public Service and Booz Allen Hamilton, *Unrealized Vision*.

277. U.S. Office of Personnel Management, *Senior Executive Service Survey Results 2008*, p. 4.

278. Donald P. Moynihan and Alasdair S. Roberts, "The Triumph of Loyalty over Competence: The Bush Administration and the Exhaustion of the Politicized Presidency," *Public Administration Review* 70 (July/August 2010), pp. 572–581. The quotation is on p. 579.

279. U.S. Office of Personnel Management, *Federal Employment Viewpoint Survey, 2010* Washington, DC: U.S. Government Printing Office, 2010, p. 39.

280. Laura Langbein, "Controlling Federal Agencies: The Contingent Impact of External Controls on Worker Discretion and Productivity," *International Public Management Journal* 12 (1, 2009), pp. 82–115. The quotation is on p. 103.

281. David K. Hamilton, "The Continuing Judicial Assault on Patronage," *Public Administration Review* 59 (January/February 1999), pp. 54–62. The first case was *Elrod* v. *Burns*, and there have been four cases since.

282. James R. Thompson, as quoted (on p. 58) in Jeffrey L. Katz, "The Slow Death of Political Patronage," *Governing* (April 1991), pp. 58–62.

283. Stephen Allred, as quoted in ibid., p. 62.

284. U.S. Bureau of the Census, *Census of Governments, 1992*, Vol. 1, No. 2 (Washington, DC: U.S. Government Printing Office, 1995). Figures are for 1992.

285. As derived from data in Tari Renner and Victor S. DeSantis, "Municipal Form of Government: Issues and Trends," *Municipal Year Book, 1998* (Washington, DC: International City/County Management Association, 1998), pp. 30–40 (the figure is on p. 34); and Evelina R. Moulder, "Municipal Form of Government: Trends in Structure, Responsibility, and Composition," *Municipal Year Book, 2008* (Washington, DC: International City/County Management Association, 2008), pp. 3–8 (the figure is on p. 7). The proportion of mayors with the exclusive power to develop and recommend budgets to the council declined from 16 percent to 11 percent, 1991–2006.

286. As derived from data in Susan A. MacManus and Charles S. Bullock, III, "The Form, Structure, and Composition of America's Municipalities in the New Millennium," *Municipal Year Book, 2003* (Washington, DC: International City/County Management Association, 2003), pp. 3–18. The proportion of mayors with the exclusive power to appoint unelected department heads declined from 27 percent to 17 percent, 1991–2001 (p. 13).

287. James Conant, "Management Consequences of the 1960–1990 'Modernization' of State Government," *Handbook of State Government Administration*, John J. Gargan, ed. (New York: Marcel Dekker, 2000), pp. 13–32. Twenty-six states reorganized their governments, 1965–1990.

288. Frank P. Sherwood and Lee J. Breyer, "Executive Personnel Systems in the States," *Public Administration Review* 47 (September/October 1987), pp. 410–416. The figure is on p. 411.

289. Julia E. Robinson, "The Role of the Independent Political Executive in State Governments: Stability in the Face of Change," *Public Administration Review* 58 (March/April 1998), pp. 119–128.

290. Mann and Doig, *The Assistant Secretaries*, p. 120. In 1964, 90 percent of the assistant secretaries and deputy agency administrators were college graduates.

291. Jeffrey L. Brudney, Cynthia J. Bowling, and Deil S. Wright, *Continuity and Change in Public Administration across the 50 States: Linking Practice, Theory, and Research through the American State Administrators Project, 1964–2008* (Auburn, AL: Center for Governmental Services, Auburn University, 2010), p. 11. Current figures are for 2008.

292. Ibid., p. 13. Figures are for 2008. Growth figures are for 1968–2008.

293. Bowman and West, "State Government 'Little Hatch Acts' in an Era of Civil Service Reform," p. 24. Figures are for 2007.

294. "Inside the Year Book," *Municipal Year Book, 2005* (Washington, DC: International City/County Management Association, 2005), p. x. Between 1945 and 1969, the number of municipalities that had the plan had burgeoned by almost three-fourths.

295. Moulder, "Municipal Form of Government," p. 4. Figure is for 2006.

296. Edgar E. Ramirez de la Cruz, "County Form of Government: Trends in Structure and Composition," *Municipal Year Book, 2009* (Washington, DC: International City/County Management Association, 2009), pp. 21–27. Figure is for 2007 (p. 24).

297. Moulder, "Municipal Form of Government," p. 7. Figures are for 2006.

298. MacManus and Bullock, "The Form, Structure, and Composition of America's Municipalities in the New Millennium," p. 12. Figures are for 2001.

299. Tanis J. Salant, "Trends in County Government Structure," *Municipal Year Book, 2004* (Washington, DC: International City/County Management Association, 2004), pp. 35–41. Figures are for 2002.

300. Killian and Choudhury, "Continuity and Change in the Role of City Managers," p. 11. Figure is for 2009.

301. Wood and Marchbanks, "What Determines How Long Political Appointees Serve?" p. 392. Figures are for 1982–2003.

302. Patricia W. Ingraham, "Building Bridges or Burning Them? The President, The Appointees, and The Bureaucracy," *Public Administration Review* 47 (September/October 1987), pp. 425–435. The figure is on p. 429.

303. David E. Lewis, *Political Appointments, Bureau Chiefs, and Federal Management Performance* (Princeton, NJ: Princeton University, Woodrow Wilson School of Public and International Affairs, 2005), p. 35. Figure is for 2004.

304. Ferrara and Ross, *Getting to Know You*, p. 9. Figure for political appointees is for 1992, and the authors provide some evidence that the percentage has not changed much since then. Figure for careerists is for 2003.

305. Wood and Marchbanks, "What Determines How Long Political Appointees Serve?" p. 392.

306. Kenneth J. Meier and Alisa Hicklin, "Employee Turnover and Organizational Performance: Testing a Hypothesis from Classical Public Administration," *Journal of Public Administration Research and Theory* 18 (October 2008), pp. 573–590. The quotation is on p. 573. This is an analysis of "data from several hundred public organizations" over nine years.

307. U.S. Government Accountability Office, *Federal Chief Information Officers: Responsibilities, Reporting Relationships, Tenure, and Challenges*, GAO-04-823 (Washington, DC: U.S. Government Printing Office, 2004), p. 22. The quotation is a summary of GAO's much broader research, U.S. General Accounting Office, *Results-Oriented Cultures: Implementation Steps to Assist Mergers and Organizational Transformations*, GAO-03-669 (Washington, DC: U.S. Government Printing Office, 2003).

308. Lewis, *Political Appointments, Bureau Chiefs, and Federal Management Performance*, pp. 4, 2. Data are for 2004. This is a seminal comparison of 242 federal bureau chiefs.

309. Andrew Douglas McNitt, "Tenure in Office of Big City Mayors," *State and Local Government*

Review 42 (Winter 2010), pp. 22–35. This is a study of mayors of nineteen major cities, 1853–1995.

310. Carolyn Cain, Enamul Choudhury, and James C. Clingermayer, "Turnover, Trust, and Transfers: An Examination of Local Government Budget Execution," *International Journal of Public Administration* 27 (August/September 2004), pp. 557–576.

311. Ferrara and Ross, *Getting to Know You*, p. 9. Figure is for 1992, but the authors provide some evidence that it is still roughly correct.

312. Lewis, *Political Appointments, Bureau Chiefs, and Federal Management Performance*, pp. 35, 4, 2. Data are for 2004.

313. As derived from data (pp. 478–479) in Claudia N. Avellaneda, "Mayoral Quality and Local Public Finance," *Public Administration Review* 69 (May/June 2009), pp. 469–486. This is an analysis of forty Colombian municipalities and their elected mayors, 2000–2004. The Colombian constitution requires a "strong-mayor" form of municipal government, so mayors are deeply involved in local administration.

314. Hugo Heclo, *A Government of Strangers: Executive Politics in Washington* (Washington, DC: Brookings, 1977).

315. Alexander Hamilton, "No. 72," *The Federalist Papers*, Clinton Rossiter, ed. (New York: New American Library, 1961), p. 436.

316. Cohen, "Amateur Government."

317. Mosher, *Democracy and the Public Service*, p. 113.

318. U.S. Merit Systems Protection Board, "Understanding the Federal Workforce: Compare with Care," *Issues of Merit* (January 2007), p. 3. Figure is for 2005.

319. U.S. Merit Systems Protection Board, *The Federal Government: A Model Employer or a Work in Progress?* p. 9. Figure is for 1983–2007.

320. As derived from data in U.S. Bureau of the Census, *Statistical Abstract of the United States, 2011*, Table 462. Figure is for 2007.

321. Ibid., Table 460. Figure is for 2008.

322. Ibid., Table 462. Figure is for 2007.

323. Franklin P. Kilpatrick, Milton C. Cummings, Jr., and M. Kent Jennings, *The Image of the Federal Service* (Washington, DC: Brookings, 1964).

324. Dwaine Marvick, *Career Perspectives in a Bureaucratic Setting*, University of Michigan Governmental Studies, No. 27 (Ann Arbor, MI: University of Michigan Press, 1954), p. 134.

325. Doyle W. Buckwalter and J. Ivan Legler, "City Managers and City Attorneys: Associates or Adversaries," *Public Administration Review* 47 (September/October 1987), pp. 393–403. The quotations are on p. 393.

326. Frederick C. Mosher and Keith Axtell, unpublished studies cited in Mosher, *Democracy and the Public Service*, pp. 136–137. Federal, state, and local agencies were analyzed.

327. Mosher, *Democracy and the Public Service*, pp. 140–141.

328. Ibid., p. 103 (both quotations).

329. Jean J. Couturier, "The Quiet Revolution in Public Personnel Laws," *Public Personnel Management* 5 (May/June 1976), pp. 150–168.

330. Mosher, *Democracy and the Public Service*, pp. 104–105.

331. Jimmy Carter, *State of the Union Message* (Washington, DC: U.S. Government Printing Office, January 19, 1978).

332. Mosher, *Democracy and the Public Service*, p. 107.

333. National Commission on the State and Local Public Service, *Hard Truths/Tough Choices: An Agenda for State and Local Reform*, First Report (Albany, NY: State University of New York, 1993), p. 27; and National Academy of Public Administration, *Modernizing Federal Classification: An Opportunity for Excellence* (Washington, DC: Author, 1991).

334. James R. Thompson, "Commentary: Pay-banding: What Have We Learned," *Federal Times.com* (June 4, 2007), http://www.federaltimes.com. Figure is for 2007.

335. National Commission on the Public Service, *Urgent Business for America*, p. 27.

336. Partnership for Public Service and Grant Thornton, *Elevating Our Federal Workforce*, p. 3. Figure is for 2008.

337. National Commission on the State and Local Public Service, *Hard Truths/Tough Choices*, p. 27.

338. Chi, "Trends in State Civil Service Systems," pp. 405–412. The data are on p. 410.

339. Cortney Whalen and Mary E. Guy, "Broadbanding Trends in the States," *Review of Public Personnel Administration* 28 (December 2008), pp. 349–366. Figures (p. 349) are for 2008.

340. Selden, *Human Capital*, p. 147. Figures are for 2007.

341. Ibid., p. 148. Data are for 2007, and refer to states that have broadbanded at least 75 percent of their workforces.

342. Jonathan West, "City Personnel Management: Issues and Reforms," *Public Personnel Management* 13 (Fall 1984), pp. 317–334. Figure, 56 percent, is for 1983.

343. U.S. Merit Systems Protection Board, *Addressing Poor Performers and the Law.*

344. Robert L. Mathis and John H. Jackson, *Human Resource Management*, 12th ed. (Mason, OH: Thomson South-Western, 2008), pp. 353–354.

345. Yang and Kassekert, "Linking Management Reform with Employee Job Satisfaction."

346. Geon Lee and Benedict S. Jimenez, "Does Performance Management Affect Job Turnover Intention in the Federal Government?" *American Review of Public Administration* 41 (March 2011), pp. 168–184. The quotation is on p. 168.

347. Berman, Bowman, West, *et al.*, *Human Resource Management in Public Service*, p. 262.

348. Selden, Ingraham, and Jacobson, "Human Resource Practices in State Government," p. 605. Rhode Island is the exception.

349. Pew Center on the States, *People Forward*, p. 5. Figure, 87 percent, is for thirty responding states in 2007.

350. Freyss, "Continuity and Change in Local Personnel Policies and Practices," p. 15. Figure is for 1995.

351. Hal G. Rainey, Carol Traut, and Barry Blunt, "Reward Expectancies and Other Work-Related Attitudes in Public and Private Organizations: A Review and Extension," *Review of Public Personnel Administration* 5 (July 1986), pp. 50–72.

352. U.S Merit Systems Protection Board, *A Call to Action*, pp. 35–36. Data are for 2009.

353. Dennis M. Daley, *Performance Appraisal in the Public Sector* (Westport, CN: Quorum, 1992).

354. "Reforming Government Pay," *Washington Post* (July 28, 2005).

355. U.S. General Accounting Office, *Results-Oriented Cultures: Insights for US Agencies from Other Countries' Performance Management Initiatives*, GAO-02-862 (Washington, DC: U.S. Government Printing Office, 2002).

356. U.S. Government Accountability Office, *Human Capital: Symposium on Designing and Managing Market-Based and More Performance-Oriented Pay Systems*, GAO-05-832SP (Washington, DC: U.S. Government Printing Office, 2005).

357. U.S. General Accounting Office, *Posthearing Questions Related to Pay for Performance*, pp. 1–2.

358. U.S. Government Accountability Office, *Human Capital: Symposium on Designing and Managing Market-Based and More Performance-Oriented Pay Systems*, Highlights page.

359. U.S. General Accounting Office, *Results-Oriented Cultures: Creating a Clear Linkage between Individual Performance and Organizational Success*, GAO-03-488 (Washington, DC: U.S. Government Printing Office, 2003), Highlights page.

360. Selden, *Human Capital*, p. 116.

361. U.S. Merit Systems Protection Board, *The Federal Government: A Model Employer or a Work in Progress?* p. 33. By 2005, 67 percent agreed with the statement.

362. U.S. Office of Personnel Management, *Federal Employee Viewpoint Survey*, 2010, p. 37.

363. Hays, "Trends and Best Practices in State and Local Human Resource Management," p. 267.

364. Heather Kerrigan, "Making Performance a Priority," *Governing* (April 2011), pp. 54–55.

365. U.S. Merit Systems Protection Board, *The Federal Workforce for the 21st Century: Results of the Merit Principles Survey 2000* (Washington, DC: U.S. Government Printing Office, 2003), p. 24.

366. Partnership for Public Service, *Asking the Wrong Questions*, p. 3.

367. Corporate Leadership Council, *Literature Review: Employee Selection Tests*, Catalog No. 070-198-213 (Washington, DC: Author, 1998).

368. Joyce Ehrlinger, Kerri Johnson, Matthew Banner, *et al.*, "Why the Unskilled Are Unaware: Further Explorations of (Absent) Self-Insight among the Incompetent," *Organizational Behavior and Human Decision Processes* 105 (January 2008), pp. 98–121. The quotations are on pp. 117–119.

369. U.S. Government Accountability Office, *Issues Related to Poor Performers in the Federal Workplace*, GAO-05-812R Poor Performers in

the Federal Workplace (Washington, DC: U.S. Government Printing Office, 2005), p. 2.

370. Light, "To Restore and Renew." Figure is for 2001.

371. U.S. Office of Personnel Management, *Poor Performers in Government: A Quest for the True Story* (Washington, DC: U.S. Government Printing Office, 1999), p. 6.

372. Ibid., p. 13.

373. U.S. Merit Systems Protection Board, *Federal Supervisors and Poor Performers* (Washington, DC: U.S. Government Printing Office, 1999), pp. 15–16, 8. Figures are for 1996.

374. Ricccucci and Naff, *Personnel Management in Government*, p. 27.

375. James B. King, then-director of the Office of Personnel Management, as cited in Frank Greve, "Civil Service Can Be a Job for Life," *Baltimore Sun* (November 29, 1993).

376. U.S. Merit Systems Protection Board, *The Probationary Period: A Critical Assessment Opportunity* (Washington, DC: U.S. Government Printing Office, 2005); and U.S. Merit Systems Protection Board, *A Call to Action.*

377. U.S. Merit Systems Protection Board, *The Probationary Period*, pp. 9, 7. Figures are for 1998–2001.

378. As derived from data in U.S. Merit Systems Protection Board, *Supervisory Probationary Period: A Missed Opportunity* (Washington, DC: U.S. Government Printing Office, 2011). Figure is for FY 2007.

379. National Commission on the Public Service, *Urgent Business for America*, pp. 40–41.

380. U.S. Equal Employment Opportunity Commission, *Annual Report on the Federal Workforce Fiscal Year 2010* (Washington, DC: U.S. Government Printing Office, 2011), Figures 7, 12. In 2010, "processing days" for a hearing averaged 332, and, for a subsequent appeal hearing, processing days averaged 292. Both numbers are rising over time. The EEOC handles the most cases, all of which are discrimination complaints.

381. Riccucci and Naff, *Personnel Management in Government*, p. 27.

382. Lisa Rein, "Fight for Job Leaves Stephen Patrick Idle and on the Federal Payroll," *Washington Post* (October 9, 2011).

383. U.S. Office of Personnel Management, *Poor Performers in Government*, p. 33.

384. U.S. Merit Systems Protection Board, *Federal Supervisors and Poor Performers*, pp. 13, 17. Figure is for 1996.

385. U.S. General Accounting Office, *Performance Management: How Well Is the Government Dealing with Poor Performers?* GAO/GGD-91-7 (Washington, DC: U.S. Government Printing Office, 1990), pp. 32–33.

386. The Future Foundation and SHL, *Getting the Edge in the New People Economy* (London and New York: Authors, 2004), p. 31. This study found that business managers in the United States spend about 13 percent of their time correcting employees' mistakes, or about five hours out of forty per week.

387. U.S. Merit Systems Protection Board, *Federal Supervisors and Poor Performers*, pp. 13, 17. Figure is for 1996.

388. U.S. Government Accountability Office, *Issues Related to Poor Performers in the Federal Workplace*, p. 11. Figure is for 2003.

389. U.S. Merit Systems Protection Board, *Federal Supervisors and Poor Performers*, p. 19. Figure is for 1996.

390. U.S. Merit Systems Protection Board, *Removing Poor Performers in the Federal Service* (Washington, DC: U.S. Government Printing Office, 1995), pp. 6–7. Figures are for 1994.

391. U.S. Merit Systems Protection Board, *A Call to Action*, pp. 36–37. Data, 21 and 22 percent, respectively, are for 2009.

392. U.S. Merit Systems Protection Board, *Federal Supervisors and Poor Performers*, p. 8 (which cites studies beginning in 1981); and U.S. Office of Personnel Management, *Federal Employee Viewpoint Survey, 2010*, p. 37.

393. Light, "The Content of Their Character," p. 15. Figures are for 2001–2002.

394. U.S. Office of Personnel Management, *Federal Employee Viewpoint Survey, 2010*, p. 28.

395. U.S. Merit Systems Protection Board, *In Search of Highly Skilled Workers*, p. 33. Figures are for 2005.

396. U.S. Office of Personnel Management, *Senior Executive Service 2008 Survey Results*, p. 2. Figures are for 2008.

397. Dennis M. Daley, "The Burdens of Dealing with Poor Performers: Wear and Tear on Supervisory Organizational Engagement," *Review of Public Personnel Administration* 28 (March 2008), pp. 44–59.

398. Selden, *Human Capital*, p. 63. "Involuntary separations" were 1.76 percent in 2007 and 1.95 percent in 2000.

399. As derived from data in U.S. Merit Systems Protection Board, *Federal Supervisors and Poor Performers*, pp. 7, 15. Figure is for 1997.

400. Selden, *Human Capital,* p. 51; and U.S. Merit Systems Protection Board, *The Probationary Period*, p. 9. Figures are 22 percent and 1.6 percent, respectively.

401. Light, "The Content of Their Character," p. 15.

402. Elling, Thompson, and Monet, "The Problematic World of State Management." Figures are for 2000–2001.

403. Pew Center on the States, *People Forward*, p. 28. Figures are for twenty-six reporting states in 2007.

404. Elling, Thompson, and Monet, "The Problematic World of State Management." Figures are for 2000–2001.

405. Hebdon, "Labor-Management Relations in the United States, 1999," pp. 22–27.

406. Ibid., p. 23.

407. U.S. Office of Personnel Management, *Adherence to the Merit Principles in the Workplace: Federal Employees' Views* (Washington, DC: U.S. Government Printing Office, 1997), p. 7.

408. Risher, *Pay for Performance*, p. 41.

409. Council for Excellence in Government, Gallup, and Accenture, *The Appeal of Public Service*, p. 5. Fifty-one percent said this in 2008.

410. U.S. Office of Personnel Management, *Adherence to the Merit Principles in the Workplace*, p. 3.

411. U.S. General Accounting Office, *Human Capital: Using Incentives to Motivate and Reward High Performance*, GAO/T-GGD-00-118 (Washington, DC: U.S. Government Printing Office, 2000).

412. Selden, *Human Capital*, p. 141. Figures are for 1980–2007.

413. National Commission on the Public Service, *Urgent Business for America*, p. 31. Figure is for 2001.

414. U.S. Government Accountability Office, *Government Performance: Lessons Learned for the Administration on Using Performance Information to Improve Results*, GAO-08-1026T (Washington, DC: U.S. Government Printing Office, 2008), p. 6. Figures are for 1997–2007.

415. Howard Risher, "We Know Performance Pay Works," *Federal Computer Week* (November 16, 2009), p. 10.

416. Selden, *Human Capital*, p. 143. Figures are for 2004–2007.

417. Pew Center on the States, *People Forward*, p. 5.

418. Freyss, "Continuity and Change in Local Personnel Policies and Practices," p. 15. Figure is for 1995.

419. Selden, "Human Resource Management in American Counties, 2002," p. 81. Figures are for 2002.

420. U.S. Merit Systems Protection Board, *The Federal Government: A Model Employer or a Work in Progress?* p. 30. The percentage of federal employees responding positively to this question has risen steadily from 17 to 49 percent, 1983–2007.

421. U.S. Office of Personnel Management, *Federal Employee Viewpoint Survey, 2010*, p. 38. In 2010, 44 percent agreed that, "Awards in my work unit depend on how well employees perform their jobs," and 26 percent agreed with the statement about pay raises.

422. J. Edward Kellough and Lloyd G. Nigro, "Pay for Performance in Georgia State Government: Employee Perspectives on GeorgiaGain after 5 Years," *Review of Public Personnel Administration* 22 (June 2002), pp. 146–166; and James S. Baldwin, Marc G. Gertz, Sally C. Gertz, *et al.*, "Civil Service Reform in Florida State Government: Employee Attitudes One Year Later," *Review of Public Personnel Administration* 23 (December 2003), pp. 286–304.

423. Richard C. Elling, "Bureaucracy: Maligned Yet Essential," *Politics in the American States: A Comparative Analysis*, 6th ed., Virginia Gray and Herbert Jacob, eds. (Washington, DC: CQ Press, 1996), pp. 286–318. The quotations are on p. 292. Figure, 51 percent, is for the "mid-1980s."

424. James L. Perry, Trent A. Engbers, and So Yun Jun, "Back to the Future? Performance-Related Pay, Empirical Research, and the Perils of Persistence," *Public Administration Review* 69 (January/February 2009), pp. 39–51. The quotations are on p. 47. This is an analysis of fifty-seven studies published, 1977–2008.

425. Antoinette Weibel, Katja Rost, and Margit Osterloh, "Pay for Performance in the Public Sector—Benefits and (Hidden) Costs," *Journal of Public Administration Research and Theory* 20 (April 2010), pp. 387–412. The quotation is on p. 387. This is "a meta-analytic review of previous experimental

studies on the effects of pay for performance on performance."

426. Gene A. Brewer and Richard M. Walker, "The Impact of Red Tape on Governmental Performance: An Empirical Analysis," *Journal of Public Administration Research and Theory* 20 (January 2010), pp. 233–257. The quotation is on p. 249. This is an analysis of 166 English local authorities.

427. Seong Soo Oh and Gregory B. Lewis, "Can Performance Appraisal Systems Inspire Intrinsically Motivated Employees?" *Review of Public Personnel Administration* 29 (June 2009), pp. 158–167. The quotation is on p. 160.

428. Wouter Vandenabeele, "The Mediating Effect of Job Satisfaction and Organizational Commitment on Self-Reported Performance: More Robust Evidence of the PSM-Performance Relationship," *International Review of Administrative Sciences* 75 (March 2009), pp. 11–34. This is a study of Belgian bureaucrats.

429. Perry, Engbers, and Jun, "Back to the Future?" p. 47.

430. Paul C. Light, "The End of the Civil Service?" *Washington Post* (May 9, 2003).

431. Henry L. Tosi, Steve Werner, Jeffrey P. Katz, et al., "How Much Does Performance Matter? A Meta-Analysis of CEO Pay Studies," *Journal of Management* 26 (2, 2000), pp. 301–339. The quotation is on p. 301.

432. Debra Mesch and Patrick M. Rooney, "Determinants of Compensation: A Study of Pay, Performance, and Gender Differences for Fundraising Professionals," *Nonprofit Management & Leadership* 18 (Summer 2008), pp. 435–463. The quotations are on pp. 441, 458.

433. Carl Dahlstrom and Victor Lapuente, "Explaining Cross-Country Differences in Performance-Related Pay in the Public Sector," *Journal of Public Administration Research and Theory* 20 (July 2010), pp. 577–600. The quotation is on p. 577. This is an analysis of twenty-five European nations.

434. Carol Rusaw, "Professionalism under the 'Performance-Based Pay' Reform: A Critical Assessment and Alternative Development Model," *Public Personnel Management* 38 (Winter 2009), pp. 35–53.

435. Perry, Engbers, and Jun, "Back to the Future?" p. 47.

436. Risher, *Pay for Performance*, p. 10.

437. Perry, Engbers, and Jun, "Back to the Future?" p. 45.

438. Partnership for Public Service and Grant Thornton, *Closing the Gap*, p. 11. Figures are for 2010.

439. Robert Roberts, "The Supreme Court and the Continuing Deconstitutionalization of Pubic Personnel Management," *Review of Public Personnel Administration* 29 (March 2009), pp. 3–19. The quotations are on pp. 4, 17.

440. The following list is based on U.S. Merit Systems Protection Board, *Managing for Engagement: Communication, Connection, and Courage* (Washington, DC: U.S. Government Printing Office, 2009), pp. 66–74.

441. U.S. Merit Systems Protection Board, *Removing Poor Performers in the Federal Service*, p. 7. Figure is for 1994.

442. Julia B. Isaacs, *Economic Mobility of Black and White Families,* and *Economic Mobility of Men and Women* (Washington, DC: Brookings, 2007).

443. We are grateful to Elling, "Administering State Programs," p. 276, for the provision of these terms.

444. Reginald Wilson, *Affirmative Action: Yesterday, Today, and Beyond* (Washington, DC: American Council on Education, 1995), p. 6.

445. Bob Zelnick, *Backfire: A Reporter's Look at Affirmative Action* (Washington, DC: Regnery, 1996), p. 29.

446. As derived from data in U.S. House of Representatives, Committee on Government Reform—Minority Staff, Special Investigations Division, Prepared for Rep. Henry A. Waxman, *Dollars, Not Sense: Government Contracting under the Bush Administration* (Washington, DC: Author, 2006).

447. Mitchell F. Rice and Maurice Mongkuo, "Did *Adarand* Kill Minority Set-Asides?" *Public Administration Review* 58 (January/February 1998), p. 85; and *Federal Register*, cited in Ann Devroy, "Affirmative Action Rules Are Revised," *Washington Post* (May 23, 1996).

448. U.S. Government Accounting Office, *New Markets Tax Credits: Minority Entities Are Less Successful in Obtaining Awards than Non-Minnority Entities*, GAO-09-536 (Washington, DC: U.S. Government Printing Office, 2009), Highlights page. The analysis is of the multi-billion-dollar Community Development Financial Institutions Fund, 2005–2008.

449. George R. La Noue and John C. Sullivan, "Race Neutral Programs in Public Contracting," *Public Administration Review* 55 (July/August 1995), pp. 348–357. The quotation is on p. 354.

450. Pan S. Kim, "Disability Policy: An Analysis of the Employment of People with Disabilities in the American Federal Government," *Public Personnel Management* 25 (Spring 1996), pp. 73–88. The quotation is on p. 73. In 1999, the Supreme Court ruled in three cases that the ADA did not apply to people whose condition could be corrected.

451. American Bar Association, as cited in: Laurie Asseo, "High Court Limits Disabilities Law," *Washington Post* (June 22, 1999).

452. Gregory B. Lewis and David W. Pitts, "Representation of Lesbians and Gay Men in Federal, State, and Local Bureaucracies," *Journal of Public Administration Research and Theory* 21 (January 2011), pp. 159–180. The quotation is on p. 169. Figures are for 2000, and refer to percentages of same-sex partners.

453. U.S. Merit Systems Protection Board, "Sexual Orientation, Workplace Treatment, and the Limitations of Survey Data," *Issues of Merit* (September 2009), p. 4. Figure is for 2005 and 2007.

454. Human Rights Campaign, *GLBT Equality at the Fortune 500* (Washington, DC: Author, 2008). Figure is for 2008.

455. Charles W. Gossett, "Lesbians and Gay Men in the Public-Sector Workforce," *Public Personnel Management: Current Concerns, Future Challenges*, 4th ed., Norma M. Riccucci, ed. (New York: Longman, 2006), pp. 76–77. Figure is for 2005.

456. U.S. Government Accountability Office, *Sexual Orientation and Gender Identity Employment Discrimination: Overview of State Statutes and Complaint Data*, GAO-10-135R Sexual Orientation/Gender Identity Employment Discrimination (U.S. Government Printing Office, 2009), p. 1. Figure is for 2009.

457. Lewis and Pitts, "Representation of Lesbians and Gay Men in Federal, State, and Local Bureaucracies," pp. 159–180. The quotation is on p. 169. Datum is for 2000.

458. U.S. General Accounting Office, *Sexual Orientation-Based Employment Discrimination: States' Experience with Statutory Prohibitions*, GAO-02-878R (Washington, DC: U.S. Government Printing Office, 2002), p. 2.

459. Gossett, "Lesbians and Gay Men in the Public-Sector Workforce." Figure is for 2005.

460. The term comes from the Equal Employment Opportunity Commission, and refers to "any person covered by [federal] antidiscrimination legislation," a standard that would appear to omit the category of sexual orientation, but cover all the remaining classes. See Riccucci and Naff, *Personnel Management in Government*, p. 406.

461. As derived from data in U.S. Bureau of the Census, *Statistical Abstract of the United States, 2011*, Table 8; and Stanley B. Malos, *Current Legal Issues in Performance Appraisal, 2006*, http://www.cob.sjsu.edu/malos_s/bookchap.htm. Figure is for 2008.

462. The case is *Smith* v. *City of Jackson*.

463. Robert N. Roberts, "Damned If You Do and Damned If You Don't: Title VII and Public Employee Promotion Disparate Treatment and Disparate Impact Litigation," *Pubic Administration Review* 70 (July/August 2010), pp. 582–590. The quotation is on p. 583.

464. U.S. Government Accountability Office, *Federal Contractors: Better Performance Information Needed to Support Agency Contract Award Decisions*, GAO-09-374 (Washington, DC: U.S. Government Printing Office, 2009), Highlights page. Figure is for FY 2007.

465. The case is *MetroBroadcasting* v. *Federal Communications Commission*.

466. Linda Greenhouse, "Justices Say Law Bars Retaliation over Bias Claims," *New York Times* (May 28, 2008).

467. The case is *CBOCS West, Inc.* v. *Humphries*.

468. The case is *Gomez-Perez* v. *Potter*.

469. Thompson, *Personnel Policy in the City*, pp. 112–130.

470. Robert J. Huntley and Robert J. McDonald, "Urban Managers: Organizational Preferences, Managerial Styles, and Social Policy Roles," *Municipal Year Book, 1975* (Washington, DC: International City Management Association, 1975), pp. 149–159. Data (for 1974) and quotation (emphasis added) are on p. 157.

471. Evelina R. Moulder, "Affirmative Action in Local Government," *Municipal Year Book 1991* (Washington, DC: International City Management Association, 1991), pp. 47–52.

472. Paul Oyer and Scott Schaefer, "Sorting, Quotas, and the Civil Rights Act of 1991: Who Hires

When It's Hard to Fire?" *Journal of Law and Economics* 45 (April 2002), pp. 41–68.

473. Paul Oyer and Scott Schaefer, "The Bias Backfire," *Harvard Business Review* 82 (November 2004), p. 26.

474. Elizabeth L. Schoenfelt and Leslie C. Pedigo, "A Review of Court Decisions on Cognitive Ability Testing, 1992–2004," *Review of Public Personnel Administration* 25 (September 2005), pp. 271–287.

475. See, for example, James L. Outtz, "The Role of Cognitive Ability Tests in Employment Selection," *Human Performance* 15 (Spring 2002), pp. 161–171; and Kevin R. Murphy, "Can Conflicting Perspectives on the Role of g in Personnel Selection Be Resolved?" pp. 173–186, in the same issue. African Americans typically score one standard deviation lower than whites on cognitive ability tests. Hispanics do somewhat better.

476. Earl Hunt, "When Should We Shoot the Messenger? Issues Involving Cognitive Testing, Public Policy, and the Law," *Psychology, Public Policy, and Law* 2 (September/December 1996), pp. 486–505.

477. Moulder, "Affirmative Action in Local Government," p. 51; and Evelina R. Moulder, "Affirmative Action: The Role Local Governments Are Playing," *Municipal Year Book 1986* (Washington, DC: International City Management Association, 1986), pp. 24–28 (the data are on p. 26).

478. The case is *Albermarle Paper Co.* v. *Moody*. The ruling was made in 1975.

479. The case is *State of Connecticut,* et al. v. *Adele*. The ruling was made in 1982.

480. Schoenfelt and Pedigo, "A Review of Court Decisions on Cognitive Ability Testing, 1992–2004," p. 272.

481. Riccucci and Naff, *Personnel Management in Government*, p. 268.

482. The 1981 decision was actually a consent decree that OPM signed in the case, *Luevano* v. *Campbell*.

483. U.S. Merit Systems Protection Board, *Federal Appointment Authorities*, p. 5.

484. Stein, "Merit Systems and Political Influence," p. 267.

485. The case is *Personnel Administrator* v. *Feeney*.

486. The case is *Chicago Firefighters Local 2,* et al. v. *City of Chicago,* et al.

487. Jean Couturier, "Court Attacks on Testing: Death Knell or Salvation for the Civil Service System," *Good Government* 88 (Winter 1971), pp. 10–12. The figure is on p. 12.

488. Couturier, "The Quiet Revolution in Public Personnel Laws." Figures are for 1971–1976.

489. Schoenfelt and Pedigo, "A Review of Court Decisions on Cognitive Ability Testing, 1992–2004." This is a study of twenty-two lawsuits heard by appellate and district courts, 1992–2004. All these suits challenged cognitive ability tests, and most were class-action, race-based claims brought by minority plaintiffs who worked in governments.

490. Leslie E. Tower and Mohamad G. Alkrady, "The Social Costs of Career Success for Women," *Review of Public Personnel Administration* 28 (June 2008), pp. 144–165. The quotation is on p. 144.

491. Mohamad G. Alkadry and Leslie E. Tower, "Covert Pay Discrimination: How Authority Predicts Pay Differences between Women and Men," *Public Administration Review* (September/November 2011), pp. 740–750. The quotation is on p. 740. This is a study of 384 public chief procurement officers.

492. Tim V. Eaton and John R. Nofsinger, "Funding Levels and Gender in Public Pension Plans," *Public Budgeting & Finance* 28 (September 2008), pp. 108–128. The quotations are on p. 108.

493. The case is *Rosenfeld* v. *Southern Pacific Co.*

494. The case is *Weeks* v. *Southern Bell Telephone and Telegraph Co.*

495. James E. Campbell and Gregory B. Lewis, "Public Support for Comparable Worth in Georgia," *Public Administration Review* 46 (September/October 1986), pp. 432–437.

496. Susan E. Gardner and Christopher Daniel, "Implementing Comparable Worth/Pay Equity: Experiences of Cutting-Edge States," *Public Personnel Management* 27 (Winter 1998), pp. 475–489.

497. N. Joseph Cayer, "Local Government Personnel Structure and Policies," *Municipal Year Book, 1991* (Washington, DC: International City/County Management Association, 1991), pp. 8–13.

498. Gardner and Daniel, "Implementing Comparable Worth/Pay Equity"; and U.S. General Accounting Office, *Pay Equity: Washington State's Efforts to Address Comparable Worth,*

GAO/GGO-92-87BR (Washington, DC: U.S. Government Printing Office, 1992).

499. Jared J. Llorens, "Uncovering the Determinants of Competitive State Government Wages," *Review of Public Personnel Administration* 28 (December 2008), pp 308–326. The quotations are on pp. 308, 321.

500. As derived from survey data in U.S. Bureau of the Census, *Statistical Abstract of the United States, 2011*, Table 315. Figure is for 2006.

501. Cynthia S. Ross and Robert E. England, "State Governments' Sexual Harassment Policy Initiatives," *Public Administration Review* 47 (May/June 1987), p. 261. Data are for 1985.

502. Cayer, "Local Government Personnel Structure and Policies," p. 12.

503. As derived from data in U.S. Equal Employment Opportunity Commission, *Charge Statistics, FY 1997 Through FY 2010*, and *Sexual Harassment Charges: EEOC and FEPAs Combined, FY 1997-FY 2010* (Washington, DC: U.S. Government Printing Office, 2011). Figures are for FY 2010.

504. As derived from data in U.S. Equal Employment Opportunity Commission, *Charge Statistics, FY 1997 Through FY 2010*, and *Sexual Harassment Charges*. Figures are for 1997–2010.

505. U.S. Merit Systems Protection Board, *Sexual Harassment in the Federal Workplace: Trends, Progress, Continuing Challenges* (Washington, DC: U.S. Government Printing Office, 1995), pp. 7, 18. In 1980, only 65 percent of male federal employees stated that pressuring a co-worker for sexual favors constituted harassment; in 1994, 93 percent said so.

506. Ibid., pp. vii, viii. Figures are for 1994.

507. Ibid., p. 19.

508. Survey by the UCLA Graduate School of Management and Korn Ferry International, as cited in ibid., p. 20.

509. The case is *Meritor Savings Bank* v. *Vinson*.

510. The case is *Franklin* v. *Gwinnett County Public Schools*.

511. *Harris* v. *Forklift System, Inc.* 510 U.S. 17, No. 92-1168 (Washington, DC: Supreme Court of the United States, 1993).

512. U.S. Merit Systems Protection Board, *Prohibited Personnel Practices: Employee Perceptions*, p. 28. Percentage fell from 13.4 to 5 percent, 1992–2010.

513. As derived from data in U.S. Merit Systems Protection Board, *Prohibited Personnel Practices: A Study Retrospective*, p. 8. Figures are for 1992–2007.

514. Ugorji O. Ugorji, "Career-Impeding Supervisory Behaviors: Perceptions of African American and European American Professionals," *Public Administration Review* 57 (May/June 1997), pp. 250–255.

515. U.S. Merit Systems Protection Board, *Fair and Equitable Treatment*, p. 60.

516. H. E. Hennessey, Jr. and H. John Bernardin, "The Relationship between Performance Appraisal Criterion Specificity and Statistical Evidence of Discrimination," *Human Resource Management* 42 (Summer 2003), pp. 143–158. The quotation is on p. 143.

517. Barry M. Goldman, Barbara A. Gutek, Jordan H. Stein, *et al.*, "Employment Discrimination in Organizations: Antecedents and Consequences," *Journal of Management* 32 (December 2006), pp. 786–830,

518. U.S. Merit Systems Protection Board, *Fair and Equitable Treatment*, p. 66.

519. Ellen V. Rubin, "The Role of Procedural Justice in Public Personnel Management: Empirical Results from the Department of Defense," *Journal of Public Administration Research and Theory* 19 (January 2009), pp. 125–143.

520. Gerald R. Ferris, Dwight D. Fink, Dharm P. S. Bhawuk, *et al.*, "Reactions of Diverse Groups to Politics in the Workplace," *Journal of Management* 22 (Spring 1996), pp. 23–44.

521. U.S. Merit Systems Protection Board, *Prohibited Personnel Practices: Employee Perceptions*, p. 28. Percentage fell from 12.2 to 3.9 percent, 1992–2010.

522. As derived from data in U.S. Merit Systems Protection Board, *Prohibited Personnel Practices: A Study Retrospective*, p. 9. Figures are for 1992–2007.

523. U.S. Merit Systems Protection Board, *Sexual Harassment in the Federal Workplace*, pp. vii, viii.

524. U.S. Merit Systems Protection Board, *The Federal Government: A Model Employer or a Work in Progress?* p. 41.

525. Richard W. Stackman, Patrick E. Connor, and Boris W. Becker, "Sectoral Ethos: An Investigation of Personal Values Systems of Female and Male Managers in the Public and Private Sectors," *Journal of Public Administration Research and Theory* 16 (October 2006), pp. 577–590. The quotation is on p. 589.

526. Leisha DeHart-Davis, Justin Marlowe, and Sanjay K. Pandey, "Gender Dimensions of Public Service Motivation," *Public Administration Review* 66 (November/December 2006), pp. 873–887.

527. Julie Dolan, "Gender Equity: Illusion or Reality for Women in the Federal Executive Service?" *Public Administration Review* 64 (May/June 2004), pp. 299–306.

528. Dennis M. Daley and Katherine C. Naff, "Gender Differences and Managerial Competencies," *Review of Public Personnel Administration* 18 (April 1998), pp. 41–56.

529. Dorothy Olsheski and Raphael Caprio, "Comparing Personal and Professional Characteristics of Men and Women State Executives: 1990 and 1993 Results," *Review of Public Personnel Administration* 16 (January 1996), pp. 31–40.

530. Daley and Naff, "Gender Differences and Managerial Competencies."

531. Michael J. Zyphur, Jayanth Narayanan, Gerald Koh, *et al.*, "Testrosterone-Status Mismatch Lowers Collective Efficacy in Groups: Evidence from a Slope-as-Predictor Multilevel Structural Equation Model," *Organizational Behavior and Human Decision Processes* 110 (November 2009), pp. 70–79. The quotation is on p. 70.

532. Marion Eals and Irwin Silverman, "The Hunter-Gatherer Theory of Spatial Sex Differences: Proximate Factors Mediating the Female Advantage in Recall of Object Arrays," *Ethology and Sociobiology* 15 (March 1994), pp. 95–105.

533. Richard A. Fox and Robert A. Schuhmann, "Gender and Local Government: A Comparison of Women and Men Managers," *Public Administration Review* 59 (May/June 1999), pp. 231–242.

534. DeHart-Davis, Marlowe, and Pandey, "Gender Dimensions of Public Service Motivation."

535. Kenneth J. Meier, Lawrence J. O'Toole, Jr., and Holly T. Goerdel, "Management Activity and Program Performance: Gender as Management Capital," *Public Administration Review* 66 (January/February 2006), pp. 24–36.

536. Willow S. Jacobson, Christine Kelleher Palus, and Cynthia J. Bowling, "A Woman's Touch? Gendered Management and Performance in State Administration," *Journal of Public Administration Research and Theory* 20 (April 2010), pp. 477–544. The quotation is on p. 477.

537. Meier, O'Toole, and. Goerdel, "Management Activity and Program Performance," p. 32.

538. Jacobson, Palus, and Bowling, "A Woman's Touch?" p. 477.

539. Victoria Bishop, Catherine Cassell, and Helge Hoel, "Preserving Masculinity in Service Work: An Exploration of the Underreporting of Customer Anti-Social Behaviour," *Human Relations* 62 (January 2009), pp. 5–25. This is a study of bus drivers.

540. Kenneth J. Meier, Sharon H. Mastracci, and Kristin Wilson, "Emotional Labor in Public Organizations: An Empirical Examination of the Link to Performance," *Public Administration Review* 66 (November/December 2006), pp. 899–909; and Kenneth J. Meier and Jill Nicholson-Crotty, "Gender, Representative Bureaucracy, and Law Enforcement: The Case of Sexual Assault," in the same issue, pp. 850–860.

541. Gregory B. Lewis, "Race, Sex, and Performance Ratings in the Federal Service," *Public Administration Review* 57 (November/December 1997), pp. 479–489. The quotation is on p. 479.

542. Meier, O'Toole, and Goerdel, "Management Activity and Program Performance," p. 32.

543. Dolan, "Gender Equity," p. 299.

544. David Fasenfest, Jason Booza, and Kurt Metzger, *Living Together: A New Look at Racial and Ethnic Integration in Metropolitan Neighborhoods, 1990–2000* (Washington, DC: Brookings, 2004).

545. *Wall Street Journal*, NBC News Poll, as cited in Gerald F. Seib and Joe Davidson, "Whites, Blacks Agree on Problems; the Issue Is How to Solve Them," *Wall Street Journal* (September 29, 1994).

546. Pew Research Center for the People and the Press, *Trends in Political Values and Core Attitudes, 1987–2007* (Washington, DC: Author, 2007), p. 40. White support for affirmative action grew from 53 to 65 percent, and black support remained steady, declining from 94 to 93 percent, 1995–2007.

547. American National Election Studies, "Aid to Blacks/Minorities 1970–2008," *The ANES Guide to Public Opinion and Electoral Behavior*, http://www.electionstudies.org/nesguide/text/t4b_4_1.txt. In 1970, 79 percent of blacks agreed that Washington should help them; in 1992, 38 percent said this, a response that has since fluctuated from 31 to 44 percent, 1994–2008.

548. Pew Research Center for the People and the Press, *Conflicted Views of Affirmative Action* (Washington, DC: Author, 2003), p. 3.

549. Miquel M. Unzueta, Brian Lowery, and Eric D. Knowles, "How Believing in Affirmative Action Quotas Protects White Men's Self-Esteem," *Organizational Behavior and Human Decision Processes* 105 (January 2008), pp. 1–13. The quotations are on p. 1.

550. Pew Research Center for the People and the Press, *Trends in Political Values and Core Attitudes, 1987–2007*, p. 40.

551. Pew Research Center for the People and the Press, *Conflicted Views of Affirmative Action*, pp. 5, 2, and 3, respectively.

552. Edward Felsenthal, "Are Civil-Rights Laws Being Interpreted Too Broadly?" *Wall Street Journal* (June 10, 1996).

553. Ralph R. Reiland, "Affirmative Action or Equal Opportunity?" *Regulation* 18 (Summer 1995), pp. 12–13.

554. "Disadvantaged Groups, Individual Rights," *The New Republic* (October 15, 1977), p. 7; and Eliot Marshall, "Race Certification," in the same issue, p. 19.

555. Pew Research Center for the People and the Press, *Conflicted Views of Affirmative Action*, p. 3.

556. Madeline E. Heilman, Caryn J. Block, and Peter Stathatos, "The Affirmative-Action Stigma of Incompetence: Effects of Performance Information Ambiguity," *Academy of Management Journal* 40 (June 1997), pp. 603–625.

557. Caitlin Knowles Myers, "A Cure for Discrimination? Affirmative Action and the Case of California's Proposition 209," *Industrial & Labor Relations Review* 60 (April 2007), pp. 379–396. The quotation is on p. 379.

558. Scott E. Page, *The Difference: How the Power of Diversity Creates Better Groups, Firms, Schools, and Societies* (Princeton, NJ: Princeton University Press, 2007), pp. xxiii, 162.

559. Cedric Herring, "Does Diversity Pay? Racial Composition of Firms and the Business Case for Diversity," *American Sociological Review* 72 (April 2009), pp. 208–224.

560. Jason A. Grissom, "The Determiniants of Conflict on Governing Boards in Public Organizations: The Case of California School Boards," *Journal of Public Administration Research and Theory* 20 (July 2010), pp. 601–628. The quotation is on p. 601.

561. Mitchell J. Chang and Alexander W. Astin, "Who Benefits from Racial Diversity in Higher Education?" *Diversity Digest* 2 (Winter 1997), http://www.diversityweb.org/Digest/W97/research.html.

562. Selden, "A Solution in Search of a Problem?" p. 918.

563. Page, *The Difference*, pp. xxiii, 314.

564. U.S. Merit Systems Protection Board, *Fair and Equitable Treatment*, p. 68. Data are for FY 2005–2008.

565. Sungjoo Choi and Hal G. Rainey, "Managing Diversity in U.S. Federal Agencies: Effects of Diversity and Diversity Management on Employee Perceptions of Organizational Performance," *Public Administration Review* 70 (January/February 2010), pp. 109–121. The quotations are on p. 116. Emphasis added. The data for gender and age diversity "produce mixed results."

566. Yongbeom Hur, Ruth Ann Strickland, and Dragan Stefanovic, "Managing Diversity: Does It Matter to Municipal Governments?" *International Journal of Public Sector Management* 23 (5, 2010), pp. 500–515.

567. Michael Kinsley, "The Spoils of Victimhood," *The New Yorker* (March 27, 1995), pp. 62–69. The quotation is on p. 67.

568. Selden, "A Solution in Search of a Problem?" p. 914.

569. As derived from data in U.S. Bureau of the Census, *Statistical Abstract of the United States, 2011*, Tables 6, and 498. Percentages have been rounded. All data are for 2007 and include persons of two or more races.

570. Carl A. Kogut and Larry E. Short, "Affirmative Action in Federal Employment: Good Intentions Run Amuck?" *Public Personnel Management* 36 (Fall 2007), pp. 197–206. The quotation is on p. 204.

571. As derived from data in U.S. Bureau of the Census, *Statistical Abstract of the United States, 2011*, Table 499. Figure is for executive branch employees in 2007, and excludes postal workers.

572. U.S. Office of Personnel Management, *Federal Civilian Workforce Statistics: The Fact Book, 2007 edition* (Washington, DC: U.S. Government Printing Office, 2010), p. 50. Data are for 2006.

573. U.S. Merit Systems Protection Board, *Women in the Federal Government: Ambitions*

and Achievements (Washington, DC: U.S. Government Printing Office, 2011), p. 15. Figures are for 1991–2009.

574. U.S. Government Accountability Office, *Women's Pay: Converging Characteristics of Men and Women in the Federal Workforce Help Explain the Narrowing Pay Gap*, GAO-09-621T (Washington, DC: U.S. Government Printing Office, 2009), Highlights page. Figures are for 1988–2007.

575. Institute for Women's Policy Research, *Fact Sheet: The Gender Wage Gap: 2008*, IPWR #C350 (Washington, DC: Author, 2009), p. 1. In 2007, the gender pay gap for year-round, full-time workers' median annual earnings in the United States was 22 percent.

576. U.S. Merit Systems Protection Board, *Women in the Federal Government*, p. 7. Figures are for median salaries, 1976–2009.

577. Ibid., p. 48. Figures are for 1991–2007.

578. As derived from data in U.S. Bureau of the Census, *Statistical Abstract of the United States, 2011*, Table 462. Figure is for 2007.

579. Jared J. Llorens, Jeffrey B. Wenger, and J. Edward Kellough, "Choosing Public Sector Employment: The Impact of Wages on the Representation of Women and Minorities in State Bureaucracies," *Journal of Public Administration Research and Theory* 18 (July 2008), pp. 397–413. The quotations are on p. 397.

580. Brudney, Bowling, and Wright, *Continuity and Change in Public Administration across the 50 States*, p. 11. Current figures are for 2008.

581. Killian and Choudhury, "Continuity and Change in the Role of City Managers," p. 12. Current figure is for 2010. Others are for 2000 and 1989.

582. Ibid. Figure is for 2007.

583. Llorens, Wenger, and Kellough, "Choosing Public Sector Employment," p. 397.

584. Llorens, "Uncovering the Determinants of Competitive State Government Wages," p. 321.

585. Brudney, Bowling, and Wright, *Continuity and Change in Public Administration across the 50 States*, p. 11. Current figure is for 2008.

586. Olsheski and Caprio, "Comparing Personal and Professional Characteristics of Men and Women State Executives."

587. Brudney, Bowling, and Wright, *Continuity and Change in Public Administration across the 50 States*, p. 11. Current figure is for 2010. Others

are for 2000, when 12 percent of city managers were women, and 1974, when 1 percent were.

588. Jerry Mitchell, "Education and Skills for Public Authority Management," *Public Administration Review* 51 (September/October 1991), pp. 429–437. Figure (p. 431) is for 1990.

589. Jessica Chao, Julia Parshall, Desiree Amador, *et al.*, *Philanthropy in a Changing Society: Achieving Effectiveness through Diversity* (New York: Rockefeller Philanthropy Advisors, 2008), pp. 6, 19. Current data are for 2006. Trend data are for 1982–2006.

590. Heather Joslyn, "A Man's World," *The Chronicle of Philanthropy* (September 17, 2009). Figure is for 2007.

591. William A. Brown and Chao Guo, "Exploring the Key Roles for Nonprofit Boards," *Nonprofit & Voluntary Sector Quarterly* 39 (June 2010), pp. 536–546. Details are in Chapter 5.

592. Mesch and Rooney, "Determinants of Compensation," p. 457. This was true for all positions studied: chief development officers, staffers, and consultants.

593. Chao, Parshall, Amador, *et al.*, *Philanthropy in a Changing Society*, p. 21. Current data are for 2006. Figures for all employees are for women of all races, 1982–2006, and data on CEOs and board chairs are for white women only, 1990–2006.

594. Joslyn, "A Man's World." Figure is for 2007.

595. Ronald G. Shaiko, "Female Participation in Association Governance and Political Representation: Women as Executive Directors, Board Members, Lobbyists, and Political Action Committee Directors," *Nonprofit Management and Leadership* 8 (Winter 1997), pp. 121–139.

596. Mesch and Rooney, "Determinants of Compensation," pp. 458–459.

597. Susan D. Sampson and Lynda L. Moore, "Is There a Glass Ceiling for Women in Development?" *Nonprofit Management & Leadership* 18 (Spring 2008), pp. 321–339. Gender gap figure is derived from data on p. 326 and is for 2005. Gap widening figure is for 1988–2005.

598. Selden, "A Solution in Search of a Problem?" p. 917.

599. Bethany G. Sneed, "Glass Walls in Bureaucracies: Examining the Difference Departmental Function Can Make," *Public Administration Review* 67 (September/October 2007), pp. 880–891. The quotations are on pp. 888, 880.

600. Eleanor V. Laudicina, "Managing Workforce Diversity in Government: An Initial Assessment," *Public Administration Quarterly* 19 (Summer 1995), pp. 170–192.

601. Nelson Dometrius and Lee Sigelman, "Assessing Progress Toward Affirmative Action Goals in State and Local Governments: A New Benchmark," *Public Administration Review* 44 (May/June 1984), pp. 244–245. Data are for 1980.

602. Ellen Simon, Associated Press, "Black CEOs: A Tiny Group Shrinks More," *USA Today* (November 5, 2007); and "Women CEOs," *Fortune,* http://www.fortune.com/fortune/fortune500/articles/. In 2007, four Fortune 500 CEOs were black. In 2011, eleven were women.

603. Alison M. Konrad and Kathy Cummings, "The Effects of Gender-Role Congruence and Statistical Discrimination on Managerial Advancement," *Human Relations* 50 (October 1997), pp. 1305–1328.

604. Kathleen Cannings and Claude Montmarquette, "Managerial Momentum: A Simultaneous Model of the Career Progression of Male and Female Managers," *Industrial and Labor Relations Review* 44 (January 1991), pp. 212–228.

605. Joyce K. Fletcher, *Disappearing Acts: Gender, Power, and Relational Practices at Work* (Cambridge, MA: MIT Press, 1999).

606. Jeffrey A. Flory, Andreas Liebbrandt, and John A. List, *Do Competitive Work Places Deter Female Workers? A Large-Scale Natural Field Experiment,* NBER Working Paper No. 16546 (Cambridge, MA: National Bureau of Economic Research, 2010), p. 31.

607. Pew Research Center for the People and the Press, *Conflicted Views of Affirmative Action,* p. 3. Figure is for 2003.

608. As derived from data in U.S. Bureau of the Census, *Statistical Abstract of the United States, 1952,* 73rd ed. (Washington, DC: U.S. Government Printing Office, 1952), Table 208. Figure is for all men in the civilian labor force, or men fourteen years old and older.

609. As derived from data in U.S. Bureau of the Census, *Statistical Abstract of the United States,* 2011, Table 585. Current figure is for 2009, and is for all men in the civilian labor force, or men sixteen years old and older.

610. Judith J. Friedman and Nancy Di Tomaso, "Myths about Diversity: What Managers Need to Know about Changes in the U.S. Labor Force," *California Management Review* 38 (Summer 1996), pp. 54–77. The datum is on p. 58.

611. As derived from data in U.S. Bureau of the Census, *Statistical Abstract of the United States, 2011,* Table 585. Current figure is for 2009. The 1980 figure does not include Asians and Asian Americans. All figures include people who are sixteen and older, but exclude persons reporting more than one race. Minority percentages were calculated by subtracting the percentages of whites in the labor force from 100 percent.

612. U.S. General Accounting Office, *The Changing Workforce: Demographic Issues Facing Employers,* GAO/T-GGD-92-61 (Washington, DC: U.S. Government Printing Office, 1992), pp. 1–7.

613. As derived from data in U.S. Bureau of the Census, *Statistical Abstract of the United States, 1952,* Table 208. Figure is for all women in the civilian labor force, or women fourteen years old and older.

614. Ibid. and U.S. Bureau of the Census, *Statistical Abstract of the United States, 2011,* Table 585. Figures for women (a 285 percent growth rate) and men (85 percent) are for 1950–2009.

615. As derived from data in U.S. Bureau of the Census, *Statistical Abstract of the United States, 2011,* Table 585. Current figure is for 2009, and refers to all women in the civilian labor force, or women who are sixteen years and older. Projection is for 2009–2018.

616. Friedman and Di Tomaso, "Myths about Diversity"; and Audrey J. Cohen, "Predictors of Public and Private Employment for Business College Graduates," *Public Personnel Management* 22 (Spring 1992), pp. 167–186.

617. U.S. Merit Systems Protection Board, *The Federal Government: A Model Employer or a Work in Progress?* pp. 19–20.

Implementing
Public Policy

In the fourth and final part of *Public Administration and Public Affairs*, we explain how to get things done. Although we touched upon certain aspects of getting things done in Chapter 4's discussion of administration in organizations, in Part IV we take a broader view.

Implementation is the execution and delivery of public policies by organizations or arrangements among organizations.

We approach the complex arena of public policy execution in slices of narrowing breadth.

Hence, in the introductory chapter to Part IV, we explain what is being implemented—that is, public policy, and how it is made and adjusted.

The following two chapters focus on the institutions that governments use to implement public policy. Their use has extended the reach of government far beyond its nominal station. The federal government spends only 7 percent of its budget on the civilian programs that federal administrators directly implement;[1] When we include in the official count of federal workers the number of civilian employees who work indirectly for the federal government through contracts, mandates, and grants, the total number of federal civilian workers is eight times greater than the official number. When we define the federal workforce to include these "indirect" employees, then about two out of every five American households has someone in them who is working for the federal government.[2]

In similar fashion, state and local governments extend their influence by using the same institutions and methods. Some have called these arrangements "government by proxy,"[3] which has resulted in a "shadow workforce" that toils in "the shadow of government."[4]

Finally, and perhaps of greatest importance, we focus on the specific area of ethical decision making by individual public administrators in the formulation and implementation of public policies, and close our book with some thoughts on the passion for public administration.

NOTES

1. Donald F. Kettl, *Government by Proxy* (Washington, DC: Congressional Quarterly Press, 1988).
2. Paul C. Light, *Fact Sheet on the New True Size of Government* (Washington, DC: Brookings, 2003), pp. 4, 3. Figures are for 2002, when the federal government directly employed nearly 1.76 million civilian employees, contracted out almost 5.17 million jobs to private employers, effectively ordered state and local governments to hire an estimated 4.65 million employees (in 1996) through mandates, and provided grant funds for these governments to hire an additional 2.86 million workers, for a total of over 14.4 million. This total does not include almost 1.46 military personnel and 875,000 Postal Service employees, which would bring the total to almost 16.77 million federal workers in 2002.
3. Kettl, *Government by Proxy*.
4. Paul C. Light, *The True Size of Government* (Washington, DC: Brookings, 1999).

Understanding and Improving Public Policy

Public policy is a course of action adopted and pursued by government. *Public policy analysis* is the study of how governmental policies are made and implemented, and the application of available knowledge to governmental policies for the purpose of improving their formulation and implementation.[1]

PUBLIC POLICY ANALYSIS: A BRIEF HISTORY

The evolution of public policy analysis has, until comparatively recently, taken two very separate tracks. One is practical, the other academic.

Public Policy and the Policymakers

Woodrow Wilson was the first president to hire social scientists in government. Herbert Hoover also used social scientists to conduct the first analyses of national economic and social trends, but Franklin Delano Roosevelt's aggressive expansion of the federal government in the 1930s resulted in numerous new federal agencies that relied on social scientists to start, implement, and often devise, new public policies.

It was President Lyndon Johnson who accorded (if inadvertently) policy analysis a permanent place in the federal establishment. Johnson's attempt in 1965 to mandate Planning-Programming-Budgeting government-wide (recall Chapter 8), though largely a failure, ultimately had a lasting impact on many agencies in that it "diffused among government practitioners...systemic procedures for rigorously testing policy alternatives."[2] The enactment of the Government Performance and Results Act of 1993 and the Office of Management and Budget's far-reaching decision in 1994 to staff its critical resource management offices with policy analysts secured the place of policy analysis in the federal structure.

Today, "policy analyst" is an official job description in the federal civil service, most state capitals, and some large local governments. Although the market for policy analysts is smaller than that for public administrators, "policy analysis is one of the established knowledge industries."[3]

It is an industry with some influence. Nonpartisan policy research organizations—"even those in highly politicized environments—have a significant impact on policymaking, mainly by providing information and analysis to decision-makers but also in influencing public policy outcomes."[4]

Public Policy and the Professoriate

Academia was left in the wake of governments' progress in policy analysis.

Origins It was only in 1951 that the first book on public policy analysis appeared.[5] The endeavor gathered intellectual steam during the 1950s and 1960s, but not in the universities. It was, rather, the preserve of engineers, operations researchers, and systems analysts, often working in think tanks that had connections with government.[6]

The universities' interest in public policy can be traced to a conference held in 1965 under the auspices of the Social Science Research Council.[7]

The emergence of public policy can be understood, in part, as political science's effort to fill the vacuum left by public administration's departure, described in Chapter 2. For a half-dozen years during the 1970s, when public administration's exodus from political science was in full flood, the number of independent schools and departments of public administration, and the number of public-policy papers presented at the annual conference of the American Political Science Association, virtually doubled.[8]

Political Science, Public Administration, and Public Policy Public policy now has three primary homes in universities, and a few secondary ones, too.[9]

One principal residence is political science departments. Political science's approach to public policy is substantive, processive, descriptive, and objective. We call it the *incrementalist paradigm*, and it relates to the first part of our definition of public policy analysis: "the study of how governmental policies are made and implemented." Its adherents are concerned with the substance of some specific issue (such as the environment, crime, whatever), and their publications often are titled, "The Politics of..." some substantive area.

A second home is public administration. Public administration's analytical approach to public policy is theoretical, effectual, prescriptive, and normative. We call it the *rationalist paradigm*, and it relates to the second part of our definition of public policy analysis: "the application of available knowledge to governmental policies for the purpose of improving their formulation and implementation." Its adherents are concerned with the development of theories of public policymaking.

Public policy's newest home is schools and other freestanding academic units of public policy, most of which emerged in the 1980s and thereafter. These schools meld both approaches.[10] Regrettably, the interest that students enrolled in these schools have in government "declines from entry to graduation," and some of these students

display "a troubling aversion to government," which "the policy training process.... may even confirm."[11]

Public policy analysis can best be understood in terms of its two paradigms: The incrementalist paradigm, favored by political scientists, and the rational paradigm, favored by public administrationists.

THE INCREMENTALIST PARADIGM OF PUBLIC POLICYMAKING

Charles E. Lindblom is, perhaps, the leading representative of the incrementalist paradigm; it was he who coined the term "disjointed incrementalism" as a description of the policymaking process.[12] *Disjointed* refers to the disconnect between the assessment of conditions and the development of responses to them. *Incrementalism* means that policymakers consider and implement—very slowly, very few, and very small—policy changes. Lindblom initially called disjointed incrementalism "muddling through,"[13] a frankly more descriptive and less pompous moniker.

The incrementalist paradigm is innately conservative; new public policies are seen as gradually evolving variations on the past. The policymaker is perceived as a person who does not have the brains, time, and money to fashion truly different policies. Incrementalist policies are nearly always more politically expedient than are policies that necessitate redistributions of social values. "What is most feasible is incremental."[14]

The Elite/Mass Model

The *elite/mass model* contends that a policymaking/policy-executing elite, whose members share common values and have more power than the mass, governs a passive mass in an environment characterized by apathy and information distortion. Public policies are designed, above all else, to preserve the *status quo*.

A classic expression of elite theory can be found in C. Wright Mills's *The Power Elite*.[15] The elite model is diagrammed in Figure 10-1.

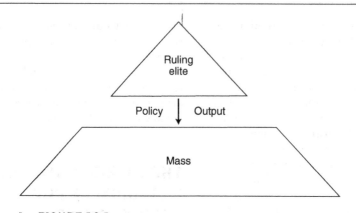

FIGURE 10-1
The Elite/Mass Model of Public Policymaking and Implementation

The Group Model

The *group model* of public policymaking is predicated on the "hydraulic theory of politics,"[16] in which the polity is conceived of as being a system of forces and pressures pushing against one another in the formulation of public policy. Although the group model usually is associated with the legislature, it also is pertinent to bureaucracies. Regulatory agencies, for example, often are "captured" by the groups that they ostensibly regulate, defining the group's interest as the public interest.[17]

An exemplary work that represents the group model is Arthur F. Bentley's *The Process of Government*.[18] Figure 10-2 illustrates the group model.

The Systems Model

The *systems model* relies on concepts of information theory (especially feedback, input, and output) and conceives of the policy process as being cyclical and unending. Policy is originated, implemented, adjusted, re-implemented, re-adjusted, *ad infinitum*. It is concerned with such questions as: What are the inputs, "withinputs," outputs, and feedback of the process? A representative author of this literary stream is David Easton's *The Political System*.[19]

The Institutionalist Model

The *institutionalist model* focuses on the organization chart of government; it describes the reporting arrangements and duties of bureaus, but ignores

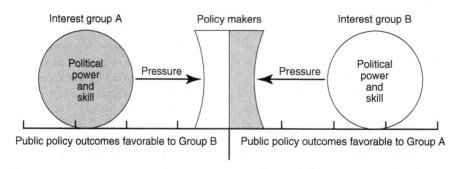

FIGURE 10-2
The Group Model of Public Policymaking and Implementation

the living linkages between them. Legalities are the objects of greatest interest. Carl J. Friedrich's *Constitutional Government and Democracy* is a representative work.[20]

The Neo-Institutionalist Model

The institutionalist model has experienced a resurrection, of a sort, that might best be described as neo-institutionalism. The *neo-institutionalist model* categorizes public policies according to policymaking subsystems and predicts institutional behavior accordingly. Theodore J. Lowi has done much of the groundbreaking thinking in the neo-institutionalist model.

Arenas of Power Lowi classifies policies by four "arenas of power." From these policy arenas emerge predictable political behaviors.

In a *redistributive power arena,* power is reallocated throughout the polity on a fundamental scale—so fundamental, in fact, that redistributive policies involve "not use of property but property itself, not equal treatment but equal possession, not behavior but being." These policies tend to be highly ideological, involving a fight between the "haves" and "have-nots," but are secretive, have low partisan visibility, and usually are centered in the bureaucracy.[21] Redistributive policies are the most difficult to administer of any policy type.[22]

The remaining three power arenas are less laden with drama. A *distributive policy* provides benefits directly to each person, but costs are not obvious; for example, the Weather Bureau's policy of providing weather reports is distributive. A *regulative policy* provides benefits to, but imposes visible costs on, particular groups; for instance, the Federal Aviation Administration enforces safety regulations and may punish the violators of those regulations. A *constituent policy* directly affects people as political actors, but does not single out individual persons for either benefits or punishments; a reapportionment statute is exemplary.

Coercion: Probability and Targets The neo-institutionalist approach is predicated on two dimensions: the probability of coercion and the target of coercion.

The *probability of coercion* may be *remote* or *immediate*. In the redistributive and regulative policy arenas, the possibility of coercion is immediate because violators of laws may be punished as individual miscreants. In the distributive and constituent arenas, by contrast, coercion is remote because logrolling and negotiation prevail.

The *target of coercion* may be *individual* or *systemic*. In distributive and regulative arenas, individual persons are targeted. In redistributive and constituent arenas, the government bypasses individuals and attempts to manipulate the conduct of the system itself.

The Organized Anarchy Model

The *organized anarchy model* of public policymaking is, at the risk of over-generalizing, an extension of the "garbage can" theory of decision making explained in Chapter 4. The model is unique in teasing out the process's messiness, humanity, and luck and is, in many ways, a very satisfying explanation of how public policy is made.

John W. Kingdon's classic, *Agendas, Alternatives, and Public Policies*, is representative of this literature.[23] The model is illustrated in Figure 10-3.

Streams of Problems, Politics, and Policies Basic to the model is the presence of three "streams" that constitute the policymaking process.

The first of these is the *problems stream*, which involves focusing the public's and policymakers' attention on a particular problem, defining the problem, and either applying a new public policy to the resolution of the problem or letting the problem fade from sight. Problems typically are defined in terms of *values*, such as conservative or liberal orientations; *comparisons*, such as the United States *versus* Iran; and *categories*—for example, is public transit for the disabled a "transportation" problem or a "civil rights" problem? Categorizing the problem becomes quite significant in how the problem is resolved.

It is in the *political stream* that the *governmental agenda*—that is, the list of issues to be resolved—is formed. The primary participants in the political stream comprise the *visible cluster*

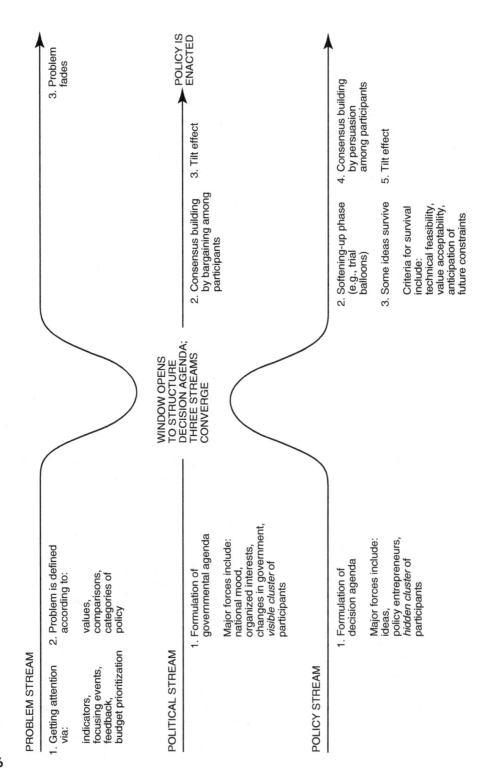

PROBLEM STREAM

1. Getting attention
   via:

   indicators,
   focusing events,
   feedback,
   budget prioritization

2. Problem is defined
   according to:

   values,
   comparisons,
   categories of
   policy

3. Problem
   fades

POLITICAL STREAM

1. Formulation of
   governmental agenda

   Major forces include:
   national mood,
   organized interests,
   changes in government,
   visible cluster of
   participants

2. Consensus building
   by bargaining among
   participants

3. Tilt effect

WINDOW OPENS
TO STRUCTURE
DECISION AGENDA;
THREE STREAMS
CONVERGE

POLICY IS
ENACTED

POLICY STREAM

1. Formulation of
   decision agenda

   Major forces include:
   ideas,
   policy entrepreneurs,
   hidden cluster of
   participants

2. Softening-up phase
   (e.g., trial
   balloons)

3. Some ideas survive

   Criteria for survival
   include:
   technical feasibility,
   value acceptability,
   anticipation of
   future constraints

4. Consensus building
   by persuasion
   among participants

5. Tilt effect

FIGURE 10-3
The Organized Anarchy Model of Public Policymaking and Implementation

of policy actors, such as high-level political appointees, members of Congress, and interest groups. A consensus is achieved by bargaining among these participants, and, at some point, a "bandwagon," or "tilt," effect occurs that is a consequence of an intensifying desire among the participants to be "dealt in" on the policy resolution.

It is in the *policy stream* that the decision agenda is formulated. The *decision agenda*, or *alternative specification*, is the list of possible policies that could resolve the issue. Here the major forces are not political, but intellectual and personal. Ideas and the role of the *policy entrepreneur*, or the person who holds a deep and abiding commitment to a particular policy change, are paramount. The major participants in the formulation of the decision agenda are the *hidden cluster* of policy actors and include career public administrators, congressional staffers, and interest groups (interest groups are powerful players in both the visible and hidden clusters).

Phases The policy stream moves from the formulation of a decision agenda to a "softening-up phase" in which "trial balloons" are released and a variety of suggestions are made about how to resolve a particular problem. These ideas survive according to whether they are technically feasible, socially acceptable, and are perceived to be free of future constraints, such as budget limitations. In both the policy and political streams, a consensus and, ultimately, a "tilt effect" occur, but the policy stream arrives at those points through rational argument, whereas the political stream does so via negotiation.

Windows and Agendas A *window* is the opportunity to change an agenda or create a policy, and a window typically is opened by a shift in the national mood. When a window opens that results in a restructuring of the *governmental agenda*, it could be solely the result of developments in either the problem stream or the political stream. But for a window to open that results in a restructuring of the *decision agenda* requires the convergence of all three streams. In this case, the role of the policy entrepreneur is critical.

THE RATIONALIST PARADIGM OF PUBLIC POLICYMAKING

Rationalism attempts to be the opposite of incrementalism. The muddled, bounded rationality of the incrementalist paradigm is eschewed in favor of methodically assigning relative weights to all social values; listing all policy alternatives and fully comprehending their consequences, costs, including opportunity costs, and benefits; and selecting the most efficient and effective policy to implement. The rationalist paradigm is concerned with the nature of public goods and services,[24] the relationships between formal decision-making structures and human propensities for both individual action[25] and collective action,[26] and the broad implications of technological innovation.[27]

Much of the rationalist paradigm deals with the devising of public policies that assure better public policies. Yehezkel Dror (as good a representative as any of the rationalists) calls this concern *metapolicy*, or policy for policymaking procedures.[28]

The rationalist paradigm conceives of public policy formation as a linear flow chart. We review three "models" of the rationalist paradigm next, although we should note that the distinctions among them are not as clear-cut as are the models comprising the incrementalist paradigm.

The Rational Choice Model

In 1963, a modest collection of scholars met to discuss, in their words, "developments in the 'no-name' fields of public administration."[29] Since then, names have been acquired, and they include *rational choice, public choice,* and *political economy.* In its more applied mode (reviewed in Chapter 12), this literature is often called *metropolitan organization,* or *local public economies.*

Rational choice basks in the sunbeam of social engineering. Consider, for example, the issue of energy and the automobile. Rather than passing a law that says little more than "Thou shalt not use too much gas," a political economist might turn instead to rigging the tax structure, reasoning that, if a taxpayer chose to purchase a Bentley rather than a Volt, the general citizenry should not have to bear the common costs of that taxpayer's choice to buy a gas guzzler. Neither, however, should taxpayers be denied Bentleys if they really want them. Thus, a special tax should be levied that taxes gas guzzlers more than compacts.

Optimality On a more sophisticated plane, rational choice is concerned with "Pareto optimality," a concept originally developed by the economist Vilfredo Pareto. Or, more exactly (and because optimality is supremely difficult to achieve in any context), rational choice concerns a *Pareto improvement*, or "a change in economic organization…that makes one or more members of society better off without making anyone worse off."[30]

Tradeoffs By *tradeoff*, rational-choice writers mean what value is being exchanged (and the social costs and benefits incurred in such an exchange) for what other value. In other words, every time Value X is achieved more fully, all other values are correspondingly reduced in achievement.

Externalities Executing public policies is a process that is far from tidy, and policies meant to solve problems in one social arena can cause problems in others. This phenomenon is called an *externality*, or *spillover effect*; that is, the impacts of a public policy in one sphere "spill over" into other spheres.

Externalities may be positive or negative, intended or unintended. For example, a *positive, intended* spillover effect of reducing corporate taxes might be to raise employment levels. A *negative,*

unintended externality of the same public policy might be to reduce the financial resources available to the government for welfare programs.

The Public Goods and Services Model

The *public goods and services model* deals with what kinds of goods and services are delivered most efficiently by government, and what kinds are delivered most efficiently by other sectors.[31] The model rests on two foundations: exclusion and consumption. Table 10-1 diagrams it.

Exclusion *Exclusion* refers to the degree of control that both the buyer and seller have over a particular commodity. *High exclusionary control* occurs when a buyer and seller must agree on a price, and it is the most common condition in the real world. *Low exclusionary control* occurs when price is not an issue. For example, all ships within sight of the lighthouse can benefit from its service.

Consumption *Consumption,* or *use,* refers to how goods are consumed and services are used. *Joint consumption* occurs when goods are consumed or services are used simultaneously by many consumers without being diminished in quality or quantity. An example is a television broadcast; all viewers may "consume" a television program "jointly" without the program being diminished. *Individual consumption* occurs when goods are

---

TABLE 10-1

Goods and Services According to the Criteria of Exclusion and Consumption

	Consumption/Use	
Exclusion	Individual Use	Joint Use
Feasible	Private goods and services (a bag of groceries, a haircut, a meal in a restaurant)	Toll goods and services (cable television, telephone service, theaters, libraries, electric power)
Unfeasible	Common-pool goods and services (water in a public well, fish in the ocean, air to breathe)	Collective, or public, goods and services (peace and security, public safety, pollution control, weather forecasts, public television, radio)

consumed or services are used by a single person and others are denied access to them. A fish is an example of individual consumption; once it is consumed by one person, it is gone.

Using the notions of exclusion and consumption, we can classify goods and services into four kinds of "pure forms" that can be applied to the sector best equipped to deliver them efficiently.[32]

Private Goods and Services *Private goods and services* are pure, individually consumed goods and individually used services for which exclusion is completely feasible. An example is any commodity in the marketplace. The private sector is the most efficient provider of private goods and services; government's role is largely limited to assuring their safety and honest representation, although government's use of vouchers and subsidies is a case of the public sector involving itself in the distribution of private goods and services.

Toll Goods and Services *Toll goods and services* are pure, jointly consumed goods and jointly used services for which exclusion is completely feasible. An example is cable television. Like private goods, toll goods generally are supplied most efficiently by the private sector, but, unlike private goods, many toll goods are natural monopolies. Hence, government's role is one of assuring that monopolies are granted in a controlled way and regulated so that suppliers do not exploit their monopolistic privileges unfairly.

Common-Pool Goods and Services *Common-pool goods and services* are pure, individually consumed goods and individually-used services for which exclusion is not feasible. Breathable air is a common-pool good; no one pays for consuming air, and no one in the private sector can prevent air from being consumed.

Common-pool goods bring us to the "tragedy of the commons."[33] Common-pool goods can be tragic because they are a "commons" that "belongs" to everyone and, consequently, are easily squandered and possibly exhausted. Because breathable air is a common good, it may be consumed not only by breathers but also by polluters, thereby destroying it. Government's logical role is thus one of regulation.

Public Goods and Services *Public*, or *collective*, *goods and services* are pure, jointly consumed goods and jointly used services for which exclusion is not feasible. An example is public safety. The marketplace cannot supply public safety because it is used simultaneously by many people, and using it does not diminish its quality or quantity. Here government is the most appropriate provider.

The Technology Assessment Model

Technology assessment, or *technological forecasting*, is the evaluation of new technical and scientific innovations in terms of their current or future spillover effects. For instance, medicine may be viewed as a technology that, in its success in extending life, has been more responsible than any other factor for the population explosion and environmental stress. Figure 10-4 illustrates the model.

In 1972, Congress created an Office of Technology Assessment, which, for twenty-three years, served as a nonpartisan agency that assisted Congress in understanding complex, technical issues affecting American society. Its 143 dedicated and talented professionals were terminated by Congress in 1995 as a cost-cutting measure. Nevertheless, technology assessment continues to be a useful, if a relatively specialized, model for policy analysts.

THE PROBLEMS WITH THE PARADIGMS

The incrementalist and rationalist paradigms have problems.

Arguments over Incrementalism

Although the two camps concur that the policy-making process is incremental, they part company over incrementalism's social desirability.

The incrementalists hold that incremental policymaking works well because the human element and political negotiation are central to it. The rationalists' restrictively technical myopia leads them to make predictions and policies that

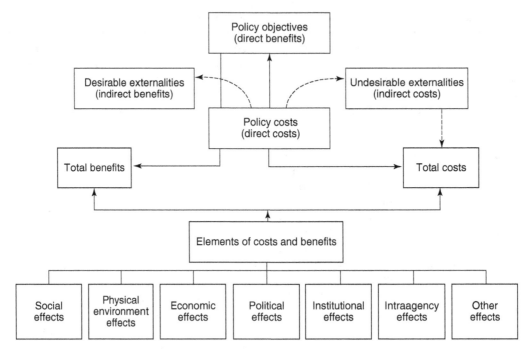

FIGURE 10-4

Technology Assessment in Public Administration

are often wrong,[34] whereas bargaining with many stakeholders results in better policy: "We can no longer profitably discuss our world and its future in simple linear terms," as the rationalists argue.[35]

The rationalists counter that poor policies are the pernicious products of the deceit that is inherent in any policymaking process that is based on bargaining, as the incrementalist paradigm is. Negotiation requires that policymaking rivals deliberately hide their real goals, and, as a result, critical realities may be overlooked. Such secrecy almost guarantees that poor public policies will result.[36] Perhaps of even greater concern, the adoption of transformational policies, even when they are clearly needed, is dismissed by the conservative incrementalists in favor of tinkering.

Incremental Policymaking? Not So Much

Another issue is that neither paradigm is as grounded in reality as it might be. Policymaking is not as incremental as both paradigms aver.

Does Incrementalism Mean Small Change?

Adherents of both paradigms contend that incremental policymaking means, in part, that public policy is the product of small changes. But just what does "small" policy change actually mean?

In an effort to answer this question, analysts found, "surprisingly," that, in the federal budget, "a low proportion of changes are small by any logical standard. During most years, more than one-fifth of budgetary changes are greater than 50 percent, and nearly half are more than 10 percent."[37] Another examination concluded that there are as many big policy changes as small ones in the formulation of public policy.[38]

Does Incrementalism Mean Slow Change?

Incrementalism also holds that making and changing public policy is a slow process. The evidence suggests, however, that policy change is not slow and can happen very quickly. A thorough study concludes that the "gradualism model" does not describe change in the policy agenda "particularly well." Instead, "a subject rather suddenly 'hits,' 'catches on,' or 'takes off,'" and the proportion of policymakers who express interest in a prospective new policy can triple from a third to nearly all within a single year.[39]

An (Unfortunate?) Absence of Incrementalism

In sum, if incremental policymaking is defined as small changes made slowly, then the empirical evidence demonstrates that few—fewer than three out of every ten—changes in public policy are made incrementally.[40] Regrettably, this is not such a good thing for the public organization, as research indicates that "budgetary incrementalism"—in other words, a stable budget—has "a beneficial effect" on its performance.[41]

A Pair of Pouting Paradigms

So here is what we are left with:

- Two paradigms of public policymaking that have utterly different goals. The incrementalists want only to understand and describe the policymaking process. The rationalists want to improve public policies by improving the process that makes them.
- Two paradigms that disagree about the quality of the policymaking process. The incrementalists think that muddling through results in policies that at least "satisfice." The rationalists worry that incrementalism imperils society.
- Two paradigms that agree that the policymaking process is incremental, when, at best and in fact, it is only partially incremental. Although the process is, indeed, disjointed, it produces at least as many big policy changes as small ones, and it can move much faster than either paradigm assumes.

What is needed is "a third approach"[42] that threads its way between the conservative, even cynical, biases of incrementalism and the radical, even utopian, perspectives of rationalism—an approach that does not substitute numbers for important intangibles, such as human emotions, but which does use computers and quantification to illuminate choices.

A THIRD APPROACH: THE STRATEGIC PLANNING PARADIGM OF PUBLIC POLICYMAKING

This third approach has acquired the title of *strategic planning*, or, less frequently, *strategic decision making* or *strategic management*. Strategic planning emerged in the world of business—Alfred Chandler, Jr., first called attention to it in 1962[43]—and it since has become a preoccupation of public organizations and, much less so, of nonprofit ones.

Public strategic planning is the identification, prioritization, and communication of major policy and administrative goals by public and nonprofit organizations, and the integration of those goals into the management, budgeting, and performance measurement systems of these organizations.

Successful Strategic Planning: Executives and Planners

To succeed, strategic planning in all sectors must start with the organization's highest decision makers. It is not done by planners. "First we ask: who is leading the planning? If it is a planner...we are in trouble."[44] Why? Because only top officers can link the three critical components of strategic planning: goals, actions, and outcomes.

Planners are more useful in providing executives with relevant information, and then assuring that they use it in making the big decisions that are the essence of strategic planning. In addition, planners are critical in keeping the planning process on track by nagging executives to make those needed decisions in a timely manner.

When top public and nonprofit executives are not involved in the planning process, the usual consequence is all too well known: irrelevant, unread plans. Many public strategic plans have been written, at high cost, only to collect dust on many shelves, a sad happenstance that is attributable not only to uninvolved executives but also to the unique challenges of planning strategically that are inherent in the public and third sectors.

Strategic Planning in Governments

Governments, which began adopting strategic plans during the 1970s, must plan in environments that are more constraining, penetrating, and tumultuous than are the environments of private and nonprofit organizations. "Success in strategic planning" by governments "is not achieved mechanistically, with one thing leading inexorably to another."[45]

"Governmental strategic planning probably should be judged by different standards than private-sector, corporate strategic planning," as governments are unable "to follow the linear, sequential planning models of the business policy textbooks, and...prepare a public-sector equivalent of the slick corporate strategic plan."[46] "A well-crafted" strategic plan in local governments amounts to a modest five to seven pages.[47]

Federal Strategic Planning The Government Performance and Results Act of 1993 requires, for the first time in federal history, that agencies submit multiyear strategic plans to Congress and the Office of Management and Budget. The first-ever government-wide strategic plan appeared in 1998, which, in the words of the act, provides "a single cohesive picture of the annual performance goals for the fiscal year."

By 2010, Washington had gained considerably more knowledge about strategic planning, and enacted the Government Performance and Results Act Modernization Act in an effort to better coordinate the planning process. The act requires, significantly, that OMB and certain congressional committees develop a handful of long-range, "cross-agency," government-wide priority goals every two years; aligns the agencies' strategic plans with presidential terms; and links annual performance goals with strategic plans.

These efforts have brought results. Seven out of ten federal managers consider "strategic goals to a great or very great extent in allocating resources," and this proportion is steadily rising.[48]

State Strategic Planning The states are enamored with strategic planning. Nearly four-fifths of state agencies have "partially or fully" implemented strategic plans, and public strategic planning has the highest rate of implementation of any of eleven managerial innovations surveyed in the states.[49] The percentage of governors who provide written "overall policy guidance" to their agencies (clearly strategic planning) in preparing agency budget requests has increased steadily from a third in 1970 to almost four-fifths today.[50]

The adoption by state agencies of strategic planning is closely related to a new governor assuming office, sound state finances, substantial state experience with the private sector, and when similar agencies in neighboring states have adopted it.[51]

Local Strategic Planning Sixty-two percent of cities and counties have strategic plans, and they gather no dust: fully half have been revised within the past eighteen months or so, a process involving not only local officials but also citizen advisory boards (in 44 percent of cities and counties), chambers of commerce (23 percent), and local educators (16 percent), among other groups.[52] More than a third of cities have completed a full cycle of at least one strategic plan over the last five years;[53] over four-fifths of cities specifically budget for their plans' goals; and almost two-thirds wed the salary increases of their administrators with accomplishing their strategic goals.[54]

Communities that succeed in their strategic plans have a "powerful process sponsor" (i.e., one or, typically, more, major figures who endorse the idea of strategic planning); a strong "process champion" (often a skilled administrator); an agency-wide expectation of disruptions and delays; and a willingness to be flexible.[55] Technical difficulties may loom even larger than political ones in implementing local planning .[56]

Strategic Planning in Nonprofit Organizations

"Many nonprofit organizations do not use strategic planning." Third-sector administrators resist its introduction because it is more difficult than in public and private organizations to attain agreement among stakeholders about what, precisely, their organization's goals are. Achieving this agreement is the single most significant internal variable in inducing independent organizations to plan strategically.[57]

The "most critical" reason why nonprofit associations plan at all, however, is external. Their donors exert "coercive pressure" to force the organization to "submit a plan of action, leading several authors to conclude that nonprofits plan when they have to plan." This is "one of the strongest research findings" in the field.[58]

Those few independent organizations that have successful strategic plans are larger; have decentralized management and sophisticated executive directors who play a "critical role" in their plan's success; are governed by boards that focus on policy issues rather than on administration; and feature high levels of trust and healthy working relationships among directors, board members, and operational units.[59] Nonprofit organizations that make strategic decision also are more likely to use performance measures and have effective governance, diverse funding sources, and a highly educated executive director.[60]

The Benefits of Strategic Planning for the Public and Third Sectors

Public strategic planning improves public and nonprofit performance and sharpens these organizations' goals, and, at least in government, its implementation is largely successful.

Improving Public Performance Although it has long been known that, "strategic planning positively influences firm performance" in the private sector,[61] it only recently has been determined that there also is a strong and positive correlation between it and improved public performance. Studies find that "logical, clearly planned strategies" in government "are a useful route to better performance"[62] and that "quantified strategic priorities lead to better organizational outcomes" in the public sector—most notably, improved performance.[63]

An intriguing study of cities found that "management and strategy do matter" in whether municipal governments are less or more efficient, even when accounting for city size, location, and wealth, among other variables that are not directly controlled by urban administrators. "A low-performing municipality tends to have a predominantly outward [strategic] orientation...whereas a higher-performing municipality...[has a] both inward and outward orientation."[64]

Public administrators agree with these researchers. Strategic planning's single most useful feature, cited by nine out of ten state agency heads, is that of "clarifying agency priorities" and "management directions."[65] Remarkably, 93 percent of senior local officials think that strategic planning is worth the time and expense that it entails, and only 2 percent say that it is not.[66] Three-fifths of "senior officials" in municipalities that have completed two or more strategic plans report that, on average, three-fifths of their plans' goals were achieved.[67]

Improving Nonprofit Performance In those relatively rare instances when nonprofit organizations seriously utilize strategic planning, their performance heightens, just as it does in private and public organizations. In addition, planning strategically in the independent sector associates positively with organizational growth, both in funding and membership; greater effectiveness in mission attainment; and improved effectiveness by their boards of directors.[68]

Perils and Problems of Public Strategic Planning

Although strategic planning has been described as a "hearty, public-sector perennial,"[69] it is a perennial that derives what heartiness it has from growing in thin and sandy soil.

Public Planning Problems: Vague Goals, Permeating Environments Despite its widespread use in government, private corporations are much more likely than public agencies to use strategic planning.[70] Why is this?

As we have observed throughout this book, agency missions are characterized by a "pervasive vagueness," and agencies themselves are wide open not only to environmental forces, but also to arbitrary time constraints, such as budget and election schedules, that can rush or delay strategic decisions in ways that they no longer are strategic.[71] City managers and mayors agree that the single greatest obstacle to successful public strategic planning is the "need to gain greater control over the external political environment."[72]

Hence, in the view of at least some observers, "normal expectations have to be that most efforts to produce fundamental decisions and actions in government through strategic planning will not succeed,"[73] and "bold moves" by public executives will be rendered "almost completely impossible."[74]

Well. Let us remind ourselves that revolutionary change is not necessarily central to successful strategic planning. Strategic planning, recall, charts "a third way" between plodding incrementalism, which resists making fundamental decisions and bold moves, and rip-roaring rationalism, which often welcomes them. The evidence suggests that public agencies use strategic planning as it should be used, scampering between these two paradigms as they adapt them to their needs.[75] Sure, strategic planning is less likely to effect rapid and significant

change in public organizations than in private ones—which may explain why it is used less in governments than in companies—but strategic planning nevertheless can sharpen agency goals, accelerate agency progress, and improve public performance.

The Symbolic Uses of Nonprofit Planning? In the third sector, strategic planning's limitations may be less a function of a vague missions and merciless environments and more a consequence of organizational cynicism. Because most of the independent associations that have strategic plans were forced by external powers to adopt them, their plans "may be largely symbolic...and the planning process may be decoupled from other strategic activities," such as improving performance.[76]

NOTES

1. Our definition is based loosely on Harold D. Lasswell, *A Pre-view of Policy Sciences* (New York: American Elsevier, 1971), pp. 1–2.
2. William N. Dunn, *Public Policy Analysis: An Introduction*, 2nd ed. (Englewood Cliffs, NJ: Prentice-Hall, 1994), p. 49.
3. Ibid., p. 50.
4. John A Hird, "Policy Analysis for What? The Effectiveness of Nonpartisan Policy Research Organizations," *Policy Studies Journal* 33 (Spring, 2005), pp. 83–105. The quotation is on p. 83.
5. Daniel Lerner and Harold D. Lasswell, eds., *The Policy Sciences: Recent Developments in Scope and Method* (Stanford, CA: Stanford University Press, 1951).
6. Dunn, *Public Policy Analysis*, p. 48.
7. Austin Ranney, "Preface," *Political Science and Public Policy*, Austin Ranney, ed. (Chicago: Markham, 1968), pp. i–xiii. The datum is on p. x.
8. Nicholas Henry, *Public Administration and Public Affairs*, 4th ed. (Englewood Cliffs, NJ: Prentice-Hall, 1989), p. 291.
9. Dunn, *Public Policy Analysis*, p. 50.
10. Steven G. Koven, Frank Goetz, and Michael Brennan, "Profiling Public Affairs Programs: The View from the Top," *Administration & Society* 40 (November 2008), pp. 691–710.
11. Carol Chetkovich, "What's in a Sector? The Shifting Career Plans of Public Policy Students," *Public Administration Review* 63 (November/December 2003), pp. 660–674. The quotations are on pp. 660, 670–671.
12. Charles E. Lindblom, *The Policy Making Process* (Englewood Cliffs, NJ: Prentice-Hall, 1968).
13. Charles E. Lindblom, "The Science of Muddling Through," *Public Administration Review* 19 (Spring 1959), pp. 79–88.
14. Ralph K. Huitt, "Political Feasibility," *Political Science and Public Policy*, pp. 263–276. The quotation is on p. 274.
15. C. Wright Mills, *The Power Elite* (New York: Oxford University Press, 1956).
16. L. Harmon Zeigler and G. Wayne Peak, *Interest Groups in American Society*, 2nd ed. (Englewood Cliffs, NJ: Prentice-Hall, 1972), p. 12.
17. Louis M. Kohlmeier, *The Regulators: Watchdog Agencies and the Public Interest* (New York: Harper & Row, 1969).
18. Arthur F. Bentley, *The Process of Government* (Bloomington, IN: Principia Press, 1949). First published in 1908.
19. David Easton, *The Political System* (New York: Knopf, 1953).
20. Carl J. Friedrich, *Constitutional Government and Democracy* (Boston: Little, Brown, 1941).
21. Theodore J. Lowi, "American Business, Public Policy, Case Studies, and Political Theory," *World Politics* 16 (July 1964), pp. 677–693. The quotation is on p. 691.

22. Thomas J. Greitens and M. Ernita Joaquin, "Policy Typology and Performance Measurement: Results from the Program Assessment Rating Tool (PART)," *Public Performance & Management Review* 33 (June 2010), pp. 555–570.

23. John W. Kingdon, *Agendas, Alternatives, and Public Policies*, 2nd ed. (New York: Longman, 2003).

24. An example is L. L. Wade and R. L. Curry, Jr., *A Logic of Public Policy: Aspects of Political Economy* (Belmont, CA: Wadsworth, 1970).

25. An example is Gordon Tullock, *The Politics of Bureaucracy* (Washington, DC: Public Affairs Press, 1965).

26. An example is Mancur Olson, *The Logic of Collective Action* (Cambridge, MA: Harvard University Press, 1965).

27. An example is Nicholas Henry, "Copyright, Public Policy, and Information Technology," *Science* 182 (February 1, 1974), pp. 384–391.

28. Yehezkel Dror, *Public Policy Making Reexamined* (San Francisco: Chandler, 1968), p. 8.

29. Vincent Ostrom "Editorial Comment: Developments in the No-Name Fields of Public Adminstration," *Public Administration Review* 24 (January/February 1964), pp. 62–63.

30. E. J. Mishan, *Economics for Social Decisions: Elements of Cost-Benefit Analysis* (New York: Praeger, 1972), p. 14.

31. Much of the following discussion is drawn from E. S. Savas, *Privatizing the Public Sector: How to Shrink Government* (Chatham, NJ: Chatham House, 1982), pp. 29–52.

32. Ibid., p. 33.

33. Garrett Hardin, "The Tragedy of the Commons," *Science* 162 (December 13, 1968), pp. 1243–1248.

34. William Ascher, "Forecasting Potential of Complex Models," *Policy Sciences* 13 (May 1981), pp. 247–267.

35. Derek Viray, *Planning and Education* (London: Routledge and Kegan Paul, 1972), p. 4.

36. Harold Enarson, "The Art of Planning," *Educational Record* 56 (Summer 1975), pp. 170–174.

37. Sarah Anderson and Laurel Harbridge, "Incrementalism in Appropriations: Small Aggregation, Big Changes," *Public Administration Review* 70 (May/June 2010), pp. 464–474. The quotation is on p. 464.

38. Kingdon, *Agendas, Alternatives, and Public Policies*, p. 81.

39. Ibid., p. 80.

40. Ibid., p. 82.

41. Simon Calmar Andersen and Peter B. Mortensen, "Policy Stability and Organizational Performance: Is There a Relationship?" *Journal of Public Administration Research and Theory* 20 (January 2010), pp. 1–22. The quotation is on p. 1.

42. Amitai Etzioni, "Mixed Scanning: A Third Approach to Decision Making," *Public Administration Review* 27 (December 1967), pp. 385–392.

43. Alfred Chandler, Jr., *Strategy and Structure: Chapters in the History of the Industrial Enterprise* (Cambridge, MA: Massachusetts Institute of Technology Press, 1962).

44. Michael Aiken and Jerald Hage, "The Organic Organization and Innovation," *Sociology* 5 (January 1971), pp. 63–82. The quotation is on p. 80.

45. Robert Backoff, Barton Weschler, and Robert E. Crew, Jr., "The Challenge of Strategic Management in Local Government," *Public Administration Quarterly* (Summer 1993), pp. 127–144. The quotation is on p. 142.

46. John M. Bryson and William D. Roering, "Initiation of Strategic Planning by Governments," *Public Administration Review* 48 (November/December 1988), pp. 995–1004. The quotation is on p. 1002.

47. International City/County Management Association, "Strategic Planning: A Guide for Public Managers," *IQ Report* 34 (August 2002), p. 9.

48. U.S. General Accounting Office, *Results-Oriented Government: GPRA Has Established a Solid Foundation for Achieving Greater Results*, GAO-04-38 (Washington, DC: U.S. Government Printing Office, 2004,), p. 43. Figure is for 2003.

49. Jeffrey L. Brudney, F. Ted Hebert, and Deil S. Wright, "Reinventing Government in the American States: Explaining Administrative Reform," *Public Administration Review* 59 (January/February 1999), pp. 19–30. The quotation is on p. 23.

50. Robert C. Burns and Robert D. Lee, Jr., "The Ups and Downs of State Budget Process Reform: Experience of Three Decades," *Public Budgeting & Finance* 24 (Fall 2004), pp. 1–19. The datum is on p. 5. Figures are for 1970–2000.

51. Frances Stokes Berry, "Innovation in Public Management: The Adoption of Strategic Planning," *Public Administration Review* 54 (July/August 1994), pp. 322–329. Figures are for 1992.

52. Evelina R. Moulder, "Citizen Engagement: An Evolving Process," *Municipal Year Book, 2010* (Washington, DC: International City/County Management Association, 2010), pp. 28–32. Data (p. 29) are for 2009.

53. Gregory Streib and Theodore H. Poister, "The Use of Strategic Planning in Municipal Governments," *Municipal Year Book, 2002* (Washington, DC: International City/County Management Association, 2002), pp. 18–25.

54. Theodore H. Poister and Gregory Streib, "Elements of Strategic Planning and Management in Municipal Government: Status after Two Decades," *Public Administration Review* 65 (January/February 2005), pp. 45–56.

55. Bryson and Roering, "Initiation of Strategic Planning by Governments."

56. George A. Boyne, Julian S. Gould-Williams, Jennifer Law, and Richard M. Walker, "Problems of Rational Planning in Public Organizations: An Empirical Assessment of the Conventional Wisdom," *Administration & Society* 36 (July 2004), pp. 328–350.

57. Melissa M. Stone, Barbara Bigelow, and William Crittenden, "Research on Strategic Management in Nonprofit Organizations: Synthesis, Analysis, and Future Directions," *Administration & Society* 31 (July 1999), pp. 378–423. The quotation is on p. 383.

58. Ibid., p. 391.

59. Ibid., pp. 406, 408–409.

60. Kelly LeRoux and Nathaniel S. Wright, "Does Performance Measurement Improve Strategic Decision Making? Findings from a National Survey of Nonprofit Social Service Agencies," *Nonprofit Leadership & Voluntary Sector Quarterly* 39 (August 2010), pp. 571–587.

61. C. Chet Miller and Laura B. Cardinal, "Strategic Planning and Firm Performance: A Synthesis of More than Two Decades of Research," *Academy of Management Journal* 37 (December 1994), pp. 1649–1665. The quotation is on p. 1649.

62. Richard M. Walker, Rhys Andrews, George A. Boyne, *et al.*, "Wakeup Call: Strategic Management, Network Alarms and Performance," *Public Administration Review* 70 (September/October 2010) pp. 731–741. The quotation is on p. 738.

63. George A. Boyne and Alex A. Chen, "Performance Targets and Public Service Improvement," *Journal of Public Administration Research and Theory* 17 (July 2007), pp. 455–478. The quotation is on p. 455.

64. Hans Knutsson, Ola Mattison, Ulf Ramberg, and Torbjorn Tagesson, "Do Strategy and Management Matter in Municipal Organisations?" *Financial Accountability & Management* 24 (August 2008), pp. 295–319. The quotations are on p. 295.

65. Frances Stokes Berry and Barton Weschler, "State Agencies' Experience with Strategic Planning: Findings from a National Survey," *Public Administration Review* 55 (March/April 1995), pp. 159–168. The quotation is on p. 165. Data are for 1992.

66. Streib and Poister, "The Use of Strategic Planning in Municipal Governments," pp. 23–24. Data are for circa 2001.

67. Poister and Streib, "Elements of Strategic Planning and Management in Municipal Government," p. 51. Figures are for circa 2001.

68. Stone, Bigelow, and Crittenden, "Research on Strategic Management in Nonprofit Organizations," p. 391.

69. Gerald J. Miller, "Unique Public-Sector Strategies," *Public Productivity & Management Review* 13 (Winter 1989), pp. 133–144. The quotation is on p. 133.

70. Richard E. Boyatzis, *The Competent Manager* (New York: Wiley, 1982).

71. Miller, "Unique Public-Sector Strategies," pp. 137–138.

72. Gregory Streib, "Strategic Capacity in Council-Manager Municipalities: Exploring Limits and Horizons," *International Journal of Public Administration* 15 (9, 1992), pp. 1737–1755. The quotation is on p. 1737.

73. Bryson and Roering, "Initiation of Strategic Planning by Governments," p. 995.

74. Miller, "Unique Public-Sector Strategies," pp. 137–138.

75. Barton Weschler and Robert W. Backoff, "Policymaking and Administration in State Agencies: Strategic Management Approaches," *Public Administration Review* 46 (July/August 1986), pp. 321–327.

76. Stone, Bigelow, and Crittenden, "Research on Strategic Management in Nonprofit Organizations," pp. 408–409.

Intersectoral Administration

Governments source. *Sourcing* is the selection of an entity and a method that public administrators judge to be the most appropriate for delivering or implementing a particular public program.

Public administrators making sourcing decisions may, in keeping with tradition, *in-source*—that is, designate their own agency as the entity to implement their agency's programs. Or not. Instead, they might choose to *outsource* some programs—that is, use an entity other than their own agency. This option includes using for-profit companies, nonprofit organizations, public authorities, special districts, government-sponsored enterprises, volunteers, and other government agencies, to name a few.

Alternative methods of policy implementation also exist. These include contracts, public–private partnerships, vouchers, grants, franchises, and mandates, among others.

Intersectoral administration is the management and coordination of the relationships among governments and organizations in the private and nonprofit sectors for the purpose of achieving specific policy goals. Figure 11-1 illustrates the major characteristics of these intersectoral configurations, and arrays them on a public–private continuum.

COLLABORATION AND PRIVATIZATION

In implementing public policy, governments collaborate with all three sectors, but they privatize with only two: the private and nonprofit sectors.

Why Collaborate?

Governments' decision, whether by design, default, or defeat, to collaborate with businesses and nonprofit organizations in implementing public policies, stems from several positive impulses (and a few negative ones).[1] They include the following:

- *Savings.* Savings often can be realized. For example, civil service rules on pay scales and benefits may be skirted by using private contractors who pay only minimum wages and offer few benefits to their employees, or by using volunteers.
- *Fiscal easements.* Collaboration with nongovernmental organizations can bypass cumbersome fiscal procedures and raise revenues in ways that more constitutional approaches inhibit.
- *Personnel easements.* Collaboration with nonpublic organizations permits the government to hire specialists and people of unusual talent, without paying as much attention to the usual and sometimes inconvenient public personnel policies.
- *Experimentation.* Using other sectors to experiment with new policies and procedures appears to be highly valued among public administrators, or at least among the more talented ones. Cities that privatize do so, in part, because they have "innovative managerial and institutional strengths."[2]
- *Lowered political risk.* Government becomes less visible when public policies are

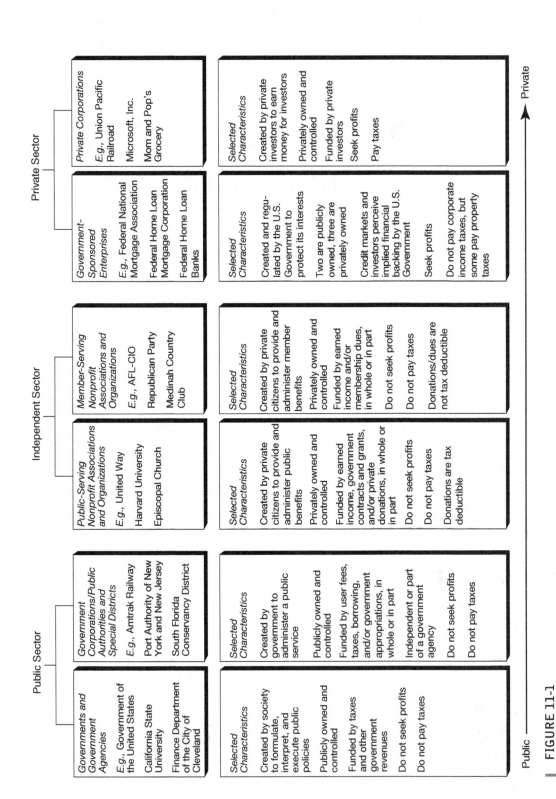

FIGURE 11-1
Organizations and Characteristics of the Public, Independent, and Private Sectors

implemented by organizations other than the government, and avoiding risk, particularly political risk that accompany "a controversial service," is a major motivation to outsource.[3]

- *Image enhancement.* Collaboration can enhance the image of lean but effective government. The personnel working for government can be expanded through agreements with other sectors, even though the official size of the civil service remains the same or is actually reduced. When government partners with businesses, in particular, an aura of businesslike efficiency extends to government, and the venerable mantra that "government should be run like a business" appears, at last, to have been addressed.

- *Greater leverage.* Collaboration permits government agencies to have their services enhanced by the existence of private- and independent-sector organizations that already may be doing what the government wishes to do.

- *Economic development.* Collaboration can assist the economic development of a jurisdiction, especially local ones, by channeling, through contracts and subsidies, public funds to companies and nonprofit organizations in the jurisdiction. These organizations can then put more people on their payrolls.

- *Emergency management.* Occasionally, government must collaborate with other sectors when emergencies occur.

- *Cost clarification.* A particular (and important) form of collaboration, contracting out the delivery of government services to the private and nonprofit sectors, clarifies the true costs of public programs by placing those programs in the competitive marketplace.

- *Incentive to improve public productivity.* The "threat of privatization," and the possible loss of their government jobs, may spur public employees to raise governmental performance.[4]

- *Pinstripe patronage.* "Pinstripe patronage," such as no-bid contracts and revolving doors, is inherent in collaborative arrangements, and it can advance public officials' legitimate and even inspiring visions of a better future, or, as we describe later, erode efficient and effective governance by sustaining conflicts of interest and graft.[5]

An American Orthodoxy

Businesses are the primary producers of public goods and, other than governments themselves, the dominant deliverers of public services. This fact of public life is called *privatization*, which occurs when government sells its assets to, or buys goods or services from, a privately owned for-profit company or nonprofit organization for the purpose of implementing specific policy goals.

In general, most Americans express doubts about the private sector's ability to deliver public services. Asked whether companies or local governments could deliver "more efficiently" six local services, Americans favored companies for delivering just one service, and then by the notably slender margin of 1 percent.[6] Only about a sixth of the general public (17 percent) and college seniors (16 percent) express "the most confidence" in businesses to deliver public services.[7] More than nine out of ten Americans "do not believe that the [federal] government gets best value from its contractors."[8]

Despite the hoi polloi's uncertainty about outsourcing, the belief that business outperforms government in conducting the public's business persists in more rarefied circles. This orthodoxy can be traced to the earliest American thinking about public administration as a profession: from Woodrow Wilson's characterization of it as "a field of business" in his founding essay of 1887 (recall Chapter 2) to the municipal research bureaus of the early twentieth century (mentioned in preceding chapters). These influential bureaus were supported by "a small number of wealthy business people," and their staffs, unsurprisingly, "gave deference in their publications to the wonders of business efficiency, regardless of the accuracy of the claim."[9]

This bias toward business has burned brightly ever since.[10] For example, when the woefully mismanaged town of Ecorse, Michigan, was restored to fiscal health in 1990, a process that was accompanied by contracting out almost every service in sight to the private sector, the resultant urban legend held that the "Ecorse experiment shows that...the private sector can respond to changing conditions much more quickly than can bureaucracies."[11]

FEDERAL PRIVATIZATION

Almost all governments privatize, but the federal government likely has set the standard.

A Forthcoming Federal Fire Sale?

Washington is profoundly into the business of purveying the people's property. The federal government is the biggest electronic vendor in the world, selling about $3.6 billion of its assets, ranging from horses to helicopters, over the Internet each year.[12]

Increasingly, Washington is interested in ridding itself of real estate, and with good reason. The federal government is the largest property owner in the United States, with 429,000 buildings, containing over 3.3 billion square feet. About a tenth of these buildings are "underutilized" (more than 10,000 are "excess" buildings), and cost taxpayers nearly $1.7 billion a year to keep up. Although Washington is disposing of these properties, each of these numbers is growing.[13]

Washington may be on the verge of igniting the fire sale of the century.

Purchasing: Primary Purpose of Federal Privatization

Impressive as federal fire sales may be, they are flighty flickers compared with federal *purchasing*, also known as *procurement* or *acquisitions*, which is government contracting with organizations in the private and nonprofit sectors to buy goods and services.

Portentous Purchasing
The extent of federal contracting is colossal. Some 4 million "contract actions" are let each year[14] to more than 160,000 contractors.[15]

Forty-four percent of federal contract dollars fund services, and 42 percent pay for supplies and equipment; the remaining expenditures, mainly for construction and information services and technology, are each in the single digits.[16] The Department of Defense, as the world's largest, richest bureaucracy, with a budget that exceeds the economies of all but a dozen nations, is Washington's Croesus of contracting. Although, with the end of the Cold War, the Pentagon's share of acquisitions has slipped from 82 percent of all federal contract dollars in 1985[17] to 72 percent today,[18] Defense's share is hardly niggling. About three-quarters of all the remaining contract dollars are spent by just a half-dozen civilian agencies.[19]

Big Bucks: Pricing Procurement
During the 2000s, federal contracting costs were "the fastest growing component of federal discretionary spending,"[20] increasing at a record rate of 171 percent,[21] or twice as fast as any other category.[22] In 2009, Washington hit its all-time record, spending an astounding $550 billion on procurement. In 2010, federal acquisition expenditures actually declined for the first time in thirteen years (if by a modest 3 percent) to $535 billion.[23] Today, federal procurement expenditures account for 42 percent of all federal discretionary spending, up by a fifth, from 35 percent, a decade earlier.[24]

Although, as we explain later, the surge in federal privatization has been of questionable utility to most citizens, it has had a transformative economic impact on many of those who reside in the country's capital. The federal contracting dollars that flow to the Washington, D.C., metropolitan area have septupled over thirty years, and currently account for a startling one-third of its gross regional product (and 15 percent of *all* contracting dollars), raising at least some of its residents' riches to the point where Washingtonians now enjoy the highest median household income of any metropolitan area in the United States.[25]

Humongous Hiring: "Indirect" Federal Employees
An estimated 7.6 million private-sector workers work indirectly for federal agencies through contracts. The number of these indirect federal employees burgeoned by 73 percent in just nine years, and amounts to considerably more than three times the federal civilian workforce.[26]

Private-sector employees who are paid through federal contracts receive 60 percent of all federal contract dollars, whether for goods or services,[27] but this apparent bounty is not as personally enriching as one might surmise. Twenty percent of federally contracted workers earn wages that place them under the poverty line, compared with 8 percent of federal civilian employees.[28]

Policies for Procurement Congress took an interest in privatization more than six decades ago, and enacted legislation that set some broad rules of the game. These include the *Armed Services Procurement Act* of 1949, which mandates advertised bidding for Defense and other agency contracts; the *Truth-in-Negotiations Act* of 1962, which requires contractors to support their bids with data; the *Competition in Contracting Act* of 1984, which established a bidding and appeals system that later was significantly simplified, but still stands in principle; and the *Procurement Integrity Act* of 1988, which prohibits contract officers from discussing employment prospects with, and slipping inside information to, contractors with whom they are negotiating.

Procuring Bureaucracies The Office of Federal Procurement Policy, established by Congress in 1974 and placed in the Office of Management and Budget (OMB), is responsible for providing overall direction for government-wide procurement policies and procedures. Title VII of the Civil Service Reform Act of 1978 authorizes administrators in all agencies to "make determinations with respect to contracting out."[29] The General Services Administration (GSA) assists agencies in purchasing and related projects with the goal of assuring that the government gets good value for the dollar.

Procurement's Personnel: The Contracting Cadres. The primary purchasing personnel are an "acquisition workforce" that numbers over 106,500, the core of which is nearly 33,000 *contracting officers* who are responsible for the business aspects of outsourcing.[30] Contracting officers can make or break federal contracts involving millions, even billions, of dollars, and their power is as subtle as it is formidable. Should the contractual environment be "politically overloaded," as it often is, especially in costlier contracts, then "the primary task of the contracting officer is to balance political demands... with budgetary restrictions and governmental needs."[31]

Regrettably, contracting officers may be ill-equipped for these responsibilities. Over a fifth of them do not have a college degree (although this figure is shrinking), and they typically occupy mid-level supervisory positions.[32] Yet, these administrators are responsible for managing a hugely complex system in the form of the Federal Acquisition Regulation, a document in excess of 1,600 pages, plus agency supplements amounting to another 2,900 pages. (By contrast, the Australian government's procurement regulations total ninety-three pages.)[33] It is all the more discouraging, therefore, that, as the dollars expended on federal contracts burgeoned by 171 percent, the number of contracting officers increased by less than a fourth.[34]

The Perils of Privatization

By 1961, federal contracting with corporations was so pervasive that President Dwight D. Eisenhower, former Supreme Commander of Allied Forces in World War II and a pro-industry Republican, in his televised farewell address to the nation, coined the term, "military-industrial complex," warned Americans of its "grave implications," and stated that its "total influence—economic, political, even spiritual—is felt in every city, every State house, every office of the Federal government."[35]

By any standard, Ike's statement not only was stunning in its implications for democratic governance, but also eerily prescient. "It is now commonplace," states the Government Accountability Office (GAO), "for agencies to use contractors to perform activities historically performed by government employees."[36] "What had once been an 'arms-length' relationship between government staff and contractors has become a relationship where these parties are virtually indistinguishable as they carry out agency missions."[37]

Today, the federal government itself describes, ominously, its administrative circumstances as "a contractor-dependent environment."[38] Why ominously? Because "the closer that contractor services come to supporting" government's core responsibilities, the greater the risk "of influencing the government's control and accountability."[39] Small wonder, perhaps, that contracting out "is negatively related to job satisfaction" among federal employees.[40]

This risk is clearly attenuating, and in the nation's most sensitive policy areas. Nearly a third of the intelligence professionals who have top secret clearances are employed by private companies, and no one seems to be particularly well informed about them. The secretary of defense candidly expressed this widespread ignorance when he admitted, "This is a terrible confession. I can't get a number on how many contractors work for the Office of the Secretary of Defense."[41] In the department most responsible for domestic safety, Homeland Security, more than four-fifths of its information resources' staffers are outside contractors, and a third of its some 600 major information systems that are currently in use "reside in contractor facilities."[42]

Philosophies of Federal Contracting

Federal contracting is best understood as a normative system of values that change over time, and these philosophies often are expressed in administrative regulations.

OMB Circular A-95 The first of these regulations appeared in 1955, when what is now the Office of Management and Budget issued Bureau of the Budget Bulletin Number 55-4, which stated straightforwardly that the government would rely on the private sector for goods and services so that it would not be competing with business.

In 1966, OMB altered this philosophy when it issued OMB Circular A-76, "Performance of Commercial Activities." The Circular reiterated that it is the government's policy "to rely on competitive private enterprise" to supply it with goods and services, but (and this is the shift from the earlier policy) the government should itself perform those functions that "are inherently governmental in nature."

Identifying "Inherently Governmental" Activities—Or Not An *inherently governmental activity* "is a function that is so intimately related to the public interest as to mandate performance by Government employees.... Governmental functions normally fall into two categories: (1) the act of governing...and (2) monetary transactions and entitlements."[43]

This description may sound crisp, clear, and concise, but, alas, it is not. Messiness emerges not when the government tries to identify its commercial activities, but, peculiarly, its governmental ones.

Consider war. Most of us think that war, which constitutionally can be declared only by Congress, is about as "inherently governmental" as it gets, but the Constitution also empowers Congress to "grant Letters of Marque and Reprisal"—that is, to authorize privateers, usually ship owners, to make war on the nation's behalf.

Today, we are witnessing a resurrection of privateers, or, at least, the privatization of war. Fifty-three percent of the Department of Defense's personnel in Afghanistan and Iraq were contracted workers.[44] More than 2,000 contractors have been killed in these conflicts, amounting to over a quarter of all American deaths; during the wars' final years, more contract employees than troops were killed.[45] It is officially projected that contractors will continue to constitute a critical component of any new American-waged wars in the future.[46]

Trying to define "inherently governmental," in sum, "is like trying to nail Jell-O to the wall; only nailing Jell-O is easier."[47]

Identifying "Commercial" Activities *Commercial activities* are those functions that are more appropriately conducted by businesses, rather than by government. Congress in 1998 passed the Federal Activities Inventory Reform Act (the FAIR Act), which requires OMB and the agencies to identify each year their commercial activities.

In contrast to the amorphous and ill-defined governmental activities, OMB now lists more than 700 specific commercial activities, and they are found throughout the federal hierarchy.[48]

Bye-Bye Bidding

Official federal data show that two-thirds of all contracts, and at least half of all contract dollars, are let *without* "full and open competition."[49] These figures actually represent improvements; during the 1970s, an estimated 85 percent of all contract dollars were let without any, or stringently limited, competition.[50]

How do agencies circumvent the bid procedure? Much of this circumvention is legal, if still questionable. Contracting officers have the power to waive bidding requirements, and they waive with gusto. Depending on the study, from about a third to nearly nine-tenths of all contracts are officially exempted from "the fair opportunity process."[51] In most cases, these waivers are granted without "fair and open competition," or with "unjustified exceptions" or "faulty justifications."[52]

In addition, agencies are not above using guile. Fully two-thirds of all federal solicitations for business have already been effectively awarded without bidding. The administrator in charge of publicizing these advertisements notes several "scams" (his word) that agencies use to avoid bids, such as miscoding a contract in the announcement so that potential bidders can never find it ("That happens pretty often"); mentioning a particular firm in the ad itself ("That's a pretty clear tip-off that there's not going to be any competition"); and mandating bidding deadlines so brief that only preselected bidders can meet them. As one federal contractor put it, "Anybody who believes you read [these ads] and get your contracts is out of it. You'd starve."[53]

Low-Balling and Lying

Even when contracts are let competitively, and even though the Federal Acquisition Regulation requires officials to do business only with "responsible sources" that have a "satisfactory record of integrity and business ethics," subterfuge and deceit remain. Contractors' initial *estimated* costs for hundreds of major projects built over nine decades in twenty countries, including the United States, on five continents, were, on average, 28 percent short of their *actual* costs![54] This gap remained quite consistent over time; indeed, the current difference between the Pentagon's contractors' first estimates for weapon systems and their final costs is a remarkably similar average of 26 percent—and rising.[55] The "overwhelming statistical significance" of these data is that "the cost estimates used to decide whether such projects should be built are highly and systematically misleading," and are "best explained by strategic misrepresentation, that is, lying."[56]

If low-balling and lying may be commonplace among companies seeking agency contracts, it is a practice in which agencies are complicit. According to a federal "cost containment expert," prospective contractors know that if they tell administrators "how much something is really going to cost, they may scrub it. And they know that if they tell the Congress how much it's really going to cost, Congress may scrub it. So you start in with both sides knowing that it is going to cost more."[57]

Lobbyland

The corporate side in this complicity hires lobbyists to garner government contracts.

More than 25,000 "Government Relations individuals," a term that includes lobbyists (current, retired, and expired[58]), political action committees, and related groups in Washington, are registered with Congress.[59] Of these individuals, nearly 13,000 are active lobbyists, and the number of active Washington lobbyists has grown by a fourth over a dozen years.[60]

The lay of the lobbying landscape is lush and loaded with lagniappe. The dollars that Washington lobbyists spend to get their way more than doubled in a decade, and now is $3.5 *billion* per annum.[61]

The Rapidly Rotating Revolving Door

Who better to lobby government than those who know it from the inside? Thus we arrive at the infamous *revolving door*, or the process by which public officials resign and then work as bag men and women for the same special interests with which they formerly dealt.

The Scope of Spin Washington's revolving door began its rapidly accelerating spin during the 1980s, and, by the late 1990s, 12 percent of Washington's registered lobbyists were former federal officials.[62] Today, nearly one in three is.[63]

When big money is involved, this figure explodes. Fifty-two percent of the 3,000 lobbyists who, in 2010, lobbied the financial reform bill were former federal employees.[64] Three-fourths of the more than 600 registered lobbyists who represent the oil and gas industry have "revolving-door connections," including "dozens of former presidential appointees."[65]

Conversely, nearly a third—a plurality—of all upper-level federal executives and professionals who are hired from outside the government were working for a federal contractor when hired.[66] Administrators in the Department of Energy, which privatizes about 90 percent of its budget and is second only to Defense in the dollars that it contracts out, "bounce," in the words of a former contracting officer in the Department, "back and forth between government and industry just like Ping-Pong balls."[67]

The revolving door is hardly the exclusive aperture of the executive branch. Over a dozen years, 43 percent of all 198 Senators (50 percent) and Representatives (42 percent) who left Congress registered as lobbyists.[68] Parallel patterns pertain for congressional staffers. In the 1970s, just 3 percent of retiring members of Congress became lobbyists.[69]

Lucre's Lure Federal officials who leave for the private sector are lured by greener pastures. Often, their salaries quadruple or even septuple.[70] In explaining why so many of her colleagues resist more meaningful lobbying reform, a congresswoman observed that "It's because there's a lot of money involved."[71] One is reminded by her observation of a phrase favored by American youth: "Duh."

But the real money is made by the special interests that hire them. Former federal employees who lobby spend a fourth of all lobbying expenditures in Washington, but more than compensate for their spendthrift ways by raking in two-thirds of all lobbying firms' fees.[72] More than half of all consulting contracts awarded by the Pentagon, less than a fifth of which are openly bid, go to former Pentagon employees. Significantly, 40 percent of these contracts are first proposed by the contractor, a figure that appears to be about twice that of civilian agencies, and more than seven out of ten of them could have been conducted in-house by federal employees.[73]

The Sin of Spin. In light of the significant number of executives who work for the companies with which they dealt as federal administrators, "the public could perceive" that these "potentially at risk" executives "may not have acted in the best interest of the government because they viewed a…contractor as a potential employer."[74]

The sin of spin is not confined to the executive branch. Retiring members of Congress who intend to become lobbyists may harbor "ambitions that potentially jeopardize the interest of the public," and certainly the evidence suggests that they do. Members who expect to voluntarily retire and become lobbyists sponsor significantly more legislation during their final term in office than do voluntarily retiring members in their final term who do not intend to become lobbyists.[75] A notoriously effective lobbyist stated that he "owned" about 100 members of Congress, an ownership that he attained by promising selected congressional staffers positions in his firm, at triple their current salaries, when they were ready to retire from federal service.[76]

Slowing the Spin In 2007, in an effort to slow the revolving door's spin, Congress passed the Honest Leadership and Open Government Act, which bans cabinet secretaries and other high-level administrators from lobbying their former agencies for two years following retirement. Congress was less forthcoming in slowing its own revolving door, although the Act does apply the same prohibition on Senators from lobbying Congress, lesser limitations on staffers, and none on Representatives. All members and senior staffers, however, must disclose any current negotiations with prospective employers.

Service Contracts and the Beltway Bandits

A *federal service contract* is a legal agreement for the provision by the private sector of training, leasing, and technical, professional, logistical, social, or managerial support to the federal government. Examples include computer programming, administrative assistance, and temporary labor.

In 1985, service contracts amounted to only 23 percent of all federal contracting dollars.[77] Today, service contracts account for four-fifths of all contracts issued by civilian agencies,[78] and for more than half of those let by the Pentagon.[79]

As an indication of their growing importance, Congress in 2003 passed the Services Acquisition Reform Act, which creates incentives for performance-based service contracts and appoints in civilian agencies "chief acquisition officers" empowered to decide whether or not contracted programs may continue and force accountability among contractors and federal managers alike. Unfortunately, these officers have yet to meet expectations.[80]

Costly Consultants An extensive and expensive use of service contracts is the hiring of private consultants, who operate in a netherworld of dank and bureaucratic murk. Although OMB states that over 52,000 private companies furnish the federal government with their expertise and advice,[81] the GAO is unable to ascertain just how much Washington spends on consultants.[82]

The indications are, however, that consultants can be costly. Had the departments of Energy and Defense used government employees instead of consultants, they would have saved significant sums—from over a fourth to more than half.[83]

More anecdotal, but revealing, evidence on the utility of the "Beltway bandits" abounds. (The derogation derives from the Beltway encircling Washington.) When a program chief received, six months late, a contracted consultation by the Stanford Research Institute, she discovered "not only that the work was poor," but that, to her dismay, the Institute had "lifted almost word for word" at least one section of its report from her own work. "Can't your staff think for itself?" she asked. Inexcusably, her office continued its $13 million contract with the Institute, despite unequivocal proof that its plagiarizing personnel were unqualified.[84] Federal contracting officers bemoan that "the public gets...maybe 10 percent of their money's worth" from consultants; that their reports amount to "gobbledygook"; and that federal administrators "are so busy trying to shovel money out the door, we don't have time to see

what happens to it after it leaves"; "as a taxpayer, I'm sick."[85]

Consultants themselves agree: "It's a game.... Government comes to us and wants help in identifying their problems, but they don't seem to be able to use the material. They could spend much less and get more for it."[86]

"It looks like a conspiracy, but really it's chaos."[87] So stated one of the nation's leading experts on governing-by-contracting, and likely he is accurate.

The Shadow Government Chaotic incompetence is one thing. Policy manipulation, however, is another.

We noted earlier that privatization in general presents serious issues of public control and accountability, but these issues attenuate when "advice" from private consultants waxes into policy executed by public administrators. In reports that date from 1961, the GAO has noted consultants' "excessive involvement in agency management" that is "influencing agencies' control of Federal policies and programs."[88] "We've seen situations where an agency contracts out so much of its data gathering and policy analysis that it thinks it has control, but the consultant is, in effect, making the decision."[89]

These are fundamental issues. They deal with who makes, and implements, public policy in an advanced democracy—representatives of the public interest or of private interests.

OMB first addressed these concerns in 1980, and it has consistently demanded that agencies retain their "inherently governmental decision-making authority" when contracting with consultants and other service contractors.[90] A decade following the initial issuance of this policy, however, over a fifth of federal contracts for consultants' services appeared to involve "inherently governmental functions."[91]

Contracting in Incompetence

Much of federal contracting is a model of efficiency. A comparison of the Defense Department's and companies' costs in buying identical electronic and engine parts, for example, found that the Pentagon paid much less than did the business sector. These savings were credited to the fact that Defense "was already using commercial practices commonly followed by large firms," including tough bargaining.[92]

Doing Kafka Proud But much is not. At least a third of the American interrogators who were implicated in the severe mistreatment of prisoners in Iraq's infamous Abu Ghraib prison were not American soldiers, but private businesspeople. They were hired not by the Pentagon, as one might reasonably assume, but through a computer services contract overseen by an Interior Department's office in Arizona. In apparent violation of federal regulations, the contract was never opened for bid, and the contract itself was written by an employee of the firm that won the contract. The process was so convoluted that the Army could not determine who wanted to hire private interrogators in the first place. Deals such as this, and there are too many of them, have been described as "possessing a logic that would do only Kafka proud."[93]

A Pervasive Problem How did these debacles happen? Unfortunately, they are examples of a far more systemic federal incompetence in privatizing.

Time is money. Federal purchases of less than $100,000 take an average of three months to complete, compared to one to four weeks in the private sector.[94]

A lack of due diligence is money. Some kinds of federal contracts require that administrators assess the past performance of prospective contractors before awarding them contracts, but, in seven out of ten of these contracts, contractors' previous performance is never assessed.[95]

A counterproductive contracting culture is money. The culture of contracting rarely places serious value on acquiring one's money's worth. Often, "the concept that the contracting officer's primary purpose is to acquire a contract that promises the highest quality at the lowest price is misleading if not false."[96] As a former procurement officer put it, "It doesn't matter if you screw everything up, as long as you keep the dollars flowing."[97]

Change is money. The Pentagon alters a whopping 63 percent of weapon systems' requirements *after* their development has begun, and this dubious

practice associates with "significant program cost increases."[98] Over the course of fourteen years, in fact, the U.S. Army spent more than $32 billion on twenty-two major weapon systems—systems that it cancelled and never built.[99]

Unused leverage is money. Federal agencies miss "opportunities to leverage the government's buying power" by failing to use interagency contracts to purchase the same goods and services from common vendors.[100] It appears that less than a tenth of contract dollars are leveraged.[101]

Senseless rules are money. Procurement regulations add cost, but not value,[102] toting up to 12 percent or more in additional contract costs.[103] Large pluralities of senior federal executives think that the "procurement process" fails to reduce waste, fraud, and abuse, or even serves "the best interests of the Government."[104]

Cost-reimbursement contracts are money. *Cost-reimbursement contracts* ask contractors to make a good-faith effort to meet estimated costs, but the government (with some restrictions, depending on the contract) will pay any costs exceeding that estimate. Cost-reimbursement contracts involve "high risk for the government because of the potential for cost escalation and because the government pays a contractor's costs of performance regardless of whether the work is completed.... The complete picture of the government's use" of these contracts "is unclear," but it appears that they account for at least a fourth of all federal contracting dollars.[105] Unfortunately, the dollars spent through cost-reimbursement contracts are growing—by 11 percent, on average, each year.[106]

Contracting in Corruption

Washington's procurement procedures are meant to assure if not efficiency then at least honesty. In this, they frequently fail.

Stiffing the Government Since 1995, sixty-eight of the top 100 federal contractors have been fined more than $19 billion for 699 "instances of misconduct," including fraud, "defective pricing," poor performance, and violations of health, tax, labor, ethics, antitrust, environmental, and human rights laws.[107]

In the Pentagon, America's biggest contractor, the Justice Department's Operation Ill Wind, exposed "America's biggest defense scandal." "No one will ever know how much the phony contracts and sweetheart deals really cost taxpayers," but it is known that they amounted to billions of dollars, and resulted in over ninety corruption convictions of contractors and federal executives.[108] Such convictions are singularly rare when the United States wages war in other countries, even though the sums involved are colossal; a "conservative estimate" of the dollars lost over nine years to "waste and fraud" in the wars in Afghanistan and Iraq "ranges from $31 billion to $60 billion," amounting from 15 to 29 percent of all contract dollars spent in the two countries.[109]

Stiffing the Law A second sort of corruption occurs when contractors violate federal laws that are unrelated to their contractual performance, but still are awarded new federal contracts.

Thirteen percent of all federal contract dollars have gone to companies convicted of labor law violations,[110] and nearly a fifth flow to corporations that have been convicted of seriously violating federal health and safety regulations, including violations that resulted in the deaths of thirty-five workers in some of those companies over the course of a single year.[111]

Of the fifty largest penalties imposed for violating health and safety laws, 16 percent were levied against seven federal contractors. Fully half of the fifty most egregious incidents of wage theft—that is, companies that had cheated their employees out of the wages due them—were perpetrated by twenty companies that held federal contracts.[112]

Stiffing the Taxpayer A particularly pernicious form of contracting corruption concerns those companies that are awarded federal contracts but fail to pay the taxes they owe.

Contented Contractors Some 33,000 contractors with all federal agencies, other than the Defense Department, owe Washington more than $3.3 billion in federal taxes.[113] When we throw in the Pentagon, more than 27,000 Defense contractors, or 14 percent of all Defense contractors, owe

another $3 billion in federal taxes.[114] Altogether, deadbeat contractors account for nearly two-fifths of all federal contractors.[115]

More than 27,000 health care providers who collect federal payments from Medicare, or 6 percent of all such providers, owe more than $2 billion (an "understated" sum) in federal back taxes.[116]

"At least" 3,700 recipients (or 5 percent of all recipients) of more than $24 billion in contracts, grants, and loans disbursed under the American Recovery and Reinvestment Act of 2009 owe more than $757 million in federal taxes (a "likely understated" amount); 55 percent of the taxes owed (or $417 million) were corporate income taxes, suggesting that these recipients were probably contractors.[117]

The states are not immune; more than 4,600 federal contractors who collected $1.8 billion in federal contracts in just one year owe their state governments $17 million in unpaid state taxes.[118]

Altogether, more than 94,700 documented contractors and health professionals owe more than $10 billion in unpaid taxes, yet receive billions more in federal contracts. Criminal acts abound in all of these instances, and surely uncounted others.

How is this possible? Because "Federal law does not prohibit the awarding of contracts or grants to entities because they owe federal taxes and does not permit IRS [Internal Revenue Service] to disclose taxpayer information, including unpaid federal taxes, to federal agencies unless the taxpayer consents."[119]

Offshore Contractors A variation on this sour theme is that of offshore contractors which are headquartered in tax-haven countries. In just one year, these offshore companies received $846 million in federal contracts, yet cost the U.S. treasury an estimated $4 *billion* in lost tax revenue.[120] "Large tax haven contractors" also are "more likely to have a tax cost advantage" in competing for federal contracts "than large domestic contractors."[121]

In short, taxpayers are stiffed twice—first by offshore contractors who pay no taxes, and then by the government that pays some of these contractors with taxpayers' money. And, to add insult to injury, federal contractors who pay their taxes and hire American workers are at a competitive disadvantage with those contractors who do not.

Why Does Corruption in Contracting Continue?

Corruption in federal contracting continues for a host of reasons.

The Structure of Contracting Corruption In part, fraud flourishes because the structure of privatization itself is unusually corruptible. Of the high risk federal operations identified by the GAO as unduly vulnerable to fraud, waste, abuse, and mismanagement, more than a third involve "large procurement operations or programs delivered mainly by third parties."[122]

Federally Fixed on Felons There is, however, another, more troubling reason why corruption permeates federal privatization: With few exceptions, Washington keeps coming back for more.

Even as federal contract costs more than doubled,[123] the number of *exclusions*—that is, suspensions and debarments—issued by all federal agencies to contractors actually *declined* by 55 percent over five years, and now amount to fewer than 4,500 per year,[124] an infinitesimal subfraction of the close to 4 million contracts that Washington lets annually.[125]

Of far greater importance, the big enchiladas of federal contracting are almost never suspended or debarred, despite long records of serious, including some criminal, violations. Not one of the twenty-five major corporations convicted of defrauding the federal government in the 1980s was banned from further contract work.[126] During the 1990s and 2000s, the top ten federal contractors shelled out almost $3 billion in fines and penalties for 280 instances of proven or alleged misconduct, but not one of them was excluded from further work.[127]

Forever Fraud At least some of the reason why federal agencies keep contracting with these high-flying felons is practical. Few, if any, other contractors could take over some of the big, complex projects that these big, complex companies manage, so firing them may not be a realistic option.[128]

Another is technical: Various glitches may conceal from agencies an astounding 99 percent of the suspensions and debarments that other agencies have levied on their prospective contractors for past violations.[129]

Yet another is managerial: Agencies sometimes fail to check the government's list of suspended and debarred companies; or the excluded companies change their identities; or, astonishingly, some agencies continue to contract with companies that they themselves excluded! Examples include the German contractor that the Army debarred because he tried to ship nuclear bomb parts to North Korea, but nevertheless needlessly continued its contract with this "morally bankrupt individual" (to quote the Army's own assessment) to the tune of another $4 million. Or the corporation that the Navy suspended because one of its employees had sabotaged repairs on an aircraft carrier that could have caused massive deaths, yet, "less than a month later, the Navy improperly awarded the company three new contracts."[130]

But much of the reason why the feds fire so few felonious firms is political. Canceling a government contract "drastically disrupts the careers of those associated with it," because the cancellation "hurts regional economies. What causes pain locally triggers congressional rescue activity."[131] Bringing Congress into the act can be a federal administrator's worst nightmare, so federal "contractual relationships may be more like treaties than contracts in that often no real separation occurs.... Once integrated into the public sector, firms tend to remain there."[132]

Does Federal Outsourcing Work?

For more than three decades, and with enormous energy, Washington tried to determine which sector, public or private, could conduct which federal functions more efficiently. In 2008, the feds effectively declared themselves defeated in this effort.[133]

Nevertheless, it is becoming increasingly apparent that the federal government usually outperforms the private sector. A stunning 84 percent of federal managers support "shrinking the contractor workforce to save money," a proportion that no other money-saving method comes remotely close to nearing.[134] And there is empirical evidence to back up these informed views. For example, bringing back into the Pentagon 30,000 outsourced jobs would save an estimated $44,000 per year for each position.[135] A careful analysis of thirty-five federal occupational classifications covering more than 550 service activities found that federal employees were less costly than contractors in thirty-three of the thirty-five categories. "Fair and reasonable" billing rates (as required by law) charged by contractors toted up to "1.83 times more than the government pays federal employees in total compensation, and more than 2 times the total compensation paid in the private sector for comparable services."[136]

Reforming Federal Privatization

Slowly, Washington has begun to act on its dawning recognition that federal privatization is flirting with fiasco.

Professionalizing Privatization's Personnel

Congress has created a Federal Acquisition Institute (in 1976), established a separate career path for the Pentagon's acquisitions specialists (1990), and founded the Defense Acquisition University (1991) all in an effort to professionalize purchasing's personnel.

Reforming the Privatization Process

During the 1990s, Congress passed four laws designed to simplify privatization procedures.

The *Government Performance and Results Act* of 1993 requires agencies to measure the performance of contractors. Nearly two decades after its passage, unfortunately, progress in implementing performance contracting remains "excruciatingly slow,"[137] and only a slender 11 percent of contracts meet performance-based criteria.[138]

In 1996, Congress passed the *Information Technology Management Reform Act,* detailed in Chapter 6; the *Federal Acquisition Streamlining Act,* which simplified the purchase of relatively low-cost items; and the *Federal Acquisition Reform Act,* which simplifies the appeals process, recasts the Federal Acquisition Regulation in terms of guidelines rather than rules, and frees administrators from selecting only the lowest bidder.

These laws have backfired, largely because they: cut back contract audits; significantly

weakened the requirement, first established by the *False Claims Act* of 1863, that companies certify their prices as being the most favorable to the government; and authorized the General Services Administration to collect "industrial funding fees"—that is, a percentage of the sales it handles—from vendors who sell to federal agencies. These changes amount to a set of incentives for GSA to overlook overcharges—the industrial funding fees alone cover GSA's budget—and the results are predictable. A decade following their passage, corporate sales to agencies that were conducted through the GSA's flagship program septupled. "Agencies have used the GSA to avoid true competition and steer work to preferred companies, resulting in cases of waste, fraud and increased cost to taxpayers" amounting to "hundreds of millions, if not billions," of dollars.[139]

During the 2000s, Congress tried yet again to gain a semblance of control over federal contracting. The *Federal Funding Accountability and Transparency Act* (the *Obama-Coburn Act*) of 2006 requires that all recipients of federal funds, certainly including contractors and subcontractors, be publicly listed. In 2008, the Federal Acquisition Regulation Council added to the Federal Acquisition Regulation new ethics rules that require mandatory disclosure when contractors violate particular laws, and expanded the grounds for excluding contractors. The *Clean Contracting Act* of 2008 limited noncompetitive contracts, and narrowed standards for what can be outsourced.

The Audacity of Hope

In 2009, almost a half century following Eisenhower's warning about the perils of privatization, the forty-fourth president of the United States, Barack Obama, on his forty-fourth day in office, delivered the second major presidential address on federal contracting, appropriately, in the Eisenhower Executive Office Building. Obama called for the reform of "our broken system of government contracting." He directed OMB to end payments to contractors who were "paid for services that were never performed, buildings that were never completed, companies that skimmed off the top," and who "have been allowed to get away with delay after delay after delay."[140]

Congress responded to the president's actions by passing three consequential bills. The *Weapon Systems Acquisition Reform Act* of 2009 beefed up weapons' cost estimating and testing; the *Fraud Enforcement and Recovery Act* of 2009 dramatically expanded the risk for institutional recipients of federal funds that engaged in mismanagement or fraud; and the *American Recovery and Reinvestment Act* of 2009 directed greater competition in awarding contracts and strengthened federal follow up.

"Government contracting is plainly entering an era of...an unprecedented level of scrutiny" and "significantly greater risk for contractors,"[141] "many" of whom went "into shock" when they learned of Obama's reforms, "and left some acquisitions experts speechless."[142]

It is undeniably encouraging that, even though the federal government remains contractor-dependent, there is an effort being undertaken at the highest levels to liberate the government's dependency and to reassert its primacy in the implementation of public policy. Perhaps, however, the more potent cure for contracting woes is the likelihood of its shrinking use in the future, a shrinkage, as we have noted, that began in 2010. It is projected that, due to squeezed budgets resulting from significantly reduced revenue and unprecedented deficit spending, federal contracting costs will grow at a compound annual rate of just 2 percent, "a very, very slow growth rate," in the foreseeable future.[143] This glacial growth rate may be the single best prospect for gaining greater public control of federal procurement.

PRIVATIZING IN THE STATES

State governments also procure and privatize.

The States Resistant

Relative to the federal and local governments, the states resist privatizing. This is not to say that state privatization is trivial. State governments spend at least a fifth of their operating budgets on procurement and contracting.[144] Nevertheless, almost two-thirds of state administrators report that their governments' privatization has stayed the same (53 percent) or declined (12 percent) over the past five years.[145] State employee associations, such as unions, and elected officials are the most commonly cited obstacles to state privatization efforts.[146]

Selling Small A modest 14 percent of state officials in just nine states report that "asset sales" are even conducted in their states,[147] and only a fraction of 1 percent of state agencies had actually sold public goods over the preceding five years.[148]

That states privatize their assets so modestly is odd in light of the facts that states and their local governments have hundreds of billions of dollars in assets (roads, parks, etc.) that, at least in theory, could be privatized,[149] and Washington has long promoted their privatization. In 1992, President George H. W. Bush issued Executive Order 12803, which terminated federal requirements that states and localities that sold or leased projects which had been built with some federal funds had to repay those funds, and, in 1996, Congress legislated that the Federal Aviation Administration encourage the privatization of state and local airports.

Privatizing Services The most favored form of privatization in the states is that of outsourcing services. Two-thirds of the states,[150] and three-fifths of all state agencies, contract with companies to deliver at least one service, and states contract more frequently with corporations than they contract with independent organizations and other government agencies to provide services.[151] Education and transportation agencies contract with companies the most, where contracting is growing, and health and social service agencies contract the least, where the practice is in decline.[152] In addition, nearly half of state administrators in twenty-two states report that their states enter into public–private partnerships to deliver services.[153]

But even in the privatization of services, states lag. A slender 5 percent of state agency heads (or possibly less[154]) report that they have fully implemented the privatization of even one major service.[155] Fully a third of the states contract with no one to deliver any of their services— not corporations, not nonprofit organizations, not other government agencies.[156]

Motives, Money, and Management

Why do states privatize? Does privatization save states' money? How well do states manage their privatization?

Motivations to Privatize More than two-thirds of the directors of state budget and legislative service agencies, and almost two-fifths of state department heads, report that "cost savings" are the primary reason that they privatize some services, followed by a lack of expertise (more than half), greater flexibility, and speedier implementation.[157]

Slim Savings State administrators' high hopes that privatization will save money are not borne out in practice. More than six out of ten directors of state budget and legislative service agencies report that any government-wide savings obtained from privatization are "unknown" (24 percent) or fail to respond, and the 18 percent who report savings (well over half of whom say that savings are 1 percent or less) is equaled by those who report no savings. Less than a fourth of state agency heads claim any savings for their departments from privatization, and a third detect no savings.[158]

Modest Management On the whole, the states' administration of privatization seems not as strong as it could be. Even though three-fourths of the states have the capacity to automatically track their vendors' performance over several contracts,[159] the states' monitoring of their contractors' performance has been described by "most" state managers as "the weakest link in their privatization process,"[160] and it may be that as many as three-quarters of them fail to track their contractors' performance.[161] Those states that privatize the most successfully have created centralized entities that manage all aspects of outsourcing.[162]

Outsourcing and Influencing

When state agencies contract with special interests to deliver services, those interests gain a unique leverage in shaping agency policies. "Contracting opens a pathway for organized interests to lobby public managers.... The influence of organized interests over state agency decision making is driven, in part, by whether an agency contracts out for public service delivery."[163]

More gravely, there also are increasing reports of conflicts of interest and less-than-open bidding in state privatization practices.[164] State administrators' propensity to socialize with contractors may be a factor in the possible deterioration of professional privatization, as such chumminess "plays a significant role" in these managers' positive perception of contractors, outweighing even state administrators' past experience in the private sector and activities that are comparable with those of their contractors.[165]

PRIVATIZING BY LOCAL GOVERNMENTS

In contrast to state governments, local governments are privatizing enthusiastically. Four-fifths of local administrators believe that "privatization will represent a primary tool to provide local government services and facilities."[166]

Buying Goods, Selling Assets

Thirty-nine states set purchasing standards for their local governments, and a dozen require their local governments to centralize their purchasing function in a single office, although centralized purchasing is the norm for almost all local governments anyway. Thirty-seven states require their local governments to competitively bid all purchases exceeding a specified amount (thirty-two), or of a designated type (five).[167]

Local governments surpass the states in their propensity to purvey their goods to private parties, but fall far short of federal levels. Less than a fourth of cities and counties sell any assets over a five-year period.[168]

Privatizing Local Services

Improving the delivery of local services to citizens is an extraordinarily vital concern of local administrators, with city managers ranking it third out of twenty-six "influences" that affect their decision making (only "budgetary constraints" and "staff input" rank higher).[169] Because of its importance, local governments have experimented aggressively with manifold methods of bettering services, one of which is outsourcing them. As in the states, the contracting out of service delivery has waxed into the dominant form of local privatization.

Cities and counties deliver 47 percent of all their services by using only their own workers, a proportion that is the lowest in a quarter-century, but which nevertheless has held steady at around half. These jurisdictions concentrate their use of their own employees on support functions (i.e., personnel, payroll, secretarial, and public relations), followed by crime control, inspections, and parking.[170]

Service contracting with for-profit firms accounts for 18 percent of all city and county services, with vehicle towing handily leading the way, followed by the operation of gas utilities, child welfare programs, and legal services. Although the privatization of local services has expanded modestly from 15 percent of all services twenty-five years earlier,[171] the practice is nearly universal: At least 99 percent of cities and counties contract out some of their services,[172] and "contracts have been used for *every* service," from parking to police, that these governments provide.[173]

Seventeen percent of municipal and county services, on average, are delivered jointly by governments' own employees and employees in the private sector—a decline of more than a fourth from twenty-five years earlier. The leaders here are parking meters and programs for the elderly.[174]

The remaining local services are delivered by nonprofit organizations, detailed later in this chapter, and by other governments, considered in Chapter 12.[175]

Outsourcing *in Extremis*

A few local governments reject the very concept of public employees, choosing instead to outsource the delivery of their services to companies, non-profit organizations, and other governments. Sandy Springs (population 90,000), Georgia, has only its public safety, judicial, and legal personnel on the public payroll; Centennial (104,000), Colorado, has fewer than thirty municipal workers;[176] and

Weston (62,000), Florida, just three.[177] In 2010, Maywood (30,000), California, faced with a fiscal crisis, threatened with cancellation of its insurance coverage, and fed up with its historically surly police force, fired all its employees, retaining only its town manager and attorney.[178]

Other localities take the opposite route, keeping all their employees and outsourcing only their topmost position, the town manager. Eight small towns in North Carolina have done this, contracting with management firms for full- or part-time town managers to manage their governments, but keeping their towns' employees on the public payroll.[179]

Why Local Governments Privatize Services

The propensity of local governments to privatize their services correlates with a surprisingly diverse conglomeration of reasoning, pressures, motives, and circumstances.

Saving Money By far the most pervasive incentive for cities and counties to privatize services is an internal desire to cut costs, a motivation cited by a notable 87 percent of local managers.[180] This response marks a dramatic change in local officials' perception, and is more than double the proportion of those who thought that privatization saved money more than three decades earlier.[181]

Saving money is an eminently rational reason to privatize services. But there are other, murkier motives for local governments to outsource.

New Services When a local government takes on new services to deliver, it often privatizes their delivery. One study found that the addition of more services was "the strongest and most reliable predictor" of local privatization.[182]

Playing Politics An analysis of national surveys found that there were indications that local "elected officials are using private contractors to...reward electoral constituencies." Partisanship also plays a prominent part, and cities that are controlled by the Republican Party contract more with the private sector than do cities in which the Democrats are in power.[183]

Good Times Money matters. In a strange twist of local officials' professed conviction that privatization cuts costs, local governments contract out their services more frequently *not* when they are facing tough financial times, but rather when they are, relatively speaking, rolling in dough.[184] Contrarily, "there is no evidence that fiscal stress induces privatization" by local governments.[185] Governmental wealth appears to trump even partisan ideology in the decision to privatize.[186]

Contracting Among Friends As with state agencies, when local governments partner with outside organizations, "social factors" count for a lot, particularly if their administrators share comparable professional experiences and have "genuine affection for each other." Social factors are more important to both parties than any economic benefits that might result from their collaborative arrangements.[187] In fact, when there is high turnover among local officials, contracting out local services to all three sectors abruptly and steeply declines, implying that there must be an existing foundation of familiarity between officials and contractors before contracts will be let.[188]

Bureaucratic Symbiosis In a perverse variant of Parkinson's Law, the more bureaucrats that there are in a school district, the more that those bureaucrats will contract with outsiders to do their jobs for them. For each 1 percent increase in central office administrators as a percentage of total employment, there is a 0.32 percentage increase in contracting by the district. "Increases in bureaucracy…generate future increases in contracting. Increases in contracting…generate future increases in bureaucracy."[189]

The presence of a small number of "administrative professionals" attenuates these correlations. Why? Because their skills were needed to process contracts and because they were more interested in making "strategic decisions rather than more trivial day-to-day decisions," and contracting out freed them to do so.[190]

Place and Circumstance A government's location, size, competitive circumstances, and the interest that its citizens have in the quality and delivery of local services, also affect its level of outsourcing.

Suburban governments contract out more services than do rural and urban governments, mostly because there are competitors for their business, which is crucial in enhancing efficiency, and their residents have at least a middling interest in services.

Rural governments (and governments with small populations[191]) outsource less than suburban ones, mainly because there is a dearth of alternative service suppliers, but also because their citizens evidence the least concern with services.

Central cities privatize the least, even though they are in the most competitive markets and their residents' interest in services is highest. But, because urban governments already govern relatively large swaths of territory, which yields them uniquely advantageous "internal economies of scale" that are denied to smaller jurisdictions, they are unable to reduce costs through outsourcing to the extent that suburban and rural governments can.[192]

Why Local Governments Do Not Privatize Services

Local reluctance to contract out services is relatively weak, and is diminishing over time. More than six out of ten cities and counties report that they encounter *no* obstacles to privatizing, and this figure rises with every survey.[193] Nevertheless, there are some serious barriers to local privatization

Employee Opposition Forty-seven percent of the two-fifths of cities and counties that have encountered impediments to outsourcing report that opposition from their own employees is the single greatest obstacle, and this is the highest percentage out of thirteen possible responses.[194] After growing for years,[195] employee resistance seems to have leveled off, and may even be declining,[196] but government workers nonetheless remain privatization's chief public enemy.

Unions Local employees' central ally in their antiprivatization posture is organized labor, no doubt in part because local privatization associates with reduced union membership.[197] Two-fifths of those local officials who encounter hurdles to privatization cite restrictive labor contracts as an obstacle; they are the second most-cited impediment and the only one that is growing over time.[198]

Contracting out services "is less likely to be supported fully by city councils in places where public employees unions are strong."[199] When unions win excessive benefits for their members, however, local governments turn to privatization in an effort to stem rising labor costs. An analysis of national polls revealed that "Contrary to our hypothesis, public unionization increased the likelihood of private for-profit delivery....Unionization may not be the barrier to privatization it was once thought to be."[200]

Pushback Politicos Thirty-nine percent of local administrators who encountered obstacles to privatization cite opposition from elected officials. It is the third most significant impediment, and it is declining as a hurdle over time.[201] Their reluctance to outsource local government jobs doubtless is a reflection of the fact that, as we detailed in Chapter 9, local government workers are unusually active in local elections.

Riffed: What Happens to Public Employees When Local Governments Privatize? In all likelihood, the most salient concern underlying the resistance to privatization is the fate of those who lose their government jobs as a consequence of contracting them out. This is an important worry. Here is what we know:

- *A relatively small number of public workers lose their jobs to privatization.* Estimates range from 5 to 7 percent of the local workforce.[202]
- *Those local workers who lose their jobs receive little public assistance.* Only three out of ten receive any benefits.[203] Only 19 percent of local governments develop programs to minimize the adverse effects of privatization on their displaced employees.[204]
- *Privatization creates jobs as well as eliminates them.* Because jobs are shifted from government to the private sector, the jobs lost and gained are essentially a wash.[205]
- *Pay by local governments and pay by local contractors is about the same, but the benefits offered by contractors are less generous.* Half of the contractors offer fewer benefits, and only 16 percent offer more.[206]
- *Local employees of color appear to lose their jobs to privatization at a faster rate than white employees.* This seems to be especially the case in cities with populations of 100,000 to 500,000.[207]

Managing Privatized Local Services

Do local governments manage privatization cost-effectively? Yes, they do, at least in comparison with the federal and state governments.

Managed Competition *Managed competition* encourages government departments to compete for service delivery contracts with private companies, nonprofit organizations, and each other. It originated in Phoenix in the 1970s, and, while we have few facts about its fiscal impact, it appears to have a salutary effect, and often involves dividing a city into competitive service districts. Although it seems to work best in large local governments, 23 percent of all cities and counties use managed competition, a slight decrease over five years.[208]

Competing for Local Contracts Competitive bidding seems to be used more frequently by local governments than by any other governmental level. Thirty-seven states require their local governments to competitively bid all purchases exceeding a specified amount (thirty-two), or of a designated type (five).[209] Only 18 percent of cities and counties select any contractors without competitive bidding, and even this low proportion is shrinking over time.[210] Cities with city managers are more likely than are cities without them to have formal bidding systems.[211]

Local administrators are wary of the private sector, and tend to privatize only those services that have a low risk of failure and limited prospects for corporate exploitation.[212] Most local governments insert "high-powered" incentives and disincentives in their long-term contracts with private firms, a practice that they almost never repeat when contracting with other governments and nonprofit organizations.[213] It is in the interest of these governments, however, to not be too heavy-handed, as "rigidly constructed legal agreements" with the private sector can distort incentives, create conflicts, and "do little" to fulfill contracted objectives.[214]

Getting a Grip Local governments appear to have a relatively firm grip on their management of private contractors. Thirty-nine states set purchasing standards for their local governments, and a dozen require their local governments to centralize their purchasing function in a single office, although centralized purchasing is the norm for almost all local governments anyway.[215]

Forty-five percent of all cities and counties,[216] and more than nine-tenths of larger local governments,[217] formally evaluate their contractors' performance. By contrast, federal agencies assess the performance of about a seventh of their contractors,[218] if even that much,[219] and as few as a fourth of state agencies formally monitor their contractors.[220]

Moreover, local governments act on their assessments. Twenty-two percent of cities and counties that privatized at least one service over the last five years brought those services back in-house for reasons of poor corporate performance.[221] Since 1997, the rate at which cities, towns, and counties bring privatized services back in-house for delivery has surpassed the rate of new contracting out.[222] Smaller, poorer communities are the most likely of all local jurisdictions to bring services back in-house when they perceive poor performance by their contractors.[223]

The Quality Question Most local administrators consistently express themselves as quite satisfied with the quality of privatized services.[224] Independent researchers are less effusive, however, and an unusually solid review concludes that "there is no discernible relationship one way or the other. In other words, as best we know at present, contracting does not reduce or increase quality, as a general rule."[225]

Still, some contractors deliver higher quality services than other contractors, and the variable that associates most positively with high contracting quality is somewhat surprising. It is: Trust.

Higher levels of trust between local officials and contractors "result not only in lower costs, but also in higher quality of services and greater responsiveness to the needs of local government."[226]

When local officials are not satisfied with the quality of outsourced services, they act with notable firmness. Of the more than a fifth of cities and counties that bring privatized services back in-house, more than six out of ten do so, at least in part, because they were dissatisfied with service quality. Perceived poor quality of service delivery is handily the leading reason why local officials engage in "reverse contracting," surpassing even insufficient savings.[227]

IS BUSINESS BETTER?

Is the American orthodoxy accurate? Is business better?

At first glance, it appears so. An analysis of essentially all empirical studies of privatization across the globe found that governments' savings derived from contracting out service delivery to the private sector never exceed 30 percent, and, on average, amount from 6 to 12 percent, with the largest savings, 19 to 30 percent, in cleaning, maintenance, and refuse collection.[228] These findings starkly question the claims of privatization zealots, who tout savings of 50 percent,[229] but, nevertheless, privatizing public service delivery correlates positively, if far from universally, with lower public costs.

Efficiency's Own Urban Legend: Business Is Better

But are those lower costs the case simply because the private sector is inherently more efficient (and, by inference, more competent) than the public sector?

This is efficiency's own urban legend—that, indeed, business is better. As with all urban legends (e.g., mile-long snakes slither in our sewers), it is not entirely factually correct.

The Cost of Service Delivery Although, as we related in Chapter 7, government is stuck with some structural problems that impede the measurement of its efficiency and make it more difficult for government to attain the same efficiencies as business, these issues appear to be less the case in the area of providing services. That same global literature review referenced earlier succinctly summarizes this reality: "Cost reductions are attained whether public or private sector organizations win contracts. This finding, that there was no general tendency for private provision to be any more cost-effective than public provision of services under contract, is a significant one."[230]

It sure is. Herbert Simon, Nobel laureate and a godfather of both public and business administration, put it well when he referred to "the falsity" of the "common claim" that public organizations "cannot, and on average do not, operate as efficiently as private businesses."[231]

Efficiency, Effectiveness, and Equity in Service Delivery
But wait. There's more.

Both public–private and public–nonprofit partnerships demonstrate no, or even negative, statistically significant relationships with greater efficiency (i.e., effectiveness increases while cost decreases), greater effectiveness (i.e., services' outputs and outcomes are improved), and greater equity (i.e., compassion and trust are raised, personal attention is given, and the special needs of the disadvantaged, excluded, and underrepresented are met) in the delivery of local public services.

In terms of efficiency, government contracts with either the private or the independent sector "may not necessarily be a suitable vehicle for enhancing cost-effectiveness" in providing public services, as both sectors display "statistically insignificant" relationships with efficiency.

The correlation between "public–private partnerships" and effectiveness "is actually negative and significant," and governments' "partnership with the voluntary sector appears to have no relationship with effectiveness, despite this being a common approach to delivering many local services."

Finally, public–private partnerships show a "negative and statistically significant" correlation with equity, and an "insignificant" association with public–nonprofit partnerships.[232]

What Really Lowers Service Delivery Costs?

If not private corporations and nonprofit organizations, then what *does* lower the cost of delivering government services?

Competition, probably.

Consider some examples. When bidders are competing for the same federal contract, some $100,000 *more* in bids per full-time equivalent contracted position is generated than when there is just one bidder.[233] A leading concern of almost three out of ten local contractors is that "competition from other firms" pushes "prices too low for their firm to compete."[234] When a new Nigerian government required competitive bidding to build public works, and then, prudently, checked those bids against bids for comparable projects listed on the Internet, the average cost of public works projects was slashed by 40 percent.[235]

There are, however, some caveats, and serious ones. When school districts award competitive contracts, it results in lower spending on the schools' "central task" of core-course instruction, and contracting out "is not positively associated with district performance."[236] An extensive study of service contracting in local governments found "only limited support for the proposition that competition improves contracting performance" (although, obviously, the study did find support).[237]

When all is said and done, however, the bulk of evidence suggests that competition correlates, and positively so, with lower costs in delivering public services.

PRACTICAL PRIVATIZATION: LESSONS LEARNED

What should public administrators keep in mind when contracting with private companies? Here are eight major lessons learned:[238]

- *Strong public support and a political champion probably are prerequisites for privatization.*
- *Select potential candidates for privatization carefully.* Public programs that have a distinctive business profile (such as lotteries, airports,

and college dormitories) are the easiest to contract out successfully.

■ *Privatize gradually.* Wholesale, rapid privatization often reduces political support.

■ *Develop an accurate costing system before contracts are solicited.* Define outputs, set benchmarks, and use *activity-based costing*, an accounting technique that covers all the expenses of providing a service.

■ *Inject the maximum amount of competition possible.*

■ *Use well-defined contracts that set performance measures and incorporate evaluation procedures.*

■ *Mitigate the impact of privatization on displaced public employees.* Advise them of benefits and help them find jobs. This not only reduces employee resistance to privatization, but also is the ethical thing to do.

■ *Recognize that the weakest links in the contracting process for all three levels of government are those of managing the contract and achieving accountability.* It is these two areas that require the greatest attention from public administrators when privatizing services.[239] Three promising steps in these regards are upgrading of the acquisition workforce's authority, resources, and talent (one analysis found that "an embedded culture of uncertainty avoidance" among senior procurement managers "invariably" led to their not using more cost-effective acquisition methods[240]); appointing agency-based chief acquisition officers who make contracting decisions in coordination with the government's central budget office; and establishing in agencies policymaking "business councils" chaired by department heads and composed of top agency officers in acquisitions, finance, and human and information resources.[241]

THE BUSINESSES OF GOVERNMENTS

We have been describing how governments *contract* with businesses to implement public policies. But governments also *create* businesses to implement

their policies. These creations are called *public enterprises*, or entities chartered by governments that provide market-oriented public services. An example is a state-supported telephone company. Often, but not always, these enterprises are meant to become self-funding.

In the United States, state-owned enterprises account for a modest 1 percent of its gross domestic product (GDP), in contrast to thirteen countries with market economies similar to that of the United States, where these enterprises account for an average of 9 percent of GDP.[242] This is not to say that American public enterprises are trivial. Although a definitive census of public enterprises is nonexistent,[243] they nonetheless are a major means by which American governments implement public policies.

Enterprising Washington

Washington has both embraced and eschewed owning businesses, but has left a legacy of some powerful federal enterprises that have unequaled power and autonomy.

The Evolution of Federal Enterprises The first federal enterprise is generally thought to be the First Bank of the United States, chartered in 1792, although President Theodore Roosevelt's purchase in 1903 of the Panama Railroad marks Washington's involvement with government enterprises as we presently understand them.

With the onslaught of the Great Depression, Washington took a renewed interest in the government enterprise, an interest that redoubled during World War II. By 1953, Washington was "the largest electric power producer in the country, the largest insurer, the largest lender and the largest borrower, the largest landlord and the largest tenant, the largest holder of grazing land and timberland, the largest owner of grain, the largest warehouse operator, the largest ship owner, and the largest truck fleet operator."[244]

Such public enterprise did not rest easily with corporate America, which launched a concerted drive in the 1950s to bar the feds from competing with business. Through a series of executive orders, most federal enterprises were reorganized or dismantled. Still, some federal enterprises remain formidable, providing electricity and other benefits to nearly 9 million people in the Tennessee Valley, a contiguous territory that spans seven states; transporting all of the nation's 25 million railroad travelers; and delivering mail to more than 300 million people.

The Federal Quasi Government

Aside from the fifteen cabinet departments, and an additional eighty-eight executive agencies and organizations, there are more than 115 federal "entities" that ooze among the government's branches and society's sectors. These entities, with the partial exception of federal corporations (discussed shortly), are specifically exempted from the sixteen major statutes that address a dozen "key" standards of governance, accountability, and transparency that apply to line departments and agencies.[245]

This "federal quasi government"[246] is as ill-understood as it is important. It is officially composed of five types of entities,[247] but commonly accepted definitions of them are rare, if not nonexistent, in Washington, and federal agencies themselves differ over which entities should be included in which category.

What is known about the five entities comprising this quasi government follows.

Services for Federal Workers

There is "a large but unknown number" of *nonappropriated fund instrumentalities* that are created and funded not by Congress, but by agencies, to provide services to federal personnel; an example is military post exchanges, which sell discounted goods to soldiers. "There is no official or commonly understood definition" of these services.[248]

Research Centers

The thirty-nine *federally funded research and development centers*, such as Argonne National Laboratory, are private organizations created by federal agencies to meet long-term federal research needs. Agencies contract with these centers to conduct research, and they are awarded a modest 14 percent of all federal expenditures for research and development.[249]

"Other"

There are fifty *other federally established organizations* that do "not fit" into any other category, have "narrowly defined" missions that "vary substantially," and include "private, nonprofit organizations, institutes, banks, funds, foundations, and other organizations."[250] Organizations in this capacious, catchall category range from Amtrak, the nation's passenger railway, to Gallaudet University.

Government Corporations

Although no official "comprehensive descriptive definition" of *federal government corporations* exists,[251] we do know that, generally speaking, they are: organizations "established by the U.S. government in a corporate form by a federal charter for a public purpose"; that this purpose is "predominantly of a business nature"; and that they are expected to "produce revenue and are potentially self-sustaining."[252] Figure 11-1 outlines some of their characteristics.

There are at least nine differing tallies of the number of federal corporations, ranging from eighteen to fifty-eight,[253] but the GAO's latest count of twenty-three strikes us as a particularly careful one.[254] Eighteen of these twenty-three, such as the Tennessee Valley Authority, are "wholly owned" by the federal government, and five, such as the Federal Deposit Insurance Corporation, have "mixed ownership" involving the feds and private parties.[255] Twenty-two "self-reported," mostly small, government corporations have annual gross outlays that exceed the combined gross outlays of the departments of Commerce, Education, and Energy.[256]

The Government Corporation Control Act of 1945 is the basic policy governing government corporations, and, by most accounts, it was conscientiously followed until the late 1970s, when special interests eroded oversight. As a consequence, "legislation has been enacted and executive action has been taken which...conflict with both the letter and spirit" of the act.[257] No federal corporation fully complies with all fifteen major statutes that pertain to ethical, open, and well-managed government, and greater oversight is direly needed.[258]

Government-Sponsored Enterprises

Although "there is no broad-based statutory definition" of a *government-sponsored enterprise (GSE)*,[259] it can be loosely defined as a financial intermediary created by Congress that directs capital to a particular sector of the economy. Figure 11-1 sketches its basic features.

Currently, there are five GSEs (although federal agencies dispute even this narrow number[260]), and their missions are to make housing or farming more affordable.[261] Although each GSE is regulated by a federal agency, none is subject to oversight under the Government Corporation Control Act, and virtually none of the regulations imposed by the Securities and Exchange Commission apply to them. None pay corporate income taxes.

One GSE is owned entirely by shareholders and sells stock on the New York Stock Exchange; two are member-owned cooperatives; and the two largest are owned (as of 2008) by the U.S. Treasury Department. Together, these five GSEs control about $7 *trillion* in financial obligations.

GSEs loan money to banks, and these loans have the "implicit guarantee" of the federal government. Hence, the risk to financial institutions is minimal if the recipients of their loans default, and this minimal risk, in turn, results in lower interest rates on loans that are backed by GSEs. Lower interest rates greatly ease buying a house or improving a farm, but Washington's implicit guarantee burdens taxpayers because it amounts to a costly public subsidization of GSEs.[262]

Ever since Congress created the first GSE, in 1916, federal officials have staunchly insisted that Washington does not back GSE loans, and that the "implicit guarantee" that it does back them is merely an unwarranted but comforting assumption by the marketplace. Nevertheless, Congress in 1987 spent more than $4 billion to bail out an over-extended GSE, the Farm Credit System, thereby undermining its contention, and, in 2008, this congressional fig leaf finally and forever fell.

In that year, the two biggest government-sponsored enterprises, the Federal National Mortgage Association (Fannie Mae) and the Federal Home Loan Mortgage Corporation (Freddie Mac), which Congress had charged with expanding home ownership, were placed into "conservatorship" by the secretary of the treasury, effectively declaring them to be bankrupt. The government guaranteed their finances with $200 billion in taxpayers' money; then doubled it to $400 billion in 2009; and then, on Christmas Eve of that year, the treasury department stuffed their stockings by announcing that it would cover over the next three years *any* losses that exceeded $400 billion—effectively

writing Fannie and Freddie a blank check. Fannie, Freddie, and, inferentially, the three other GSEs, "now in effect have an explicit U.S. government guarantee behind them."[263]

Fannie, Freddie, Fraud, and Fear

Congress created Fannie in 1938 as a federal agency, but in 1968, in a cynical ploy to lower, at least technically, federal deficits, the president and Congress converted it into a government-sponsored enterprise, owned by stockholders, thus removing its finances from the government's books. (It worked, at least for a while; in 1969 there was actually a modest budget surplus of about $3 billion.) When Fannie came on line as a GSE in 1970, Congress chartered Freddie as its shareholder-owned competitor.

The Rise of Fannie and Freddie Both GSEs quickly prospered. During the three decades preceding their bankruptcies, they roughly doubled their mortgage holdings and mortgage-backed securities every five years,[264] and, by the early 2000s, they owned more than four-fifths of all the assets owned by all GSEs combined.[265]

How they achieved such dominance, however, is another story. In an effort to burnish their stocks' image, and thereby raise their executives' multi-million dollar bonuses, Fannie and Freddie were engaging in criminal accountancy that paralleled practices in other businesses that were exposed in 2002, causing the bankruptcies of Enron and other major firms. Their regulatory body responded by firing Freddie's corporate officers and fining it $125 million in 2003, and firing Fannie's executives and fining it $400 million in 2004.

Fannie and Freddie were unfazed. Both GSEs, which for years had numbered among the top twenty lobbying spenders in Washington,[266] lobbied Congress so heavily to lighten even further their already featherweight regulations that, in 2006, the Federal Election Commission fined Freddie a record sum for violating election laws.

The Fall of Fannie and Freddie In part because of their criminal records, the treasury secretary did more in 2008 than merely rescue Fannie and

Freddie from looming bankruptcy. He also fired their top officers; abolished their boards of directors; convinced Congress to close down and replace their regulatory agency; ended dividends to stockholders and stripped them of their right to govern (although both GSEs could continue to sell stock); and, mercifully, banned them from lobbying.

Why did they fail? Certainly the meltdown of the housing market that began in 2007 was a factor; Fannie's and Freddie's stock prices plunged by more than 90 percent in just twelve months. Of greater significance, decades of increasingly lax regulation, abetted by Congress, attenuated their "risk-management deficiencies," which, in turn "compromised their safety and soundness"[267] But the root cause was that each GSE had always been saddled with two, diametrically opposed missions: To make as many home loans as possible, and to make as much money as possible for themselves and their shareholders. "The conflict between these two goals caused the companies to nearly collapse."[268]

Worse, throughout their entire life spans prior to their being place into conservatorship, their warring missions resulted in, to quote the GAO's delicate phrase, "a mixed record on achieving housing mission objectives."[269] Astoundingly, Fannie and Freddie managed to attain this pathetic record even though they were endowed with huge federal subsidies in the forms of tax exemptions and an implicit guarantee of their loans, and even though they were largely unfettered by federal oversight and routinely committed crimes to inflate profits. In 2011, a major rating agency lowered Fannie's and Freddie's credit ratings (and those of the remaining three GSEs, in whole or part, as well).

Why did the government salvage them? Because they were too big to fail. Fannie and Freddie are the nation's biggest source of housing finance. Historically, they held or guaranteed nearly half of all home mortgages in the United States,[270] a proportion that, with the advent of a steep recession beginning in 2007 and concomitant tight lending by private lenders, has burgeoned to 65 percent. At $6.7 trillion, the financial obligations of these two government-sponsored enterprises are so gigantic, amounting to almost half of the gross federal debt and more than a third of

the nation's GDP, that their default could place the entire economy in crisis.[271]

In 2011, the administration proposed to Congress three options, each of which called for withdrawing much of Fannie's and Freddie's market presence, and relying far more on private lenders to finance housing.[272] It seems clear that, within a decade, Fannie and Freddie will no longer be the almost omnipotent behemoths that they once were.

State and Local Enterprises and the Public Authority

State and local enterprises precede their introduction in federal circles by at least 200 years, and continue to be a vibrant part of governing at the grassroots.

What Are Public Authorities?
Grassroots enterprises are managed by public authorities, which are the state or local equivalents of Washington's government corporations. More formally, a *public authority* is a corporate form of special purpose government, or part of a public agency, that is chartered by one or more state or general purpose local governments, or by popular vote, to fulfill a business-oriented public mission.

The rub in this definition is the confounding presence of *special districts*, which replicate almost all the characteristics of public authorities, except that they are (at least in theory) governmental in form and are charged with noncommercial public missions. Figure 11-1 lists some of the characteristics that public authorities and special districts have in common.

Confusingly, about half of the allegedly more communal, political, and governmental special districts conduct businesslike services, such as waterworks, that are, supposedly, the sole preserve of the more managerial, technical, and commercial public authorities. The obverse is equally present. Disney World, a market-oriented enterprise by any standard, is not a public authority but is a special district—the Reedy Creek Improvement District.

Public authorities and special districts are blithely unbothered by these definitional debates and, as a practical matter, define themselves in terms of whatever works. "While it might not seem right to equate government corporations [i.e., public authorities] with special districts, there is also nothing exactly wrong with this equation."[273]

A Slippery Slew In light of the confusion surrounding public authorities, it is not surprising that we know little about them, including how many there are. Although "many scholars have suggested that there are between 10,000 to 12,000,"[274] no one really knows, and at least five differing counts range, astonishingly, from 5,000 to 18,000.[275] The number of public authorities, however, likely is much more. Once again, those pesky special districts are the issue. The Census Bureau has given us an impressively precise, and big, tally of independent special districts: There are 37,381 of them, a count that does *not* include an unknown, but large, number of special districts that are parts of public agencies.[276]

What Do Public Authorities Do? Public authorities are responsible for a surprisingly broad array of public enterprises. Almost half, 45 percent, own and manage public housing; 18 percent are engaged in environmental protection, principally sewerage, solid waste disposal, and pollution control; 14 percent are involved in economic development; 7 percent run public-use facilities, such as gardens, galleries, golf courses, parks, parking garages, stadiums, museums, and zoos; 4 percent deal with transportation, including not only bridges and roads, but also mass transit; 3 percent manage health care facilities; 2 percent administer ports; and 1 percent each own and operate utilities or finance educational programs, primarily student loans and campus construction. Five percent of public authorities operate more than one enterprise.[277]

Pervasive Public Authorities The scope of these businesses is daunting. They invest more dollars in new capital facilities than all state and municipal governments combined.[278]

Local governments own and operate essentially all of the nation's commercial airports, 85 percent of the country's municipal water supplies and wastewater plants, four-fifths of all local public transportation systems, a fourth of the nation's electrical plants (more than 2,000 electric utilities serving over 16 million customers), and 800 municipal natural gas utilities that are bankrolled by nearly 4 million customer accounts.[279]

The Evolution of the Public Authority

Public authorities not only have broad branches, but also deep roots.

Origins In the eighteenth century, and likely earlier, various kinds of cooperative associations arose in states and communities that could reasonably be identified as prototype public authorities.[280] The "fountain societies," for instance, were publicly owned water supply companies, and other precursors of public authorities dealt with civic, educational, and even ecclesiastical affairs.

In the early 1800s, state governments dramatically accelerated their use of public authorities, and chartered "bodies corporate" to build bridges, turnpikes, and canals, including New York's massive Erie Canal system. State legislatures chartered *all* bodies corporate, whether public or private, and the demarcation between the two was dim. Not infrequently, state legislators and corporate executives would expedite, through graft, the granting of charters for businesses, including businesses that invested public funds in private enterprises. When these businesses failed, as they often did, states and localities would default on the debts that they had incurred by investing in them; in the 1870s, "approximately one-fourth of the indebtedness of major local governments was in default."[281] These scandals persisted well into the 1920s.

A Progressive Push As a consequence of these state and local defaults, the reformers comprising the Progressive Movement inserted in virtually all state constitutions prohibitions against lending public money. Of course, the grassroots governments still needed to finance their various enterprises, and, to accommodate this necessity (as well as their desire to extricate partisan patronage from government[282]), the Progressives pushed through the first incorporation laws, which, for the first time, delineated the differences between public and private corporations. The Port Authority of New York and New Jersey, with over 9,000 employees, was established during this period, and "the history of the modern-day government corporation truly began" with its founding in 1921.[283]

The Federal Factor Even though the Progressive Movement was a momentous motivator, it was the federal government, under President Franklin Delano Roosevelt, that gave a huge impetus to public authorities. FDR saw in them a major means of battling the Great Depression.

Accordingly, in 1934, Roosevelt drafted "model legislation" for state and local governments to follow in creating pubic authorities. By 1948, forty-one of the forty-eight states had adopted variants of FDR's model legislation.[284]

Of deeper impact, Roosevelt greatly eased the financing of public authorities' infrastructure projects by energizing municipal bonds, specifically, money-generating revenue bonds (discussed in Chapter 8), which public authorities relied on (and still do) almost exclusively to fund their construction projects.

First, Roosevelt made revenue bonds more marketable by broadening and strengthening their federal income tax exemption. The Securities Act of 1933 and the Securities Exchange Act of 1934 were his vehicles of choice in this respect.

Simultaneously, he made state and local authorities an offer they could not refuse. He, in effect, said that Washington would buy all the revenue bonds that they could issue. And he meant it; in 1933, the Reconstruction Finance Corporation, one of two federal agencies that bought these bonds, accounted for more than half of *all* federal outlays.[285] Between 1931 and 1936, the number of states permitting the sale of revenue bonds rose from thirty-one to forty.[286] Today, all states allow their use.

Crossroads and Motivations By the end of World War II, state and local authorities stood at the head of several crossroads. One option was that, as their federal patron had intended, they could "self-liquidate," or close down after their capital costs were paid off and turn their functions over to state or local governments. Another alternative

was that they could continue charging users for their services, and the revenues could be deposited in state and local general funds. Or, public authorities could keep the user fees flowing into their own coffers and use those revenues to finance new projects. If they took this final route, public authorities would emerge as independent agencies.

For the most part, they chose the final route. Even though FDR's bureaucracy for financing grassroots authorities was dismantled during the 1950s, state and local authorities that the feds had originally underwritten, and thousands more since, live on and prosper in their mostly monopolistic marketplaces.

Creating, Governing, and Administering Public Authorities

Over the centuries, public authorities have evolved into powerful enterprises that vary widely in their founding, governance, and administration.

Creating Public Authorities "Authorities have from their inception been extremely 'ad hoc' in nature."[287]

New York and Pennsylvania developed the two basic models for creating public authorities. In New York, public authorities are individually chartered by the state legislature. In Pennsylvania, however, local governments can create public authorities through a number of different devices, and with little or no interference from the state. More than two-thirds of the states use the Pennsylvanian approach; in fact, only New York and Maine require that the state legislature enact specific legislation to establish each public authority.[288]

Governing Public Authorities Public authorities function in an astonishingly unconstrained environment. They often have vague geographic boundaries, and may lack a specific constituency.[289]

In most states, no single department even maintains an accurate listing of active public authorities, nor do authorities report their finances to the Securities and Exchange Commission—which private businesses must do.[290] In fact, the municipal bond market—the second largest securities market in the nation, which has as its foundation the public authority—is the only major securities market that remains virtually free from oversight by the Securities and Exchange Commission.[291]

State and local authorities are headed by boards of directors, typically of "three or more citizens," who usually serve without compensation. Most are appointed by elected officials, or by the board itself. Board members serve staggered, fixed terms, and almost never may be fired by the officials who appointed them, nor by anyone else, except for cause (i.e., by breaking the law).[292]

Board directors tend to have business or professional backgrounds, and the lack of interest among many of them in the affairs of the authorities that they head has been amply documented, with a significant number appointing surrogates to attend board meetings, but who, in fact, rarely attend. Vacancies on these boards are frequent.[293]

Although there are some signs that these boards are trying, tepidly, to engage more citizens,[294] public oversight is minimal. Many board meetings are not announced; about six citizens, on average, attend these meetings (not surprising, as authorities "typically hold their meetings on weekday mornings.... and the opportunities for average citizens to speak are extremely limited"[295]); and the press does not regularly attend nearly two-thirds of board meetings (for over a third of the authorities, in fact, the media never attend meetings).[296]

Administering Authorities Public authorities are managed by executive directors, over four-fifths of whom are appointed by their boards and the remainder by the chief elected executive or legislature of the government that chartered the authority.[297]

Independently conducted surveys, all taken at roughly the same time, confirm that these executive directors, in comparison with city managers (who are among their closest counterparts), have much more secure jobs,[298] are considerably less educated,[299] and are significantly less experienced in their professions.[300] "In a fundamental difference...authority executives deal with fewer competing demands and expectations" than do city managers.[301] Majorities of both authority executives and city and county managers agree (unusually so, for they agree on nothing else) that authority executives are far freer of political pressures than are city

and county managers. Small wonder, perhaps, that not one of the responding senior managers of 217 large special districts expressed an iota of dissatisfaction with his or her job.[302]

Public Power and Quasi Governments

There is little doubt that the administrators of federal corporations and state and local authorities have power. How well have they used it?

Libertine Liberties At the federal level, it is clear that some major government enterprises have failed to meet their ostensible missions of becoming financially self-sustaining. Every year, Congress directly allocates, on average, more than $60 billion to eighteen of its twenty-three government corporations, or nearly four-fifths of them, and more than $4 billion to seventeen, a third, of its fifty "other" federal enterprises.[303]

In the states and communities, the unique freedom enjoyed by authority executives appears to have some deleterious economic consequences. The per-capita costs of services provided by special purpose governments generally are higher than the same services provided by general purpose governments.[304]

Authority costs are high, at least in part, because of incompetent management. Here are some examples:[305]

- The Port Authority of New York and New Jersey built a $21 million luggage tunnel at a major airport without first checking if the airlines wanted it. They did not. The tunnel remains unused and boarded up.
- New York's Dormitory Authority awarded millions of dollars in construction contracts to firms banned by other public agencies because of the firms' ties to organized crime and their long records of violations.
- Public housing, which engages the energies of close to half of all public authorities, is a particular administrative sore point. In the early 1990s, Washington unilaterally took over the nation's worst public housing, expelling in the process the local housing authorities that had managed them with an awesome ineptness. Examples include the chair of the New York

City authority who redecorated her office in pink at a cost of $350,000, and the one fourth of public housing units in New Orleans that were vacant because they were unfit for human habitation (and this was *before* Hurricane Katrina struck).[306]

Corruption is present as well, and numerous instances of fraud, kickbacks, extortion, embezzlement, and other crimes have been documented that involved millions of dollars and which had been committed by board members, executive directors, or employees of public authorities at all levels of government.[307]

Has there been a misuse of managerial freedom by public authorities? Yes; the examples are too legion to conclude otherwise. Is this misuse endemic? We do not know.

Infrastructure or Accountability? Without question, public authorities have left large legacies—roads, skyscrapers, power grids, to name a few—that might not otherwise be present because some lazy, lugubrious general purpose governments were not fulfilling their responsibilities. It is telling in this regard that, in states with centralized state governments and local governments that proactively provide services, there are often fewer authorities and districts, and they clearly engage in "less governmental activity."[308]

Still, public authorities present persistent problems of accountability. Despite attacks from both the left and right, "public authorities have withstood such assaults practically unscathed and continue to claim rights of independent management."[309]

THE INDEPENDENT SECTOR: EXPERIENCES IN INTERDEPENDENCE

Perhaps no sector in the maze of intersectoral administration has become more prominent more quickly than has the independent sector. As we explained in the introduction to Part II, the *independent sector* is composed of those organizations that are created by private interests, are privately owned, and do not seek profits. Figure 11-1 provides details.

Nine out of ten American adults[310] belong to at least one of America's 1.8 million nonprofit associations.[311] The independent sector owns about 5 percent of all net worth in the private sector; accounts for close to 6 percent of GDP;[312] employs more than 9 percent of the civilian workforce;[313] and its employment growth significantly outpaces those in the private and public sectors.[314]

Serving Themselves or Serving Others

There are two principal types of nonprofit associations. *Member-serving organizations* include labor unions, political parties, and private clubs, among others, and they exist to provide benefits to their members. There are about 500,000 of them. *Public-serving*, or *public-benefit, organizations*, include universities, foundations, charities, and churches, among others, and they exist to provide benefits to the people. There are about 1.3 million of them.[315]

Public-serving organizations dominate the third sector. Nine out of ten of all full-time employees in the independent sector are employed by public-serving nonprofit organizations,[316] and their revenues account for about two-thirds of all nonprofit revenue.[317] The primary revenue sources of public-benefit organizations are fees (such as the tuition paid by students at independent colleges), at 51 percent, a proportion that has held remarkably steady over twenty years; government grants and contracts, at 37 percent and rising; and private giving, at a modest 12 percent and falling.[318]

Both public-serving and member-serving nonprofit organizations are exempt from federal, state, and local taxes. Public-serving associations, however, benefit from a unique tax policy that applies only to them. Under Section 501 (c) (3) of the U.S. Internal Revenue Code, federal taxpayers who donate to public-serving organizations may deduct from their taxable income the value of their donations, and state and local governments have followed the federal lead in adopting this policy.

Governments and the Independent Sector

Privatization applies not only to for-profit businesses, but also to nonprofit organizations.

Washington and the Independent Sector

Independent organizations are "key partners in delivering federal programs and services," and it appears that federal funding of the third sector is significant.[319] Analysts estimate that Washington transfers, either directly or through third parties, about the same amount of money to the independent sector that it contracts out to the private sector.[320]

Federal fiscal support of independent organizations has more than doubled in real buying power over twenty-four years. The increase is attributable to the growth in Medicare, Medicaid, and some indexed income assistance programs, such as public housing and food stamps. This doubling came at a price: Federal spending on the remaining programs that habitually rely on nonprofit organizations to deliver publicly funded services declined by nearly a fifth over the same period.[321]

Although a database has been under development since 2006, it remains the case that there are no comprehensive statistical data that track federal support to nonprofit organizations.[322] Figure 11-2 illustrates why this is: The bulk of federal funding ends up in nonprofit coffers only after it has been handled by many hands.

Some federal funds, such as Medicare's subsidies to the elderly, are transferred to nonprofit organizations because individual recipients have chosen to use their services; the feds annually channel perhaps $145 billion to independent organizations in these "fee-for-service payments." Some, such as many federal grants to the states, are passed through the states to nonprofit organizations, or to local governments that then send them to nonprofit organizations; each year, the emerging sector receives an estimated $55 billion in this fashion from just two federal grant programs. And some, such as research grants to independent universities, flow directly from federal agencies to third-sector organizations; Washington annually disburses $25 billion in grants (federal grants comprise nearly 10 percent of public-benefit organizations' total income[323]), and $10 billion in contracts, directly to independent recipients. In addition, each year the feds provide them with "approximately $2.5 billion in loan guarantees and $450 million in loans."[324]

Washington also supports the third sector indirectly, and foregoes "approximately $50 billion" in annual federal tax revenues as a result of its policy of exempting nonprofit organizations from taxation.[325]

The States and the Independent Sector States and their local governments transfer well over $100 billion in grants and contracts each year directly to nonprofit organizations. Three-quarters of this sum comes from the federal government in the form of pass-through grants (explained in Chapter 8) to the states.[326]

More than seven out of ten of all state agencies contract with nonprofit associations to deliver

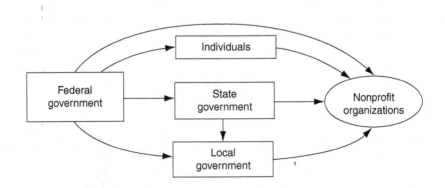

FIGURE 11-2

Paths of Federal Funds to Nonprofit Organizations

Source: U.S. Government Accountability Office, *Nonprofit Sector: Increasing Numbers and Key Role in Delivering Federal Services*, GAO-07-1084T (Washington, DC: U.S. Government Printing Office, 2007), p. 8.

services.[327] Those states that make available greater levels of funding for nonprofit organizations also have more nonprofit organizations overall, and more nonprofit organizations of large size.[328]

Perhaps of greater significance, state governments, like the federal government, also subsidize the independent sector through their tax policies. Every state exempts charities from the local property tax, saving them from $9 to $15 billion per year; two dozen of the forty-five states with a sales tax do not tax purchases by charitable organizations, and another sixteen provide limited exemptions, totaling about $2.5 billion annually; and the states' relief of charities from the corporate income tax, levied by forty-five states, nets the independent sector close to $4 billion per annum.[329]

Nonprofit organizations' fundraising activities can affect the availability to themselves of state funds.[330] It seems likely that this funding could continue with relative ease, as state administrators rely less on quantitative measures to determine the performance of their nonprofit contractors, at least compared with their for-profit contractors, and rely more on qualitative judgments.[331]

Communities and the Independent Sector

Cities and counties contract out 8 percent of all their services to independent organizations,[332] the same percentage as twenty-five years earlier.[333] Even though these governments are somewhat leery about contracting with third-sector associations, and prefer contracting out to them services that have little likelihood of failing,[334] they are more satisfied with how nonprofit organizations deliver their services than they are with how for-profit corporations provide them. Although cities and counties bring back in-house 24 percent of the contracts that they have with independent organizations, they reel in 33 percent, or almost two-fifths more, of the contracts that they sign with private companies.[335]

Like their state counterparts, local administrators favor qualitative measures of their nonprofit contractors' performance over quantitative ones, which they reserve for their business contractors.[336] Unlike their dealings with private companies, local governments shy away from inserting formal rewards and penalties into their contracts with third-sector organizations, preferring to rectify

problems of productivity through conversation and, less so, with technical assistance.[337]

But contracts do not tell the whole story, and it appears that *most* (52 percent) nonprofit organizations that collaborate with local agencies do not bother with contracts at all, but rely instead on informal cooperative arrangements. Astonishingly, "although (as expected) local governments are more likely to provide funding and equipment with formal agreements than without," a fourth of local public dollars that flow to the third sector "still are provided outside the contracting area."[338]

That independent-sector executives are able to induce local administrators to furnish on faith a fourth of their funding of nonprofits is impressive testimony to their powers of persuasion. It is even more impressive that they do so in light of the fact that "nonprofit executives generally exhibit a stronger current of negativity toward intersectoral partnership than do their public sector counterparts" in local governments.[339] Those independent organizations that are smaller and younger, and those organizations with executive directors who are men, or who have never been employed by government, or whose attitudes toward collaboration with government were negatively shaped by past experience, are the most resistant to collaborating with local governments.[340]

Who Benefits?

The public and nonprofit sectors "demonstrate a remarkable similarity in the benefits they seek" from each other, in that "the motivation to partner is driven by a desire to secure those resources most scarce for the respective sector." For the public sector, those scarce resources are expertise and the capacity to govern; for the independent sector, it is money.[341]

The leading emerging-sector recipients of governments' contracts and grants are those that work in human services, a mission to which half of all nonprofit organizations dedicate themselves.[342] *Human services* are a classification of government policy that encompasses health, culture, recreation, post-secondary education, and social services. *Social services* refer to job training; day care; and, by far the fiscally dominant category, "individual and family services"—that is, welfare.[343]

Seventy percent of the revenue collected from all sources by public-serving nonprofit organizations flows to those that deliver human services,[344] and governments play a large role in this figure—more than two-fifths of *all* governmental spending on human services is disbursed to nonprofit organizations.[345] Governments' contribution to the total revenues of third-sector associations that provide these services range from a tenth for arts and cultural programs to more than half for social services.[346]

▶ A CASE OF INDEPENDENT GOVERNANCE

Neighborhoods Renascent

How does government by the nonprofit sector work in practice? Neighborhood governance, *or the participation by community-based nonprofit organizations in local governments' policymaking and administration as it pertains to their communities, exemplifies the interrelationships among the sectors in implementing public policy.*

Neighborhood governance takes several forms. Neighborhood associations *are informal groups of community residents that work with local governments to improve their communities. They got their start with the Housing Act of 1949, which required citizen participation in public hearings. Over time, particularly during the 1960s and 1970s, Congress or federal agencies inserted no fewer than 155 provisos federal intergovernmental grants programs that mandated citizen participation in local governmental decision making (U.S. Advisory Council on Intergovernmental Relations, 1979, p. 4).*

Another form is community development corporations, *or organizations that are chartered under state law, created and led by the residents of depressed communities, and link public subsidies with private investment for the purpose of revitalizing those communities, particularly housing. They were created by the Economic Opportunity Act of 1964 and the Demonstration Cities and Metropolitan Development Act of 1966. There are 235 of them (NeighborWorks).*

When it comes to governing neighborhoods, however, the home-grown colossus (it was denied the founding impetus of Congressional legislation) is the residential community association.

Residential community associations, community associations, or common-interest communities, are nonprofit organizations of homeowners or (in a small number of cases) long-term leaseholders that are governed under local real estate contract laws. They have been called "private governments" that are "a cross between local government and the assistant principal for discipline at a very strict high school" (White).

The present form of residential community associations owes no small debt to a public administrationist, Charles Stern Archer, who was central in their creation at "a time when the greatest minds in public administration were interested in the modern form of homeowners associations—when they invented them in 1928" (McKenzie, p. 543).

By 1960, there were fewer than a thousand common-interest communities, but today there are nearly 310,000. In 1970, they were responsible for barely 700,000 housing units and just over 2 million residents; today, there are almost 25 million housing units sheltering 62 million people who are governed by community associations. Since 1980, fully half of all new housing has been placed under the rule of common-interest communities. A fifth of all Americans are members. About 3 percent of the membership serves on their governing boards, and control almost $42 billion in associations' budgets (Community Associations Institute).

There are three types of common-interest communities: *condominium associations,* in which residents of a complex own their own apartments, account for 38 to 42 percent of them; 52 to 55 percent are *homeowners' associations* and other planned communities, composed of owners of detached houses or townhouses, are found mostly in the suburbs; and 5 to 7 percent are *cooperatives,* or *co-ops,* which are associations of residents who lease their apartments and own no part of the building that they inhabit (Community Associations Institute). Residential community associations impose mandatory fees on their members and directly deliver services—most commonly, landscaping, garbage collection, water, sewer, street lights, and

(continued)

(continued)

street maintenance—that are the traditional duties of municipal governments; the typical residential community association, in fact, delivers ten local services (U.S. Advisory Commission on Intergovernmental Relations, 1989, p. 13).

Seven out of every ten residents are satisfied with the services that community associations provide; nearly nine out of ten residents think that their elected governing board members try to satisfy residents; and more than four-fifths believe that they get a "good" or "great" return on their association assessments (Zogby International and Community Associations Institute, pp. 4, 6). As we reviewed in Chapter 1, and discuss further in Chapter 12, these are far higher positives than citizens grant their governments along comparable dimensions.

Most local governments have established formal relations with neighborhood governance groups, and almost seven out of ten cities allocate funds to train neighborhood groups in making decisions for their own neighborhoods, a growing practice (Kearney, p. 30). A small proportion of about a third of all local governments' services is delivered by neighborhood groups to their own neighborhoods, either as a result of government encouragement (3 percent, with crime prevention patrols and programs for the elderly and the arts leading the way) or actual contracts (2 percent, with libraries and child day care the leaders) (Morley, pp. 44, 40).

Despite their intrusion into areas that have been exclusively governmental preserves, 56 percent of their officers report that the level of cooperation between their associations and local governments is good, and 71 percent state that they had been treated fairly by local officials (U.S. Advisory Commission on Intergovernmental Relations, 1989, p. 20). However, 87 percent, a rising proportion, of community association residents would not "want to see more government control" of their associations (Zogby International and Community Associations Institute, p. 5)

If there is a lesson to be drawn from neighborhood governments, perhaps it is this: Smaller governing can be better governance. ■

Note: Figure for community development corporations is for 2011. Data for residents' opinions regarding community associations are for 2009, and data on the numbers of association-governed communities, housing units, residents, boards, and budgets are for 2010.

Sources: U.S. Advisory Commission on Intergovernmental Relations, *Citizen Participation in the American Federal System,* A-73 (Washington, DC: U.S. Government Printing Office, 1979); NeighborWorks, *NeighborWorks Lookup* (Washington, DC: Author, 2011), www.nw.org/network/utilities/NWOlookup/asp; Otis White, "Otis White's Urban Notebook," *Governing* (February 2006), p. 17; Evan McKenzie, "Present at the Creation: The Public Administration Profession and Residential Private Government," *Public Administration Review* 71 (July/August 2011), pp. 543–545; Community Associations Institute, *Industry Data* (Falls Church, VA: Author, 2011), http://www.caionline.org/about/facts.cfm; Zogby International and Community Associations Institute, *What Do Americans Say about Their Community Associations? You Might Be Surprised* (New York and Falls Church, VA: Authors, 2009); Richard C. Kearney, "Reinventing Government and Battling Budget Crises: Manager and Municipal Government Actions in 2003," *Municipal Year Book, 2005* (Washington, DC: International City/County Management Association, 2005), pp. 27–32; Elaine Morley, "Patterns in the Use of Alternative Service Delivery Approaches," *Municipal Year Book, 1989* (Washington, DC: International City Management Association, 1989), pp. 33–44; and U.S. Advisory Commission on Intergovernmental Relations, *Residential Community Associations: Private Governments in the Intergovernmental System?* A-112 (Washington, DC: U.S. Government Printing Office, 1989).

The Third Sector and the Other Two

There is some systematic research (not a lot) that yields insight on how the third sector compares with the private sector, and how it interacts with the public sector, in delivering services. We close our discussion of the emerging sector with a brief review of some of these findings.

■ *Citizens' confidence in the third sector's ability to deliver public policies is high.* When asked in whom they had "the most confidence to deliver services on the public's behalf," 42 percent of the general public said government, 29 percent cited nonprofits, and a modest 17 percent said "private contractors."[347] Paradoxically, although government agencies have shorter (or no) waiting lists of prospective clients than nonprofit organizations, and charge lower (or no) fees to clients, the clients of government agencies are less satisfied with the services they receive than are the clients of comparable nonprofit organizations.[348]

- *Nonprofit organizations and for-profit companies perform at comparable levels of quality in delivering public services.* Nonprofit service centers are *not* more likely (as one might reasonably assume) than for-profit centers to serve more disadvantaged clients; neither type of center is consistently more effective in increasing their clients' earning and employment rates; and both types perform better when monetary incentives are included in their government contracts.[349]

- *Elites value the third sector more than the other two.* Federal and business managers were asked to identify which institution— the federal government, state and local governments, businesses, or nonprofit organizations— would they have "the most confidence in" to implement four publicly relevant functions. Nonprofit organizations essentially swept the field, with federal and business managers typically giving higher ratings to the independent sector than they gave even to their own sectors.[350] Similarly, a stunning 44 percent of college seniors cited the nonprofit sector as the institution in which they had the most confidence to deliver services, followed by government contractors, at 16 percent, and with government at a screechingly bottom-scraping 6 percent.[351] University students also express more trust in nonprofit organizations than government and companies, volunteer for them more frequently, and are more likely to buy health care and education services from them.[352]

- *Prestige and networking matter.* Third-sector organizations that rely heavily on private contributions grow "at a faster rate" if they have "high status, more ties to urban elites," and are more central in networks of organizations.[353]

- *Independent-sector organizations significantly improve their odds for attaining government funding by collaborating with other nonprofit organizations, professionalizing their staffs, and adopting "standard management strategies" for achieving their missions.*[354]

- *Public funding of nonprofit organizations in the form of grants, rather than contracts, may produce superior results.* Contract-based funding forces nonprofit organizations, in contrast to private companies, to hire less professional "temporary staff for core service delivery in government-funded programs," which, in turn, reduces "the effectiveness of the services the agency [provides] to the community."[355]

Fortunately, it appears that governments generally rely heavily on grants when dealing with independent organizations. Recall that federal agencies use two-and-a-half times more grants than contracts (at least as measured in dollars) when hiring nonprofit organizations.[356] There are no data that directly show a heavier use of grants over contracts when state and local governments partner with third-sector organizations, but there is considerable indirect evidence suggesting that this is the case.[357]

- *Governments can manipulate the regulatory environment of the independent sector in ways that affect nonprofit organizations' number, size, diversity, and even the personal characteristics of their executives.*[358]

- *Government funding has a significant, and positive, impact on third-sector organizations.*

Perhaps most notably, a "higher level of government support" for a nonprofit, public-serving organization correlates positively with more dollars donated by individuals, corporations, and foundations relative to charities with proportionately fewer public dollars in their budgets. "A 1 percent increase in government funding is followed by 0.122 percent of rise in public support."[359]

Government funding does many more good things that are even more fundamental to the independent sector's longer term health. The larger the percentage of government funds relative to charitable donations in a nonprofit organization's budget, the more likely that the organization will be: Larger in membership yet leaner in both its board size and its administrative staff; use fewer volunteers; be less dependent on its own earned income; be more racially diverse in its volunteers, staff, and (probably[360]) its board;[361] be more likely to collaborate with other organizations;[362] be less administratively complex,[363] and be "substantially" likelier to "embrace participatory governance practices."[364]

IMPLEMENTATION BY INDIVIDUALS: VOLUNTEERS AND VOUCHERS

Some public policies are implemented directly by people.

Volunteering for Government

Almost three out of ten American adults do volunteer work, devoting fifty median hours to such service per year.[365] Over a fourth of volunteers volunteer for governments, and more than six out of ten work in the independent sector.[366] Regardless of sector, however, many volunteers dedicate their energies to governmentally related missions. Over a fourth of these 63 million volunteers are involved with "educational or youth services," 14 percent work in "social or community service," 6 percent volunteer for "civic and political" affairs, and 1 percent for "public safety."[367] Over a fourth of Americans report that they have participated in community crime watches.[368]

Washington's Volunteers

Congress prohibits the federal government from using volunteers except in unusual or specific circumstances, such as during emergencies or to further the educational goals of students.

A paradox: federal policymakers enthusiastically have subsidized millions of volunteers to work everywhere but in federal agencies. In 1961, the Peace Corps was formed, sending American volunteers abroad; in 1965, VISTA, now AmeriCorps, began channeling volunteers to needy American communities. Since then, the Police Corps, Volunteers for Prosperity, Senior Corps, Learn and Serve America, Community Emergency Response Teams, Neighborhood Watch Programs, Volunteers in Police Service, a Medical Reserve Corps, and a Fire Corps have been founded as federally sponsored volunteer agencies.

State and Local Volunteers

State agencies score a bit better on the use of volunteers than do the feds, but not by much. Twelve percent of state administrators in only seven states report that any volunteers are used in their governments.[369] Not even 2 percent of state agencies use volunteers, and their use is in decline. Corrections and transportation agencies use volunteers the most frequently.[370]

About 70 percent of cities report that they use volunteers in delivering public programs,[371] but volunteers deliver an average of barely 5 percent of twenty-seven municipal and county services, or two-fifths of all local services.[372] This is a decline of nearly two-fifths from twenty-five years earlier, when volunteers helped deliver 8 percent of nearly half of all local services.[373] Volunteers are used most frequently in the operation of cultural and arts programs, museums, and fire prevention.[374]

Volunteers: Productive and Pricey

Volunteers can make possible governmental accomplishments that would not be possible without them.[375] When organizations are well-structured and mix volunteers with paid employees, volunteers' attitudes and commitment to the organization match those of paid employees.[376] In contrast to employees, however, volunteers also donate money to the organizations that they serve.[377]

Contrary to their popular image, however, volunteers can be costly. Consider volunteer firefighters. When the annual costs of recruiting, training, and managing them exceed a relatively small sum (less than $1,000 per firefighter[378]), then "the use of volunteers should be reconsidered" because it is more cost-effective to start adding full-time paid professionals.[379]

Alas, there is no free lunch.

Vouching for Citizen Service

Vouchers are coupons with a dollar value that governments distribute to citizens needing a service; the citizen can choose a provider from competing organizations that the government has selected as eligible, and the government reimburses the organization at a preset rate. Federal, state, and local vouchers are used in "a wide and diverse range of program areas," led by child care, criminal justice, education, employment and training, environmental protection, general assistance, health care, housing, nutrition, and transportation.[380]

Washington's Voluminous Vouchers The Food Stamp Program, initiated in 1964, and Medicare, started in 1965, are the federal government's two principal voucher programs.

Under the Food Stamp Program, the Agriculture Department issues to poor people coupons, which they may use to buy groceries at any store accepting food stamps, and receive a federal discount in the process. More than 33 million people receive over $50 billion in food stamps each year.[381]

Medicare distributes $500 billion in annual health benefits to 50 million people who are sixty-five or older.[382] The Tax Equity and Fiscal Responsibility Act of 1982 allowed participants the option of using a voucher that lets them choose a health maintenance organization from preapproved list, and nearly a third of Medicare recipients use it.[383]

Lesser known federal vouchers (which Washington usually dubs "certificates," a less politically loaded term) focus on a variety of domestic programs. The Workforce Investment Act of 1998 introduced vouchers to federal targeted training programs.[384] Childcare services use vouchers so extensively that they have become the nation's "primary method" of financing child care.[385]

The Department of Housing and Urban Development's Housing Choice Voucher Program (also known as "Section 8," after the section in the Housing Act that authorized it), introduced in 1974, accounts for almost a fourth of the housing units in federally assisted low-income housing programs[386] and helps more than 2 million households pay rent. Washington's use of housing vouchers "reflects a major shift," and their use associates with better outcomes for children, families leaving and avoiding welfare, and workplace success for breadwinners.[387]

State and Local Vouchers State and local governments use vouchers, too, but far from extensively.

Six percent of state administrators in just three states report that their governments use vouchers.[388] Not even 1 percent of all state agencies actually use vouchers, however, and their use is in decline. Social service agencies use them the most.[389]

A modest 3 percent of cities and counties use vouchers to deliver twenty-two local services (over a third of all local services), although their use is increasing. Favored areas are the operation of food programs and shelters for the homeless.[390]

Education, or *school, vouchers*, originated in Milwaukee in 1990, are coupons issued by governments that parents can apply toward the tuition charged by a private school; their children are not required to attend the public school assigned to them by their school district. Although these vouchers come with a high and controversial profile, their impact, though slowly expanding, remains limited. A small fraction of 1 percent of pupils use vouchers to attend private schools. Nearly two dozen "school choice programs," a term that includes tax breaks and privately endowed scholarships, as well as vouchers, are found in sixteen states and the District of Columbia.[391]

NOTES

1. Unless noted otherwise, the following discussion is drawn largely from: Ira Sharkansky, "Government Contracting," *State Government* 53 (Winter 1980), pp. 23–24; Donna Wilson Kirchheimer, "Entrepreneurial Implementation in the U.S. Welfare State," Paper Presented at the 1986 Annual Meeting of the American Political Science Association, Washington, DC, August 28–31, 1986; Jeffrey D. Greene, *Cities and Privatization: Prospects for the New Century* (Upper Saddle River, NJ: Prentice Hall, 2002), p. 8; and some of the author's own thoughts.

2. Gerald W. Johnson and John G. Heilman, "Metapolicy Transition and Policy Implementation: New Federalism and Privatization," *Public Administration Review* 47 (November/December 1987), pp. 468–478. The quotation is on p. 468.

3. James C. Clingermayer, Richard C. Feiock, and Christopher Stream, "Governmental Uncertainty and Leadership Turnover: Influences on Contracting and Sector Choice for Local Services," *State and Local Government Review* 35 (Fall 2003), pp. 150–160. The quotation is on p. 150.

4. Byron E. Price, "The Threat of Privatization: The Impetus Behind Government Performance," *International Journal of Public Administration* 30 (November 2007), pp. 1141–1155. This is a literature review.

5. Martin Tolchin and Susan J. Tolchin, *Pinstripe Patronage: Political Favoritism from the Clubhouse to the White House and Beyond* (Boulder, CO: Paradigm Publishers, 2010).

6. U.S. Advisory Commission on Intergovernmental Relations, *Changing Public Attitudes on Government and Taxes, 1985*, S-14 (Washington, DC: U.S. Government Printing Office, 1985), pp. 28–29.

7. Brookings Institution, as cited in Partnership for Public Service, *Public Opinion on Public Service* (Washington, DC: Author, 2005), p. 6. Public's response is for 1998, and seniors' is for 2002.

8. Primavera Systems, *America, Inc.—Annual Shareholder Management Report* (Crystal City, VA: Author, 2007), p. 1. Figure, 92 percent, is for 2007.

9. Irene S. Rubin, "Who Invented Budgeting in the United States?" *Public Administration Review* 53 (September/October 1993), pp. 438–444. The quotation is on p. 443.

10. Annmarie Hauk Walsh, *The Public's Business: The Politics and Practices of Government Corporations* (Cambridge, MA: MIT Press, 1978), p. 40.

11. Robert T. Kleiman and Anandi P. Sahu, "Privatization as a Viable Alternative for Local Governments: The Case of a Failed Michigan Town," *Contracting Out Government Services*, Paul Seidenstat, ed. (Westport, CN: Praeger, 1999), pp. 151–165. The quotation is on p. 163.

12. Graeme Browning, "Dot.gov Goes Retail," *Federal Computer Week* (May 28, 2001), pp. 21–27. Figure is for 2001. Amazon.com, the largest private Internet vendor, sold $2.8 billion worth of products in 2001.

13. Federal Real Property Council, *FY 2009 Federal Real Property Report: An Overview of the U.S. Federal Government's Real Property Assets* (Washington, DC: U.S. Government Printing Office, 2010), pp. 4–5.

14. Federal Procurement Data System—Next Generation, *Federal Procurement Report, FY 2007, Section III, Agency Views* (Washington, DC: U.S Government Printing Office, 2008), p. 1. Figure includes letter contracts, but not "modifications."

15. U.S. Government Accountability Office, *Federal Contractors: Better Performance Information Needed to Support Agency Contract Award Decisions*, GAO-09-374 (Washington, DC: U.S. Government Printing Office, 2009), Highlights page. Figure is for FY 2007.

16. As derived from data in Federal Procurement Data System—Next Generation, *Federal Procurement Report, FY 2007, Section III*, p. 6.

17. As derived from data in U.S. General Accounting Office, *Federal Acquisition: Trends, Reforms, and Challenges*, GAO/T-OCG-00-7 (Washington, DC: U.S. Government Printing Office, 2000), p. 2.

18. As derived from data in Federal Procurement Data System—Next Generation, *Federal Procurement Report, FY 2007, Section III*, p. 54.

19. U.S. General Accounting Office, *Acquisition Workforce: Status of Agency Efforts to Address Future Needs*, GAO-03-55 (Washington, DC: U.S. Government Printing Office, 2002), p. 1.

20. U.S. House of Representatives, Committee on Government Reform, Minority Staff, Special Investigations Division, *Dollars, Not Sense: Government Contracting Under the*

Bush Administration (Washington, DC: U.S Government Printing Office, 2006), p. i.

21. As derived from data in ibid., p. 3; and Robert Brodsky, "Contracting Spending Dips for the First Time in 13 Years," *Government Executive* (February 3, 2011), http://www.govexec.com. Federal contract dollars increased from $203 billion to $550 billion, 2000–2009.

22. U.S. House of Representatives, Committee on Government Reform, Minority Staff, Special Investigations Division, *Dollars, Not Sense*, p. i.

23. As derived from data in Brodsky, "Contracting Spending Dips for the First Time in 13 Years." Figures are for fiscal years.

24. As derived from data in ibid.; U.S. House of Representatives, Committee on Government Reform, Minority Staff, Special Investigations Division, *Dollars, Not Sense*, p. i; and U.S. Office of Management and Budget, "Historical Tables," *The President's Budget for Fiscal Year 2012* (Washington, DC: U.S. Government Printing Office, 2011), Table 5.4. Figures are for FY 2000–FY 2010.

25. Annie Gowen, "Government Dollars Fuel Wealth: D.C. Enclaves Reap Rewards of Contracting Boom," *Washington Post* (August 15, 2011). Contracting dollars' growth, controlled for inflation, is for 1980–2010. Fifteen percent figure is for 2010 and is derived from data in this source and in Brodsky, "Contracting Spending Dips for the First Time in 13 Years."

26. As derived from data in Paul C. Light, *Creating High Performance Government: A Once-in-a-Generation Opportunity* (New York: Robert F. Wagner School of Public Service, New York University, 2011), p. 24. Federal contract employees grew from an estimated 4.4 million to 7.6 million, 1999–2008.

27. U.S. Office of Management and Budget, as cited in Louis Peck, "America's $320 Billion Shadow Government," *Fiscal Times* (September 28, 2011). Figure is for FY 2010.

28. Kathryn Edwards and Kai Filion, "Outsourcing Poverty: Federal Contracting Pushes Down Wages and Benefits," *Issue Brief*, #250 (Washington, DC: Economic Policy Institute, 2009), p. 1. Figures are for 2006.

29. U.S. General Accounting Office, *Government Contractors: Are Service Contractors Performing Inherently Governmental Functions?* GAO/GGD-92-11 (Washington, DC: U.S. Government Printing Office, 1991), p. 19.

30. Federal Acquisition Institute, *FY 2009 Annual Report on the Federal Acquisition Workforce* (Washington, DC: U.S. Government Printing Office, 2010), Table 9-1.

31. Phillip J. Cooper, "Government Contracts in Public Administration: The Role and Environment of the Contracting Officer," *Public Administration Review* 40 (September/October 1980), pp. 459–468. The quotation is on p. 462.

32. Federal Acquisition Institute, *FY 2009 Annual Report on the Federal Acquisition Workforce*, Table 9-2. In FY 2009, 78 percent were college graduates (in FY 1999, 59 percent were), and most were GS-11 employees.

33. Al Gore, *From Red Tape to Results: Creating a Government That Works Better and Costs Less, Reinventing Federal Procurement* (Washington, DC: U.S. Government Printing Office, 1993), p. 3.

34. As derived from figures in Federal Acquisition Institute, *FY 2009 Annual Report on the Federal Acquisition Workforce*, Table 9-2. Figure, 23 percent, is for FY 2000–FY 2009. More than half of this increase occurred FY 2008–FY 2009.

35. Dwight D. Eisenhower, *Farewell Address to the Nation* (Washington, DC: U.S. Government Printing Office, January 17, 1961), p. 2.

36. U.S. Government Accountability Office, *Sourcing Policy: Initial Agency Efforts to Balance the Government to Contractor Mix in the Multisector Workforce*, GAO-10-744T (Washington, DC: U.S. Government Printing Office, 2010), p. 3.

37. Allan V. Burman, "Six Practical Steps to Improve Contracting," *The Business of Government* (Spring 2009), pp. 62–66. The quotation is on p. 65.

38. U.S. Government Accountability Office, *Federal Acquisition Challenges and Opportunities in the 21st Century*, GAO-07-45SP (Washington, DC: U.S. Government Printing Office, 2006), p. 15.

39. U.S. Government Accountability Office, *Sourcing Policy: Initial Agency Efforts to Balance the Government to Contractor Mix in the Multisector Workforce*, p. 3.

40. Kaifeng Yang and Anthony Kassekert, "Linking Management Reform with Employee Job Satisfaction: Evidence from Federal Agencies," *Journal of Public Administration Research and Theory* 20 (April 2010), pp. 413–436. The quotation is on p. 413.

41. As derived from data in Dana Priest and William M. Arkin, "National Security Inc." *Washington Post* (July 20, 2010). Figure (31 percent) is an estimate for 2010. Robert Gates is quoted.

42. Booz Allen Hamilton and Partnership for Public Service, *Cyber In-Security: Strengthening the Federal Cybersecurity Workforce* (Washington, DC: Authors, 2009), p. 2. Figures are for 2009.

43. U.S. Office of Management and Budget, *Policy Letter 92-1: Inherently Governmental Functions* (Washington, DC: Author, September 23, 1992).

44. Amber Corrin, "Public vs. Private: A Coalition of the Willing?" *Federal Computer Week* (January 10, 2010), p. 36. Figure is for 2010.

45. As derived from data in Steven L. Schooner and Collin D. Swan, "Contractors and the Ultimate Sacrifice," *Service Contractor* (September 2010), pp. 16–18. Figures are for 2001–2010.

46. U.S. Commission on Wartime Contracting in Iraq and Afghanistan, *Transforming Wartime Contracting: Controlling Costs, Reducing Risks,* Final Report to Congress (Washington, DC: U.S. Government Printing Office, 2011). Death ratio figure is since January 2010.

47. David Isenberg, as quoted in Peter G. Tuttle, "Don't Cut Corners While Outsourcing," *Federal Computer Week* (June 28, 2010), p. 15.

48. U.S. Government Accountability Office, *Department of Labor: Better Cost Assessments and Department wide Performance Tracking Are Needed to Effectively Manage Competitive Sourcing Program,* GAO-09-14 (Washington, DC: U.S. Government Printing Office, 2008), p. 8.

49. As derived from data in Federal Procurement Data System—Next Generation, *Federal Procurement Report, FY 2007, Section III,* p. 1.

50. Cooper, "Government Contracts in Public Administration," p. 463.

51. As derived from data in U.S. General Accounting Office, *Contract Management: Civilian Agency Compliance with Revised Task and Delivery Order Regulations,* GAO-03-983 (Washington, DC: U.S. Government Printing Office, 2003), pp. 22–24; and U.S. Government Accountability Office, *Contract Management: Guidance Needed to Promote Competition for Defense Task Orders,* GAO-04-874 (Washington, DC: U.S. Government Printing Office, 2004), p. 3.

52. U.S. General Accounting Office, *Contract Management: Civilian Agency Compliance with Revised Task and Delivery Order Regulations,* pp. 22–23.

53. John O'Mally, editor of *Commerce Business Daily* (replaced in 2002 by the portal, FedBiz Opps) and Vince Villa, consultant, as quoted in "Most Ads for Contractors Meaningless," *Washington Post* (June 25, 1980).

54. Bent Flyvberg, Mette Skamris Holm, and Soren Buhl, "Underestimating Costs in Public Works Projects: Error or Lie?" *Journal of the American Planning Association* 68 (Summer 2002), pp. 279–295. This is a study of 258 railway, road, bridge, and tunnel projects that were built between 1910 and 1998.

55. U.S. Government Accountability Office, *Defense Acquisitions: Assessments of Selected Weapon Programs,* GAO-08-467SP (Washington, DC: U.S. Government Printing Office, 2008), Highlights page. Figure is for FY 2007.

56. Flyvberg, Skamris Holm, and Buhl, "Underestimating Costs in Public Works Projects," p. 279.

57. Gordon Rule, quoted in William Proxmire, *Report from the Wasteland: America's Military Industrial Complex* (New York: Praeger, 1970), p. 83.

58. Debra Mayberry, "37,000? 39,402? 11,500? Just How Many Lobbyists Are There in Washington, Anyway?" *Washington Post* (January 29, 2006).

59. Lobbyists.info, http://www.lobbyists.info/faq.aspx. Figure is for 2010.

60. As derived from data in OpenSecrets.org, Center for Responsive Politics, http://www.opensecrets.org/lobby/index.php. Figure is for 1998–2010.

61. Ibid. Growth figure is for 1998–2010. Expenditure figure is for 2010.

62. Elizabeth Brown, *More Than 2,000 Spin Through Revolving Door* (Washington, DC: Center for Public Integrity, 2005), p. 2. Figure is "for the period between1998 and mid-2004."

63. Center for Responsive Politics, as cited in Dan Eggen and Kimberly Kindy, "Three of Every Four Oil and Gas Lobbyists Worked for Federal Government," *Washington Post* (July 22, 2010). Figure is for 2009.

64. Caitlin Ginley and Michael B. Pell, *On Financial Reform Bill, 52% of Lobbyists Worked in Government* (Washington, DC: Center for Public Integrity, 2010), http://www.publicinteg-

rity.org/articles/entry/2142/. The legislation is the Restoring America's Financial Stability Act of 2010.

65. Eggen and Kindy, "Three of Every Four Oil and Gas Lobbyists Worked for Federal Government."

66. As derived from data in U.S. Merit Systems Protection Board, *In Search of Highly Skilled Workers: A Study on the Hiring of Upper Level Employees from Outside the Federal Government* (Washington, DC: U.S. Government Printing Office, 2008), p. 13. Upper-level hires refer to Grades 12–15 in the General Schedule. Figure, 32 percent, is for 2005.

67. Newchy Mignone, as quoted in Jonathan Neumann and Ted Gup, "The Revolving Door: Industry Plums Await Retired U.S. Officials," *Washington Post* (June 25, 1980).

68. Public Citizen, *Congressional Revolving Doors: The Journey from Congress to K Street* (Washington, DC: Author, 2005), p. 1. Figures are for 1992–2004.

69. Jill Abramson, "The Business of Persuasion Thrives in Nation's Capitol," *New York Times* (September 29, 1998).

70. Ibid., and Susan Baer, " 'Revolving Door' Spins Fast as Ever for Ex-Clintonites," *Baltimore Sun* (December 1, 1996).

71. Representative Marcy Kaptur, as quoted in Gary Lee, "Trade, National Security, and the Revolving Door," *Washington Post* (April 13, 1992).

72. Brown, *More Than 2,000 Spin Through Revolving Door*, p. 2. Figures are for 1998–2004. We should note that former federal officials almost always are listed in these forms as members of lobbying teams that typically include lobbyists who did not serve in the federal government.

73. U.S. General Accounting Office, *DOD Use of Consultant Service Contracts*, 115083 (Washington, DC: U.S. Government Printing Office, 1981). The GAO reviewed 256 contracts for management support services valued at $175 million.

74. U.S. General Accounting Office, *DOD Revolving Door: Post-DOD Employment May Raise Concerns*, GAO/NSIAD-87-116 (Washington, DC: U.S. Government Printing Office, 1987), p. 12.

75. Adolfo Santos, "Post-Congressional Lobbying and Legislative Sponsorship: Do Members of Congress Reward Their Future Employers?" *LBJ Journal of Public Affairs* 16 (Fall 2003), pp. 56–64. The quotation is on p. 62. Congresspersons who retired voluntarily to work as lobbyists sponsored in their final term 2.2 more bills, on average, than those who did not, a "statistically significant" difference, 1984–1996.

76. Jack Abramoff, appearing on "The Lobbyist's Playbook," *60 Minutes*, CBS Television Network (November 6, 2011).

77. U.S. General Accounting Office, *Federal Acquisition: Trends, Reforms, and Challenges*, GAO-T-OCG-00-7 (Washington, DC: U.S. Government Printing Office, 2000), p. 6.

78. U.S. Government Accountability Office, *Acquisition Planning: Opportunities to Build Strong Foundations for Better Service Contracts*, GAO-11-672 (Washington, DC: U.S. Government Printing Office, 2011), Highlights page. Figure is for FY 2010.

79. U.S. Government Accountability Office, *Defense Acquisition Workforce: Better Identification, Development, and Oversight Needed for Personnel Involved in Acquiring Services*, GAO-11-892 (Washington, DC: U.S. Government Printing Office, 2011), p. 1. Figure is for FY 2010.

80. Burman, "Six Practical Steps to Improve Contracting," p. 65.

81. U.S. Office of Management and Budget, as cited in Frank Greve, "Hired Guns Running the U.S.," *Philadelphia Inquirer* (May 19, 1992). Figure is for 1992.

82. U.S. General Accounting Office, as cited in Stuart Auerbach, "Disclosure Rules on Consultants Held Insufficient," *Washington Post* (November 2, 1990).

83. As derived from data in U.S. General Accounting Office, *Government Contractors: Measuring Costs of Service Contractors Versus Federal Employees*, GGD-94-95 (Washington, DC: U.S. Government Printing Office, 1994), Appendix IV.

84. Response of Dr. Lois Ellen Datta, chief, Headstart Evaluation Branch, Office of Education, in a 1970 letter to the Stanford Research Institute, as quoted in Daniel Guttman and Daniel Willner, *The Shadow Government: The Government's*

Multi-Billion Dollar Giveaway of its Decision-Making Powers to Private Management Consultants, "Experts," and Think Tanks (New York: Pantheon, 1976), p. 167.

85. Three federal contract administrators, as quoted in Jonathan Neumann and Ted Gup, "An Epidemic of Waste in U.S. Consulting, Research," *Washington Post* (July 22, 1980).

86. Board member William Farris, Institute of Management Consultants, quoted in ibid.

87. Daniel Guttman, appearing on the program *60 Minutes*, CBS Television Network (November 30, 1982).

88. U.S. General Accounting Office, *Civil Servants and Contract Employees: Who Should Do What for the Federal Government?* FPCD-81-43 (Washington, DC: U.S. Government Printing Office, 1981), p. 6.

89. Al Stapleton of the GAO, as quoted in "Consultants: New Target for Budget Trimmers," *U.S. News & World Report* (December 1, 1981), p. 40.

90. U.S. Office of Management and Budget, *Policy Letter No. 93-1 (Reissued), Management Oversight of Service Contracting* (Washington, DC: Author, 1994). This directive, issued in 1993, replaced OMB Circular A-120 of 1980.

91. U.S. General Accounting Office, *Government Contractors: Are Service Contractors Performing Inherently Governmental Functions?* p. 5.

92. Joseph Besselman, Ashish Arora, and Patrick Larkey, "Buying in a Businesslike Fashion—and Paying More," *Public Administration Review* 60 (September/October 2000), pp. 421–434. The quotation is on p. 421. The Pentagon bought 676,000 parts, amounting to more than $60 million, and paid over 14 percent less for electronics and nearly 32 percent less for engine parts.

93. Peter Warren Singer, "Nation Builders and Low Bidders in Iraq," *New York Times* (June 15, 2004), for the quotation and some material; and Peter Warren Singer, "A Contract the U. S. Military Needs to Break," *Washington Post* (September 12, 2004).

94. Gore, *From Red Tape to Results*, pp. 28, 1. Figures are for the early 1990s.

95. U.S. Government Accountability Office, *Federal Contractors: Better Performance Information Needed to Support Agency Contract Award Decisions*, Highlights page. Figure, 69 percent, is for FY 2007.

96. Cooper, "Government Contracts in Public Administration," p. 462.

97. Quoted in Russell Mitchell, "It Was Mr. Fixit Vs. The Pentagon—and the Pentagon Won," *Business Week* (December 24, 1990), p. 52.

98. U.S. Government Accountability Office, *Defense Acquisitions: Assessments of Selected Weapon Programs*, Highlights page. Figure is for FY 2007.

99. "Not publicly released," Army-commissioned report, as cited in Marjorie Censer, "Army Report: Military Has Spent $32 Billion since '95 on Abandoned Weapons Programs," *Washington Post* (May 27, 2011). Figures are for 1995–2009.

100. U.S. Government Accountability Office, *Contracting Strategies: Data and Oversight Problems Hamper Opportunities to Leverage Value of Interagency and Enterprise wide Contracts*, GAO-10-367 (Washington, DC: U.S. Government Printing Office, 2010), Highlights page.

101. As derived from data in Brodsky, "Contracting Spending Dips for the First Time in 13 Years," and U.S. Government Accountability Office, *Interagency Contracting: Improvements Needed in Setting Fee Rates for Selected Programs*, GAO-11-784 (Washington, DC: U.S. Government Printing Office, 2011), Highlights page.

102. Center for Strategic and International Studies, *Integrating Civilian and Military Technologies: An Industry Survey* (Washington, DC: Author, 1993).

103. U.S. Defense Systems Management College, as cited in Gore, *From Red Tape to Results*, p. 80.

104. U.S. Merit Systems Protection Board, *Workforce Quality and Federal Procurement: An Assessment* (Washington, DC: U.S. Government Printing Office, 1992), p. 40.

105. U.S. Government Accountability Office, *Contract Management: Extent of Federal Spending under Cost-Reimbursement Contracts Unclear and Key Controls Not Always Used*, GAO-09-921 (Washington, DC: U.S. Government Printing Office, 2009), Highlights page. Figure, 26 percent, is for 2008. The other two main types of federal contracts are *fixed-cost*, in which the contractor is not reimbursed for costs that surpass the agreed-upon cost, and *time-and-materials*, in which the government pays fixed, per-hour rates for all expenses within a pre-established ceiling.

106. As derived from data in Light, *Creating High Performance Government*, p. 3. Figure is for 2000–2008.

107. As derived from data in Project on Government Oversight, *Federal Contractor Misconduct Database* (Washington, DC: Author, 2010), http://www.contractormisconduct.org/. Figures are for 1995–2009. "Top 100 contractors" is for FY 2009.

108. Andy Pasztor, *When the Pentagon Was for Sale: Inside America's Biggest Defense Scandal* (New York: Scribner, 1995), p. 38.

109. U.S. Commission on Wartime Contracting in Iraq and Afghanistan, *Transforming Wartime Contracting*, pp. 5, 22. Figures are for FY 2002–FY 2011.

110. U.S. General Accounting Office, *Worker Protection: Federal Contractors and Violations of Federal Labor Law*, GAO/HEHS-96-8 (Washington, DC: U.S. Government Printing Office, 1995), p. 1. In 1993, $23 billion in federal contracts was awarded to eighty companies that had violated federal labor laws.

111. U.S. General Accounting Office, *Occupational Safety and Health: Violations of Safety and Health Regulations by Federal Contractors*, GAO/HEHS-96-157 (Washington, DC: U.S. Government Printing Office, 1996), p. 3. In 1994, $38 billion in federal contracts were awarded to 261 companies that had seriously violated federal health and safety laws.

112. As derived from data in U.S. Government Accountability Office, *Federal Contracting: Assessments and Citations of Federal Labor Law Violations by Selected Federal Contractors*, GAO-10-1033 (Washington, DC: U.S. Government Printing Office, 2010), Highlights page. Figures are for 2005–2009.

113. U.S. Government Accountability Office, *Financial Management: Thousands of Civilian Agency Contractors Abuse the Federal Tax System with Little Consequence*, GAO-05-637 (Washington, DC: U.S. Government Printing Office, 2005). Figures are for 2004.

114. U.S. General Accounting Office, *Financial Management: Some DOD Contractors Abuse the Federal Tax System with Little Consequence*, GAO-04-95 (Washington, DC: U.S. Government Printing Office, 2004), p. 13. Figures are for 2002.

115. As derived from data in: Ibid. and U.S. Government Accountability Office, *Federal Contractors: Better Performance Information Needed to Support Agency Contract Award Decisions*, Highlights page.

116. U.S. Government Accountability Office, *Medicare: Thousands of Medicare Providers Abuse the Federal Tax System*, GAO-08-618 (Washington, DC: U.S. Government Printing Office, 2008). Figures are for 2006.

117. U.S. Government Accountability Office, *Recovery Act: Thousands of Recovery Act Contract and Grant Recipients Owe Hundreds of Millions in Federal Taxes*, GAO-11-485 (Washington, DC: U.S. Government Printing Office, 2011), Highlights page, p. 8. Recipients include "subrecipients" and vendors. Funds disbursed are for 2010. Taxes owed are for 2009.

118. U.S. Government Accountability Office, *Financial Management: State and Federal Governments Are Not Taking Action to Collect Unpaid Debt through Reciprocal Agreements*, GAO-05-697R Reciprocal Agreements for Collecting Unpaid Debt (Washington, DC: U.S. Government Printing Office, 2005), p. 2. Figures are for 2004.

119. U.S. Government Accountability Office, *Recovery Act: Thousands of Recovery Act Contract and Grant Recipients Owe Hundreds of Millions in Federal Taxes*, Highlights page.

120. Democratic staff, House Ways and Means Committee, as cited in Jonathan D. Salant, Associated Press, "Companies Relocate to Escape Taxes," *Savannah Morning News* (May 27, 2003). Figures are for 2001.

121. U.S. General Accounting Office, *International Taxation: Tax Haven Companies Were More Likely to Have a Tax Cost Advantage in Federal Contracting*, GAO-04-856 (Washington, DC: U.S. Government Printing Office, 2004), Highlights page.

122. Stephen Goldsmith and William D. Eggers, "Government for Hire," *New York Times* (February 21, 2005).

123. As derived from data in Brodsky, "Contracting Spending Dips for the First Time in 13 Years," and U.S. House of Representatives, Committee on Government Reform, Minority Staff, Special Investigations Division, *Dollars, Not Sense*, p. i. Figures are for FY 2000–FY 2009.

124. As derived from data in Council of the Inspectors General on Integrity and Efficiency,

A Progress Report to the President, Fiscal Year 2009 (Washington, DC: U.S. Government Printing Office, 2010), Table 10. Suspensions and debarments declined from 9,918 to 4,485, 2005–2009. A *suspension* is a temporary exclusion of a contractor pending the completion of investigation or legal proceedings. A contractor can be suspended if he or she has been indicted, other federal agencies are conducting an investigation, or a serious accusation has been made. A *debarment* is a fixed-term exclusion, usually not exceeding three years. A contractor can be debarred if he or she has been convicted of fraud, other crimes, or a "willful failure to perform." It appears that perhaps two-thirds, of "excluded" contractors are debarred.

125. Federal Procurement Data System—Next Generation, *Federal Procurement Report, FY 2007, Section III,* p. 1.

126. Richard W. Stevenson, "Many Caught but Few Are Hurt For Arms Contract Fraud in U.S.," *Washington Post* (November 12, 1990). The period was 1983–1990.

127. Scott Amey, "Suspension and Disbarment: The Record Shows That the System Is Broken," *Federal Times* (March 21, 2005), http://www.federaltimes.com. Figures are for 1990–2003. By contrast, in 2003 and 2004, 43,000 firms, all of them small, had been banned from further federal contracts.

128. Anne Marie Squeo, "Are Firms Too Big to Debar?" *Wall Street Journal* (June 10, 2003).

129. U.S. Government Accountability Office, *Federal Procurement: Additional Data Reporting Could Improve the Suspension and Debarment Process,* pp. 2–3. Figure is for 2003.

130. U.S. Government Accountability Office, *Excluded Parties List System: Suspended and Debarred Businesses and Individuals Improperly Receive Federal Funds,* GAO-09-174 (Washington, DC: U.S. Government Printing Office, 2009), Highlights page.

131. William Henry Lambright, *Governing Science and Technology* (New York: Oxford University Press, 1976), p. 123.

132. Cooper, "Government Contracts in Public Administration," pp. 462–463.

133. Clay Johnson III, *Memorandum for the President's Management Council: Subject, Plans for Commercial Services Management* (Washington, DC: U.S. Office of Management and Budget, July 11, 2008), p. 1.

134. Kellie Lunney, "Federal Managers Support Program Cuts, Fewer Contractors," *Government Executive* (November 7, 2011), http://govexec.com/story_page_pf.cfm?articleid=49270&.

135. U.S. House Appropriations Committee, as cited in Corrin, "Public vs. Private," p. 36.

136. Project on Government Oversight, *Bad Business: Billions of Taxpayer Dollars Wasted on Hiring Contractors* (Washington, DC: Author, 2011), http://pogo.org.

137. Steve Kelman, "The Way to Better Contracts," *Federal Computer Week* (May 10, 2010), p. 16.

138. U.S. General Accounting Office, *Contract Management: Guidance Needed for Using Performance-Based Service Contracting,* GAO-02-1049 (Washington, DC: U.S. Government Printing Office, 2002), p. 3. Figure is for 2001.

139. Robert O'Harrow, Jr. and Scott Higham, "Changes Spurred Buying, Abuses." Agency sales conducted through GSA's Multiple Award Schedules rose from $5 billion to $35 billion, 1996–2006.

140. Barack Obama, *Remarks by the President on Procurement* (Washington, DC: The White House, 2009), p. 3.

141. Vinson and Elkins LLP, "Recovery Act Includes Unprecedented Accountability and Transparency Provisions," *V&E Litigation Update* (Houston, TX: Author, 2009), http://www.vinson-elkins.com.

142. John Monroe, "2009 Year in Review," *Federal Computer Week* (December 7, 2010), pp. 20–26. The quotations are on p. 22.

143. Ray Bjorklund of FedSources, as quoted in Elise Castelli, "Contract Spending Expected to Flatten," *Federal Times.com* (June 8, 2009), http://www.federaltimes.com. Projection is for 2008–2014.

144. John R. Bartle and Ronnie LaCourse Korosec, *Procurement and Contracting in State Government, 2000* (Syracuse, NY: Syracuse University Government Performance Project, 2001), p. iv. Figure is for 2000, and is higher when state-delivered Medicaid benefits are included.

145. Keon S. Chi, Kelley A. Arnold, and Heather M. Perkins, "Privatization in State Government: Trends and Issues," *Book of the States, 2004,* (Lexington, KY: Council of State Governments, 2004), pp. 465–482. Figure (p. 465) is for 2002.

146. Keon S. Chi and Cindy Jasper, *Private Practices: A Review of Privatization in State Government* (Lexington, KY: Council of State Governments, 1998), p. 8. Data are for 1997. See also U.S. General Accounting Office, *Privatization: Lessons Learned by State and Local Governments*, GAO/GGD-97-48 (Washington, DC: U.S. Government Printing Office, 1997), which found the same obstacles to state privatization.

147. Chi, Arnold, and Perkins, "Privatization in State Government," pp. 468, 479. Figures are for 2002.

148. Chi and Jasper, *Private Practices*, p. 14. Figure is for 1997.

149. Robert W. Poole, Jr., David Haarmeyer, and Lynn Scarlett, *Mining the Government Balance Sheet: What Cities and States Have To Sell*, Policy Study No. 139 (Washington, DC: Reason Public Policy Institute, 1992), p. 2. The "preliminary estimate" was $227 billion in 1992.

150. As derived from data in Chi, Arnold, and Perkins, "Privatization in State Government," p. 479. Figure, thirty-three states, is for 2002. Fourteen states did not respond, and we assume in this calculation that their lack of response indicates a lack of contracting.

151. As derived from data in Yoo-Sung Choi, Chung-Lae Cho, Deil S. Wright, and Jeffrey L. Brudney, "Dimensions of Contracting for Service Delivery by American State Administrative Agencies: Exploring Linkages between and Intergovernmental Relations and Intersectoral Administration," *Public Performance & Management Review* 29 (September 2005), pp. 46–66. The information is for 1998 and is derived from data on p. 50

152. Chi and Jasper, *Private Practices*, p. 14. Data are for 1997.

153. Chi, Arnold, and Perkins, "Privatization in State Government," pp. 468, 479. Figure is for 2002.

154. Chi and Jasper, *Private Practices*, p. 14.

155. Jeffrey L. Brudney, F. Ted Hebert, and Deil S. Wright, "Reinventing Government in the American States: Measuring and Explaining Administrative Reform," *Public Administration Review* 59 (January/February 1999), p. 23. Data are for 1995. Chi and Jasper, *Private Practices*, found comparable levels of privatization: 43 percent of agency heads had privatized *less* than 5 percent of their services.

156. Chi, Arnold, and Perkins, "Privatization in State Government," pp. 479, 465. Between 1998 and 2002, seventeen states did no contracting out of services; 25 percent of state agency heads said privatization had increased, and 11 percent did not respond.

157. Ibid., p. 467. Figures are for 2002.

158. As derived from data in ibid., pp. 468–469. Figures are for 2002. An earlier, 1998, study found that slightly more state agency heads, a third, reported some savings deriving from program privatization. See Jeffrey L. Brudney, Sergio Fernandez, Jay Eungha Ryu, and Deil S. Wright, "Exploring and Explaining Contracting Out: Patterns among the American States," *Journal of Public Administration Research and Theory* 15 (July 2005), pp. 394–420.

159. National Association of State Procurement Officials, as cited in Matthew Potoski, "State and Local Government Procurement and the Winter Commission," *Public Administration Review*, Supplement to Vol. 68 (December 2008), pp. S58–S69. Figure is for 2000.

160. U.S. General Accounting Office, *Privatization: Lessons Learned by State and Local Governments*, p. 6.

161. As derived from data in Chi and Jasper, *Private Practices*, p. 8. Our estimate assumes that the more than half of the respondents who did not respond to this question did so because they had no monitoring systems.

162. Russell Nichols, "Selling Out," *Governing* (December 2010), pp. 39–40.

163. Christine A. Kelleher and Susan Webb Yackee, "A Political Consequence of Contracting: Organized Interests and State Agency Decision Making," *Journal of Public Administration Research and Theory* 19 (July 2009), pp. 579–602. The quotations are on p. 579.

164. Alan Greenblatt, "Sweetheart Deals," *Governing* (December 2004), http://governing.com. The article notes that these problems also are occurring in local governments.

165. Mary K. Feeney and Craig R. Smith, "Social Embeddedness in Outsourcing: What Shapes Public Managers' Perceptions?" *Public Performance & Management Review* 31 (June 2008), pp. 517–546 (the quotation is on p. 541); and Leisha DeHart-Davis and Gordon Kingsley, "Managerial Perceptions of

Privatization: Evidence from a State Department of Transportation," *State and Local Government Review* 37 (March, 2005), pp. 228–241. Both sources are studies of the Georgia Department of Transportation.

166. Irwin T. David, "Privatization in America," *Municipal Year Book, 1988* (Washington, DC: International City Management Association, 1988), pp. 43–55. Figure is for 1987. The quotation is on p. 43.

167. U.S. Advisory Commission on Intergovernmental Relations, *State Laws Governing Local Government Structure and Administration*, M-186 (Washington, DC: U.S. Government Printing Office, 1993), p. 43. Figures are for 1990.

168. David, "Privatization in America," p. 52. In 1982–1987, 24 percent of cities and counties sold assets.

169. Jerri Killian and Enamul Choudhury, "Continuity and Change in the Role of City Managers," *Municipal Year Book, 2010* (Washington, DC: International City/County Management Association, 2010), pp. 10–18. The ranking (p. 13) is for 2010.

170. Mildred Warner and Amir Hefetz, "Pragmatism over Politics: Alternative Service Delivery in Local Governments, 1992–2002," *Municipal Year Book, 2002* (Washington, DC: International City/County Management Association, 2004), pp. 8–16 (data are on p. 13), and as derived from data in Harry P. Hatry and Carl F. Valente, "Alternative Service Delivery Approaches Involving Increased Use of the Private Sector," *Municipal Year Book, 1983* (Washington, DC: International City Management Association, 1983), pp. 199–217 (data are on pp. 216–217). Current figure and in-house services are for 2007. Figure has ranged from 47 to 52 percent, 1982–2007. "All local services" refers to sixty services surveyed in 1982 and sixty-seven in 2007.

171. Ibid. (both citations), p. 14 and as derived from data on pp. 216–217, respectively. Current figures and privatized services are for 2007. Trend figures are for 1982–2007.

172. David, "Privatization in America," p. 44.

173. Rowan Miranda and Karlyn Andersen, "Alternative Service Delivery in Local Government, 1982–1992" *Municipal Year Book, 1994* (Washington, DC: International City/County Management Association, 1994), pp. 26–35. The quotation is on p. 28. Emphasis added.

174. Mildred E. Warner and Amir Hefetz, "Cooperative Competition: Alternative Service Delivery, 2002–2007," *Municipal Year Book, 2009* (Washington, DC: International City/County Management Association, 2009), pp. 11–20. The data are on p. 13, and as derived from data in Hatry and Valente, "Alternative Service Delivery Approaches Involving Increased Use of the Private Sector," pp. 216–217. Figure has ranged from 17 to 23 percent, 1982–2007.

175. Categories total more than 100 percent because the "ICMA treats the data on service provision separately from the data on service delivery." See Warner and Hefetz, "Cooperative Competition," p. 12.

176. Alan Greenblatt, "Observer," *Governing* (February 2006), pp.17–18.

177. Jonas Prager, "Contract City Redux: Weston, Florida, as the Ultimate New Public Management Model City," *Public Administration Review* 68 (January/February 2008), pp.167–180.

178. David Streitfeld, "A City Outsources Everything. Sky Does Not Fall," *New York Times* (July 19, 2010).

179. Mark D. Bradbury and G. David Waechter, "Extreme Outsourcing in Local Government: At the Top and All But the Top," *Review of Public Personnel Administration* 29 (September 2009), pp. 230–248. Figure is for 2009.

180. Ibid., p.16. Figure is for 2007.

181. Patricia M. Florestano and Stephen B. Gordon, "A Survey of City and County Use of Private Contracting," *The Urban Interest* 3 (Spring 1981), pp. 22–29. In 1980, 43 percent of 225 local purchasing officials thought that privatization saved money (p. 25).

182. Roland Zullo, "Does Fiscal Stress Induce Privatization? Correlates of Private and Intermunicipal Contracting, 1992–2002," *Governance* 22 (July 2009), pp. 459–481. The quotation is on p. 459. This is a study of American counties.

183. Clingermayer, Feiock, and Stream, "Governmental Uncertainty and Leadership Turnover," p. 157. Services examined were confined to elderly and mental health programs.

184. Timothy B. Krebs and John P. Peliserro, "What Influences City Council Adoption and Support for Reinventing Government? Environmental or Institutional Factors?" *Public Administration Review* 70 (March/April 2010), pp. 258–267.

185. Zullo, "Does Fiscal Stress Induce Privatization?" p. 459.

186. Germa Bel and Xavier Fageda, "Why Do Local Governments Privatise Public Services? A Survey of Empirical Studies," *Local Government Studies* 33 (August 2007), pp. 517–534.

187. Mary M. Shaw, "Successful Collaboration between the Nonprofit and Public Sectors," *Nonprofit Management and Leadership* 14 (Fall 2003), pp. 107–120. The quotation is on p. 107.

188. Clingermayer, Feiock, and Stream, "Governmental Uncertainty and Leadership Turnover," p. 156.

189. Laurence J. O'Toole, Jr. and Kenneth J. Meier, "Parkinson's Law and the New Public Management? Contracting Determinants and Service-Quality Consequences in Public Education," *Public Administration Review* 64 (May/June 2004), pp. 342–352. The quotations are on pp. 348–349.

190. Yosef Bhatti, Asmus Leth Olsen, and Lene Holm Pedersen, "The Effects of Administrative Professionals on Contracting Out," *Governance* 22 (January 2009), pp. 121–137. The quotations are on pp. 121, 125–126. This is a study of Danish municipalities.

191. Robert Mohr and Steven C. Deller, "Alternative Methods of Service Delivery in Small and Rural Municipalities," *Public Administration Review* 70 (November/December 2010), pp. 894–905.

192. Mildred E. Warner and Amir Hefetz, "Service Characteristics and Contracting: The Importance of Citizen Interest and Competition," *Municipal Year Book, 2010* (Washington, DC: International City/County Management Association, 2010), pp. 19–27. The quotation is on p. 26.

193. Warner and Hefetz, "Cooperative Competition," p. 17. Figure, 61 percent, is for 2007. In 1992, 48 percent of local governments reported that they had encountered no obstacles in implementing a private service delivery. See Mildred Warner and Amir Hefetz, "Pragmatism over Politics: Alternative Service Delivery in Local Governments, 1992–2002," *Municipal Year Book, 2004* (Washington, DC: International City/County Management Association, 2004), pp. 8–16. The figure is on p. 14.

194. Warner and Hefetz, "Cooperative Competition," p. 17. Figures are for 2007.

195. As derived from data in Ibid. and David, "Privatization in America," pp. 43–47.

196. Warner and Hefetz, "Cooperative Competition," p. 17. Local employee resistance declined from 41 to 39 percent, 2002–2007.

197. Timothy Chandler and Peter Ferrille, "Municipal Unions and Privatization," *Public Administration Review* 51 (January/February 1991), pp. 15–22.

198. Warner and Hefetz, "Cooperative Competition," p. 17. Figure is for 2007.

199. Krebs and Peliserro, "What Influences City Council Adoption and Support for Reinventing Government?" p. 263. Chandler and Ferrille, "Municipal Unions and Privatization," also found this to be the case two decades earlier.

200. Clingermayer, Feiock, and Stream, "Governmental Uncertainty and Leadership Turnover," p. 156.

201. Warner and Hefetz, "Cooperative Competition," p. 17. Respondents citing this obstacle declined from 44 to 39 percent, 2002–2007.

202. James D. Ward, "Exploring Unintended Consequences of Privatization, 1979 to 1999," paper presented at the National Conference of the American Society for Public Administration (San Diego, 2000), p. 3.

203. Stephen Moore, "How Contracting Out City Services Impacts Public Employees," *Contracting Out Government Services*, Paul Seidenstat, ed. (Westport, CN: Praeger, 1999), pp. 211–218.

204. Warner and Hefetz, "Cooperative Competition," p. 18. Figure is for 2007.

205. Moore, "How Contracting out City Services Impacts Public Employees," p. 214.

206. Ibid.

207. Ward, "Exploring Unintended Consequences of Privatization, 1979 to 1999" p. 6.

208. Warner and Hefetz, "Cooperative Competition," p. 18. Figure is for 2007. In 2002, the figure was 27 percent.

209. U.S. Advisory Commission on Intergovernmental Relations, *State Laws Governing Local Government Structure and Administration*, p. 43. Figures are for 1990.

210. Sergio Fernandez and Hal G. Rainey, "Local Government Contract Management and Performance Survey: A Report," *Municipal Year Book, 2005* (Washington, DC: International City/County Management Association, 2005), pp. 3–4. Figure is for 2003–2004. Twenty-two percent of cities and counties used sole-source bids in 1987. See David, "Privatization in America," p. 51.

211. Henry George Frederickson, Gary Alan Johnson, and Curtis Wood, "The Changing Structure of American Cities: A Study of the Diffusion of Innovation," *Public Administration Review* 64 (May/June 2004), pp. 320–330. Datum is on p. 324.

212. Trevor L. Brown, "The Dynamics of Government-to-Government Contracts," *Public Performance & Management Review* 31 (March 2008), pp. 364–386. This is an analysis of data drawn from the 1992 and 1997 ICMA alternative service delivery surveys. It compares public works and transportation services (low-risk areas) with health and human services (high-risk areas).

213. Mary K. Marvel and Howard P. Marvel, "Shaping the Provision of Outsourced Public Services: Incentive Efficacy and Service Delivery," *Public Performance & Management Review* 33 (December 2009), pp. 183–213. This is an analysis of 135 cities and counties in Ohio, which do not insert these provisions in their short-term contracts with companies.

214. Janice Johnson Dias and Steven Maynard-Moody, "For-Profit Welfare: Contracts, Conflicts, and the Performance Paradox," *Journal of Public Administration Research and Theory* 17 (April 2007), pp. 189–211. The quotations are on p. 189.

215. U.S. Advisory Commission on Intergovernmental Relations, *State Laws Governing Local Government Structure and Administration*, p. 43. Figures are for 1990.

216. Warner and Hefetz, "Cooperative Competition," p. 19. Figure is for 2007.

217. Robert Jay Dilger, Randolph R. Moffett, and Linda Struyk, "Privatization of Municipal Services in America's Largest Cities," *Public Administration Review* 57 (January/February 1997), pp. 21–26.

218. As derived from data in U.S. General Accounting Office, *Contract Management: Civilian Agency Compliance with the Revised Task and Delivery Order Regulations*, Highlights page and p. 22.

219. U.S. General Accounting Office, *Contract Management: Guidance Needed for Using Performance-Based Service Contracting*, p. 3. This study found that only 11 percent of federal contracts were assessed for performance. And recall that, in 69 percent of contracts that require performance assessments, no assessment

is done. See U.S. Government Accountability Office, *Federal Contractors: Better Performance Information Needed to Support Agency Contract Award Decisions.*

220. As derived from data in Chi and Jasper, *Private Practices*, p. 8. Our calculation assumes that the more than half of respondents who did not respond to this question did so because they had no monitoring system.

221. Warner and Hefetz, "Cooperative Competition," p. 20. Figure is for 2002 and 2007.

222. Scott Lamothe and Meeyoung Lamothe, "The Dynamics of Local Service Delivery Arrangements and the Role of Nonprofits," *International Journal of Public Administration* 29 (October/November, 2006), pp. 769–797.

223. Pascale Joassart-Marcelli and Juliet Musso, "Municipal Service Provision Choices within a Metropolitan Area," *Urban Affairs Review* 40 (March 2005), pp. 492–519. The data are on p. 515.

224. Dilger, Moffet, and Struyk, "Privatization of Municipal Services in America's Largest Cities," p. 23, and David Osborne and Ted Gaebler, *Reinventing Government: How the Entrepreneurial Spirit Is Transforming the Public Sector* (Reading, MA: Addison-Wesley, 1992), p. 89.

225. Graeme A. Hodge, *Privatization: An International Review of Performance* (Boulder, CO: Westview, 2000), p. 156.

226. Sergio Fernandez, "Understanding Contracting Performance," *Administration & Society* 41 (March 2009), pp. 67–100. The quotation is on p. 92. This is a study of more than 400 "contractual relationships" between American local governments and private service providers.

227. Warner and Hefetz, "Cooperative Competition," p. 20. Figure, 61 percent, is for 2007.

228. Hodge, *Privatization*, p. 155. This impressive source is likely the most comprehensive review of the literature.

229. William D. Eggers, *Rightsizing the Government: Lessons from America's Public Sector Innovators* (Los Angeles, CA: Reason Foundation, 1993).

230. Hodges, *Privatization*, p. 119.

231. Herbert A. Simon, "Why Public Administration?" *Journal of Public Administration Research and Theory* 8 (Winter 1998), pp. 1–11. The quotation is on p. 11.

232. Rhys Andrews and Tom Entwistle, "Does Cross-Sectoral Partnership Deliver? An Empirical Exploration of Public Service Effectiveness, Efficiency, and Equity," *Journal of Public Administration Research and Theory* 20 (July 2010), pp. 679–701. The quotations are on pp. 691, 689, 692, respectively. This is a study of forty-six broadly representative local government service departments in Wales.

233. OMB study, as cited in David Perera, "OMB: Competitive Sourcing Spends $1 to Save $20," *Federal Computer Week* (September 27, 2005), http://www.fcw.com.

234. Susan A. MacManus, "Why Businesses are Reluctant to Sell to Governments," *Public Administration Review* 51 (July/August 1991), pp. 328–346. The quotation is on p. 334. Figure, 29 percent, is for 1990.

235. Sebastian Mallaby, "The Democracy Trap," *Washington Post* (April 25, 2005).

236. O'Toole and Meier, "Parkinson's Law and the New Public Management?" p. 342.

237. Fernandez, "Understanding Contracting Performance," p. 93.

238. Unless noted otherwise, this discussion is based on Paul Seidenstat, "Theory and Practice of Contracting Out in the United States," *Contracting Out Government Services Paul Seidenstat, ed.*, (Westport, CN: Praeger, 1999), pp. 3–26.

239. Mark Considine, "The End of the Line? Accountable Governance in the Age of Networks, Partnerships, and Joined-Up Services," *Governance* 15 (January 2002), pp. 21–41.

240. Peter E.D. Love, Peter R. Davis, David J. Edwards, and David Baccarini, "Uncertainty Avoidance: Public Sector Clients and Procurement Selection," *International Journal of Public Sector Management* 21 (July, 2008), pp. 753–776. The quotation is on p. 753. This is an experiment involving focus groups composed of Australian senior managers involved with procurement.

241. These recommendations are based on Burman, "Six Practical Steps to Improve Contracting," pp. 62–63.

242. E. S. Savas, *Privatization and Public-Private Partnerships* (New York: Chatham House, 2000), p. 9.

243. Jerry Mitchell, *The American Experiment with Government Corporations* (Armonk, NY: M. E. Sharpe, 1998) p. 19.

244. Walsh, *The Public's Business*, p. 29.

245. As derived from data in U.S. Government Accountability Office, *Federally Created Entities: An Overview of Key Attributes*, GAO-10-97 (Washington, DC: U.S. Government Printing Office, 2009), pp. 9, 25, 26, 34. Data are for 2009.

246. Ronald C. Moe, "The Emerging Federal Quasi Government: Issues of Management and Accountability," *Public Administration Review* 61 (May/June 2001), pp. 290–312.

247. U.S. Government Accountability Office, *Federally Created Entities: An Overview of Key Attributes*, pp. 9, 18. Data are for 2009.

248. Ibid., p. 16.

249. U.S. Government Accountability Office, *Federal Research: Opportunities Exist to Improve the Management and Oversight of Federally Funded Research and Development Centers*, GAO-09-15 (Washington, DC: U.S. Government Printing Office, 2008), Highlights page. Figure, $13 billion, is for 2006.

250. U.S. Government Accountability Office, *Federally Created Entities: An Overview of Key Attributes*, p. 21.

251. U.S. General Accounting Office, *Government Corporations: Profiles of Existing Government Corporations*, GAO/GGD-96-14 (Washington, DC: U.S. Government Printing Office, 1995), p. 2.

252. U.S. Government Accountability Office, *Federally Created Entities: An Overview of Key Attributes*, pp. 13–14.

253. For reasons of space, we shall not list the first eight of these tallies and their sources, but they can be found in the tenth edition of this book (2007), p. 344, Note 205. The ninth count is ibid.

254. U.S. Government Accountability Office, *Federally Created Entities: An Overview of Key Attributes*, pp. 13–16. Figure is for 2009.

255. Ibid., pp. 13–16. Figures are for 2009.

256. U.S. General Accounting Office, *Government Corporations: Profiles of Existing Government Corporations*, p. 6. Data are for 1994.

257. Harold Siedman, "United States Experience: The Need to Reassert the Government Corporation Control Act of 1945," *Public Administration and Development* 18 (August 1998), pp. 295–299. The quotation is on p. 297.

258. U. S. General Accounting Office, *Government Corporations: Profiles of Existing Government Corporations*, pp. 2–3.

259. U.S. Government Accountability Office, *Federally Created Entities: An Overview of Key Attributes*, p. 18.

260. Ibid. and U.S. Office of Management and Budget, "Government-Sponsored Enterprises," *The President's Budget for Fiscal Year 2010* (Washington, DC: U.S. Government Printing Office, 2009), pp. 1339–1344. The GAO counts three, and OMB tallies five.

261. U.S. Office of Management and Budget, "Government-Sponsored Enterprises," pp. 1339–1344.

The Farm Credit System (FCS, founded in 1916) is a member-owned cooperative that provides privately financed credit to rural areas, and includes the Agricultural Credit Bank, the Farm Credit Banks, and direct lender associations. They are regulated by the Farm Credit Administration (FCA), an independent federal agency.

The Federal Home Loan Bank System (FHLBanks, 1932) is a member-owned cooperative composed of twelve Federal Home Loan Banks that facilitates the extension of credit to all banks and other financial institutions. FHLBanks were regulated by the Federal Housing Finance Board until it was replaced by the Federal Housing Finance Agency (FHFA), an independent board created in 2008 by the Federal Housing Finance Reform Act (Division A of the Housing and Economic Recovery Act of 2008), which combined the Federal Housing Finance Board with the Office of Federal Housing Enterprise Oversight. Both regulators expired in 2009, and were succeeded by the FHFA.

Fannie Mae and Freddie Mac, owned by the federal government, were regulated by the Department of Housing and Urban Development's Office of Federal Housing Enterprise Oversight until 2009, when it was replaced by the FHFA.

The Federal Agricultural Mortgage Corporation (Farmer Mac, 1988), owned by shareholders, facilitates mortgages for farms and rural homes. It is supervised by the FCA.

262. Marvin Phaup, "Federal Use of Implied Guarantees: Some Preliminary Lesson from the Current Financial Distress," *Public Administration Review* 69 (July/August 2009), pp. 651–659.

263. Neil Irwin and Zachary A. Goldfarb, "U.S. Seizes Control of Mortgage Giants," *Washington Post* (September 8, 2008).

264. Thomas H. Stanton, "The Life Cycle of the Government-Sponsored Enterprise: Lessons for Design and Accountability," *Public Administration Review* 67 (September/October 2007), pp. 837–860. Figure is for 1975–2005 (p. 839).

265. As derived from data in U.S. General Accounting Office, *Government-Sponsored Enterprises: A Framework for Strengthening GSE Governance and Oversight*, GAO-04-269T (Washington, DC: U.S Government Printing Office, 2004), p. 4. In 2003, Fannie and Freddie accounted for 81 percent of all GSE financial obligations.

266. Tom Raum and Jim Drinkard, Associated Press, "Fannie Mae, Freddie Mac, Spent Millions on Lobbying," *USA Today* (July 17, 2008). Freddie was fined $3.8 million.

267. U.S. Government Accountability Office, *Fannie Mae and Freddie Mac: Analysis of Options for Revising the Housing Enterprises' Long-term Structures*, GAO-09-782 (Washington, DC: U.S. Government Printing Office, 2009), p. 10.

268. Rob Cyran, "Let's Wind Fannie and Freddie Down," *New York Times* (August 30, 2009).

269. U.S. Government Accountability Office, *Fannie Mae and Freddie Mac: Analysis of Options for Revising the Housing Enterprises' Long-term Structures*, p. 10.

270. "How Fannie and Freddie Make Their Money," *Wall Street Journal* (May 3, 2004). In 2003, the two GSEs held or guaranteed over 47 percent of all residential mortgages in the United States.

271. U.S. Federal Housing Finance Agency, *About FHFA*, http://www.fhfa.gov. Figures are for September 2010, and include Federal Home Loan Banks.

272. U.S. Department of the Treasury and U.S. Department of Housing and Urban Development, *Reforming America's Housing Finance Market: A Report to Congress* (Washington, DC: Authors, 2011).

273. Mitchell, *The American Experiment with Government Corporations*, p. 14.

274. Jerry Mitchell, "Education and Skills for Public Authority Management," *Public Administration Review* 51 (September/October 1991), pp. 429–437. The quotation is on p. 436.

275. For reasons of space, we shall not list each of these five tallies and their sources, but they can be found in the tenth edition of this book (2007), p. 345, Note 219.

276. U.S. Bureau of the Census, *Local Governments and Public School Systems by Type and State: 2007*, http://ftp2.census.gov/govs/cog/GovOrgTab03ss.xls. Figure is for 2007.

277. Jerry Mitchell, "The Policy Activities of Public Authorities," *Policy Studies Journal* 18 (Summer 1990), pp. 928–942. Figures are for 1989. This is likely the most thorough survey of public authorities.

278. Walsh, *The Public's Business*, p. 6.

279. Robert W. Poole, Jr., *Revitalizing State and Local Infrastructure: Empowering Cities and States to Tap Private Capital and Rebuild America*, Policy Study No. 190 (Washington, DC: Reason Public Policy Institute, 1995), pp. 3–4; and Denning and Olson, "Public Enterprise and the Emerging Character of State Service Provisions," pp. 6, 9.

280. Unless noted otherwise, the following discussion is largely drawn from Walsh, *The Public's Business*.

281. U.S. Advisory Commission on Intergovernmental Relations, *Bankruptcies, Defaults, and Other Local Financial Emergencies*, A-99 (Washington, DC: U.S. Government Printing Office, 1985), p. 2.

282. Jerry Mitchell, "Public Authorities and Government Debt: Practices and Issues," *Handbook of Debt Management*, Gerald J. Miller, ed. (New York: Marcel Dekker, 1996), pp. 141–160.

283. Mitchell, *The American Experiment with Government Corporations*, p. 27.

284. Walsh, *The Public's Business*, pp. 27–29.

285. Ann Crittenden, "The Hoover Way to Help Sick Companies," *New York Times* (January 24, 1982). Ironically, the two agencies that FDR used to buy revenue bonds had been created in 1932 by President Herbert Hoover; the other was the Public Works Administration.

286. Walsh, *The Public's Business*, pp. 27–29.

287. Osborne M. Reynolds, Jr., *Local Government Law*, 3rd ed. (St Paul, MN: West, 2009), p. 39.

288. Walsh, *The Public's Business*, p. 6.

289. Reynolds, *Local Government Law*, p. 39.

290. Walsh, *The Public's Business*, p. 289.

291. George L. Shepard, "Let There Be Light: The SEC's New Regulations for the Municipal Securities Market," *Public Budgeting & Finance* 16 (Summer 1996), pp. 133–141.

292. Jerry Mitchell, "Policy Functions and Issues for Public Authorities," *Public Authorities and Public Policy: The Business of Government*, Jerry Mitchell, ed. (Westport, CN: Praeger, 1992), pp. 1–14. The quotation is on p. 5.

293. John Carver, *Boards That Make a Difference* (San Francisco, CA: Jossey-Bass, 1990); and Mitchell, *The American Experiment with Government Corporations*, p. 95.

294. Tanya Heikkila and Kimberley Roussin Isett, "Citizen Involvement and Performance Management in Special-Purpose Governments," *Public Administration Review* 67 (March/April 2007), pp. 238–248.

295. Mitchell, *The American Experiment with Government Corporations*, p. 95.

296. Donald T. Wells and Richard Scheff, "Performance Issues for Public Authorities in Georgia," *Public Authorities and Public Policy*, p. 172. Ninety-five public authorities in Georgia were examined.

297. Mitchell, "Education and Skills for Public Authority Management," pp. 429–437.

298. Ibid. and Tari Renner, "Appointed Local Government Managers: Stability and Change," *Municipal Year Book, 1990* (Washington, DC: International City Management Association, 1990), pp. 30–35. Authority executives had tenures of nearly eight years, compared to over five for city managers.

299. Mitchell, "Education and Skills for Public Authority Management"; and De Santis and Newell, "Local Government Managers' Career Paths," *Municipal Year Book, 1996*, p. 5. Eighteen percent of authority executives had not completed college, compared to 4 percent of local government managers.

300. Ibid. (both citations). Only 38 percent of authority executives had been previously employed by an authority compared to 100 percent of city managers who had worked for a city.

301. Mitchell, "Education and Skills for Public Authority Management," pp. 434–435.

302. Jonathan P. West, "Job Satisfaction of Public Managers in Special Districts," *Review of Public*

Personnel Administration 29 (December 2009), pp. 327–353. Data are for 2008.

303. U.S. Government Accountability Office, *Federally Created Entities: An Overview of Key Attributes*, pp. 39–41. Figures are annual averages for FY 2005–2008.

304. Kathryn A. Foster, *The Political Economy of Special-Purpose Governments* (Washington, DC: Georgetown University Press, 2007), pp. 219–221.

305. The following examples are drawn from: Mitchell, *The American Experiment with Government Corporations*, pp. 96, 107, 116, and 117, respectively.

306. Ibid., p. 108. The U.S. Department of Housing and Urban Development began taking over public housing from local public authorities and began managing them directly in the 1990s.

307. Ibid., pp. 112–127; Donald Axelrod, *Shadow Government: The Hidden World of Public Authorities—and How They Control over $1 Trillion of Your Money* (New York: Wiley, 1992); and Diana Henriques, *The Machinery of Greed: Public Authority Abuse and What to Do about It* (Lexington, MA: Lexington Books, 1986).

308. George Ross Stephens and Nelson Wikstrom, "Trends in Special Districts," *State and Local Government Review* 30 (Spring 1998), pp. 120–138. The quotation is on p. 133.

309. Walsh, *The Public's Business*, p. 4.

310. American Association of Retired Persons survey, as cited in: American Society of Association Executives, *Why Are Associations So Important?* http://www.asaenet.org.

311. U.S. Government Accountability Office, *Nonprofit Sector: Significant Federal Funds Reach the Sector through Various Mechanisms, but More Complete and Reliable Funding Data Are Needed*, GAO-09-193 (Washington, DC: U.S. Government Printing Office, 2009), p. 5. Figure, an estimate, is for 2007.

312. C. Eugene Steuerle and Virginia K. Hodgkinson, "Meeting Social Needs: Comparing Independent Sector and Government Resources," *Nonprofits & Government: Collaboration & Conflict*, 2nd ed., Elizabeth T. Boris and C. Eugene Steuerle, eds. (Washington, DC: Urban Institute Press, 2006), pp. 81–106. Figures are for 2002.

313. Ibid. Figure is for 2002.

314. Independent Sector, *Employment in the Nonprofit Sector* (Washington, DC: Author, 2004).

315. As derived from data in U.S. Government Accountability Office, *Nonprofit Sector: Significant Federal Funds Reach the Sector through Various Mechanisms, but More Complete and Reliable Funding Data Are Needed*, p. 5. Figures are for 2007.

316. Lester M. Salamon, *America's Nonprofit Sector: A Primer*, 2nd ed. (New York: The Foundation Center, 1999), p. 22. Figures are for 1995–1996 and exclude volunteers.

317. Ibid., p. 36.

318. Lester M. Salamon, *The Resilient Sector: The State of Nonprofit America* (Washington, DC: Brookings, 2003), p. 52. Figures are for 1977–1997.

319. U.S. Government Accountability Office, *Nonprofit Sector: Significant Federal Funds Reach the Sector through Various Mechanisms, but More Complete and Reliable Funding Data Are Needed*, Highlights page.

320. Alan J. Abramson, Lester M. Salamon, and C. Eugene Steuerle, "Federal Spending and Tax Policies: Their Implications for the Nonprofit Sector," *Nonprofits & Government: Collaboration & Conflict*, 2nd ed., Elizabeth T. Boris and C. Eugene Steuerle, eds. (Washington, DC: Urban Institute Press, 2006), pp. 107–140. The data are on p. 118. These researchers estimate that Washington directed $317 billion to the nonprofit sector in FY 2004, when Washington spent more than $305 billion on private-sector contracts. See Federal Procurement Data System, *Federal Procurement Report* (Washington, DC: Author, 2004).

321. As derived from data in Abramson, Salamon, and Steuerle, "Federal Spending and Tax Policies," pp. 118, 111, 117, 113. Data are for 1980–2004.

322. The Federal Funding Accountability and Transparency Act of 2006 requires the collecting and reporting of data concerning "subawards," or those federal expenditures that end up with nonprofits and other recipients after being funneled through those entities that received federal money directly.

323. As derived from data in U.S. Internal Revenue Service, "Table 1. Form 990 Returns of 501 (3) (c) Organizations: Balance Sheet and Income Statement Items, by Asset Size, Tax Year 2008,"

SOI Tax Stats—Charities & Other Tax Exempt Organizations Statistics (Washington, DC: Author, 2011), http://www.irs.gov/taxstats/charitablestats/article/0,id=97176,00.html. Figure is for 2008.

324. U.S. Government Accountability Office, *Nonprofit Sector: Significant Federal Funds Reach the Sector through Various Mechanisms, but More Complete and Reliable Funding Data Are Needed*, Highlights page. Figures are for 2006. This is an analysis of "nonprofit organizations' roles in 19 federal programs."

325. Ibid. Figure is for 2006.

326. Woods Bowman and Marion R. Fremont-Smith, "Nonprofits and State and Local Government," *Nonprofits & Government: Collaboration & Conflict*, 2nd ed., Elizabeth T. Boris and C. Eugene Steuerle, eds. (Washington, DC: Urban Institute Press, 2006), pp. 181–218, p. 194. In 2001–2002, state and local governments provided an estimated $112 billion directly to nonprofit organizations, of which $84 billion was in the form of federal pass-through money.

327. Choi, Cho, Wright, and Brudney, "Dimensions of Contracting for Service Delivery by American State Administrative Agencies," p. 50. Figure, 71 percent, is for 1998 (n = 850).

328. William Luksetich, "Government Funding and Nonprofit Organizations," *Nonprofit and Voluntary Sector Quarterly* 37 (September 2008), pp. 434–442. This is a study of all the states over fourteen years.

329. Bowman and Fremont-Smith, "Nonprofits and State and Local Government," pp. 201–207. Figures are for 2001–2002.

330. Luksetich, "Government Funding and Nonprofit Organizations."

331. Anna A. Amirkhanyan, "Monitoring across Sectors: Examining the Effect of Nonprofit and For-Profit Contractor Ownership on Performance Monitoring in State and Local Contracts," *Public Administration Review* 70 (September/October 2010), pp. 742–755.

332. Warner and Hefetz, "Cooperative Competition," p. 14. Figure is for 2007.

333. As derived from data in Hatry and Valente, "Alternative Service Delivery Approaches Involving Increased Use of the Private Sector," pp. 216–217.

334. Brown, "The Dynamics of Government-to-Government Contracts."

335. Lamothe and Lamothe, "The Dynamics of Local Service Delivery Arrangements and the Role of Nonprofits," p. 791.

336. Amirkhanyan, "Monitoring across Sectors."

337. Marvel and Marvel, "Shaping the Provision of Outsourced Public Services," p. 197.

338. Beth Gazley, "Beyond the Contract: The Scope and Nature of Informal Government-Nonprofit Partnerships," *Public Administration Review* 68 (January/February 2008), pp. 141–154. The figure is on p. 144; the quotation is on p. 146. This is a study of two large, comparable samples of municipal and county officials and nonprofit executives in Georgia conducted in 2003.

339. Beth Gazley and Jeffrey L. Brudney, "The Purpose (and Perils) of Government-Nonprofit Partnerships," *Nonprofit and Voluntary Sector Quarterly* 36 (September 2007), pp. 389–415. The quotation is on p. 389. This is a study of two large, comparable samples of municipal and county officials and nonprofit executives in Georgia conducted in 2003.

340. Beth Gazley, "Why *Not* Partner With Local Government? Nonprofit Managerial Perceptions of Collaborative Disadvantage," *Nonprofit and Voluntary Sector Quarterly* 39 (February 2010), pp. 51–76. This is a survey of 285 responding executive directors of nonprofit organizations in Georgia conducted in 2004.

341. Gazley and Brudney, "The Purpose (and Perils) of Government-Nonprofit Partnerships," p. 389.

342. As derived from data in Elizabeth T. Boris, "Introduction: Nonprofit Organizations in a Democracy—Roles and Responsibilities," *Nonprofits & Government: Collaboration & Conflict*, 2nd ed., Elizabeth T. Boris and C. Eugene Steuerle, eds. (Washington, DC: Urban Institute Press, 2006), pp. 1–36. The data are on p. 9. Figure is for 2004, and combines "Health" and "Human Services."

343. Salamon, *America's Nonprofit Sector*, p. 55.

344. As derived from data in Steuerle and Hodgkinson, "Meeting Social Needs," p. 101. Figure is for 2003, and includes "Health," which accounted for 57 percent of the total.

345. Lester M. Salamon, "Government and the Voluntary Sector in an Era of Retrenchment: The American Experience," *Journal of Public Policy* 6 (January–March 1986), pp. 1–20. Figure, 42 percent (p. 7) is for 1982.

346. Salamon, *The Resilient Sector*, p. 54. Figures are for 1997.

347. Brookings Institution, as cited in Partnership for Public Service, *Public Opinion and Public Service* (Washington, DC: Author, 2005), p. 6. Figures are for 1998.

348. Kanika Kapur and Burton D. Weisbrod, "The Roles of Government and Nonprofit Suppliers in Mixed Industries," *Public Finance Review* 60 (July/August 2000), pp. 275–308.

349. Carolyn J. Heinrich, "Organizational Form and Performance: An Empirical Investigation of Nonprofit and For-Profit Job-Training Service Providers," *Journal of Policy Analysis and Management* 19 (Spring 2000), pp. 233–261; and Kristen Gronsberg, "Poverty and Nonprofit Organization Behavior," *Social Science Review* 64 (June 1990), pp. 208–241.

350. Princeton Survey Research Associates and Brookings Institution, *Health of the Public Service* (Washington, DC: Authors, 2001).

351. Brookings Institution as cited in Ibid. Figures are for 2002.

352. Fernida Handy, Stephanie Seto, Armanda Wakaruk, *et al.*, "The Discerning Consumer: Is Nonprofit Status a Factor?" *Nonprofit and Voluntary Sector Quarterly* 39 (October 2010), pp. 866–883.

353. Joseph Galaskiewicz, Wolfgang Bielefeld, and Myron Dowell, "Networks and Organizational Growth: A Study of Community-Based Nonprofits," *Administrative Science Quarterly* 51 (September 2006), pp. 337–380. The quotation is on p. 337.

354. David F. Suarez, "Collaboration and Professionalization: The Contours of Public Sector Funding for Nonprofit Organizations," *Journal of Public Administration Research and Theory* 21 (April 2011), pp. 307–326. The quotation is on p. 307. This summarizes 200 interviews with leaders of nonprofit organizations in the San Francisco Bay Area.

355. Kunle Akingbola, "Staffing, Retention, and Government Funding: A Case Study," *Nonprofit Management & Leadership* 14 (Summer 2004), pp. 453–465. The quotations are on pp. 463, 453.

356. U.S. Government Accountability Office, *Nonprofit Sector: Significant Federal Funds Reach the Sector through Various Mechanisms, but More Complete and Reliable Funding Data Are Needed*, Highlights page. Figure is for 2006.

357. A third of all state agencies outsource by awarding "grants and subsidies," and they are the third most-used method of privatization employed by the states. See Chi, Arnold, and Perkins, "Privatization in State Government," p. 468. In addition, those state and local agencies that rely most heavily on the independent sector to deliver their services are also the leading awarders of state and local grants. This conclusion is derived from data in: Salamon, "Government and the Voluntary Sector in an Era of Retrenchment," p. 7; Choi, Cho, Wright, and Brudney, "Dimensions of Contracting for Service Delivery by American State Administrative Agencies," p. 50; Chi and Jasper, *Private Practices*, p. 14; and Warner and Hefetz, "Cooperative Competition," pp. 14–15.

358. Eleanor Brown and Kaitlyn Caughlin, "Donors, Ideologues, and Bureaucrats: Government Objectives and the Performance of the Nonprofit Sector," *Financial Accountability & Management* 25 (February 2009), pp. 99–114.

359. Greg Chen, "Does Meeting Standards Affect Charitable Giving? An Empirical Study of New York Metropolitan Charities," *Nonprofit Management & Leadership* 19 (Spring 2009), pp. 349–365. The quotations are on p. 360. This is an analysis of the Better Business Bureau's Charity Review program.

360. In contrast to the analysis cited, another quantitative study found that "reliance on government funding decreases the likelihood that nonprofit organizations will develop strong, representative boards" (p. 468). See Chao Guo, "When Government Becomes the Principal Philanthropist: The Effects of Public Funding on Patterns of Nonprofit Governance," *Public Administration Review* 67 (May/June 2007), pp. 458–473.

361. Melissa Middleton Stone, Mark A. Hager, and Jennifer J. Griffin, "Organizational Characteristics and Funding Environments: A Study of a Population of United Way-Affiliated Nonprofits," *Public Administration Review* 61 (May/June 2001), pp. 276–289. This is an analysis of 191 of these affiliates in Massachusetts.

362. Hee Soun Jang and Richard C. Feiock, "Public versus Private Funding of Nonprofit Organizations," *Public Performance & Management Review* 31 (December 2007), pp. 174–190.

363. Stone, Hager, and Griffin, "Organizational Characteristics and Funding Environments," pp. 276, 285.

364. Kelly LeRoux, "Paternalistic or Participatory Governance? Examining Opportunities for Client Participation in Nonprofit Social Service Organizations," *Public Administration Review* 69 (May/June 2009), pp. 504–517. The quotations are on pp. 513, 504.

365. U.S. Bureau the Census, *Statistical Abstract of the United States, 2011*, 130th ed. (Washington, DC: U.S. Government Printing Office, 2011), Table 583. Figure, 28 percent, is for 2009.

366. Murray Weitzman, Nadine Jalandoni, Linda Lampkin, and Thomas Pollack, *The New Nonprofit Almanac and Desk Reference* (San Francisco, CA: Jossey-Bass, 2002), pp. 18–19. Figures are for 1998.

367. U.S. Bureau the Census, *Statistical Abstract of the United States, 2011*, Table 583. Figures are for 2009.

368. Council for Excellence in Government and Hart-Teeter Poll, *America Unplugged Citizens and Their Government* (Washington, DC: Authors, 1999), p. 5. In 1999, 27 percent had participated.

369. Chi, Arnold, and Perkins, "Privatization in State Government," pp. 468, 479. Figures are for 2002.

370. Chi and Jasper, *Private Practices*, p. 14. Data are for 1997.

371. Sydney Duncombe, "Volunteers in City Government: Advantages, Disadvantages, and Uses," *National Civic Review* 74 (September 1985), pp. 356–364.

372. As derived from data in Warner and Hefetz, "Cooperative Competition," p. 15. Figures are for 2007.

373. As derived from data in Hatry and Valente, "Alternative Service Delivery Approaches Involving Increased Use of Private Sector," pp. 216–217. Figures are for 1982.

374. Warner and Hefetz, "Cooperative Competition," p. 15. Data are for 2007.

375. Robert S. Montjoy and Jeffrey L. Brudney, "Volunteers in the Delivery of Public Services, Hidden Costs...and Benefits," *American Review of Public Administration* 21 (December 1991), pp. 327–344.

376. Matthew A. Liao-Troth, "Attitude Differences Between Paid Workers and Volunteers," *Nonprofit Management and Leadership* 11 (Summer 2001), pp. 423–442.

377. David M. Van Slyke and Janet L. Johnson, "Nonprofit Organizational Performance and Resource Development Strategies: Exploring the Link between Individual Volunteering and Giving," *Public Performance & Management Review* 29 (June 2006), pp. 467–496.

378. William D. Duncombe and Jeffrey L. Brudney, "The Optimal Mix for Volunteers and Paid Staff in Local Governments: An Application to Municipal Fire Departments," *Public Finance Quarterly* 23 (July 1995), pp. 356–384.

379. Jeffrey L. Brudney and William D. Duncombe, "An Economic Evaluation of Paid, Volunteer, and Mixed Staffing Options for Public Services," *Public Administration Review* 52 (September/October 1992), pp. 474–481. The quotation is on p. 474.

380. Paul Posner, Robert Yetvin, Mark Schneiderman, et al., "A Survey of Voucher Use: Variation and Common Elements," *Vouchers and the Provision of Public Services*, C. Eugene Steuerle, Van Doorn Ooms, George Peterson, and Robert D. Reischauer, eds. (Washington, DC: Brookings, Committee for Economic Development, and Urban Institute, 2000), pp. 503–540.

381. U.S. Bureau of the Census, *Statistical Abstract of the United States, 2011*, Table 569. Figures are for 2009.

382. Ibid., Tables 140, 142. Figures are for 2009.

383. U.S. Congressional Budget Office, *An Analysis of the President's Budgetary Proposals for Fiscal Year 2000* (Washington, DC: U.S. Government Printing Office, 1999), Table 3-2. This figure is a projection.

384. Burt R. Brown, "Vouchers for Federal Targeted Training Programs," *Vouchers and the Provision of Public Services*, C. Eugene Steuerle, Van Doorn Ooms, George Peterson, and Robert D. Reischauer, eds. (Washington, DC: Brookings, Committee for Economic Development, and Urban Institute, 2000), pp. 224–250.

385. U.S. Department of Health and Human Services, Office of the Inspector General, *States' Child Care Certificate Systems: An Early Assessment of Vulnerabilities and Barriers* (Washington, DC: Author, 1998), p. 3.

386. George E. Peterson, "Housing Vouchers: The U.S. Experience," *Vouchers and the Provision of Public Services*, C. Eugene Steuerle, Van Doorn Ooms, George Peterson, and Robert D. Reischauer, eds. (Washington, DC: Brookings, Committee for Economic Development, and Urban Institute, 2000), pp. 139–175.

387. Center on Budget and Policy Priorities, *Introduction to the Housing Voucher Program* (Washington, DC, Author, 2003), p. 2.

388. Chi, Arnold, and Perkins, "Privatization in State Government," pp. 468, 479. Figures are for 2002.

389. Chi and Jasper, *Private Practices*, p. 14. Data are for 1997.

390. As derived from data in Elaine Morley, "Patterns in the Use of Alternative Service Delivery Approaches," *Municipal Year Book, 1989* (Washington, DC: International City Management Association, 1989), pp. 33–44 and Hatry and Valente, "Alternative Delivery Approaches Involving Increased Use of the Public Sector," pp. 216–217. Figures and services (p. 39) are for 1988. Trend data are for 1982–1988.

391. As derived from data in The Foundation for Educational Choice, *The ABCs of School Choice, 2011 edition* (Indianapolis, IN: Author, 2011), p. 8. We have excluded from this count of twenty-three school choice programs two "town tuitioning programs" in Maine and Vermont. These programs exist simply because some towns have no schools, and therefore must send their pupils to schools in other towns.

Intergovernmental Administration

The administration of a "single" domestic policy often involves a pastiche of funding sources and public administrators interacting through all governmental levels. This pastiche is called *intergovernmental relations*, or the series of financial, legal, political, and administrative relationships established among all units of government that possess varying degrees of authority and jurisdictional autonomy. These relationships are called *federalism* when applied more narrowly to the federal government's relations with state governments, and the states' relationships with each other, although, in this book, we usually use these terms interchangeably. *Intergovernmental administration,* sometimes called *intergovernmental management,* is the management and coordination of the relationships among governments for the purpose of achieving specific policy goals.

SOME SYSTEMIC FINDINGS ABOUT FEDERALISM

The United States, of course, has a federal system of governance. It is not unique in this respect; and cross-country studies, as well as a few analyses of the fifty American states, find that national and state intergovernmental systems share some characteristics that differentiate them from unitary systems. A few of these findings follow:

- As we noted in the introduction to Part III, nations with federal governmental structures associate with less political corruption[1] and smaller shadow economies[2] than do those with unitary structures.
- As we detailed in Chapter 7, federal systems deliver services and tax more efficiently than unitary ones.[3]
- Total public-sector employment is lower in countries with federal structures than in those with unitary ones.[4]
- The greater the degree of fiscal decentralization in a nation (a condition that is common in federal systems, but is essentially absent in unitary ones), the fewer public employees there are in the national government, but the more employees there are in subnational governments and in total.[5]
- The greater the degree of fiscal decentralization in a country, the slower that public expenditures, tax burdens, and governments grow.[6]
- However, the more that public *spending* is decentralized (in contrast to revenue collecting) throughout a nation, the *faster* that its governments grow.[7]
- The greater the degree of fiscal decentralization in a country, the smaller the public sector's share of the nation's gross domestic product (GDP). This is especially true when there are also many competing governments in the country.[8]
- The greater degree of fiscal decentralization in an American state, the higher the level of public trust in government. A single standard deviation increase in either revenue decentralization or expenditure decentralization correlates with a nearly 4 percent increase in trusting people.[9]

- The more governments that there are in an American state, the higher the level of public trust in government. A single standard deviation in the number of governments correlates with an almost 2.5 percent increase in the number of trusting people.[10]
- Federalism fosters policy innovation. More than four-fifths of all "creativity in government" is found in states and communities.[11] The American states are "laboratories of democracy" in that states adopt innovative policies that are originated by other states.[12] Insofar as the U.S. Government is concerned, however, the states are no laboratories of democracy. There is little connection in the aggregate between changes in state policy agendas and "national patterns of policy attention."[13]

All in all, federal systems of government and decentralized governance appear to be less corrupt, more efficient, less costly, more responsive, more innovative, and have more trusting citizens than do unitary systems and centralized governance.

AMERICAN FEDERALISM, THE CONSTITUTION, AND THE COURTS

Americans are governed by a lot of governments, and their number grows.

America's Proliferating Governments

Table 12-1 identifies the 89,451 governments in the United States by type and indicates their fluctuations in twenty-year increments since 1942.

Most of the proliferation of cities and towns occurred in the years following World War II and was largely due to unplanned metropolitan growth. For instance, New Squier, New York, was established so that a kosher slaughterhouse could be operated, and Gardena, California, was founded so that its residents could play poker legally.[14]

Special purpose governments evidence the greatest flux. School districts, as a consequence of the school consolidation movement, have withered by 88 percent to less than an eighth of their number sixty-five years earlier. Special districts, largely as a result of popular resistance to consolidating general purpose local governments, have more than quadrupled.

The Constitution: The Functions of Federalism

The constitution focuses on three facets of federalism.[15]

Separate National and State Identities Most fundamentally, the Constitution establishes separate identities for the nation and the states. For the

TABLE 12-1				
Number of Governmental Units, by Type: 1942, 1962, 1982, and 2007				
Type of Government	1942	1962	1982	2007
Total	155,116	91,237	81,831	89,451
U.S. government	1	1	1	1
State governments	48	50	50	50
Local governments	155,067	91,186	81,780	89,476
Counties	3,050	3,043	3,041	3,033
Municipalities	16,220	18,000	19,076	19,492
Townships	18,919	17,142	16,734	16,519
School districts	108,579	34,678	14,851	13,051
Special districts	8,299	18,323	28,078	37,381

Source: U.S. Bureau of the Census, *Local Governments and Public School Systems by Type and State: 2007*, http://ftp2.census.gov/Gov/cog/GovOrgTab03ss.xls.

nation, perhaps the most significant statement is in *Article VI*: "This Constitution and the Laws of the United States...shall be the Supreme Law of the Land." The most important clause for the states is *Section 3, Article IV*, which stipulates that state legislatures may prohibit the formation of new states, or parts of new states, within their boundaries.

Distinct National and State Responsibilities   Four portions of the Constitution distinguish national and state responsibilities. *Section 8, Article I*, delegates seventeen specific powers to the national government, including defense, general welfare, and commerce, and leaves the remaining powers to the states. The *Tenth Amendment*, which was added hastily in response to such populist rabble rousers as Patrick Henry, specifies that these remaining powers are "reserved to the States...or to the people," thereby drawing a darker line that the federal government could not, presumably, cross. *Article I*'s *Section 9* prohibits the national government from exercising certain powers, such as taxing state exports, and its *Section 10* forbids the states from undertaking certain responsibilities, such as coining money.

Integrating Nation and States   Finally, the Constitution deals with the integration of the national and state governments by providing for collaboration among them in the performance of some vital functions. For example, the federal and state governments cooperate in amending the Constitution, electing a president, and, through Congress, enacting laws.

The Courts: Necessary and Proper Implied Powers

The Constitution's federal features have been and are being refined by the courts. Without question, the most influential single case in this process is *McCulloch* v. *Maryland*, which was settled by the Supreme Court in 1819.

The case involved the state of Maryland's attempt to tax the second U.S. Bank, which was located in Maryland, but soon waxed into an argument over whether the United States could even form a bank. The federal government argued that a national bank could be established because it was an "implied power" under the Constitution, even though the Constitution did not specifically authorize such policies as the establishment of the bank.

Chief Justice John Marshall and his colleagues concurred, citing the final sentence of Section 8, Article I, which accords the federal government the authority "To make all Laws which shall be necessary and proper for carrying into Execution...all the Powers vested by this Constitution in the Government of the United States." Hence, Congress had the power to do whatever is "necessary and proper to implement its specified functions."

THE EVOLUTION OF INTERGOVERNMENTAL ADMINISTRATION

Operating within the formal rules of the game established by the Constitution and by subsequent judicial interpretation, America's governments have gone through five phases in their administrative relationships. Early scholars identified the first two of these phases with lasting metaphors involving pastry, which we, with admittedly dubious judgment, have extended.

The Layer Cake: Dual Federalism, 1789–1932

The Constitution recognizes only two levels of government: national and state. Hence, the terms "dual federalism" and "layer cake federalism" indicate that, during the nation's first 140 years, the federal and state governments stuck to their very separate knitting. For example, when Congress in 1854 did try (unusually) to transfer funds to the states to help them treat their indigent insane, the president vetoed the bill on the logic that to encourage the states to "become humble suppliants for the bounty of the Federal Government" would reverse "their true relation to this Union."[16]

In the aftermath of the Civil War, however, the nation entered a period of dented dual federalism. From 1865 to 1869, the country (at least the victorious northern half of it) enacted the Thirteenth, Fourteenth, and Fifteenth Amendments to the Constitution. These new civil rights policies legitimized federal involvement in heretofore sacrosanct state affairs.

The federal judiciary also began to penetrate state sovereignty. Between 1794 and 1860, the Supreme Court voided, on average, about one state law per year. Between 1860 and 1937 (the year when the Court radically reversed course and actively sanctioned a dramatic expansion of federal power), however, the Court overruled nearly seven per year. Dual federalism, if dinged and dented, still survived, but "the pitiful position in 1860 of the national government was ended."[17]

The Marble Cake: Cooperative Federalism, 1933–1960

With the ascension of Franklin Delano Roosevelt to the presidency in 1933, the layer cake sagged and whorled into "marble cake federalism," marking a radical expansion of Washington's intergovernmental power.

As we detail later, federal financial aid to state and local governments burgeoned. Perhaps of even greater significance, governments trusted each other to act in the common interest, and governments occupying higher levels in the federal hierarchy imposed few restrictions on governments at the lower levels. By 1960, only two "major" intergovernmental mandates had been imposed by Washington.[18]

The Pound Cake: Co-Optive Federalism, 1961–1980

In our third phase of federalism, the federal government grew more domineering and demanding in the intergovernmental construct. Perhaps "pound cake" best describes federalism during its co-optive phase, because state and local governments were being pounded by Washington.

When John F. Kennedy became president in 1961, Washington pragmatists addressed federalism. Problems—many of which festered not in Washington but in subnational jurisdictions—had to be solved, and the federal government was the government to solve them. It did this by hurling money,

in the form of hundreds of highly specialized grants that had thousands of regulatory strings attached, at state capitols and town halls.

States and communities were more than willing to pay the price of federal largesse. As an acerbic observer noted during this period, "If Washington offered grants for cancer implants, cities would line up to apply."[19] By the end of the 1970s, federal co-optation had replaced intergovernmental cooperation, and state and local governments verged on truly becoming "humble suppliants" of a federal satrap.

The Crumble Cake: Competitive Federalism, 1980–2008

Around 1980, there were signs that the intergovernmental cake was beginning to loosen, and deteriorate, into a "crumble cake."

Fending for Oneself During the 1980s, much of the federal fiscal assistance to states and localities was withdrawn, and, with it, "the network of federal offices and agencies that was established to improve and rationalize intergovernmental management" was "diminished, disbanded," and politicized.[20] Fitful, but not unsuccessful, efforts initiated in the 1930s to form a coherent national policy for localities dribbled away in the 1980s, and by the 2000s "the era of federal urban policy" was, "like, way over."[21]

The consequence of Washington's three decades of indifference to state and local concerns was the debut of "Competitive," or "Fend-for-Yourself," federalism.[22] "Competitive," however, no longer referred to state and local governments competing among themselves for federal grants, as it did during Co-Optive Federalism. Instead, competition meant that all governments, including the federal one, were competing with each other for revenue. In just three years during the 1980s, state tax collections rose by one-third.[23]

Faltering Faith in the Feds Washington, at least in the popular mind, has lost this competition. Over thirty-five years, the plurality of Americans who thought that they got "the *most* for their money" from Washington (not quite two-fifths of Americans), rather than from state and local governments,[24] flipped, and became the plurality who thought that they got "the *least* for their money" from the feds (slightly more than two-fifths).[25]

Americans also have greater "trust and confidence" in the grassroots governments than in Washington. Just 53 percent of Americans express a "great deal" or a "fair" amount of trust and confidence in the federal government (55 percent say this for the states, and 62 percent for localities), and 47 percent say they have "little" or "none" (44 percent for the states, and 37 percent for local governments).[26] Another reputable poll found that only 22 percent of the American public "trust the government in Washington almost always or most of the time," an astoundingly low proportion.[27]

The Angel Food Cake: Manna-from-Heaven Federalism, 2009–Present

In 2009, President Barack Obama, "the first genuine big-city president the country has had for nearly a century,"[28] radically reversed course. He created an Office of Urban Affairs and an Office of Intergovernmental Affairs, and placed both in the White House.

Both offices symbolized a wider turnaround. Obama took on the twin pillars of federal intergovernmental policy, fiscal federalism and regulatory federalism. As we review later, he poured money into state and local coffers and lifted those governments out of much of the mire of regulations and red tape into which they had slowly sunk over five decades.

FISCAL FEDERALISM

The old question in politics of who gets what, when, where, and how is nowhere more evident than in the intergovernmental money game. This game is called *fiscal federalism*, or the granting of funds by one government to other governments for the purpose of achieving specific policy goals. It would be useful to recheck Chapter 8's Figure 8-1, which charts the rivers and rivulets of intergovernmental revenue.

A World Turned Upside Down: A Century of Fiscal Change

At the beginning of the twentieth century, local governments dominated public finance, accounting for 58 percent of all governmental expenditures. (When we delete national defense and diplomacy, localities accounted for an astounding 72 percent of all governments' spending.) Washington spent 34 percent of all public outlays, and the states a nominal 8 percent.[29] Local governments retained their fiscal prominence until 1934.[30]

In 1913, the Constitution's Sixteenth Amendment, which permitted the federal government to collect taxes on incomes, was ratified, and intergovernmental finance would never be the same. In just a quarter century, Washington emerged as the reigning figure in public finance, the states had doubled their portion of all public outlays, and local governments' share had declined by nearly a third.[31]

Spending by the federal government surpassed all state and local spending in 1970, a pattern that has continued unabated ever since.[32] Today, Washington spends 55 percent of all governments' outlays. The fifty states spend 25 percent, and the nation's 89,476 local governments account for 20 percent.[33]

It is a world turned upside down.

The Grant-in-Aid: Foundation of Fiscal Federalism

Policymakers realized that the new realities of intergovernmental finance required that richer governments help poorer ones. Hence, the emergence of fiscal federalism, the cornerstone of which is the *grant-in-aid,* or a conditional "gift" from one government to another that subsidizes an existing program or encourages new ones.

Getting Theirs: Lobbying by Governments   The federal government distributes these gifts more lavishly than any other, so it is understandable that thirty-five states maintain offices in Washington,[34] and that the states spend from $7 million to $10 million each year in taxpayers' dollars lobbying Congress and federal agencies.[35] More than 1,400 local governments[36] spend about $60 million annually to hire Washington lobbyists, a figure that doubled in less than a decade.[37] "Of the 250 top-grossing [lobbying] firms in Washington, 48 have state, local and tribal governments as their leading source of revenue, far more than any other sector."[38]

State capitals are not spared. "Legislative liaisons" for local governments, state agencies, and other governmental entities comprise an estimated 25–35 percent of all lobbyists in the capitals of "most states."[39]

The Purposes of Federal Grants Forty-five percent of all federal grant dollars sent to state and local governments is for health care; 93 percent of this growing area is devoted to Medicaid, a health program for the poor, the costs of which are shared between Washington and the states. Nineteen percent is devoted to welfare, notably grants for needy families and food stamps; 17 percent pertains to education, training, employment, and social services; and 11 percent supports transportation projects, more than half of which is funneled to highways.[40]

Federal Categorical Grants Washington sends more than four-fifths of its grant dollars to state and local governments as *categorical grants*, or grants-in-aid that address narrow policy issues, and which rigidly stipulate precisely how federal money is to be expended.[41] Ninety-eight percent of federal grant programs are categorical grants,[42] and there are three kinds.

Project, or *discretionary*, *grants* are grants that are distributed at the discretion of federal administrators. Eighty-six percent of all federal grant programs are project grants.[43]

Formula grants are grants distributed by an administratively or legislatively prescribed formula, and the federal government pays without limit (unless one is contained in the formula) according to the formula. Although barely 13 percent of all federal grant programs are formula grants,[44] a whopping 85 percent of all federal grant dollars are distributed by formulas.[45]

Finally, there are *formula/project grants*, which are awarded at the discretion of federal administrators, but within the bounds of a formula, such as the amount of dollars that may be awarded to a

state. Just 2 percent of all federal grant programs are formula/project grants.[46]

Federal Block Grants The remaining federal assistance funds are in *block grants*, which are a type of formula grant that allows the recipient more discretion than categorical grants. Block grants were unknown until 1966, and have consistently emphasized economic development. In part because of congressional distrust of the grassroots, block grants never have accounted for more than a fifth of all federal aid dollars, and their funding long has been sporadically declining.[47]

Congress' Categorical Favorite: Fragmentation Three-fourths of all grants programs administer less than 2 percent of all grant dollars, and a fifth of all programs are responsible for less than 1 percent of all grant dollars.[48]

This is intergovernmental fragmentation of a rare order. To their credit, federal officials have attempted to address the implications of grants fragmentation, but these efforts, extending over eighty years, have come to naught, largely because of congressional resistance,[49] a phenomenon that has been aptly described as "creeping categorization."[50]

A Shaky Helping Hand: The Erratic Federal Role in State and Local Budgets

Like a libertine, Congress has toyed with state and local governments, sometimes showering them with presents and other times shriveling them with parsimony. Here, we trace the ups and downs of the federal Ferris wheel of fiscal federalism.

Down, 1789–1932 Although the federal government has allocated grants to subnational governments since the eighteenth century, they never amounted to much during the nation's first 140 years or so. Even during the opening thirty years of the twentieth century, federal intergovernmental grants accounted for less than one-half of 1 percent of the national economy; their modest number ranged from five to twelve;[51] and they constituted about 3 percent of all federal outlays,[52] one-half of 1 percent of total revenue (i.e., general revenue and other than general revenue, as described in Chapter 8) in the states and a trace amount of total revenue in local governments.[53]

Up, 1933–1940 President Roosevelt assumed office in 1933 and quickly set about revolutionizing fiscal federalism. Federal assistance shot from a fraction of 1 percent of the economy to almost 4 percent in 1934 and never sank below 2 percent for the remainder of the decade.[54] The number of federal grants programs more than doubled during the 1930s,[55] and their funding flexed by a phenomenal factor of fifteen.[56] By 1939, federal grants accounted for almost two-fifths of *all* federal spending,[57] a record sum of nearly $3 billion that would not be equaled for more than a decade.[58]

The impact of this fiscal revolution was stunning. Federal grants expanded exponentially from a sliver of 1 percent of total state revenue in 1932 to a head-turning 27 percent by 1934. Direct federal grants quadrupled their contribution to all local revenue from 1 percent in 1934 to nearly 4 percent by 1940.[59]

Down, 1941–1958 During the 1940s and 1950s, federal grant dollars slipped significantly, and rarely exceeded 1 percent of the national economy.[60] Even by the early 1950s, federal grant programs numbered fewer than forty,[61] and throughout almost all of the fifties, they accounted from 5 to 6 percent of federal outlays.[62] On average, about 14 percent of total state revenue, and 1 percent of all local revenue, were provided by direct federal grants.[63]

Up. Way Up, 1959–1978 Beginning in 1959, federal grants exploded, and this explosion thundered on throughout the next two decades.

Federal grants-in-aid peaked during this period in 1978, when 492 grants programs[64] accounted for almost 4 percent of the economy,[65] a proportion that had not been seen since 1934, and 17 percent of all federal expenditures.[66] Between 1959 and 1978, federally furnished funding as a portion of state and local budgets more than doubled, attaining nearly 28 percent of these governments' total outlays and an astonishing 47 percent of their own source spending.[67]

Between 1957 and 1978, the dollars that federal grants contributed to total state revenue burgeoned by more than a third to 22 percent.[68] In 1978, three-fourths of all state agencies received federal grants, up from just a third in 1964,[69] and these grants made up *at least half* of the budgets in more than a fourth of all state agencies![70]

Between 1960 and 1978, the portion of federal assistance allocated directly to local governments more than tripled, from 8 to 29 percent.[71] Direct federal aid as a share of total local revenue jumped nine-fold, from 1 percent in 1957 to over 9 percent in 1978.[72] When we combine this direct federal aid with federal pass-through grants to the states that were earmarked for local uses, estimated federal assistance as a share of local budgets more than tripled, from 5 to 16 percent.[73]

Down. Way Down, 1979–1989 After 1978, federal assistance to states and communities plummeted—precipitously. Within a decade, Washington's intergovernmental aid as a share of GDP had fallen by almost half to 2 percent; federal assistance as a portion of federal outlays declined by more than a third to 11 percent; and direct federal grants as a share of total state revenue slipped by nearly a fourth to 17 percent, and by a startling two-thirds to 3 percent of all local revenue.[74]

Up, Down, Whatever, 1990–2008 After 1990, Washington began to reinfuse states and localities with federal funds. By the mid-2000s, there were more grants programs than ever—some 1,200,[75] sponsored by at least twenty-nine federal agencies.[76] Federal grants accounted for over 3 percent of GDP and 16 percent of all federal outlays.[77]

A record proportion—four-fifths—of all state agencies received federal assistance.[78] Direct federal grants contributed 20 percent of all state revenue, slightly higher than in the 1980s, and 4 percent of total local revenue, up by a fourth from the 1980s. When direct federal grants to localities are combined with federal pass-through grants to the states, they comprised an estimated 13 percent of all local revenue.[79]

All in all, the 1990s and 2000s appeared to be mostly good grants news for the grassroots governments. But appearances can be deceiving.

Grants for Payments for Individuals One such deception that emerged during this period concerned *grants for payments for individuals*, which are federal grants to state governments that are earmarked for particular federal programs—typically, welfare programs—that channel federal funds through state governments to state residents.

Grants for payments for individuals butter no parsnips for state and local governments. They do not fund state or local programs; they fund only federal ones. By the end of the 2000s, grants for payments for individuals accounted for almost two-thirds of federal grant dollars,[80] twice their proportion in 1978, when they amounted to less than a third.[81] (Following the introduction of massive recession-recovery funds into federal grants [detailed shortly], however, grants for payments to individuals declined slightly to 60 percent of all federal grant dollars, but this decline is probably a temporary one.[82])

Medicaid and Monetary Misery Medicaid, the health care grant for the poor, is the gorilla of grants for payments for individuals.

From the 1980s through the 2000s, the dollars in all federal intergovernmental grants for each and every purpose steadily declined—with one exception: Medicaid.[83] Medicaid's share of federal grants is so huge, accounting for more than two-fifths of *all* grant dollars, that its presence obscured this shrinkage. In addition, Medicaid's growth was so formidable (two decades earlier, Medicaid's share of grant dollars was a relatively modest 30 percent) that it also veiled the fact that the overall long-term fiscal trend in federal grants was not one of growth, but of stasis.[84]

During the 2000s, even the growth in Medicaid's funding shrank. By 2006, the shrinkage in Washington's intergovernmental grants no longer could be hidden, and federal grants, including Medicaid, as measured in constant dollars, were in overall decline, sinking by 4 percent over three years.[85]

Grants, Taxes, and Corruption The shrinkage in federal grant dollars for state and local programs veiled another serious and growing deception in Washington's grants system: corruption. Billions

of federal grant dollars were being sent to tax cheats, many of whom had committed other federal crimes, who exploited federal confidentiality policies about tax data.

About 39,000 recipients of $124 billion in federal grants, or 4 percent of those recipients who directly received just a fifth of all federal grant dollars, owe $790 million in federal taxes.[86] Two percent the nearly 55,000 income-tax-exempt organizations that owe Washington almost $1 billion in unpaid, primarily payroll, taxes were awarded $14 billion in direct federal grants.[87]

Each of these unpaid tax amounts is "understated," some substantially so. More than four-fifths of these tax-cheating, grant-awarded scofflaws had not disclosed that they owed back taxes when they applied for their grants, a clear violation of federal law and an equally clear indicator of their criminal motivation.[88]

In sum, the 1990s and 2000s were the "whatever" decades of fiscal federalism.

Up, Up, and Awa-a-ay, 2009–Present Rescue, however, was at hand as Washington began channeling to state and local governments hundreds of billions of dollars in new funding that were being pumped into the economy to avert additional economic meltdown.

From 1990 to 2008, federal intergovernmental grant dollars grew, on average, by 6 percent annually,[89] but, beginning in 2009, the average growth rate of these dollars more than doubled to 15 percent per year. Federal aid to state and local governments, which had averaged $295 billion a year from 1990 to 2008, would more than double to an actual or projected average of $614 billion over each of the ensuing eight years.[90]

Currently, there are "over 1,670 federal grant programs" sponsored by twenty-three "federal grant-making departments and agencies." Federal grant dollars, having grown by 350 percent from 1990 to 2010, now constitute "over one-fifth of the federal budget"[91] and account for 4 percent of GDP,[92] surpassing their apexes of 1934 and 1978, when they attained 3.7 percent of the economy.[93]

These actions were soon felt at the grassroots. Twenty-eight percent of total state and local spending, and a third of state and local own source spending, is being funded by federal grants.[94] Whether these increased subsidies will continue into the foreseeable future, however, is an open question. The Budget Control Act of 2011 (described in Chapter 8), which cut spending and laid the groundwork for further cuts, will reduce the dollars in many of Washington's intergovernmental grants. An important exception is the massive Medicaid grant, which the act exempts from cuts.

The Unfunded Mandates Mess

A rancorous wrinkle that pervades fiscal federalism is the infamous *unfunded mandate*, which is an order given by the federal government or a state government to another government, but with no funds provided to implement that order.

The Impact of Unfunded Federal Mandates A majority of Americans believe that the costs of federal mandates should be shared among all governmental levels.[95] The feds themselves acknowledge that "the nation's state, local, and tribal governments urgently need relief from the burdens of unfunded federal mandates."[96]

State and local officials are so upset by unfunded federal mandates that they declared a National Unfunded Mandates Day, and understandably so. "Up to 10 percent of a state's general fund budget goes to filling in gaps in federal unfunded mandates,"[97] costing all the states, on average, more than $26 billion (and rising) per year.[98]

Local governments, however, appear to bear the brunt of unfunded federal mandates. Implementing just ten to twelve of them cost cities and counties 12 percent of their local tax revenue.[99]

Reforming Unfunded Federal Mandates In 1995, Congress passed the Unfunded Mandates Reform Act, which bans any unfunded mandate, whether contained in legislation or in agency-issued rules, that costs states, localities, or the private sector $50 million (in 1996 dollars) or more per year to implement.

It has not been particularly effective. Congress has passed perhaps as many as eleven laws,[100]

and federal agencies have issued at least one rule,[101] that affect state and local governments but which violate the act's unenforceable threshold. Worse, the law's procedures are so complex that it is extremely difficult for agency administrators to recognize that they are inadvertently inserting into their new rules provisos that "nonfederal parties…might perceive as unfunded mandates." In fact, more than half (sixty-five) of all 113 "final major rules" issued by federal agencies over two years "had not triggered" the Unfunded Mandates Reform Act.[102]

Fiscal Federalism in the States

Fiscal federalism flourishes within the states, too, and, since we are in the midst of discussing unfunded mandates, let us conclude that discussion with a review of unfunded state mandates.

Unfunded State Mandates Determining the fiscal burden of unfunded state mandates on local governments has been described as a "fool's errand," but their costs are considerable,[103] and the states have tried a variety of methods, some less cynical than others, to alleviate their impact.

Forty-two states require that each state mandate's probable fiscal impact on their local governments be determined before the legislature imposes them,[104] and seventeen legislatures purport to reimburse their communities for the costs of implementing their mandates, but these reforms are often bypassed and have provided scant relief.[105] Voters in ten states, however, have ratified constitutional amendments requiring that any unfunded mandate must command a "super-majority" vote, ranging from two-thirds or three-fifths, by state legislators to be enacted, and this has been "the best anti-mandates strategy" to date.[106]

The Purposes of State Grants States concentrate their grants to local government on education (66 percent, with most going to school districts); welfare (12 percent, almost all of which goes to counties); general local government support (7 percent); health and highways (4 percent each); and "miscellaneous" assistance (8 percent),[107] much of it for corrections and public housing.[108]

The Sensitive States? With the exception of imposing unfunded mandates, the states have shown themselves to be reasonably well attuned to the needs of their local governments.

State grants-in-aid have only rarely accounted for less than 30 percent of total local revenue since 1970—a tribute to the states' constancy of purpose.[109] A study of 162 large cities found that, over twenty-four years, federal intergovernmental aid per capita dropped by almost three-fifths, but state aid per capita rose by close to half.[110] Of course, the federal government, through its pass-through grants, plays a large fiscal role in the states' support, and an estimated two-fifths of all the intergovernmental revenue that localities receive are actually provided by Washington.[111]

Intriguingly, the states also are growing more aware of the financial needs of their more distressed cities, a remarkable development because, "at a time when central cities are more dependent on their states than ever, there is considerable evidence that their clout in state legislatures is eroding."[112] State aid to needy cities is increasingly comparable to federal aid in that it is targeted toward the most distressed areas and poorest people, although federal aid seems to be slightly more focused on meeting the needs of the most dysfunctional inner cities.[113]

Governments and Grants: There Is No Free Lunch

Governmental "gifts" of "free money" cost the governments that get them. Beginning in 1911, Congress required that some of its modest grants be matched by state or local contributions,[114] and today more than half of all federal grants programs and, of greater significance, over three-quarters of grant dollars, involve some form of matching requirements.[115]

But the heavier price of grant funds is more subtle and profound. Sixteen percent of *all* state-and-local workers are working for these governments solely because federal grants pay the equivalent of their salaries,[116] and these federal "grantee jobs" have grown by 18 percent over twelve years.[117] This formidable federal fiscal presence in grassroots bureaucracies undermines their administration and perverts their policies.

Money's Managerial Monkey Wrench State and local governments suffer, as well as benefit, from intergovernmental aid.

In State Governments Federal aid has a disproportionately large, and likely negative, impact on state administrative autonomy, flexibility, and effectiveness. During the 1970s, when federal assistance attained record shares of state budgets, governors devoted far more time to "state-federal" matters than they had during the 1960s,[118] and over half of their top administrators contacted federal personnel monthly, weekly, or even daily.[119]

As these patterns imply, the more federal money in state coffers, the more that federal managers will displace state executives in state bureaucracies. In almost every survey taken over thirty-four years, "roughly half" of state agency heads report that "federal aid fosters special 'semi-exempt' status" from oversight by the governor, legislature, or both.[120]

It gets worse. Those state governments that are the most competitively disadvantaged in winning federal grants also have the weakest managerial capacities—they are the "most in need" but are the "least equipped to capture grants." As a consequence, they are trapped in an inequitable and malignant cycle of ever-diminishing management capacity.[121]

In Local Governments The same disruptive administrative patterns that occur in the states are found in local governments. A decade after Washington's intergovernmental aid had peaked, and direct federal grants as a share of local budgets had been slashed by two-thirds,[122] local officials' contacts with federal administrators had fallen off by nearly two-fifths,[123] suggesting that intergovernmental funds displace local executives in favor of federal and state managers.

Intergovernmental grants cost local governments more than managerially. Administering just five federal grant programs costs cities the equivalent of nearly a fifth of *all* their federal aid.[124] Yet, local governments appear unable to escape their "consistent dependence" on both federal and state grants, even though they have diversified their own revenue sources and "significantly altered" their structures for handling these grants.[125]

Policy Perversities Intergovernmental revenue can not only weaken grassroots management, it also can distort state and local policy and policymaking.

In 1928, when federal grants to the states did not attain even 1 percent of state budgets,[126] 6 percent of state agency heads nonetheless reported that "Federal aid led to National interference in affairs that are the appropriate domain of the State."[127] In 1974, when federal aid to the states accounted for 22 percent of state budgets,[128] over four-fifths of these executives bemoaned federal intrusion.[129] By the close of the 2000s, when federal funding had reached new lows, just 38 percent of state agency heads thought that federal "aid imbalance" was skewing state programs, handily the lowest percentage ever recorded in all eight surveys taken over thirty-four years.[130]

The pattern in these "roller coaster" figures is clear: The more federal funds that states receive, the more likely that state executives will perceive a lower level of "state *policy* autonomy."[131]

Similar patterns pertain in local governments. When federal funds were flush, about two-thirds of municipal administrators and approximately four-fifths of county managers would have made *different* budgetary—that is, policy—decisions had federal funds *not* been present.[132]

The Flypaper Effect State and local officials would be even more irked than they are about grant money skewing their policies if they knew that, when grant funds are spent to support a particular policy, spending for that policy continues at substantially higher levels and for longer periods of time than when grant money is not, or never has been, a factor.[133] Larger and longer spending for the policy may roll on even after the grant is gone because revenue from other sources frequently fills the void. This is known as the *flypaper effect*, because grant dollars stick where they land.

In the states, federal policy-specific grants have "a much stronger effect" on state policies than does any other financial variable, and they continue to stick to a particular policy area "for several years" after the grant money is gone.[134]

The same holds true at the local level. State grants to cities have a "positive flypaper effect" in eight out of ten policy categories.[135]

Those Rascally Recipients! At least some of all that "creativity in government" that is occurring at the grassroots,[136] noted earlier, seems to be in the form of wile that these governments devote to skirting Washington's wishes over how its grants are used.

The states withdraw so much of their own money from programs supported by federal grants that, on average, a program actually receives only forty more cents for every federal dollar granted to it. In other words, states effectively skim the equivalent of 60 percent of federal aid and use it for purposes other than the feds intended.[137]

Local governments, by contrast, look for loopholes. In general, communities favor using federal funds less for social services and poor people and more for construction projects and muzzling taxes.[138] The less specific the grant, the more likely that local governments will use it for "luxury" services, such as recreational programs, and the less likely that it will be spent for "normal" services, such as public safety.[139] Federal grants clearly meant for antipoverty programs have been used (quite legally) by local governments to subsidize developers in building luxury hotels and up-market department stores.[140]

REGULATORY FEDERALISM

In part because state and local recipients of federal grants have been so slippery in how they spend them, Washington increasingly has turned to tightening their use and limiting other subnational activities that have little to do with grants management. The imposition by governments of rules and mandates on other governments is called *regulatory federalism*.[141]

Ruling Robustly

Both the federal and state governments regulate their subservient governments with relish.

Washington Rules "During the 1960s and 1970s, state and local governments, for the first time, were brought under extensive federal regulatory controls."[142] Unilateral federal preemptions of state and local authority enacted during the 1970s account for almost a quarter of all preemptions imposed during the entire twentieth century,[143] and by the 1980s Washington's regulations outnumbered its grant programs.[144]

Washington's rules now dominate intergovernmental administration. Every year, Congress enacts more than eight statutes, on average, that clearly encroach on subnational governance;[145] federal courts make more than 3,500 decisions relating to over 100 federal laws that affect state and local governments;[146] and federal agencies issue about 4,250 "final rules" that apply to state and local governments, a number that grows by a tenth each year.[147] Nearly three out of ten state and local workers are employed solely because federal regulations require their presence, a proportion that is almost twice that of those grassroots employees who are funded by federal grants.[148]

The States Regulate

On average, a fifth of the hundreds of measures introduced each year in state legislatures directly affect the authority, procedures, and finances of local governments,[149] with counties bearing the brunt (at least relative to cities) of state regulation.[150] States impose on their local governments some 4,300 laws that deal with more than 200 local functions, and these laws are proliferating.[151] Sometimes this state regulatory oversight can be miasmic in detail, and legislatures have been known to legislate the procedures for paving city sidewalks, the methods for removing local weeds, and the design of county stationery.[152]

States concentrate on five broad areas of local affairs: financial management (described in Chapters 1 and 8); human resources management (reviewed in Chapter 9); changing local boundaries (explained at the close of this chapter); administrative operations (focusing primarily on the assurance of transparent governance); and local elections (all states set voter qualifications and registration procedures, and forty-six impose campaign finance disclosure requirements). Only in the area of elections have state laws governing localities decreased; the greatest growth in these laws has occurred in human resources and financial management.[153]

The Mandates Maw

The bulk of intergovernmental rules issued by the federal and state governments deal with what one would expect in the way of assuring fiscal accountability and programmatic propriety, but not all. Some are highly intrusive mandates.

A *mandate* is a far-reaching intergovernmental regulation imposed by one government on another government that requires the receiving government to advance specific goals or meet certain standards. Usually, but not always, mandates are linked to grants-in-aid. The demarcation between mandate and regulation is often dim, and one person's transmogrifying mandate can be another's pettifogging rule.

Federal Mandates

"There is no universally accepted definition of a federal mandate, and surprisingly little consensus on the matter."[154] Accordingly, just how many federal mandates there are is unknown, and counts range from 36[155] to 439.[156]

Three of the four kinds of federal mandates are bound in the federal grants system; should a recipient government ignore or violate them, it risks losing its grants. These mandates include the following:[157] *Crosscutting requirements*, found in virtually all federal grants programs, stipulate compliance with specific federal policies, such as nondiscrimination, by all governments receiving federal assistance. *Partial preemptions* deny, in limited ways, traditional prerogatives of subnational jurisdictions because Washington demands that they adopt federal standards. *Crossover sanctions* permit the federal government to punish a state or community by reducing or withdrawing federal aid in one or more programs if its standards are not being satisfied in another program.

A fourth type of federal mandate, *direct orders*, are instructions from Washington to state or local governments that, if not followed, can result in civil or criminal penalties. An example is Congress's 1977 order to cities to stop dumping sewage at sea. Direct orders have little to do with grants and involve the constitutionally problematic prospect of stand-offs between federal and state governments.

All four sorts of federal mandates have proliferated since 1960, with the greatest growth in crossover sanctions and direct orders, "the two most openly coercive" types.[158] Federal mandates are not necessarily capricious exercises of power. Many, in fact, are entirely responsible, such as those mandates that assure civil rights and honest elections, and these kinds of mandates are rarely resisted by the governments on which they are imposed.[159] Indeed, some have been welcomed by subnational officials as improving intergovernmental cooperation.[160]

State Mandates   The states also mandate, and these mandates matter—more so, apparently, than federal ones. City managers report that state "mandates/policies" influence their decision making nearly twice as forcefully as federal mandates and policies.[161]

There is a significant and positive correlation between a state's high affluence, strong partisan competitiveness, public administrative excellence, and a state's propensity to impose many mandates on its local governments.[162] When local governments dominate a state's finances (i.e., when they account for more than half of all state and local tax revenue), the state legislature imposes more mandates on them, suggesting that legislators want to keep their wealthy local governments in check; when states dominate, by contrast, they enact fewer mandates.[163]

The Wreckage of Regulatory Federalism

Just as intergovernmental regulations and mandates are proliferating, so are their costs.

Budgetary Burdens   The many estimates of the growing weight of "federal actions," notably regulations, on state and local governments range "from 2 to 3 percent" of their annual budgets "to 20 percent or more," costs that could become "a serious challenge to federalism."[164]

For local governments, stewing at the bottom of the federal hierarchy, the regulatory costs foisted on them by both the federal and state governments can be crushing. "From a range of studies, it appears localities dedicate anywhere from 20 percent to 90 percent of their expenditures" to implementing both federal and state rules and mandates.[165]

Preempting Power at the Grassroots   Just as fiscal federalism warps state and local administration and policymaking, so does regulatory federalism, except that regulatory federalism does so more directly.

Seventy percent of the 520 federal laws enacted since 1790 that substitute national policies for state and local ones, or prohibit states and communities from exercising powers that had previously been theirs, were imposed after 1960 and "will likely continue to grow." This "dangerous trend" has broadened from a traditional concentration on interstate commerce to health, banking, civil rights, and the environment, and "has already caused a significant shift in the balance of powers and responsibilities" that substitutes subnational self-determination with federal will.[166] Large majorities or pluralities of state officials report that federal agencies have overridden state decisions and prevented their states from pursuing preferred policies "several times."[167]

Perhaps three-quarters of federal intergovernmental regulations apply only to local governments or directly affect local governments through the states.[168] Two-fifths of local officeholders believe that federal regulations result in Washington playing "an inappropriate role" in their affairs, and two-thirds think that "federal agency implementation" of their own regulations "is inefficient, making compliance difficult," with half attributing this problem to Washington's micromanagement and "unrealistic" standards.[169]

State intervention prods similar reactions from local officials, who, as we noted earlier, evidence a much greater concern over state mandates than federal ones.[170] Although more than nine out of ten county officeholders say that the responsibilities of their governments have increased markedly, not even a third of them think that they have been granted adequate authority by their states to execute their duties and meet local needs.[171]

Deregulating Regulatory Federalism?

The national and state capitals have tried to reduce the burdens of their intergovernmental regulations, but with uncertain effect.

Federal Efforts   Washington became concerned with how federal rules were undermining state and local governance in the 1980s. The *Paperwork Reduction Act* of 1980; the *Regulatory Flexibility Act* of 1980; the *State and Local Government Cost*

Estimate Act of 1981; *Executive Order 12612*, issued in 1987; *Executive Order 12875* of 1993; and the *Federal Financial Assistance Management Improvement Act* of 1999 were designed, at least in part, to provide regulatory relief to the grassroots governments.

All in all, these efforts have had "little effect on agencies' rulemaking activities." Of 11,414 final intergovernmental rules issued by federal agencies over thirty-three months, a whopping total of five contained a legally required assessment of their impact on subnational governments.[172]

State Efforts   Beginning in 2008, with the advent of the "Great Recession," many states (California, Massachusetts, Michigan, and North Carolina are among the more prominent) lifted regulations on their local governments and endowed them with new powers, particularly revenue raising powers. These actions have been hailed as "Fend-for-Yourself Localism."[173]

When states deregulate their communities, the results are generally positive. Most local officials report that, when the state accords them the authority to raise their own revenue, their governments' fiscal health markedly improves, and they are convinced that local fiscal autonomy is "the solution to many of the problems that municipalities face."[174]

MONEY, MANDATES, AND WASHINGTON: NOW WHAT?

Nearly three-fifths of Americans believe that Washington "is interfering too much in state and local matters," an increase of almost a fifth over close to a half-century.[175] Are they right? Probably so.

Another Fine Mess

Federal intergovernmental management is not merely, in Oliver Hardy's (of Laurel and Hardy) memorable phrase, "another fine mess," but several fine messes.

Another Fine Managerial Mess   Substantive federal policies are fraught with inconsistencies of intergov-

ernmental administration. Federal environmental policy, for instance, long has been characterized by less money and more mandates than education and health care policies. Because federal waivers are more common in the environmental arena than in education and health care, federal intergovernmental policies for the environment experience heavier litigation than the other two.[176]

As this manic mix of managerial rigidities and flexibilities implies, "federal oversight has been inconsistent across states and communities, thus compounding local problems such as fiscal inequities and administrative inefficiencies.... flawed the system of grantee accountability.... limited the imposition of federal sanctions regarding grant performance and fraud...[and] have further complicated the ability of both states and localities to adapt to changes in requirements." These problems "have plagued federal grant programming for the last several decades."[177]

Another Fine Fiscal Mess   Federal oversight of federal grant dollars is somewhat shaky. At the end of a year, for example, there is "about $1 billion" remaining in federal grant accounts that have expired, but which, strangely, nevertheless remain open. These left-over dollars have not been disbursed to their federally designated recipients. Moreover, the undisbursed $1 billion languishing in expired but still-open federal accounts is not the whole story; the sum reflects only 70 percent of all federal grant disbursements.[178]

Another consequence of shaky fiscal oversight is that *improper payments*, or government checks with incorrectly calculated sums, or which are sent to the wrong recipients, such as dead people (we sketched their dimensions in Chapter 6), permeate the federal grants system. Five of the ten federal programs that account for 94 percent of the dollars lost to improper payments (or $118 billion) are intergovernmental grant programs. These five programs alone are responsible for 38 percent of that $118 billion.[179]

Another Fine Judicial Mess   Adding to these managerial and financial messes is the courts' often inconsistent intervention in intergovernmental administration and relations.

The judiciary judges the intergovernmental system in two broad dimensions.

Pick Your Policy One is the policy area, an area in which the courts seem to rule not by invoking an overarching principle, but instead by tailoring their decisions to the policy in question. In general, federal courts are more supportive of the federal government in intergovernmental matters that concern environmental and educational policies, and less forthcoming in health care, an intergovernmental policy area in which they tilt toward states and localities.[180]

Nation or State? The other dimension is more fundamental and concerns the federal government's relations with the states.

In 1995, a revolution of sorts took place in the Supreme Court's opinion about these relations. In that year, the Supreme Court, in *United States v. Lopez,* reversed nearly six decades of its own constitutional interpretations and held that the Constitution's interstate commerce clause no longer was sufficient justification for inserting the federal government into the affairs of states.

For the next seven years, *Lopez* was followed by nine five-to-four rulings, all made by the same five justices, who displayed a remarkable "determination to reconfigure the balance between state and federal authority in favor of the states [by] thrusting the doctrine of state sovereignty well beyond existing boundaries."[181] Perhaps the most notable upshot of these decisions is that, because the states have "sovereign immunity" (a phrase not to be found in the Constitution), states cannot be sued in federal or state courts when they violate certain federal laws. (But not local governments; the Court ruled unanimously, in 2006, that local governments are *not* protected from being sued.[182])

From 2003 onwards, however, the Court shuffled and muffled this series of decision; three rulings seemed to reassert some federal power over the states,[183] and at least one favored state sovereignty.[184] Overall, it appears that "the Court has moved not so much to grant more power to the states as to prune back the power of Congress."[185]

The Capable States

Despite the judiciary's ambivalence about federal and state relations, the states have made enormous progress on their own since the mid-twentieth century, when the states were described as "the tawdriest, most incompetent, most stultifying unit in the nation's political structure."[186] State governments now boast "progressive administrative results that border on the revolutionary."[187]

The states' *policy scope*—that is, the amount and variety of programs that the states conduct—has expanded enormously over the past half-century. The number of different "common administrative agencies" in the states, each with a unique policy mission, has more than doubled since 1959, and now averages 111 in each state.[188] State governments are the largest single employer in most states[189] and "were a key force in the growth of the national and local governments" during the final half of the twentieth century.[190]

As we observed in Chapter 9, the professionalism of state administrators has improved dramatically. A periodic "report card" on state management accords the states a bare "B-minus,"[191] a grade that puts state governments on a par with the nation's thirty-five largest and wealthiest cities,[192] and is slightly higher than that of forty similar counties.[193]

In sum, state governments are doing more things and doing them more ably than ever before.

Sorting Out Federalism: Who Should Do What?

This brings us to the question of which levels of government should be responsible for what areas of public policy, a question that has consumed scholars and policymakers since at least 1940.[194] What is surprising about these efforts is that, currently, at least, the views of experts, citizens, and public officials are mostly in harmony.

Who Should Do What? Scholars' Views Sorting out federalism is subject to rational thinking, and here is what scholars of intergovernmental relations recommend.

By far the greatest budgetary burden on the states is health care, described in Chapter 8, the costs of which typically are shared between Washington and the states. It makes sense for the federal government to relieve the states of this shared responsibility, and fully take it over.[195] Other areas that rationally should be retained as federal functions include welfare for the most impoverished Americans, research and development, central information gathering, and interstate highways.[196]

Areas that make sense to share between the federal and state governments are environmental and natural resources programs and higher education; student grants and loans should be mostly a federal responsibility, and managing campuses should be a state one.[197]

States should be "clearly in charge" of those areas that require tailoring and adapting to local conditions—that is, skills training, housing, child care, infrastructures, rural services, and economic development. Whether the states wish to support these programs is the states' call: "Federal programs in these areas are devolved to the states or just wither away."[198]

Local governments should have primary responsibility for roads, sanitation, and public safety.[199] Authorities disagree about elementary and secondary education, with some holding that it should be a largely local affair,[200] and others arguing that it should be entirely a state responsibility.[201]

Who Should Do What? Citizens' Views   Citizens largely concur with the experts. Most Americans agree that Washington should "take the lead" in managing health care and environmental protection, and that the states lead in the delivery of education and economic development. A plurality of people differ, if marginally, with the experts only in their belief that the states, rather than Washington, should manage anti-poverty programs. "The American public has very reasonable and consistent ideas about the policy responsibilities of the national, state, and local governments."[202]

Who Is Doing What?   Is any of this near-universal agreement between scholars and citizens reflected in which governments actually do what?

Happily, yes. Federal, state, and local budgets largely correspond with public administrationists' advice and Americans' preferences about which

governments should do what across nineteen different policy areas.

"Public preferences about the national government's role in specific policy areas are mirrored very closely by the national government's actual [budgetary] commitment in each of these areas," and, for nine of these areas, the percentages of public opinion and federal spending are "nearly linear"—that is, almost identical.

The same holds true for state and local spending, although "the patterns are not as clearly linear as at the national level." Nevertheless, overall, "the distribution of citizen preferences conforms closely to the relative efforts of the various governmental levels within the respective policy areas."[203]

A Federal Reset?

Without doubt, Washington continues "to hold much of the power and significance" that, beginning in the 1930s, it gained over state and local governments,[204] and, for the last thirty or so years, the federal government arguably did not use much of that power wisely. From 1986 through 2008, "the financial burdens imposed by federal laws and regulations" on state and local governments grew "faster than the growth of federal financial aid."[205]

In the 2010s, a reset in intergovernmental relations may be occurring. In 2009, a year that could become a watershed year in federalism, Washington not only more than doubled the dollars in its grants to the grassroots governments, but it also initiated a concerted and continuing effort to assist states and localities in their management of federal grants, and to lighten the feds' heavy regulatory hand in grassroots' administration and policymaking. Washington accomplished this through the American Recovery and Reinvestment Act of that year, which not only pumped most of the new funding into federal grants, but also established a Recovery Accountability and Transparency Board that functions as central point of contact.

The board and other innovations have greatly improved relations between the federal government and the grassroots.[206]

FEDERALISM AMONG EQUALS: THE STATES

If the semi-sovereign states occasionally verge on being "humble suppliants" of Washington, they can be preening peacocks when dealing with each other.

Interstate Cooperation

The Constitution requires that "full faith and credit shall be given in each state to the public acts, records, and judicial proceedings of every state," and, as a partial consequence, four devices of interstate cooperation have emerged that are designed to solve their common problems.

Interstate Compacts and Commissions The granddaddy of interstate cooperation is the *interstate compact,* which is a formal agreement between two or more states that normally requires congressional approval.

There are more than 200 interstate compacts in operation, but only thirty-six were agreed to during the nation's first 131 years, so states evidently are finding them increasingly useful. The typical state has entered into twenty-five interstate compacts.[207] These compacts have spawned 116 interstate commissions to enforce their provisions in education, transportation, rivers, fisheries, and energy, among other fields.[208]

Uniform State Laws Another golden oldie, begun in 1892, is *uniform state laws,* which are virtually identical statutes that have been enacted in two or more states, often in an attempt to preempt national legislation that could deepen the federal government's involvement in state affairs.

States that have a low level of administrative capability favor enacting uniform laws.[209]

National and Regional Associations Since the nineteenth century, state governments and a passel of state professionals have founded dozens of national organizations to exchange ideas and advance their interests with Washington.

During the 1970s, thirty-three states formed three interstate organizations that promote regional interests in the Southeast, Northeast, and West.

In Congress, states have banded together in five regional coalitions.

Multistate Legal Actions The newest wrinkle in interstate cooperation is *multistate legal actions,* which refer to states, working through the National Association of Attorneys General, entering into lawsuits with other states against a common adversary, such as, recently, the tobacco industry.

Larger states with a high level of administrative capacity favor their use.[210]

Interstate Conflict

Despite these manifold methods of interstate cooperation, the states remain competitive, and, occasionally, conflictive.[211] For example, nineteen states impose some sort of *severance tax*—that is, a tariff on natural resources exported to other states.[212]

Other statewide "exports," such as costly social problems, are free of severance taxes. South Dakota gave ninety-three people charged with felonies the choice of facing prosecution or moving to California; all ninety-three moved to the Golden State, whose officials promptly dubbed South Dakota's actions as outrageous. Following congressional devolution of welfare in 1996, Kentucky established a program for moving its most impoverished denizens to wealthier areas—including to wealthier states.[213]

All is not happy in the realm of the American states.

INTERGOVERNMENTAL ADMINISTRATION IN THE STATES

The states deal with each other as equals, but their relationships with their own local governments are quite different.

Creatures of the State

Because the Constitution is silent on the subject of local governments, and because they nonetheless multiplied, the judiciary eventually was forced to clarify their relationship to their states. The Supreme Court first did so in 1845, holding in *Maryland* v. *Baltimore and Ohio Railroad* that "counties are nothing more than certain portions of the territory into which the state is divided for more convenient exercise of the powers of the government," and, in 1907, the Court ruled in *Hunter* v. *City of Pittsburgh* that a state legislature could decide municipal boundaries as it saw fit, regardless of the preferences of affected citizens.

Both of these landmark cases cast local governments as "creatures of the state," a phrase given to us in 1868 by Judge John F. Dillon of the Iowa supreme court that is now known as "Dillon's rule." Judge Dillon held that local governments have no independence beyond what the state grants them, and no justice has questioned him.

The Insidious Introduction of Home Rule

Despite the powerful presence of Dillon's rule, local governments, slowly, steadily, and stealthily, have accreted for themselves *home rule,* or "all forms of local or regional self-determination."[214]

Missouri gave home rule political meaning when it adopted a constitution in 1875 that delegated to the people of St. Louis a power that, until that year, had been the exclusive prerogative of the state legislature: "the power to make a charter." Today, forty-eight states grant some form of home rule authority to their municipalities (Alabama and Vermont are the exceptions), and thirty-seven states offer it to their counties.[215] Only New Mexico denies any form of home rule to its local jurisdictions.[216]

A Steadier Helping Hand

Besides providing their localities with steady fiscal support, all the states furnish them with expertise in the form of departments of community affairs. Thirteen states have enacted laws to control urban sprawl, which have proven to be modestly successful,[217] or have adopted formal procedures for helping local governments in fiscal stress,[218] a wise precaution in light the

fact that these jurisdictions in thirty-six states have weathered such crises during their "recent history."[219]

Intergovernmental cooperation within the states also occurs at levels lower than that of government-to-government. State and local agencies collaborate, too, and the single strongest factor in predicting local cooperation with state agencies is a large presence of "professional incentives," most notably annual performance evaluations of local administrators that emphasize their collaboration with other agencies. A smaller local budget also associates positively with a greater local willingness to collaborate with state agencies.[220]

A Slow Centralization of State Power

Overall, there has been a steady, if slow, centralization of state power—that is, "the state controls basic public policy, allocates and delivers public services" at the expense of local governments.[221] In 1932, no state was categorized as "centralized," but today a third are. In 1902, all states were "decentralized," but by 1977, none were. Larger states tend to be more decentralized, and smaller states are more centralized.[222]

INTERGOVERNMENTAL ADMINISTRATION AMONG LOCAL GOVERNMENTS

Local governments are getting on famously with each other. As with the states, beginning in the late 1800s they have formed numerous national organizations, several of which have waxed into forceful advocates of local interests with the federal and state governments. There are in Congress caucuses for the suburbs and rural and metropolitan areas, which function as local interests' counterparts to the states' regional congressional alliances.

Recurring Regionalism

Regional governance within the states' boundaries has a somewhat tumultuous record.

Washington and Regional Governance Congress entered this thicket in 1959, with an amendment to Section 701 of the Housing Act of 1954, which channeled over twenty-three years more than $200 million in "701 planning funds" to state, regional, and local planning agencies. Of even greater significance, however, was the issuance of Office of Management and Budget (OMB) Circular A-95 in 1969, which established regional governmental councils as gate-keepers for federal planning grants, a power that was singularly comprehensive. Between the mid-1960s and mid-1970s, federal grants supporting state and local planning burgeoned from 9 to 160,[223] and regional councils of government rocketed from fewer than fifty in the mid-1950s to 669 by 1976.[224]

By the mid-1970s, federal regulations and legislation had created some 2,000 regional policy and planning bodies,[225] including councils for solid waste disposal, economic development, air quality, disaster assistance, the elderly, transportation, crime, health, and airports.

The Great Washington Walk-Away In 1982, Congress abruptly terminated its 701 planning grants and President Ronald Reagan's Executive Order 12372 eliminated OMB Circular A-95.

Both actions reduced by roughly a fifth the number of regional councils to about 500[226] and, among those councils that survived, cut their staffs and the federal grants programs that they administered by approximately a third.[227] Although Congress remains the largest single source of revenue for the typical regional council, followed by state grants and membership dues,[228] federal support is at least a third less than it was before 1982.[229] A decade following the great Washington walk-away, ten states had discarded the regional planning process altogether.[230]

Reducing Regional Governance Today, most regional councils within the states engage in a "dual planning and service role," focusing on economic development, transportation, solid waste, and land use. From a third to a half of these councils directly deliver these and other services to regional residents.[231]

Increasingly, regional councils are being challenged by "other entities seeking regional authority,"[232] most forcefully by corporate alliances with regional agendas that work closely with local governments.[233] The heads of regional councils report, tellingly, that "most key decisions in their regions are made *outside* of their councils,"[234] and they are "somewhat tentative about the future of their councils as dominant regional structures."[235]

Local Collaboration and Service Delivery

With the encouragement of their state governments (forty-two states have enacted legislation that specifically authorizes their local governments to enter into agreements with each other to provide services, a growing trend[236]), cities, counties, and special purpose governments have entered into *interlocal service arrangements*, or agreements among local governments to deliver services to their citizens.

These arrangements got their start with the "Lakewood Plan," when, in 1954, the just-incorporated city of Lakewood, California, contracted with Los Angeles County and some special districts to provide a plethora of public services in the city. "The City without a Payroll," as it became known because it had so few employees,[237] waxed into a model for other local governments. "Eighty per cent of the state's newly incorporating municipalities have now adopted the template."[238]

There are four major variants of interlocal service arrangements.

Intergovernmental Service Contracts An *intergovernmental service contract* occurs when one jurisdiction pays another to deliver a service to its residents.

Intergovernmental service contracts are used more frequently than any other method of outsourcing service delivery, including privatization. A full fifth of all city and county services—led by welfare eligibilities determination, job training, and mental health programs—are delivered through these agreements,[239] an increase of more than half from a quarter-century earlier, when they provided just 13 percent of a bit more than four-fifths of all local services.[240] Over half of cities and counties use intergovernmental service contracts.[241]

Local government officials rely almost exclusively on "informal discussions" to enforce these contracts, but the "perceived effectiveness" of these discussions "diminishes with the length of the contract."[242] Understandably, local administrators prefer "not to use other governments for services that require extensive monitoring."[243]

Joint Service Agreements A *joint service agreement* is the cooperative delivery by two or more governments of a local service to the residents of the participating jurisdictions. More than half of local governments deliver services jointly. Libraries and public safety communication are the most popular areas.[244]

Shared Service Agreements A *shared service agreement* is the consolidation of functions (support services, led by information technology, are favored) "from several agencies into a single, stand-alone entity." Public administrators find that their most bountiful benefits are improved and standardized services and increased collaboration.[245]

Intergovernmental Service Transfers An *intergovernmental service transfer* is "the permanent transfer of total responsibility for the provision of a service from one governmental unit to another." Forty percent of cities and counties have transferred services, and 34 percent of cities and counties have received such transfers. Sanitation services are transferred most frequently.[246]

Why Communities Cooperate: Governments, Who Need Governments...

In contrast to local governments' dealings with the private sector, in which commerce and competition are prominent, when governments deal with each other, community and collaboration prevail.

Buffeted Budgets Just as saving money is the leading reason why local governments contract with the private sector to deliver services (recall Chapter 11), so it is with interlocal collaboration, with 80 percent of cities and counties citing it.[247]

We observed as well in Chapter 11 that those local governments which contract out a high proportion of their services to the private sector are wealthier governments, but this is far from the case among those localities that enter into relatively large numbers of interlocal service arrangements. These governments are generally poorer governments,[248] shoulder large local debt levels, have assumed responsibility for delivering new services,[249] and are burdened with many service duties and employees.[250]

The Logic of Efficiency Coming in at a close second to savings is the similar "achieving economies of scale," with 77 percent of cities and counties citing it.[251] It has long been a singular prod. Some thirty years ago, economies of scale was the reason "cited almost overwhelmingly in all service categories by both cities and counties" to enter into interlocal service arrangements of all types.[252]

Collaboration and Regionalism The third-ranking motivator for working with other governments is the strengthening of "collaborative intergovernmental relations," cited by almost two-thirds of local managers, followed, at three-fifths, by the promotion of "regional service integration."[253] Both of these interrelated motivations have been strongly cited by these administrators for more than three decades.[254]

State Policies State policies also can influence their localities' desire to collaborate with one another. In those states that have made municipal annexation more difficult, imposed local revenue limitations, and curtailed the creation of new local governments, especially special districts and public authorities, there is a much higher probability that their local governments will cooperate with each other in funding and providing local services.[255]

Professionalism Is Primary The local manager who is most likely to collaborate with other governments in delivering services networks extensively in regional associations of governments[256] (the smaller the association, the likelier it is that the manager's government will participate in "interlocal service delivery"[257]); is professionally well connected; has a master of public administration degree; shares "a common set of professional norms" with colleagues in other governments;[258] possesses "specific managerial skills"; and leads a "high-capacity" agency.[259] City managers who harbor abnormally high levels of professional ambition are more likely to sell their city's services to other local governments but are much less likely buy services from other jurisdictions.[260]

Trust Me   Trust plays a part, too. Local governments are much more likely to contract out to other governments those services that have high risks for "opportunism leading to contract failure," and much less likely to outsource high-risk services to private or nonprofit organizations, "suggesting that governments view other governments as trusted contract vendors."[261]

Concerns over Collaboration: Community Counts

Whereas the leading obstacle for contracting out services to the private sector is employee opposition, the chief impediment for contracting with other governments is a "concern about loss of community control," a worry cited by 64 percent of local officials.

Employee opposition ranks a distant second, at 43 percent, followed by contract-monitoring misgivings, at 32 percent, as reasons not to collaborate with other local governments.[262]

Consolidating and Centralizing Local Services

These concerns have not dissuaded local governments from embracing the efficiencies that derive from greater economies of scale. Just as Washington is co-opting state and local authority, and just as state governments are centralizing power over their local jurisdictions, larger local governments are taking over the responsibilities of smaller ones.

Fifty-six percent of all intergovernmental service contracts let by cities are awarded to counties, which also are the principal providers for more than half of all services that are delivered through joint service agreements.[263]

Of greater significance, larger local governments are *permanently* taking over the traditional duties of smaller governments, *and at the request* of those governments. Two-thirds of cities and counties with populations of at least 250,000 receive intergovernmental service transfers, compared to less than a fifth of local jurisdictions with fewer than 10,000 people.[264] Fifty-four percent of all intergovernmental service transfers from cities go to counties, and 14 percent (the next highest) to regional organizations of governments.[265] These trends have persisted for at least five decades,[266] and there are recent signs that cities are transferring their services to special districts at greater rates than in the past.[267]

Government-to-Government: The Most Productive Collaboration

In Chapter 11, we observed that local public-to-private and public-to-nonprofit partnerships bore negative statistical correlations, or there were no correlations, with efficiency, effectiveness, and equity in the delivery of local services. Is this also the case with public-to-public partnering?

Hardly. Consider efficiency. Intergovernmental service arrangements usually are successful in lowering the per-unit costs of delivering local services.[268] In fact, it appears from unavoidably limited data that, when governments contract out services to the private sector, they save an average of 14 percent, but, when they contract with the public sector, they save over a third more: 22 percent.[269] There is a "positive and significant" statistical relationship between a local "public–public partnership" and efficiency, "indicating that these arrangements appear to increase efficiency."[270]

Government-to-government contracts also correlate, strongly and positively, with the effective and equitable provision of local services, a correlation that, as we detailed in Chapter 11, is negative or absent in local governments' contracts with both private companies and nonprofit organizations.

"Public–public partnerships outperform their sectoral cousins across all three dimensions of performance," and this holds true "even when controlling for past performance, service expenditure, and organizational environments."[271]

PLACE, PEOPLE, AND POWER: THE PUZZLE OF METROPOLITAN GOVERNANCE

Over the past seven decades, the number of *metropolitan statistical areas*, or cities of at least 50,000 people and their suburbs, more than doubled to 366.[272] Metropolises cover a fifth of America's land[273] and contain more than four-fifths of its people.[274]

Area and Power

A vexing question facing metropolises is that of matching their public's problems with the appropriate scope, jurisdiction, functions, and even number of governments that would deal most efficiently and justly with those problems. "A great deal of intellectual energy, spanning several decades, has gone into efforts to determine the correct pattern of organization for metropolitan areas."[275]

What is the best way, in other words, of reconciling area with power?

No question is more central—and wholly unique—to public administration than is this one.

The City: In Sickness and in Health

The populations of almost all central cities are shrinking, and this has grave implications for not only them, but also for their surrounding metropolises.

Urban Hemorrhaging In just forty years (1950–1990), the population density of the nation's 522 largest central cities plummeted, on average, by an astounding 50 percent. These cities lost their citizens almost entirely to their surrounding suburbs. In 1950, less than 70 percent of Americans in the major metropolises lived in their central cities; by 1990, more than 60 percent dwelt in their suburbs.[276] This trend accelerated during the 1990s,[277] and showed some signs of reversing in the 2000s,[278] but most cities still remain thinly populated relative to their suburbs, a condition that has some worrisome consequences.

Urbs, 'Burbs, and Economics Of greatest significance, any government that loses population also loses wealth. Average per capita income in the cities, which had been somewhat higher than in the suburbs, began to decline in 1960, and, by 1990, had hit 85 percent of what suburbanites earned, where it has remained ever since.[279] Nearly twice as many "primary-city residents" live in poverty (more than 18 percent) than suburban residents (less than 10 percent).[280] When income gaps between cities and suburbs are wide, cities deteriorate. Housing, education, and family structure in the cities slide, while crime climbs.[281]

Diversity and Elasticity To stanch urban hemorrhaging, both in population and in wealth, cities must grow. To grow, cities must be diverse and elastic.

Ethnic diversity is central to urban population growth. The fastest-growing cities are those that draw from all racial groups,[282] so it follows that it is in cities' self-interest to cultivate diversity.

Urban population growth also depends on *elasticity*, which is a city's ability to grow by in-filling vacant areas with people, or by expanding its boundaries to include people living in its suburbs, or both.

"The first law of urban dynamics" is that "*only elastic cities grow*."[283] Inelastic cities lose population. Compared with elastic cities, inelastic cities are older; more racially segregated; less prudently managed and fiscally viable; less able to adjust to economic change; and less effective in advancing the prosperity of the entire metropolitan area.[284]

Regrettably, urban elasticity is a rare commodity. Three national surveys of city managers conducted over ten years consistently found that "the two major economic development barriers" are the availability of land, followed by its cost. From two-fifths to more than half cite these impediments to elasticity.[285]

The Metropolis: Lots of Little, Layered, Local Governments

Thus far, we have been concentrating mostly on how municipal variables affect the fortunes of urban denizens. But metropolitan factors affect them, too, and the most important one is the degree of ultralocalist governance in a metro area. *Ultralocalism*[286] (an admittedly loaded word), or, more conventionally, *governmental fragmentation, decentralization,* or *differentiation,* is "the number of governmental units per 10,000 residents in a metropolitan area."[287] The more governments per 10,000 residents, the more governmentally fragmented the metropolis.

Most metropolitan areas, 85 percent, are highly fragmented.[288]

Lots of Little Local Governments Ultralocalist metropolises reflect some deeply entrenched American values. In essence, those values are the more governments the merrier, and the smaller governments the better.

There are, on average, in each metro area about 100 local governments,[289] a growing number. Since 1942, the proportion of all local governments found in metropolitan areas has nearly quadrupled, and some two-fifths of all local jurisdictions are now in them.[290] These governments govern few citizens—fewer than 6,000 on average.[291]

Layered Local Governments Focusing only on the proliferating number of local jurisdictions and their small populations does not do justice to the confusing and overlapping nature of governmental fragmentation. More than six out of ten Americans are governed, and taxed, by two or more layers of the nation's 39,044 counties, municipalities, and townships at once. In thirty-eight states, citizens are governed and taxed by up to two layers of general purpose local governments simultaneously, and in ten states some residents are governed and taxed by *three* layers of them![292]

These counts do *not* include America's 50,432 special purpose governments, which also tax or charge fees for vital services. Residents of metropolitan areas fall under the jurisdiction of a half-dozen or more of the country's 37,381 special districts, a figure that excludes its 13,051 school districts.[293] The boundaries of at least two–fifths of special districts, and two-thirds of school districts, are not coterminous with those of general-purpose local governments, and meander over them or within them.[294]

Ultralocalism: The Quest for Urban Efficiency

There is a large literature that justifies—even, occasionally, celebrates—the *status quo* of metropolitan fragmentation. It is known as "metropolitan organization," or "local public economies," and is written by a segment of the rational choice crowd that we reviewed in Chapter 10. These scholars argue that ultralocalism (or what they sometimes call "polycentric" or "multinucleated political systems"[295]) provides the most efficient governance in metropolitan regions.[296]

Ultralocalism: The Theory How does ultralocalism induce efficiency? Governmental efficiency is achieved in fragmented metropolises because many governments are competing and collaborating to serve metropolitan citizens. The presence of a plethora of cheek-by-jowl governments, as these theorists tirelessly remind us, empowers metropolitans to "vote with their feet," moving easily from one community to another if they are dissatisfied with local governing. This potential mobility, and its attendant loss of tax revenue, spurs greater governmental efficiencies. By contrast, a single, metropolitan-wide government is less efficient, just as a corporate monopoly is less likely to provide its customers with the best goods and services at the best price in a marketplace that it controls.[297]

Ideas have power. By the 1980s, even long-standing federal friends of coherent subnational governance had turned "from being a champion of strong regional governance to an advocate of public choice with its tacit acceptance that fragmentation is good,"[298] and Washington abandoned its "few national inducements to metropolitan coherence."[299]

Ultralocalism: The Practice Public choice theorists have buttressed their rhetoric with empirical research, and much of this literature agrees on the following:[300]

- Researchers generally find that metropolitan areas with more local governments provide more cost-effective services, and a greater variety of services and delivery mechanisms, than metropolises with fewer local governments.

- Local governments in highly fragmented metro areas spend less, and their rate of expenditure growth is slower, than local governments in less fragmented metropolises.

- Smaller local governments generally are more efficient than larger local governments.

Issues with Ultralocalism

There has long been a persistent perception among local public administrators that "polycentric" polities do not cut it. Why? Because ultralocalism encourages governmental confusion and irresponsibility, lowers citizen satisfaction, and supports social inequities.

Ultralocalism as Confusion

In ultralocalist metropolitan areas, confusion flourishes.

An example: In Louisiana, a speeding motorist was followed by police from no fewer than seven cities before he rolled to a stop.

Another: When St. Louis County plainclothes detectives were conducting a gambling raid, they were promptly arrested by police from the town of Wellston, who were staging their own raid.[301]

Ultralocalism as Irresponsibility

In fragmented metropolises, buck passing is greatly eased.

An example: "A woman tourist who stopped overnight at a motel near Miami had to telephone three police departments to report a suspected prowler outside her door." We do not know if any of these departments responded to her call.

Another: There was a fire in a house less than three blocks from a fire station in Las Vegas, Nevada, but just beyond the city limits. Las Vegas firefighters had been instructed to prevent the fire from reaching city property, so they carefully watched the house burn until county fire engines arrived. Angry neighborhood residents hurled rocks at the immobile city fire engines, causing substantial damage.[302]

Ultralocalism as Dissatisfaction

Although, as we noted earlier, local services may be delivered more cost-effectively in highly fragmented metro areas than in less fragmented ones, centrist metro governments correlate with higher citizen satisfaction

with public services.[303] This holds true for citizens of color as well as white citizens.[304]

Metropolitans do vote with their feet, just as the ultralocalists insist. But their implication that metro residents move to other towns only because they are unhappy with local tax rates seems, at best, incomplete, especially when we recall from Chapter 8 that citizens display a marked willingness to pay for local services.[305] Effective and well-managed government may matter more than tax rates.

Ultralocalism as Inequity

"In general, the more highly fragmented a metro area is, the more segregated it is racially and economically."[306] Highly fragmented metropolises have far wider income gaps between inner city and outer suburb and more concentrated areas of poverty, which is "the single most important indicator of an urban area's social health,"[307] than do more centralized metro areas. Ominously, after a decade of dramatic decline during the 1990s, *concentrated areas of poverty*—that is, poor people clustered in very impoverished communities—are expanding.[308]

Ominously? Yes, because concentrated poverty comprises a "critical mass" of "social tinder"[309] that can ignite, and ignition is most likely to crackle in ultralocalist metropolises and inelastic municipalities. The three most disastrous urban race riots of the 1960s—in Los Angeles in 1965 and in Newark and Detroit in 1967, in which 100 people died—all occurred in highly fragmented metropolitan areas and in cities with ratings of "zero elasticity" (Newark and Detroit) or "low elasticity" (Los Angeles, which re-exploded in 1992 at a cost of fifty-five lives). These are the lowest two of the five elasticity rankings. Miami's wrenching race riot in 1980, in which eighteen died, and Cincinnati's three-day riot in 2001, also erupted in cities with zero elasticity.[310] Fragmented metro areas and inelastic cities associate with civic anger.

Gargantua: The Quest for Urban Efficiency—and Equity

Dissatisfaction with the ultralocalist *status quo* has produced an effort to reform fragmented metropolitan governance. One political scientist has labeled, memorably, this movement "gargantua."[311] As with ultralocalism, "gargantua" is also an admittedly loaded word, and the more common phrases are *centralized government* and *centrism*, *regional government* and *regionalism*, and *metropolitan*, or *metro, government*.

A *metropolitan government* is a general-purpose local government with "all of the powers of a municipality under state law" (especially "key planning and zoning powers"), which contains within its limits at least 60 percent of the people living in its metropolitan area, and most (but ideally all) of the area's major cities. A metro government "must exercise exclusive powers within its jurisdiction."[312]

Gargantua is predicated on the premise that sweeping away slews of stunted local governments and establishing in their place a comprehensive regional government "is much better than trying to get multiple local governments to *act* like a metropolitan government," as is the norm today.[313] There is, after all, a reason why more than half of America's 39,044 cities, towns, and counties collaborate with one another to deliver services more cost-effectively than they can deliver them by themselves.[314] There is as reason why cooperative arrangements among localities surpass every other form of outsourcing service provision, including contracting with companies and nonprofit organizations, and continue to grow.[315] And there is a reason why larger local governments and regional organizations are taking over duties that once were the preserves of smaller jurisdictions, and with their blessing.[316]

That reason is greater efficiency.[317] But the advocates of metro government offer more.

The Grails of Gargantua

At root, the ultralocalists are concerned with only one value: efficiency in the delivery of local services.

So, too, are the gargantuans. There is a long history of practical analyses that promote efficiency in local governance through local governmental consolidation.[318] Recall also that the "overwhelming" reasons why local officials enter into interlocal service arrangements are "economies of scale."[319]

So the gargantuans fully understand and appreciate governmental efficiency. But, in contrast to the ultralocalists, the gargantuans also hold that coherent, robust governance and an ennobling civic culture must be at least as central as efficiency in the debate over how to better govern metropolitan areas.

Fixating solely on governmental efficiency when so many metro areas are in advanced states of division, decay, and degradation smacks of rearranging the deck chairs on the *Titanic*. "Reversing the fragmentation of urban areas is an *essential* step in ending severe racial and economic segregation.... Areas characterized by geographically large, multipowered governments," by contrast, "tend to promote more racial and economic integration and achieve greater social mobility."[320]

Metro government, by definition, radically reduces, even eliminates, fragmentation. It recognizes that central cities and their suburbs are mutually dependent for success on each other.[321]

The public choice theorists, by focusing exclusively on efficiency, may have deflected policymakers from confronting these larger concerns. If so, then the friends of fragmentation have done the nation a disservice.

Is Gargantua All That Inefficient?

There are growing indicators that gargantua may be more efficient than the ultralocalists contend. As we detailed in Chapter 11, central cities outsource services much less frequently than any other type of general-purpose local government, even though these cities are *far* more characterized by conditions that strongly correlate with greater outsourcing, such as competitive private sectors and taxpayer pressure for cost-effective services. The factor that trumps all others, however, is scale, and central cities, uniquely, have it. Because central cities, on average, govern many more people and much more territory than other sorts of local government, they can achieve far greater economies of scale. So, because economies of scale render big cities more structurally, or "internally," efficient than the others, the draw of outsourcing fades.[322]

These patterns make our point: Economy of scale is an essential structural key to efficient governance, and gargantuan governments have that key—built in and in spades. Ultralocalist governments also can acquire that key, kind of, but only through enervating, time consuming, and ultimately inefficient bargaining, contracting, and collaborating with companies, nonprofit organizations, and other governments. It is not the same.

Moving Mincingly Toward Metro

The creation of metro governments has much room for progress. Only 15 percent of metropolitan areas are served by metro governments in twenty-one states, and most of these are medium-sized communities; only 3 percent of the four-fifths of Americans living in metro areas live in areas served by metro governments.[323]

Reformers have developed two main approaches to extend regionalism's reach.

City-County Consolidation *City-county consolidation* is the unification of the governments of one or more cities with the surrounding county in which the boundary lines of the jurisdictions involved become coterminous. More than four-fifths of all metropolitan areas, in which more than two-fifths of all Americans reside, are in a single county,[324] so city-county consolidation would seem to be a promising route toward metropolitan-wide government.

As a practical matter, however, consolidations have not made much progress, and there are only thirty-eight consolidated governments in the United States, or about 1 percent of all county governments.[325] The first nine city-county consolidations (1805–1907), and two in 1969 and 1998, were executed by legislative fiats,[326] an option that remains "fully within the legal powers of most state legislatures, even if at present such sweeping urban reorganization is beyond legislatures' desires and political powers."[327] The remainder were implemented by popular referenda.[328]

Although the perfunctory pace of city-county consolidations is quickening (more than three-fourths have been achieved since 1947[329]), citizens are not enthusiastic about them. Of the 166 consolidation attempts initiated since 1800, only 22 percent have been successful.[330]

Why is this? One reason is state legislative reluctance. Only fourteen states, a declining number, specifically authorize their cities and counties

to consolidate.[331] Another is klutzy consolidation campaigns. Consolidation campaigns that advocate greater governmental efficiency and economies of scale (which, of course, are valid reasons to consolidate) almost always fail; those that win share a "common element," which is defining a vision of regional economic development, and then convincing voters that the "existing political structure" is unable to fulfill it.[332]

Municipal Annexation An incremental approach usually is more successful in moving toward metro government, and the paramount piecemeal procedure is *municipal annexation*, initiated in 1854 by Philadelphia, in which cities extend their boundaries to subsume their surrounding territories.

States allow their municipalities to annex in five ways. Ten states rely on legislatively created special boards, and their use has held steady over time. The two simplest methods, unilateral annexations authorized by state legislatures or city councils, have declined over three decades to six and eight states, respectively, but the two most problematic procedures, popular referenda (used in twenty states) and judicial determination (six states), have grown.[333]

Even though the states "have made annexation more difficult,"[334] cities are annexing more than ever. About nine out of ten central cities that can annex do so,[335] and, each decade, cities annex considerably more land and people than in the previous decade.[336] On average, more than 60,000 municipal annexations are executed every ten years,[337] expanding the boundaries of more than four-fifths of the 522 largest cities by a minimum of 10 percent.[338]

For the past half century, fragmentation's friends have formed mainstream thinking about urban administration. Today, this is changing, and the result is a renewed regionalism that might have been stillborn without recent research on the relations between metropolitan efficiency and citizen equity.

Ideas have power.

NOTES

1. Rajeev K. Goel and Michael A. Nelson, *Causes of Corruption: History, Geography and Government* (Helsinki, Finland: Bank of Finland Institute for Economies in Transition, 2008).

2. Desiree Teobaldelli, "Federalism and the Shadow Economy," *Public Choice* 146 (March 2011), pp. 269–289.

3. Ibid.

4. Jorge Martinez-Vazquez and Ming-Hung Yao, "Fiscal Decentralization and Public Sector Employment," *Public Finance Review* 37 (September 2009), pp. 539–571.

5. Ibid.

6. Silika Prohl and Friedrich Schneider, "Does Decentralization Reduce Government Size? A Quantitative Study of the Decentralization Hypothesis," *Public Finance Review* 37 (November 2009), pp. 639–664.

7. Jason Sorens, "The Institutions of Fiscal Federalism," *Publius* 41 (March 2011), pp. 207–231.

8. Ibid.

9. Oguzhan Dincer, "Fiscal Decentralization and Trust," *Public Finance Review* 38 (March 2010), pp. 178–192.

10. Ibid.

11. Nandhini Rangarajan, "Evidence of Different Types of Creativity in Government: A Multimethod Assessment," *Public Performance & Management Review* 32 (September 2008), pp. 132–163. This is an analysis of the 119 recipients of the Ford Foundation's Innovations in Government awards, 1990–2001.

12. Jack L. Walker, "The Diffusion of Innovation in the American States," *American Political Science Review* 63 (September 1969), pp. 880–899.

13. David Lowery, Virginia Gray, and Frank R. Baumgartner, "Policy Attention in State and Nation: Is Anyone Listening to the Laboratories of Democracy?" *Publius* 41 (March 2011), pp. 286–310. The quotation is on p. 286.

14. Henry S. Reuss, *Revenue-Sharing: Crutch or Catalyst for State and Local Governments?* (New York: Praeger, 1970), pp. 53–56.

15. This discussion is drawn largely from: Kenneth N. Vines, "The Federal Setting of State Politics," *Politics in the American States*, 3rd ed., Herbert Jacob and Kenneth N. Vines, eds. (Boston: Little, Brown, 1976), pp. 3–48, especially pp. 4–9.

16. President Franklin Pierce, quoted in David B. Walker, *The Rebirth of Federalism: Slouching Toward Washington*, 2nd ed. (New York: Chatham House, 2000), p. 69.

17. As derived from data in ibid., p. 74. The quotation is on p. 75.

18. Ibid., p. 7.

19. Norton Long, as quoted in William R. Barnes, "Beyond Federal Urban Policy," *Urban Affairs Review* 40 (May 2005), pp. 575–589. The quotation is on p. 578.

20. Tim Conlan, "From Cooperative to Opportunistic Federalism: Reflections on the Half-Century Anniversary of the Commission on Intergovernmental Relations," *Public Administration Review* 66 (September/October 2006), pp. 663–676. The quotation is on p. 668.

21. Barnes, "Beyond Federal Urban Policy," pp. 576, 582, 575, respectively.

22. John Shannon, "Competitive Federalism—Three Driving Forces," *Intergovernmental Perspective* 15 (Fall 1989), pp. 17–18.

23. Alan Greenblatt, "The Hand-off," *Governing* (April 2011), pp. 24–28. Figure (p. 26) is for 1983–1986.

24. U.S. Advisory Commission on Intergovernmental Relations, *Changing Public Attitudes on Government and Taxes, 1992*, S-22 (Washington, DC: U.S. Government Printing Office, 1993), p. 4. Emphasis added.

25. John Kincaid and Richard L. Cole, "Citizen Attitudes Toward Issues of Federalism in Canada, Mexico, and the United States," *Publius* 41 (Winter 2011), pp. 53–75. The quotations and data are on p. 64. Emphasis added. Figure, 41 percent, is for 2007.

26. Ibid., p. 61. Figures are for 2009. We should note that the National Election Study, cited in Chapter 1's Figure 1-1, finds consistently lower scores in its more comprehensive trust in government index, which we ascribe to differing methodologies.

27. Pew Center for the People and the Press, *The People and Their Government: Distrust, Discontent, Anger and Partisan Rancor* (Washington, DC: Author, 2010), p. 2. Figure is for 2010.

28. Alan Greenblatt, "Obama and the Cities," *Governing* (April 2009), pp. 23–28. The quotation is on p. 24.

29. Vines, "The Federal Setting of State Politics," p. 16. Figures are for 1902. To avoid double counting, these and the following figures in this section do not include intergovernmental grants. The figures that follow do include federal military and foreign relations spending

30. Russell L. Hanson, "Intergovernmental Relations," *Politics in the American States: A Comparative Analysis*, 9th ed., Virginia Gray and Russell L. Hanson, eds. (Washington, DC: CQ Press, 2008), pp. 30–60. The datum is on p. 37.

31. Vines, "The Federal Setting of State Politics," p. 16. Figures are for 1938.

32. Hanson, "Intergovernmental Relations," p. 37.

33. As derived from data in U.S. Bureau of the Census, *Statistical Abstract of the United States, 2011*, 130th ed. (Washington, DC: U.S. Government Printing Office, 2011), Tables 454, 453, 452, 450, 471. Figures are for 2007.

34. National Association of State Budget Officers, *Budget Processes in the States* (Washington, DC: Author, 2008), p. 3. Figure is for 2008.

35. Phil Kerpen, *Taxpayer-Funded Lobbying: Big Government Growth Machine* (Washington, DC: Americans for Prosperity Foundation, 2007), p. 2. Figures are for 1998–2006.

36. Julia DiLaura, *Your Tax Dollars at Work—on K Street* (Washington, DC: Center for Public Integrity, 2006), p. 1. Figure is for 1998–2003.

37. Kerpen, *Taxpayer-Funded Lobbying*, p. 2. Figures are for 1998–2006 and do not include more than $19 million spent by transportation authorities, and $15 million by local waterworks, in 2006 on lobbying the federal government; both spending figures more than doubled, 1998–2006.

38. Center for Public Integrity, as cited in Jodi Rudoren and Aron Pilhofer, "Hiring Federal Lobbyists, Towns Learn Money Talks," *New York Times* (July 2, 2006). Figures are for 2006.

39. Anthony J. Nownes, Clive S. Thomas, and Ronald J. Hrebenar, "Interest Groups in the States," *Politics in the American States: A Comparative Analysis,* 9th ed., Virginia Gray and Russell L. Hanson, eds. (Washington, DC: CQ Press, 2008), pp. 98–128. The quotation is on p. 111.

40. As derived from data in U.S. Bureau of the Census, *Statistical Abstract of the United States, 2011*, Table 430. Figures are for 2010 (estimated).

41. Walker, *The Rebirth of Federalism*, p. 9. Figure is for 1997.

42. U.S. Advisory Commission on Intergovernmental Relations, *Federal Grant Profile, 1995: A Report on ACIR's Federal Grant Fragmentation Index*, SR-20 (Washington, DC: U.S. Government Printing Office, 1995), p. 1. Figure is for 1995.

43. As derived from data in U.S. Government Accountability Office, *Federal Grants: Improvements Needed in Oversight and Accountability Processes*, GAO-11-773T (Washington, DC: U.S. Government Printing Office, 2011), pp. 3–4. Figure is for 2011.

44. As derived from data in ibid. Figure is for 2011.

45. U.S. Government Accountability Office, *2010 Census: Population Measures Are Important for Federal Funding Allocations*, GAO-08-230T (Washington, DC: U.S. Government Printing Office, 2007), Highlights page. Figure is for 2000.

46. As derived from data in U.S. Government Accountability Office, *Federal Grants: Improvements Needed in Oversight and Accountability Processes*, pp. 3–4. Figure is for 2011.

47. Kenneth Finegold, Laura Wherry, and Stephanie Schardin, *Block Grants: Historical Overview and Lessons Learned*, No. A-63 (Washington, DC: Urban Institute, 2004).

48. As derived from data in U.S. General Accounting Office, *Federal Assistance: Grant System Continues to Be Highly Fragmented*, GAO-03-718T (Washington, DC: U.S. Government Printing Office, 2003), p. 5. Figures are for 2001.

49. Ibid., p. 15.

50. Finegold, Wherry, and Schardin, *Block Grants*, p. 4.

51. U.S. Advisory Commission on Intergovernmental Relations, *The Federal Role in the Federal System: The Dynamics of Growth, A Crisis of Confidence and Competence*, A-77 (Washington, DC: U.S. Government Printing Office, 1980), pp. 120–121.

52. Barbara Floersch, "Federal Grantmaking: The Long View of History," *Grantsmanship Magazine* (Summer 2001), pp. 1–12. Figure (p. 3) is for 1929.

53. As derived from data in American Council on Intergovernmental Relations, *Significant Features of Fiscal Federalism, 1995*, Vol. 2 (Washington, DC: Author, 1998), p. 52.

54. U.S. Advisory Commission on Intergovernmental Relations, *The Federal Role in the Federal System*, pp. 120–121.

55. Ibid., p. 121. In 1932 there were twelve federal grants, in 1937 there were twenty-six, and 1946, twenty-eight.

56. Walker, *The Rebirth of Federalism*, p. 99. Figure is for 1933–1939.

57. Floersch, "Federal Grantmaking," pp. 3, 5. In 1939, federal grants accounted for 39 percent of all federal outlays, or $2.9 billion.

58. U.S. Advisory Commission on Intergovernmental Relations, *The Federal Role in the Federal System*, p. 120. In 1950, federal aid to state and local governments hit $3 billion.

59. As derived from data in American Council on Intergovernmental Relations, *Significant Features of Fiscal Federalism, 1995*, Vol. 2, p. 52.

60. U.S. Advisory Commission on Intergovernmental Relations, *The Federal Role in the Federal System*, p. 120. Figure for GNP covers 1950 and 1952–1958.

61. Ibid., p. 121.

62. Ibid., p. 120; and American Council on Intergovernmental Relations, *Significant Features of Fiscal Federalism, 1995*, Vol. 2, p. 38.

63. As derived from data in American Council on Intergovernmental Relations, *Significant Features of Fiscal Federalism, 1995*, Vol. 2, p. 52. Figures are for 1952 and 1957.

64. Walker, *The Rebirth of Federalism*, p. 6.

65. U.S. Advisory Commission on Intergovernmental Relations, *The Federal Role in the Federal System*, p. 120.

66. American Council on Intergovernmental Relations, *Significant Features of Fiscal Federalism, 1995*, Vol. 2, p. 38.

67. Ibid.

68. As derived from data in ibid., p. 52.

69. Chung-Lae Cho and Deil S. Wright, "Perceptions of Federal Aid Impacts on State Agencies: Patterns, Trends, and Variations across the 20th Century," *Publius* 37 (Winter 2007), pp. 110–130. The data are on p. 111.

70. U.S. Advisory Commission on Intergovernmental Relations, *The Federal Role in the Federal System*, p. 121.

71. Walker, *The Rebirth of Federalism*, p. 7.

72. As derived from data in American Council on Intergovernmental Relations, *Significant Features of Fiscal Federalism, 1995*, Vol. 2, p. 52.

73. As derived from data in ibid. and Walker, *The Rebirth of Federalism,* p. 227. Figures are for 1957 and 1977. Data are not available for 1978.

74. A derived from data in American Council on Intergovernmental Relations, *Significant Features of Fiscal Federalism, 1995*, Vol. 2, pp. 38, 52. Data are for 1978–1988. With some exceptions, these benchmarks continued their decline through 1990.

75. U.S. Government Accountability Office, *Federal Assistance: Illustrative Simulations of Using Statistical Population Estimates for Reallocate a Certain Federal Funding*, GAO-06-567 (Washington, DC: U.S. Government Printing

76. Office, 2006), Highlights page. In FY 2004, there were 1,172 federal grants programs.

77. U.S. General Accounting Office, *Electronic Government: Initiatives Sponsored by the Office of Management and Budget Have Made Mixed Progress*, GAO-04-561T (Washington, DC: U.S. Government Printing Office, 2004), p. 7.

77. U.S. Bureau of the Census, *Statistical Abstract of the United States, 2011*, Table 429. Figures are for 2008.

78. Jeffrey L. Brudney, Cynthia J. Bowling, and Deil S. Wright, *Continuity and Change in Public Administration Across the 50 States: Linking Practice, Theory, and Research through the American State Administrators Project, 1964–2008* (Auburn, AL: Center for Governmental Services, Auburn University, 2010), p. 22. Figure, 79 percent, is for 2004.

79. As derived from data in U.S. Bureau of the Census, "Table 1. Summary of State and Local Finances by Level of Government: 2006–2007," *Census of Governments, 2007* (Washington, DC: U.S. Government Printing Office, 2009), http://www2.census.gov/govs/estimate/0700ussl_1.txt. Figures are for 2006–2007. Figure for federal pass-through grants to localities assumes that these grants continue to account for about one-third of federal grants to the states.

80. U.S. Bureau of the Census, *Statistical Abstract of the United States, 2011*, Table 429. Figure, 66 percent, is for 2009, when grants for payments for individuals' share of grant dollars peaked.

81. American Council on Intergovernmental Relations, *Significant Features of Fiscal Federalism, 1995*, Vol. 2, p. 38.

82. U.S. Bureau of the Census, *Statistical Abstract of the United States, 2011*, Table 429.

83. Iris J. Lav, "Piling on Problems: How Federal Policies Affect State Fiscal Conditions," *National Tax Journal* 56 (September 2003), pp. 535–554.

84. As derived from data in U.S. Bureau of the Census, *Statistical Abstract of the United States, 2011*, Table 430. Current figure is for 2010 (estimated). Earlier figure is for 1990.

85. As derived from data in ibid., Table 429. Figure is in constant (2000) dollars, 2005–2008.

86. U.S. Government Accountability Office, *Tax Compliance: Federal Grant and Direct Assistance Recipients Who Abuse the Federal Tax System*, GAO-08-31 (Washington, DC: U.S. Government

Printing Office, 2007), Highlights page. Figures are for 2006.

87. U.S. Government Accountability Office, *Tax Compliance: Thousands of Organizations Exempt from Federal Income Tax Owe Nearly $1 Billion in Payroll and Other Taxes*, GAO-07-563 (Washington, DC: U.S. Government Printing Office, 2007), pp. 8, 18. Figure is for FY 2006.

88. As derived from data in ibid., p. 19.

89. As derived from data in U.S. Bureau of the Census, *Statistical Abstract of the United States, 2011*, Table 429.

90. As derived from data in U.S. Office of Management and Budget, "Historical Tables," *The President's Budget for Fiscal Year 2012* (Washington, DC: U.S. Government Printing Office, 2011), Table 12.1. The 15 percent average annual growth rate is for 2008–2010. Average annual figures for federal intergovernmental expenditures include actual expenditures of $538 billion in 2009 and $608 billion in 2010, and projections for 2011–2016.

91. U.S. Government Accountability Office, *Federal Grants: Improvements Needed in Oversight Accountability Processes*, p. 3. Figures are for 2010.

92. U.S. Office of Management and Budget, "Historical Tables," Table 12.1. Figures are averages for FY 2009–2010.

93. U.S. Advisory Commission on Intergovernmental Relations, *The Federal Role in the Federal System*, pp. 120–121.

94. As derived from data in U.S. Bureau of the Census, *Statistical Abstract of the United States, 2011*, Tables 428, 429. Figures are for 2009. At this writing, separate figures for state and local governments are unavailable.

95. U.S. Advisory Commission on Intergovernmental Relations, *Changing Public Attitudes on Governments and Taxes, 1991*, S-20 (Washington, DC: U.S. Government Printing Office, 1991), p. 10.

96. U.S. Advisory Commission on Intergovernmental Relations, *Federal Mandate Relief for State, Local, and Tribal Governments*, A-129 (Washington, DC: U.S. Government Printing Office, 1995), p. 4.

97. Richard T. Moore and Don Balfour, National Conference of State Legislatures, "Unfunded Federal Mandates," Memorandum of November 16, 2010, to Senator Lamar Alexander.

98. National Conference of State Legislatures, *Mandate Monitor* (Washington, DC: Author, November 17, 2010), p. 1.

99. U.S. Conference of Mayors/Price Waterhouse, *Impact of Unfunded Mandates on U.S. Cities: A 314 City Survey* (Washington, DC: U.S. Conference of Mayors, 1993), p. 2; and National Association of Counties/Price Waterhouse, *NACo Unfunded Mandates Survey* (Washington, DC: National Association of Counties, 1993).

100. National Conference of State Legislatures, *Mandate Monitor*, p. 1. Figure is for 2010.

101. U.S. Government Accountability Office, *Federal Mandates: Identification Process Is Complex and Agency Rules Vary*, GAO-05-401T (Washington, DC: U.S. Government Printing Office, 2005), p. 14. Figure is for 2001–2002.

102. U.S. Government Accountability Office, *Federal Mandates: Few Rules Trigger Unfunded Mandates Reform Act*, GAO-11-385T (Washington, DC: U.S. Government Printing Office, 2011) Highlights page. Figures are for 2001–2002.

103. Janet Kelly, "Unfunded Mandates: The View from the States," *Public Administration Review* 54 (July/August 1994), pp. 405–408. The quotation is on p. 405.

104. U.S. Advisory Commission on Intergovernmental Relations, *Mandates: Cases in State-Local Relations*, M-173 (Washington, DC: U.S. Government Printing Office, 1990), p. 7.

105. Kelly, "Unfunded Mandates," pp. 405–406; and Janet M. Kelly, "Lessons from the States on Unfunded Mandates," *National Civic Review* 84 (Spring 1995), p. 138.

106. Linda Wagar, "A Declaration of War," *State Government News* (April 1993), p. 18.

107. As derived from data in Council of State Governments, *Book of the States, 2011* (Lexington, KY: Author, 2011), Table 2.3. Figures are for 2008.

108. Walker, *The Rebirth of Federalism*, p. 228.

109. As derived from data in American Council on Intergovernmental Relations, *Significant Features of Fiscal Federalism, 1995*, Vol. 2, p. 52, for 1970–1994 data; and U.S. Bureau of the Census, "Table 1" (2004 and 2009). In 2006–2007, state aid to localities accounted for more than 29 percent of local income.

110. Bruce A. Wallin, *Budgeting for Basics: The Changing Landscape of City Finances* (Washington, DC: Brookings, 2005), p. 5. Per capita federal aid to these cities decreased by 59

percent, and state aid increased by 46 percent, 1977–2000.

111. As derived from data in Walker, *The Rebirth of Federalism*, p. 227; and U.S. Bureau of the Census, "Table 1" (2009). Figure is for 2006–2007. We have computed this rough estimate on the assumption that Washington continues to earmark about one-third of its assistance to the states as pass-through grants.

112. Hal Wolman, Todd Swanstrom, Margaret Weir, *et al.*, *The Calculus of Coalitions: Cities and States and the Metropolitan Agenda* (Washington, DC: Brookings, 2004), p. 20.

113. John Yinger, "States to the Rescue? Aid to Central Cities Under the New Federalism," *Public Budgeting & Finance* 10 (Summer 1990), pp. 27–44.

114. Floersch, "Federal Grantmaking," p. 2.

115. U.S. Advisory Commission on Intergovernmental Relations, *Federal Grant Profile, 1995*, p. 7.

116. Paul C. Light, *Fact Sheet on the New True Size of Government* (Washington, DC: Center for Public Service, Brookings Institution, 2003), p. 4; and as derived from data in U.S. Bureau of the Census, *Statistical Abstract of the United States, 2004–2005*, 124th ed. (Washington, DC: U.S. Government Printing Office, 2004), Table 454. In 2002, 2.86 million federal grantee jobs were in state and local governments.

117. As derived from data in Light, *Fact Sheet on the New True Size of Government*, p. 5. Grantee jobs grew by 444,000, 1990–2002.

118. Dennis O. Grady, "American Governors and State-Federal Relations: Attitudes and Activities, 1960-1980," *State Government* 57 (3, 1984), pp. 106–112.

119. U.S. Advisory Commission on Intergovernmental Relations, *State Administrators' Opinions on Administrative Change, Federal Aid, Federal Relationships*, M-120 (Washington, DC: U.S. Government Printing Office, 1980), pp. 52, 45. Figures are for 1978.

120. Brudney, Bowling, and Wright, *Continuity and Change in Public Administration Across the 50 States*, pp. 23–24. In seven of the eight surveys, 1974–2004, 45 to 58 percent said this. In 2008, 36 percent said this, which "may reflect the greater scrutiny agencies typically receive during economic downturns."

121. Brian K. Collins, "Redistributive Policy and Devolution: Is State Administration a Road Block (Grant) to Equitable Access to Federal Funds?" *Journal of Public Administration Research and Theory* 16 (October 2006), pp. 613–632. The quotations are on p. 613.

122. As derived from data in American Council on Intergovernmental Relations, *Significant Features of Fiscal Federalism, 1995*, Vol. 2, p. 52. Figure is for 1978–1988.

123. Robert W. Gage, "Intergovernmental Change: A Denver Area Perspective," *Intergovernmental Perspective* 14 (Summer 1988), pp. 14–17.

124. Thomas Muller and Michael Fix, "The Impact of Selected Federal Actions on Municipal Outlays," in Joint Economic Committee, U.S. Congress, *Government Regulation: Achieving Social and Economic Balance*, Vol. 5 of *Special Study on Economic Change* (Washington, DC: U.S. Government Printing Office, 1980), pp. 327, 330, 368.

125. Deborah A. Carroll, Robert J. Eger, III, and Justin Marlowe, "Managing Local Intergovernmental Revenues: The Imperative of Diversification," *International Journal of Public Administration* 26 (December 2003), pp. 1495–1519.

126. As derived from data in American Council on Intergovernmental Relations, *Significant Features of Fiscal Federalism, 1995*, Vol. 2, p. 52.

127. Quoted in Cho and Wright, "Perceptions of Federal Aid Impacts on State Agencies," p. 108.

128. As derived from data in American Council on Intergovernmental Relations, *Significant Features of Fiscal Federalism, 1995*, Vol. 2, p. 52.

129. Brudney, Bowling, and Wright, *Continuity and Change in Public Administration Across the 50 States*, p. 24.

130. Ibid. Current figure is for 2008.

131. Ibid. Emphasis is original.

132. Albert J. Richter, "Federal Grants Management: The City and County View," *Municipal Year Book, 1977* (Washington, DC: International City Management Association, 1977), pp. 180–192. Figures (pp. 183–184) are for 1976.

133. James R. Hines, Jr. and Richard H. Thaler, "The Flypaper Effect," *Journal of Economic Perspectives* 9 (Winter 1995), pp. 217–226.

134. Therese A. McCarty and Stephen J. Schmidt, "Dynamic Patterns in State Government Finance," *Public Finance Review* 29 (July 2001), pp. 208–222. The quotation is on p. 220.

135. Steven C. Deller and Craig S. Maher, "Categorical Municipal Expenditures with a Focus on the Flypaper Effect," *Public Budgeting & Finance* 25 (September 2005), pp. 73–90.

136. Rangarajan, "Evidence of Different Types of Creativity in Government."

137. U.S. General Accounting Office, *Federal Grants: Design Improvements Could Help Federal Resources Go Further*, GAO/AIMD-97-7 (Washington, DC: U.S. Government Printing Office, 1996), p. 2.

138. U.S. Government Accountability Office, *Community Development Block Grants: Program Offers Recipients Flexibility but Oversight Can Be Improved*, GAO-06-732 (Washington, DC: U.S. Government Printing Office, 2006).

139. Deller and Maher, "Categorical Municipal Expenditures with a Focus on the Flypaper Effect."

140. Donald F. Kettl, "Boutiques for the Poor," *Governing* (June 1999), p. 14.

141. U.S. Advisory Commission on Intergovernmental Relations, *Regulatory Federalism: Policy, Process, Impact, and Reform*, A-95 (Washington, DC: U.S. Government Printing Office, 1984).

142. U.S. Advisory Commission on Intergovernmental Relations, *Federal Regulation of State and Local Governments: The Mixed Record of the 1980s*, A-126 (Washington, DC: U.S. Government Printing Office, 1993), p. v.

143. As derived from data in National Academy of Public Administration, *Beyond Preemptions: Intergovernmental Partnerships to Enhance the New Economy* (Washington, DC: Author, 2006), p.16.

144. U.S. Advisory Commission on Intergovernmental Relations, *Federal Regulation of State and Local Governments*, p. 56.

145. As derived from data in National Academy of Public Administration, *Beyond Preemptions*, p. 16.

146. U.S. Advisory Commission on Intergovernmental Relations, *Federal Court Rulings Involving State, Local, and Tribal Governments, Calendar Year 1994*, M-196 (Washington, DC: U.S. Government Printing Office, 1995).

147. As derived from data in U.S. General Accounting Office, *Federalism: Comments on S.1214-The Federalism Accountability Act of 1999*, GAO/T-GGD-99-143 (Washington, DC: U.S. Government Printing Office, 1999), p. 4. Figures are for 1996–1998.

148. As derived from data in: Light, *Fact Sheet on the New True Size of Government*, p. 4; and U.S. Bureau of the Census, *Statistical Abstract of the United States, 1999*, 119th ed. (Washington, DC: U.S. Government Printing Office, 1999), Table 534. Figure, 28 percent, is for 1996–1997.

149. David R. Berman, "State-Local Relations: Authority, Policies, Cooperation," *Municipal Year Book, 1999* (Washington, DC: International City/County Management Association, 1999), pp. 47–61. Data are on p. 50.

150. Joseph Zimmerman, "The Discretionary Authority of Local Governments," *Urban Data Service Reports* 13 (November 1981), pp. 1–13. Datum is on p. 11.

151. Osbin L. Ervin, "Understanding American Local Government: Recent Census Bureau and ACIR Contributions," *Public Administration Review* 55 (March/April 1995), pp. 209–212. Figures (p. 210) are for 1978–1990.

152. Berman, "State-Local Relations: Authority, Policies, Cooperation," p. 49.

153. U.S. Advisory Commission on Intergovernmental Relations, *State Laws Governing Local Government and Administration*, M-186 (Washington, DC: U.S. Government Printing Office, 1993), p. 20.

154. U.S. Advisory Commission on Intergovernmental Relations, *Federally Induced Costs Affecting State and Local Governments*, M-193 (Washington, DC: U.S. Government Printing Office, 1994), p. 3.

155. U.S. Advisory Commission on Intergovernmental Relations, *Regulatory Federalism*, Appendix I.

156. U.S. Advisory Commission on Intergovernmental Relations, *Federal Statutory Preemption of State and Local Authority: History, Inventory, and Issues*, A-121 (Washington, DC: U.S. Government Printing Office, 1992), p. 9.

157. The following typology is described more fully in U.S. Advisory Commission on Intergovernmental Relations, *Regulatory Federalism*, pp. 7–10.

158. Timothy J. Conlan and David R. Beam, "Federal Mandates: The Record of Reform and Future Prospects," *Intergovernmental Perspective* 18 (Fall 1992), p. 8.

159. Kelly, "Lessons from the States on Unfunded Mandates," pp. 133–139.

160. Kiki Caruson and Susan A. MacManus, "Mandates and Management Challenges in the Trenches: An Intergovernmental Perspective on Homeland Security," *Public Administration Review* 66 (July/August 2006), pp. 522–536.

161. As derived from data in Jerri Killian and Enamul Choudhury, "Continuity and Change in the Role of City Managers," *Municipal Year Book, 2010* (Washington, DC: International City/County Management Association, 2010), pp. 10–18. In 2010, state mandates ranked ninth as an "influence," and federal ones ranked sixteenth (p. 13).

162. Rodney E. Hero and Jody L. Fitzpatrick, "State Mandating of Local Government Activities: An Exploration," Paper Presented at the Annual Meeting of the American Political Science Association, Washington, DC, August 28–31, 1986, p. 18.

163. U.S. Advisory Commission on Intergovernmental Relations, *State Mandating of Local Expenditures*, A-67 (Washington, DC: U.S. Government Printing Office, 1978), p. 41. Data are for 1976.

164. U.S. Advisory Commission on Intergovernmental Relations, *Federally Induced Costs Affecting State and Local Governments*, p. 7.

165. David R. Berman, "State-Local Relations: Authority, Finances, Cooperation," *Municipal Year Book, 2002* (Washington, DC: International City/County Management Association, 2002), pp. 45–61. The quotation is on pp. 49–50.

166. As derived from data in National Academy of Public Administration, *Beyond Preemptions*, p. 16. Data are for 1790–2004. The quotations are on pp. 1–2.

167. U.S. Advisory Commission on Intergovernmental Relations, *Federal Statutory Preemption of State and Local Authority*, p. 34. Data are for 1988.

168. Catherine H. Lovell, *et al., Federal and State Mandating on Local Governments: An Exploration of Issues and Impacts* (Riverside: Graduate School of Administration, University of California, 1979), p. 82.

169. U.S. Advisory Commission on Intergovernmental Relations, *Regulatory Federalism*, p. 175. Figures are for 1981.

170. Killian and Choudhury, "Continuity and Change in the Role of City Managers," p. 13.

171. Gregory Streib and William L. Waugh, Jr., "The Changing Responsibilities of County Governments: Data from a Survey of County Leaders," *American Review of Public Administration* 21 (June 1991), pp. 139–156, 144. Figures (p. 144), 93 and 31 percent, respectively, are for 1989.

172. U.S. General Accounting Office, *Federalism: Comments on S.1214-The Federalism Accountability Act of 1999*, p. 4. Data are for 1996–1998. "Federalism assessments" are required by the Unfunded Mandates Reform Act and Executive Order 12612.

173. Greenblatt, "The Hand-off," p. 26.

174. Victoria Gordon, "Home Rule and Improved Fiscal Health: Perception or Reality?" *Municipal Year Book, 2006* (Washington, DC: International City/County Management Association, 2006), pp. 33–38. The quotation is on p. 37.

175. Pew Research Center for the People & the Press, *Distrust, Discontent, Anger, and Partisan Rancor: The People and Their Government* (Washington, DC: Author, 2010), Section 2, http://people-press.org/report/606/trust-in-government. Data are for 1964, when 40 percent thought this, and 2010, when 58 percent did.

176. William T. Gormley, Jr., "Money and Mandates: The Politics of Intergovernmental Conflict," *Publius* 36 (Fall 2006), pp. 523–540.

177. Donna Milam Handley, "Strengthening the Intergovernmental Grant System: Long-Term Lessons for the Federal-Local Relationship," *Public Administration Review* 68 (January/February 2008), pp. 126–136. The quotation is on pp. 126–127.

178. U.S. Government Printing Office, *Federal Grants: Improvements Needed in Oversight and Accountability Processes*, GAO-11-773T (Washington, DC: U.S. Government Printing Office, 2011), pp. 10–11. Figures are for 2006.

179. U.S. Government Printing Office, *Improper Payments: Recent Efforts to Address Improper Payments and Remaining Challenges*, GAO-11-575T (Washington, DC: U.S. Government Printing Office, 2011), p. 3. Figures are for FY 2010.

180. Gormley, "Money and Mandates."

181. Linda Greenhouse, "States Are Given New Legal Shield by Supreme Court," *New York*

Times (June 24, 1999). The Court's pro-states' rights cases decided during this period are: *Seminole Tribe* v. *Florida* (1996); *Printz* v. *United States* (1997); *Alden* v. *Maine* (1999); *Florida* v. *College Savings Bank* (1999); *College Savings Bank* v. *Florida* (1999); *United States* v. *Morrison* (2000); *University of Alabama* v. *Garrett* (2001); *Alexander* v. *Sandoval* (2001); and *Federal Maritime Commission* v. *South Carolina State Ports Authority* (2002).

182. The case is *Northern Insurance Company of New York* v. *Chatham County.*

183. The Court's pro-federal-power cases are *Nevada* v. *Hibbs* (2003); *Tennessee* v. *Lane* (2004); and *Gonzales* v. *Raich* (2005).

184. The case is *Gonzales* v. *Oregon* (2006).

185. Dale Krane and Heidi Koenig, "The State of American Federalism, 2004: Is Federalism Still a Core Value?" *Publius* 35 (Winter 2005), pp. 1–40. The quotation is on p. 1.

186. Robert S. Allen, ed., *Our Sovereign State* (New York: Vanguard, 1949), p. vii.

187. Brudney, Bowling, and Wright, *Continuity and Change in Public Administration Across the 50 States*, p. 4.

188. Ibid., p. 3. Figure is for 2008. In 1959, there were an average of fifty-one agencies per state.

189. Ibid., p. 2.

190. John Bohte and Kenneth J. Meier, "The Marble Cake: Introducing Federalism to the Government Growth Equation," *Publius* 30 (Summer 2000), pp. 35–46. The quotation is on p. 44.

191. As derived from data in Katherine Barrett and Richard Greene, "Grading the States: The Mandate to Measure," *Governing* (March 2008), pp. 24–93. Grade is for 2008.

192. As derived from data in Katherine Barrett and Richard Greene, "Grading the Cities: A Management Report Card," *Governing* (February 2000), pp. 22–91. Grade, B–, is for 2000.

193. Katherine Barrett, Richard Greene, and Michelle Mariani, "Grading the Counties: A Management Report Card," *Governing* (February 2002), pp. 20–89. Grade, C+, is for 2002.

194. For details of this history, see U.S. General Accounting Office, *Federal Assistance: Grant System continues to be Highly Fragmented*, p. 3; Floersch, "Federal Grantmaking," p. 4; and Bruce D. McDowell, "Grant Reform Reconsidered," *Intergovernmental Perspective* 17 (Summer 1991), pp. 8–11.

195. Alice M. Rivlin, "A New Vision of American Federalism," *Public Administration Review* 52 (July/August 1992), pp. 315–320.

196. Paul E. Peterson, "Who Should Do What? Divided Responsibility in the Federal System," *Brookings Review* 13 (Spring 1995), pp. 6–11.

197. Ibid.

198. Rivlin, "A New Vision of American Federalism," p. 320.

199. Peterson, "Who Should Do What?"

200. Ibid.

201. Rivlin, "A New Vision of American Federalism."

202. As derived from data in Saundra K. Schneider, William G. Jacoby, and Daniel C. Lewis, "Public Opinion Toward Intergovernmental Policy Responsibilities," *Publius* 41 (Winter 2011), pp. 1–30. Data and quotation are on pp. 9, 21, respectively. Figures are for 2006.

203. Ibid., pp. 10, 21. Data are for 2006.

204. Sanford F. Schram and Carol S. Weissert, "The State of American Federalism, 1996–1997," *Publius* 27 (Spring 1997), pp. 1–26. The quotation is on p. 1.

205. U.S. Advisory Commission on Intergovernmental Relations, *Federal Regulation of State and Local Governments*, pp. 67–68.

206. Katherine Barrett and Richard Greene, "Overseeing the Stimulus," *Governing* (January 2011), pp. 42–43.

207. National Center for Interstate Compacts, *Understanding Interstate Compacts* (Lexington, KY: Council of State Governments, 2009), p. 3. Figures are for 2009.

208. William Kevin Voit, *Interstate Compacts and Agencies, 1998* (Lexington, KY: Council of State Governments, 1999).

209. Ann O'M. Bowman, "Horizontal Federalism: Exploring Interstate Interactions," *Journal of Public Administration Research and Theory* 14 (October 2004), pp. 535–546. The data are on pp. 538, 541–542, 544.

210. Ibid., pp. 538, 540–541, 544. The years were 1992–1999.

211. Much of the following discussion on interstate conflict is drawn from Joanne Omang, "In This Economic Slump, It's a State-Eat-State Nation," *Washington Post* (June 14, 1982); and Richard Benedetto, "States Skirmish in 'Border War,'" *USA Today* (February 24, 1984).

212. As derived from data in Council of State Governments, *Book of the States, 2011*, Table 7.15. Figure is for 2009.

213. Roger Alford, "Kentucky Program Pays Moving Expenses to Relocate Welfare Recipients," *Savannah Morning News* (June 21, 2001).

214. William B. Munro, "Home Rule," *Encyclopedia of the Social Sciences*, Vol. 4 (New York: Macmillan, 1930), p. 434.

215. U.S. Advisory Commission on Intergovernmental Relations, *State Laws Governing Local Government and Administration*, p. 20. Figures are for 1990.

216. Adam Coester, *Dillon's Rule or Not?* (Washington, DC: National Association of Counties, 2004), p. 3.

217. Jerry Anthony, "Do State Growth Management Regulations Reduce Sprawl?" *Urban Affairs Review* 39 (January 2004), pp. 376–397.

218. Anthony G. Cahill and Joseph A. James, "State Response to Local Fiscal Stress," *Municipal Year Book, 1996* (Washington, DC: International City/County Management Association, 1996), pp. 60–70.

219. Beth Walter Honadle, "The State's Role in U.S. Local Government Fiscal Crises: A Theoretical Model and Results of a National Survey," *International Journal of Public Administration* 26 (January 2003), pp. 1431–1473.

220. Megan Mullin and Dorothy M. Daley, "Working with the State: Exploring Interagency Collaboration within a Federalist System," *Journal of Public Administration Research and Theory* 20 (October 2010), pp. 757–778.

221. G. Ross Stephens, "State Centralization and the Erosion of Local Autonomy," *Journal of Politics* 36 (February 1974), pp. 44–76.

222. Ibid.; and G. Ross Stephens, "Patterns of State Centralization/Decentralization during the Last Half of the Twentieth Century, Paper presented at the Annual Meeting of the Southwestern Political Science Association (Austin, TX, March 18–21, 1992). By 1992, sixteen states were "centralized."

223. Allan D. Wallis, "Inventing Regionalism: The First Two Waves," *National Civic Review* 83 (Spring 1994), pp. 168–169. Figures are for 1964–1977.

224. Patricia S. Atkins and Laura Wilson Gentry, "An Etiquette for the 1990s Regional Council," *National Civic Review* 81 (Fall/Winter 1992), pp. 466–487.

225. David B. Walker and Albert J. Richter, "Regionalism and the Counties," *County Year Book, 1975* (Washington, DC: National Association of Counties and International City Management Association, 1975), pp. 14–19. The data are on p. 15.

226. Sherman W. Wyman, "Profiles and Prospects: Regional Councils and Their Executive Duties," *Municipal Year Book, 1994* (Washington, DC: International City/County Management Association, 1994), p. 53. Figure is for 1990.

227. Richard Hartman, *A Report to the Membership* (Washington, DC: National Association of Regional Councils, 1979), p. 4.

228. Wyman, "Profiles and Prospects," p. 49. Data are for 1990.

229. Patricia S. Atkins, "From the Mauling to the Malling of Regionalism," *Public Administration Review* 53 (November/December 1993), pp. 583–586. In 1977, federal support accounted for 75 percent of councils' budgets, and in 1988, 45 percent.

230. J. Eugene Grigsby, III, "Regional Governance and Regional Councils," *National Civic Review* 85 (Spring/Summer 1996), pp. 53–58. Figure (p. 55) is for 1992.

231. Wyman, "Profiles and Prospects," pp. 52–53. Figures are for 1990.

232. Ibid., p. 56.

233. Allan D. Wallis, "The Third Wave: Trends in Regional Governance," *National Civic Review* 83 (Summer–Fall 1994), pp. 294–298.

234. Neal R. Peirce, Curtis W. Johnson, and John Stuart Hall, *Citistates: How America Can Prosper in a Competitive World* (Santa Ana, CA: Seven Locks Press, 1993), p. 318. Emphasis is original. Figure is for 1990.

235. Wyman, "Profiles and Prospects," p. 56.

236. U.S. Advisory Commission on Intergovernmental Relations, *State Laws Governing Local Government Structure and Administration*, M-186 (Washington, DC: U.S. Government Printing Office, 1993), p. 9. Figure is for 1990. In 1978, thirty-nine states did so.

237. City of Lakewood, *Lakewood Plan (Part 1 of 3): Lakewood City Government Breaks New Ground*, http://www.lakewoodcity.org.

238. Tad Friend, "Contract City," *The New Yorker* (September 5, 2011), pp. 34–40. The quotation is on p. 36.

239. Mildred E. Warner and Amir Hefetz, "Cooperative Competition: Alternative Service Delivery, 2002–2007," *Municipal Year Book, 2009* (Washington, DC: International City/County Management Association, 2009), pp. 11–20. The data are on pp. 13–14. Figure is for 2007. Although it is unclear, we suspect that "intergovernmental service contracts" include joint and shared service agreements, discussed next.

240. As derived from data in Rowan Miranda and Karlyn Andersen, "Alternative Service Delivery in Local Government, 1982–1992," *Municipal Year Book, 1994* (Washington, DC: International City/County Management Association, 1994), pp. 11–35. Data (p. 31) are for 1982.

241. Lori M. Henderson, "Intergovernmental Service Arrangements and the Transfer of Functions," *Municipal Year Book, 1985* (Washington, DC: International City Management Association, 1985), p. 195. Figure, 52 percent, is for 1983.

242. Mary K. Marvel and Howard P. Marvel, "Shaping the Provision of Outsourced Public Services: Incentive Efficacy and Service Delivery," *Public Performance & Management Review* 33 (December 2009), pp. 183–213. The quotations are on p. 202.

243. Mary K. Marvel and Howard P. Marvel, "Government-to-Government Contracting: Stewardship, Agency, and Substitution," *International Public Management Journal* 11 (2, 2008), pp. 171–192. The quotation is on p. 171.

244. Henderson, "Intergovernmental Service Arrangements and the Transfer of Functions," pp. 197–198. Figure, 55 percent, is for 1983.

245. Timothy J. Burns and Kathryn G. Yeaton, *Success Factors for Implementing Shared Services in Government* (Washington, DC: IBM Center for the Business of Government, 2008), pp. 6, 16, 18, 34. Forty-six respondents, or 15 percent, at all governmental levels in several countries (a majority were Americans) were surveyed.

246. U.S. Advisory Commission on Intergovernmental Relations, *Intergovernmental Service Arrangements for Delivering Local Public Services: Update 1983*, A-103 (Washington, DC: U.S. Government Printing Office, 1985), pp. 2, 55, 62. Figures are for 1976–1983, and include some transfers from and to companies, nonprofit agencies, and other governments, such as special districts and states.

247. Warner and Hefetz, "Cooperative Competition," p. 19. Figure refers to "intergovernmental contracting" in 2007, but research states or strongly suggests that savings also are the leading motivation to enter into the other forms of intergovernmental service arrangements.

248. Pascale Joassart-Marcelli and Juliet Musso, "Municipal Service Provision Choices within a Metropolitan Area," *Urban Affairs Review* 14 (March 2005), pp. 492–519. The data are on p. 516.

249. Roland Zullo, "Does Fiscal Stress Induce Privatization? Correlates of Private and Intermunicipal Contracting, 1992–2002," *Governance* 22 (July 2009), pp. 459–481.

250. James C. Clingermayer, Richard C. Feiock, and Christopher Stream, "Governmental Uncertainty and Leadership Turnover: Influences on Contracting and Sector Choices for Local Services," *State and Local Government Review* 35 (Fall 2003), pp. 150–160. The data are on p. 158.

251. Warner and Hefetz, "Cooperative Competition," p. 19. Figure refers to "intergovernmental contracting" in 2007.

252. Henderson, "Intergovernmental Service Arrangements and the Transfer of Functions," p. 196. Figure is for 1983.

253. Warner and Hefetz, "Cooperative Competition," p. 19. Figures, 64 and 59 percent, respectively, are for 2007.

254. Henderson, "Intergovernmental Service Arrangements and the Transfer of Functions," p. 196. Datum is for 1983.

255. Skip Krueger and Ethan M. Bernick, "State Rules and Local Governance Choices," *Publius* 40 (October 2010), pp. 697–718.

256. Kelly LeRoux, Paul W. Brandenburger, and Sanjay K. Pandey, "Interlocal Service Cooperation in U.S. Cities: A Social Network Explanation," *Public Administration Review* 70 (March/April 2010), pp. 268–278. The quotation is on p. 273.

257. Kelly LeRoux, "Nonprofit Community Conferences: The Role of Alternative Regional Institutions in Interlocal Service Delivery," *State and Local Government Review* 40 (Fall 2008), pp. 160–172.

258. LeRoux, Brandenburger, and Pandey, "Interlocal Service Cooperation in U.S. Cities," pp. 273, 268.

259. Michael McGuire and Chris Silvia, "The Effect of Problem Severity, Managerial and Organizational Capacity, and Agency Structure on Intergovernmental Collaboration: Evidence from Local Emergency Management," *Public Administration Review* 70 (March/April 2010), pp. 279–288. The quotations are on p. 279.

260. Kelley LeRoux and Sanjay K. Pandey, "City Managers, Career Incentives, and Municipal Service Decisions: The Effects of Managerial Progressive Ambition on Interlocal Service Delivery," *Public Administration Review* 71 (July/August 2011), pp. 627–636.

261. Trevor L. Brown, "The Dynamics of Government-to-Government Contracts," *Public Performance & Management Review* 31 (March 2008), pp. 364–386.

262. Warner and Hefetz, "Cooperative Competition," p. 19. Figure refers to "intergovernmental contracting" in 2007.

263. Henderson, "Intergovernmental Service Arrangements and the Transfer of Functions," pp. 196,198. Data are for 1983.

264. U.S. Advisory Commission on Intergovernmental Relations, *Intergovernmental Service Arrangements for Delivering Local Public Services*, p. 62. Data are for 1972–1983.

265. Henderson, "Intergovernmental Service Arrangements and the Transfer of Functions," p. 202. Figures are for 1983.

266. U.S. Advisory Commission on Intergovernmental Relations, *Intergovernmental Service Arrangements for Delivering Local Public* Services, p. 97, tracks these trends for 1965–1983; and Joassart-Marcelli and Musso, "Municipal Service Provision Choices within a Metropolitan Area," p. 516, continues the tracking, at least among local governments in Southern California, for 1982–1997.

267. Joassart-Marcelli and Musso, "Municipal Service Provision Choices within a Metropolitan Area," p. 516.

268. U.S. Advisory Commission on Intergovernmental Relations, *Intergovernmental Service Arrangements for Delivering Local Public Services*, pp. 43–44.

269. Graeme A. Hodge, *Privatization: An International Review of Performance* (Boulder, CO: Westview, 2000), p. 99.

270. Rhys Andrews and Tom Entwistle, "Does Cross-Sectoral Partnership Deliver? An Empirical Exploration of Public Service Effectiveness, Efficiency, and Equity," *Journal of Public Administration Research and Theory* 20 (July 2010), pp. 679–701. The quotation is on p. 691.

271. Ibid., pp. 692–693.

272. U.S. Advisory Commission on Inter-governmental Relations, *Metropolitan Organization: Comparison of the Allegheny and St Louis Case Studies*, SR-15 (Washington, DC: U.S. Government Printing Office, 1993), p. 3; and U.S. Bureau of the Census, *Statistical Abstract of the United States, 2011*, Appendix II, p. 900. Current figure is for 2009. In 1942, there were 140 standard metropolitan statistical areas.

273. U.S. Bureau of the Census, *Statistical Abstract of the United States, 2001*, 120th ed. (Washington, DC: U.S. Government Printing Office, 2001), Table 31. Figure is for 1998.

274. As derived from data in U.S. Bureau of the Census, *Statistical Abstract of the United States, 2011*, Table 24. Figure, 84 percent, is for 2009.

275. U.S. Advisory Commission on Intergovernmental Relations, *The Organization of Local Public Economies*, A-109 (Washington, DC: U.S. Government Printing Office, 1987), p. 49.

276. David Rusk, *Cities Without Suburbs* (Washington, DC: Woodrow Wilson Center Press, 1993), p. 5.

277. Bruce Katz and Jennifer Bradley, "Divided We Sprawl," *Atlantic Monthly* 284 (December 1999), pp. 26–34.

278. Brookings Institution, *The State of Metropolitan America: On the Front Line of Demographic Transition* (Washington, DC: Author, 2010), p. 46. Figure is for 2000–2008.

279. Todd Swanstrom, Colleen Casey, Robert Flack, et al., *Pulling Apart: Economic Segregation among Suburbs and Central Cities in Major Metropolitan Areas* (Washington, DC: Brookings, 2004), p. 4.

280. Brookings Institution, *The State of Metropolitan America*, p. 139. Data are for 1999–2008.

281. Amy L. Nelson, Kent P. Schwirian, and Patricia M. Schwirian, "Social and Economic Distress in Large Cities, 1970–1990: A Test of the Urban Crisis Thesis," *Social Science Research* 27 (December 1998), pp. 410–431.

282. Brookings Institution, *Racial Change in the Nation's Largest Cities: Evidence From the*

2000 Census (Washington, DC: Author, 2001), p. 4.

283. Rusk, *Cities Without Suburbs*, p. 10. Emphasis is original.

284. Ibid., pp. 5–44.

285. Lingwen Zheng and Mildred E. Warner, "Local Economic Development, 1994–2004: Broadening Strategies, Increasing Accountability," *Municipal Year Book, 2010* (Washington, DC: International City/County Management Association, 2010), pp. 3–9. The quotation is on p. 7, and the data are on p. 9.

286. The term is Reuss's, in *Revenue-Sharing*.

287. U.S. Advisory Commission on Intergovernmental Relations, *Metropolitan Organization*, p. 5.

288. Rusk, *Cities Without Suburbs*, p. 95. Figure is for 1990.

289. U.S. Advisory Commission on Intergovernmental Relations, *Metropolitan Organization*, p. 3; and U.S. Bureau of the Census, *1992 Census of Governments: Government Organization*, Vol. 1, No. 1 (Washington, DC: U.S. Government Printing Office, 1994), Table 26. Figures cover 1942–1992.

290. U.S. Advisory Commission on Intergovernmental Relations, *Metropolitan Organization*, p. 3. In 1942, 10 percent of all local governments were in metropolitan areas, and in 1992, 38 percent were.

291. As derived from data in U.S. Bureau of the Census, *Statistical Abstract of the United States, 1994*, 114th ed. (Washington, DC: U.S. Government Printing Office, 1994), Tables 462 and 39; and U.S. Bureau of the Census, *1992 Census of Governments*, Table 26. Figures are for 1992.

292. Donald Boyd, *Layering of Local Governments & City-County Mergers* (Albany, NY: Nelson A. Rockefeller Institute of Government, 2008), pp. 5–7. Figures are for 2000, except for the number of general purpose local governments, which is for 2007.

293. Osborne M. Reynolds, Jr., *Local Government Law*, 3rd ed. (St Paul, MN: West, 2009), p. 33.

294. As derived from data in U.S. Bureau of the Census, *2002 Census of Governments, Vol. 1, No. 1, Government Organization* (Washington, DC: U.S. Government Printing Office, 2002), Tables 10, 15. Figures are for 2002, and include dependent school systems. Thirty-seven percent of special districts and 15 percent of "public school systems" (or school districts plus dependent school systems) did not respond to this question.

295. Vincent Ostrom, Charles M. Tiebout, and Robert Warren, "The Organization of Government in Metropolitan Areas: Theoretical Inquiry." *American Political Science Review* 55 (December 1961), pp. 831–842.

296. Charles M. Tiebout is generally thought to be the progenitor of this school. See his "A Pure Theory of Local Expenditures," *Journal of Political Economy* 64 (April 1956), pp. 416–424.

297. Ostrom, Tiebout, and Warren, "The Organization of Government in Metropolitan Areas," p. 834.

298. Grigsby, "Regional Governance and Regional Councils," p. 55.

299. Neal R. Pierce, with Curtis W. Johnson and John Stuart Hall, *Citistates: How Urban America Can Prosper in a Competitive World* (Washington, DC: Seven Locks Press, 1993), p. 6.

300. The following points are drawn from four excellent reviews of the literature: U.S. Advisory Commission on Intergovernmental Relations, *The Organization of Local Public Economies* and *Metropolitan Organization*; Robert Bish and Elinor Ostrom, *Local Government in the United States* (San Francisco: ICS Press, 1988); and Darcy Rollins and Antoniya Owens, *Empirical Evidence of the Effects of Government Fragmentation* (Boston: New England Public Policy Center, Federal Reserve Bank of Boston, 2006).

301. Reuss, *Revenue-Sharing*, pp. 59–60.

302. Ibid., pp. 58–59. The quotation is on p. 59.

303. James A. Christianson and Carolyn E. Sachs, "The Impact of Government Size and Number of Administrative Units on the Quality of Public Services," *Administrative Science Quarterly* 25 (March 1980), pp. 89–101.

304. Ruth Hoogland De Hoog, David Lowery, and William A. Lyons, "Metropolitan Fragmentation and Suburban Ghettos: Some Empirical Observations on Institutional Racism," *Journal of Urban Affairs* 13 (October 2008), pp. 479–493.

305. Nicholas O. Alozie and Catherine McNamara, "Gender Differences in Willingness to Pay for Urban Public Services," *Urban Affairs Review* 45 (January 2010), pp. 377–390.

306. Rusk, *Cities Without Suburbs*, p. 34.

307. Ibid., p. 31.

308. Elizabeth Kneebone and Alan Berube, *Reversal of Fortune: A New Look at Concentrated Poverty in the 2000s* (Washington, DC: Brookings, 2008).

309. Rusk, *Cities Without Suburbs*, p. 43.

310. Ibid., pp. 56–57. Since 1957, Miami-Dade County, Florida, has been governed by an unusual "two-tiered federation" that falls short of an actual city-county consolidated government (the Twin Cities and Toronto have similar structures), but, with thirty-five municipal governments in a metro area of nearly 2.5 million people, is relatively regional in its governance. The Cincinnati, Detroit, Los Angeles, and Newark metro areas are highly fragmented.

311. Robert C. Wood, "The New Metropolises: Green Belt, Grass Roots versus Gargantua," *American Political Science Review* 52 (March 1958), pp. 108–122.

312. Rusk, *Cities Without Suburbs*, p. 89.

313. Ibid., pp. 89, 88. Emphasis added.

314. Henderson, "Intergovernmental Service Arrangements and the Transfer of Functions," p. 195.

315. Warner and Hefetz, "Cooperative Competition," pp. 13–14.

316. U.S. Advisory Commission on Intergovernmental Relations, *Intergovernmental Service Arrangements for Delivering Local Public Services,* p. 62.

317. Warner and Hefetz, "Cooperative Competition," p. 19.

318. For a summary of early reports, many of them issued by governments, that argue regionalism is more efficient than fragmentation, see Reuss, *Revenue-Sharing*, pp. 55–63. For a more current example, see New York State Commission on Local Government Efficiency & Competitiveness, *21st Century Local Government* (Albany, NY: Author, 2008).

319. Henderson, "Intergovernmental Service Arrangements and the Transfer of Functions," pp. 196, 198, 201.

320. Rusk, *Cities Without Suburbs*, pp. 85, 34. Emphasis added. A more recent analysis also finds that metropolitan fragmentation associates with hardship. See David J. Wright and Lisa M. Montiel, *Divided They Fall: Hardship in America's Cities and Suburbs*

321. Rusk, *Cities Without Suburbs*, pp. 40–41.

322. Mildred E. Warner and Amir Hefetz, "Service Characteristics and Contracting: The Importance of Citizen Interest and Competition," *Municipal Year Book, 2010* (Washington, DC: International City/County Management Association, 2010), pp. 19–27. The quotation is on p. 26.

323. Rusk, *Cities Without Suburbs*, p. 95. Figures are for 1990. We are using Rusk's definition of metro government, and a universe of all 320 metro areas as of 1990.

324. Rusk, *Cities Without Suburbs*, p. 96.

325. Suzanne M. Leland and Kurt Thurmaier, "Lessons from 35 Years of City-County Consolidation Attempts," *Municipal Year Book, 2006* (Washington, DC: International City/County Management Association, 2006), pp. 3–10. Figure is for 2004.

326. Ibid., p. 4. The 1805–1907 count includes two consolidations involving the five boroughs comprising New York City mandated by the New York state legislature in 1874 and 1898.

327. Rusk, *Cities Without Suburbs*, p. 92.

328. Leland and Thurmaier, "Lessons from 35 Years of City-County Consolidation Attempts," p. 4.

329. As derived from data in ibid. Twenty-nine consolidations occurred, 1947–2004.

330. Boyd, *Layering of Local Governments & City-County Mergers*, p. 19. Figures are for 1800–2006.

331. U.S. Advisory Commission on Intergovernmental Relations, *State Laws Governing Local Government Structure and Administration*, pp. 25–26. Data are for 1990.

332. Leland and Thurmaier, "Lessons from 35 Years of City-County Consolidation Attempts," p. 9.

333. Jamie L. Palmer and Greg Lindsey, "Classifying State Approaches to Annexation," *State and Local Government Review* 33 (Winter 2001), pp. 60–73. Data are for "the 1970s" (p. 67), 1997.

334. Ibid., p. 68.

335. David Rusk, *Annexation and the Fiscal Fate of Cities* (Washington, DC: Brookings, 2006), p. 1.

336. As derived from data in Walker, *The Rebirth of Federalism*, p. 292; and Rodger Johnson, Marc Perry, and Lisa Lollock, "Annexation

and Population Growth in American Cities, 1990–2000," *Municipal Year Book, 2004* (Washington, DC: International City/County Management Association, 2004), pp. 3–7. During the 1990s, cities annexed 36 percent more land and 62 percent more people than they did, on average, in each of the preceding two decades.

337. Walker, *The Rebirth of Federalism*, p. 292. Figure is for 1970–1989.

338. Rusk, *Cities Without Suburbs,* p. 10. Figure is for 1950–1990.

Toward a
Bureaucratic Ethic

Public administration has been, in comparison with other professions, slow to recognize its own ethical practices. Prior to the abandonment of the politics/administration dichotomy and the principles of administration (recall Chapter 2), a public administrator needed morality no more than a hotel clerk carrying out his or her daily duties.

CODES AND COMMISSIONS: THE RISE OF PUBLIC SECTOR ETHICS

This perspective began to change in the United States in the early twentieth century.

Ethics for the Public Professions

What is now the International City/County Management Association adopted the first code of ethics for a public profession in 1924. The code reflected the anticorruption values of the municipal reform movement of the period, and essentially held up efficiency as its ethical touchstone. Despite its initial narrowness, the city managers' code was groundbreaking and other public professions followed suit. All the associations that represent the profession's major specializations now have codes of, and provide training in, ethics for their members.

That critical component of professionalism, the universities, also have recognized the importance of public ethics. The field's national accrediting body requires graduate education in ethics, and all introductory public administration textbooks include a discussion of ethics.[1]

Ethics for Governments

Governments lagged behind the public professions in recognizing ethics, but by the mid-twentieth century they were catching up. Today, more government workers (47 percent) than either nonprofit employees (44 percent) or businesspeople (38 percent) report that their organization has a full ethics and compliance program in place.[2]

Federal Ethics   Congress first imposed a general code of ethics on federal administrators in 1958, and, twenty years later, with the passage of the Ethics in Government Act of 1978, expanded the code and founded the Office of Government Ethics.

Federal ethics regulations focus mostly on conflicts of financial interest and impartiality, consume about forty pages, and command the attention of nearly 9,000 federal employees who work, at least sometimes, in ethics programs.[3] "Congress has enacted laws and presidents have issued executive orders that have produced a deeply layered and extraordinarily cumbersome regulatory scheme designed to insure the integrity of federal employees," and clarity, simplicity, and straightforwardness suffer.[4]

Grass-Roots' Ethics The first general code of state ethics was legislated in 1954 by the New York general assembly, and now forty-seven states have some form of written ethics code. Most are characterized by some serious omissions, and, in more than half the states, codes do not address even as many as four out of six basic areas of ethics legislation; to wit: the presence of an ethics code (pretty basic, that); mandatory financial disclosure; and limits on honoraria, gifts from lobbyists, post-government employment, and representation of clients before state agencies.[5]

Thirty-six states have established commissions to oversee ethics issues.[6] Most are largely toothless, vulnerable, reactive, fragmented, symbolic, and underfunded. Perhaps not even 10 percent of all financial disclosure forms submitted by public officials receive a "substantive review" due to a lack of funds.[7]

Local elected officials in twenty states, a growing number, are subject to state-imposed ethics codes.[8] Almost seven out of ten cities have codes of ethics, and a third of all cities regularly review their employees' ethical conduct.[9]

PRACTICING ETHICAL PUBLIC ADMINISTRATION

Practicing public ethics has its own unique challenges.

The Ethical Environment of the Public Administrator

It is unarguably heartening to learn that 56 percent of federal employees think that "my organization's leaders maintain high standards of honesty and integrity," and 62 percent feel that they can "disclose a suspected violation of law, rule or regulation without fear of reprisal"; both percentages are rising over time.[10] It is even more encouraging to learn that 100 percent of high-level municipal officials report that their managers "demonstrate" ethical conduct.[11]

Despite these gratifying findings, however, public administrators toil on slippery ethical slopes. For nearly two decades, virtually all public administrators in federal, state, and local governments have agreed that they "encounter ethical dilemmas at work."[12]

Fourteen percent of civil servants at all governmental levels feel that they are pressured to compromise ethical standards in the course of their jobs (markedly more public administrators say this than either nonprofit employees, at 11 percent,[13] and businesspeople, at 10 percent[14]), and this percentage is an increase of two-fifths from four years earlier.[15]

Committing to a Higher Standard

Public administrators are committed to ethics. More than three-quarters of federal, state, and local managers believe that "ethical concerns can be empowering in organizations" (only 7 percent disagree), up from two-thirds a decade earlier.[16] City managers display a solid knowledge of their profession's code of ethics,[17] and, happily, the number of city managers with higher ethics ("about one-third," who also possess higher levels of education and professionalism) is twice that of managers who have lower levels (17 percent).[18]

A Higher Ethical Standard Public administrators see themselves as adhering to a higher ethical standard than their corporate compatriots, and nearly nine out of every ten consistently spurn the notion that "government morality in America is lower than business morality."[19] Public administrators appear to hold themselves to a higher ethical standard than do even the taxpayers who pay their salaries, and register even greater umbrage over governmental scandals than does the general public.[20]

Walking the Ethical Walk More than half of all public employees, almost exactly the same proportion as in the nonprofit and private sectors, state that they have observed "misconduct," ranging from "Internet abuse" to theft, in their workplaces during the previous year. What is important in this context is that government workers are much more likely to report such misconduct to appropriate authorities than are their nonprofit and business counterparts, and their willingness to do so is steadily growing. Seventy percent, up from 60 percent seven years earlier, of public employees alert a responsible party of misconduct, compared with 62 percent of independent-sector workers and just 42 percent of private-sector employees.[21]

Public administrators are not only talking the ethical talk, but also are walking the ethical walk.

DO MORALS MATTER?

Do ethics matter? Are governments and public administrators more effective because they are ethical?

Ethics and the Effective Government

Among governments, a low "ethical climate" associates with greater damage and injury to citizens and businesses, and more complaints from the public. By contrast, a high ethical climate (i.e., managers who set a good ethical example, and communicate and enforce high ethical standards) correlates with fewer employees who take sick leave and take less of it, and workers who are more likely to think that their departments provide customers with better value for their money and who plan to keep working in those departments.[22]

Top public executives who have a deep sense of ethics administer governments that have fewer lawsuits, better bond ratings, and are more likely to implement state-of-the-art productivity improvements than those governments that are managed by administrators whose ethical senses are less ingrained and who, as a result, "pursue innovation but disregard accountability and responsiveness."[23]

Ethics and the Effective Public Administrator

As these studies suggest, solid ethics and successful careers waltz gracefully together. An experiment in "getting one's way in policy debates" among public administrators found that, while some shrewd tactics help, the most critical and effective tactic is that of honestly presenting one's argument.[24] Graduates of the top public administration

programs in the United States rank "maintaining ethical standards" as the single most important "skill," by far, for achieving success, regardless of where they are employed—governments, businesses, or nonprofit organizations.[25]

And ethics are indeed a skill. An empirical analysis of public administrators concludes that "the concepts of virtue and competence are, in practice, very similar.... because virtue is an integral feature of managerial competencies."[26]

In short, high ethics associate with better governance and more successful public careers.

BUREAUCRACY'S BANE: DETERMINING THE PUBLIC INTEREST

Central to a bureaucratic ethic is this singular question: How do public administrators determine what is in "the public interest"? Regrettably, "little of the literature of public administration reflects on the nature of the public interest."[27]

In the legislature, the public interest is defined by majority vote. In the courts, *stare decisis*, or judicial precedent, provides an evolutionary system of legal principles through which the public interest is fulfilled. When we approach government's executive branch, however, we find no similarly clear-cut method of determining the public's interest, though public administrationists have tried to both rationalize that such a method is unnecessary and to develop such a method.

Bureaucratic Accountability

The academic effort to skirt the question of how public administrators should make decisions that are in the public interest is called *bureaucratic accountability*, or the study of how various restraints safely hem and channel bureaucrats into making decisions that are democratic, ethical, legal, and fair. Hence, not to worry; nothing more is needed.

Internal Constraints and External Controls Just what these restraints are depends on the public-administration scholar. Some argue that internal constraints, whether founded on their professional socialization[28] or stemming from their own "moral foundations,"[29] inhibit public administrators from committing unethical acts. Others contend that external controls—laws,[30] courts,[31] publicity,[32] legislative surveillance,[33] bureaucratic decentralization,[34] and citizen participation in bureaucratic decision making[35]—assure ethical behavior. Still others maintain that a combination of internal and external variables reinforce one another to the benefit of the public interest.[36]

What Do Public Administrators Use? How reflective this literature is of the real bureaucratic world is, at best, unclear. Some research finds that internal inhibitors are salient; those agencies in which the values of efficiency, effectiveness, quality, excellence, and teamwork are dominant associate with high ethical expectations and standards.[37] Another investigation concludes the opposite, finding that public administrators rely heavily on an external control, the law itself, as their principal guide in dealing with ethical issues; internal constraints—personal belief systems and professional values—run a distant second.[38]

A Missed Point The bureaucratic-accountability writers have usefully listed attitudes and mechanisms that may prevent, correct, or punish public administrators for making decisions that are not in the public interest. But they have not recommended any systematic and proactive practice (and certainly none with the elegant simplicity and practical utility of majority vote and judicial precedent) that bureaucrats actually could use to make such decisions. Moreover, as the scant empirical evidence on the topic suggests, there *is* no systematic practice.

Organizational Humanism

In contrast to the students of bureaucratic accountability, another band of public administrationists does posit a systemic ethical framework for bureaucratic decision making. These are the organizational humanists.

The Ultimate Bureaucratic Value *Organizational humanism* is a philosophy of public ethics that is founded on the precept that personal dignity is "the

ultimate value," and it defines in operational terms precisely what the public interest is. *The* public interest is to always treat each person humanely.[39]

Organizational humanism, in its more candid mode, "forwards the proposition that the ends of man are the ends of man.... it is not willing to compromise its human values on any grounds.... [and] calls for the ultimate capitulation of operational mechanics and political strategies to a concept of the public interest based on man as the most important concern of bureaucratic power."[40]

The organizational humanists are attractive because they make no bones about what they think is important. Its problem lies in its application. Devils always lurk in the details.

Applying Organizational Humanism: A Non-Starter Consider, for example, how organizational humanism would treat affirmative action. There are two, value-based positions in this controversy.

One is that government should make special efforts, including the reduction of entrance and promotion standards, to hire and advance members of those segments of society that have endured unfair discrimination through no fault of their own.

The other position is that no "lowering of standards" should be considered, regardless of the applicant's past tribulations, because government owes the best governance possible to *all* the governed, deprived groups included.

Would organizational humanism be for or against affirmative action? Who knows?

Organizational humanism states only that "the ultimate value" in bureaucratic decision making is "the ends of man." Is humanity best served by hiring or promoting a deprived-group member who does not execute his or her duties satisfactorily, or is it best served by not hiring or by holding back that same person? This dilemma can be rendered even more exquisite when the incompetent, or even just less competent, deprived-group member applies to an agency charged with ending discrimination against deprived groups.

It is reasonably apparent that organizational humanism does not offer much of a guide to the public administrator in formulating a decision that is in the public interest.

CAN NORMATIVE THEORY HELP? FOUR PHILOSOPHIES OF THE PUBLIC INTEREST

So the essential problem still remains: The public administrator needs a simple and operational articulation of the public interest that permits him or her to make a decision, based on rational thinking, that is in the public interest.

Should we move beyond the confines of the scholarly community of public administration in addressing this issue? Can the world's great philosophers help?

There are four philosophies of the public interest that are relevant to bureaucratic decision making.

Intuitionism: Morally Muddling Through

One such philosophy is intuitionism, advocated by Aristotle, among others. *Intuitionism* expounds a plurality of first principles, all of them, no doubt, admirable. As a practical matter, however, these principles can conflict with one another when applied to specific situations, and intuitionism offers no particular method (other than one's intuition), much less a rational and systemic one, for choosing which principle should take precedence.

Intuitionism amounts to morally muddling through.

Would intuitionism help us in resolving our dilemma of affirmative action? As with organizational humanism, who knows?

Perfectionism: Promoting Perfect People

Another germane philosophy is perfectionism, which, in contrast to intuitionism, has no problem of ambiguity. *Perfectionism* contends that the sole principle in determining the public interest should be the promotion of excellence in art, science, and culture. Any misfortune for society's less fortunate, and less talented, segments that results is morally justified because the entire society is lifted that much nearer to perfection.

Friedrich Nietzsche is exemplary of a perfectionist perspective. As Nietzsche put it so pithily, the deepest meaning that can be given to the human experience is "your living for the rarest and most valuable specimens,"[41] and Nietzsche evidently included himself among those specimens.

Unsurprisingly, perfectionism's opinion of affirmative action is clear: To hell with it.

Utilitarianism: The Most Benefits for the Most People

A third ethical framework for the determination of the public interest is utilitarianism, represented by John Stuart Mill, among others.

Utilitarianism differs from intuitionism in that it is systematic in logic, and from perfectionism in that it is democratic in values. *Utilitarianism* holds that, if a public policy makes most people better off, even if some people are left worse off, then the public interest is served.

An example of a utilitarian policy would be one that raised everyone's taxes and sent the new revenues that they generated to physicians. Such a policy would make everyone healthier (i.e., better off) by encouraging more people to enter the medical profession. Even though society's least well-off taxpayers would lose money under this arrangement, the policy nonetheless would be ethical and in the public interest because everyone's net balance of health would be enhanced, including that of the least well off.

Utilitarians would reject affirmative action as a policy reflective of the public interest because it does not, in theory, make everyone better off. Under utilitarianism's economic criteria, affirmative action makes only certain groups better off.

Fairness: A Theory of Justice

Utilitarianism has much going for it, but there remains the gnawing issue of what to do about the bottom of society, a stratum that utilitarian policies slap in the chops.

In 1945, Karl Popper suggested that "Instead of the greatest happiness for the greatest number [as the utilitarians advocate], one should demand, more modestly, the least amount of avoidable suffering for all; and further, that unavoidable suffering ... should be distributed as equally as possible."[42]

A generation later, John Rawls extended Popper's ideas, contending that the public interest can be discerned in most situations by applying two "principles of justice": (1) that "each person is to have an equal right to the most extensive basic liberty compatible with a similar liberty for others," and (2) that "social and economic inequalities are to be arranged so that they are both (a) reasonably expected to be to everyone's advantage, and (b) attached to positions and offices open to all."[43] Should these principles come into conflict, the second is expected to yield to the first; thus, just as in organizational humanism, the dignity of the individual person is of paramount importance.

Rawls's theory of justice goes further, however. His principles necessarily lead to the conclusion that inequalities of wealth, authority, and social opportunity "are just only if they result in compensating benefits for everyone, and in particular for the least advantaged members of society. These principles rule out justifying institutions on the grounds that the hardships of some are offset by a greater good in the aggregate. It may be expedient but it is not just that some should have less in order that others may prosper."[44]

In short, as Rawls observes, his principles in essence are a rigorous statement of the traditional Anglo-Saxon concept of fairness.

Applying Fairness: A Real Starter How would Rawls's and Popper's theories deal with affirmative action? They would, by the inevitability of their logic, argue for it on these grounds:

- *Not* hiring and promoting society's least well off would be further depriving society's most deprived groups.
- Hiring and promoting them would facilitate the full realization of their "basic liberty" (or personal dignity) without encroaching on the basic liberty of others.
- Hiring and promoting them helps assure that all positions and offices are open to all.
- Hiring and promoting them helps assure that privileges innate to such offices continue to work toward the advantage of all in a reasonably equal way, because the privileges and positions are being extended to the less well off in society.

The Unique Utility of Fairness as the Public Interest When applied with the rigor brought by Rawls and Popper, fairness offers the public administrator a workable, rational way for determining the public interest. So, for that matter, do perfectionism and utilitarianism (but not organizational humanism and intuitionism, which have severe problems of workability or logic). We think that perfectionism and utilitarianism are not appropriate for American public administrators, however, because the former's values are incompatible with the dominant values of American society, and the latter's logic permits the least advantaged people in society to be disadvantaged further.

Does Philosophy Matter?

We have reviewed four philosophies of the public interest. So what? Does the ivory tower matter in the corridors of power?

We remind those who might sneer, No, in answering this question that to be both cynical and unworldly is a particularly unattractive combination. Philosophy does, in fact, affect bureaucratic decision making and public policy, and it does so in deep and meaningful ways.

Aristotle's intuitionism pervades the public sector. Its popularity, however, is not due to its intellectual force. Rather, intuitionism is singularly easy to choose as a theory of the public interest, in part because most public administrators are unaware that they are choosing it. Most public administrators, like most of us, make decisions on the basis of what seems to be the most nearly right at the time. This, in essence, is what intuitionism is all about.

Nietzsche's perfectionism has been consciously selected by the National Science Foundation as its operating philosophy of the public interest. The Foundation's mission of financing "pure" scientific research—that science should be funded for the sake of science—is a clear expression of the perfectionist principle.

Utilitarianism is the official, if unacknowledged, premise on which policy choices are made by the U.S. Army Corps of Engineers, and likely by many other agencies, too. The Corps has adopted "benefit/cost analysis" as its method of deciding which engineering projects are in the best interests of the nation, and benefits and costs are cast in terms of dollars saved or lost. Hence, proposed projects, such as flood control, that protect trailer parks and poor people, rather than McMansions and rich people, would not make the cut because manors are worth more than mobile homes. To protect cheaper homes at the expense of costlier ones would violate benefit/cost precepts—and utilitarian precepts as well.[45]

Rawls's and Popper's theory of justice is widely implemented; it furnishes the philosophic foundation for the vast majority of American governments that levy a progressive tax on personal income, and no government imposes a regressive income tax, whether personal or corporate. Mainstream personal income tax codes are purposely designed to assure that the least well off are not made less well off, a principle that is central to Rawls's and Popper's theory.

Even in the recesses of governmental bureaucracies, philosophy flourishes.

The Passion of Public Administration

Although, as we observed at the beginning of this book, constraint is the dominating characteristic in the culture immersing America's public administrators, they nonetheless make large—sometimes very large—decisions. Consider the case, and the ethics, of New York's Robert Moses, who transitioned from dreamy idealist to one of the preeminent power brokers of the twentieth century.

Robert Moses is sometimes called "America's greatest builder," and the term is not hyperbolic. He confided to friends his grand plans to transmogrify New York as early as 1914, while still in his twenties, and began his career as a "Goo-Goo," that dismissive term used by Tammany Hall politicians to describe "good government" reformers.

Throughout his entire career (1924–1968), Moses never held an elected office. Instead, he secured appointments to head numerous public authorities, basking in such modestly-titled positions as "Coordinator," or as an authority's board member—but often its *only* member. At his peak, Moses headed fourteen state and city authorities at once. Moses added to the city 416 miles of parkways; 15,000 acres through his shoreline projects; and over a thousand apartment buildings housing more people than lived in Minneapolis.

In the state, Moses built all but one of its major expressways; seven of the nine bridges linking Manhattan with the mainland; a number of huge power

dams; and parks. By the time Moses had finished, New York owned 45 percent of all the nation's acreage devoted to state parks.

Nationally, Moses was instrumental in drafting the life-changing Interstate Highway Act and the controversial Urban Renewal program. His interest in Urban Renewal was understandable: Moses, who controlled all such projects in New York, spent more than twice the amount of federal Urban Renewal dollars than did all other cities *combined*.

As the urban scholar, Lewis Mumford, one of Moses's most tenacious foes, stated, "In the twentieth century, the influence of Robert Moses on the cities of America was greater than that of any other person" (Caro, *The Power Broker*, p. 12).

Was Moses good or bad for New York—and the nation?

To his everlasting credit, Moses rammed through titanic projects that employed thousands, moved hundreds of thousands, and created greenswards enjoyed by millions. And "rammed" is the apt verb. Moses manifested a "savage energy" that would erupt into a "fury" when his plans were frustrated. He "would lunge out of his chair and begin, as one aide put it, 'waving his arms, just wild,' pick up the old-fashioned inkwell on his desk and hurl it at aides so that it shattered against a wall; how he would

(continued)

(*continued*)

pound his clenched fists into the walls hard enough to scrape the skin off them, in a rage beyond the perception of pain" (Caro, "The City Shaper," pp. 48–49).

There was, however, a dark side to his genius. To build, Moses destroyed. His projects, which, with few exceptions, were built for the middle class and the wealthy, required razing the homes of a half-million people, most of them poor. Asked if he had ever considered altering his projects to save their homes, Moses retorted, "'Nah' ... I can still hear the scorn in his voice as he said it ... scorn for me who had thought it necessary to ask about them" (Caro, "The City Shaper," p. 52).

Moses routinely employed deception, slander, libel, blackmail, and thinly-veiled bribery to achieve his goals, tactics that resulted in "some of the greatest scandals of twentieth century New York, scandals almost incredible ... for the colossal scale of their corruption." Moses boasted (jokingly, one hopes) that "nothing I have ever done has been tinged with legality" (Caro, "The City Shaper," p. 42). Though personally "money honest" (to employ a term for a complex reality that only New Yorkers could express so succinctly), his "Moses men," his closest allies and administrators, became multimillionaires.

Being money honest, however, did not mean that this particular bureaucrat subsisted in a low-profile life of genteel modesty. Indeed, Moses's positions came with a multitude of expensive and enviable perks, including a yacht, skippered by three captains, for his personal use, and four dining rooms scattered around the city, each with its own full-time staff, who served only Moses and his guests. The *secretaries* who worked in his authorities were not only paid more than New York City's commissioners, but also were given bigger cars, driven by chauffeurs who were on call twenty-four/seven.

Through some adroit, if ethically questionable, maneuvering by New York's governor, Moses lost all his power in 1968. But Moses never gave up. As a labor leader put it, "They want him to get tired and to go away and get lost. But I say, 'Forget it!' This guy don't blow away" (Caro, "The City Shaper," p. 53).

Robert Moses died in 1981. He was ninety-two, still a fighter. ■

Sources: Robert A. Cairo, *The Power Broker: Robert Moses and the Fall of New York* (New York: Knopf, 1974) and Robert A. Cairo, "The City Shaper," *The New Yorker* (January 5, 1998), pp. 42–53.

WHAT IS TO BE DONE? IMPLEMENTING ETHICAL ADMINISTRATION

In 1902, the Russian Communist V. I. Lenin demanded, "What is to be done?" about the plight of the proletariat, and promptly answered his own question with this word: *Revolution!*

Something akin to a revolution may be needed to cope with government's most egregious and destructive form of unethical behavior, corruption, a suppurating public pustule that inspired the founding of public administration itself. Perhaps it is time to return to our roots.

Only in Washington

An irony in the endless American effort to curtail corruption is that its locus seems to have shifted over the course of the twentieth century from state and local governments to the federal one. The nearly universal professionalizing of state civil services and the dominance of the council-manager plan in local governments clearly correlate with declining corruption in these jurisdictions. Washington, however, appears to be awash in conflicts of interest and special-interest influence.

A glaringly shameful example is the moral corrosion of federal governance caused by Washington's revolving door (reviewed in Chapter 11), a door that is virtually nonexistent in state and local governments.

Fewer than 15 percent of state agency heads,[46] or just a fourth of the comparable percentage for their closest federal counterparts,[47] are hired directly from corporations. Nor do they quickly skedaddle back to the private sector. State agency directors have a median tenure of six years and rising in their present positions,[48] or twice the average tenure of federal agency heads who are careerists,[49] and four times longer than that of federal political appointees.[50]

In local governments, even these faint connections are utterly absent. *All* city and county chief administrative officers are hired either from within their own government (21 percent) or from another local government (79 percent),[51] and they have spent an average of nearly seven years in their current positions.[52]

If Congress is serious about cleaning up Washington's bureaucracy—and itself—then it must address the federal revolving door in terms far stiffer than it has. We hear, with increasing frequency, disturbing anecdotes about administrators who have joined the federal service solely to boost their prospects for more lucrative careers as lobbyists.

Trust, Esteem, and Pay

We are not suggesting that all state and local governments are angelic; far too many have yet to ascend to purgatory. But the grassroots governments do seem to have cultivated, more successfully than their federal cousin, two qualities that are vital to ethical—and effective—governing. They are public trust in government, and popular esteem for those who govern.

We discussed in Chapter 1 how both factors correlate with superior governing. Regrettably, deepening the public's trust is a tough challenge in a culture that, perhaps more than any other, constrains its governments' role in society.

Nevertheless, it is a challenge that can be met, and a straightforward way of doing so, at least to some extent, would be to pay public administrators more competitively, as higher salaries associate not only with higher social status, but also with better governing.

State and local governments seem to understand these correlations better than Washington. As we noted in Chapter 9, the salaries of state and local administrators often surpass those of their federal counterparts, and, as we explained in Chapter 12, Americans also hold their state and local governments in higher esteem than the federal one.

Research shows that greater pay reduces corruptive temptations, particularly among those public administrators who are at the forefront of protecting the public interest from the predations of private interests.[53] This problem is especially acute in the federal government, where regulation and privatization—two huge and sprawling areas that are uniquely susceptible to graft—expanded radically during the twentieth century and into this one. Regulators, contract officers, and other public administrators whose positions render them vulnerable to being compromised, should have their pay raised to levels that are more competitive with their corporate counterparts. The costs would be relatively trivial (their salaries need not be in lockstep with the private sector), and the benefits would be unambiguously immense.

The city-state of Singapore exemplifies the public benefits brought by competitive public salaries. Its government's ministers (i.e., cabinet-level executives) are paid more than $1 million, with comparably competitive salaries down the line. With just 5 million people, Singapore has impressively vast financial reserves of about $250 billion[54] (a starkly solid sign of good governance), and boasts "one of the world's least corrupt and most efficient bureaucracies."[55]

The challenge of raising public pay equals that of raising the public's trust of government and its respect for those who work in it: Only 13 percent of the citizenry think that the salaries of public administrators should be raised "to encourage the best people to go into government."[56] Yet, for the sake of that very citizenry, both challenges must be faced.

BIG BUREAUCRACY, BIG DECISIONS

It is fitting to close this book with a thought about the ultimate duty of the public administrator. That duty is to make ethical decisions. Public administrators' decisions can be immensely far-reaching, or affect just one person. But each of them changes people, for good or ill.

We request that, if you enter the field, you remember to ask yourself how people will be helped or hurt by your decisions. Few questions are more important in any context, but in the context of the public life of your nation, none is more important.

NOTES

1. James S. Bowman, Evan M. Berman, and Jonathan P. West, "The Profession of Public Administration: An Ethics Edge in Introductory Textbooks?" *Public Administration Review* 61 (March/April 2001), pp. 194–205.

2. Ethics Resource Center, *National Nonprofit Ethics Survey: An Inside View of Nonprofit Sector Ethics* (Arlington, VA: Author, 2008), pp. 2, 22. Figures are for 2007.

3. Robert W. Smith, "Corporate Ethics Officers and Government Ethics Administrators: Comparing Apples with Oranges or a Lesson to Be Learned?" *Administration & Society* 34 (January 2003), pp. 632–652. The quotation is on p. 639. Figure is for 1998.

4. National Commission on the Public Service, *Urgent Business for America: Revitalizing the Federal Government for the 21st Century* (Washington, DC: U.S. Government Printing Office, 2003), pp. 21–22.

5. Beth A. Rosenson, *Shadowlands of Conduct: Ethics and State Politics* (Washington, DC: Georgetown University Press, 2005), pp. 5, 10–11. Data are for 1996.

6. Fran Burke and George C. S. Benson, "State Ethics Codes, Commissions, and Conflicts," *State Government Review* 10 (May 1989), pp. 195–198.

7. Robert W. Smith, "Enforcement or Ethical Capacity: Considering the Role of State Ethics Commissions at the Millennium," *Public Administration Review* 63 (May/June 2003), pp. 283–295. The quotations are on pp. 283 and 292. This is a study of sixty "ethics officials and stakeholders" in Connecticut, Florida, and New York.

8. U.S. Advisory Commission on Intergovernmental Relations, *State Laws Governing Local Government Structure and Administration*, M-186 (Washington, DC: U.S. Government Printing Office, 1993), p. 33. Figure is for 1990. In 1978, seventeen states imposed ethics codes.

9. Mary Ann Feldheim and Xiaohu Wang, "Ethics and Public Trust: Results from a National Survey," *Public Integrity* 6 (Winter 2003–2004), pp. 63–75. Figures are for 2000.

10. U.S. Office of Personnel Management, *Federal Employee Viewpoint Survey, 2010* (Washington, DC: U.S. Government Printing Office, 2009), p. 39.

11. Feldheim and Wang, "Ethics and Public Trust," p. 70. Figures are for 2000.

12. James S. Bowman and Claire Connolly Knox, "Ethics in Government: No Matter How Long and Dark the Night," *Public Administration Review* 68 (July/August 2008), pp. 627–639. The quotation is on p. 628. Ninety-seven percent said this in 1989, 1996, and 2006.

13. Ethics Resource Center, *National Nonprofit Ethics Survey*, p. 16. Figure is for 2007.

14. Ethics Resource Center, *National Business Ethics Survey: An Inside View of Private Sector Ethics* (Arlington, VA: Author, 2008), p. 16. Figure is for 2007.

15. Ethics Resource Center, *National Government Ethics Survey: An Inside View of Public Sector Ethics* (Arlington, VA: Author, 2008), p. 6. Figure is for 2007. In 2003, 10 percent of government workers said this.

16. Bowman and Knox, "Ethics in Government," p. 628. Figures are for 2006 and 1996.

17. Greg Streib and Mark Rivera, "Assessing the Ethical Knowledge of City Managers," *Public Integrity* 12 (Winter 2009/2010), pp. 9–23.

18. Evan M. Berman and Jonathan P. West, "Responsible Risk-Taking," *Public Administration Review* 58 (July/August 1998), pp. 346–352.

19. Bowman and Knox, "Ethics in Government," p. 629. From 85 to 88 percent said this in 1989, 1996, and 2006.

20. James S. Bowman, "Ethics in Government: A National Survey of Public Administrators," *Public Administration Review* 50 (May/June 1990), pp. 345–353.

21. Ethics Resource Center, *National Nonprofit Ethics Survey*, pp. 3–4; *National Government Ethics Survey*, pp. 7, 19, 20, 25, 31, 32; and *National Business Ethics Survey*, p. 3. Figures are for 2007.

22. Colleen G. Waring and C'Anne Daugherty, "Auditing Ethics—Make Them an Offer They Can't Refuse," *Journal of Government Financial Management* 53 (Spring 2004), pp. 34–40.

23. Berman and West, "Responsible Risk-Taking," p. 349.

24. Jason L. Jenson, "Getting One's Way in Policy Debates: Influence Tactics Used in Group Decision-Making Settings," *Public Administration Review* 67 (March/April 2007), pp. 216–227.

25. Paul C. Light, *The New Public Service* (Washington, DC: Brookings, 1999), p. 110

26. Michael Macaulay and Alan Lawton, "From Virtue to Competence: Changing the Principles of Public Service," *Public Administration Review* 66 (September/October 2006), pp. 702–710. The quotations are on pp. 701, 709.

27. Eugene D. Dvorin and Robert H. Simmons, *From Amoral to Humane Bureaucracy* (San Francisco, CA: Canfield Press, 1972), p. 61.

28. Carl J. Friedrich and Taylor Cole, *Responsible Bureaucracy* (Cambridge, MA: Harvard University Press, 1949).

29. Kathryn Denhardt, "Unearthing the Moral Foundations of Public Administration: Honor, Benevolence, and Justice," *Ethical Frontiers in Public Management*, pp. 256–283.

30. John A. Rohr, *Ethics for Bureaucrats: An Essay on Law and Values*, 2nd ed. (New York: Marcel Dekker, 1989).

31. K. C. Davis, *Administrative Law* (St. Paul, MN: West Publishing, 1951).

32. Gordon Tullock, *The Politics of Bureaucracy* (Washington, DC: Public Affairs Press, 1965).

33. Charles S. Hyneman, *Bureaucracy* (New York: Harper & Row, 1950).

34. Dwight Waldo, "Development of a Theory of Democratic Administration," *American Political Science Review* 46 (March 1952), pp. 81–103.

35. Ludwig Von Mises, *Bureaucracy* (New Haven, CT: Yale University Press, 1944).

36. Terry L. Cooper, *The Responsible Administrator* (San Francisco, CA: Jossey-Bass, 1990).

37. Donald C. Menzel, "The Ethical Environment of Local Government Managers," *American Review of Public Administration* 25 (September 1995), pp. 247–261.

38. Harold F. Gortner, *Ethics for Public Managers* (New York: Praeger, 1991).

39. Dvorin and Simmons, *From Amoral to Humane Bureaucracy*, p. 61.

40. Ibid., pp. 60–61. The authors are explaining what they call "radical humanism," which appears to be a more plainly-spoken version of organizational humanism.

41. Friedrich Nietzsche, as quoted in J. R. Hollingsdale, *Nietzsche: The Man and His Philosophy* (Baton Rouge, LA: Louisiana State University Press, 1965), p. 127.

42. Karl Popper, *The Open Society and Its Enemies: Vol. I, The Spell of Plato*, 5th ed. (Princeton, NJ: Princeton University Press, 1966), p. 285. The set first was published in 1945.

43. John Rawls, *A Theory of Justice* (Cambridge, MA: Belknap Press of Harvard University Press, 1971), p. 60.

44. Ibid., pp. 14–15.

45. Laura Mumford, "Policy Analysis and the U.S. Army Corps of Engineers." Paper submitted to a graduate course in public administration, December 11, 1984, School of Public Affairs, College of Public Programs, Arizona State University, Tempe, Arizona, Nicholas Henry, instructor.

46. Jeffrey L. Brudney, Cynthia J. Bowling, and Deil S. Wright, *Continuity and Change in Public Administration Across the 50 States: Linking Practice, Theory, and Research through the American State Administrators Project, 1964–2008* (Auburn, AL: Center for Governmental Services, Auburn University, 2010), pp. 13–14. This is an analysis of some 1,000 state agency directors. Private-sector figure is for 1994–2008; "fewer than 15 percent" is for the 2000s.

47. As derived from data in U.S. Merit Systems Protection Board, *In Search of Highly Skilled Workers: A Study on the Hiring of Upper Level Employees from Outside the Federal Government* (Washington, DC: U.S. Government Printing Office, 2008), p. 13. Chapter 11 has details.

48. Brudney, Bowling, and Wright, *Continuity and Change in Public Administration Across the 50 States*, p. 13.

49. David E. Lewis, *Political Appointments, Bureau Chiefs, and Federal Management Performance* (Princeton, NJ: Princeton University, Woodrow Wilson School of Public and International Affairs, 2005), p. 35. Chapter 9 has details.

50. Patricia W. Ingraham, "Building Bridges or Burning Them? The President, The Appointees, and The Bureaucracy," *Public Administration Review* 47 (September/October 1987), pp. 425–435. Chapter 9 has details.

51. Victor S. DeSantis and Charldean Newell, "Local Government Managers' Career Paths," *Municipal Year Book, 1996* (Washington, DC: International City/County Management Association, 1996), pp. 3–10. The data are on p. 6.

52. Jerri Killian and Enamul Choudhury, "Continuity and Change in the Role of City Managers," *Municipal Year Book, 2010* (Washington, DC: International City/County Management Association, 2010), pp. 10–18. Figure, 6.8 years (p. 11), is for 2010.

53. Gary S. Becker and George J. Stigler, "Law Enforcement, Malfeasance, and Compensation of Enforcers," *Journal of Legal Studies* 3 (January 1974), pp. 1–18.

54. Monetary Authority of Singapore, *Official Foreign Reserves*, http://www.mas.gov.sg/data_room/reserves_statistics/Official_Foreign_Reserves.html. Figure is for 2011.

55. James Surowiecki, "The Regulation Crisis," *The New Yorker* (June 14 & 21, 2010), p. 56.

56. Kevin Merida, "Americans Want a Direct Say in Political Decision-Making, Pollsters Find," *Washington Post* (April 17, 1994).

Becoming a Public or Nonprofit Administrator

Now that you have read about public and nonprofit administration, why not consider working in one or the other, too?

HOW MANY JOBS? HOW MUCH PAY?

Jobs in government and the independent sector are plentiful, exciting, and fulfilling.

Employment in the Public Sector

Government positions are many and manifold. *The Public Administration Career Directory* (Library of Congress Call Number JK716.P1815) is a good introduction to the large array of public professions.[1]

There are nearly twenty-two and a half million civilian public employees, or about one for every six workers. Most, 64 percent, are in local government; state government accounts for 23 percent of public employment, and the federal government for 12 percent.[2]

Positions The 2000s were not a decade of significant growth in public employment.

From 2000 to 2008, federal employees working under the General Schedule grew by a modest half of one percent per year, on average, and, between 2008 and 2009, these employees actually declined by

14 percent.[3] The good news for prospective federal managers in these depressing trends is that 44 percent of all federal new hires were hired into professional and administrative positions.[4]

State and local employment each increased by about 1 percent per year.[5]

Pay Governmental pay during the 2000s grew faster than hiring.

From 2000 to 2008, federal pay in the General Schedule increased by more than 4 percent annually, on average, but, between 2008 and 2009, salaries declined by nearly 14 percent.[6] In late 2010, President Barack Obama announced a two-year freeze of federal civilian salaries.

During the 2000s, state wages and salaries grew by slightly more than 4 percent a year, and local pay increased by close to 5 percent annually, on average.[7] Public authorities and special districts appear to offer consistently higher salaries, including entry-level salaries, for comparable positions than those offered by general purpose governments, whether federal, state, or local.[8]

Federal Public Administration

More than 2.1 million people[9] work in over 800 different occupations[10] in the federal civilian workforce. Nearly six out of ten of these employees have administrative or policy responsibilities.[11]

The feds are hiring about 80,000 new, entry-level employees annually.[12] Between 2010 and 2015, more than one-third of all federal civilian workers, or some 600,000 employees, will be eligible to retire,[13] and Washington predicts that 57 percent of them will do so; supervisors and managers are "far more likely to retire" than are other employees.[14]

Although federal salaries are locality based, Grade 7, which most new recruits enter, starts at over $40,000, on average. The top grades, Grade 13 through 15, range from about $90,000 to over $155,000. Salaries for the 8,000 Senior Executive Service positions range from $120,000 to $180,000.[15]

For the absolutely latest information on federal salaries, check the Office of Personnel Management's website at http://www.opm.gov/oca/.

State Public Administration

There are nearly 5.3 million state employees, almost half of whom work in education.[16] Prospects for positions are good, as 27 percent of state employees are eligible to retire.[17]

About $70,000 to more than $110,000 seems to be the salary level for appointed state administrators (excluding higher education, which pays considerably more). Even in the least populated states, it is rare to find the top salaries at less than $70,000. Southern states tend to pay their public administrators the least, followed by Eastern states; Western states generally pay the most. Finance, social services, environmental protection, and health are among the highest paying fields, and planning, purchasing, solid waste management, tourism, and transportation are among the lowest.[18]

The Book of the States (Library of Congress Call Number JK2403.B6), published annually, lists the average salaries for fifty-one state government positions by state and region.

Local Public Administration

Local governments employ more than 14.4 million people, nearly three-fifths of whom work in education.[19]

City and town managers command an average salary of $101,000, ranging from $68,000 in the smallest towns, those with fewer than 2,500 people, to $231,000 in cities with populations of at least one million. The average pay of directors of personnel, finance, and information services range, respectively, from the low-to-mid $80,000s, and heads of purchasing are paid in the upper $60,000s. Western governments pay their public administrators the most; Northeastern cities and towns pay the least—often a third less than Western cities.[20]

County salaries generally are somewhat higher than are municipal pay rates for comparable positions. County managers earn an average salary of $121,000. The average pay of directors of personnel, information services, and finance, range, respectively, from the high $70,000s to the high $80,000s, and heads of purchasing earn in the mid-$70,000s. Western counties pay the most, and North Central counties the least.[21]

The Municipal Year Book (Library of Congress Call Number JS342.A2152), published annually, publishes average salaries for twenty-odd (the number varies with each edition) city and county positions by region, form of government, city type, and population.

Nonprofit Administration

The 1.3 million or so public-serving nonprofit organizations in the United States employ an estimated 9.5 million people. Member-serving nonprofit organizations amount to another 500,000 associations and 1.4 million employees.[22]

The median salary for a chief executive officer in a nonprofit, public-benefitting organization is nearly $135,000.[23] Chief executive officers' salaries generally are highest in foundations and nonprofit organizations with a medical mission, ranging from $500,000 to more that $4 million in the better endowed ones. Youth and religious organizations also pay well.[24] Program officers in these organizations have a median salary of almost $77,000.[25]

Fundraisers are crucial in nonprofit organizations. Those chief development officers who earn more than their colleagues are: older (up to a point: "diminishing returns" kick in as one ages); have some graduate education (however, a bachelor's degree gives the officer no salary advantage over those who have only a high school diploma, or even no diploma); more fundraising experience; and longer tenure in office (although both experience and tenure have only "a marginally significant and small effect on the bonuses" of these officers). Race and professional certifications have essentially no impact on salary. The most important variable in assuring that a chief development officer has a larger salary is that the officer be male.[26]

PREPARING FOR A POSITION: EDUCATION, RÉSUMÉS, NETWORKING, AND INTERNING

There are many ways to prepare for a management position in the public and independent sectors.

Gaining a Gainful Education: The Master of Public Administration Degree

The single best educational qualification for a management position in the public and nonprofit sectors is the Master of Public Administration (M.P.A.) degree.

The New Degree of Choice

Graduate degrees in public administration are held by 12 percent of state agency heads (only business administration ranks higher),[27] and by a plurality—27 percent and rising—of state budget officers.[28] More than half of all city managers,[29] and 8 percent of "senior managers" in large special districts, have an M.P.A.[30]

The M.P.A. also is the primary degree for those entering the independent sector. Nearly 200 universities offer masters degrees or concentrations in nonprofit management. The M.P.A. accounts for half of all these programs, and, when we include M.P.A.-related degrees, such as those in public policy, the proportion shoots to 64 percent. None of the percentages for the remaining programs, such as those in social work or stand-alone degrees, surmount single digits.[31]

The MPA and Career Advancement

People with a master's degree have median incomes that are 17 percent higher than those with just a bachelor's degree,[32] and this gap widens among public administrators: About ten years ago, more

than half of those with the M.P.A. earned at least $50,000, compared to fewer than a fourth who had only a baccalaureate degree.[33]

Nearly three-quarters of government supervisors rate the performance of their M.P.A. holders to be superior to those with other sorts of advanced degrees. Unsurprisingly, four-fifths of these employees think that the M.P.A. has been more beneficial to them as professionals than any other kind of master's degree.[34] Among federal employees, the M.P.A. holders advance faster, rank higher, and earn more than do holders of any other graduate degree (with the sole exception of those with law degrees).[35]

Getting Started To learn more about the Master of Public Administration and related degrees, contact the National Association of Schools of Public Affairs and Administration at http://www.naspaa.org.

To learn what current students think of their M.P.A. experience, check Facebook's new site, at http://www.naspaa.org/facebook/facebook2.26.htm.

Financing an Education in Public or Nonprofit Administration

There are several ways to help finance your graduate education in the field.

Federal Financial Assistance Qualified graduate students can borrow more than $20,000 in federal Stafford Loans. To apply, go to www.fafsa.ed.gov, or contact your university's student financial aid office.

Three income tax credits—American Opportunity, Hope, and Lifetime Learning—shield certain education-related expenses from taxation. In addition, the income derived from most scholarships and grants is tax exempt. Federal policies also allow deductions for: tuition and fees (up to a point); the interest paid on student loans; the interest gained from selected U.S. Savings Bonds when used for education; some expenses for work-related education, and more than $5,000 in employer-provided educational assistance.[36]

Take full advantage of these tax breaks. Nearly a fifth of taxpayers (or more than 400,000 of them) who are eligible for higher-education tax credits or tuition deductions do not claim them.[37] So claim them.

Campus Opportunities Increasingly, universities are offering scholarships in public and nonprofit administration, so check with your M.P.A. director, university foundation, and student financial aid office, where part-time employment opportunities also may be found.

Truman Scholars The richest of the national scholarships in pubic administration is the Truman Scholars (http://www.truman.gov). This highly competitive national scholarship program is geared exclusively to supporting the graduate studies of sixty to eighty college seniors planning to enter the public service. Stipends are up to $30,000 per year, and the application deadline is in early February.

Robertson Fellowships The Robertson Foundation for Government (info@rffg.org), founded in 2010, offers forty to fifty fellowships for applicants to selected graduate schools who are committed to federal careers in international relations and national security. Fellows are expected to be proficient in a second language.

American Society for Public Administration Many local chapters of the American Society for Public Administration (ASPA, http://www.aspanet.org) offer modest scholarships for M.P.A. students. ASPA's national headquarters maintains no guide to them. Your best bet is to join ASPA (dues are low for students), attend your chapter's meetings, and apply.

Labor Relations Each year, the National Public Employer Labor Relations Association Foundation offers from two to four Anthony C. Russo Scholarships, valued at $3,000 each and rising, for graduate students in public administration, but especially those with an interest in labor and employee relations. The deadline is usually September 30, and an application may be completed and submitted at http://www.npelra.org/about_foundation.asp.

Public Service The Public Employees Roundtable offers eight to ten Public Service Scholarships per year to graduate and undergraduate students. Applicants must have at least a 3.5 grade point average, and preference is given to those who have worked or volunteered for government. Applications may be completed and submitted at http://www.theroundtable.org.

Public Finance The Government Finance Officers Association offers five annual scholarships for undergraduate or graduate students interested in public finance, including one that is reserved for students of color. Awards range from $2,500 to $10,000. The website is http://www.gfoa.org/services/scholarships.shtml.

Public Works The regional and state chapters of the American Public Works Association (APWA) offer a spate of scholarships for undergraduate and graduate students in public administration with a public works emphasis. Check APWA's website at http://apwa.net, although Googling "APWA scholarships" works just as well, if not better.

Urban and Land Use Planning The American Planning Association (APA) offers a variety of scholarships in urban and regional planning. Several are targeted at students of color and women, and the deadline for all of them is April 30. In addition, state APA chapters in Arizona, California, Connecticut, Ohio, and Texas offer their own scholarships. Deadlines vary by chapter. Awards for national and state APA scholarships usually are around $2,000 per year. APA's website, at http://www.planning.org/institutions/scholarship.htm?project, provides full information on these and related scholarships.

The Lambda Alpha International Land Economics Foundation Scholarship (LAI@lai.org) is a renewable, $3,000 scholarship for a graduate student in the United States, Britain, or Canada in public administration, planning, and urban studies, among other fields.

The National Forum for Black Public Administrators (http://www.nfbpa.org/) offers a $3,000 Land-Use Planning Scholarship for an African-American graduate student in urban planning and related fields. The deadline is in February.

Students of Color In addition to its planning scholarship, the National Forum for Black Public Administrators offers at least half a dozen scholarships for African-American undergraduate or graduate students that range from $1,000 to $10,000, with most at $5,000. The deadline is in February.

The Congressional Hispanic Caucus Institute awards one-time scholarships ranging from $1,000 to $5,000 to Hispanic high school and college students "who have a history" of community service. The deadline is March 1. Applications are available at www.chicyouth.org.

The Hampton Roads Chapter of the Conference of Minority Public Administrators offers an annual scholarship of $1,000. The deadline is March 31, and applications may be completed at http://www.compahr.org/mserver/Awards.aspx.

Women Students The Center for Women in Government and Civil Society offers $9,000 Fellowships on Women and Public Policy. Recipients study policy issues at the State University of New York in Albany, and also are assigned "policy-related placements in New York State agencies." Applications are due in mid-May. The website is http://www.cwig.albany.edu/fellow.htm.

Almost all colleges have university women's clubs composed of the colleges' employees and spouses. Often, these clubs sponsor scholarships for non-traditional women students. The university's foundation office usually has information.

Writing Your Résumé

Public employers, who often are inundated by applications following a job announcement, take about thirty seconds to decide whether to keep or trash a résumé,[38] so it is critical that you design your résumé with its reader uppermost in mind.

Be Clear Your job is to make your résumé easy to understand, absorb, and remember. Whether your résumé is submitted in hard copy or online, a colored type and a fancy font are not the ways to make it memorable, as they send a message of idiosyncrasy. Use black type and a standard font of readable size, such as Times New Roman, size 12.

Positions held and educational attainments always are listed in reverse chronological order.

Obsess over Errors of Spelling, Grammar, and Punctuation An estimated 20 percent of résumés contain at least one typographical error.[39] Forty percent of résumé readers discard résumés when they notice one typo, and 76 percent toss them when they spot two.[40] Enough said.

Tell a Story What is most significant about your story? Begin each point with an active verb. List each project that you have directed, designed, developed, implemented, researched, reported, managed, controlled, planned, organized, edited, or built.

Tailor Your Story to the Job Think how your experiences and qualifications relate to the job description. Use in your résumé the same verbs and nouns found in that description and in the organization's other literature.

Make It Human Rather than, for example, stating that you are a "results-oriented professional," write instead that, "I enjoy solving tough problems." Include professional or student publications or papers (avoid going overboard with this), and/or a strong reference.

References First, think through carefully who will give you a strong, positive reference. This pool is invariably small. Family and friends usually do not qualify, but those who can assess your professionalism, such as professors, past and present employers, and civic group leaders, often do. Then be sure to *ask* your prospective references if they will oblige. Three references are a minimum, and employers increasingly are requesting five.

It is perfectly appropriate to note that references are available on request, or you can list them on your résumé. Be sure to include not only your reference's name, but also title, postal address, telephone number, including area code, and e-mail address. State briefly your relationship to your reference, such as "Reported to...." Even better, if possible, quote your references (with their permission), especially employers, in your résumé when they say glowing things about you.

Don't Get Personal The résumé reader may be safely assumed to conclude that your health is "excellent" without being told as much, and your age, gender, and marital status are your own business. Listing hobbies and pastimes can be a plus if they can be construed as giving you an edge for a job, but noting that you like "reading" probably is a waste of space.

Be sure, however, to list everything that you think may enhance your qualifications for the job. It is appropriate to include indicators of your high character and sociability, such as memberships in civic organizations, under its own heading.

Hardening Your Résumé If you send a hard copy of your résumé, use a heavy, high-quality, cream-colored (not a pastel) stationery to help it stand out. Be consistent in your overall format. "Bullets" also can be clarifying and useful. Justify the right-hand margin; doing so presents a neater appearance.

Most professionals advise that a résumé be limited to a single page, especially for those who are new to the marketplace. If yours is a one-pager, it is appropriate to list references on the reverse side or on a second page. If your résumé is more than one page, number the pages and write your name, title, and/or organization in bold italics in an upper corner of each page. This keeps your name and identity in front of your reader at all times.

Be sure to include a separate cover letter. Summarize your credentials, and explain only what you can do for your prospective employer, not what it can do for you. Limit it to one page. Justify the right-hand margin. And make it punchy. It is your opening, and best, shot.

Electrifying Your Résumé Of course, some employers insist that a résumé be e-mailed. If at all possible, however, submit a hard copy (but not both; one will be discarded). Check the "How to Apply" section of the job announcement to determine which version you will submit.

Hard copies are preferable because, in electronic résumés, density and dullness dominate. Some online systems convert into gibberish varying typefaces and other devices that render your hard-copy résumé more readable. Avoid invalid characters by using only numbers and letters; asterisks instead of bullets; and spaces rather than tabs.[41]

Perhaps 80 percent of e-mailed résumés are electronically searched for keywords before a human eye ever sees them, and résumés without those keywords die a quiet death. Just as you would do when writing a hard-copy résumé, scan the organization's (and comparable organizations') job advertisements, job descriptions, and websites for words and phrases that represent particular skills and experiences that your prospective employer thinks are important, then plug them into your online résumé. Because computers count the number of times that keywords are used, repeat keywords moderately throughout your résumé to assure that your résumé survives its electronic culling.[42]

Do not e-mail your résumé as an attachment. Employers increasingly are shifting away from accepting attachments as a means of protecting themselves from computer viruses. Instead, create a plain-text version of your résumé, and paste it into the text of your e-mail.

Avoid titling the "Subject" of your e-mail with the humdrum, "Résumé," and use something spiffier, such as "Award-Winning Human Resources Manager." Get the reader's attention.

"Knowledge, Skills, and Abilities" Some public employers require that applicants complete "knowledge, skills, and abilities" (or KSA) sections as a part their résumés. (The federal government abandoned KSAs in 2010, and now accepts résumés instead.) "If you're asked to rate your level of experience via multiple choice or true-false questions, remember that only applicants who receive the highest ratings...qualify for most jobs.... Give yourself the highest rating you can without lying." If you are required to write an essay, identify the problem you addressed and how you solved it, describe your very successful results, and list any kudos and compliments received. Limit each of your answers to one page or its equivalent, and do not feel obligated to fill the space provided, especially if you can make your case economically.[43]

The Partnership for Public Service offers useful insights about writing KSAs, at http://www.makingthedifference.org/federaljobs/ksawriting.shtml.

Get Help Do not be shy in asking for help in polishing up your résumé. Your campus's career services office can be a genuine asset in developing a presentable résumé.

USA Jobs (http://www.usajobs.gov), the federal job announcement website, offers an Online Résumé Builder that focuses on the applicant's abilities for a specific federal job.

Networking

You have written your résumé, and are completing your M.P.A. Now is the time to network.

Start with Your Friends Set up a free LinkedIn profile URL (LinkedIn is a global network of more than forty million professionals) of your job qualifications, and then include, in your outgoing e-mails' signature line, www.linkedin.com/in/yourname. Doing this will remind your e-mail recipients that you are looking for a job. Use Twitter to remind acquaintances of your job search, but make two accounts, one for friends and the other for your job search, which uses your real name and a headshot of yourself—well groomed and in a suit. Assure that your Facebook or MySpace page (if you lack one, make one) is chock-a-block with information relevant to your job search, and tighten its privacy settings to assure that only your friends can see comments and photos. Ninety percent of recruiters check out applicants on Google, so Google yourself to know what is out there.[44]

Who Is Whom? Knowing who is whom is essential to being an effective networker. You can find out by perusing the *Congressional Yellow Book*, *Federal Yellow Book*, *Government Affairs Yellow Book*, *Federal Regional Yellow Book*, *Municipal Year Book*, *Nonprofit Sector Yellow Book*, *State and Local Source Book*, and *State Yellow Book*.

Join Professional Networks Several professional associations are organized as state, regional, or local chapters, and these chapters offer excellent opportunities to develop contacts and establish relationships that could pay off as internships and jobs.

Perhaps the most promising of these chapter-based associations is the American Society for Public Administration. ASPA has more than ninety local chapters across the country composed of public administrators from all governmental levels and specializations, and this generalist approach to the field renders ASPA uniquely useful as a network. Typically, ASPA chapters sponsor monthly luncheons and regional conferences where new contacts are easily made. To learn how to join, ask your course instructor, or contact ASPA directly.

Launched in 2008, GovLoop (http://www.govloop.com) is a social networking government website composed of some 15,000 public administrators, academics, and contractors, and it sponsors about 400 events annually. Members post job openings on it.

Young Government Leaders (http://www.younggovernmentleaders.org) has 1,800 members who are federal administrators and professionals and six chapters in the United States.

The National League of Cities (http://www.nlc.org) is the nation's largest organization of municipal governments, and it sponsors state municipal leagues in every state except Hawaii.

The National Association of Counties (http://www.naco.org) has fifty-three state associations in forty-seven states, representing more than 2,000 counties in which four-fifths of Americans dwell. Most hold annual meetings.

Other specialized, chapter-based associations include the American Public Works Association (http://www.pubworks.org), the National Contract Management Association (http://www.ncmahq.org), and the National Institute of Governmental Purchasing (http://www.nigp.org), each with about seventy chapters in the United States and Canada, and the National Public Employer Labor Relations Association (http://www.npelra.org), with chapters in fifteen states and the Rocky Mountain region. Blacks in Government (http://www.bignet.org) has more than sixty chapters in the states and in federal agencies.

Interning

An internship, paid or voluntary, can be an important step toward acquiring relevant work experience for students lacking it, and frequently can lead to a full-time job in the organization in which one interns. Check with appropriate faculty members and your university's career services office about internship possibilities.

Internships in Professional Associations The International City/County Management Association's (http://www.icma.org) Local Government Management Fellowship Program aims to place 100 M.P.A. students in "management-track positions" in local governments each year. Applications are available in late summer.

The International Hispanic Network (http://www.internationalhispanicnetwork.org) offers twenty Public Policy Fellowships that provide "hands-on" experience in the District of Columbia for Hispanic college graduates and graduate students. Thirty Congressional Internships are available for Hispanic undergraduate students; summer housing, airfare, and a $2,000 stipend are included.

The National League of Cities (http://www.nlc.org) offers internships in a wide variety of areas that relate to urban governance. They and other internships are listed under "Job Announcements." Just contact the League at employment@nlc.org if you spot one that is of interest.

Federal Internships There is a slew of internship programs available in federal agencies. Information about all of them—long-term and short-term, paid and unpaid—can be accessed at the Partnership for Pubic Service's portal, http://www.makingthe difference.org/federalinternships/search. It also has information on student employment opportunities and co-op programs.

There are three major federal internships that pay stipends, and which are designed to lead to permanent federal employment.

The largest internship, with nearly 23,000 interns, is the Federal Career Intern Program (http://opm.gov/careerintern/index.asp). It allows agencies to hire applicants at General Schedule Grades 5, 7, and 9, after spending a two-year training internship in the agency. It has waxed into the main employment route for new federal hires. Agencies set their own application deadlines.

The Student Career Experience Program (SCEP, www.opm.gov/employ/students/intro.asp) has about 15,000 participants. Regrettably, only 27 percent of SCEP interns are permanently hired by federal agencies. Undergraduate and graduate students are eligible. To participate, your university and the pertinent federal agency must have a formal agreement; to find out if they do, check with your university's student financial aid office or the agency.

The Presidential Management Fellows (PMF, http://www.pmf.opm.gov/) offers about 400 fellowships annually. Applicants must be in their final year of graduate school and be nominated by their university. Fellows receive two-year appointments at Grades 9, 10, or 12, and routinely convert to regular civil service appointments, often at Grade 13, upon the successful completion of the internship. Senior PMFs are available for more experienced applicants. The deadline for application is generally in October.

State, Local, and Nonprofit Internships The National Society for Experiential Education (http://www.nsee.org) notes internship opportunities in the public and nonprofit sectors.

PA Times (http://www.aspanet.org/publications/patimes) advertises internships at all governmental levels for subscribers and ASPA members.

State, local, and a few other kinds of internships are listed by the Placement Office of the LBJ School at the University of Texas (http://www.utexas.edu/lbj/internships/links.php). The portal is excellent.

To locate internships in local governments, it can be bountifully fruitful to surf the Web, as many local governments offer internships.

Some 150 internships and 6,000 volunteering opportunities in the independent sector are listed at Action without Borders (http://idealist.org). The list is global.

FINDING A POSITION

Perhaps the most comprehensive portal listing available government positions is http://www.markosweb.com/www/careersingovernment.com/. It covers all governmental levels, and lists separately executive and entry-level jobs.

Never discount your own campus's resources when job hunting. Often the public administration program has its own contacts with those who hire, and your campus's career services office also can be very helpful.

A number of professional associations provide accessible and free lists of public and nonprofit jobs. Be sure to check these websites; a third of all job seekers find their jobs on Internet job boards.[45]

The following listing does not repeat website information when it has been provided earlier.

Federal Sources

Some 60,000 federal (and a number of state and local) positions are listed through the U.S. Office of Personnel Management's USA Jobs; the list is worldwide and updated daily. USA Jobs' electronic bulletin board may be reached by modem at (912) 757-3100 or Telnet, fjob.opm.gov. By calling (912) 757-3000, one connects with voice mail and may request an application form.

The Partnership for Public Service (http://www.makingthedifference.org/federaljobs/) is an excellent source for pursuing federal employment.

State and Local Sources

The American Society for Public Administration, the National Association of Schools of Public Affairs and Administration, and the Association of Public Policy Analysis and Management have pooled their resources to create PublicService-Careers.org, a portal that offers "the most comprehensive and useful information about careers in the field."

PA Times contains advertisements for positions at all levels of government, plus some in the nonprofit and private sectors, by state, portals, specialization, and governmental level. It is open only to subscribers and members of ASPA.

The LBJ School at the University of Texas lists public and nonprofit jobs on a first-rate website that is separate from its internship site. Check http://www.utexas.edu/lbj/careers/links/.

The Public Sector Job Bulletin (http://govtjobs.com) lists state and local government jobs by type from "A" (Administration and Management) to "U" (Utilities).

The Council of State Governments (http://www.statesnews.org/other_resources/classifieds.html) lists state government jobs by state, and its own job availabilities in its Washington and four regional offices.

GovtJob.Net (http://www.govtjob.net/) specializes in state and local job opportunities.

The best single source for local government databases offering employment opportunities is the National City Government Resource Center, which lists about a dozen job *databases* in the public and nonprofit sectors, with an emphasis on local governments. Click "Job Opportunities."

The National League of Cities' "Job Opportunities" page lists jobs (as well as internships) in the nation's cities. One may send a résumé to the League for specific positions listed on the site. The site provides postal and e-mail addresses, and telephone and fax numbers.

The National Association of Counties provides job possibilities in county governments on its "JobsOnline."

Independent Sector Sources

Action without Borders' website lists about 1,500 jobs and information about job fairs and careers.

The Chronicle of Philanthropy (http://philanthropy.com/jobs/) advertises virtually every job available in philanthropic circles—typically, several hundred.

The Independent Sector (http://www.independentsector/jobs_postings.htm) lists job opportunities available in its member nonprofit organizations, and these are numerous.

THE APPLICATION

Avoid submitting your credentials to an online general job-hunting service, but, if you do, be wary. Read the site's privacy policy carefully. Do not provide it with any personal information, including your full name; note instead that they are available on request. You may receive a vaguely-worded "job offer" that asks for a fee or private information. Ignore it Assure that you can delete your résumé from the site after you accept a job.

It is far preferable to post a hard copy of your application, or, next best, e-mail it, to a specific employer.

Then follow up. A remarkable 94 percent of corporate executives recommend that candidates do so, as it demonstrates initiative and interest in the position that can help you stand out.[46] Reiterate your continuing interest in the position, state your professional accomplishments that relate specifically to the job, and, above all, be brief.

More than four-fifths of business executives suggest that one should initiate a follow-up within two weeks after the application has been submitted. E-mailing one's follow-up is suggested by a plurality, 38 percent, of corporate executives.

A telephone call is recommended by 33 percent. Practice what you are going to say, place your call when the person is most likely to be free (often in the early morning or late afternoon), and do not leave a voice mail until at least your third call fails to make personal contact.

A handwritten note (23 percent of executives favor this route) expresses genuine interest in the job and suggests that you have not blanketed the market with your résumés.

THE INTERVIEW

The final step in securing a job is the interview, and it is a critical step. Almost seven out of every ten federal supervisors rely to a "great" or "moderate" extent on the interview in making their decisions to offer a job to a candidate. With the marginal exception of prior work experience (which, in the opinions of federal supervisors, leads the interview by just 2 percent), no other variable even comes close to the interview in deciding a candidate's fate.[47]

Be aware that first impressions last. And by "first," we mean the first one-tenth of one second. People do not really change their impression of a person after that first tenth of a second, and this holds true "for all judgments—attractiveness, likeability, trustworthiness, competence, and aggressiveness."[48]

Preparing for the Interview

Preparing for an interview is straightforward. Here are the basics.

Do Your Homework First and foremost, do your homework. Learn all that you can about the needs of the organization and the person or people who will be interviewing you. The Internet is an invaluable resource for tracking this down. And read all the material that they send you. If you have not received a mission statement, strategic plan, financial summary (for nonprofit organizations), or the

name(s) and position(s) of your interviewer(s) prior to your interview, request them and any other information that you may need.

Know Names Learn the names and positions of your interviewers before the interview, and memorize them. This is, admittedly, more easily recommended than done when there are many interviewers, but try anyway. Little will advance your career more effectively than remembering names.

Practice, Practice, Practice The interview is a splendid example of the axiom, practice makes perfect. Tap a close and patient friend to help you formulate answers to specific questions that are almost certain to be asked, and then practice your answers with him or her out loud. Try to keep your answers to about two minutes.

It is highly likely that you will be asked the following questions: Would you tell us about yourself? (Avoid reciting your résumé, dates, and chronologies; focus on the important and relevant things that you have done.) Why do you want this job? Why do you think that you are qualified for it? What will you bring to the job? What are the most pressing needs that you think confront our organization? What are your greatest strengths and weaknesses as a manager? (Select a "weakness" that is really a strength, such as tending to get ahead of yourself, providing an excess of opportunities for subordinates, or over-enthusiasm for projects. Think through your answer to this question carefully; interviewers are increasingly aware of this ruse.)

Interviewees who have had jobs should also be prepared for such questions as: Why did you leave your last job? What was your greatest career achievement? And how would your last boss describe you?

Sixty percent of employers check applicants' credit ratings.[49] If you have a creditworthiness issue (and if you still have made it to the interview), be prepared to answer questions concerning it honestly and openly.

Most campus career services offices offer interview practice sessions that often include videotaping so that you can see for yourself your own interviewing persona, and improve it. Take full advantage of this free service.

Scheduling Your Interview   Schedule your interview with two objectives in mind. If possible, avoid the after-lunch-time slot, and shoot for the first or final interview, which interviewers remember more clearly than the mull in the middle.

Dress for Success   The interview is not the place to make a fashion statement. Unless you have information to the contrary, wear a dark suit; it conveys respect for your interviewer.

A conservative tie and white long-sleeved shirts should be worn by men. Women safely can add some color. Avoid distractive garb. Neither men nor women should wear dangling jewelry, women should wear subdued nail polish, and everyone should shine their shoes.

Being Interviewed

There are a number of pointers that will increase your chances in an interview.

Bring Copies   Bring a copy of your résumé and references to your interview. Yes, your interviewer is supposed to have all this, but always prepare for the worst.

Avoid the Obvious   Interviewees have been known to chew gum, accept phone calls, text messages, or slip off their shoes during an interview. Lose the gum and the phone, but keep the shoes—on. Under no circumstance indicate a lack of interest or arrogance of any stripe. Never curse or relate an even slightly off-color joke; doing so will kill your chances, even if you are being interviewed by drunken sailors.

Shake Hands and Smile   This is standard procedure when one is being interviewed by a single person, but many interviews are conducted by panels of multiple participants. Shake hands with all of them, preferably before the interview begins so that you can warm up your crowd. If you have learned who holds what position in the organization, say something like, "Ah, yes, the comptroller," after they have given you their name.

Body Language   Maintain eye contact with your questioner. Smile. Sit erectly, tilting slightly forward, with your hands folded on the table or resting on your chair's arms. Do not fold your arms over your chest. Men should keep both feet planted firmly on the floor. Women may cross their ankles. Use your hands to illustrate a point.

Be Succinct, Interesting, and Observant   Keep your answers succinct and pointed, but not dry. Use personal examples to illustrate what you are trying to say. After you have answered a question, ask, at least occasionally, if you answered the question. Be cognizant of your interviewer's, or interviewers', attention. Should you notice eyes glazing over, or panelists nodding off, bring your answer to a quick close.

A trick that interviewers occasionally use is the silent treatment—that is, they say nothing after you have finished your answer in an effort to rattle you. Do not fall for it. Remain silent yourself. When this game has gone on long enough, ask, "Is there anything that I can add?"

Interview's End   Toward the end of your interview, you will be asked if you have any questions. Have some, preferably questions that demonstrate that you have done your homework about the organization. If, by some fluke, you are not asked if you have questions, politely ask if you may ask a couple.

Do not ask about pay and benefits; doing so indicates that you have not done your homework and that you are a money-grubber to boot. These questions should be asked if you receive a job offer. If you have questions about travel reimbursement, ask the interviewer's assistant.

At the close of the interview, thank your interviewer for his or her time. Express your genuine interest in the job. With a single interviewer, shake hands. With a panel of interviewers, shake their hands if you have not already done so; if you shook their hands earlier, play it by ear as to whether you want to initiate a second round. If you can recall the panelists' names, however, it is most impressive to shake hands with each one and thank them by name just before you leave.

After the Interview

Following the interview, you may be invited to join your interviewers or other employees for a drink or meal. By all means, join them, even if it means rescheduling your travel. But watch yourself. Be under no illusion that the interview is over.

Within twenty-four hours of the completion of the interview, write a thank-you note to your interviewer(s), and again express your interest in the job and the value that you can bring to the organization. Eighty-eight percent of business executives think that a thank-you note "can boost a job seeker's chances of landing the position," but corporate hiring managers estimate that 49 percent of job interviewees fail to send them.[50] So write them. If you were interviewed by more than one person sequentially, thank each of them individually. If you were interviewed by a panel, writing only to the chair of the panel usually is sufficient, but, if you developed a rapport with someone, then thank him or her, too.

If you have remotely legible handwriting, a fountain pen (a roller-ball will do), and good stationery, write a brief note by hand; this conveys your personal interest. If your handwriting can be understood only by code breakers, type it on good stationery, sign it, and post it; avoid e-mailing it, as it is more satisfying to the recipient to receive a personally signed letter. If the time between your interview and a decision date is very short, then, of course, e-mail your thanks. But follow up with a handwritten note.

Then wait to learn if you have been hired. And be patient. It takes more than three months, on average, to hire a federal employee,[51] and state and local governments average four months.[52]

If you were selected, congratulations, but do not accept the offer until you are comfortable that you fully understand all aspects of the position, such as pay, benefits, travel, and responsibilities. Ask for twenty-four hours to think it over. (A tip: If your prospective boss over-stressed the importance of loyalty during the interview, then be very cautious about accepting an offer.) If you were not hired, it is not inappropriate to call your interviewer and ask, extremely politely, how you could improve your qualifications and presentation. If you still have an interest in working for the organization, write another note to your interviewer(s) expressing how honored you were to be a finalist, and that your interest in their fine organization remains keen.

Be aware that some organizations and interviewers are insensitive, impolite, and boorish. They may fail to notify you if you were not selected; or they may do so very late; or they may notify you with scant, if any, courtesy. In these cases, count your blessings.

NOTES

1. Morgan J. Bradley, *The Public Administration Career Directory* (Detroit, MI: Visible Ink, 1994).
2. As derived from data in U.S. Bureau of the Census, *Statistical Abstract of the United States, 2011*, 130th ed. (Washington, DC: U.S. Government Printing Office, 2011), Table 459.
3. As derived from data in ibid., Table 495.
4. U.S. Merit Systems Protection Board, "Credentialed But Not Qualified," *Issues of Merit* (Washington, DC, U.S. Government Printing Office, April 2011), p. 4. Figure is for 2010.
5. As derived from data in U.S. Bureau of the Census, *Statistical Abstract of the United States, 2011*, Table 459. Figure is the average for all employees, 2000–2008.
6. As derived from data in ibid., Table 495.
7. As derived from data in ibid., Table 459. Figures are for all employees, 2000–2008.
8. International Personnel Management Association, *Pay Rates in the Public Service: Survey of 62 Common Job Classes in the Public Sector* (Washington, DC: Author, 1985).
9. U.S. Bureau of the Census, *Statistical Abstract of the United States, 2011*, Table 497. Figure is for 2009 and does not include the Postal Service (703,698 employees) and intelligence agencies.
10. U.S. Merit Systems Protection Board, *The Federal Selection Interview: Unrealized Potential* (Washington, DC: U.S. Government Printing Office, 2003), p. 6.
11. U.S. Office of Personnel Management, *The Fact Book, 2007* (Washington, DC: U.S. Government Printing Office, 2010), p. 14. Figure is for 2006.

12. U.S. Merit Systems Protection Board, *Attracting the Next Generation: A Look at Federal Entry-Level New Hires* (Washington, DC: U.S. Government Printing Office, 2008), p. 6.

13. "The Memo That Roared," *Washington Post* (June 19, 2009).

14. U.S. Merit Systems Protection Board, *As Supervisors Retire: An Opportunity to Reshape Organizations* (Washington, DC: U.S. Government Printing Office, 2009), p. ii.

15. U.S. Office of Personnel Management, *2011 Salary Tables and Related Information*, http://www.opm.gov/oca/11tables/index.asp. Figures are for 2011.

16. As derived from data in U.S. Bureau of the Census, *Statistical Abstract of the United States, 2011*, Table 460. Figures are for 2008.

17. Leslie Scott, "States Anticipate Talent Shortage," *Book of the States, 2008* (Lexington, KY: Council of State Governments, 2008), pp. 455–457. Figure is a projection for 2012.

18. As derived from data in Council of State Governments, *Book of the States, 2010* (Lexington, KY: Author, 2010), Table 4.11. Data are for 2010.

19. As derived from data in U.S. Bureau of the Census, *Statistical Abstract of the United States, 2011*, Table 460. Figures are for 2008.

20. Rollie O. Waters and Joyce C. Powell, "Salaries of Municipal Officials, 2009," *Municipal Year Book, 2010* (Washington, DC: International City/County Management Association, 2010), pp. 75–96.

21. Ibid., pp. 97–114.

22. Organizational counts are for 2007, and are derived from U.S. Government Accountability Office, *Nonprofit Sector: Significant Federal Funds Reach the Sector through Various Mechanisms, but More Complete and Reliable Funding Data Are Needed*, GAO-09-193 (Washington, DC: U.S. Government Printing Office, 2009), p. 5. Membership counts are for 1996, and are found in Lester M. Salamon, *America's Nonprofit Sector: A Primer*, 2nd ed. (New York: The Foundation Center, 1999), p. 22.

23. Council on Foundations, "Executive Summary," *2008 Grantsmakers Salary and Benefits Report* (Washington, DC: Author, 2008), p. 1. Figure is for 2008.

24. As derived from data in Chronicle of Philanthropy, *Executive Compensation Data* (Washington, DC: Author, 2011). Data are for 2010.

25. Council on Foundations, "Executive Summary," p. 1. Figure is for 2008.

26. Debra Mesch and Patrick M. Rooney, "Determinants of Compensation: A Study of Pay, Performance, and Gender Differences for Fundraising Professionals," *Nonprofit Management & Leadership* 18 (Summer 2008), pp. 435–463. The data and quotation are on p. 447.

27. Jeffrey L. Brudney, Cynthia J. Bowling, and Deil S. Wright, *Continuity and Change in Public Administration Across the 50 States: Linking Practice, Theory, and Research through the American State Administrators Project, 1964–2008* (Auburn, AL: Center for Governmental Services, Auburn University, 2010), p. 12. Figure is for 2008.

28. Robert C. Burns and Robert D. Lee, Jr., "The Ups and Downs State Budget Process Reform: Experience of Three Decades," *Public Budgeting & Finance* 24 (Fall 2004), pp. 1–19. Figure (p. 15) is for 2000.

29. As derived from data in Jerri Killian and Enamul Choudhury, "Continuity and Change in the Role of City Managers," *Municipal Year Book, 2010* (Washington, DC: International City/County Management Association, 2010), pp. 10–18. Figure, 51 percent, is for 2009.

30. Jonathan P. West and Evan M. Berman, "Job Satisfaction of Public Managers in Special Districts," *Review of Public Personnel Administration* 29 (December 2009), pp. 327–353. Datum (p. 336) is for 2008.

31. As derived from data in Roseanne M. Mirabella, *Nonprofit Management Education*, http://academic.shu.edu/npo/list.php?sort=degree&type=gnoc. Figures are for 2011.

32. As derived from data in Sandy Baum, Jennifer Ma, and Kathleen Payea, *Education Pays 2010: The Benefits of Higher Education for Individuals and Society* (Washington, DC: The College Board, 2010), p. 11, Figure 1.1. Figure is for 2010.

33. National Association of Schools of Public Affairs and Administration, *Salary Information for MPAs/MPPs* (Washington, DC: Author, 2008), p. 2. Figures are for 2003.

34. George Grode and Marc Holzer, "The Perceived Utility of MPA Degrees," *Public Administration Review* 35 (July/August, 1975), pp. 403–412.

35. Gregory B. Lewis, "How Much Is an MPA Worth? Public Administration Education and

Federal Career Success," *International Journal of Public Administration* 9 (April 1987), pp. 397–415. This is a study of a large sample of federal employees.

36. U.S. Internal Revenue Service, *Tax Benefits for Education*, Publication 970 (Washington, DC: U.S. Government Printing Office, 2011). Data are for 2010.

37. U.S. Government Accountability Office, *Tax Gap: Complexity and Taxpayer Compliance*, GAO-11-747T (Washington, DC: U.S. Government Printing Office, 2011), Highlights page. Figure, 19 percent, is for 2005.

38. Lily Whiteman, "The Write Stuff," *PA Times* (January/February 2010), pp. 10, 13–14.

39. Jeff Wuorio, "5 Ways to Make Your Résumé Shine," *USA Weekend* (September 16–18, 2011), p. 4.

40. Arlinda Smith Broady, "Sharpen Your Interview Skills," *Savannah Morning News* (May 5, 2010).

41. Ibid.

42. Richard Beatty, *The Ultimate Job Search: Intelligent Strategies to Get the Right Job Fast* (Indianapolis: Jist Works, 2006).

43. Whiteman, "The Write Stuff," pp. 13–14.

44. These suggestions are drawn from Liz Ryan, at liz@asklizryan.com and Alyssa Bailey, "Use Social Networking for a Career," *USA Weekend* (May 20, 2010).

45. Peter Weddle, as cited in Selena Dehne, "Perfecting Your Digital Résumé," *Savannah Morning News* (December 17, 2006).

46. Almost all of the information in the following discussion is drawn from a survey conducted by Robert Half International, *Don't Be a Stranger* (Menlo Park, CA: Author, 2006). Data are for 2006.

47. U.S. Merit Systems Protection Board, *The Federal Selection Interview*, p. 7.

48. Janine Willis and Alexander Todorov, "First Impressions: Making Up Your Mind After a 100-Ms Exposure to a Face," *Psychological Science* 17 (July 2006), pp. 592–598. The quotation is on p. 592.

49. *Washington Times*, as cited in ARA Content, "What You Should Know about 'Strategic Default,'" *Savannah Morning News* (July 31, 2011).

50. Survey by Robert Half International, as cited in Career Builder, *A Simple "Thank You" Can Land the Job*, http://www.careerbuilder.ca/CA/JobSeeker/CareerAdvice/ViewArticle.aspx? Data are for 2007.

51. U.S. General Accounting Office, *Human Capital: Opportunities to Improve Executive Agencies' Hiring Processes*, GAO-03-450 (Washington, DC: U.S. Government Printing Office, 2003), p. 3. Figure, 102 days, is for 2002.

52. Sally Coleman Selden, *Human Capital: Tools and Strategies for the Public Sector* (Washington, DC: CQ Press, 2009), p. 56. Figure is for 2006.

INDEX